CAN MIGHT MAKE RIGHTS?

This book looks at why it is so difficult to create "the rule of law" in post-conflict societies such as Iraq and Afghanistan and offers critical insights into how policymakers and field-workers can improve future rule of law efforts. Aimed at policymakers, field-workers, journalists, and students trying to make sense of the international community's problems in Iraq and elsewhere, this book shows how a narrow focus on building institutions such as courts and legislatures misses the more complex political and cultural issues that affect societal commitment to the values associated with the rule of law. The authors place the rule of law in context, showing the interconnectedness between the rule of law and other post-conflict priorities, from reestablishing security to revitalizing civil society. The authors outline a pragmatic, synergistic approach to the rule of law that promises to reinvigorate debates about transitions to democracy and post-conflict reconstruction.

Jane Stromseth is a professor of law at Georgetown University Law Center, where she teaches in the fields of international law and constitutional law. She has written widely on international law governing the use of force, humanitarian intervention, accountability for human rights atrocities, and constitutional war powers. She has served in government as a director for Multilateral and Humanitarian Affairs at the National Security Council and as an attorney-advisor in the Office of the Legal Adviser at the U.S. Department of State. She serves on the editorial board of the *American Journal of International Law*.

David Wippman is Vice Provost for International Relations, Cornell University, and a professor of law at Cornell University Law School. He previously served as a partner at Reichler, Appelbaum, & Wippman, a firm specializing in the representation of developing countries, and as a director for Multilateral and Humanitarian Affairs at the National Security Council. Wippman is coauthor (with Steve Ratner and Jeff Dunoff) of *International Law: Norms, Actors, Process* (2d ed. 2006).

Rosa Brooks is a professor of law at Georgetown University Law Center, currently on leave while serving as Special Counsel at the Open Society Institute. Before entering academia, Brooks served as a senior advisor at the U.S. Department of State's Bureau of Democracy, Human Rights and Labor and as a consultant for Human Rights Watch and other nongovernmental organizations. She serves on the executive council of the American Society of International Law, and she writes a weekly opinion column for the *Los Angeles Times*.

Can Might Make Rights?

BUILDING THE RULE OF LAW
AFTER MILITARY INTERVENTIONS

Jane Stromseth
Georgetown University Law Center

David Wippman
Cornell Law School

Rosa Brooks
Georgetown University Law Center

A project of the American Society
of International Law

CAMBRIDGE UNIVERSITY PRESS
Cambridge, New York, Melbourne, Madrid, Cape Town, Singapore, São Paulo

Cambridge University Press
32 Avenue of the Americas, New York, NY 10013-2473, USA

www.cambridge.org
Information on this title: www.cambridge.org/9780521860895

First published 2006
Reprinted 2007

Printed in the United States of America

A catalog record for this publication is available from the British Library.

Library of Congress Cataloging in Publication Data

Stromseth, Jane E.
Can might make rights? : building the rule of law after military interventions / Jane Stromseth,
David Wippman, Rosa Brooks.
    p. cm.
Includes bibliographical references and index.
ISBN-13: 978-0-521-86089-5 (hardback)
ISBN-10: 0-521-86089-X (hardback)
ISBN-13: 978-0-521-67801-8 (pbk.)
ISBN-10: 0-521-67801-3 (pbk.)
1. Rule of law. 2. Humanitarian intervention. 3. Peace-building. I. Wippman, David,
1954– II. Brooks, Rosa. III. Title.
K3171.S77 2006
341.5′84 – dc22   2006012924

ISBN 978-0-521-86089-5 hardback
ISBN 978-0-521-67801-8 paperback

For our families

Contents

Acknowledgments

The American Society of International Law sponsored this book project, and we are permanently indebted to Charlotte Ku, Rick LaRue, and Sandra Liebel for their generous assistance during the book's long incubation period. We also thank the U.S. Institute of Peace and the Carnegie Corporation for their generous financial support of this project, and John Berger at Cambridge University Press for shepherding this book into print.

We also benefited from exceptional research assistance provided by law students at Georgetown University Law Center, University of Virginia School of Law, and Cornell Law School. In particular, we would like to thank Gabe Rottman, Maya Goldstein-Bolocan, Milan Markovic, Ruthanne Deutsch, and Elizabeth Keyes at Georgetown; Kevin Donohue and Leah Edmunds at Virginia; and Melissa Baker, Sarah Bernett, Ilana Buschkin, Heidi Craig, Jennifer Filanowski, Cailin Hammer, Ralph Mamiya, Miles Norton, and Ulysses Smith at Cornell. Pam Finnigan, Anne Cahanin, and Susan Potts all provided extremely helpful secretarial support.

James Schear, John Ehrenreich, and Peter Brooks provided numerous valuable comments and suggestions along the way; and Stephen Scher provided excellent editorial assistance. Michele Brandt, Charles Call, Scott Carlson, Deborah Isser, Seth Jones, Rama Mani, David Marshall, Brett McGurk, Laurel Miller, Marina S. Ottaway, Michele Schimpp, Eric Schwartz, and Taylor Seybolt all read an early draft of the manuscript and provided comments at a workshop held in November 2004 at the American Society of International Law; we apologize for not always heeding their advice.

We are also grateful to the dozens of people in Iraq, East Timor, Sierra Leone, Kosovo, Bosnia, Washington, New York, Geneva, Brussels, Amsterdam, and The Hague who patiently discussed their work and ideas with us. For assistance in East Timor, we are particularly grateful to Kim Hunter, Asia Foundation Country Representative in East Timor; Annelise

Parr, Executive Assistant to the Special Representative of the U.N. Secretary-General; Foreign Minister Jose Ramos-Horta; and U.S. Ambassador G. Joseph Rees. In Sierra Leone, special thanks are due to David Crane, Prosecutor of the Special Court for Sierra Leone; and Eric Witte, Special Assistant to the Prosecutor.

CHAPTER ONE

Introduction: A New Imperialism?

It is hard to find anything good to say about imperialism. Fueled by greed and an easy assumption of racial and cultural superiority, the imperialism of the 19th-century European powers left in its wake embittered subject populations and despoiled landscapes. Traditional governance structures (some just, some unjust) were displaced by European implants, indigenous cultural practices suppressed, and natural resources ruthlessly exploited for the benefit of colonial elites and distant European overlords. Although imperialist ideologies and practices were frequently justified by reference to lofty ideals (the need to bring civilization, industry, or Christian values to more primitive nations, for instance), today there are few who would defend imperialism.

Until quite recently, most scholars were content to declare that the age of imperialism was over and good riddance to it. After World War II, strong international norms emerged favoring self-determination, democracy, and human rights and condemning wars of expansion and aggression. In the 1950s and 1960s, independence movements in colonized regions gained strength and moral credibility. As the possession of colonies increasingly became a political liability, most of the former imperial powers divested themselves of the trappings of empire. Some did so with almost unseemly haste, with a quick election, a ceremonial changing of the flag, and a series of bows and handshakes sufficing to transfer governmental power from foreign hands to those of the indigenous leaders.

By the time the Cold War ended, *imperialism* seemed a relic of a bygone era. The term remained handy as a disparaging metaphor used by those inclined to criticize American foreign policy muscle-flexing, but for the most part, imperialism seemed to be as extinct as the dodo bird: it had collapsed under its own weight, a victim of greed, sloth, and insufficient brainpower. Although the former imperialist powers continued to dominate the world stage militarily and economically, they had gone out of the business of invading and exercising permanent military control over foreign lands.

But something odd happened in the years since the early 1990s. For reasons that are complex, many of the same powerful western states that contritely rejected imperialism a few short decades ago today are increasingly resorting to military force to intervene in the territories of other states, and in many cases, they are remaining on as de facto governments years after the fighting ends. Consider the past decade's interventions in Bosnia, Haiti, Kosovo, East Timor, Liberia, Sierra Leone, Afghanistan, and Iraq. Ironically, these recent military interventions have generally been made in the name of the very same values that led to the rapid dismantling of imperialist structures in the second half of the 20th century: human rights, democracy, and a rejection of the use of aggressive war as an instrument of foreign policy. Although most of the recent interventions have been engaged in on behalf of "the international community," or at least some sizeable subset thereof, most of the intervening states have been western states – mainly the United States and the North Atlantic Treaty Organization (NATO) powers. Not entirely coincidentally, most of the states intervened in (the "failed states" like Sierra Leone and the "rogue" states like Iraq) have been states formerly subject to imperialist rule.

Some of these recent interventions are usually seen as having been essentially humanitarian in nature (Kosovo, East Timor). Others were motivated primarily by national and international security considerations, with humanitarian concerns very much a secondary motive (Afghanistan, Iraq). Each of these recent interventions has had both passionate defenders and passionate detractors, and there is little question that from the perspective of international law, some recent interventions have been more justifiable than others.

Nonetheless, whether they are justifiable or unjustifiable, wise or unwise, such military interventions will almost certainly be a fact of life for some time to come. The "international community" – and the United States, as the most significant military and economic power in the world today – will likely engage in, or assist, many more such interventions, at least in instances where there appears to be a clear threat to U.S. security.

In part, this is because the events of September 11, 2001 left the United States and many of its NATO allies determined to root out terrorism and other global security threats wherever they can be found, through the use of military force when necessary. The desire to incapacitate the terrorist al-Qaeda network drove the U.S.-led military intervention in Afghanistan; the perceived threat of weapons of mass destruction was the primary driver of the subsequent U.S.-dominated intervention in Iraq. Military interventions (and the deployment of peacekeeping forces) will also continue to be motivated in part by broader humanitarian concerns, such as the need to prevent genocide and other mass atrocities and the need to restore peace and stability in regions devastated by civil war.

Frequently, of course, the motives behind military interventions will be complex and mixed. In Haiti, for instance, U.S. military interventions (both in 1994 and in 2004) were motivated partly by humanitarian considerations (a concern about political repression and indiscriminate bloodshed) and partly by more pragmatic (and self-interested) considerations: the desire to prevent a massive influx of refugees from Haiti to the United States, for instance. In the age of globalization, there can often be no neat distinction between "humanitarian" concerns and "security" concerns. Repression, poverty, and injustice can fuel terrorism, instability, civil war, and organized crime, and these in turn can lead to still more repression, poverty, and injustice. In the future, many military interventions are likely to arise jointly out of humanitarian concerns and security concerns.

The military interventions driven by interwoven humanitarian and security concerns have often been compared – and contrasted – to traditional imperialism. Indeed, many commentators – some approving, some less so – have referred to recent interventions as "liberal imperialism" or "the new imperialism." Unlike earlier imperial powers, those western states and regional powers that have backed recent military interventions have explicitly (and, on the whole, credibly) disclaimed any desire to exercise permanent control over defeated populations and territories or to gain economically from their military ventures. Also, today's interventions tend to be multilateral in nature, often (though not always) authorized by the United Nations (UN) or parallel regional structures. But like earlier imperial powers, today's interventionists find themselves acting as de facto governments in dysfunctional and war-torn states.

This may be inevitable. Creating durable solutions to humanitarian and security problems requires a long-term commitment to rebuilding and reforming repressive or conflict-ridden societies. In particular, long-term solutions require rebuilding (or building from scratch) the rule of law: fostering effective, inclusive, and transparent indigenous governance structures; creating fair and independent judicial systems and responsible security forces; reforming and updating legal codes; and creating a widely shared public commitment to human rights and to using the new or reformed civic structures rather than relying on violence or self-help to resolve problems. Yet these tasks often cannot simply be left entirely to local populations, because in the immediate wake of interventions, such societies usually continue to be riven by the same conflicts and problems that motivated the intervention in the first place. After genocide, ethnic cleansing, or war, few societies are immediately able to "get back on their feet." Most need – and many demand – substantial outside assistance in reestablishing security and reconstructing governance and economic institutions. Post-conflict reconstruction is slow, expensive, and fraught with difficulty, and in part for that reason, today's "liberal imperialists" are often somewhat reluctant imperialists. If the main goals of the old imperialists were territorial expansion and economic gain, and imperialist governing elites enjoyed broad support from their domestic constituencies, the architects of today's military interventions find themselves in a far different situation. Interventions are a costly and dangerous business, diverting government resources away from domestic priorities and risking the lives of the intervening power's soldiers. The electorates of western nations are often loathe to support expensive, risky foreign ventures that offer few clear short-term domestic dividends. Because modern international and domestic norms forbid interventions designed explicitly to exploit the resources of other states, today's interventionists must generally make a public commitment to building just, democratic, peaceful, and prosperous societies in the areas that they control, if they are to avoid worldwide condemnation. Yet building just and prosperous societies is complex and requires intervening powers to make virtually open-ended commitments of resources and people to post-intervention societies – which is, again, likely to be less than popular with domestic constituencies concerned about how their tax dollars are spent.

Thus, while a potentially critical world watches events unfold in real time on the Internet and CNN, today's "new imperialists" must pledge themselves to ensuring peace and stability, rebuilding damaged infrastructures and economies, protecting vulnerable populations, nurturing a strong civil society, fostering legitimate indigenous leaders, and supporting democratic state institutions. Since today's interventionists generally intervene in the name of global order and "the rule of law," they must consequently strive to build the rule of law in the societies in which they intervene, at risk of losing their own global credibility. They must work closely with regional and international organizations and with a wide range of nongovernmental actors (from human rights groups to humanitarian aid organizations). At the same time, they must satisfy domestic constituencies concerned about costs and domestic social and economic priorities.

This is no easy task. Building the rule of law is no simple matter, although triumphal interventionist rhetoric occasionally implies that it is. The idea of the rule of law is often used as a handy shorthand way to describe the extremely complex bundle of cultural commitments and institutional structures that support peace, human rights, democracy, and prosperity. On the institutional level, the rule of law involves courts, legislatures, statutes, executive agencies, elections, a strong educational system, a free press, and independent nongovernmental organizations (NGOs) such as bar associations, civic associations, political parties, and the like. On the cultural level, the rule of law requires human beings who are willing to give their labor and their loyalty to these institutions, eschewing self-help solutions and violence in favor of democratic and civil participation.

Especially in societies in which state institutions and the law itself have been deeply discredited by repressive or ineffectual governments, persuading people to buy into rule of law ideals is difficult. Both institutionally and culturally, building the rule of law also requires extensive human and financial resources, careful policy coordination between numerous international actors and national players, and at the same time an ability to respond quickly, creatively, and sensitively to unpredictable developments on the ground.

Today's interventionism presents a mix of old and new problems. In the age of human rights, what goals, if any, justify military interventions? In what ways do the values and methods of the new interventionism constrain and complicate the process of achieving the new imperialism's goals? Just what is it that we mean when we talk about "the rule of law"? Concretely, how does one go about creating the rule of law? How can one tell when the rule of law has successfully been established? At what stage do interveners have an obligation to stick around, and at what stage do they instead have an obligation to go home and leave local actors to determine their own destinies?

These are difficult questions, and none of them can be easily answered. We believe, however, that answers need to be attempted nonetheless. The new interventionism will probably be a feature of the global order for years to come, and the stakes are too high to shrug off the hard questions as unanswerable, or to continue to address these dilemmas in an ad hoc and ill-considered fashion.

This book was initially conceptualized in early 2001, before the events of September 11 shook up the global legal order. In the first months of 2001, looking back on the recent international interventions in Bosnia, Haiti, Kosovo, Liberia, East Timor, and Sierra Leone, it seemed to us that a book on humanitarian interventions would make a useful contribution to U.S. and international policy debates. We initially planned to write a book that would focus in part on establishing clear legal and pragmatic criteria for humanitarian interventions and in part on the issue of post-intervention efforts to rebuild the rule of law in conflict-ridden societies. When we first began to plan this book, we took it for granted that most humanitarian interventions would have broad, if not universal, international support and that the intervening powers would also enjoy a reasonably high degree of support from the local population in post-conflict societies.

The events that followed the September 11 terrorist attacks challenged these assumptions. Although the U.S.-led invasions of Afghanistan and Iraq had humanitarian dimensions (ousting the repressive and murderous Taliban and Baathist regimes), both interventions were motivated mainly by perceived national security imperatives (eliminating terrorist bases in

Afghanistan and preventing the acquisition of weapons of mass destruction by Iraq).

For the most part the international community supported the intervention in Afghanistan and accepted the invasion's legality. In the case of Iraq, however, there was no such acquiescence; the invasion's legal legitimacy rested on a highly contested claim of authority. Even many traditional U.S. allies openly criticized it, and UN Secretary-General Kofi Annan publicly called it illegal. The U.S.-led invasion of Iraq found only limited and ambivalent international support, and global skepticism of the intervention has only been exacerbated by the subsequent failure to find weapons of mass destruction within Iraq, despite the prewar claims of the U.S. government. All this has fed a popular perception in the greater Middle East that the U.S. intervention was motivated by little more than a desire for regional domination and control of Iraqi oil resources. Inside Iraq, public attitudes toward the intervention vary substantially among the different segments of the population. Although most Iraqis are happy to see Saddam Hussein gone, there has been widespread criticism of American inability to restore basic security in key parts of Iraq. Iraqi mistrust of the U.S.-led intervention has been further exacerbated by popular perceptions of U.S. military heavy-handedness, combined with the global scandal sparked by revelations about the abuse of Iraqi prisoners at Abu Ghraib and elsewhere.

These two post–9/11 interventions posed a dilemma for our initial conception of this book. After 9/11, a book focusing entirely on humanitarian interventions no longer seemed to make much sense, because the U.S. and international discourse had moved on to a very different place. The U.S.-led invasions of Afghanistan and Iraq seemed like a far cry from the international humanitarian interventions in places like Kosovo and East Timor. Nonetheless, as events in Afghanistan and Iraq unfolded, it became increasingly clear to us that however different these various military interventions were on the front end, post-conflict issues in Afghanistan and Iraq had a great deal in common with post-conflict issues in Kosovo, East Timor, or any of the other societies subject to international humanitarian interventions before 9/11.

Regardless of the motivations behind particular past military interventions – regardless of whether they were justifiable or unjustifiable, popular or unpopular, wise or unwise – all post-intervention societies face many similar challenges. Although Kosovo, East Timor, and Iraq are dramatically different societies, for instance, with divergent histories and cultures, they all had similar needs when the main phase of the fighting ended. All had damaged infrastructures – bombed roads, burnt-out homes and offices, devastated electrical and sanitation systems. All had significant populations in desperate need of humanitarian assistance such as food, shelter, and medical care. All had public institutions that either barely functioned or entirely lacked popular credibility and a population that had to one extent or another been cut off from access to critical skills or the outside world. All faced the challenge of ensuring accountability for past human rights abuses and preventing future abuses.

In a broad sense, then, there is much that all these post-intervention societies have in common. As a result, intervening powers face grave and similar responsibilities when the bombs stop falling, regardless of the intervention's underlying legitimacy or motives.

Interveners may be tempted to cut and run after the initial military phase of an intervention ends, getting out with as little loss of life and money as possible. Yet both moral and pragmatic considerations suggest that taking a longer-term view is better in the end.

In part, this is because even the United States, as the sole remaining superpower, needs to maintain some degree of international legitimacy and support. Although the United States may be willing and able to accept the costs of going it alone (or almost alone) when it comes to perceived national security imperatives, the United States still faces significant political and diplomatic pressure to be a good global neighbor and a responsible superpower. U.S. domestic and international commitments to democracy and human rights force even reluctant American politicians to promise that American power will be used for the benefit of the people in post-intervention societies, as well as for U.S. benefit.

In addition, military interventions that do not ultimately rebuild the rule of law in post-conflict societies are doomed to undermine their own goals. This is true whether the interventions were undertaken initially for humanitarian reasons, security reasons, or a complicated mix of the two. Unless the rule of law can be created in post-intervention societies, military interventions will not fully eradicate the dysfunctional conditions that necessitated intervention in the first place. Without the rule of law, human rights abuses and violence will recur and continue unchecked, posing ongoing threats not only to residents of post-conflict societies but also to global peace and security – and perhaps necessitating another intervention a few years down the road.

Haiti is a case in point: ten years after sending in U.S. and UN troops to restore a democratically elected leader to power, the United States recently found itself, ironically, complicit in removing the very same leader and forced to send in troops to ensure a peaceful transition to a new government. Had the United States and the international community made a more sustained investment in rebuilding the rule of law in Haiti and maintained the pressure for reform, many abuses might have been prevented, and there might have been no need to send in the Marines a second time around. As of this writing, there is little reason to believe that the United States has yet learned this lesson from the first U.S.-led intervention in Haiti: once again, U.S. troops were quickly withdrawn, and U.S. promises of meaningful reconstruction assistance have amounted to little.

East Timor provides another recent example. Just one year after the termination of the UN peacekeeping operation sent to restore order and establish democratic institutions, the newly independent state was forced in May 2006 to declare a state of emergency and invite a new international peacekeeping force back into the country to stop rapidly escalating local violence. The inability of the Timorese government to maintain order on its own revealed the fragility of its democratic institutions and political culture, and exposed fault lines and grievances within Timorese society that will continue to fester if left unaddressed. It also highlighted the failure of the UN Transitional Administration in East Timor (UNTAET) and other international actors to create adequate preconditions for stability and the rule of law during the period in which all legislative, administrative, and executive power rested with the interveners. As in Haiti, interveners scaled back their commitment too soon, and so were forced to return.

Unfortunately, Haiti and East Timor are hardly atypical. Time and again, interveners have underestimated the time, effort, and resources needed for the rule of law to take root. The temptation to undertake interventions "on the cheap" has undercut longer-term policy goals for the United States and other major international and regional powers. Resource and other constraints often lead to a reluctance to intervene in the early stages of a humanitarian or security crisis, even when all the warning signs point to the dangers of remaining passive. Military interventions – especially those primarily humanitarian in nature – often involve too little force, too late, followed by an even more minimal commitment of resources to the post-intervention rebuilding phase. When the "immediate crisis" is past, public attention dwindles, and so does donor support; post-conflict, interveners often then find it difficult to provide enough troops, civilian police, reconstruction funds, and so on to make much of a dent in post-conflict problems.

The lack of resources in turn often comes to shape post-intervention aims, as initially ambitious reconstruction plans are scaled down to reflect diminishing resources. This often forces unappealing compromises with local power-brokers or "spoilers" (such as warlords in Afghanistan or the KLA in Kosovo), who must be relied on to "make the trains run on time" in the absence of viable alternatives structures, abandoned because they cost too much. Needless to say, compromises with spoilers and conflict entrepreneurs usually come back to haunt interveners a short way down the road, and conflict may well ultimately break out again – requiring another cycle of interventions, lofty promises, and a rapid retreat from initial commitments.

Thus, even if moral considerations are insufficient to persuade some policymakers of the importance of building the rule of law in post-conflict settings, Haiti and similar examples should suggest that what goes around, comes around: the failure to invest adequately in interventions to build the rule of law in the first place has long-term negative consequences for human rights, human security, and global security.

This book consequently proceeds from two premises. The first is that the United States and the international community will continue to engage in military interventions followed by post-conflict efforts to rebuild the rule of law. The second is that all post-conflict reconstruction efforts face many similar challenges, regardless of the rationale behind the original intervention. In this book, we thus try to analyze the common lessons that interventions from Bosnia to Iraq hold for future post-conflict reconstruction efforts.

Concretely, this book seeks to examine what we know and what we don't know about rebuilding the rule of law in the wake of military interventions. The bad news, which will come as no surprise either to foreign policy professionals or to careful newspaper readers, is that the track record of the international community in general, and the United States in particular, is not very impressive. From Bosnia and Haiti to Afghanistan and Iraq, post-intervention efforts to build the rule of law have been haphazard, under-resourced, and at times internally contradictory, with as many failures as successes. This is in part because post-conflict societies tend to be inhospitable environments for efforts to promote the rule of law. Post-conflict societies are often characterized by high levels of violence and human need, damaged physical and civic infrastructures, and sometimes little or no historical rule of law traditions. But to some degree, the poor track record of rule of law promotion efforts is due to the failure of interveners to appreciate the complexities of the project of creating the rule of law.

The good news is that the international community is finally beginning to have a sense of "best practices," an increasingly nuanced understanding of what works and what doesn't in post-conflict settings. The Iraq experience has underlined the critical importance of immediately reestablishing basic security in the wake of military interventions. This in turn requires that the international community plan in advance for the rapid deployment of civilian police in the post-conflict period – something that was neglected in Iraq, with costs that continue to be felt today. The Iraq experience also underlines the fact that effectively reestablishing security means far more than simply ensuring that looting and violent crime are kept in check: it also involves ensuring that basic daily needs are met and that people have adequate food, water, shelter, medical care, and so on. After more than a decade of well-intentioned but flawed interventions, it has become increasingly clear that the various aspects of post-conflict reconstruction must be addressed in a *coordinated* way: when security, economic issues, civil society, and governmental issues are all dealt with by separate offices operating on more or less separate tracks, confusion and problems easily multiply. Perhaps most critically of all, we know from past failures that there is no "one size fits all" template for rebuilding the rule of law in post-conflict settings: to be successful, programs to rebuild the rule of law must respect and respond to the unique cultural characteristics and needs of each post-intervention society.

Much of this may sound obvious, and on some level it is. Nonetheless, the international community and the U.S. foreign policy establishment have been slow to learn these lessons, and slower still to turn abstract insight into concrete policy changes. Much has already been written on the subject of post-conflict reconstruction, but this book strives to fill a need that still remains unmet: to have a single volume available that pulls together the disparate bits of knowledge we have gained in the past decade, particularly regarding the central challenge of building the rule of law, broadly construed to include both the operation of the law itself and the background social and political institutions required to stabilize and promote it. Our goal in this book is to offer enough theoretical, legal, and historical background to enable readers to contextualize and understand the basic dilemmas inherent in interventions designed to build the rule of law, while also offering concrete suggestions for getting it right in the future.

This book is not a how-to manual, but its focus is fundamentally pragmatic: we are less concerned with political and legal theory than with what seems to work on the ground, and what does not. Nonetheless, when it come to creating "the rule of law" in post-intervention settings, we are convinced that understanding what does and doesn't work requires some basic historical and theoretical insights. We present those insights here in what we hope is a straightforward and readable manner before moving on to a detailed analysis of concrete challenges and positive practices.

Although building the rule of law may seem like a rather abstract idea, it can be useful to think of it in the same way we think about building a house. To build a house – and not just any house, but a house that will be sturdy, functional, beautiful, affordable, and appropriate to its geographic and cultural setting – one needs a mix of different insights and skills. First of all, one needs some historical and theoretical background: one will want to know at least a bit about the various ways in which people have designed houses in the past; one will want to understand that houses can be built in many different styles. One will want to understand what the other houses in the area look like: if they all have peaked roofs, there may be a good reason (to enable heavy snow to slide off the roofs easily, for instance). One needs to understand the trade-offs between, for instance, letting in lots of light and ensuring that the house is neither too cold in winter nor too hot in summer. One also needs to know a bit about the physics of houses: how much weight can be borne by walls of different materials? How big of a furnace is necessary to heat a particular space?

At some point, such insights and questions lead to a basic conception of the kind of house it makes sense to build in a particular place. From this more abstract kind of knowledge, one must move through some very practical steps. An architect must create a design for the house: a preliminary blueprint showing how the different rooms will fit together, what will go where, and so on. Good building materials must be obtained as well: solid wood or bricks and mortar and the like. One also needs enough money to pay for the whole edifice, and a contractor who can work well with various subcontractors, with the architect, and with the future occupants. And, most obviously, one must convince the future occupants that this new house is a useful thing to have in the first place – and that being patient during the lengthy construction process is worth the wait.

None of these things is "more important" than the others; the building project will fail if any one of them is ignored, and throughout the planning and building process, continuous attention must be paid to each element. The blueprint needs to be based on an understanding of history, geography, good design principles, and the physics of construction. Building materials need to be appropriate to the blueprint, and everything needs to be matched to the available resources. One needs the right mix of people, personalities, and skills, coordinated well enough to ensure that the mason arrives before the plumber and that the house has a roof before the flooring is installed. Adjustments may have to be made on the fly as unexpected problems and opportunities arise, and all the players must somehow be kept on board throughout the inevitable complications and delays.

This metaphor is elaborate, but apt. When it comes to creating the rule of law, one needs a basic theoretical and historical background, a blueprint, building blocks, money, appropriately skilled people, and a cultural commitment to the underlying project. In efforts to build the rule of law in post-intervention societies, the minimally necessary historical and theoretical background consists of a basic understanding of the legal and historical context in which military interventions occur and an awareness that the rule of law is a complex and culturally situated idea, consisting both of institutions and of a particular set of normative cultural commitments. The "blueprint" for building the rule of law in post-intervention societies is the overarching structural and constitutional arrangement: electoral rules, power-sharing arrangements between political factions or ethnic groups, the division of power between different branches and levels of government, and so on. The "building blocks" for the rule of law might be said to be courts, police, prisons, legislatures, schools, the press, bar associations, and the like. Of course, unlike the bricks and timber that go into physical structures, the institutional building blocks on which the rule of law depends are themselves made up of human beings, with their own hopes, fears, and attitudes, and this makes creating the institutional aspects of the rule of law as complex as any other venture that relies on mobilizing multiple individuals in a common enterprise.

When it comes to the rule of law, there is no neat way to separate out the creation of new or reformed institutions from the creation of new cultural commitments. For that reason, we discuss the ways in which past interventions have been justified and perceived by interveners, bystanders, and "intervenees," for people's beliefs about the legitimacy of a military intervention have a strong effect on their attitudes toward post-conflict projects. When we consider efforts to promote the rule of law, this is particularly true. If an intervention's legality and legitimacy is widely contested, as was the case with the U.S.-led intervention in Iraq, this can complicate postwar efforts to build the rule of law, as we will elaborate. Although legality and legitimacy are not always one and the same – and success can create its own post hoc legitimacy – the stronger the legal basis for an intervention, the greater the prospects that an intervener will enjoy widespread international support for its post-conflict rebuilding efforts.

The problem of resources is more straightforward. Most rule of law efforts are funded by foreign donors, who are often unable or unwilling to make their financial assistance quite match their rhetorical commitment to the rule of law. Problems of coordination are also readily intelligible: to successfully create the rule of law, governments, NGOs, civil society institutions, politicians, and ordinary people must all work together cooperatively and efficiently. And finally, as noted above, there is the role of culture. Just as 19th-century Egyptian governmental efforts to "better" the lot of nomadic tribespeople by constructing houses for them failed when it turned out that the nomads did not particularly value staying in one place and living in houses, so too efforts to build the rule of law in post-intervention societies will inevitably fail if ordinary people lack an underlying cultural commitment to the values associated with the rule of law.

Building the rule of law is a holistic process, and it is almost inevitably marked by internal contradictions. Short-term interests may genuinely conflict with long-term interests (for instance, collaboration with local warlords or militias may be useful in establishing security in the short term but may dangerously empower "spoilers" in the long term). Fostering "local ownership" and respecting local cultural norms may conflict with efficiency interests and international standards. Satisfying minority political participation interests may conflict with satisfying majorities. Promoting the rule of law is not politically neutral, although interveners often like to imagine that it is. In practice, the decisions interveners make necessarily empower some local actors at the expense of others. This incites opposition (sometimes violent), which can in turn force interveners to respond with coercion, which then generates more opposition.

Building the rule of law requires a constant balancing act. As a result, movement toward the rule of law often is not linear, but back and forth. Interveners must constantly make choices among problematic alternatives. But interveners, precisely because they are interveners (and so don't fully understand local culture, interests, or institutions), are often not well positioned to make such choices and may not fully understand the likely consequences.

This does not mean that building the rule of law is a fool's errand. It does mean that is far more difficult than is generally understood. The evidence suggests, however, that interveners can achieve moderate success if they take these complexities into account and plan accordingly. The goal of this book is to help interested actors understand the difficulties of post-conflict rule of law promotion and the conditions, time, energy, resources, and skills required for success. We argue that a constructive approach to building the rule of law must be *ends-based and strategic, adaptive and dynamic, and systemic.* We call this the *synergistic approach* to post-intervention rule of law, and we think it offers a helpful framework for planning, implementing, and evaluating rule of law-related projects.

The structure of this book is straightforward and flows from the architectural metaphor elaborated above. Following this first introductory chapter, we have two chapters containing background historical, legal, and theoretical discussions.

Chapter 2 discusses the international legal framework governing the use of force and its impact on understandings of when military intervention is justified. We examine how the framework set forth in the United Nations Charter has functioned and evolved in practice from the Cold War to the post–9/11 era, noting in particular the growing influence of human rights principles in shaping international understandings of legitimate military intervention. This legal and historical analysis illuminates how international perceptions of an intervention's legitimacy can significantly influence the willingness of states to contribute to post-conflict reconstruction. The chapter also examines the complex question of local perceptions of an intervention's legitimacy and the extent to which intervener compliance with international law is one, among many, contributing factors. Given that promoting the rule of law after military intervention is, in no small part, an effort to convince local actors that law matters, Chapter 2 argues that how interveners conduct themselves – and their ability to maximize their legitimacy among the local population – invariably will influence the success of these efforts.

Building on this, Chapter 3 discusses the elusive idea of the "rule of law." Most scholars and policymakers agree that the rule of law is what protects people against anarchy and arbitrary exercises of power, but there is less agreement about whether the rule of law consists primarily in certain formal structures and processes (elections, constitutions, courts, fair trial guarantees, etc.) or whether the rule of law is a matter mainly of certain substantive commitments (to human rights, for example). Chapter 3 briefly explores this debate and ultimately argues for a very pragmatic conception of the rule of law. A pragmatic conception of the rule of law acknowledges the importance both of institutions and substantive commitments, and relies on international human rights norms as the touchstone for evaluating whether particular practices comport with the rule of law. In Chapter 3, we discuss what it means to conceptualize rule of law programs *synergistically*. The synergistic approach has three main components: (1) we emphasize that rule of law programs must be *ends based and strategic* rather than formalistic or rigidly institutionalist; (2) we argue that rule of law programs must be *adaptive and dynamic*. Because no two societies are alike, programs must be built around local needs and issues and must be flexible enough to change as conditions change; and (3) we also emphasize that building the rule of law requires looking at *systemic* issues. Fair, independent, and efficient courts can contribute to the rule of law only if they are part of a system in which all other components also function, for instance. Thus, narrow and uncoordinated rule of law programs will have little positive effect.

In Chapter 4, we turn from these background questions to more pragmatic considerations. Chapter 4 focuses on blueprints for governance in post-intervention settings: the macro-level political bargains that define what a post-conflict society should look like. Will it be a unitary or a federal state? How will power be shared between various groups? What structures will best balance the interests of majorities with the rights of minorities? The chapter argues that although there is no "one size fits all" blueprint possible, nonetheless there are common features and common problems that recur across particular blueprint types. The chapter explains why blueprints requiring bargains over state identity are more difficult to implement than blueprints settling conflicts over power and resources, and offers suggestions for blueprint design and implementation in future cases.

In Chapters 5 to 7, we turn to the issue of building blocks. Chapter 5 focuses in particular on the critical challenge of ensuring security, broadly defined: meeting basic human needs, getting well-trained civilian police out quickly in the wake of conflicts, and creating the stability that will enable the subsequent development of credible courts and other institutions. We argue that reestablishing a secure environment is a necessary first step to rebuilding the rule of law and that timing is everything: when major fighting ends, there is a critical window of opportunity in which intervening forces can demonstrate that a new sheriff is in town. The failure to move aggressively to establish security early on emboldens spoilers, weakens public confidence, and jeopardizes reconstruction efforts, in a vicious circle. We note that military forces alone possess the capacity to restore security in the immediate wake of an intervention, but military forces lack the capacity for genuine policing, making it crucial to bring in civilian police and rebuild indigenous policing capacity.

Chapter 6 focuses on those aspects of rule of law promotion that may be most familiar to readers: the justice system, including courts, law enforcement, and prisons. But Chapter 6 emphasizes that too many existing rule of law programs view one or more aspects of justice systems in isolation. Instead, they need to be understood as interrelated parts of an exceptionally complex whole. We urge a synergistic approach to justice system reform that focuses on the *ends* that the rule of law should serve, that adaptively and dynamically builds upon existing cultural foundations, and that works for balanced reform in justice institutions, viewed as a system. Courts cannot contribute to the rule of law without police and prisons that also function well, and institutions alone cannot alter the assumptions, habits, and cultural commitments of the actors within them. Moreover, courts, prisons, and police are embedded in the larger society, and creating effective justice systems also requires a focus on access to justice, civil society, education, and informal dispute resolution mechanisms, all of which can sustain (or undermine) the justice system itself.

Chapter 7 looks at the unique challenge of seeking accountability for past atrocities and the impact of these efforts on building the rule of law prospectively. Severe atrocities marked most of the conflicts we examine in this book, and interveners and local leaders alike have faced difficult decisions regarding the importance of criminal accountability, reparations, reconciliation, and other goals, and regarding institutional mechanisms to advance these aims. This chapter explores how international and national priorities can sometimes conflict, and how choices about accountability mechanisms – international tribunals, mixed national/international courts, domestic courts, truth and reconciliation commissions, among others – can influence efforts to rebuild the rule of law in post-conflict societies in a number of ways, including through demonstration effects and domestic capacity-building. We argue that pursuing accountability for the past should be understood as part of a larger effort to strengthen the rule of law prospectively and that accountability processes should be designed with this aim in mind.

Chapter 8 returns to the thorny question of how a substantive commitment to the values underlying the rule of law can be created. In the long term, restructured institutions and reformed legal codes will be effective only if they are buttressed by a widespread cultural commitment to the rule of law on the part of elites and ordinary people alike. This chapter looks more closely at the issue of how rule of law cultures can be created in societies in which law and governance structures have been badly discredited. It notes that interveners can unintentionally undermine the rule of law through poorly planned programs, and outlines several ways interveners can ensure that they at least "do no harm." It then focuses on several issues of particular importance to building rule of law cultures: the role of NGOs and civil society; the role of legal education, including clinics; and programs designed to increase awareness of rights and governance issues, such as community organizing programs, access to justice initiatives, and programs that make use of paralegals and other nonlegally trained advocates and mediators. It emphasizes the importance, in some societies, of traditional informal dispute settlement procedures, especially in poorer and rural communities. Finally, Chapter 8 outlines key issues in creating rule of law cultures: getting to the grassroots; creating a thriving civil society; shaping the next generation;

giving people a stake in rule of law reforms; involving marginalized groups such as women, youth, and minorities; and a willingness to use creative methods and synergies between, for instance, rule of law and antipoverty programs.

Chapter 9 takes on the issue of improving the planning and delivery of international rule of law assistance. It is easy to identify good practices in the abstract, but promoting rule of law in post-conflict societies occurs in a particular institutional context. In the real world, states, international organizations, and NGOs compete, resources are limited, and political constraints are stark and often shifting. This chapter looks at the way these factors shape the capacity of various actors to build the rule of law in the aftermath of military intervention. Among other things, the chapter considers ways to achieve unity of effort among international actors, possible improvements to existing planning mechanisms, means to facilitate donor coordination, and the vital importance of involving local actors and building indigenous capacity in post-conflict reconstruction efforts. Finally, Chapter 10 offers brief concluding observations.

Because of our conviction that building the rule of law requires an integrated approach, we have organized this book thematically, rather than around specific country case studies. Nonetheless, throughout the book we discuss specific examples of failures and successes from recent interventions, to ensure that the discussion remains grounded at all times in the practical.

Much of the important writing on rule of law promotion that has been done in the past has focused on reform efforts in transitional and developing societies, rather than on rule of law in post-intervention societies. Although this book occasionally draws on that literature and mentions examples from such developing and transitional societies, the cases and examples we offer are drawn mainly from societies that have been the subject of major post–Cold War military interventions: Somalia, Haiti, Bosnia, Kosovo, East Timor, Sierra Leone, Liberia, Afghanistan, and Iraq. Such interventions differ in some notable ways from the many ongoing projects to strengthen the rule of law in developing or transitioning societies. On the one hand, the emergency circumstances that trigger intervention, the frequent devastation of institutions in post-conflict settings, and the presence of armed interveners all pose special and distinctive dilemmas for building the rule of law. On the other hand, these very factors – and the dramatic infusion of resources that often characterizes post-intervention societies, at least initially – also offer unique opportunities; governance structures and institutions can often be radically remade in ways that would otherwise be impossible.

Of course, just as post-conflict societies differ from transitional and developing societies, they also differ substantially from one another. Throughout this book, we stress the critical importance of understanding the unique historical and cultural terrain for building the rule of law in each particular country, even as we also aim to provide a thematic discussion of many of the recurring challenges and common elements involved in strengthening the rule of law after interventions. Indeed, although our focus is on intervention and its aftermath, we also hope that the insights we offer in this book may be of relevance to those working to build the rule of law in a broader set of circumstances as well.

All of the authors teach in U.S. law schools, but we approach the issue of post-intervention reconstruction not solely as academics but also as practitioners. We have all served in U.S. government foreign policy positions as well as carving out careers in academia, and some of us have served in the private and NGO sectors as well. Between the three of us, we have experience on the ground in Haiti, Bosnia, Kosovo, East Timor, Liberia, Sierra Leone, and Iraq. In this book we draw on our personal experiences as well as on the experience and insights of many others, because we are convinced that the joint store of knowledge that we and others have built up over the years is worth sharing and discussing.

This book owes a great deal to the hundreds of people we have interviewed over the past few years. Our interviews have taken us from Washington, DC, and New York to Geneva, Brussels, Amsterdam, The Hague, Nigeria, Sierra Leone, Kosovo, Bosnia, Iraq, and East Timor; interviewees have ranged from high-level local, UN, EU, NATO, and U.S. government officials to experts from NGOs and think tanks to soldiers, activists, judges, lawyers, journalists, and others working on the ground in various post-conflict societies. None of this would have been possible without generous financial support from the U.S. Institute of Peace and the Carnegie Corporation, and we remain grateful to both organizations.

This book represents our effort to contribute to the ongoing conversation about how to ensure that military interventions lead to societies that are genuinely better off after the interventions than they were before. It is intended as a resource for foreign policy, military, and humanitarian professionals, for students, for journalists, and for those many "nonexperts" who simply want to understand the world around them, and the reasons for success and failure in the challenging task of rebuilding the rule of law after military interventions.

CHAPTER TWO

Interventions and International Law: Legality and Legitimacy

Armed interventions levy enormous burdens, not least upon those with the capacity and will to mount them. When U.S. Secretary of State Colin Powell, referring to Iraq, opined to the president – "If we break it, sir, we will own it" – he was voicing a practical reality: interveners face far greater pressure today than in earlier eras to help stabilize and rebuild war-torn countries after major combat ends.

As a consequence, decisions to commit forces and resources to foreign interventions are among the most difficult ones that national leaderships face, especially in democratic countries. Governments must be convinced that contributing troops and other personnel serves their national interests and values, that the intervention has a reasonable prospect of success, that lesser strategies – for example, containment – cannot deliver the desired results, and in a larger sense that the benefits of the action outweigh its costs and risks. Recent experience in Iraq and elsewhere has also shown that states are far more likely to participate in an intervention – and contribute to post-conflict reconstruction – if they view the underlying intervention itself as legitimate.

The perceived legitimacy of an intervention will turn on many factors, including how urgent and compelling the circumstances are in the target state. Are terrorist groups using the territory to train operatives and launch attacks on other countries, with the support of the local regime? Are state actors or nonstate groups perpetrating horrific atrocities, in violation of fundamental norms of international law? Are threats to national and regional security increasing? Have diplomatic efforts to address the situation proved unavailing?

Without question, the presence of clear legal authority to intervene will also be highly significant in convincing other states that military action is legitimate. That sense of legitimacy can, in turn, substantially influence the willingness of governments to support or contribute to the intervention. Legality by itself is no guarantee of support, to be sure. But the *absence* of agreed legal authority can undermine the chances of building or sustaining a committed coalition. The fact that the U.S. military intervention in Afghanistan in 2001 was widely viewed as lawful self-defense, for example, made it easier for other states to contribute forces and resources than in the highly contested 2003 Iraq War. In general, the further interventions are from the two clear agreed legal bases for using force under the United Nations (UN) Charter – in self-defense or with Security Council authorization – the greater the risk that other governments will dispute their legitimacy and be reluctant to support them.

Legality and legitimacy, of course, are not precisely the same thing. Some interventions – such NATO's use of force in Kosovo or the intervention by a coalition of Nigerian-led forces in Liberia – were widely viewed as legitimate even though they were neither authorized by the Security Council in advance nor undertaken in self-defense. In the case of Kosovo, for instance, a substantial majority of the countries on the Security Council regarded the intervention as justified even though it was not possible, given the positions of Russia and China, to obtain the Council's authorization. Furthermore, in cases where an intervention succeeds in suppressing widely recognized dangers or abuses, the very fact of its success will tend to overshadow the question of its technical legality. To a degree, success creates its own legitimacy.

The problem is that few interventions are ever so straightforward, and the prospects of keeping critical states engaged in the midst of the inevitable setbacks are greater if they are convinced of the legality and legitimacy of the enterprise at the outset. Legality and legitimacy at the front end can reinforce the willingness of states to stay the course when the going gets tough. Given that interventions increasingly involve long-term efforts at political, social, and economic transformation, their legitimacy will constantly be reassessed by relevant actors as circumstances evolve on the ground; a strong consensus about the intervention's legitimacy from the beginning can increase the prospects for ongoing cooperation from both local and international actors. Furthermore, in the face of inevitable skepticism regarding the motives of those most inclined to prosecute an intervention, a broad-based multilateral coalition can be critical in conveying the message that the action reflects more than just the self-interest of one or a few nations, however powerful.

The concrete objectives that interveners pursue will also profoundly shape perceptions of the intervention's legitimacy. Here again international legal norms are relevant. Whatever factors trigger states to intervene in the first place, they increasingly face international pressure to help build governance structures and institutions that advance self-determination and protect the basic international human rights of the local population, while respecting the unique culture of the people whose future is directly at stake. Gone are the days when countries could intervene to seek territory and resources for themselves without regard for the aspirations and needs of the local population. Moreover, the ability of intervening states to act in a manner consistent with fundamental principles of international law – including human rights and international humanitarian law – will influence not only international support for but also local acceptance of the intervention's legitimacy.

Indeed, the presence or absence of perceived legitimacy is particularly crucial at the local level. The interveners, after all, need the local population not merely to participate in the hard work of rebuilding but to assume responsibility for their own destinies over the longer term. As we argue below, however, local perceptions in post-conflict situations can often be highly volatile – driven by bouts of euphoria, disappointment, relief, and resentment – and interveners cannot presume local goodwill and support for their actions, however well intentioned.[1]

Interveners who aim to strengthen the rule of law in conflict-ridden societies ignore local and international perceptions of legitimacy at their peril. If interveners want to be successful in building the rule of law after intervention, they will need to take seriously the international legal norms that, as noted earlier, will shape perceptions about whether the intervention is legitimate and worth supporting. That sense of legitimacy may be critical in building and sustaining multilateral coalitions that can help to ameliorate domestic skepticism of outside interveners in the difficult, long-term process of strengthening the rule of law after the fighting stops.

Our present way of understanding the relevant international legal norms – concerning the use of force, the justifications for military interventions, and the constraints upon their legitimate objectives – emerged from and evolved out of the post-World War II institutional and legal framework of the United Nations and its Charter. As we shall see, international law concerning intervention is by no means static. Strategic realities have continually affected both how states have interpreted the basic rules of the UN Charter and the extent to which human rights principles have influenced the fact or character of interventions. Thus, we will examine how the international legal framework has functioned and evolved in practice from the Cold War era to the immediate post–Cold War years to the exceedingly difficult period since 9/11. With a special emphasis on the years since the end of the Cold War, we discuss the growing influence of human rights principles in shaping international understandings of legitimate military intervention. We also examine the complex question of local perceptions of an intervention's legitimacy and the extent to which intervener compliance with international law is one, among many, contributing factors. Because promoting the rule of law after military intervention is, in part, an effort to convince local actors that

---

[1] For a useful discussion of one particular case, *see* James A. Schear, *Bosnia's Post-Dayton Traumas,* 104 FOREIGN POLICY 87 (1996).

law matters, the interveners' own conduct – and their ability to maximize their legitimacy among the local population – inescapably will influence the outcome of the intervention.

The legal and historical analysis presented in this chapter provides the context for the rest of the book in two important respects. Quite straightforwardly, the legal and historical materials discussed here provide the substantive framework for what follows. The issues and problems analyzed in this chapter recur, in one way or another, in every subsequent chapter. Just as importantly, however, what we hope to illustrate here is the complex interaction of international law with the social and political realities on the ground, both locally and internationally. For it is this complex and ever changing interaction that must be understood and taken into account if social and political stability – and with it, the rule of law – are to be achieved in the wake of military intervention.

I. THE INTERNATIONAL LEGAL FRAMEWORK: THE UN CHARTER AND THE USE OF FORCE

The United Nations Charter has been the centerpiece of the international legal framework governing the use of force since 1945. The Charter represents an effort to construct effective barriers against aggression and to subject intervention to agreed upon international rules – an effort that stands out against the larger swath of human history during which states were largely free to resort to war as a matter of state policy.[2] The Charter's founders aimed, above all, "to save succeeding generations from the scourge

---

[2] The concept of war as a sovereign right of states largely prevailed from 1648, when the system of secular nation-states developed in Europe following the Peace of Westphalia, until 1914. The devastation of World War I led states to establish the League of Nations, which aimed to limit the resort to force in international relations. The League's Covenant, which took effect in 1920, placed some restrictions on force but did not categorically prohibit resort to war. The members of the League agreed, for example, to settle their disputes by peaceful means through arbitration, judicial settlement, or action by the League's Council, and they agreed not to resort to war until three months after a decision had been reached – a cooling-off period designed to slow any rush to war. Members also agreed not to go to war if the other state complied with the decision. If a member resorted to war in violation of the Covenant, the League of Nations envisioned that member states would take collective action, such as economic and diplomatic sanctions; but the League Council only had the power to recommend that its members contribute military forces. In short, the League lacked an effective enforcement mechanism as subsequent events would so clearly show. The 1928 Kellogg–Briand Pact was more categorical than the League Covenant: it condemned resort to war for the solution of international disputes or as an instrument of national policy, and the parties pledged to resolve their disputes peacefully. But the Kellogg–Briand Pact failed to clearly address the question of the use of force short of war, and it established no enforcement mechanism. The clear limitations of these instruments, and the horrors of World War II, spurred renewed efforts to place international legal limits on the use of force.

of war" and "to ensure, by the acceptance of principles and the institution of methods, that armed force shall not be used, save in the common interest."[3] Two hardheaded and realistic leaders, President Franklin Delano Roosevelt and Prime Minister Winston Churchill, led the effort to create an organization that could act effectively and collectively against aggression and other threats to the peace, within a framework that placed constraints on the unilateral use of force.

The Charter's fundamental principles include the central nonintervention norm set forth in Article 2(4), which affirms that states "shall refrain in their international relations from the threat or use of force against the territorial integrity or political independence of any state, or in any other manner inconsistent with the Purposes of the United Nations." But the Charter's architects understood that rules limiting the use of force were insufficient without a robust enforcement mechanism that could draw on the military and economic resources of the great powers, whose forces together had been necessary to defeat Hitler.

Thus, the Charter gave a body of states – the United Nations Security Council – primary responsibility for maintaining international peace and security, as well as far-reaching enforcement authority for that purpose. Chapter VII of the Charter explicitly empowers the Security Council to respond, with military force if necessary, to threats to the peace, breaches of the peace, or acts of aggression, in order to restore and maintain international peace and security. The Charter also clearly recognizes the right of states to take immediate action in self-defense and affirms, in Article 51, that "Nothing in the present Charter shall impair the inherent right of individual or collective self-defense if an armed attack occurs against a Member of the United Nations...." The prospect of reliance on regional self-defense alliances was clearly encompassed by this affirmation of the right of "collective" as well as individual self-defense. In addition, in Chapter VIII, the UN Charter encourages regional arrangements – consistent with the United Nations' purposes and principles – to resolve local disputes peacefully or, if necessary, to take "enforcement action" with the Security Council's authorization. The Charter, in short, provides for the lawful use of force in two clear situations: when authorized by the Security Council under its Chapter VII authority or in exercise of the right of self-defense under Article 51.

The Charter was designed to be both stabilizing and empowering. The very existence of the Charter – and the core prohibition on aggression reflected in Article 2(4) – forced states to explain and justify their decisions to use force and provided at least some limitation on the purposes for which force could be used.[4] At the same time, the Charter empowered the

[3] Preamble to United Nations Charter.

[4] Professor Louis Henkin put it this way: "The occasions and the causes of war remain. What has become obsolete is the notion that nations are as free to indulge it as ever, and the death

Security Council to use force collectively in the common interest to protect international peace and security.

The Charter, though ambitious, was a creature of its time in many respects. Interstate aggression was the primary threat on the minds of the Charter's framers. The big powers of the day were expected to contribute significant forces to protect the peace, and they received the critical veto power on the Security Council – a privilege that generated controversy from the start. Thus, no effective enforcement action could be taken against the Council's five permanent members – the United States, Britain, China, Russia, and France – or their interests.[5] The Charter's strong nonintervention principle, moreover, was clearly weighted in favor of the status quo. Change in the state order was to be achieved peacefully, not through the use of force. The Charter also expressly affirmed that the United Nations was "based on the principle of the sovereign equality" of states – notwithstanding their vastly differing governmental structures and internal conditions – and the Charter made clear that the UN's authority to intervene in "matters which are essentially within the domestic jurisdiction of any state" had limits.[6]

Yet the UN Charter was also designed to be flexible and capable of adapting to new circumstances and threats. The Security Council's power to respond to "threats to the peace," for instance, is far-reaching: the Council can act preemptively *to prevent* emerging "*threats* to the peace" and is not limited to responding only to "breaches of the peace" or "acts of aggression." Moreover, the Charter does not limit or define these terms, leaving to the Security Council the flexibility to make these determinations in concrete circumstances.[7] Also, the Security Council's authority to take action is broad and includes a wide spectrum of potential responses, from diplomatic measures to economic sanctions to the use of force. The only limits on the Council

---

of that notion is accepted in the Charter." Louis Henkin, *The Reports of the Death of Article 2(4) Are Greatly Exaggerated*, 65 AM. J. INT'L. L. 544, 545 (1971).

[5] Since the Charter was adopted, the Chinese seat, originally held by the Nationalist government of Taiwan, was assumed by the People's Republic of China, and Russia assumed the seat originally held by the Soviet Union upon its dissolution.

[6] UN Charter, Art. 2(1), Art. 2(7).

[7] The Charter's founders left it to the Security Council to make these judgments in light of the circumstances. Ruth Russell, A HISTORY OF THE UNITED NATIONS CHARTER (1958), at 464–465, 669–672. In 1945 Britain's Lord Halifax stressed the importance of giving the United Nations and its members the flexibility to deal with new situations that could not be foreseen. As he explained, "instead of trying to govern the actions of the members and the organs of the United Nations by precise and intricate codes of procedure, we have preferred to lay down purposes and principles under which they are to act. And by that means, we hope to insure that they act in conformity with the express desires of the nations assembled here, while, at the same time, we give them freedom to accommodate their actions to circumstances which today no man can foresee. We all want our Organization to have life.... We want it to be free to deal with all the situations that may arise in international relations. We do not want to lay down rules which may, in the future, be the signpost for the guilty and a trap for the innocent." UNCIO Selected Documents (1945), at 537.

are that it act consistently with the "purposes and principles" of the United Nations.[8]

Promoting respect for human rights is one of these fundamental purposes,[9] and the UN's members expressly agreed in the Charter to advance this goal.[10] A number of states argued, moreover, that extreme violations of human rights could create a threat to the peace warranting a Security Council response.[11] But the Charter's drafters did not create a "humanitarian intervention" exception to the UN Charter's limits on the *unilateral* use of force.[12] Indeed, the Charter's principles of nonintervention and state sovereignty were at odds with any claimed unilateral right to use force in response to another state's human rights violations.

The UN's member states did commit themselves, however, "to take joint and separate action" in cooperation with the United Nations to promote "universal respect for, and observance of, human rights."[13] Over time, the UN Charter's human rights provisions were supplemented by a growing body of international human rights instruments. In 1948, the UN General Assembly adopted the Universal Declaration of Human Rights, affirming core civil and political rights as well as economic and social rights, and expressly affirming the equal rights of men and women.[14] The Universal Declaration

---

[8] UN Charter, Art. 24(2).

[9] Specifically, Article 1(3) of the UN Charter affirms that it is a purpose of the United Nations "To achieve international cooperation in . . . promoting and encouraging respect for human rights and for fundamental freedoms for all without distinction as to race, sex, language, or religion. . . ."

[10] Article 55 provides that the United Nations shall promote "universal respect for, and observance of, human rights," and all member states pledge, in Article 56, to "take joint and separate action" to achieve that purpose.

[11] The discussions regarding Article 2(7) at San Francisco in 1945 reveal considerable awareness that internal conditions within a country, including grievous violations of human rights, could potentially pose a threat to peace and security and thus give rise to enforcement action by the United Nations. Sensitivity on this point is not surprising given the recent horrors of the Holocaust. The Report of the Subcommittee on the UN's purposes and principles recognized that if human rights and fundamental freedoms "were grievously outraged so as to create conditions which threaten peace or to obstruct the application of provisions of the Charter, then they cease to be the sole concern of each state." Doc. 723, I/1/A/19, *Report of Rapporteur, Subcommittee I/1/A to Committee I/1 (Preamble, Purposes and Principles), Documents of the United Nations Conference on International Organization, San Francisco 1945*, Vol. 6, June 1, 1945, at 705.

[12] Sean Murphy, HUMANITARIAN INTERVENTION (1996), at 70–75. In previous eras, some states had claimed a right of humanitarian intervention – that is, a right to use force in response to severe human rights abuses within another state, without the consent of its government. But this doctrine was controversial and fraught with potential for abuse. Intervening states frequently had other goals and motivations in using force, and other states generally rejected claims of humanitarian intervention.

[13] UN Charter, Arts. 55, 56.

[14] Forty-eight states voted in favor, no states opposed, and eight countries, including the Soviet Union, abstained. A landmark development, the Universal Declaration affirms core civil and political rights, such as a right to liberty; freedom of thought, expression, and association;

was followed by a series of major multilateral human rights treaties drafted under UN sponsorship and now ratified by the vast majority of states. These treaties include the Genocide Convention of 1948; the International Convention on the Elimination of All Forms of Racial Discrimination, adopted by the General Assembly in 1965; followed in 1966 by the International Covenant on Civil and Political Rights, and the International Covenant on Economic, Social and Cultural Rights; the Convention on the Elimination of All Forms of Discrimination Against Women adopted in 1979, followed in 1984 by the Convention Against Torture, in 1989 by the Convention on the Rights of the Child, and in 2000 by an important protocol restricting the use of child soldiers.[15] In the decades following the Universal Declaration, parallel human rights developments also occurred at the regional level.[16] Together with customary international law principles, including fundamental norms binding on all states, these multilateral human rights treaties provide the legal framework for the protection of international human rights.[17]

Another critical legal development during the 20th century that bears directly on the use of force is the international law of armed conflict. This body of law – which governs *how* force is used and the treatment of both combatants and noncombatants – has developed substantially since the Hague Regulations at the turn of the 20th century; it now includes the four Geneva Conventions of 1949, the 1977 protocols, and statutes adopted in the 1990s establishing international tribunals to prosecute perpetrators of

prohibition against slavery; freedom of religion; right to a fair and public trial; presumption of innocence; prohibition against torture or cruel and inhuman treatment or punishment; protection against arbitrary interference with privacy, family, home, or correspondence; and prohibition against arbitrary arrest. Thanks to the efforts of Eleanor Roosevelt, it also goes further and provides for the equal rights of men and women. The Universal Declaration also enumerates certain economic and social rights, such as the right to work, to equal pay for equal work, to join trade unions, and to a decent standard of living, including adequate health care, food, clothing, and housing, the right to education, and the right to participate fully in the cultural life of the community.

[15] These treaties are available on the Web site of the Office of the UN High Commissioner for Human Rights, at http://www.ohchr.org/.

[16] The European Convention for the Protection of Human Rights and Fundamental Freedoms was signed in 1950 and took effect three years later. In Latin America, the Charter of the Organization of American States (OAS), which took effect in 1951, provided for the establishment of an Inter-American Commission on Human Rights, which was subsequently formed in 1960. The American Convention on Human Rights entered into force in 1978. The Organization of African Unity adopted the African Charter on Human and Peoples' Rights in 1981, which entered into force five years later.

[17] Multilateral treaties, at both the international and regional levels, are one of the main sources of human rights law. In addition there is customary international law as well as decisions and actions by UN organs and other international and regional bodies, including judicial tribunals. Substantively, international human rights standards include *jus cogens* norms – that is, rules binding on all states – such as the prohibition against slavery, against genocide, and against torture.

war crimes, crimes against humanity, and genocide.[18] As the International Court of Justice – itself a creation of the United Nations – has underscored, the "cardinal principles" of the international law of armed conflict are the principle of distinction between combatants and civilians – that civilians should not be made the object of attack – and the principle that combatants should not be caused unnecessary suffering.[19] States have a powerful interest in reciprocal treatment by other states, which can serve as an important incentive to comply with these international legal rules. But violations are all too frequent, and holding perpetrators of atrocities accountable remains an enormous challenge, as we discuss in Chapter 7.

When viewed in a longer-term perspective, the developments in international law achieved by the end of the 20th century are quite remarkable. Despite setbacks and continuing problems of noncompliance, states had nevertheless agreed to fundamental international legal rules governing the use of force and protecting human rights. These fundamental international legal developments of the 20th century together represent a growing, if imperfect, "rule of law" internationally that, at a minimum, sets basic parameters on how states should behave toward each other and internally.

The challenge, of course, is how to enforce these basic rules, and this has long been the most difficult issue in international law. States committing egregious human rights violations generally reject criticism of their behavior and stubbornly defend their own sovereignty.[20] States and nonstate

---

[18] *See* Adam Roberts & Richard Guelff, DOCUMENTS ON THE LAWS OF WAR (3rd ed. 2000). These statutes include the 1998 Rome Statute of the International Criminal Court. Id. at 667.

[19] International Court of Justice, Legality of the Threat or Use of Nuclear Weapons, Advisory Opinion of 8 July 1996, para. 78. As the Court wrote: "The cardinal principles contained in the texts constituting the fabric of humanitarian law are the following. The first is aimed at the protection of the civilian population and civilian objects and establishes the distinction between combatants and non-combatants; States must never make civilians the object of attack and must consequently never use weapons that are incapable of distinguishing between civilian and military targets. According to the second principle, it is prohibited to cause unnecessary suffering to combatants: it is accordingly prohibited to use weapons causing them such harm or uselessly aggravating their suffering. In application of that second principle, States do not have unlimited freedom of choice in the weapons they use."

[20] The challenge of securing greater protection for basic human rights around the globe is enormous. International human rights standards and institutions have made a significant contribution, but enduring protection clearly depends critically on changes in national legislation and legal institutions as well as in social, political, and economic conditions. Human rights violations are frequently rooted in deep and "longstanding political, economic, and social ills" often fueled by "[p]rejudice, ignorance, hunger, disease, greed, and political corruption." Thomas Buergenthal, *International Human Rights Law and Institutions: Accomplishments and Prospects*, 63 WASH. L. REV. 1, 18 (1988). *See also* Richard Bilder, *An Overview of International Human Rights Law*, in GUIDE TO INTERNATIONAL HUMAN RIGHTS PRACTICES (H. Hanum, ed. 1983), at 17. Autocratic and corrupt governments often inflict violations on their citizens. In addition, in many parts of the globe, failed states, in which

actors alike have used force in ways that have violated fundamental rules of international law and have led to enormous suffering. Furthermore, the simultaneous development of international norms limiting the use of force and norms protecting human rights paradoxically contained the seeds of a tension – a potential clash between the UN Charter's rules restricting military intervention, without Security Council authorization, in response to internal conflicts, on the one hand, and human rights norms that clearly prohibit atrocities within states, on the other. In the last decade of the 20th century, the Security Council responded to this tension, in some cases at least, by authorizing collective interventions in response to threats to peace and security that did not involve external aggression but rather internal or mixed conflicts with dire humanitarian consequences. Examples include the interventions in Somalia and Haiti.[21] But there were clear limits on the willingness of key Security Council members – determined to protect state sovereignty and vulnerable themselves to criticism on human rights grounds – to authorize military action in situations that did not involve cross-border conflict. This tension came to the fore in Kosovo when NATO states, responding to a humanitarian emergency and seeking to halt grave human rights abuses, used force without authorization from the Security Council.

Whether the Security Council is capable of agreed, effective action has always been shaped fundamentally by the attitudes of its five permanent members and by their relationships with one another. These relationships have evolved since the difficult Cold War period, but substantial challenges to forging agreement on interventions in the "common interest" persist even as new threats to peace and security have clearly emerged.

basic security and law and order have broken down, pose severe threats to human rights, with rapes, kidnappings, summary executions, and arbitrary exercise of power by local warlords denying people the most basic protections of life. *See* Michael Ignatieff, *State Failure and Nation-Building*, in HUMANITARIAN INTERVENTION: ETHICAL, LEGAL, AND POLITICAL DILEMMAS (J. L. Holzgrefe & Robert O. Keohane, eds., 2003). In the face of very limited resources and ongoing instability, the challenge of establishing the basic security that is a precondition for the protection of human rights can be enormous. Effective responses can take many years of effort and substantial resources. Despite the obstacles and enormous challenges to protecting even the most basic of human rights in many countries, international human rights law and institutions – including international and regional tribunals, UN special rapporteurs, and other mechanisms – have contributed concretely over time to the development of standards that enable states, individuals, and nongovernmental organizations to shine a critical spotlight on abusive practices and galvanize support to change those practices.

[21] *See* discussion in Part II of this chapter. Additional examples of mixed conflicts include Bosnia, Liberia, and Sierra Leone, discussed below. We disagree, as has the Security Council itself through its practice, with Michael Glennon's narrow reading of the scope of the Council's authority under Chapter VII to respond to threats to the peace. Michael J. Glennon, LIMITS OF LAW, PREROGATIVES OF POWER: INTERVENTIONISM AFTER KOSOVO (2001), at 101–143.

II. FROM THE COLD WAR TO THE POST–COLD WAR PERIOD: INTERVENTION IN AN EVOLVING STRATEGIC CONTEXT

The Cold War's strategic realities – marked by the U.S.–Soviet superpower confrontation – constrained the effective operation of the UN Charter system from the start. With the exception of Korea in 1950, the Security Council was largely stalemated from taking action in conflicts touching the interests of the major powers.[22] Regional security alliances, such as NATO, functioned as the primary bulwark of international security during the Cold War period. The Security Council was able to authorize peacekeeping missions in a number of situations when the major powers found this to be in their interest, and agreed parameters for successful peacekeeping developed over time.[23] But the Security Council's role in major crises remained severely limited.

Despite numerous interventions and counterinterventions during the bitter Cold War years, no clear agreed basis for using force (other than in self-defense) emerged during this period. The Soviet Union made dubious claims of intervention by "invitation" in its sphere of influence in Eastern Europe. U.S. arguments in favor of prodemocratic intervention engendered controversy.[24] Some military interventions with a humanitarian effect – such as Tanzania's intervention in Uganda to remove the brutal Idi Amin from power – were tolerated or supported by states because they occurred outside the sphere of great power interest and were viewed as arguably in the common interest. But states declined to embrace "humanitarian intervention" as a new legal basis for using force unilaterally – as opposed to seeing it as a potentially excusable breach of the Charter in exceptional circumstances.[25]

Even if states, on occasion, tolerated some interventions with a humanitarian purpose or effect, no *collective* efforts to rebuild the rule of law or reshape governmental authority structures after intervention were possible during the Cold War years. Both strategic and normative factors constrained any such efforts. Strategically, as the divisive experience in the Congo illustrated,

---

[22] Even the UN-authorized response to North Korea's invasion of South Korea was made possible only by the temporary absence of the Soviet Union from the Security Council. Once the Soviets returned, the General Assembly recommended subsequent measures in Korea under the Uniting for Peace Resolution.

[23] These include the consent of the parties, impartiality of the operation, nonuse of force except in self-defense, a clear and workable mandate, and adequate personnel and financing. *See* United Nations Department of Public Information, THE BLUE HELMETS: A REVIEW OF UNITED NATIONS PEACE-KEEPING (1985), at 3–5; THE EVOLUTION OF UN PEACEKEEPING: CASE STUDIES AND COMPARATIVE ANALYSIS (William J. Durch, ed. 1993).

[24] Louis Henkin, *The Use of Force: Law and U.S. Policy*, in RIGHT V. MIGHT: INTERNATIONAL LAW AND THE USE OF FORCE (1991), at 44, 54–56.

[25] For analysis, *see* Murphy, HUMANITARIAN INTERVENTION, *supra* note 12, at 142–143; Tom J. Farer, *An Inquiry into the Legitimacy of Humanitarian Intervention*, in LAW AND FORCE IN THE NEW INTERNATIONAL ORDER (Lori F. Damrosch & David J. Scheffer, eds., 1991), at 185–201.

each side in the Cold War standoff viewed interventions by the other side or its allies as an effort to seek strategic advantage; this reality precluded any long-term cooperation on nation-building. Normatively, the decolonization movement and the end of the UN trusteeship system was fueled by the belief that states should be free to govern themselves without undue outside inter-ference. Even scholars writing in support of "humanitarian intervention" during the Cold War period tended to argue for modest intervention with only a limited impact on authority structures.[26] This would change, however, when a new strategic and normative environment made possible collective efforts to rebuild troubled states.

The end of the Cold War transformed the strategic context in which inter-ventions have occurred. No longer mortal enemies competing for strategic strongholds around the globe, the United States and Russia began to reassess deployments and to selectively disengage from some conflict zones. In east-ern Europe, new possibilities for democracy emerged, and in western Europe the movement toward integration gained new momentum. At the same time, in many parts of the world, conflicts previously overshadowed by the Cold War broke sharply into focus.

With the Cold War over, the prospects for international agreement on particular interventions improved. No longer frozen by the U.S.–Soviet con-frontation, the UN Security Council was able to authorize collective military intervention in a variety of circumstances. The major powers did not always provide needed forces, but the ending of the Cold War opened the door to broader possibilities for agreed action just as a more diverse array of threats to the peace – brutal civil wars, ethnic strife, and desperate humanitarian emergencies – galvanized international attention.

Normative trends also influenced international responses to these threats. A growing emphasis on the human rights of individuals increasingly chal-lenged traditional conceptions of state sovereignty – particularly since the major powers no longer viewed every conflict through the restrictive prism of Cold War tensions. Under the human rights treaties adopted in the decades following World War II, states took on clear duties not to commit genocide or torture or to otherwise violate the fundamental human rights of those within their borders. States that egregiously abridged human rights became increasingly subject to criticism from other states and from a growing global network of nongovernmental organizations. Time and again, moreover, a globalized media and international NGOs spotlighted attention on violent conflicts throughout the world, increasing normative pressures for some kind of international response to escalating humanitarian emergencies that spilled over across borders or involved extreme atrocities. But a related challenge

---

[26] *See, e.g.,* Michael J. Bazyler, *Reexamining the Doctrine of Humanitarian Intervention in Light of the Atrocities in Kampuchea and Ethiopia,* 23 STAN. J. INT'L L. 547, 604–606 (1987).

soon emerged: to what extent could the international community agree on intervention in the common interest, or follow through to help rebuild shattered states after intervention?

A. UN Security Council-Authorized Interventions

The 1990s revealed both new possibilities for agreed international intervention under the UN Charter system and clear limitations on those possibilities. The Security Council's unified response to Iraq's 1990 invasion of Kuwait inaugurated the decade on an auspicious note. Authorizing "all necessary means" to liberate Kuwait and "restore international peace and security in the area,"[27] the states on the Council responded to a classic case of aggression with a clear authorization of collective force. The aftermath of the war, however, particularly the question of how to respond to Saddam Hussein's repression of the Kurds in northern Iraq, foreshadowed the difficult challenges that would soon preoccupy the Council in addressing internal conflicts, even those with cross-border effects. The Council demanded that Saddam Hussein stop repressing Iraqi civilians and called on states to assist in providing humanitarian relief, but the Council stopped short of invoking its Chapter VII authority to authorize force.[28] Moreover, the Council's unity in imposing clear disarmament obligations on Saddam Hussein in 1991 at the end of the Persian Gulf War was not matched by unity of response as Saddam defied and materially breached those duties in the years that followed.

The Security Council did forge agreement on international intervention in a significant number of cases during the 1990s, however. The Council's authorizations in the cases of Somalia, Haiti, Bosnia, and East Timor, for instance, showed far more varied and flexible understandings of "threats to the peace" as a basis for collective action than classic aggression, even if some states were wary about moving in this direction. These authorizations underscored both the greater political latitude for agreement in the post–Cold War period and the adaptability of the Charter system to new circumstances.

In the case of Somalia, the Council in 1992 authorized a coalition of predominantly American forces to establish "a secure environment for humanitarian relief operations" after finding that the "magnitude of the human tragedy" in Somalia was a threat to international peace and security.[29] Later, once relief was flowing, the Council authorized a far more ambitious "nation-building" operation, which – in the face of hostile local warlords

---

[27] S.C. Res. 678 (1990), at para. 2.

[28] *See* S.C. Res. 688 (1991); Jane E. Stromseth, *Iraq's Repression of Its Civilian Population: Collective Responses and Continuing Challenges*, in ENFORCING RESTRAINT: COLLECTIVE INTERVENTION IN INTERNAL CONFLICTS (Lori Fisler Damrosch, ed., 1993), at 77–117.

[29] S.C. Res. 794 (1992).

and insufficient international resources – ultimately failed dramatically to achieve its goals.[30]

In Haiti, after determining in 1994 that the deteriorating situation threatened peace and security in the region, the Security Council authorized military intervention to "facilitate the departure" of the de facto regime of General Raoul Cedras and restore the government of elected President Jean-Bertrand Aristide to power.[31] A follow-on peacekeeping and reconstruction effort made some headway, but subsequent political developments in Haiti brought that country full circle to the brink of anarchy. Then, a decade after Aristide was restored to power, he resigned and departed under pressure, as rebel forces approached the capital; and the Security Council authorized a multinational force to provide security to support "the constitutional political process under way in Haiti" and to facilitate humanitarian and other international assistance.[32]

In Bosnia-Herzegovina, which dissolved into a brutal civil war after the breakup of the former Yugoslavia, the Security Council in 1993 authorized NATO to use its air power to help protect UN-designated safe areas from attack.[33] Later, in the face of escalating "ethnic cleansing" by Bosnian Serb

---

[30] S.C. Res. 814 (1993). With the Clinton Administration's support, the Council in March 1993 authorized the United Nations Operation in Somalia (UNOSOM II) to replace the U.S.-commanded operation and to engage in a number of tasks. In addition to emphasizing the disarmament of Somali factions, the Security Council also authorized UNOSOM II to assist in the economic rehabilitation of Somalia, promote political reconciliation, and help reestablish political institutions and civil administration throughout the country. S.C. Res. 814, section B, para. 7, section A, para. 4. Control of the Somalia operation passed from the United States to the United Nations in May 1993. But the more ambitious goals were not matched with adequate forces, and a series of disasters, including the brutal murder of Pakistani peacekeepers by Somali forces, a subsequent unsuccessful campaign to arrest warlord General Aideed, and the loss of sixteen American soldiers in an ill-fated raid on an Aideed stronghold, led in 1994 to the withdrawal of U.S. forces, the subsequent withdrawal of other international forces, and an end to this ambitious nation-building exercise. *See generally* John L. Hirsch & Robert B. Oakley, SOMALIA AND OPERATION RESTORE HOPE (1995); Jane E. Stromseth, *Collective Force and Constitutional Responsibility: War Powers in the Post-Cold War Era,* 50 U. MIAMI L. REV. 145, 170–171 (1996).

[31] S.C. Res. 940 (1994), at 2. The Council also authorized UN member states "to establish and maintain a secure and stable environment that will permit implementation of the Governors Island Agreement," id., in which the military regime of General Raoul Cedras had agreed to relinquish power.

[32] S.C. Res. 1529 (2004), para. 2.

[33] S.C. Res. 836 (1993). More precisely, this resolution authorized the United Nations Protection Force (UNPROFOR) in former Yugoslavia "to deter attacks against the safe areas," id., para. 5, and "acting in self-defence, to take the necessary measures, including the use of force, in reply to bombardments against the safe areas by any of the parties or to armed incursion into them." Id., para. 9. In addition, the Security Council in Resolution 836 decided that "Member states, acting nationally or through regional organizations or arrangements, may take, under the authority of the Security Council and subject to close coordination with the Secretary-General and UNPROFOR, all necessary measures, through the use of air power, in and around the safe areas in the Republic of Bosnia and Herzegovina, to support

forces and the shelling of civilians in Sarajevo, NATO air forces took more decisive military action leading to the 1995 Dayton Accords.[34]

At the end of the decade, Australian-led forces authorized by the Security Council (with begrudging Indonesian consent) helped bring stability to East Timor after its historic referendum in favor of independence.[35] The Council also authorized the UN Transitional Administration in East Timor (UNTAET) and gave it far-reaching executive and legislative power as the United Nations assisted the self-determination of the Timorese people by supporting their transition to independent statehood.[36]

These UN-authorized interventions in the 1990s demonstrated the Security Council's willingness to define "threats to the peace" more broadly and flexibly than ever before to include humanitarian emergencies, the overthrow of democratically elected leaders, extreme repression of civilian populations and cross-border refugee flows threatening regional security, and failure to hold perpetrators of major atrocities accountable.[37] The Security Council, in short, was prepared, at least in some cases, to authorize military intervention in response to anarchy, humanitarian emergencies, and threats to democracy – invoking reasons for intervention that went well beyond aggression or classic cross-border threats to peace and security.

The key to these authorizations was the willingness of a major power or regional organization to contribute significant forces – *and* agreement by the Council's five permanent members not to oppose collective action. But even in cases of severe atrocities and desperate humanitarian need, these conditions were not always present. Rwanda illustrated this dramatically.

When a devastating genocide engulfed Rwanda in 1994, the members of the United Nations failed dramatically to act effectively to stop the killing.[38] This collective failure to intervene left hundreds of thousands of desperate human beings with no hope of survival. The minimal international response, and the reluctance of the member states of the Security Council to commit significant forces even in the face of such overwhelming need, made at least

UNPROFOR in the performance of its mandate set out in paragraphs 5 and 9 above." Id., para. 10.

[34] *See* Richard Holbrooke, To End a War (1998).

[35] S.C. Res. 1264 (1999) (INTERFET).

[36] S.C. Res. 1272 (1999) (UNTAET). Upon attaining independence in May 2002, East Timor became the Democratic Republic of Timor Leste. Because this book and chapter refer to multiple time periods, pre and post independence, we use the term East Timor for ease of reference, but we recognize that Timor Leste is the country's preferred English name today.

[37] *See* Lori Fisler Damrosch, *Introduction* and *Concluding Reflections,* in Enforcing Restraint: Collective Intervention in Internal Conflicts, *supra* note 28, at 12–13, 356–359; Murphy, Humanitarian Intervention, *supra* note 12, at 282–290.

[38] Samantha Power, "A Problem from Hell": America and the Age of Genocide (2002), at 329–389; S/1999/1257, *Report of the Independent Inquiry into the Actions of the United Nations during the 1994 Genocide in Rwanda,* December 16, 1999.

some states and leaders consider whether, if such a situation arose again, they should be prepared to act even without formal Security Council authority – perhaps through regional organizations.

B. Regional Interventions and the Common Interest

In fact, both before and after Rwanda's genocide, groups of states intervened in several long-festering conflicts when the Security Council proved unwilling or unable to agree on a clear collective response. Regional organizations, in particular – ECOWAS in Liberia and Sierra Leone, and NATO in Kosovo – decided to deploy military forces during the 1990s without prior authority from the Security Council when they concluded that urgent humanitarian and security circumstances in their region required it. But squaring these interventions with the UN Charter's provisions on the use of force proved difficult to varying degrees.

The UN Charter, to be sure, envisions that regional organizations will play a significant role in conflict resolution. Indeed, the Charter encourages states to use regional arrangements to peacefully resolve regional disputes before bringing matters to the Security Council.[39] But the Charter's drafters sought to strike a balance that would not jeopardize the UN's primary role in protecting international peace and security.[40] On the one hand, in cases of self-defense, states clearly can respond to armed attacks through regional self-defense arrangements if they choose, reporting to the Security Council after the fact. On the other hand, if regional organizations engage in "enforcement action" in situations that do not involve self-defense, they must obtain Security Council authorization. As Charter Article 53 states: "no enforcement action shall be taken under regional arrangements or by regional agencies without the authorization of the Security Council...."[41] Although the term *enforcement action* is not defined in the Charter, few would dispute that the use of force on the territory of another state without its consent would qualify.

Yet several interventions by the Economic Community of West African States (ECOWAS) during the 1990s enjoyed substantial international legitimacy, despite the absence of prior authority from the Security Council. ECOWAS forces, the preponderance from Nigeria, intervened in Liberia and later in Sierra Leone after the Security Council failed to forge an agreed international response.[42] In both cases, the Security Council subsequently

---

[39] UN Charter, Art. 52.

[40] Anthony Clark Arend, *The United Nations, Regional Organizations, and Military Operations: The Past and the Present*, 7 DUKE J. COMP. & INT'L L. 3 (1996).

[41] UN Charter, Art. 53(1).

[42] *See* David Wippman, *Enforcing the Peace: ECOWAS and the Liberian Civil War*, in ENFORCING RESTRAINT, *supra* note 28, at 157–203; Lee Berger, *State Practice Evidence of the*

commended the action taken by ECOWAS but sought to monitor and provide some international oversight.[43] In short, the ECOWAS interventions were tolerated and endorsed retrospectively but with a clear message that some degree of Council oversight was critical to the Council's willingness to support the interventions, even if the effectiveness and extent of that oversight proved problematic on the ground.

ECOWAS is unique in that its members have agreed by treaty – in a special Protocol – to establish a Mediation and Security Council with the legal capacity to authorize intervention in a wide range of circumstances. The Protocol, for instance, provides for intervention in situations of internal conflict that "threaten[] to trigger a humanitarian disaster" or "pose[] a serious threat to peace and security in the sub-region" and in the "event of serious and massive violation of human rights and the rule of law."[44] Although interventions by consent, pursuant to this Protocol, on the territory of ECOWAS members are not necessarily in tension with the Charter's nonintervention norm,[45] the ECOWAS Protocol does illustrate that the process of determining what is in the "common interest" is becoming more multidimensional: Organizations other than the UN Security Council are prepared to act in the face of the Council's inability or unwillingness to forge a collective response.

The ECOWAS interventions in Liberia and Sierra Leone revealed the Security Council's own willingness to accept regional action first with Council endorsement after the fact. But there is reason for caution in generalizing too far from this experience. As the intense controversy among the Security Council's permanent members over Kosovo showed, regional enforcement action without advance Council authorization can also generate strong disagreement – at least in cases that touch directly on the interests of those members. Kosovo also raised the complex and contested issue of "humanitarian intervention" – that is, the use of force by a state or group of states to protect individuals in another state from severe human rights abuses without the consent of that state's government.

Humanitarian Intervention Doctrine: The ECOWAS Intervention in Sierra Leone, 11 IND. INT'L & COMP. L. REV. 605 (2001).

[43] S.C. Res. 788 (1992) (Liberia); S.C. Res. 1132 (1997) (Sierra Leone).

[44] Protocol Relating to the Mechanism for Conflict Prevention, Management, Resolution, Peace-Keeping and Security (1999), Art. 25, Art. 10. The Protocol also provides for intervention in "cases of aggression or conflict in any Member State or threat thereof"; in "case of conflict between two or several Member States"; in "the event of an overthrow or attempted overthrow of a democratically elected government"; and in "[a]ny other situation as may be decided by the Mediation and Security Council." Art. 25.

[45] For a nuanced analysis, *see* David Wippman, *Military Intervention, Regional Organizations, and Host-State Consent*, 7 DUKE J. COMP. & INT'L L. 209 (1996); David Wippman, *Pro-Democratic Intervention by Invitation*, in DEMOCRATIC GOVERNANCE & INTERNATIONAL LAW (Gregory H. Fox & Brad R. Roth, eds. 2000).

C. Kosovo and the Dilemma of "Humanitarian Intervention"

When NATO governments decided to intervene with force in response to the escalating crisis in Kosovo, they faced a difficult dilemma. On the one hand, violence in the province was increasing, security forces were targeting civilians, refugee flows were accelerating, and a humanitarian crisis was mounting. The Milosevic regime was violating Security Council resolutions calling on the former Yugoslavia to halt hostilities against the civilian population of Kosovo and to avert an "impending humanitarian catastrophe,"[46] and no prospect of a diplomatic resolution of the conflict was in sight. On the other hand, Russia and China were not prepared to authorize collective military action in response to the situation, so the Security Council was at an impasse. Although NATO governments could point to numerous factors that supported the legitimacy of military action, NATO states could not invoke either of the two clear, agreed legal bases for using force under the UN Charter: NATO's use of force was neither an exercise of the right of self-defense nor authorized by the Security Council. The Kosovo crisis, in short, pitted fundamental human rights principles affirmed by the UN Charter against the Charter's rules limiting the resort to force – confronting NATO with the dilemma of either acting without Council authorization or tolerating severe human rights abuses in a desperate and escalating humanitarian crisis in Europe.

NATO ultimately chose to use force in response to the extraordinary circumstances in Kosovo. Even so, most NATO states were reluctant to claim a legal "right" of "humanitarian intervention." Most NATO members instead defended their intervention in Kosovo more narrowly as an action consistent with objectives set forth in Security Council resolutions, even if not expressly authorized by the Council.[47] Germany, for example, argued that NATO's action was consistent with the "sense and logic" of Council resolutions.[48] France likewise emphasized Milosevic's noncompliance with Security Council resolutions and argued that "the legitimacy of NATO's action lies in the authority of the Security Council."[49] Britain came closest in March 1999 to invoking humanitarian intervention as a distinct legal basis for NATO's military action, arguing that force could be justified "as an exceptional measure on grounds of overwhelming humanitarian

---

[46] S.C. Res. 1199 (1998). *See also* Bruno Simma, *NATO, the UN and the Use of Force: Legal Aspects*, 10 Eur. J. Int'l L. 1–22 (1999); Catherine Guicherd, *International Law and Kosovo*, 41 Survival 27–28 (1999).

[47] This section draws directly on Jane Stromseth, *Rethinking Humanitarian Intervention: The Case for Incremental Change*, in Humanitarian Intervention: Legal, Political, and Ethical Dilemmas (J. L. Holzgrefe & Robert O. Keohane, eds., 2003), at 232.

[48] Simma, *NATO, the UN and the Use of Force, supra* note 46, at 12.

[49] Press release, French Foreign Ministry, March 25, 1999.

necessity."[50] Other British statements, however, linked the justification for NATO's military intervention more directly to purposes articulated in UN Security Council resolutions.[51] The United States made no reference to "humanitarian intervention" as a legal concept but instead emphasized the unique factual circumstances at hand, including "Belgrade's brutal persecution of Kosovar Albanians, violations of international law, excessive and indiscriminate use of force, refusal to negotiate to resolve the issue peacefully, and recent military build-up in Kosovo – all of which foreshadow a humanitarian catastrophe of immense proportions."[52] In short, NATO states, in sometimes differing ways, explained why they viewed their military action as "lawful" – as having a legal basis within the normative framework of international law, a framework that includes fundamental human rights norms as well as resolutions adopted by the Security Council under Chapter VII of the Charter.

Despite the controversy provoked by NATO's intervention in Kosovo, many other states also concluded that the intervention was justified. The Security Council itself decisively rejected a resolution, supported by Russia and China, that called NATO's intervention a flagrant violation of the UN

[50] Statement of Sir Jeremy Greenstock to the Security Council, March 24, 1999, in S/PV.3988, at 12. Belgium was prepared to take a few more steps down this road in proceedings before the International Court of Justice. Defending against FRY charges of illegality, Belgium argued in May 1999 that NATO's action was a "lawful armed humanitarian intervention." Argument of Belgium before the International Court of Justice, May 10, 1999, at 7, *available at* www.icj-cij.org. Belgium also argued, in the alternative, that NATO's action was excusable under "a state of necessity ... which justifies the violation of a binding rule in order to safeguard, in face of grave and imminent peril, values which are higher than those protected by the rule which has been breached." Id., at 8.

[51] As Prime Minister Tony Blair stated in April 1999: "Under international law a limited use of force can be justifiable in support of purposes laid down by the Security Council but without the Council's express authorization when that is the only means to avert an immediate and overwhelming humanitarian catastrophe. Any such case would in the nature of things be exceptional and would depend on an objective assessment of the factual circumstances at the time and on the terms of relevant decisions of the Security Council bearing on the situation in question." Prime Minister Tony Blair, *Written Answer for House of Commons*, April 29, 1999, Hansard, Col. 245.

[52] Statement of Ambassador A. Peter Burleigh to the Security Council, March 24, 1999, S/PV.3988, 3988th Meeting of the Security Council, at 4. The United States also stressed the implications of the developing refugee crisis for regional security and invoked the Security Council resolutions that called the situation a threat to peace and security. In this context, in the face of Belgrade's persistent refusal to honor its commitments or negotiate a peaceful solution, the United States ultimately concluded that NATO military action was "justified and necessary to stop the violence and prevent an even greater humanitarian disaster." Id., at 5. Other NATO states likewise avoided any general doctrinal justification for NATO's action and emphasized instead both the extraordinary circumstances surrounding the intervention and the Security Council's resolutions. Guicherd, *International Law and Kosovo*, *supra* note 46, at 26–28.

Charter and a threat to peace and security.[53] Only one other state – Namibia – voted in favor of this resolution. All the other states on the Security Council – countries large and small from every region of the world – essentially concurred in NATO's conclusion that force was necessary in these exceptional circumstances. UN Secretary-General Kofi Annan also refused to condemn NATO's military action, stating instead that there "are times when the use of force may be *legitimate* in the pursuit of peace."[54] To be sure, many states deeply regretted the Security Council's failure to act, but many also concluded that allowing the Milosevic regime's actions to go unchecked would lead to a humanitarian catastrophe and would condone "systematic and brutal violations" of the Council's own resolutions.[55] In short, most Security Council members reached the same conclusion NATO reached: that in these extraordinary circumstances, intervention was necessary and legitimate even if it did not fit comfortably within the strictures of the UN Charter's provisions governing force. Moreover, even the states that opposed the intervention came together afterwards in voting for Resolution 1244, which authorized an international security force and an international "civil presence" in Kosovo with far-reaching responsibilities.[56]

The perceived legitimacy of the Kosovo intervention – in the view of NATO governments and of many other states as well – contributed to their willingness to commit forces and resources to the intervention and to the difficult follow-on tasks of stabilization and post-conflict reconstruction. Twenty-five NATO nations and twelve non-NATO states contribute to the Kosovo Force (KFOR) responsible for maintaining security in Kosovo.[57] The broad-based international support for KFOR and in particular for the UN Mission in Kosovo (UNMIK) has helped to mobilize a greater array of resources in the face of the inevitable difficulties of post-conflict reconstruction.

---

[53] S/1999/328, March 26, 1999; S/PV.3989, 3989th Meeting of the UN Security Council, March 26, 1999, at 6.

[54] Kofi A. Annan, THE QUESTION OF INTERVENTION: STATEMENTS BY THE SECRETARY-GENERAL (1999), at 33 (emphasis added). The Secretary-General was remarkably supportive of NATO's decision in this situation. Annan and many of his top advisers had experienced directly the horrific consequences of UN neutrality in Bosnia in the face of systematic ethnic cleansing and recurring atrocities, and they regarded a similar posture in Kosovo as unacceptable. In a strong speech in Geneva before the UN Commission on Human Rights, the Secretary-General made clear that "ethnic cleansers" and those "guilty of gross and shocking violations of human rights" will find no justification or refuge in the UN Charter. Id. At the same time, the Secretary-General also stressed the Security Council's primary responsibility for maintaining peace and security and the urgent need for unified, effective Council action in defense of human rights in the future.

[55] Statement by Danilo Turk, Permanent Representative of Slovenia, in S/PV.3988, March 24, 1999, at 6.

[56] S.C. Res. 1244 (1999), paras. 7–11.

[57] *See* http://www.nato.int/kfor/kfor/nations/default.htm (last accessed January 19, 2006).

Even so, the legal basis for humanitarian intervention remained deeply contested in the aftermath of the Kosovo intervention. Supporting a particular intervention based on its unique factual circumstances was one thing; developing a more far-reaching legal doctrine was quite another. The overwhelming majority of states declined to embrace any doctrine or legal right of humanitarian intervention in the absence of Security Council authorization. And despite the strong encouragement of Secretary-General Annan, it continued to be an uphill battle to develop agreed criteria for Security Council responses to severe atrocities and humanitarian emergencies.[58]

Nevertheless, based on the experience in Kosovo and in other interventions during the 1990s (such as the intervention to protect the Iraqi Kurds after the 1991 Gulf War), one can reasonably argue that the normative status of intervention to protect individuals from severe atrocities is in a state of evolution. At the very least, for many states and legal scholars, Kosovo was an example of an "excusable breach" of the formal rules of the UN Charter. It may be premature to claim that a new legal norm in support of humanitarian intervention in exceptional cases has emerged in any clear or uncontested way, but elements of a normative consensus may be developing gradually.[59] In a situation like Rwanda – or Darfur, Sudan – a collective

---

[58] Secretary-General Annan and the British government have led these efforts. For a fuller discussion, see Stromseth, *Rethinking Humanitarian Intervention*, supra note 47, at 261–267. UN Secretary-General Kofi Annan made the issue of intervention the centerpiece of his address to the UN General Assembly in September 1999. He focused on the tragic dilemma confronting the international community when the UN Charter's rules regarding the lawful use of force are in tension with human rights imperatives in concrete situations such as Kosovo. On the one hand, as Annan stressed, military intervention without Security Council authorization may erode the legal framework governing the use of force and undermine the Council's authority by setting potentially dangerous precedents. On the other hand, the Council's failure to act in the face of horrific atrocities betrays the human rights principles of the Charter and erodes respect for the UN as an institution. To avoid such problems in the future, the Secretary-General has emphasized the need to ensure that the Security Council can rise to the occasion and agree on effective action in defense of human rights. Indeed, he has argued that the "core challenge to the Security Council and to the United Nations as a whole in the next century" is "to forge unity behind the principle that massive and systematic violations of human rights – wherever they take place – should not be allowed to stand." Kofi Annan, Address to the 54th Session of the UN General Assembly, September 20, 1999, *reprinted in* Annan, THE QUESTION OF INTERVENTION, *supra* note 54, at 39. Governments, commissions, foreign affairs institutes, nongovernmental organizations, and scholars have taken up the Secretary-General's challenge, in a number of initiatives that address the difficult issues raised by Kosovo and by failures to act in other desperate situations. *See, e.g., The Responsibility to Protect, Report of the International Commission on Intervention and State Sovereignty,* December, 2001, *available at* www.iciss.ca/report-en.asp; The Danish Institute of International Affairs, HUMANITARIAN INTERVENTION: LEGAL AND POLITICAL ASPECTS (1999); and Adam Roberts, *The So-Called Right of Humanitarian Intervention,* 3 YB. INT'L L. 3–51 (2001).

[59] An emerging norm in support of humanitarian intervention as lawful in truly exceptional circumstances may be developing gradually over time, case by case. For instance, a careful

humanitarian intervention by a regional organization or a group of states may well enjoy wide legitimacy in the absence of effective action by the Security Council. Even if the formal rules remain the same, human rights principles will influence how the UN Charter is understood and applied in concrete cases.

A stronger international consensus clearly has emerged regarding the duties of states to protect their own populations from severe atrocities and human rights abuses.[60] The Secretary-General's High-Level Panel on Threats, Challenges and Change, for instance, concurred not only that states have such a responsibility but also that "there is a collective international responsibility to protect, exercisable by the Security Council authorizing military intervention as a last resort, in the event of genocide and other large-scale killing, ethnic cleansing or serious violations of international humanitarian law which sovereign Governments have proved powerless or unwilling to prevent."[61] Likewise, when heads of state gathered at the United Nations General Assembly in September 2005, they agreed that each state "has the responsibility to protect its populations from genocide, war crimes, ethnic cleansing and crimes against humanity" – a responsibility that entails "prevention of such crimes."[62] In addition, the heads of state expressed willingness to take collective action, including Security Council

examination and comparison of the Kosovo intervention and the intervention to protect the Iraqi Kurds in the immediate aftermath of the 1991 Gulf War reveal common elements. These include serious violations of fundamental human rights involving loss of life perpetrated by a government that showed no willingness to stop; the inability of the UN Security Council to authorize military action, despite ongoing Council concern about the clear threat to peace and security; under the circumstances, force was necessary to stop the human rights abuses committed by government forces; the military actions taken were proportional to the end of stopping the atrocities; the interventions were undertaken by a coalition of states acting collectively; both interventions focused on stopping the atrocities, protecting individuals at risk, and stabilizing a situation that risked further humanitarian catastrophe; and the states taking military action defended their action as legally justified. In addition, both interventions were welcomed by the population at risk, and neither intervention was condemned by the Security Council. To be sure, thoughtful scholars will differ on the degree to which they find any normative consensus emerging from recent practice. Nevertheless, the effort to identify potentially developing custom from recent practice is a promising one. *See* Stromseth, *Rethinking Humanitarian Intervention, supra* note 47, at 244–255. Although a very strong preference for Security Council authorization clearly remains, in extraordinary and desperate circumstances an intervention may be widely accepted as legitimate and as consistent with the human rights purposes of the UN Charter – and indeed as lawful – even if it is not expressly authorized by the Security Council. But whether humanitarian intervention is viewed as an "excusable breach" or as an emerging norm in very narrow circumstances, states clearly continue to reject any broad right of humanitarian intervention.

[60] *See, e.g., The Responsibility to Protect, Report of the International Commission on Intervention and State Sovereignty, supra* note 58.

[61] *Report of the Secretary-General's High-Level Panel on Threats, Challenges and Change, A More Secure World: Our Shared Responsibility*, December 2004, at 66 (para. 203).

[62] 2005 World Summit Outcome, UNGA Resolution A/60/L.1, September 20, 2005, para. 138.

action under Chapter VII of the UN Charter, "should peaceful means be inadequate and national authorities are manifestly failing to protect their populations from genocide, war crimes, ethnic cleansing and crimes against humanity."[63] Whether states on the Security Council will actually be prepared to take decisive action, however, remains a difficult problem, as the situation in Darfur so desperately illustrates.

But because humanitarian intervention without Security Council authorization remains deeply controversial, states intervening in response to severe atrocities and other humanitarian emergencies without a clear Council mandate will face enormous pressure to demonstrate that they are really acting in the common interest. Interveners also must take seriously the tremendous challenge of sustaining legitimacy – both in building coalitions to assist in post-conflict reconstruction and in maintaining the support of local populations. This imperative has continued in the difficult post–9/11 period – in interventions triggered more directly by threats to national security.

III. AFTER 9/11: INTERVENTION IN THE FACE OF NEW THREATS TO SECURITY

The horrific terrorist attacks on September 11, 2001 demonstrated dramatically that the strategic realities of the post–Cold War era had changed forever. A nonstate actor – a terrorist network of global scope – violated the most fundamental norms of international law by targeting innocent civilians for brutal destruction, unconstrained by notions of reciprocity or by the need to protect sovereign territory, and determined to attack again with potentially even more devastating results. Counterterrorism became a paramount national security focus for the United States as it responded, with its allies, to the September 11 attacks and the prospect of even more al-Qaeda attacks in the future.

A. Self-Defense against Terrorism

The international community came together immediately after September 11 to denounce the terrorist attacks emphatically. The UN Security Council unanimously and "unequivocally" condemned the attacks "in the strongest terms," stressing that "such acts, like any act of international terrorism, [are] a threat to international peace and security."[64] The Council, it is fair to say, recognized that these attacks were of such magnitude that both military action in self-defense and cooperative law enforcement could be justified responses. In Resolution 1368, the Council affirmed "the inherent right of individual or collective self-defense in accordance with the Charter"[65]

---

[63] Id., para. 139.
[64] S.C. Res.1368 (2001), operative para. 1.
[65] Id., preambular para. 3.

an important recognition of the applicability of the right of self-defense in response to terrorist attacks.[66] The Council, at the same time, also called on all states "to work together urgently to bring to justice the perpetrators, organizers and sponsors of these terrorist attacks" and "*stress[ed]* that those responsible for aiding, supporting or harbouring the perpetrators, organizers and sponsors of these acts will be held accountable."[67] In addition, the Council affirmed its own readiness to respond to the 9/11 attacks and "to combat all forms of terrorism."[68] Later, in Resolution 1373, the Council imposed far-reaching counterterrorism duties on all states.[69]

America's allies were even more explicit in recognizing the right of self-defense in response to the attacks. NATO invoked the collective self-defense provisions in Article 5 of the North Atlantic Treaty for the first time in the alliance's history.[70] Likewise, Australia, acting under the ANZUS Treaty, invoked its collective self-defense provisions for the first time.[71] The members of the Rio Pact also responded jointly.[72]

Although terrorist attacks by nonstate actors can raise difficult issues of state responsibility,[73] the facts in this case were such that the U.S. intervention

---

[66] The Security Council's affirmation of the right of self-defense in response to the September 11 terrorist attacks was a significant development, given earlier disagreements over uses of force in response to terrorist acts. *See* Michael Byers, *Preemptive Self-Defense: Hegemony, Equality and Strategies of Legal Change*, 11 J. POLIT. PHIL. 171, 177–179 (2003); Thomas M. Franck, *Editorial Comment: Terrorism and the Right of Self-Defense*, 95 AM. J. INT'L L. 839 (2001).

[67] S.C. Res. 1368, operative para. 3.

[68] Id., para. 5.

[69] S.C. Res. 1373 (2001). Resolution 1373 obligates all states to "[r]efrain from providing any form of support, active or passive, to entities or persons involved in terrorist acts," to "[t]ake the necessary steps to prevent the commission of terrorist acts," to "eliminate[e] the supply of weapons to terrorists," among other duties. Id., para. 2.

[70] Statement by the North Atlantic Council, September 12, 2001, press release (2001) 124, *available at* http://www.nato.int/docu/pr/2001/p01–124e.htm.

[71] The Australia, New Zealand, United States (ANZUS) security alliance originally involved Australia, New Zealand, and the United States, but today it involves active defense commitments only between Australia and the United States. In 1986, as a result of disagreement over New Zealand's stance on nuclear warships in its ports, the United States unilaterally suspended its obligations to New Zealand under the ANZUS treaty, and New Zealand's role is described as "dormant." *See* Luke Peter, New Zealand's Dormant Role in ANZUS Unchanged Since 80s-PM, Christchurch Press, September 20, 2001, at 3. After the September 11 attacks, Australia invoked the collective self-defense provisions of the ANZUS treaty for the first time in the alliance's fifty-year history. *See Howard Government Invokes ANZUS Treaty*, September 14, 2001, *available at* http://www.australianpolitics.com/news/2001/01–09–14c.shtml. *See* Art. IV of Security Treaty (ANZUS), 3 U.S.T. 3420, 131 U.N.T.S. 83, signed September 1, 1951, entered into force April 29, 1952.

[72] Meeting of Consultation of Ministers of Foreign Affairs, Resolution on Terrorist Threat to the Americas, September 21, 2001 (invoking relevant provisions of the Rio Treaty), *available at* http://www.oas.org/oaspage/crisis/RC.24e.htm.

[73] *See, e.g.,* Richard J. Erickson, LEGITIMATE USE OF FORCE AGAINST STATE-SPONSORED TERRORISM (1989), at 95–106.

in Afghanistan was widely regarded by other states as lawful self-defense.[74] Afghanistan's Taliban regime had long defied Security Council demands that it turn over Osama bin Laden and cease its support for al-Qaeda. In light of this history, the nature of the attacks, and the Taliban's continued violation of its international duties, the U.S. military action was broadly supported as a defensive action to combat terrorism.

In commencing military action in Afghanistan in October 2001, the United States and its allies explicitly invoked the legal right of self-defense. The U.S. government emphasized that it had "clear and compelling information that the Al-Qaeda organization, which is supported by the Taliban regime in Afghanistan, had a central role in the attacks" of September 11. Moreover, the United States stressed, "[d]espite every effort by the United States and the international community, the Taliban regime has refused to change its policy"; instead, al-Qaeda continued to operate from the territory of Afghanistan, training and supporting "agents of terror who attack innocent people throughout the world and target United States nationals and interests in the United States and abroad."[75] Thus, the United States did not seek Security Council authorization but instead exercised its inherent right of self-defense "to prevent and deter further attacks on the United States." At the same time, the United States emphasized that its actions were directed against the Taliban and al-Qaeda, not against the Afghan people, and that U.S. "humanitarian efforts to alleviate the suffering of the people of Afghanistan" would continue.

The immediate military operation in Afghanistan, which removed the Taliban from power, led to the much more difficult and long-term challenge of stabilizing and rebuilding that country – an effort requiring substantial resources and the support of allies and partners. The fact that many states regarded the intervention itself as a legitimate act of self-defense reinforced their willingness to contribute to the demanding reconstruction effort. With the Security Council's subsequent support for the Bonn Agreement (a UN-brokered roadmap for transitional governance and national elections) and for post-conflict rebuilding, many states and organizations have been willing to help – at least to some degree – with various aspects of the daunting struggle to bring greater security, political stability, and economic assistance to Afghanistan's exceedingly difficult political terrain. A substantial number of countries have contributed forces to the U.S.-led Operation Enduring

---

[74] See Jack M. Beard, *America's New War on Terror: The Case for Self-Defense Under International Law*, 25 Harv. J. L. & Pub. Pol. 559 (2002).

[75] Letter dated October 7, 2001 from the Permanent Representative of the United States of America to the United Nations addressed to the President of the Security Council, S/2001/946.

Freedom, aimed at defeating Taliban and al-Qaeda remnants,[76] while thirty-five NATO and non-NATO countries contribute troops to the international security assistance force (ISAF) in Afghanistan.[77]

B. The Controversy over "Preemption"

Although many states are working together to thwart terrorist attacks and to bring terrorists to justice, the decision of the Bush Administration to articulate a high-profile doctrine of preemptive action has been a lightening rod for controversy. First unveiled in presidential and vice presidential speeches in summer 2002, the doctrine saw its fullest articulation in the Bush Administration's National Security Strategy document of September 2002.[78] There, the Bush Administration indicated that the United States must be prepared to preempt "emerging threats before they are fully formed."[79] Rather than quietly keeping preemption as a possible option in extreme situations, as previous administrations had done, the very public articulation of a new "doctrine" alarmed even close U.S. allies. In its expansive form, the doctrine poses a challenge to the UN Charter framework itself[80] and has the potential to be destabilizing.[81]

---

[76] See http://www.globalsecurity.org/military/ops/enduring-freedom.htm (last accessed January 19, 2006) ("By 2002 the coalition had grown to more than 68 nations, with 27 nations having representatives at CENTCOM headquarters.").

[77] See http://www.nato.int/issues/afghanistan (last accessed January 19, 2006).

[78] National Security Strategy of the United States of America, September 17, 2002 (hereinafter *National Security Strategy*), Section V, *available at* http://www.whitehouse.gov/nsc/nss.html.

[79] Introduction to id. Our discussion of preemption draws on Jane E. Stromseth, *Law and Force after Iraq: A Transitional Moment*, 97 AM. J. INT'L L. 628, 634–639 (2003).

[80] As discussed in the National Security Strategy, the doctrine would apply even if there is no imminent armed attack. More precisely what the administration means by "imminent *threat*" or "grave threat" and whether the administration would be prepared to present a situation to the Security Council in the first instance, when circumstances permit, has yet to be clarified. Whether the doctrine would, in fact, conflict with the UN Charter would depend on how it is implemented in practice.

[81] See W. Michael Reisman, *Editorial Comment: Assessing Claims to Revise the Laws of War*, 97 AM. J. INT'L L. 82, 89 (2003) ("The danger presented by the installation of a doctrine of preemptive self-defense is systemic: if writ large and generally available in international law, it is even more likely than anticipatory self-defense to lead to greater resort to international violence by lowering the threshold for unilaterally determined contingencies that warrant acts of self-defense. This potential could create an imperative for all latent adversaries to strike sooner so as to strike first, raising the expectation of violence and the likelihood of its eventuation."). *See also* Ivo Daalder, *Policy Implications of the Bush Doctrine on Preemption*, November 16, 2002, *available at* http://www.cfr.org/publication.php?id=5251 ("The doctrine of preemption . . . [i]f taken seriously by others . . . will exacerbate the security dilemma among hostile states, by raising the incentive of all states to initiate military action before others do. The result is to undermine whatever stability might exist in a military standoff.").

It is true that the precise scope of the right of self-defense has long been a subject of dispute. Ever since the UN Charter was adopted in 1945, states and scholars have debated whether the right of self-defense, affirmed in Article 51, is triggered only by an armed attack or whether a state faced with an *imminent* threat of attack can lawfully use force to defend itself anticipatorily before it is the victim of an attack.[82] Our view, in light of the history and text of the Charter, the customary international law that preceded it, and subsequent state practice, is that a right of *anticipatory self-defense* to an imminent attack reasonably falls within the right of self-defense affirmed by the UN Charter.[83]

Yet rather than initiating a more focused attempt to refine the concept of anticipatory self-defense – and working with allies to rethink the concept of imminent attack in light of the realities of terrorism – the Bush Administration articulated a doctrine of preemption whose parameters are uncertain and that is potentially very broad in scope. On the one hand, the administration's 2002 National Security Strategy grapples frankly and openly with the exceedingly difficult security challenges posed by terrorists seeking weapons of mass destruction (WMD), possibly enabled by rogue or failed states. The strategy stresses the vital need to prevent these weapons from ever being used against the United States and its allies and friends.[84] On the other hand, the strategy's counter to this danger is not simply preemption against specifically

---

[82] Article 51 of the Charter affirms that "[n]othing in the present Charter shall impair the *inherent* right of individual or collective self-defense if an *armed attack* occurs against a Member of the United Nations . . ." (emphasis added). Those who argue in favor of a limited right of anticipatory self-defense point to the Charter's reference to the "inherent right" of self-defense and to the scope of the right of self-defense prior to the Charter, which included a right of anticipatory self-defense. Those who argue that an armed attack must have already begun point to the "if an armed attack occurs" language in Article 51 and to the purpose of limiting unilateral resort to force.

[83] *See* Oscar Schachter, *The Right of States to Use Armed Force*, 82 MICH. L. REV. 1620, 1634–1635 (1984) (arguing that a limited right of anticipatory self-defense to imminent attack is consistent with Article 51 of the UN Charter, citing the criteria set forth by U.S. Secretary of State Daniel Webster in the *Caroline* case). *See also* Anthony Clark Arend & Robert J. Beck, INTERNATIONAL LAW AND THE USE OF FORCE (1993), at 71–79 (discussing differing views regarding anticipatory self-defense, but concluding that it is not prohibited). Although the debate continues among scholars, the history of state behavior and UN Security Council responses under the Charter – including repeated reference to criteria for anticipatory self-defense articulated by U.S. Secretary of State Daniel Webster in the *Caroline* case – suggest that many states do, in fact, support a limited right of anticipatory self-defense to imminent attack, dependent on the facts of the situation.

[84] As the National Security Strategy explains: "new deadly challenges have emerged from rogue states and terrorists . . . and the greater likelihood that they will use weapons of mass destruction against us, make[s] today's security environment more dangerous and complex." "We must be prepared to stop rogue states and their terrorist clients before they are able to threaten or use weapons of mass destruction against the United States and our allies and friends. . . . We must deter and defend against the threat before it is unleashed." National Security Strategy, *supra* note 78, at 13–14.

identified terrorist threats in anticipatory self-defense but also, potentially, the use of force to preempt "hostile acts"[85] and "emerging threats before they are fully formed"[86] – in particular to prevent "rogue states" from acquiring weapons of mass destruction. The very uncertainty of the doctrine's scope,[87] coupled with the subjective and often precarious nature of judgments about future threats, has made the doctrine highly controversial, raising doubts in many parts of the world about the reassuring nature of U.S. power.[88]

Even the Bush Administration seems to have walked back its original broad doctrinal pronouncements somewhat.[89] Secretary of State Colin Powell argued that preemption is primarily aimed at terrorists,[90] and other

---

[85] Id., at 15.

[86] Introduction, in id. The National Security Strategy argues that "[f]or rogue states," weapons of mass destruction "are tools of intimidation and military aggression against their neighbors. These weapons may also allow these states to attempt to blackmail the United States and our allies to prevent us from deterring or repelling the aggressive behavior of rogue states." Id. Although "[t]he United States will not use force in all cases to preempt emerging threats, nor should nations use preemption as a pretext for aggression . . . the United States cannot remain idle while dangers gather." Id. As the president put it in the Introduction to the National Security Strategy: "as a matter of common sense and self-defense, America will act against such emerging threats before they are fully formed."

[87] The boundaries of the Bush Administration's doctrine – as articulated in the National Security Strategy and by the president and other high officials – are unclear and potentially far-reaching. Although it is true that the preemption doctrine focuses on "the particular issue of rogue states seeking to acquire WMD," Walter B. Slocombe, *Force, Pre-emption and Legitimacy*, 45 SURVIVAL 117, 124 (2003), the circumstances in which the administration envisions taking preventive military action remain open ended: The United States may act, for instance, "before threats have fully materialized." Condoleezza Rice, Wriston Lecture, October 1, 2002, *available at* http://www.whitehouse.gov/news/releases/2002/10/print/20021001-6.html. Rice did add some qualifications: "[T]his approach . . . does not give a green light – to the United States or any other nation – to act first without exhausting other means, including diplomacy. . . . The threat must be very grave. And the risks of waiting must far outweigh the risks of action." But, as discussed in the National Security Strategy, the doctrine does not require an actual or an imminent armed attack. National Security Strategy, *supra* note 78, at 15.

[88] For a more wide-ranging survey of global public opinion in the aftermath of the 2003 Iraq War, discussing, among other things, attitudes toward the United States and its foreign policy, *see* Pew Research Center for the People & the Press, *Views of A Changing World 2003*, June 3, 2003, *available at* http://people-press.org/reports/display.php3?ReportID=185. For a thoughtful critique of the preemption doctrine, *see* Miriam Sapiro, *Iraq: The Shifting Sands of Preemptive Self-Defense*, 97 AM. J. INT'L L. 599 (2003).

[89] The 2006 U.S. National Security Strategy has a somewhat different tone than the 2002 version and emphasizes a "strong preference" for "address[ing] proliferation concerns through international diplomacy, in concert with key allies and regional partners." National Security Strategy of the United States of America, March 16, 2006, at 23, *available at* http://www.whitehouse.gov/nsc/nss/2006/. The 2006 strategy also states, however, that "[t]he place of preemption in our national security strategy remains the same." Id.

[90] Colin L. Powell, *A Strategy of Partnerships*, 83 FOREIGN AFFAIRS 24 (2004) ("As to preemption's scope, it applies only to the undeterrable threats that come from nonstate actors such as terrorist groups").

officials also suggested limits on the doctrine.[91] This is important because although most U.S. allies understand the unique challenges involved in effective self-defense against terrorists,[92] they are less likely to support "preemptive" force to prevent states from developing military capabilities. The further the United States moves from self-defense to actual or imminent armed attack, the harder it will likely be to convince others of the legitimacy of military intervention[93] or to secure broad international support for post-conflict reconstruction, as the recent experience in Iraq so clearly illustrates.

C. The 2003 War in Iraq

Although the Bush Administration's high-profile preemption doctrine no doubt fueled the controversy surrounding its decision to go to war against Iraq in March 2003, the intense international discord over that war had much deeper roots. In fact, the U.S. and British decision to resort to force against Iraq in the face of a deeply divided UN Security Council was the culmination of long-standing differences among Council members over Iraq's persistent violations of the disarmament obligations imposed at the end of the 1991 Persian Gulf War. The Security Council's own failure to stand up to

[91] The State Department Legal Adviser, for example, offered an interpretation of the legal basis for preemptive military action that sought to place it more clearly within parameters of anticipatory self-defense. *See* William H. Taft, IV, Legal Adviser, Department of State, *The Legal Basis for Preemption*, published by the Council on Foreign Relations, November 18, 2003, *available at* http://www.cfr.org/publication.php?id=5250. Taft wrote that "The President's National Security Strategy relies upon the same legal framework applied to the British in *Caroline* and to Israel in 1981. The United States reserves the right to use force preemptively in self-defense when faced with *an imminent threat*. While the definition of imminent must recognize the threat posed by weapons of mass destruction and the intentions of those who possess them, the decision to undertake any action must meet the test of necessity. *After the exhaustion of peaceful remedies* and a careful, deliberate consideration of the consequences, in the face of *overwhelming evidence of an imminent threat*, a nation may take preemptive action *to defend its nationals from unimaginable harm*." Id., at 5–6 (emphasis added).

[92] Because terrorists generally provide no warning and are not deterrable in the way that state actors might be, disrupting terrorist networks before they can attack and preventing them from acquiring weapons of mass destruction is necessary to exercising a meaning right of self-defense. In the case of al-Qaeda, its previous attacks and clear policies indicate an ongoing plan to attack and raise a clear presumption of future attacks. More generally, because of terrorists' disregard for the rules of international law and their use of stealth and deception to attack innocents, less certainty regarding the imminence or precise time and place of their attack is needed to act in self-defense. Working cooperatively with states, when possible, to disrupt terrorist cells on their territory nevertheless remains critically important. For discussion of self-defense in response to terrorism, *see* Jane E. Stromseth, *New Paradigms for the Jus ad Bellum?*, 38 GEO. WASH. INT'L L. REV. 561 (2006); Terrence Taylor, *The End of Imminence,* WASH. Q. (Autumn 2004), at 57; Christopher Greenwood, *International Law and Pre-emptive Use of Force: Afghanistan, Al-Qaida, and Iraq*, 4 SAN DIEGO INT'L L. J. 7 (2003).

[93] *See Report of the Secretary-General's High-Level Panel on Threats, Challenges and Change*, *supra* note 61, at 63 (distinguishing military action when a "threatened attack is *imminent*" from preventive military action against "a non-imminent or non-proximate" threat).

Saddam Hussein's defiance had undermined the effectiveness and credibility of the Council's disarmament mandates and inspection regime for years.

In making the political case for war, the United States, Britain, and their allies argued that they were intervening to enforce Security Council mandates against a brutal dictator who had used weapons of mass destruction against his own people and another state and who, they argued, was harboring and rebuilding WMD capabilities. The Bush Administration stressed the danger posed by Saddam Hussein to the security of the United States, but the degree of imminence of this "continuing" or "gathering" threat was never made clear. The three other permanent members of the Security Council – France, Russia, and China – joined by other states, strongly disputed the political case for war, at least absent a more sustained effort to give the newly revived international inspections process a chance to clarify the WMD situation on the ground in Iraq.

The intense political disagreement over the legitimacy of going to war against Iraq deprived the intervention of the undisputed legality that explicit Security Council authorization would have provided. Instead, the major protagonists on the Security Council differed strongly over the legality of the war.[94] The United States and Britain argued, as they had throughout the 1990s, that Iraq's violation of the Gulf War cease-fire terms set forth in Resolution 687 constituted a "material breach" that reactivated Resolution 678's authorization to use force.[95] Invoking this theory, the United States and Britain – joined by France – used force against Iraq in 1993.[96] In 1998, after the Security Council found Iraq in "flagrant violation of resolution 687," the United States and Britain again acted on this theory.[97] Other Security

---

[94] The paragraphs that follow draw on Stromseth, *Law and Force after Iraq, supra* note 79, at 629–631.

[95] *See* Jules Lobel & Michael Ratner, *Bypassing the Security Council: Ambiguous Authorizations to Use Force, Cease-Fires and the Iraqi Inspection Regime*, 93 AM. J. INT'L L. 124, 150–152 (1999); Ruth Wedgwood, *The Enforcement of Security Council Resolution 687: The Threat of Force Against Iraq's Weapons of Mass Destruction*, 92 AM J. INT'L L. 724 (1998).

[96] Lobel & Ratner, *Bypassing the Security Council, supra* note 95, at 150–151. This use of force was in response to Iraq's obstruction of inspections and was preceded by statements by the president of the Security Council denouncing Iraq's actions as a "material breach" of Resolution 687 and warning of "serious consequences" for "continued defiance." Id., at 151; Wedgwood, *The Enforcement of Security Council Resolution 687, supra* note 95, at 727. The UN Secretary-General subsequently stated that the military action "was carried out in accordance with a mandate from the Security Council under resolution 678 (1991)" and "was in accordance with the resolutions of the Security Council and the Charter of the United Nations." U.N. Doc.SG/SM/4902/Rev.1, *Transcript of Press Conference by Secretary-General, Boutros Boutros-Ghali, Following Diplomatic Press Club Luncheon in Paris on January 14, 1993*, U.N. Doc. SG/SM/4902/Rev.1, at 1 (1993).

[97] S.C. Res. 1205, para. 1 (November 5, 1998) (UN resolutions *are available at* http://www.un.org); Lobel & Ratner, *Bypassing the Security Council, supra* note 95, at 154; *see* also Wedgwood, *The Enforcement of Security Council Resolution 687, supra* note 95, at 726–728.

Council members contested this view, and the question whether a "material breach" by Iraq gave a coalition of willing states a right to use force to disarm Iraq was hotly debated in the final months of 2002 during Security Council deliberations. The United States and Britain sought a resolution that would maximize the chances of effective coercive diplomacy to disarm Iraq and that would not require a second resolution to authorize force. France sought to ensure an additional Security Council opportunity to determine what response should follow from Iraqi noncompliance.

Adopted unanimously in November 2002, Security Council Resolution 1441 was a "split the difference" solution. The United States and Britain got a Council decision that "Iraq has been and remains in material breach" of its disarmament obligations under Resolution 687, a decision that any Iraqi failures to comply with Resolution 1441 would "constitute a further material breach," and a reiteration of "serious consequences" for noncompliance.[98] France, for its part, got an obligation that Iraqi violations would be "reported to the Council for assessment" and that the Council would "convene immediately . . . in order to consider the situation and the need for full compliance with all of the relevant Council resolutions in order to secure international peace and security."[99]

Resolution 1441, in short, gave something to each of the contending camps and was essentially an agreement to disagree over the need for an additional Security Council resolution authorizing force. French Ambassador to the United States Jean-David Levitte admitted as much in recounting how he advised *against* introducing the so-called "second resolution" that the British, Americans, and Spanish later sought on Iraq.[100] But the British, as well as other U.S. allies, viewed such an additional resolution as extremely important politically; they wanted to make a concerted final effort to achieve Council consensus, which clearly would have enhanced the legitimacy of any subsequent action. Express Council authorization would have been far

---

[98] S.C. Res. 1441, paras. 1, 4, 13 (November 8, 2002). Resolution 1441 offered Iraq "a final opportunity to comply with its disarmament obligations" and established "an enhanced inspection regime with the aim of bringing to full and verified completion the disarmament process" established by Resolution 687 and subsequent Council resolutions. Id., para. 2.

[99] Id., paras. 4, 12.

[100] "Weeks before it was tabled," Ambassador Levitte has stated, "I went to the State Department and to the White House to say, don't do it. First, because you'll split the Council and second, because you don't need it. Let's agree to disagree between gentlemen, as we did on Kosovo, before the war in Kosovo. . . ." Jean-David Levitte, *France, Germany and the U.S.: Putting the Pieces Back Together*, address at the Council on Foreign Relations (March 25, 2003), at 14, *available at* http://www.cfr.org/publication.php?id=5774. In Kosovo, NATO members used force in response to the deteriorating humanitarian situation there without seeking Council authorization in the face of the publicly stated opposition of Russia and China. *See* Stromseth, *Rethinking Humanitarian Intervention, supra* note 47, at 234.

preferable legally as well. In the end, however, the Security Council's unwillingness to adopt the proposed "second resolution" reflected the lack of broad international support for commencing military action against Iraq – at least without giving the recently revived inspections process a more sustained effort.

The 2003 Iraq War thus began without the strong political support and uncontested legal authority that marked the 1991 Gulf War.[101] Not only was there no explicit Security Council authorization,[102] but there was also no actual or imminent armed attack by Iraq that would place a forcible response clearly within well-accepted parameters for self-defense.[103] Instead, consistent with their long-standing position, the United States and Britain argued that Resolution 678 provided continuing authority to use force in the face of material breaches by Iraq of its disarmament obligations. But the sharp international disagreement over the war's legality and legitimacy demonstrably affected the willingness of states to contribute forces both to the combat phase and to the critically important follow-on mission to stabilize Iraq and support the transition to a viable and representative government.

Britain contributed significant forces to the intervention, and a number of other states – Spain, Poland, Italy, among others – contributed forces for stabilization missions close on the heels of the end of major combat. But key NATO allies that had participated in the Kosovo intervention – France and Germany, in particular – declined to participate. What is more, although the Security Council, in May 2003, affirmed the authority of the occupying powers in Iraq – and invited other states to contribute to postwar

---

[101] For a wide range of viewpoints about the lawfulness of the military action against Iraq, *see Agora: Future Implications of the Iraq Conflict*, 97 AM J. INT'L L. 553 (2003).

[102] The United States, Britain, and Spain withdrew the so-called "second resolution" in the face of a French threat to veto it and a broader lack of support. Even the second resolution fell short of an explicit authorization of force. It would, however, have affirmed that Iraq had failed to take the final opportunity to disarm afforded by Resolution 1441. *See U.S.-British Draft Resolution Stating Position on Iraq*, THE NEW YORK TIMES, Feb. 25, 2003, at A14.

[103] Neither the United Kingdom nor Australia invoked self-defense as a legal justification for military action against Iraq. *See* UK Attorney General Lord Peter Henry Goldsmith, *Legal Basis for Use of Force Against Iraq* (March 17, 2003), *available at* http://www.ukonline.gov.uk; *see also* the Australian Attorney General's Department and the Department of Foreign Affairs and Trade, Memorandum of Advice on the Use of Force Against Iraq (March 18, 2003), *available at* http://www.smh.com.au/articles/2003/03/19/1047749818043.html. Nor did the United States invoke its inherent right of self-defense under Article 51 of the UN Charter in the legal justification it submitted to the UN Security Council. *Letter Dated March 20, 2003 from the Permanent Representative of the United States of America to the United Nations Addressed to the President of the Security Council*, U.N. Doc. S/2003/351, March 21, 2003 [arguing that "[t]he actions being taken are authorized under existing Council resolutions, including its resolutions 678 (1990) and 687 (1991)"]. Moreover, despite references to preemption in President Bush's speech to the nation on the eve of war, the United States declined to present such a legal rationale to the Security Council.

tasks – many states, including India, Pakistan, Turkey, France, Germany, Russia, and various Arab states – made it clear that they wanted a stronger and more explicit UN mandate before committing their troops and resources. Even after a clearer UN authorization was provided, the lack of a leading UN role, persistent insecurity on the ground in Iraq, and ongoing disagreement over the decision to go to war in the first place have continued to undermine U.S. efforts to seek greater international involvement in Iraq.

Despite the disputed legality of the intervention itself, circumstances on the ground might have led to a greater sense of legitimacy over time. Certainly, the perceived legitimacy of the U.S.-led intervention would have been greatly bolstered if large numbers of WMD had been seized in Iraq after the invasion. Instead, the lack of WMD, and the ongoing instability and violence in Iraq, fueled by a sustained insurgency against the occupation and the subsequent transitional governments, have undercut the intervention's legitimacy in the eyes of many governments and publics around the world. Although legality at the outset is no guarantee either of success or of sustainable international contributions and support, it does provide a degree of protection against a negative spiraling effect of international criticism and withdrawal when conditions on the ground get tough, as they so often do in ambitious interventions that seek to stabilize and rebuild countries after conflict.

IV. INTERNATIONAL LAW AND LEGITIMATE OBJECTIVES OF INTERVENTION

Just as clear international legal authority can influence whether states are prepared to join or support an intervention, international law also has an impact on the overarching goals that intervening states legitimately can pursue. Interveners can no longer seek political dominion and territorial aggrandizement without regard to international opinion or the views of the local population. Today, principles of self-determination and international human rights law constrain the objectives that interveners legitimately can seek to advance. Whether interveners assist in ushering in independence, as Australian-led forces did in East Timor, or depose the repressive Taliban regime as a necessary step to unraveling al-Qaeda's hold on Afghanistan, as U.S.-led forces did at the end of 2001, interveners face strong international expectations that they will help build democratic, representative, and human rights-respecting governance structures and legal institutions in the wake of military action. In many instances, the Security Council has adopted resolutions expressly affirming such objectives.

Even in recent interventions whose legal basis has been controversial, international legal norms have influenced the objectives of the intervention. NATO's intervention in Kosovo and the U.S.-led intervention in Iraq in 2003, for instance, were not carried out for reasons of territorial aggrandizement or dominion. On the contrary, in both cases the interveners have sought to establish security and to help build governance structures that advance fundamental goals of self-determination and protection of human rights, although Kosovo's unresolved political status has complicated matters considerably. In both cases, moreover, the interveners sought subsequent resolutions from the Security Council to bolster international support for their post-conflict rebuilding efforts, though in Iraq the United States was reluctant to cede any significant authority to the United Nations.

Not only the overarching goals of an intervention, but also more specific reconstruction efforts, are influenced in concrete ways by international legal norms. Interveners must take fundamental international human rights principles into account both in their own conduct and in building legal and political institutions in post-conflict societies. In assisting local leaders as they draft constitutions, for instance, interveners have stressed the protection of minority rights and the rights of women. Likewise, in establishing police forces, interveners have sought to provide training and guidelines for action that respect fundamental human rights. Pursuing legal accountability for atrocities in a way that meets international standards of due process has been an important goal in many recent interventions.

Interveners must operate within an accepted legal framework as they engage in post-conflict reconstruction and work to strengthen the rule of law. In most of the cases studied in this book, interveners have sought and obtained clear Security Council authorization under Chapter VII of the UN Charter to engage in a range of post-conflict rebuilding activities. In some cases, as in Iraq, interveners have operated under the law of occupation, supplemented by Security Council resolutions.[104] Whether they seek Security Council authorization, host state consent, or operate under principles of occupation law, interveners will need to take seriously the question of legal authority as they work to rebuild and even transform legal and political institutions in post-conflict societies.[105]

Finally, interveners themselves must comport with international standards of conduct or they will be soundly and justifiably criticized. The abusive misconduct of some U.S. personnel in the Abu Ghraib prison in Iraq, for example, shows the understandable outrage that will erupt when interveners fail to abide by fundamental standards of international law. If interveners seek to strengthen the rule of law domestically – and encourage lawful behavior by local authorities – they must not undermine their own credibility by violating basic legal norms themselves.

---

[104] For analysis, *see* David J. Scheffer, *Beyond Occupation Law*, 97 AM. J. INT'L L. 842 (2003); Gregory H. Fox, *The Occupation of Iraq*, 36 GEO. J. INT'L L. 195 (2005).

[105] *See* Bruce M. Oswald, *Model Codes for Criminal Justice and Peace Operations: Some Legal Issues*, 9 J. CONFLICT & SECURITY L. 253 (2004) (discussing legal authority based on Security Council resolutions under Chapter VII, host country consent, and occupation law).

V. LOCAL PERCEPTIONS OF AN INTERVENTION'S LEGITIMACY

Local perceptions of an intervention's legitimacy are, of course, critical in building support for new or reformed institutions that aim to advance the rule of law. In many cases, interveners find themselves climbing a steep wall of local skepticism. Even if they are fairly seen as liberators from tyranny or a bulwark against further civil war, there is no honor for domestic populations in being the object of an intervention. Local gratitude can be quickly vitiated by a sense of humiliation or disappointed expectations if foreign occupiers fail to deliver an improved quality of life.

Though perhaps not of crucial interest to the local population, disputes about an intervention's legality can have a significant impact on an intervention and its ultimate, long-term success. For one thing, other states that might help rebuild a war-torn country may be less likely to contribute if the intervention's legality and legitimacy is contested. In the case of Iraq, this was important to European and other governments, and the refusal of many states to participate made the occupation primarily American, complicating legitimacy within Iraq. Broad-based coalitions with clear international legal authority can help to reassure skeptical domestic audiences about an intervention's purposes, giving domestic spoilers less latitude to opportunistically undermine reconstruction efforts or to appeal to potential regional spoilers. And regional actors themselves will face more unified international pressure not to undermine post-conflict reconstruction.

The domestic legitimacy of an intervention will turn on many additional factors, including the character of the previous regime or situation. Depending largely on what preceded it, international interventions will begin with different baselines of legitimacy among the local population. In Afghanistan, historic hostility toward outside intervention was mitigated by comparison with the brutal Taliban regime and decades of bitter civil war, giving the U.S.-led intervention a very strong base of domestic support.[106] Likewise, Kosovo's majority Albanian population, subjected to long-standing discrimination, welcomed NATO's intervention. But various groups within a country will view an intervention differently depending on their interests. Kosovo's Serb population, for instance, has a very different view of NATO's intervention; likewise, in Iraq, the Kurdish population overwhelmingly supported the U.S-led intervention in contrast to opposition by a majority of Iraq's Sunni population.[107] Different domestic groups will usually be advantaged, or

---

[106] In a January 2006 poll, 82 percent of Afghans surveyed said that "overthrowing the Taliban government was a good thing for Afghanistan" and 83 percent expressed a favorable view of "the US military forces in our country." *New WPO Poll: Afghan Public Overwhelmingly Rejects al-Qaeda, Taliban*, January 11, 2006, *available at* http://www.worldpublicopinion.org.

[107] For public opinion surveys in Iraq, *see* the Brookings Iraq Index, January 17, 2006, at 38, *available at* http://www.brookings.edu/fp/saban/iraq/index.pdf (citing October/November

disadvantaged, by an intervention, and a persistent or widening gap between "winners" and "losers" can seriously undermine the prospects for ultimate success.

The legitimacy of an intervention in local eyes will also depend on the goals that interveners pursue and their effectiveness in meeting local needs. Are interveners able to establish basic security quickly and deal credibly and robustly with violent obstructionists? Can interveners address concrete needs for food, water, electricity, health care, and so forth? As we discuss in later chapters, interveners have a window of opportunity to demonstrate that conditions are changing for the better – an opportunity to build momentum and domestic support for reform. But this window closes quickly. Moreover, the first impressions made by interveners can be critical in building public confidence and enlisting domestic support for longer-term reform. Furthermore, how interveners conduct themselves – including whether they abide by basic standards of human rights and human decency – will shape local perceptions of legitimacy and can leave a lasting imprint on domestic populations.

Just as interveners must do their best to adhere to international standards of conduct and avoid undercutting their rule of law message, they must also understand and show respect for local culture if they hope to gain the support and confidence of domestic audiences. A "cultural dilemma" can arise, however, presenting interveners with difficult choices. Local cultural mores and traditions that enjoy strong popular legitimacy may at times be in tension with international human rights principles and objectives. This raises hard questions: how much transformative change can realistically be "imprinted" upon a post-conflict society by outsiders? And where gaps do appear – especially in the areas surrounding the rule of law (e.g., governance, minority protections, women's rights) – how can the seeds of reform be planted and sustained so that when change does occur it will enjoy domestic legitimacy? Ways in which international and local leaders, as well as international organizations, have grappled with these difficult challenges are examined in various places throughout this book.

CONCLUSION

In each of the post–Cold War military interventions that we address, the question of legal authority to intervene has been an important one. The UN Security Council expressly authorized some of these interventions and articulated agreed objectives. Other interventions were undertaken in self-defense, with strong international support. Even in cases where the legal basis for action was sharply contested, as in the 2003 Iraq War and NATO's 1999

2005 *Time*–ABC News Poll, in which 80 percent of those surveyed in the Kurdish area said the United States "was right to invade Iraq," in contrast to 16 percent in the Sunni area and 58 percent in the Shi'ite area).

intervention in Kosovo, the intervening states argued that their decision to use force was consistent with Security Council resolutions and objectives. In contrast to much earlier historical periods, in which states were largely free to use force to further their own territorial and political ambitions, and to conduct interventions however they saw fit, states using force in the post–Cold War era have sought to defend the lawfulness and legitimacy of their interventions in relation to fundamental international legal norms, including not only the UN Charter but also fundamental principles of international human rights law.

Indeed, despite international discord over some recent military interventions, the UN Charter remains the agreed international legal framework under which states seek to defend and evaluate decisions to use force.[108] If anything, the need to explain and justify one's actions in relation to the Charter's norms governing force is becoming more important in building effective coalitions with democratic allies whose domestic publics take these norms seriously – as the United States found in working with Britain and other allies in Iraq. The issue of justification may become increasingly more important in an information age in which publics are exposed to broader arrays of critical information and are more easily mobilized.

The widespread acceptance of the Charter framework – and the fact that states using force seek to explain and justify their actions within that framework – does not preclude strong disagreements about what the Charter permits or prohibits. An intervention's legality, moreover, is only one of many factors – most fundamentally, national security interests and political priorities – that bear on state decisions to use force or to assist in post-conflict reconstruction. Governments need to be convinced that participation serves their national interests and values and that the effort itself has some reasonable prospect of success. But the Charter's norms are such a fundamental part of the architecture of international law that intervening states ignore them at their peril, particularly if those states want other countries to assist in interventions and in subsequent post-conflict rebuilding. The terrorist threats of the post-9/11 era – demanding as they are – have not fundamentally changed this reality.[109]

---

[108] Although the inability to forge common ground on the UN Security Council over Iraq and over Kosovo before intervention were low moments for the UN system, it is exaggerated and premature to claim that the UN Charter is "dead," as some commentators have done. *See* Michael J. Glennon, *Why the Security Council Failed*, 82 FOREIGN AFFAIRS 16–18, 24 (May/June 2003). For a critique of Glennon's argument, *see* Stromseth, *Law and Force after Iraq*, *supra* note 79, at 632–634.

[109] Thwarting terrorist networks bent on acquiring weapons of mass destruction will require the active cooperation and assistance of many allies. So finding common ground on the legitimate scope of military action in self-defense and the appropriate role of law enforcement will be important to effectively countering this threat. *See* Stromseth, *Law and Force after Iraq*, *supra* note 79, at 637–640.

International law – particularly human rights law and principles of self-determination – also influences the goals that interveners can legitimately pursue as they work to rebuild war-torn countries. The demands of post-conflict reconstruction, and the specific challenges of building the rule of law after intervention, are enormous. Not only tremendous patience, persistence, and considerable resources but also the support and contributions of many states and organizations will generally be vital to success. Acting consistently with fundamental norms of international law may not guarantee international support or assure domestic legitimacy, but violating agreed principles of international law can certainly undercut both. Moreover, precisely because building the rule of law after intervention depends on strengthening cultural commitments to – and public confidence in – *the very idea of law*, the perceived legitimacy of the interveners' own conduct inevitably will influence the effectiveness of their efforts.

In the chapters that follow we explore the many complex challenges – social, political, normative, institutional – confronting interveners and domestic reformers who seek to strengthen the rule of law in post-conflict societies. But before we do, we must first address the most fundamental question of all: what does it mean to build "the rule of law"? This vital and difficult question is addressed in Chapter 3.

CHAPTER THREE

What Is the Rule of Law?: A Pragmatic Definition and a Synergistic Approach

I. THE RULE OF LAW: "I KNOW IT WHEN I SEE IT"?

The late Potter Stewart, a justice on the U.S. Supreme Court, once famously remarked that there was no need for the court to define the term *obscenity*: when it came to obscenity, Stewart said, "I know it when I see it." For many people, the phrase *the rule of law* often seems to have a similar quality.

In its colloquial sense, the phrase *the rule of law* implies a rather vague cluster of concepts: fairness, justice, predictability, equality under law. When we think of the rule of law, we may think of the phrase first made famous by Aristotle and often cited by the founders of the American republic: the rule of law involves a "government of laws, not men." More concretely, we may think of the rule of law as having something to do with certain kinds of institutions and structures: well-functioning, respected courts, judicial review, fair and adequate legal codes, well-trained lawyers, and so on. To some extent, we may also equate the rule of law with respect for basic civil and political rights.

For the most part, even those of us who work on rule of law issues would be hard pressed to go beyond these intuitions and offer a precise definition of the rule of law. Yet like Justice Stewart, we are nonetheless pretty sure that we know it when we see it. Thus, we would likely say confidently that the United States is a nation under the rule of law; so is Sweden, so is Botswana, so is Japan, and so are most stable, prosperous democratic nations, despite their varying legal systems and despite occasional problems. However, most people would not hesitate to say that postwar Iraq is still quite lacking when it comes to the rule of law, as are Liberia, North Korea, and Afghanistan.

In the foreign policy world, most policymakers and practitioners take it for granted that the rule of law is something everyone needs in post-conflict and post-intervention societies, something that is clearly worth pursuing through a variety of more and less coercive projects – even in the absence of a precise and agreed-on definition. Indeed, as observers such as the

Carnegie Endowment for International Peace's Tom Carothers have noted, "the rule of law" has become something of a foreign policy mantra over the past decade.

Perhaps precisely *because* of its elusive definition, the importance of the rule of law is something everyone can agree on, from World Bank experts and human rights activists to military officials. From the president of the United States to the UN Secretary-General, from U.S. Defense Secretary Donald Rumsfeld to the habitués of Davos, policymakers and pundits insist that creating the rule of law must be a top international priority in post-intervention societies. As President George W. Bush put it in his 2002 State of the Union speech, the rule of law is one of the "non-negotiable demands of human dignity," for which "America will always stand firm."[1] In his 2005 inaugural speech, President Bush emphasized that that "freedom" must be "sustained by the rule of law...."[2]

This chapter suggests, however, that *the idea of the rule of law is not nearly as simple as many people would like to assume.* The notion that the rule of law has an "I know it when I see it" quality captures something powerful, because we *do* know it when we see it, and we most certainly know it when we *don't* see it.

But as a guide to making intelligent policy decisions, "I know it when I see it" is not terribly effective. Indeed, naïve and superficial understandings of the rule of law can lead to foreign policy embarrassments, as the United States and the international community become embroiled in projects that are ultimately self-undermining.

In truth, the rule of law is a complex, fragile, and to some extent inherently unrealizable goal. Nonetheless, projects that are self-conscious about the nuances and paradoxes of the rule of law are much more likely to be successful than projects that rely entirely on the old "I know it when I see it" standard.

This chapter outlines some of the ways in which the concept of the rule of law is deployed by various actors in the foreign policy debate, from human rights advocates to economic policy analysts to national security experts. It then briefly describes and takes stock of the recent history of rule of law-promotion efforts in troubled societies.

Taking a step back, this chapter then explores some of the efforts scholars and policy analysts have made to define the elusive idea of the rule of law, and suggests some reasons for the disappointing outcomes of past rule of law-promotion efforts.

Finally, this chapter proposes a pragmatic definition of the rule of law to help guide future discussions and suggests that policymakers adopt what

[1] President George W. Bush, State of the Union Address, January 29, 2002.
[2] President George W. Bush, Inaugural Address, January 20, 2005.

we term the *synergistic approach* to the rule of law – an approach that emphasizes the degree to which the rule of law involves numerous moving but interlocking parts, each of which is indispensable, and each of which helps make the rule of law far more than just the sum of its parts.

II. BACKGROUND: RULE OF LAW PROMOTION: A GROWTH INDUSTRY

The past decade has seen a surge in American and international efforts to promote the rule of law around the globe, especially in post-intervention and "transitional" societies. As Tom Carothers remarked in a provocative 1998 *Foreign Affairs* article, "One cannot get through a foreign policy debate these days without someone proposing the rule of law as a solution to the world's troubles."[3] Nearly a decade later, this remains true. Like apple pie and ice cream, the rule of law is a concept no one can dislike, and even institutional actors who normally find little common ground generally agree on the value of the rule of law.

The World Bank and multinational corporations want the rule of law, because the sanctity of private property and the enforcement of contracts are critical to modern conceptions of the free market. One former World Bank economist notes wryly that "it sometimes seems like the phrases 'capitalism' and 'the rule of law' go together 'like the phrases love and marriage.'"[4] Another commentator observes that the "conventional wisdom in the international development community" is that "a crucial, if not decisive, factor in enticing investment is a stable, consistent, fair and transparent legal system";[5] still another asserts that "simply put, formal law is the foundation of the market system, essential to the development of corporations, limited liability contracts and an adequate business environment."[6] Most in the economic development and corporate communities assume that the rule of law entails or produces sensible, intelligible regulations, effective

---

[3] Thomas Carothers, *The Rule of Law Revival*, 77 FOREIGN AFFAIRS 95 (March/April 1998). Cf. Paul Kahn, THE CULTURAL STUDY OF LAW: RECONSTRUCTING LEGAL SCHOLARSHIP (1999): "When we look . . . at recent developments in Eastern Europe and Latin America, we speak of the progressive transition from dictatorial systems to the rule of law. We measure their progress – or lack of it – against our end. When we observe third world countries, we see the absence of law's rule as a pathological condition. We have a missionary zeal, believing our truth to be revealed truth. . . . Not to see the end of social order as the rule of law strikes us as unnatural."

[4] Memorandum from Ruthanne Deutsch, (Re)constructing the Rule of Law in Post-Conflict Societies (2002; on file with authors).

[5] John Hewko, *Foreign Direct Investment: Does the Rule of Law Matter?*, Carnegie Endowment for International Peace, Rule of Law Series, Working Paper No. 26, April 2002. Hewko is skeptical of the conventional wisdom, arguing that "the philosophical framework the international development community has traditionally used to carry out its legislative and institutional reform efforts . . . is incomplete. . . ." Id., at 6.

[6] Hernando de Soto, *Preface*, in THE LAW AND ECONOMICS OF DEVELOPMENT (Edgardo Buscaglia et al., eds., 1997), at xiv.

dispute resolution mechanisms, and a predictable, fair legal framework in which property interests can effectively be protected. Thus, for those concerned with the creation of a stable, favorable business climate and with new investment and market opportunities, the rule of law is often conceptualized as a necessary prerequisite.

Human rights advocates, though not typically allies of multinational corporations, business interests, or international financial institutions, are similarly enthusiastic about the rule of law. As Yale Law School professor Owen Fiss has observed, the "rule of law revival we are experiencing today" can be partly "traced to the triumph of human rights...there has been an increasing demand for law, or, more specifically, for the treatment of human rights as justiciable claims rather than mere aspirations, and for legal institutions that are able to enforce these claims."[7] The human rights-oriented conception of the rule of law involves, at a minimum, due process, equality before law, and judicial checks on executive power, for most human rights advocates regard these as essential prerequisites to the protection of substantive human rights. To human rights advocates, where the rule of law is absent, human rights violations flourish: without the rule of law, arrests and detentions are arbitrary, there is no effective mechanism for preventing torture or extrajudicial execution; individuals or groups may be free to take the law into their own hands in abusive and violent ways, and abuses go unpunished in a climate of impunity. Other rights such as freedom of expression and freedom of conscience also cannot be realized without a protective network of laws to sustain them. Promoting the rule of law thus seems to most human rights advocates like a critical component of protecting fundamental human rights.

Increasingly, international and national security experts also want to promote the rule of law, seeing it as a key aspect of preventing terrorism.[8]

---

[7] See, e.g., Owen Fiss, The Autonomy of Law, in SELA 2000, SEMINARIO EN LATINOAMERICA DE TEROIA CONSTITUCIONAL Y POLITICA: THE RULE OF LAW (JUNE 8–11, 2000), at I-26: "The rule of law revival that we are experiencing today is not just a product of the neoliberal development paradigm but can also be traced to the triumph of human rights.... It extends throughout the world. It represents, as Michael Ignatieff has said, a revolution in human consciousness. As part of this revolution, there has been an increasing demand for law, or, more specifically, for the treatment of human rights as justiciable claims rather than mere aspirations, and for legal institutions that are able to enforce these claims."

In the wake of September 11, the human rights community has redoubled its commitment to promoting "the rule of law," although many within the human rights community have grown increasingly concerned by the apparent willingness of some democratic governments to value national security concerns over strict adherence to domestic and international legal norms. See, e.g., Lawyers Committee for Human Rights, Imbalance of Powers: How Changes to U.S. Law and Security Since 9/11 Erode Human Rights and Civil Liberties (2003). Security Council.

[8] See, e.g., Council on Foreign Relations, Iraq: The Day After (2003). See also Robert Kaiser, U.S. Plants Footprint in Shaky Central Asia, THE WASHINGTON POST, August 27, 2002, at A1. See also Thomas Carothers, The New Aid, THE WASHINGTON POST, April 16, 2002, at A19. See also Thomas Carothers, Promoting Democracy and Fighting Terror, 82 FOREIGN

Especially since September 11, 2001, military and intelligence analysts have drawn attention to the ways in which the absence of the rule of law can lead to instability and violence and create fertile recruiting grounds for terrorist organizations. The logic here is straightforward: although the roots of terrorism are complex, misery and repression create fertile ground for terrorist recruiters. If the rule of law is necessary to economic growth and to eliminating egregious human rights abuses, then by extension the rule of law plays a key role in eliminating the conditions that give rise to violence and terror.

Given their differing motivations and priorities, human rights advocates, economic analysts, and those concerned primarily with national and international security naturally differ on the proper law reform priorities for transitional societies. They quarrel over whether commercial law reform should precede criminal law reform, whether the creation of courts to sort out property disputes (often a major post-intervention concern) should take priority over the creation of human rights and war crimes courts, and whether judicial reform ought to come before police and military reform.

How to allocate resources inevitably causes tensions between the groups, and since September 11, 2001, the three groups have also disagreed about the imperatives of the "war on terror," which many rights advocates see as privileging short-term security concerns over longer-term commitments to promoting human rights.[9] Nonetheless, the three groups (which can overlap) share the basic assumption that the rule of law is central to stable and modern democratic society.[10]

AFFAIRS Jan./Feb. 2003), noting that "The United States faces two contradictory imperatives: on the one hand, the fight against al Qaeda tempts Washington to put aside its democratic scruples and seek closer ties with autocracies throughout the Middle East and Asia. On the other hand, U.S. officials and policy experts have increasingly come to believe that it is precisely the lack of democracy in many of these countries that helps breed Islamic extremism." Post-September 11 events have undeniably raised new questions about whether even democratic cultures share a universal conception of "the rule of law" and its relative importance vis-à-vis national security.

Nevertheless, rhetorical commitments to "the rule of law" also continue to be made by numerous governmental actors. *See, e.g.,* George W. Bush, State of the Union Address, January 29, 2002: "America will always stand firm for the non-negotiable demands of human dignity: the rule of law; limits on the power of the state; respect for women; private property; free speech; equal justice; and religious tolerance." Similarly, the U.S. Department of State puts news releases related to the treatment of Iraqi prisoners of war and Guantanamo detainees in a section of its Web site titled, *The Rule of Law. See* http://usinfo.state.gov/dhr/democracy/rule_of_law.html (last accessed May 10, 2003). As this chapter discusses, the concept of "the rule of law" is amorphous and undertheorized; perhaps for this reason, groups as otherwise disparate as free market advocates, human rights activists, and national security hawks have all been eager to embrace the concept.

[9] *See, e.g.,* Human Rights Watch, *Anti-Terror Campaign Cloaking Human Rights Abuse,* January 16, 2002, *available at* http://www.hrw.org/press/2002/01/wr2002.htm.

[10] What's more, despite tussles over priorities, all three groups often assume that creating the rule of law in one sphere will have automatic positive spillover effects in the other: that is, if a given society has functioning judicial bodies that enforce contracts fairly and protect

The widespread agreement on the importance of the rule of law has led to a range of ambitious international projects designed to promote the rule of law in troubled or "transitional" societies. Many of the early rule of law promotion efforts were in Latin America, beginning in the 1970s and 1980s, as foreign donors sought to speed democratic transitions in formerly autocratic and repressive Latin American nations.[11] Foreign donors, and particularly the U.S. Agency for International Development (USAID), poured resources into training programs for judges, the provision of external experts (often American law professors) to help nations "modernize" their laws, and similar programs throughout Latin America.

The pace and funding levels of international rule of law programs increased dramatically in the early 1990s, as the collapse of the Soviet Union and the toppling of totalitarian regimes in other parts of the globe dramatically energized rule of law assistance.[12] In the wake of the Soviet Union's collapse, one commentator described a veritable "explosion of rule-of-law assistance" around the world.[13] In both Latin America and the former Soviet states, the focus of rule of law programs was democratization and decentralization, on the elimination of state abuses (in Latin America, anticommunism had fueled numerous state abuses; in the former Soviet states, of course, communist ideology itself fueled the abuses). Despite opposing ideologies, similarly top-down governance styles led to arbitrariness and abuse of power in Latin America and in the former Soviet bloc. In both cases, rule of law promotion efforts were linked simultaneously to efforts to eliminate abusive state policies (torture, arbitrary detention, and extrajudicial execution, for instance) and to efforts to promote capitalism and market-oriented reforms.

---

property rights, that society will ultimately also protect basic civil and political rights and vice versa. *See* Carothers, *The Rule of Law Revival*, *supra* note 3. There is, to our knowledge, little empirical evidence to support this assumption, and some work that calls it into question. *See, e.g.,* Susan Rose-Ackerman, *Political Corruption and Democracy*, 14 CONN J. INT'L L. 363 (1999); *see also* Hewko, *supra* note 5.

[11] *See* Linn Hammergren, *Applying Rule of Law Lessons from Latin America*, USAID Center for Democracy and Governance, Fall 1997, *available at* http://www.usaid.gov/our_work/democracy_and_governance/publications/pdfs/ddfallwin97_fi.pdf, for a description and analysis of many of these early programs. *See also* Linn Hammergren, *Do Judicial Councils Further Judicial Reform?: Lessons from Latin America*, 28 CARNEGIE ENDOWMENT FOR INT'L PEACE (June 2002).

[12] *See* Carothers, *The Rule Of Law Revival*, *supra* note 3.

[13] Thomas Carothers, AIDING DEMOCRACY ABROAD: THE LEARNING CURVE (1999), at 165. For some similar observations, *see* Mark Tushnet, *Returning with Interest: Observations on Some Putative Benefits of Studying Comparative Constitutional Law*, 1 U. PA. J. CONST. L. 325 (1998), noting "the upsurge of interest in comparative constitutional law among U.S. constitutional scholars," which "may be the result of the break-up of the Soviet Union, and the rapid and widespread transformation of non-democratic regimes in proto-democratic or democratic nation-states. A byproduct of the rapidity with which the change occurred was the proliferation of efforts by U.S. constitutionalists to instruct people elsewhere on what a well-designed constitution should look like."

By the mid-1990s, an increasing number of "failed states," civil wars, and human rights crises also fueled enthusiasm for rule of law promotion efforts as a way to rebuild shattered societies broken apart by civil wars and ethnic conflicts. Crises in Bosnia, Rwanda, Kosovo, East Timor, and Sierra Leone led to rule of law promotion efforts designed to rebuild (or at times build up from scratch) legal institutions, restore functioning governments, provide accountability for abuses and war crimes, and permit gradual economic recovery.

Most recently, in Afghanistan and Iraq, U.S.-dominated military interventions, though primarily motivated by national security concerns, have led to post-intervention programs to restore the rule of law. Like earlier programs in Latin America and the former Soviet states, these programs have focused to a significant extent on the rewriting of constitutions and key legislation, support to law enforcement and courts, and the provision of other forms of structural and technical assistance.

Promoting the rule of law has been an expensive enterprise. Although we argue, throughout this book, that many past rule of law efforts have suffered by being underresourced relative to their actual needs, even underresourced programs have had large price tags. Since 1990, the United States and other bilateral and multilateral donors have spent literally billions of dollars on "promoting the rule of law," and those huge governmental sums have been matched by similarly large donations from private foundations.[14] Because the "war on terrorism" has given further impetus to U.S. and international enthusiasm for rule of law promotion, millions more have been budgeted for rule of law programs in post-Taliban Afghanistan[15] and postwar Iraq.[16]

---

[14] It is impossible to offer a precise figure, however, given the many nations and agencies, public and private, involved in rule of law efforts and the definitional issues (e.g., should all democracy promotion be seen as "rule of law"?). *See, e.g.*, Peter Baker, *Funding Scarce for Export of Democracy – Outside Mideast, U.S. Effort Lags*, THE WASHINGTON POST, March 18, 2005, at A1. "Measuring how much Washington spends on democracy promotion is difficult because the money is scattered among programs and much of it is embedded in grants by the U.S. Agency for International Development. But recent trends have been clear. USAID spending on democracy and governance programs alone shot up from $671 million in 2002 to $1.2 billion in 2004, but almost all of that increase was devoted to Iraq and Afghanistan. Without those two countries, the USAID democracy spending in 2004 was $685 million, virtually unchanged from two years earlier." *See also* http://www.whitehouse.gov/omb/budget/fy2006/state.html. (In 2004, the United States provided approximately $38.5 million in FREEDOM Support Act funds to strengthen democracy, human rights, and the rule of law in Central Asia, including assistance with legislative drafting; training judges, prosecutors, and public defenders; and providing advisors for judicial and prison reform.) *See also* Carothers, *The Rule of Law Revival*, *supra* note 3.

[15] *See, e.g., USAID: Rebuilding Afghanistan: the U.S. Commitment, available at* http://www. usaid.gov/about/afghanistan/rebuilding_afghanistan.pdf (last accessed August 23, 2002).

[16] *See, e.g., FY06 OMB Budget Proposal, available at* http://www.whitehouse.gov/omb/pdf/ Diplomacy-06.pdf. Under promoting global democracy and prosperity: $360 million in economic assistance to help the Iraqi government deliver basic services to its people,

This book's central concern is with an *obvious and major shift in the nature of much rule of law assistance* over the course of the past decade. Until the mid-1990s, rule of law assistance generally involved aid packages designed to encourage governmental law reform initiatives undertaken by indigenous authorities and to support law-related NGOs.[17] In recent years, however, with the upsurge in United Nations and NATO peacekeeping operations, and the post-September 11 military interventions by the United States, there have been more and more situations in which the United States, UN, and other key actors – the European Union, the Organization for Security and Cooperation in Europe (OSCE), etc. – have ended up wholly or partially administering a society in crisis.

Thus, in Kosovo, the United Nations, the European Union, the OSCE, and NATO still collaborate to administer Kosovo under a UN umbrella, assisting the fledgling Kosovar governance structure.[18] In East Timor, the UN was the central government until the elections leading to East Timor's emergence as an independent country, and the UN continued to play a substantial supporting role in East Timor.[19] In Sierra Leone, where it took thousands of UN peacekeepers, as well as British soldiers, to help stop a brutal civil war, the fragile indigenous government relied heavily on external interveners for over half a decade to maintain security and help with everything from education, health care, and food aid to legal and judicial reform.[20]

In Afghanistan, the Bush Administration's early determination to resist "nation-building" adventures collapsed in the wake of September 11; even today, more than five years later, the new post-Taliban government survives only with massive external support provided by the U.S.-led coalition, the United Nations, the European Union, and dozens of international nongovernmental organizations. International experts inspect Afghan prisons,

collect revenues, and develop a free-market system capable of joining the global economy; $120 million for the Middle East Partnership Initiative to expand democracy, support political, economic, and social reform, and improve access to education, information, and jobs; $80 million, an increase of $20 million over 2005 levels, for the National Endowment for Democracy (NED) to provide grants to private groups and organizations that build and strengthen democratic institutions and promote the rule of law, human rights, civic education, and a free press; a $10 million contribution to the United Nations Democracy Fund to provide technical assistance to nations adopting democratic reforms.

[17] *See* Carothers, *The Rule of Law Revival*, *supra* note 3.

[18] *See* S.C. Res. 1244, U.N. Doc.S/RES/1244, June 10, 1999 (establishing the international administrative and security presence in Kosovo).

[19] The United Nations concluded its mission to East Timor in May 2005, but a small UN office continues to provide some assistance. *See* U.N. Doc.S/2005/310, *The Secretary-General, End of Mandate Report of the Secretary-General on the United Nations Mission in Support of East Timor*, U.N. Doc. May 12, 2005.

[20] As in East Timor, the UN continues to play a reduced role following the December 2005 withdrawal of its mission in Sierra Leone. *See* U.N. Doc.S/2005/777, *The Secretary-General, Twenty-Seventh Report of the Secretary-General on the United Nations Mission in Sierra Leone*, U.N. Doc. December 12, 2005.

train police and judges, plan elections, and help rewrite the laws. A NATO-led international security assistance force patrols the streets of Kabul, and American soldiers continue military operations to root out residual (and in some areas resurgent) al-Qaeda and Taliban elements in the south and east of the country.[21]

In Iraq, the U.S.-led coalition was an occupying power under the laws of war, and UN Security Council Resolution 1483 gave the United States full authority to run postwar Iraq, pending a transition to a democratically elected Iraqi government.[22] Today, even after the formal transfer of sovereignty to the Iraqis and subsequent parliamentary elections, the United States still exercises great influence over the fledgling Iraqi government and maintains a massive troop presence on the ground. Although continuing problems in Iraq have left the United States searching for escape routes, for the foreseeable future the U.S. government remains ambivalently committed to the project of recreating postwar Iraq, in much the same way that U.S. occupying forces recreated post–World War II Germany and Japan.

From Kosovo and East Timor to Afghanistan and Iraq, promoting the rule of law has become what some commentators have dubbed a neocolonialist or neoimperialist enterprise, in which foreign administrators backed by large armies govern societies that have been pronounced "unready" to take on the task of governing themselves.[23] This near-wholesale appropriation by outsiders of key internal governance tasks raises a host of issues. It also creates both new opportunities and new challenges of a type the United States has not seen since the post–World War II era, with the Allied occupations of Germany and Japan. Arguably, however, the challenges are far greater in today's global age.

---

[21] Sam Zia-Zarifi, Human Rights Watch, *World Report 2004: Losing the Peace in Afghanistan*, January 2004, *available at* http://www.hrw.org/wr2k4/5.htm. *See generally* Consortium for Response to the Afghanistan Transition, *Report: Filling the Vacuum: Prerequisites to Security in Afghanistan*, March 2002. Many critics charge that the international community has nevertheless put too few resources into rebuilding Afghanistan and that lawlessness prevails in much of the country. *See, e.g., Afghanistan*, HUMAN RIGHTS WATCH WORLD REPORT 2006, 220–226, *available at* http://hrw.org/wr2k6/wr2006.pdf. *See also* interview with William H. Spencer, Senior Advisor, International Resource Group, August 26, 2002 (notes on file with authors); U.N. Doc.A/60/224-S/2005/525, *The Secretary-General, The Situation in Afghanistan and its Implications for International Peace and Security – Emergency International Assistance for Peace, Normalcy, and Reconstruction of War-Stricken Afghanistan*, delivered to the Security Council and the General Assembly, para. 3, U.N. Doc. August 12, 2005. News reports confirm these sources. *See, e.g.*, Belquis Ahmadi, *Reality Gap in Afghanistan*, THE WASHINGTON POST, July 8, 2002; Carlotta Gall, *As NATO Forces Ease Role of G.I.'s in Afghanistan, the Taliban Steps up Attacks*, THE NEW YORK TIMES, December 11, 2005.

[22] S.C. Res. 1483, U.N. Doc.S/RES/1483, May 22, 2003.

[23] For a critical commentary on America's role in these increasingly imperialist enterprises, *see, e.g.*, Michael Ignatieff, *The American Empire: The Burden*, THE NEW YORK TIMES MAGAZINE, January 25, 2003, at 22.

As the previous chapter noted, there are profound questions about the legality and legitimacy of some recent interventions. But the track record of recent interventions raises equally profound questions about the capacity of outsiders to have a significant positive impact on troubled societies. *Although elaborate rhetorical and financial commitments to rule of law programs have grown more and more common over the past decade, it remains to be seen how much impact most of these programs will actually have.* Indeed, despite billions of aid dollars, the initial impact of most programs to promote the rule of law have ranged from mixed to disappointing, with the prospect for real long-term change still profoundly unclear.[24] In Latin America, for instance, many commentators have concluded that the earlier era of rule of law promotion programs have had little lasting impact.[25] In Russia, more than a decade after a massive infusion of foreign aid began, there have been few unequivocal "rule of law" success stories.[26] Organized

[24] *See, e.g.*, Stephen Holmes, *Can Foreign Aid Promote the Rule of Law?* 8 EAST EUR. CONST. REV. 68(1999); *see also* Carothers, *The Rule of Law Revival, supra* note 3; Carothers, *Promoting the Rule of Law Abroad: The Problem of Knowledge*, Carnegie Endowment for International Peace, Rule of Law Series, Working Paper No. 34, January 2003; *see also* Stephen Golub, *Beyond Rule of Law Orthodoxy: The Legal Empowerment Alternative*, Carnegie Endowment for International Peace, Paper No. 41, October 2003. *See also* Hansjörg Strohmeyer, *Making Multilateral Interventions Work: The U.N. and the Creation of Transitional Justice Systems in Kosovo and East Timor*, 107 FLETCHER F. WORLD AFF. 107, 112 (2001); Anthony J. Miller, *Keynote Address: UNMIK: Lessons from the Early Institution-Building Phase*, 39 NEW ENG. L. REV. 9, 17 (2004); Karla Hoff & Joseph E. Stiglitz, *After the Big Bang?: Obstacles to the Emergence to the Rule of Law in Post-Communist Societies*, World Bank, Working Paper No. 9282, October 2002; Ronald J. Daniels & Michael Trebilcock, *The Political Economy of Rule of Law Reform in Developing Countries*, 26 MICH. J. INT'L L. 99 (2004); Christian Ahlund, *Major Obstacles to Building the Rule of Law in a Post-Conflict Environment*, 39 NEW ENG. L. REV. 39 (2004).

[25] *See, e.g.*, Linn Hammergren, *Applying Rule of Law Lessons from Latin America; see also* Carothers, *The Rule of Law Revival, supra* note 3; *see also* GAO, Foreign Assistance, Report GAO/NSAID-93-140, *Promoting Judicial Reform to Strengthen Democracies*, 1993; Golub, 2004. *See also* Jose E. Alvarez, *Promoting the 'Rule of Law' in Latin America: Problems and Prospects*, 25 GEO. WASH. J. INT'L L. ECON. 281 (1991).

[26] *See* Matthew Spence, *The Complexity of Success: The U.S. Role in Russian Rule of Law Reform*, July 2005, *available at* http://www.carnegieendowment.org/files/CP60.spence. FINAL.pdf, for a fine discussion of the complex history of rule of law efforts in Russia, including a subtle analysis of a recent success, the adoption of the Russian Criminal Procedure Code. *See* Leon Aron, *Russia Reinvents the Rule of Law*, 2002, *at* http://www.aei.org/publications/pubID.13781/pub_detail.asp.; Karla Hoff & Joseph E. Stiglitz, *After the Big Bang?: Obstacles to the Emergence to the Rule of Law in Post-Communist Societies*, World Bank, Working Paper No. 9282, October 2002. "When Russia launched mass privatization, it was widely believed that it would create a powerful constituency for the rule of law. That didn't happen." *See, e.g.*, Jeffrey D. Sachs & Katharina Pistor, *Introduction: Progress, Pitfalls, Scenarios, and Lost Opportunities, in* THE RULE OF LAW AND ECONOMIC REFORM IN RUSSIA (Jeffrey Sachs & Katharina Pistor, eds., 1997). *See, e.g.*, Walter Dellinger & Samuel P. Fried, *Promoting the Rule of Law Abroad: How the U.S. Legal and Business Communities Can Help*, XX WORLD POLICY JOURNAL 79 (2003):

crime continues to play an enormous role in the economy; corruption among public officials shows little sign of abating; economic hardship continues for millions; life expectancy remains lower than it was under communism; the prisons are overcrowded and allegations of abuse routine; and Russia's ill-starred military campaign in Chechnya has killed thousands, including many civilians who died as a result of massive Russian bombardments in Grozny.[27]

In Kosovo, grave problems still remain, despite the fact that the international community literally took over the province's administration in 1999, after a massive NATO bombing campaign ended a Serbian ethnic cleansing campaign. Kosovo is still home to nearly 17,000 NATO troops and a civilian UN administration adds hundreds of additional foreigners (including NGO representatives, civilian police, and OSCE and EU staff).[28] This is down from the 50,000 internationals based in Kosovo in 2001 (40,000 KFOR troops and 10,000 civilians), which worked out to roughly one foreigner for every thirty-six Kosovars, a ratio of foreign occupiers to locals that would have inspired the envy of 19th-century colonial powers. But despite the heavy international involvement, few would assert that the rule of law has been successfully recreated in Kosovo. Although some progress has been made in a number of areas,[29] ethnic intolerance continues to rage; thuggishness and organized crime still flourish.[30] The fledgling UN-sponsored Kosovar

---

" . . . America's efforts to promote the rule of law have met with mixed success. For example, after the fall of communism, the United States embarked on an effort to develop a constitution, modernize legal codes, and protect property rights in Russia. While those efforts yielded some positive results, few would deny that rampant corruption still plagues the Russian legal system."

[27] *See* Anatol Lieven, CHECHNYA: TOMBSTONE OF RUSSIAN POWER (1998). *See* Carothers, AIDING DEMOCRACY ABROAD, *supra* note 13, at 171–172: "In other parts of the world where the U.S. has invested significantly in rule of law aid, disappointment is also common. Some ten years later, the lack of rule of law in Russia is an open sore. . . . " *See also* Holmes, *supra* note 24.

[28] *See* NATO: KFOR Information, available on the Web at http://www.nato.int/kfor/kfor/kfor_hq.htm (updated 1/06); The Secretary-General, *Monthly Report to the United Nations on the Operations of the Kosovo Force, delivered to the Security Council*, U.N. DOC.S/2005/348 (May 27, 2005).

[29] *See, e.g.,* Seth G. Jones, Jeremy M. Wilson, Andrew Rathmell, K. Jack Riley ESTABLISHING LAW AND ORDER AFTER CONFLICT (2005), Chapter 3, noting limited successes in Kosovo. *See also* Colette Rausch, *From Elation to Disappointment: Justice and Security Reform in Kosovo*, in CONSTRUCTING JUSTICE AND SECURITY AFTER WAR (Charles T. Call, ed., 2006).

[30] *See, e.g., Organization for Security and Cooperation in Europe, Mission in Kosovo Department of Human Rights and rule of law, The Response of the Justice System to the March 2004 Riots*, December 2005, *available at* http://www.osce.org/documents/mik/2005/12/17177_en.pdf; *see also Organization for Security and Cooperation in Europe, Mission in Kosovo Department of Human Rights and rule of law, Review of the Criminal Justice System*, April 2003–October 2004, *available at* http://www.osce.org/documents/mik/2004/12/3984_en.pdf.

judicial system remains hard-pressed to offer even reasonably speedy trials, much less consistently independent rulings.[31]

Other interventions have also had disappointing results. In Haiti, for instance, the UN-sponsored, U.S.-led military intervention of the early 1990s led to an early spurt of support for rule of law efforts, but international interest soon flagged, and by 2004 Haiti was once again in crisis. When armed rebels – many associated with serious rights abuses in the past – seemed likely to topple President Aristide, who had himself been badly discredited, the U.S. military intervened once more, this time to help get rid of the elected president the United States had once helped restore to power.[32] In Sierra Leone, peacekeeping troops have completed their mission and the prospects for peace look somewhat brighter, but corruption and police abuse remains widespread, and barriers to obtaining accountability for past abuses persist, despite some progress.[33]

In East Timor, where UN peacekeepers withdrew in 2005, the Timorese government, still aided by UN police advisors, military trainers, and legal experts, is struggling in the face of escalating political violence, economic hardship, development challenges, and an uneven accountability process.[34] In May 2006, the government's ability to maintain law and order collapsed in

---

[31] *See, e.g.,* id., *The Response of the Justice System to the March 2004 Riots. See also* Anthony J. Miller, *Keynote Address: UNMIK: Lessons from the Early Institution-Building Phase,* 39 NEW ENG. L. REV. 9, 17 (2004).

[32] *See, e.g.,* U.N. DOC.S/2005/302, UN Security Council, *Report of the Security Council Mission to Haiti, 13 to 16 April 2005,* U.N. DOC. May 2005; Sean. D. Murphy, ed., *Contemporary Practice of the United States Relating to International Law: Replacement of U.S.-Led Force in Haiti with UN Peacekeeping Mission,* 98 AM. J. INT'L L. 586 (2004). *See also* press release, *U.S. Department of State, Resignation of President Jean-Bertrand Aristide of Haiti,* February 29, 2004, *at* http://www.state.gov; Daniel Balint Kurt, *Aristide Calls for "Peaceful Resistance"; Haitian Insists He's Still President,* THE WASHINGTON POST, March 9, 2004, at A17; press release, UN News Centre, *UN Launches Peacekeeping Operation in Haiti,* June 1, 2004, *available at* http://www.un.org; International Crisis Group, 2005, *Haiti's Transition: Hanging in the Balance;* International Crisis Group, 2005, *available at* http://www.crisisgroup.org/home/index.cfm?id=3255&l=1; *Spoiling Security in Haiti,* International Crisis Group, 2005, *available at* http://www.crisisgroup.org/home/index.cfm?id=3371&l=1.

[33] *See, e.g.,* Human Rights Watch, *Sierra Leone Indictments Welcomed,* March 11, 2003, *available at* http://www.hrw.org/press/2003/03/sleone031103.htm, noting that despite recent indictments issued by the Special Court for Sierra Leone, "[b]ecause the Special Court is anticipated to prosecute around twenty persons, it will leave many crimes unaddressed." *See* James Cockayne, *The Fraying Shoestring: Rethinking Hybrid War Crimes Tribunals,* 28 FORDHAM INT'L L.J. 616 (2005).

[34] *See United Nations: UNMISET Facts and Figures, available at* www.un.org/peace/timor/unmisetF.htm (last accessed August 28, 2002); *see also The Secretary-General, End of Mandate Report of the Secretary-General on the United Nations Mission in Support of East Timor, delivered to the Security Council,* U.N. DOC.S/2005/310, May 12, 2005. *See also Open Society Justice Initiative and Coalition for International Justice, Unfulfilled Promises: Achieving Justice for Crimes Against Humanity in East Timor,* 2004.

the face of violent protests and gang warfare that followed the government's dismissal of 600 disgruntled soldiers. As a result, the Timorese government was forced to declare a state of emergency and request the dispatch of a new international peacekeeping force to restore order, with the outcome still uncertain at the time this book went to press.

In Afghanistan, the indicators so far are sobering: the delivery of aid funds has been delayed; local communities in many parts of the country are still vulnerable to pressure from warlords, organized criminal gangs, or interethnic strife; in much of the country women reportedly face serious retaliation if they fail to wear the burqa; prison conditions are reportedly appalling; and in some instances, Taliban-era regulations, although technically no longer valid, are still enforced. Many parts of Afghanistan have also seen a recent resurgence in Taliban activity.[35]

In Iraq, too, the preliminary indications remain discouraging; a majority of courts were destroyed by looters in the immediate postwar period, and both ordinary crime (robbery, rapes, murders, etc.) and attacks on coalition forces have greatly increased, rather than decreased, in the nearly three years since the "military phase" of the intervention in Iraq ended. Outside the Kurdish areas, a majority of Iraqis say they oppose the presence of Coalition forces and report that they view the security situation as worse in Iraq, not improved, as a result of the U.S. invasion.[36] The trial of Saddam Hussein and other former leaders face continuing delays and challenges to their credibility.[37]

III. DEFINITIONS AND REASONS

With so much consensus on the value of building the rule of law in troubled societies, why have rule of law promotion efforts been so disappointing? Are efforts by foreign interveners to promote the rule of law inevitably doomed?

[35] *See, e.g.,* Human Rights Watch, *Afghanistan: Protect Women Candidates,* Aug. 17, 2005, *available at* http://hrw.org/english/docs/2005/08/16/afghan11633.htm; James Phillips, Heritage Foundation, *Afghanistan's Elections and the Resurgent Taliban,* September 16, 2005. News reports confirm these sources. *See also* Human Rights Watch, *Between Hope and Fear: Intimidation and Attacks against Women in Public Life in Afghanistan,* Oct. 2004, *available at* https://www.hrw.org/backgrounder/asia/afghanistan1004/.

[36] *See, e.g.,* The Brookings Institution, *Iraq Index at* 37, 38, 43, December 15, 2005, containing information on security indicators and public opinion polls, *available at* http://www.brookings.edu/fp/saban/iraq/index.pdf.

[37] *See, e.g.,* Amnesty International, *Iraqi Special Tribunal: Fair Trials Not Guaranteed,* May 13, 2005; Human Rights Watch, *The New Iraq?: Torture and Ill-Treatment of Detainees in Iraqi Custody,* Jan. 2005; Robert M. Perito, United States Institute of Peace, *The Coalition Provisional Authority's Experience With Public Security in Iraq,* April 2005, *available at* www.iraqfoundation.org/reports/pol/2005/sr137.pdf; Michael P. Scharf, *Is It International Enough? A Critique of the Iraqi Special Tribunal in Light of the Goals of International Justice,* 2 J. INT'L CRIM. JUST. 330 (2004).

At some times and in some places, the answer may be yes: there may well be circumstances in which outsiders are likely to do more harm than good, and we take up this question later on in this book. But for the most part, we believe that it *is* possible for outsiders to work constructively with local populations to promote the rule of law, providing skills and funds that are unavailable locally.

If most rule of law projects so far have been disappointing, we think it is in part because of the sheer (yet often underappreciated) complexity of the task and in part because of resource and bureaucratic constraints. Thus, although the international community has spent billions on rule of law projects, some projects have been underfunded whereas others have been overfunded, and funding and planning have often been carried out in an uncoordinated fashion. These issues are taken up in Chapter 9. This chapter, however, focuses on a root cause of the many other difficulties that have plagued most rule of law programs: *the failure of many policymakers to examine or fully understand the very concept of "the rule of law."*[38]

When policymakers speak of the rule of law, they usually have in mind a certain end-state, characterized by well-functioning, respected courts, fair and adequate legal codes, well-trained police, and respect for civil and political rights. This end-state is rarely clearly defined, however; as noted at the beginning of this chapter, when pressed, many policymakers fall back on an "I know it when I see it" characterization of the rule of law. This "I know it when I see it" quality has some virtues, to be sure: it enables consensus, because it leaves everyone free to interpret the rule of law in his or her own way, with little need to confront or resolve areas of disagreement. But it also permits a superficiality and obtuseness that has badly limited the efficacy of many rule of law promotion efforts.

Just what is the rule of law, then? Scholars, philosophers, and lawyers have debated this for centuries, and although there is no one definition everyone agrees upon, it is probably fair to say that most scholarly conceptions of the rule of law at least share a similar sense of the *goals* of the rule of law. Richard Fallon of Harvard Law School has thoughtfully analyzed competing theoretical conceptions of the rule of law. Fallon argues that *virtually all understandings of the rule of law share three purposes, or values: the rule of law serves to protect people against anarchy; to allow people to plan their affairs with confidence because they know the legal consequences of their actions; and to protect people from the arbitrary exercise of power by public*

---

[38] *See, e.g.,* Carothers, AIDING DEMOCRACY ABROAD, *supra* note 13, at 165: "Aid providers interested in promoting the rule of law have not, for the most part, agonized much about the complexity and even ineffability of the concept. They have concentrated on two of its most tangible manifestations – the state institutions that play a central role in the enforcement of law and the written laws themselves." Cf. George P. Fletcher, BASIC CONCEPTS OF LEGAL THOUGHT 12 (1996): "[W]e are never quite sure what we mean by 'the rule of law.'"

officials.[39] When the rule of law exists, life is reasonably orderly and stable, and no one needs to fear unfair persecution or abuse by the authorities.

But although most conceptions of the rule of law take for granted these broad *purposes,* there are *still two qualitatively different ways of conceptualizing the rule of law.* Traditionally, many scholars defined the rule of law in a *"formal" or "minimalist"* manner, whereas much more recent scholarship has argued for a thicker, more *"substantive," "maximalist"* account of the rule of law.[40]

The minimalist conception of the rule of law emphasizes the rule of law's formal and structural components, rather than the substantive content of the laws. In other words, the rule of law involves rules and practices that are routinely followed; this conception of the rule of law echoes the Aristotelian precept that there should be a "government of laws, not men" (or, as U.S. Supreme Court Justice Antonin Scalia put it, the rule of law is "a law of rules").[41] In the 19th century, the influential British thinker A. V. Dicey emphasized that under the rule of law, no one can be punished except for violating preexisting laws and after sentencing by regular courts; everyone, including government officials, has equal status under law (no one is "above" the law), and general constitutional principles protecting rights result from ordinary legal processes.

Some minimalist theories of the rule of law also emphasize the importance of having laws that are both created through some sort of democratic process and that predate their application; when government decision-makers are bound by laws that predate them, opportunities for unfairness are limited, and the laws may have a historical legitimacy that predates their enforcement. Others theorists emphasize the importance of having laws that are universal in form, consistently applied, and sufficiently well known that citizens can plan their lives around them.[42] Still others emphasize the importance of *process* to the rule of law, insisting that the rule of law involves and requires accessible, transparent mechanisms for legal and political change. Various formal, minimalist conceptions of the rule of law have come to be associated not only with the older Aristotelian and British traditions, but also more recently with the work of scholars such as Friedrich von Hayek, Joseph Raz, and Richard Posner.[43]

---

[39] Richard H. Fallon, *"The Rule of Law" as a Concept in International Discourse,* 97 COLUM. L. REV. 1, 7 (1997).

[40] Cf. Paul Craig, *Formal and Substantive Conceptions of the Rule of Law: An Analytical Framework,* PUB. L. 467 (1997).

[41] Antonin Scalia, *The Rule of Law as a Law of Rules,* 56 U. CHI. L. REV. 1175, (1989).

[42] *See, e.g.,* Jeremy Waldron, *One Law for All? The Logic of Cultural Accommodation,* 59 WASH. & LEE L. REV. 3 (2002).

[43] *See* Friedrich A. von Hayek, THE CONSTITUTION OF LIBERTY (1960); Joseph Raz, *The Rule of Law and Its Virtue,* in THE AUTHORITY OF LAW: ESSAYS ON LAW AND MORALITY (1979); Richard A. Posner, LAW, PRAGMATISM, AND DEMOCRACY (2003).

The primary alternative to a formal, minimalist conception of the rule of law is a thicker, more "substantive" account. *A substantive account of the rule of law does not necessarily reject the notion that the rule of law has important structural and formal elements – predictability, universality, nonarbitrariness, and so on – but it insists that true rule of law also requires particular substantive commitments:* to human rights, for instance.[44]

Those who favor substantive theories of the rule of law argue that formal theories cannot be fully adequate, because it is easy to imagine a horrifically abusive government that might fully comply with the purely formal dimensions of the rule of law. Imagine, for instance, a state in which a minority group is considered inferior by the majority; duly and democratically passed laws mandate discriminatory treatment for the minority; elected officials obediently enforce the laws.... Or, alternatively, consider a state that favors gruesome and harsh punishments for minor crimes: shoplifters are flogged to death; adulterers are publicly stoned.

In either of these hypothetical states (and readers will readily think of real-life examples), the formal elements of most minimalist definitions of the rule of law might well be satisfied. The laws might not be arbitrary; they might be enforced in a consistent fashion; people could plan around them; they might even have been adopted through some fair and democratic voting process. Nevertheless, most of us would consider these states unjust in some fundamental ways, and those who favor more substantive accounts of the rule of law insist that injustice is incompatible with true rule of law.

Just as there is a range of slightly different but overlapping formal conceptions of the rule of law, there are numerous and often overlapping substantive conceptions of the rule of law, some emphasizing justice or equality, some emphasizing freedom, some emphasizing protection of minority rights, and so on.[45] But if formal conceptions of the rule of law are vulnerable to the criticism that they are devoid of moral and ethical content, and can therefore coexist comfortably with appalling human rights abuses and injustices, substantive conceptions of the rule of law have their own vulnerabilities.

Who should decide, for instance, *which* substantive values must be embodied in law for the rule of law to be satisfied? What neutral principle can be invoked to resolve disputes over competing conceptions of justice and

---

[44] *See also* Robert S. Summers, *A Formal Theory of the Rule of Law*, 6 RATIO JURIS 127, 135 (1993): "A substantive theory is characterized mainly by the greater substantive content it incorporates. Thus it incorporates to some degree one or more of the following: rules securing minimum welfare..., rules securing some variety of the market economy, rules protecting at least some basic human rights, and rules institutionalizing democratic governance. Here, the contrast with formal theories of the rule of law is stark."

[45] *See, e.g.*, Ronald Dworkin, A MATTER OF PRINCIPLE 162 (1985). Also cf. Judith N. Shklar, *Political Theory and the Rule of Law, in* THE RULE OF LAW (A. Hutchinson & P. Monahan, eds., 1987), *reprinted in* Judith N. Shklar, POLITICAL THOUGHT & POLITICAL THINKERS (Chicago: University of Chicago Press, 1998).

rights? Thus, although everyone might agree that Nazi Germany's Jewish laws were horrifically unjust, what about the laws that remain on the books in many countries of the world that grant women greatly reduced political and social rights? Would it be possible for a state such as Saudi Arabia to continue its policies that discriminate against women but still satisfy the main substantive requirements of the rule of law? Can a state that grants preferential treatment to one religious or ethnic group comply fully with the rule of law? Can a state base its law on religiously "revealed" truths (such as Shariah) still satisfy rule of law requirements?

Some critics of substantive conceptions of the rule of law argue that more minimalist conceptions of the rule of law are superior to substantive conceptions precisely *because* of their "emptiness." Robert Summers, for instance, argues that only more formal accounts of the rule of law can generate support from across the political spectrum, because formal accounts do not require consensus on potentially divisive questions about rights.[46] Around the globe, people may legitimately differ on questions relating to which rights are fundamental, but perhaps all people can at least agree on the formal, process dimensions of the rule of law, which are minimalist enough to permit different societies to develop different substantive rules.

To Summers, formal accounts of the rule of law have at least an analytic clarity that substantive accounts cannot replicate; if the rule of law has *any* distinct meaning, and is not just a convenient and vacuous shorthand for "democracy and human rights and other values I happen to like," it is best to keep it minimal and formal. If we think of the rule of law in a purely formal and minimalist way, this argument goes, at least we can be reasonably clear about what we are talking about when we talk about the rule of law. But adherents of a more substantive view of the rule of law would, of course, contest the adequacy of such minimalist approaches.

This discussion of varying conceptions of the rule of law inevitably oversimplifies. There is a wide range of formal conceptions of the rule of law, each emphasizing slightly different elements and a similarly wide range of substantive accounts. What's more, some definitions of the rule of law try to combine formal and substantive elements, whereas others look to historicity[47] or legal process to define key rule of law elements.[48] But though

---

[46] Robert Summers, *The Principles of the Rule of Law*, 74 NOTRE DAME L. REV. 1691 (1999).

[47] *See also* Rainer Grote, *Rule of Law, Rechtsstaat and 'Etat de Droit,'* in CONSTITUTIONALISM, UNIVERSALISM AND DEMOCRACY – A COMPARATIVE ANALYSIS (Christian Starck, ed., 1999).

[48] Legal scholars have offered varying definitions of the rule of law. *See, e.g.,* William Whitford, *The Rule of Law*, 2000 WISC. L. REV. 723 (2000); *see also* Richard Fallon, *supra* note 39 at 7–9, distinguishing between formalist, historicist, substantive, and legal process "ideal types" of the rule of law concept. Most of the varying conceptions contain at least some overlapping components, however, as do the varying conceptions of the rule of law drawn on by the foreign policy community. Most assume that the rule of law has both a formal component (statutes, rules known in advance, courts, politically independent judiciary with

brief, this discussion should serve to convey the enormous complexity of the idea of the rule of law and something of the scholarly controversy over its meaning.

Given the complexity and controversy over the true nature of the rule of law, it is perhaps no surprise that most policymakers tend to shrug aside the scholarly debate, and fall back on "I know it when I see it." If even philosophers and legal scholars can't agree on a definition of the rule of law, why should policymakers be troubled by definitional questions? Why not fall back on a rough-and-ready intuitive understanding of rule of law?

But although precise definitions may be impossible, this lack of clarity on the part of most policymakers can be very damaging, especially in fragile post-intervention societies, for it allows policymakers and practitioners to pursue poorly thought-through and often internally contradictory programs. Indeed, one legal scholar argues that it inevitably "detracts from the quality of the debate for anybody to invoke an emotionally laden phrase like rule of law."[49]

Because many decision-makers ignore the question of whether it is best to conceptualize the rule of law in a formal or substantive way, many rule of law programs simply conflate the two potentially very different facets of rule of law in a simplistic manner, assuming that substance will naturally flow from form – or that a normative commitment to substantive values (such as respect for individual and minority rights, a commitment to nonviolent means of resolving disputes, etc.) will naturally flow from structurally independent courts and from newly drafted legislation that highlights those values.[50]

powers of judicial review, etc.) and a substantive component that implicitly is nonpositivist: to most in the foreign policy community, the rule of law also involves laws that comport with basic notions of human rights. Fallon notes that most conceptions of the rule of law share three purposes or values: protection against anarchy and the Hobbesian war of all against all, creation of conditions in which people can plan their affairs with reasonable confidence that they can know in advance the legal consequences of their actions, and protection against some types of official arbitrariness. Beyond these purposes of the rule of law, Fallon notes that most conceptions of the rule of law emphasize five basic elements: (1) people must be able to understand and comply with the law (thus, the rule of law must involve the existence of some set of legal rules, standards, and principles that can guide people); (2) the law *should* actually guide people; (3) the law should be reasonably stable; (4) the law should be supreme, ruling officials and judges as well as ordinary citizens; and (5) there should exist "instrumentalities of impartial justice": that is, the rule of law requires courts which employ fair procedures.

49 Whitford, id., at 12.

50 Rachel Kleinfeld makes a similar point in an excellent article written for the Carnegie Endowment for International Peace's Rule of Law Series. Kleinfeld notes that the rule of law is "not a single, unified good" but is composed of five separate ends, which she defines as (1) a government bound by law, (2) equality before law, (3) law and order, (4) predictable and efficient rulings, and (5) human rights. She notes that although these ends can be mutually reinforcing, they are distinct: they can "meet different types of support or resistance within countries undergoing reforms," and these ends are "often in tension with one another." Kleinfeld notes than many rule of law practitioners assume that creating

This conflation of the formal and substantive aspects of the rule of law has led to a simplistic emphasis on structures, institutions, and the "modernization" of legal codes, in a cookie-cutter way that has generally taken little account of the differences between societies.[51] In his 1999 book, AIDING DEMOCRACY ABROAD, Tom Carothers of the Carnegie Endowment criticizes what he calls the "Rule of Law Assistance Standard Menu": it includes "reforming institutions" (judicial reform, legislative strengthening, police and prison reform, etc.), "[r]ewriting laws" (modernizing criminal, civil, and commercial laws), "[u]pgrading the legal profession through support for stronger bar associations and law schools, and "[i]ncreasing legal access and advocacy" through the support of legal advocacy NGOs, law school clinics, and so on.[52] From Latin America to the former Soviet States to Bosnia, Kosovo, East Timor and Iraq, most rule of law programs have followed precisely this "standard menu."[53]

As this chapter has already noted, however, this model has not worked particularly well in any of the places in which it has been used.[54] Despite the outpouring of foreign money and talent on rule of law programs, the results have often been disappointing. Whether we look at Russia or Guatemala,

---

law-related institutions will reliably lead to the achievement of these various desirable ends but that this assumption is far too simplistic. Kleinfeld, *Competing Definitions of the Rule of Law: Implications for Practitioners,* January 2005, *available at* http://www.carnegieendowment.org/files/CP55.Kleinfeld.FINAL.pdf. Both common sense and the academic literature warn against the easy assumption that formalistic transplants such as constitutions and legal institutions will automatically produce the desired changes in culture and behavior. *See, e.g.,* A. E. Dick Howard, *The Indeterminacy of Constitutions,* 31 WAKE FOREST L. REV. 383, 403 (1996) (warning that "planting a [constitutional] proposition in a different cultural, historical, or traditional context may lead to results quite different from those one finds in the country from which the proposition was borrowed"). This is all the more true when the thing to be transplanted is as capacious as the very idea of "the rule of law." Nonetheless, in practice, the same formalistic mistakes are made time and again. Cf. Steven G. Calabresi, *The Historical Origins of the Rule of Law in the American Constitutional Order,* 28 HARV. J. L. & PUB. POL'Y 273 (2004).

[51] *See* Carothers, AIDING DEMOCRACY ABROAD, *supra* note 13, at 176, noting: "As aid providers attempt judicial reform work in previously uncharted regions, they seem determined to repeat mistakes made in other places." More than anyone else, Carothers has spearheaded efforts to rethink rule of law promotion (and democracy promotion, more broadly). His book makes an excellent starting point for those concerned with these issues, and the Carnegie Endowment's Democracy and Rule of Law Program, which Carothers heads, has produced numerous provocative and thoughtful reports on rule of law reform.

[52] Id., at 165, 168.

[53] *See* Wade Channell, CARNEGIE ENDOWMENT FOR INTERNATIONAL PEACE, *Lessons Not Learned: Problems with Western Aid for Law Reform in Postcommunist Countries,* RULE OF LAW SERIES, No. 57 (May 2005).

[54] *See* Carothers, AIDING DEMOCRACY ABROAD, *supra* note 13, at 170: "What stands out about U.S. rule of law assistance since the mid-1980s is how difficult and often disappointing such work is." *See also* Stephen Golub, *Beyond Rule of Law Orthodoxy: The Legal Empowerment Alternative,* Carnegie Endowment for International Peace, Working Paper No. 41, October 2003.

Kosovo or Afghanistan, there is little basis for concluding that following such a "Rule of Law Assistance Standard Menu," by itself, has actually produced anything most of us would, in fact, recognize as the rule of law.[55]

To a significant extent, what such a rough-and-ready institutionally oriented approach fails to recognize is that *"promoting the rule of law" is an issue of norm creation and cultural change as much as an issue of creating new institutions and legal codes.*[56] This is most obviously true when we consider the so-called "substantive" dimensions of the rule of law: respect for minority rights, for instance, or the rights of women. In the United States, with a history of slavery and racism, citizens know very well that there can be de jure "equality" on the books and a well-functioning legal system but that this can coexist with enormous de facto discrimination. Eliminating the discriminatory legacy of racism requires going well beyond making changes to formal law, structures, and institutions, although changes to formal law can of course play an important role in promoting genuine cultural change. But eliminating discrimination is a matter of attitudes and beliefs as much as it is a matter of law and structure. Inevitably, putting into place new and improved institutions and legal codes will not automatically succeed in creating substantive cultural commitments to equality and rights.

Building the rule of law is also an issue of norm creation in a much deeper sense, however, a sense that is usually overlooked even by those who insist that their definition of the rule of law is purely formal rather than substantive. For even in its formal sense, the rule of law requires a particular set of cultural commitments. *Most fundamentally, even the most formal, minimalist conception of the rule of law requires a normative commitment to the project of law itself*, a commitment to the orderly and nonviolent resolution of disputes and a willingness to be bound by the outcome of legal rules and processes.

This normative commitment to the idea of law itself is not something that comes "naturally" to human beings, although residents of most advanced democracies take it for granted. In the United States, for instance, citizens have the luxury of living in a rule of law culture, in which vigilantism, personality-driven rule, noncompliance with legal process, and public corruption are the exceptions that seem to us to prove the general rule that we

---

[55] Golub, *supra* note 54; *see also* Frank Upham, *Mythmaking in the Rule of Law Orthodoxy*, Carnegie Endowment for International Peace, Working Paper No. 30, September 2002.

[56] *See, e.g,* John Norton Moore, *Toward a New Paradigm: Enhanced Effectiveness in United Nations Peacekeeping, Collective Security, and War Avoidance*, 37 VA. J. INT'L L. 811, 860 (1997), noting that democracy building "is a goal to be assisted through norm-creation, education, electoral observation, and other modes of peaceful engagement. [It is not] a charter for an intolerant one-size-fits-all dogma. Room must always be left for the many paths to the same bottom line which honor local conditions and wishes." Outside of the academy, however, these insights are given a certain amount of lip service, but they rarely bring decision-makers to reexamine the thrust of rule of law promotion efforts.

are a law-bound society. But the American rule of law culture was not a natural and inevitable development; it is the product of a particular history, of liberal, enlightenment traditions; it evolved over centuries and has been facilitated by a relatively high degree of prosperity.[57]

Without a widely shared cultural commitment to the idea of the rule of law, courts are just buildings, judges are just bureaucrats, and constitutions are just pieces of paper. This poses particular problems in troubled societies, with a history of repressive governments or brutal wars: why *should* anyone care about laws and courts and judges and constitutions?

In most post-intervention and post-intervention societies, it has been a long time since there was a fair and well-functioning legal system, if one ever existed at all; there may be only a weak tradition of using law to resolve disputes or no such tradition at all. Formal law may have been discredited by abuses or inefficiencies, or formal law may have barely existed for most people. In such societies, well-intentioned efforts by outsiders to build the rule of law solely by creating formal structures and rewriting constitutions and statutes often have little or no impact.[58]

There is a story, perhaps apocryphal, that has some relevance here. During the 19th and early 20th centuries, some Middle Eastern governments were anxious to "improve" the lot of nomadic tribespeople, who roamed from place to place, living in tents, rarely having reliable access to clean water or health care or schools. (Governmental desire to regulate and control nomadic populations also played a role, of course.) The governments built new houses for the nomads in cities and towns and gave them to the tribes for free, confidently expecting that the nomads would immediately transform themselves into ordinary townspeople. But although the nomads appreciated the new houses, they promptly quartered their camels in the fine shelters and then lived themselves in their old tents, outside the houses, to the government's great consternation. The houses soon deteriorated (they were not designed with the needs of camels in mind), and after a season or two,

---

[57] As recent events suggest, post 9/11, it is even more fragile and culturally contingent than most of us probably think.

[58] *See* Daniel Berkowitz, Katharina Pistor, and Jean-Francois Richard, *Economic Development, Legality, and the Transplant Effect* (unpublished draft, 2000), reporting on a study finding that how a country's legal system developed is a better predictor of legality than the substance of the laws in place. *See also* Jianfu Chen, *Market Economy and the Internationalisation of Civil and Commercial Law in the People's Republic of China,* in LAW, CAPITALISM AND POWER IN ASIA: THE RULE OF LAW AND LEGAL INSTITUTIONS 69 (J. Kaniskha Jayasuriya, ed., 1999); Ugo Mattei, *The New Ethiopian Constitution: First Thoughts on Ethnical Federalism and the Reception of Western Institutions,* in TRANSPLANTS, INNOVATION, AND LEGAL TRADITION IN THE HORN OF AFRICA 111 (Elisabetta Grande, ed., 1995); Jennifer Widner, *Building Judicial Independence in Common Law Africa,* in THE SELF-RESTRAINING STATE: POWER AND ACCOUNTABILITY IN NEW DEMOCRACIES (Andreas Schedler, Larry Diamond, & Mark F. Plattner, eds., 1999).

most of the nomads abandoned the new houses and returned to their wanderings, leaving behind a cadre of baffled and irritated government officials. The nomads, it turned out, did not particularly want to live in one place.

Efforts to create the rule of law in societies that lack a rule of law tradition can run into similar problems. Many Americans take the value of the rule of law for granted and assume that "if you build it, they will come" applies to courts as much as to baseball fields. But courts and constitutions do not occupy the same place in every culture that they occupy in American (or European) culture, and as a result, efforts to build the rule of law in post-intervention societies can appear irrelevant to the concerns of ordinary people – or, at worst, incoherent, arrogant, and hypocritical.[59]

When this occurs, such approaches may not only fail to create the rule of law – but as Chapter 8 discusses, such blinkered approaches may also actually undermine the rule of law.

IV. A PRAGMATIC DEFINITION OF THE RULE OF LAW

If we consider interventions to promote human rights and the rule of law to be justifiable and important at times, whether for moral reasons, economic reasons, or security reasons, we are faced with some very fundamental questions, to which neither scholars nor policymakers have as yet paid sufficient attention. What precisely are the cultural conditions in which law and legal institutions matter? What are the circumstances in which "legal" rules become enforceable and accepted as legitimate? Under what conditions can law play a role in shaping cultural understandings of violence? When and how can "outsiders" help create those conditions in a given society?

These questions are taken up in greater detail in Chapter 8. For now, it is enough to note that these are all issues of norm creation. Although social norms are tightly linked to law in some societies, they are not at all linked in others. When they are delinked, changing "the law" will have little effect by itself; only an explicit simultaneous focus on norm creation is likely to lead to the possibility of the rule of law.

It is easy to state this, of course, but less easy to know what to do about it. This chapter began by noting that the concept of the rule of law is much less simple than most policymakers and practitioners think. Centuries of legal theorists have been unable to agree wholly on its contours, and few rule of law theorists have grappled with the issue of *how* rule of law cultures can be created.

---

[59] Cf Yash Gai, *The Rule of Law, Legitimacy, and Governance*, 14 INT'L J. SOCIOL. OF L. 179 (1986); Herman Slaats & Keren Portier *The Implementation of State Law Though Folk Law: Karo Batak Village Elections*, 23 J. LEGAL PLURALISM 153 (1985).

Is there any way to acknowledge the complexity of the idea of the rule of law but nonetheless develop a pragmatic understanding that will allow us to move forward and create thoughtful programs in post-intervention societies?

We think that there is. First, we offer a definition of the rule of law that, though imperfect, helps capture what most people regard as the fundamental goals of rule of law promotion. Second, we offer a framework for thinking about building the rule of law, which we call the synergistic approach.

For our purposes, it is most useful to define the rule of law in the following way:

> The "rule of law" describes a state of affairs in which the state successfully monopolizes the means of violence, and in which most people, most of the time, choose to resolve disputes in a manner consistent with procedurally fair, neutral, and universally applicable rules, and in a manner that respects fundamental human rights norms (such as prohibitions on racial, ethnic, religious and gender discrimination, torture, slavery, prolonged arbitrary detentions, and extrajudicial killings). In the context of today's globally interconnected world, this requires modern and effective legal institutions and codes, and it also requires a widely shared cultural and political commitment to the values underlying these institutions and codes.

This definition is primarily *descriptive and pragmatic*. It is not intended to stand up to rigorous philosophical critiques or settle arguments about first-order and second-order rule-making or resolve questions relating to the universality of rights. Instead, this working definition seeks simply to identify *what it is that most policymakers are looking for* when they talk about the rule of law in post-intervention societies.

- By noting that the rule of law requires the state to successfully monopolize the means of violence this definition recognizes that *extreme insecurity (insurrection, civil war, frequent terrorist attacks) makes it virtually impossible for societies to sustain the rule of law.*
- By noting that the rule of law involves not merely the existence of formal rules and rights but also the existence of people who voluntarily *choose* to respect those rules and rights, this definition emphasizes that *the rule of law is a matter of cultural commitments as well as institutions and legal codes.*
- By noting that the rule of law requires that people choose to resolve disputes in a manner that is *consistent* with rules and rights, rather than defining the rule of law solely as the actual use of certain kinds of legal institutions, this definition emphasizes that *much conflict resolution occurs "in the shadow of the law."* Actual court use, even in famously litigious societies such as America, can be rare, but the rule of law exists

as long as both private and public actors accept the ultimate legitimacy of legal institutions and rules and internalize these rules into their everyday behavior and expectations.

- By noting that the rule of law exists when *most people, most of the time,* act in accordance with rules and rights, this definition emphasizes that *the rule of law is a long-term project that is always aspirational to some extent.* Even in the United States and other states with strong rule of law traditions, not every citizen and not every official respects legal rules and institutions. In post-intervention societies, expectations of perfection will never be met; this definition emphasizes the importance of significant, but not necessarily total, buy-in.

- By emphasizing that the rule of law requires respect for fundamental human rights, *we adopt an unabashedly substantive conception of the rule of law.* Here, too, we make no effort to justify this on philosophical grounds; it is enough, for our purposes, to say that we think this definition accurately describes the implicit *goals* of most rule of law programs. *By listing only those norms that are usually understood to have gained near universal acceptance, however, we take a deliberately minimalist stand.* These norms are widely accepted in part because they are relatively bare bones and allow ample room for different societies to define rights in different ways, provided they respect core principles such as prohibitions against racial, ethnic, religious and gender discrimination, torture, slavery, prolonged arbitrary detentions, and extrajudicial killings.

  These norms are enunciated in the Universal Declaration of Human Rights, and they have since been codified in international treaties such as the International Covenant on Civil and Political Rights,[60] the Convention on the Elimination of All Forms of Discrimination Against Women,[61] the International Convention on the Elimination of All Forms of Racial Discrimination,[62] and the Convention Against Torture,[63] each of which has been signed or ratified by virtually all nations in the world. These universally accepted norms are also usually seen as having attained the status of customary international law, binding even on nonsignatories to the treaties listed above.

- Finally, this definition acknowledges that *although formal law and institutions alone cannot create the rule of law, modern codes and institutions are nonetheless essential in this era of globalization.* One can readily imagine

---

[60] *Available at* http://www.unhchr.ch/html/menu3/b/a_ccpr.htm; has been ratified by 152 countries.

[61] *Available at* http://www.un.org/womenwatch/daw/cedaw/text/econvention.htm; has been ratified by 177 countries.

[62] *Available at* http://www.unhchr.ch/html/menu3/b/d_icerd.htm; has been ratified by 169 countries.

[63] *Available at* http://www.hrweb.org/legal/cat.html; has been ratified by seventy-two countries.

a peaceful, stable, and orderly society with few or no formal legal institutions (and the anthropological literature is replete with examples). Today, however, the fate of each nation is bound up with the fate of the global community, and realistically, nations cannot participate in the global economic or political system without legal institutions that are reasonably consistent with those of other modern nations. This does not lessen the degree to which creating the rule of law remains also a matter of fostering cultural commitment to the values underlying the rule of law, however.

V. THE SYNERGISTIC APPROACH

This chapter has suggested that many past rule of law programs have been disappointing in part because they have not grappled with the complexities inherent in the idea of the rule of law, but have instead proceeded on a sort of "I know it when I see it" autopilot. Unfortunately, possessing a more nuanced understanding of the rule of law is still no guarantee of success on the ground.

What does our definition mean for practitioners on the ground, who are working with local leaders to build and strengthen the rule of law in the wake of military intervention? Our definition describes the strategic goals of the rule of law but does not tell practitioners how to achieve these goals. A framework for combining the two must be developed – a framework that can help practitioners link ends and means more effectively.

We think a *synergistic approach* to building the rule of law can provide such a framework, and we spell out this approach here in an abstract way. Future chapters apply this approach to the varying challenges of building the rule of law on the ground.

Synergism, in biological terms, refers to *"the action of two or more substances, organs, or organisms to achieve an effect of which each is individually incapable."*[64] This term captures important features of a constructive approach to building the rule of law: it is *ends-based and strategic* in that it aims to achieve certain clear overarching objectives or effects. It is *adaptive and dynamic* in that it aims to build upon existing cultural and institutional resources for the rule of law and move them in a constructive direction, but it recognizes, at the same time, that the rule of law is always a work in progress, requiring continual maintenance and reevaluation. It is *systemic* because it emphasizes interrelationships between the various components of a functioning justice system, highlighting the necessity of an integrated approach to reform to achieve effects not possible by focusing on single institutions in isolation.

[64] THE AMERICAN HERITAGE DICTIONARY OF THE ENGLISH LANGUAGE 1233 (2nd College ed. 1982).

Borrowing a term from biology is a useful way to remind ourselves that building the rule of law is a profoundly human endeavor. Both the commitments of leaders and perceptions of legitimacy among the broader population will be critical to success. Indeed, an overly technical focus on reforming institutions or on training and supporting state elites, and a failure to pay sufficient attention to how ordinary citizens perceive and interact with them or to understand the political stakes and interests of government officials, will undermine the prospects for achieving the desired objectives.

The word *synergism* has a theological meaning as well. Theologically, synergism is *a theory that both human effort and divine grace are needed to achieve regeneration.*[65] Regardless of one's theological views, this meaning of synergism helps serve as reminder of the need for *humility* in efforts to build the rule of law. Although thoughtful planning plays a critical role in the success or failure of rule of law programs, there is art as well as science to rule of law efforts, and not every factor can be planned or controlled. For all our sophistication, our understanding of how societies develop and change is still shallow. Despite the best efforts of interveners and local partners, larger factors – unexpected developments, timing, relationships – are also at work in the complex endeavor of building the rule of law.

Let's unpack the three key features of the synergistic approach – its ends-based, adaptive, and systemic elements – and explore their concrete implications for building the rule of law after conflict.

- *First, the synergistic approach is ends-based and strategic.* A "synergistic" approach to building and strengthening the rule of law starts with a clear articulation of strategic objectives. Improved institutions can help to achieve certain aims of the rule of law – such as securing law and order, or protecting human rights – but the institutions are not the ends in themselves. At the very least, this insight means that reformers should focus clearly on the ultimate goals of building the rule of law and resist an overly narrow concentration on institutions alone. Keeping these overarching aims in mind, practitioners can also ask what kinds of *cross-cutting programs* are needed to advance their objectives in the face of existing resources and obstacles. Particularly in post-intervention societies with limited resources and fragile stability, some of these overarching aims may be in tension: for instance, in societies that traditionally subordinate women, emphasis on fundamental rights – including the principle of nondiscrimination – may appear to be in conflict with the goal of achieving buy-in from local populations. This should not mean that practitioners should abandon either their commitment to gender equality or their commitment to local ownership, but it does require practitioners to recognize

---

[65] Id.

that not all good things can necessarily advance equally together at the same pace. Although in a developed legal system, these ends ideally should be mutually reinforcing, achieving such a state can take decades.[66]

- *Second, the synergistic approach is adaptive and dynamic.* By this, we mean that the "synergistic" approach recognizes the need to build on what's there and move it in constructive directions – and we also recognize that the rule of law is never permanently "achieved." It must be continuously and creatively sustained.

The rule of law cannot be imported wholesale; it needs to be built on preexisting cultural commitments. Using the cultural, political, human, and material resources available, critical institutions need to be developed and strengthened. Some basic functioning legal institutions are essential: basic laws and law-making capacity, police, courts, supporting institutions and legal professionals, and prisons. But institutions that don't enjoy popular legitimacy, or that don't build on solid cultural foundations, will not be sustainable.

The emphasis on adaptive intervention encourages a focus on the perceptions and needs of ordinary people, on the consumers of the law. Interveners must be attuned to deeply rooted grievances that fuel conflict and also nurture grassroots demand for sustainable legal reform. Those engaged in building justice systems also need to understand both the appeal and the limitations of customary systems of dispute resolution and how they can be adapted and moved in constructive directions.

By noting that the synergistic approach is also dynamic, we mean that the rule of law is always a work in progress. New achievements create new challenges, and efforts to build the rule of law must continuously evolve as circumstances change.

- *Third, the synergistic approach is systemic.* A synergistic approach to strengthening the rule of law takes a systemic and holistic perspective. Appreciating how institutions intersect and operate *as a system* is vital to designing effective and balanced programs for reform. Interveners need to appreciate failures and challenges in the legal system as a whole. They need to understand the interrelationships between the various components and how they impact each other. They need to take a holistic approach to reform, working toward a balanced development of the component parts of a functioning legal system. The priorities in any given situation will depend on the areas of greatest need, with the overall aim of balanced and mutually reinforcing improvements.

Reformers also need to recognize that rule of law reform inevitably is deeply political. On a *micro* level, reformers need to be savvy about the particular political interests that are advanced, or impeded, by different

---

[66] *See* Kleinfeld, *Competing Definitions of the Rule of Law, supra* note 50.

kinds of reforms. Whether police are being trained and empowered to enforce the law, or judges are given additional resources, training, and facilities, or legislators are assisted in drafting substantive legal codes, rule of law reform involves the allocation of political power. There are winners and losers in terms of opportunities, resources, power, and status. Interveners need to be savvy about who they are promoting and about who is likely to have an interest in sabotaging reform or moving it in counterproductive directions.

Similarly, on a *macro* level, interveners need to understand the broader political impact of building up state justice institutions and civil society institutions. When interveners focus on state institutions, powerful elites may acquire more effective tools to advance their own interests at the expense of the weak if there is insufficient governance reform or inadequate mechanisms for accountability. When interveners focus on civil society, they may risk inadvertently undermining fragile governance structures by pouring resources instead into the nongovernmental sector, which can be unaccountable in different ways.

Interveners need to be honest, moreover, about how politics enters into their own reform efforts – including which pet projects they advance, which substantive laws they place priority on, and so forth.

To sum up, the synergistic approach to strengthening justice institutions is explicitly strategic, adaptive, and systemic. This approach identifies and pursues fundamental, overarching goals; works to adapt existing institutional resources in constructive directions; addresses and develops critical linkages and relationships among justice institutions; and appreciates how they are embedded in, and function within, a larger political system. This approach recognizes, moreover, that effective long-term justice reform must focus not only on critical formal institutions, such as police, courts, and prisons, but also on ordinary people and their urgent needs; it must include effective local participation in decision-making, recognize the inevitable political impact of reform efforts, and take seriously vital cultural foundations for strengthening the rule of law.

The chapters that follow this discuss the many practical challenges associated with building the rule of law, from creating adequate governance blueprints and reestablishing security to strengthening legal and judicial institutions and creating a cultural commitment to the rule of law. Our proposed definition of the rule of law and our focus on the synergistic approach reflect the unavoidable complexity of the project of building and sustaining the rule of law. Successfully building the rule of law in troubled, post-intervention societies requires interveners to keep many balls in the air at once, while struggling with coordination issues, resource constraints, and a host of other challenges.

This will always be a project fraught with difficulties. Building the rule of law will never be easy, and complete success may not even be possible in many situations. But while there is no silver bullet, our pragmatic definition of the rule of law and the synergistic approach that accompanies it offer a framework for sorting through the thorny and recurring problems that face all rule of law projects.

CHAPTER FOUR

Blueprints for Post-Conflict Governance

In most of the cases studied in this book, interveners have felt compelled to press for some set of political and institutional arrangements that will enable them to leave the country in which they have intervened in better political condition than they found it. More specifically, they have sought to negotiate or impose procedures for creating order within the affected state, selecting a new government, and establishing the basic political and legal limits within which that government will operate. These new arrangements amount to nothing less than a blueprint for the political reconstruction of the affected country.

From a rule of law standpoint, the blueprints reflect the proposed macro-political and legal underpinnings of a new or transformed state; they represent an attempt to design a new political and legal order within which other elements of a rule of law system, such as police and courts, must operate. Blueprints lay out the critical steps interveners and their local partners expect to take to move a state from the shock of military intervention to self-government under the rule of law. Typically, they include provisions for maintaining security, forming an interim government, conducting elections to choose a new government, and in many cases, drafting the constitution under which that government will operate. In some cases, the blueprint may take the form of a more or less coherent political package. The Dayton Accords, for example, addressed the military aspects of the post-conflict period, boundary issues, elections, policing, and human rights and included a new constitution designed to share power among Bosnia's contending communities. In most cases, however, the blueprint emerges only gradually and from some combination of different sources, including agreements among warring parties, UN Security Council resolutions, transitional government arrangements, and new constitutions. Moreover, blueprints constantly evolve, as conditions within the affected state change.

Blueprints also vary widely from country to country. Everyone acknowledges that political reconstruction cannot proceed on a "one size fits all" basis. At the same time, there are common features among blueprints, some specific to the nature of the problems that give rise to intervention; others dictated by preexisting international norms. The approach taken in any given case depends on the circumstances of the country at issue and the identity, resources, and commitment of both interveners and local actors.

In most of the cases considered in this volume, military intervention has followed, and been triggered by, internal conflicts that broadly described fall into one of two categories: (1) disputes over control of state resources and political power in states characterized by extremely weak state institutions and central authority, as in Liberia and Sierra Leone, and (2) disputes over national identity in which two or more distinct ethnic groups fight over territory or governance issues, as in Bosnia, Kosovo, and Rwanda. Of course, the distinction is in many respects artificial. Conflicts that center on control of state resources often also involve ethnic divisions, and ethnic conflicts (the term itself is contested) can be characterized as struggles over resources and power. Thus, there is often considerable overlap between the categories. Rwanda had both high levels of interethnic conflict and weak state institutions; Liberia had an ethnic overlay to what was principally a struggle over resources and power. Nonetheless, the differences in the nature of these conflicts are both real and important.

In two recent cases, Afghanistan and Iraq, the political and security interests of the interveners prompted intervention even in the absence of large-scale internal conflict. Yet even in these two cases, weak state institutions and ethnic and sectarian divisions have shaped the blueprints adopted in ways that raise many of the same issues as the other cases considered.

In general, conflicts driven by weak state institutions and disputes over resources and political power may be more amenable to resolution through externally driven political arrangements than conflicts that center on national identity. For conflicts in the former category, interveners have commonly pushed a fairly standard settlement blueprint. That blueprint consists of cease-fires, demobilization of combatants, and the establishment of a transitional government, all in support of internationally monitored elections leading to the formation of a new government. This approach to settlement presumes that the antecedent civil strife represents only a temporary break in the unity of the political community of the state, which can be overcome by the legitimacy that will attach to any popularly elected government.

For conflicts that center on national identity, interveners usually follow a blueprint that is similar in some respects but different in others from the one just described. As in ordinary civil conflicts, interveners may urge the parties to accept cease-fires and demobilization of combatants as a preliminary step to a political resolution. But such conflicts are seldom amenable to resolution through majoritarian electoral politics. In countries torn by conflict over national identity, voting resembles census-taking, and numerically weaker groups will not be satisfied by any solution predicated simply on majority rule. Indeed, it is precisely the prospect of majority rule that has touched off conflict in places such as Bosnia and Kosovo. In such cases, interveners and local actors may be forced to pursue more complicated political bargains, designed to share (or divide) power among the competing ethnic groups. Tinkering with existing constitutions and laws will not suffice; instead, post-conflict blueprints usually entail the drafting of a whole new set of governing arrangements, which may be embodied in a new constitution designed to share power among the state's principal ethnic or sectarian groups.

The alternatives to sharing power as a solution to identity-based conflicts are limited. They consist principally of the separation of the contending parties by granting partial or total independence to one group, as in East Timor, or the outright victory of one party over another, with the consequent vesting of political power in the victor, as in Rwanda. In such cases, power-sharing largely disappears as an issue for both internal and external actors. Efforts may be made to offer minorities legal protections short of power-sharing, but the focus, at least for external actors, shifts to many of the same issues faced in connection with states emerging from more conventional conflicts over resources and power, in particular, how to build viable state institutions that will govern in accordance with international standards and the rule of law.

In general, blueprints premised on majoritarian electoral politics seem to be both easier to design and more likely to endure than blueprints based on intercommunal power sharing. Electoral settlements have worked tolerably well in ideologically divided countries such as Cambodia, El Salvador, Nicaragua, and Mozambique, though they have so far generated only mixed results in the resource-driven conflicts of Liberia and Sierra Leone. But even in those latter conflicts, the issues up for debate, for example, disarmament, control of the interim government, and the timing of elections, are comparatively straightforward.

By contrast, attempts to promote enduring settlements to identity-based conflicts seem less promising. In conflicts of this sort, it is not simply a question of building institutional capacity and holding elections to determine the will of the population as a whole. Instead, interveners have to consider in addition intractable and divisive questions pertaining to control over territory, the extent of local autonomy, the scope of minority veto powers, the extent of minority participation in national political organs, and similar issues. Even when agreements on such issues can be reached, political arrangements predicated on intercommunal power sharing are often complicated and unstable.

In both kinds of cases, the process by which a blueprint is reached may prove as important as the blueprint itself, especially when a new constitution plays a central role in the blueprint. A broadly inclusive process may help transcend internal differences and forge a new national consensus. By contrast, a poorly conceived process that leaves important actors feeling marginalized or fails to foster a sense of local ownership will exacerbate existing tensions. The difficulties in devising workable blueprints are discussed below; the difficulties in building upon the rule of law aspects of those blueprints are considered in subsequent chapters.

I. THE PROCESS OF BLUEPRINT DESIGN

The creation of post-intervention blueprints entails a complicated process involving a mixture of coercion, bargaining, and concessions among a host of parties, including interveners, warring factions, civil society, and neighboring states. This process unfolds over time and evolves as the interests and even the identities of the parties change. Part A below discusses a series of problems – the pitfalls of bargaining, the short time horizons of interveners, the periodic divergence between international standards and local preferences, and the inevitable emergence of spoilers – inherent in post-conflict blueprint processes. Part B considers some of the problems specific to the drafting of post-conflict constitutions.

A. Problems Common to Post-Conflict Blueprints

The drafters of the various agreements and other instruments constituting blueprints for post-conflict state-building may find guidance in general principles reflecting minimum international standards. But these principles (for example, respect for minority rights, free elections, accountability), on which agreement usually exists only at a high level of generality, must be operationalized in the context of an ongoing conflict with its own history, conditions, and characteristics. And they must be operationalized in a way that secures a minimum level of acceptance among the various and often shifting parties with the power to thwart or seriously obstruct the process, and under severe time constraints.

In general, interveners lack the will, the expertise, and the power simply to impose some preconceived "ideal" blueprint. And even if they could design and impose such a blueprint, its imposition would lack local legitimacy and undercut the most basic principles of the rule of law. Accordingly, interveners must strive to achieve a set of locally acceptable political arrangements that will meet international standards. This entails a complex process of identifying and bargaining with key local actors. What emerges from this bargaining process necessarily falls far short of anyone's ideal, coherent design;[1] instead, it represents what could be cobbled together under very

---

[1] Donald Horowitz makes this point in connection with the process of constitutional design and efforts to import constitutional expertise through comparative analysis. He notes that

difficult circumstances and in response to widely varying, fast-changing, and often conflicting interests.

Unfortunately, bargaining tends to produce agreements with provisions that run at cross-purposes or provisions that gloss over (for later solution) critical differences among the parties. This problem is exacerbated by the short time horizons and limited strategic interests of the typical interveners. Under pressure to end the fighting, and to minimize their own post-conflict involvement, interveners often support blueprints that satisfy the immediate minimum demands of the contending parties, but in so doing undercut future efforts at transcending the issues dividing those parties. At the same time, internal actors, recognizing the short-term nature of the interveners' commitments, constantly work to modify blueprints in their favor and to position themselves to take power on the interveners' eventual departure. The development of workable blueprints is further handicapped by the interveners' often tenuous knowledge of local history, actors, and cultural conditions and by the limited resources that interveners are prepared to devote to stabilizing and then rebuilding war-torn societies.

The pitfalls of bargaining are readily apparent, particularly in conflicts that turn on issues of ethnic and national identity. In Bosnia, for example, interveners' overriding imperative in 1995 was to stop the fighting. When the Dayton Accords were negotiated, each of the three principal communities in Bosnia retained its own army and its own external backers. The Dayton Accords reflected this balance of power and represented a compromise between the interests of Muslims in building a unitary state with strong central authority and the interest of Croats and especially Serbs in ensuring strong regional autonomy and a weak central government. The net result was an agreement at war with itself. Provisions designed to protect the interests of Croats and Serbs divided the state along ethnic lines, rendered the central government prone to gridlock, and undercut efforts to achieve a state governed by the rule of law. Interveners could easily have designed a more workable constitution. Indeed, in late 2005, the United States among others began to urge Bosnia's political leadership to amend the Dayton constitution in fundamental ways. But in 1995, interveners were unwilling to pay the price that would have been required to impose a more viable constitution.

The reluctance of interveners to take the steps necessary to create (and implement) viable post-conflict blueprints is readily understandable. Interveners find it hard to mobilize political support for military intervention until

---

in most cases, among other things "[t]he sheer proliferation of participants makes it less, rather than more, likely that a design, with its consistent and interlocking parts, will be produced at the outset and adopted at the conclusion." Donald Horowitz, *Constitutional Design: Proposals Versus Processes*, in THE ARCHITECTURE OF DEMOCRACY: CONSTITUTIONAL DESIGN, CONFLICT MANAGEMENT, AND DEMOCRACY (A. Reynolds, ed., 2002), at 15, 16.

a crisis is obvious, usually long after the point at which a relatively modest intervention might have proven effective. When intervention finally occurs, interveners (particularly those from western states sensitive to public opinion) seek to minimize their costs by keeping force sizes, casualties, and time in country to a minimum. As a result, interveners are reluctant to confront powerful and entrenched local forces. In the short run, it is far less costly to accommodate and to the extent possible work with such forces. Although this approach has important advantages – coercion may undermine local acceptance of the proposed blueprint and even generate violent resistance – the approach also has substantial costs. In particular, it tends to generate a least-common-denominator attitude to blueprint creation and implementation. It is far easier to take a minimalist approach to demobilization and disarmament, for example, than to pay the price required to ensure that the various warring factions actually encamp and disarm. But attempts to superimpose democratic institutions on countries where the government not only lacks a monopoly on the exercise of coercive power but also is often outgunned by private armies opens the door to continued civil war, as in Liberia and Sierra Leone; the ascendance of regional warlords, as in Afghanistan; and the interpenetration of organized paramilitary criminal networks and government, as in Bosnia and Kosovo.

To make matters still more challenging, interveners when designing blueprints must find ways to reconcile international standards and the interveners' own cultural predispositions with local beliefs and cultural norms. In some cases, the two may not match. For example, as we discuss later in this chapter, the constitution in post-conflict Afghanistan privileges Islam in ways that may end up limiting religious freedom and women's rights in significant ways, even though international human rights norms prohibit discrimination on the basis of religion and gender. Interveners who seek to impose international standards in such contexts risk undermining their own efforts to demonstrate that governance should not be arbitrary or unresponsive and may jeopardize local acceptance of the overall blueprint. But interveners who accept institutions and laws that discriminate violate some of the substantive precepts of their own international rule of law reconstruction model. In short, interveners and local actors may disagree on what is best for the country's political future. Autocratic imposition of interveners' preferences, although often tempting for efficiency, security, and other reasons and sometimes necessary to meet international standards, may impede the achievement of other blueprint goals. Successful blueprints thus require interveners and their local allies to strike a careful balance between the ideal and the feasible, and the flexibility to evolve over time as new norms take root.

Creating blueprints requires prioritizing some actors' interests over others, creating winners and losers in the post-conflict reconstruction process.

Parties who conclude they can gain more from obstruction will find ways to do so. Interveners will therefore constantly be forced to police all aspects of the creation and implementation of the blueprint. In many cases this will require coercion, the natural follow-on to most instances of military intervention. Coercion is often necessary to maintain security, particularly when spoilers use violence to disrupt reconstruction efforts, but it undercuts a central premise of all blueprints, that the affected population must be free to determine its own political future. Of course, the interests of all parties, and consequently perceptions of advantage and disadvantage, will shift over time as local conditions change. Blueprints should therefore not be seen as fixed instruments but rather as flexible guidelines subject to amendment, evolution, and reinterpretation as circumstances dictate. Although it may seem counterintuitive, such flexibility is particularly important in the process of shaping a new constitutional order. As discussed below, it is generally best if that new order begins with interim principles and evolves over time.

B. The Process of Constitutional Design

Process problems are particularly acute, and particularly important, when it comes to designing a new constitution. Constitutions are founding documents, intended in theory to embody a national consensus on the basic principles and institutions of governance. At their core, constitutions are about the allocation of power, rights, and responsibilities among members of a national political community. Constitutions provide the rules of the game; they specify how power is to be exercised, by whom, and within what limits; they specify how laws are to be adopted and how disagreements within the public sphere are to be managed and resolved. In the post-conflict context, constitutions often address directly some or all of the key issues that gave rise to the conflict, through provisions aimed at managing ethnic, sectarian, regional, and other differences or placing checks on the exercise of central government power.

But constitutions are not only about the allocation of power, the design of governance institutions, or the management of conflict. They are also about reflecting and fostering a shared sense of political community and national identity among a state's citizens. In this sense, a well-designed constitution literally helps constitute the body politic and in so doing renders possible good governance and the rule of law, which ultimately depend on a social consensus on the legitimacy of governing institutions and rules.

But however well designed a constitution may be, if the process by which it is drafted and adopted is not equally well designed and managed, the constitution may lack the popular support necessary for it to prove effective. Indeed, the central insight of a recent study sponsored by the United Nations Development Programme (UNDP) and the United States Institute of Peace (USIP), based on case studies of constitution formation in nineteen post-conflict societies since the early 1970s, is that process matters.[2] What in the abstract may appear the perfect division of powers and responsibilities, or the ideal institutional balance among competing ethnic or sectarian interests, may be worth little more than the paper it appears on if the body politic to which the constitution is addressed rejects it as the product of foreign intervention or exclusionary politics. Worse, a badly conceived or implemented process may actually aggravate the divisions the new constitution is intended to overcome.

The margin for error available to today's post-conflict constitution drafters depends in large part on the nature and extent of divisions within the state. In some cases, such as Iraq, deep ethnic, sectarian, and other divisions will render the process of drafting a constitution extremely sensitive. In other cases, such as East Timor, a broad social consensus may already exist on the identity and basic political parameters of the state. In such cases, problems with constitutional process (and substance) will matter far less, at least in the near term. We discuss below some common process issues in post-conflict constitution making and pitfalls encountered in several recent cases.

1. Pursuing a Phased Constitutional Process

In some cases, constitutional bargains emerge as part of the peace process, sometimes as the product of a deal struck in haste by a small set of internal and external actors. Bosnia offers an extreme example. The current Bosnian Constitution was drafted in haste by lawyers in the U.S. Department of State and presented to the warring parties, in English, as Annex 4 to the Dayton Agreement. The negotiations at Dayton largely excluded the Bosnian Serbs, who were only nominally represented by the Federal Republic of Yugoslavia. Not surprisingly, the resulting constitution commanded little legitimacy and less support in the Republika Srpska.

In most recent cases, however, much greater attention has been paid to constitutional process in general and to issues of inclusion and exclusion in particular. The UNDP and USIP study of constitution formation outlines a phased constitution-making process that, with country-specific variation, has been employed with varying degrees of success by different post-conflict societies since the early 1970s. In general, the most successful instances of constitution-making – South Africa is the most widely cited model in this regard – begin with agreement on a "set of rules to govern the process" itself. This set of procedural ground rules "facilitates greater transparency and public credibility," because all parties know what to expect and can plan their own role accordingly.[3] Such agreements on procedure are usually

---

[2] USIP Special Report, *Iraq's Constitutional Process: Shaping a Vision for the Country's Future*, February 2005, at 2 (hereinafter *Iraq's Constitutional Process*); *see also* Jamal Benomar, *Constitution-Making after Conflict: Lessons for Iraq*, 15 J. DEMOCRACY 81, 82 (2004).

[3] *Iraq's Constitutional Process*, *supra* note 2, at 3.

accompanied by agreements on "a set of fundamental principles to guide the nation during the constitutional process and to be enshrined in the new constitution."[4] South Africa, for example, adopted an interim constitution that set out the rules by which a permanent constitution would be drafted and adopted, provided for the operation of an interim Government of National Unity, and specified fundamental constitutional principles that would be included in the final constitution.

To ensure some measure of public participation and democratic legitimacy, many transitional states utilize an elected constituent assembly or comparable body to develop, review, and approve a draft permanent constitution. Because large assemblies cannot easily debate constitutional niceties, many states utilize subcommittees or bodies of experts to develop constitutional drafts for subsequent discussion in the larger constituent assembly or parliament. Constitutional commissions and similar bodies can play critical roles in vetting proposals, soliciting input from diverse segments of society, and providing technical expertise (often with the help of international experts) that elected bodies may lack. If constitutional commissions are broadly representative of the country's major political groupings and encourage wide public participation in their work, the legitimacy of the eventual draft will be greatly enhanced. Indeed, the members of such commissions may shift over time "from serving primarily as advocates for their respective interest group into a more cohesive group with a greater focus on the needs of the whole society."[5]

The draft constitution that ultimately emerges from such a process may either be adopted by the constituent assembly or parliament, if those bodies are deemed adequately representative of the larger political community, or it may be subject to final approval in a national referendum. In either case, contemporary constitution making generally involves substantial efforts to generate broad public participation in the constitutional process, both to solicit suggestions on important constitutional issues and to generate public support for the new constitution and the institutions it establishes. Increasingly, post-conflict constitution making involves civic education campaigns, public dialogues, media outreach, and similar mechanisms.

The phased approach described above, when done well, can provide an orderly structure for immediate post-conflict governance and relieve some of the high-stakes pressure often felt by participants in constitutional negotiations. By specifying some constitutional principles at the outset while still leaving room for negotiation on others, the parties to the constitutional

---

[4] Id.
[5] Neil Kritz, *Constitution-Making Process: Lessons for Iraq*, Testimony before a joint hearing of the Senate Committee on the Judiciary, Subcommittee on the Constitution, Civil Rights, and Property Rights; and the Senate Committee on Foreign Relations, Subcommittee on Near Eastern and South Asian Affairs, June 25, 2003, *available at* http://www.usip.org/aboutus/congress/testimony/2003/0625_kritz.html (last accessed January 26, 2006).

bargain can reach agreement on key issues without feeling that everything must be resolved at once and with finality.

A phased process also creates room for balanced participation by political elites and society at large. Although broad public participation is now viewed by many experts as a key to achieving a sense of local ownership of post-conflict constitutions, the benefits of participation will depend on who participates and when and how they participate. As Carolyn McCool points out, "[t]he principle of inclusion is a guide, but is by itself of no particular merit."[6] Cultural, political, and resource constraints must all be factored into determining how inclusive the constitutional process should be at any given moment. Trying to accommodate too many participants with widely divergent goals "can produce an agreement that contains no common vision of the state's future, or a short-term accord that serves elites at the expense of strong democratic institutions. . . ."[7] Moreover, excluding potential spoilers may sometimes be essential to maintaining the integrity of the constitution-making process.

In many cases, interveners may also conclude that the exclusion or marginalization of some actors is essential to achieving interveners' own goals in the post-conflict period. In Iraq, for example, the United States sought to limit the involvement of groups closely allied to Iran, fearing that their participation might further polarize religious politics in Iraq and even lead to the formation of a quasi-theocratic government hostile to U.S. interests.[8] Such efforts may easily backfire, however, if the local populace sees them as evidence of undue foreign interference. The U.S. efforts to disempower Iraqi cleric Moqtada al-Sadr, for example, seem only to have enhanced his local stature.

Timing is usually a crucial determinant in decisions about participation. In the immediate aftermath of conflict, powerful political factions (typically the principal warring parties, though sometimes only the victorious warring parties) will often seek to dominate the constitution-making process. If allowed to do so, the constitution will "simply reflect[] division of the spoils between such factions."[9] However, political elites and powerful political factions necessarily must play a prominent role in the post-conflict constitution-making process, unless interveners are prepared to impose their own preferred model, which is both impractical and unwise. Thus interveners face something of a dilemma: excluding or marginalizing powerful local actors may create

---

[6] Carolyn McCool, *The Role of Constitution-Building Processes in Democratization*, International IDEA, at 4 (2004).

[7] Benomar, *supra* note 2, at 84.

[8] *See* Seymour Hersch, *Get Out The Vote: Did Washington Try to Manipulate Iraq's Election?*, THE NEW YORKER, July 25, 2005, *available at* http://www.newyorker.com/fact/content/articles/050725fa_fact.

[9] Kritz, *supra* note 5.

spoilers, but excessive deference to such actors may permit them to hijack the constitutional process for self-interested ends. The trick is to strike the right balance between these two approaches and to do so in a dynamic and adaptive way that is flexible enough to accommodate shifts in local power relations.

By permitting political elites to play a major but not an exclusive role in the early phases of constitutional process, it may be possible to reach critical near-term compromises on the allocation of power, for example, on the composition of an interim government, while still allowing time for the emergence and participation of more broadly based political parties and civil society groups. Moreover, critical compromises may be easier to reach early and in private, among political elites who may have incentives to compromise but feel they are unable to do so in a more public process. In South Africa, for example, the government and African National Congress representatives reached agreement in closed discussions on interim constitutional principles; the process was only opened to broad public participation after critical compromises had been made by both sides.

At some point, however, the process must be opened to broader public participation to generate the wide political support essential for a durable new constitutional order. As the UNDP–USIP study has found, "[i]n the past few decades, those cases in which the entire constitution-making process remained secretive and closed have permitted deal making among elites but have not typically produced either the most vibrant of constitutional democracies or the most stable governments over the long term."[10] Good-faith efforts at civic education, broad public dialogue, and widespread consultation may generate helpful input into the drafting process, build public support for the constitution, and foster a culture in which contending groups come to see dialogue and compromise as the appropriate means for resolving political differences.

2. The Pitfalls of Poorly Managed Constitutional Process

Every post-conflict constitution-making process is different and must follow to some extent the dictates of local conditions. Nonetheless, it is possible to learn across cases and to identify both strengths and weaknesses in recent constitution-formation processes that may provide useful lessons for the future.

Perhaps the most common problem has been haste. Interveners understandably wish to exit post-conflict states as early as possible and may see the adoption of a new constitution, followed by elections for a new government chosen under that constitution, as the key to the door home. Moreover, interveners may find it necessary to demonstrate progress to their home

---

[10] *Iraq's Constitutional Process, supra* note 2, at 6.

audiences by setting and reaching milestones in the constitutional process. The local political elites working with interveners may possess short-term advantages arising out of their role in the conflict that lead them to press hard for a quick adoption of a constitution and an early election, while their advantages remain intact. Yet it takes a substantial amount of time to conduct a well managed constitution-drafting process. In South Africa, depending on the date one chooses to mark as the beginning of the process, it took five to seven years to move from early negotiations to agreement on interim principles to a final constitution.

When the process is rushed, the constitution that emerges is likely to reflect elite interests at the expense of the larger public interest and may lack the popular legitimacy needed to survive the inevitable vicissitudes of the early post-conflict period. The 1995 Bosnian constitution is the clearest example. Drafted in haste, it represented an imposed inter-elite settlement; little effort was made to engage the wider Bosnian public. But the Bosnian constitution was probably never intended to endure as a permanent constitution. Instead, it was adopted purely as a conflict-termination device, and discussions are now underway about how to modify it in ways that will permit Bosnia to function effectively as a modern European state.

In Iraq, the constitutional process proceeded by fits and starts, as the United States and its allies surrendered more and more control over the process to Iraqi political elites. Although the United States originally thought it could install a transitional military authority, supervise the drafting and adoption of a democratic constitution, hold elections, and depart, the reality turned out to be far more complex and far more difficult to manage. Eventually, the United States yielded to demands from within Iraq for a quick transfer of sovereignty and worked with the United Nations and others to broker a fast and, to many, rigid timetable for the formation of a constitution and the election of a new government. When constitutional negotiations between Iraq's three main sectarian factions bogged down because of Sunni concerns over process and substance, the United States, eager to show progress to its critics at home, insisted on strict adherence to the timetable, even though the agreement governing the process permitted a six-month extension. Iraqi Shiites and Kurds, eager to move forward with a constitution that favored their interests, also rejected an extension. Partly as a result, the constitution, adopted over substantial Sunni opposition, did not represent a national consensus on Iraq's future and may do more to exacerbate intergroup conflict than to ameliorate it.

Typically, the feature of constitutional process most likely to be short-changed is that of public participation. In East Timor, for example, the national assembly "had a mere ninety days to deliberate on a constitution," and despite civil society and UN efforts to educate the population and to foster public participation, "the assembly ignored these efforts and the public showed little awareness of the constitutional draft."[11] Similarly, in Afghanistan, despite substantial efforts to solicit the views and involvement of a broad cross-section of society, the time and resources available were simply not sufficient to reach effectively a "vast home-bound and village-bound population...."[12]

Of course, even if adequate time is allotted to each phase of a post-conflict constitutional process, much can still go wrong. The greatest threat is that the constitutional process will be dominated by one or two parties to the detriment of other segments of the post-conflict society. In East Timor, for example, Fretilin's dominant role in the process risked placing the country on the path to a one-party state. In Afghanistan, the dominance of the early phases of the constitutional process by parties affiliated with the victorious Northern Alliance shaped the substance of the constitution, centralizing power in the hands of President Karzai and his allies.

Problems of process tend to be particularly acute in countries divided along ethnic or sectarian lines. The more politics comes to be viewed as a zero-sum game, the more difficult it is for politically weaker groups to feel, and to be, fairly included in discussions over the future allocation of political power. In Iraq, most Sunnis boycotted the elections establishing the National Assembly; as a result, when the constitutional commission was formed, it included only two Sunnis among its fifty-five members. Under pressure from the United States, the United Nations, and others, Shiites and Kurds grudgingly invited an additional fifteen Sunnis into the drafting process, but many Shiites and Kurds considered the Sunnis obstructionist and largely excluded Sunnis from much of the substantive discussions.[13] To make matters worse, the Shiite and Kurd dominated government made a last-minute change to the rules governing the constitutional referendum in an effort to ensure that disgruntled Sunnis could not block adoption of the proposed constitution. Although the rule change was revoked following heavy international criticism, the tactic, and the drafting process as a whole, helped confirm for many Sunnis their fear that they would face political marginalization in the majoritarian-rule system contemplated by the new constitution. Not surprisingly, Sunnis overwhelmingly voted no in the referendum, and although they could not defeat the adoption of the constitution, it is plain that the constitutional process in Iraq did more to hinder than to help foster national unity.

In light of the many challenges interveners face in designing post-conflict blueprints, it should come as no surprise that instances in which a blueprint has been successfully implemented are few. Indeed, the only unambiguous

---

[11] Benomar, *supra* note 2, at 90.

[12] McCool, *supra* note 6, at 14.

[13] *See* David L. Phillips, *Constitution Process Risks a Civil War*, NEWSDAY, August 26, 2005, at A45.

successes date from World War II, when the United States, Britain, and France helped transform Germany, and the United States helped transform Japan, into liberal democratic states with western-style constitutions and strong rule of law cultures. Some recent attempts to design and implement blueprints for post-conflict reconstruction have clearly failed, as in Somalia and the early efforts in Liberia and Sierra Leone; others are ongoing but clearly troubled, as in Afghanistan and Iraq; still others show substantial progress but are by no means out of the woods, as in Bosnia and Kosovo. East Timor is perhaps the most successful recent example, but its achievement of independence makes it a special case, and violence in May 2006 called into question the stability of the post-independence order.

We should be wary, however, about drawing firm conclusions from a small number of cases. Interveners have clearly learned (though not as much as might be hoped) from past experiences, and future blueprints will be designed with that experience in mind. Moreover, we should not let the best become the enemy of the good. Considerable progress toward democracy and the rule of law has been made in places such as East Timor, Bosnia, Kosovo, and Sierra Leone. Even if the full transformation envisioned in the blueprints for those states is never achieved, they are better off for the efforts that have been made.

II. BLUEPRINTS FOR MANAGING STATE FAILURE

In most of the cases considered in this volume, external intervention has occurred in states with national institutions too weak to maintain internal order. In such cases, interveners have typically opted for a relatively simple blueprint: separate, disarm, and demobilize the combatants; form a transitional government; and then hold elections to form a new government. The problem with this approach is that elections serve a country well only when functioning democratic institutions and a larger rule of law culture are already in place or at least being put into place. Otherwise, elections consecrate a winner, with more or less credibility depending on the circumstances surrounding the election at issue, but do not necessarily lead to good governance or dissuade the losers from continuing to seek power by whatever means are available. Simply put, elections by themselves will not overcome state failure and should not be seen in the abstract as a viable exit strategy.

The cases of Liberia and East Timor represent ends of a spectrum. In Liberia, elections were held in 1997 even in the absence of substantial efforts to build institutional capacity and respect for the rule of law. The results were disastrous. In East Timor, elections followed substantial efforts at capacity building and rule of law promotion. The results, though far from ideal, are generally positive. Although the difference in approach explains only part of the difference in outcome, it does illustrate the critical importance of laying adequate groundwork for an electoral solution.

A. Liberia: Failing Elections

With the backing of Burkina Faso and Cote d'Ivoire, Charles Taylor invaded Liberia on December 24, 1989, with approximately 150 men. Taylor's insurgency spread rapidly. By early June, half of the country's 2.6 million people were displaced; thousands had been killed. When rebel forces, including both Taylor's National Patriotic Front of Liberia (NPFL) and a rival, splinter force, reached Monrovia, Liberia's neighbors decided to intervene. On August 23, 1990, armed forces from Nigeria, Ghana, Guinea, Gambia, and Sierra Leone, operating as the Economic Community of West African States Monitoring Group (ECOMOG), deployed to Monrovia to stop the fighting and to deny Taylor his victory.

The ECOWAS blueprint for resolving the Liberian crisis was straightforward: establish a cease-fire; inaugurate an interim government chosen through an inclusive consultative process; and conduct free and fair elections to establish a new and generally accepted government. But ECOWAS was never prepared to take the steps necessary to render an electoral exit strategy viable. To establish a stable democratic government in Liberia, one committed to the rule of law, would have been an enormously challenging task. State institutions in Liberia collapsed entirely during the course of Taylor's insurrection. At a minimum, ECOMOG would have had to defeat Taylor militarily to pave the way for a successful interim administration. In addition, it would have been necessary to help create viable state institutions that could form the foundation on which an elected government could build. More broadly, ECOWAS would have had to transform Liberian political culture through civic education and measures to revitalize civil society. Even a united ECOWAS, with strong support from the United Nations, would have found so broad a mission daunting. But a divided ECOWAS, which received only modest assistance in the form of UN sanctions directed against Taylor and the NPFL, could not pursue so ambitious a policy.

With an appropriate mandate, ECOMOG might at the outset have overwhelmed and defeated Taylor's forces. Instead, ECOMOG sought a negotiated cease-fire. ECOMOG abandoned its posture of neutrality and drove Taylor's troops from Monrovia only after attacks by NPFL forces on ECOMOG troops. But instead of pursuing Taylor, ECOMOG contented itself with securing Monrovia, leaving Taylor in control of the rest of Liberia.[14]

---

[14] For discussion of the early years of ECOWAS involvement in the Liberian conflict, *see* David Wippman, *Enforcing the Peace: ECOWAS and the Liberian Civil War*, in ENFORCING RESTRAINT: COLLECTIVE INTERVENTION IN INTERNAL CONFLICTS (Lori F. Damrosch, ed., 1993), at 157.

On August 27, 1990, ECOWAS convened an "All Liberia Conference" of seventeen Liberian political parties and interest groups. The conference selected an interim government and entrusted it with the task of promoting national reconciliation and holding new elections. But the new Interim Government of National Unity (IGNU) had no army and few material resources. Its writ did not extend beyond Monrovia, and it remained wholly dependent on ECOMOG for its continued existence.

Taylor refused to acknowledge IGNU's legitimacy and established his own government in his own capital city of Gbargna. From the outset, Taylor worked to strip Liberia of its minerals, timber, and other assets and supported dissident forces seeking to overthrow the governments of neighboring countries. After years of sporadic warfare and numerous broken cease-fire agreements, ECOWAS reached an accommodation with Taylor in the 1995 and 1996 Abuja agreements, which called for internationally monitored elections to determine Liberia's future government. In 1997, Taylor was elected President by an 83 percent majority. Although the elections took place "in an atmosphere of intimidation," international monitors judged them free and fair.[15] But Liberians seem to have voted for Taylor primarily because he "had openly threatened to return the country to war if not elected."[16]

Taylor ruled through "intimidation, patronage, and corruption," running the country "as a personal fiefdom."[17] Taylor and his cronies grew rich in a country in which 80 percent of the population lived on less than a dollar a day and that has not had running water or electricity for more than a decade.[18] The political opposition was unable to unify behind a single candidate, and Taylor succeeded in buying off or coopting many opposition politicians.

Unfortunately, Taylor's kleptocracy was not entirely an anomaly. It prospered in substantial part because of a pathological political culture in a country that has never known democracy or responsible government. Politics in Liberia is "intensely personalized and mercenary"; it is "organized not around issues, causes, or agendas, but rather the elevation to power of individual candidates, supported by networks of people who stand to personally benefit."[19] The opposition in Liberia could not unify because each party leader sought office for him- or herself, most intending to exploit it for personal gain much as Doe and Taylor did. In this context, an elections-based

---

[15] International Crisis Group, *Liberia: The Key to Ending Regional Instability,* April 24, 2002, at 13.

[16] Id.

[17] Id.

[18] U.S. Department of State Bureau of Democracy, Human Rights, and Labor, *Liberia: Country Reports on Human Rights Practices – 2003*, February 25, 2004, *available at* http://www.state.gov/g/drl/rls/hrrpt/2003/27735.htm (last accessed January 27, 2006).

[19] *Liberia: The Key to Ending Regional Instability, supra* note 15, at 18.

exit strategy clearly could not in 1997, and cannot today, succeed without a fundamental transformation of Liberian political institutions and culture.

Eventually, Taylor himself was driven from office by rebel forces supported by Guinea, Cote d'Ivoire, and, to a lesser extent, Sierra Leone. Various international actors – the UN, ECOWAS, the African Union (AU), and the International Contact Group for Liberia (ICGL) – then pushed the warring forces into signing a peace agreement in August 2003. The agreement led to the creation of a new National Transitional Government. Shortly afterwards, the Security Council authorized the deployment of 15,000 peacekeepers with a strong Chapter VII mandate to restore peace, disarm the warring factions, and assist the transitional government in reestablishing national authority throughout the country, leading to elections in late 2005.

Unfortunately, the transitional government "contain[ed] an unsavoury mix of nominees of the warring factions, plus some of the same politicians who [were] responsible for the country's decline."[20] Their interest was in securing jobs for themselves and their allies, not in governing Liberia. To make matters worse, "each warring faction was given key public corporations and autonomous agencies, which promises to allow them to continue old habits of siphoning off state resources."[21]

By mid-2005, however, pressure from Liberian civil society activists led to an anticorruption campaign by ECOWAS and the European Community.[22] As a result, a number of Liberian ministers and officials have found themselves accused of malfeasance and subject to investigation.[23] In addition, donors imposed a Governance and Economic Management Assistance Program (GEMAP), requiring Liberia to take certain legal and administrative steps to "improve financial and fiscal administration, transparency and accountability" as conditions for aid.[24]

On October 11, 2005, Liberians turned out en masse to vote in presidential and congressional elections, electing Ellen Johnson-Sirleaf, the first woman head of state in Africa.[25] By all accounts, these elections were generally free and fair. Nonetheless, after decades of war and state decay, daunting problems remain: "[p]etty corruption manifests itself at the most ordinary level in Liberia."[26] Ex-combatants and their business associates continue to strip Liberia of its minerals, timber, and other natural resources, security

---

[20] International Crisis Group, *Liberia: Security Challenges*, November 3, 2003, at 2.
[21] Id., at 3.
[22] International Crisis Group, *Liberia's Elections: Necessary but Not Sufficient*, September 7, 2005, at 2.
[23] Id., at 2.
[24] *See* GEMAP, at 2, *available at* http://siteresources.worldbank.org/LIBERIAEXTN/Resources/GEMAP.pdf (last accessed January 27, 2006).
[25] Polgreen, Lydia, *In First for Africa, Woman Wins Election as President of Liberia*, THE NEW YORK TIMES, November 12, 2005.
[26] *Liberia's Elections, supra* note 22, at 15.

sector reform has failed to weed out human rights abusers, Liberia's culture of impunity remains strong,[27] and state institutions remain extremely weak. Thus, "[e]lections are but a small, early step in a lengthy reconstruction process."[28]

In this environment, Liberia's newly elected government is unlikely to succeed unless interveners insist on fundamental institutional reforms, sufficient to enable the growth of issue-oriented political parties and a civil society that is neither intimidated nor co-opted by a corrupt political leadership. This would seem to require the kind of pervasive institution-building undertaken by the United Nations Mission in Kosovo (UNMIK) and other UN peace missions. The GEMAP, with its provisions for training of Liberian officials, anticorruption laws and procedures, and the insertion of international experts and judges into Liberian institutions, offers a useful starting point for the long-term work of institution-building.[29] Thus far, however, little has been done to move that work forward, and GEMAP's more intrusive measures have already proven controversial among Liberians.

Moreover, it will not be sufficient to address Liberia's own institutional deficiencies and political culture. To succeed in Liberia, interveners and their local partners must also deal with the regional security aspects of the problem. ECOWAS and the UN, with critical support from the United Kingdom, have managed to stabilize Sierra Leone. French intervention has similarly managed to stabilize Cote d'Ivoire,[30] and the United States has increased its assistance to Guinea. But all states in the region, including Burkina Faso and its patron, Libya, must be dissuaded from continuing to use the multiple warring factions in the region to undermine local opposition and subvert neighboring states.

To date, the international community has shown little stomach for the large-scale effort required to render viable its own blueprint for peace. Despite the progress demonstrated in the recent elections and the GEMAP agreement, Liberia remains in dire straits. Treating the recent elections as a panacea will not only doom Liberia to a continuation of its present miseries, but it also may well undo the progress that has been made in neighboring states.

---

[27] *See* Global Witness, *An Architecture of Instability: How the Critical Link Between Natural Resources and Conflict Remains Unbroken*, December 2005, *available at* http://www.globalwitness.org/reports/show.php/en.00083.htm/.

[28] *Liberia's Elections, supra* note 22, at i.

[29] Id., at 12. Specifically, international experts with "co-signatory" power (co-veto power) are to be inserted at certain state-owned corporations; procurement processes are to be revised and the Contract and Monopolies Commission is to be strengthened; an independent Anti-Corruption Commission is to be established; an external auditor is to work alongside the General Auditing Office; training for judges will be introduced; and foreign judges are to "support and advise" their Liberian colleagues. Id.

[30] *Liberia: Security Challenges, supra* note 20, at 3.

B. East Timor and the Advantages of Independence

East Timor is a case of decolonization. The challenge in post-intervention East Timor was not to reconcile ethnic groups with radically different views concerning the identity and even the existence of the state. Rather, the challenge was to build effective and democratic institutions in a newly independent country with no history of democracy and no functioning state institutions.

On October 25, 1999, the UN Security Council adopted Resolution 1272, which established the United Nations Transitional Administration in East Timor (UNTAET). Resolution 1272 endowed UNTAET with "overall responsibility for the administration of East Timor" and gave it the right "to exercise all legislative and executive authority, including the administration of justice." UNTAET's broad mandate reflected the Security Council's view that comprehensive authority was needed to maintain order, rebuild the territory's ruined infrastructure, and establish basic institutions of governance. Local capacity to carry out such tasks was limited, given Indonesia's virtually total exclusion of East Timorese from government during the years of Indonesian control. Nonetheless, Resolution 1272 instructed UNTAET "to consult and cooperate closely with the East Timorese people in order to carry out its mandate effectively, with a view to the development of local democratic institutions . . . and the transfer to these institutions of its administrative and public service functions."

Thus, in many respects UNTAET's mission (and the blueprint for East Timor) was similar to UNMIK's mission in Kosovo: establish order and democratic institutions and then transfer control to local actors chosen by UN-conducted elections. UNTAET's great advantage in carrying out this mission was that all parties in East Timor agreed on the blueprint. Unlike the UN mission in Bosnia, UNTAET did not face a state divided against itself; unlike UNMIK, UNTAET was not impeded by an unresolved final status. More than anything else, this consensus on objectives may account for UNTAET's relative success. East Timor is now independent, with a functioning government.

It does not follow, though, that East Timor is an untrammeled success story. Critics describe the UN state-building operation in East Timor as "a series of missed opportunities and wastage."[31] Others go further and accuse UNTAET of giving birth to a "failed state," given East Timor's standing as the poorest state in Asia. The central criticism is that UNTAET's mandate to exercise complete legislative, executive, and judicial authority conflicted with its mandate to develop democratic institutions and transfer power to

---

[31] Simon Chesterman, *No Strategy without an Exit? Elections and Exit Strategies in East Timor, Kosovo, and Beyond,* October 2001, at 3, *available at* http://www.ipacademy.org/PDF_Reports/no_strategy_without_an_exit_for_web.pdf.

East Timorese.[32] UNTAET, originally structured as a peacekeeping mission along the lines of UNMIK, tended to centralize decision-making and focused on building the capacity of international actors to deliver necessary services. Doing so came at the cost of local capacity-building. East Timorese were largely excluded from the transitional administration. As criticism of UNTAET and its reliance on foreign staff escalated, UNTAET initiated a process of "Timorization" in 2000, but the process was carried out with inadequate oversight and insufficient training. According to Jarat Chopra, who served for a time as head of UNTAET's Office of District Administration, "UNTAET's implicit agenda bore the ominous hallmarks of a typical UN 'exit strategy' by avoiding committed engagement in problem-solving; holding a face-saving election after a reasonable period; and withdrawing without having built adequate local capacity."[33]

UNTAET did consult with Timorese political leaders, particularly through the Timorese National Resistance Council (CNRT), an umbrella organization of East Timorese resistance groups, and later through an unelected advisory council, the National Consultative Council (NCC). Though the NCC reviewed UNTAET regulations, the Special Representative of the Secretary-General (SRSG) retained full authority to promulgate and implement them on his own if necessary. And as the SRSG later acknowledged, the NCC "came under increasing scrutiny for not being representative enough of East Timorese society, and not transparent enough in its deliberations."[34] In the summer of 2000, a National Council was formed to bring East Timorese into the interim government and to confer on them several portfolios in what has been described as "co-government," but no powers were actually transferred to Timorese leaders.[35]

In August 2001, UNTAET organized elections to select an eighty-eight-member constituent assembly to draft a constitution and to serve as a provisional legislature. But the new Assembly largely approved a draft constitution already prepared by CNRT. Although the constitution is unremarkable in most respects (it is based on Portuguese and Angolan models), the deference

[32] See, e.g., Aurel Croissant, International Interim Governments, Democratization, and Post-Conflict Peace-Building: Lessons from Cambodia and East Timor, 5 STRATEGIC INSIGHTS (2006), available at http://www.ccc.nps.navy.mil/si/2006/Jan/croissantJan06.asp (last accessed January 27, 2006); Jarat Chopra, Building State Failure in East Timor, in DEVELOPMENT AND CHANGE (2002), at 979, 985.

[33] Jarat Chopra, The UN's Kingdom in East Timor, 42 SURVIVAL 31 (2000).

[34] Sergio de Mello, quoted in Simon Chesterman, East Timor in Transition: From Conflict Prevention to State-Building, May 2001, available at http://www.ipacademy.org/Publications/Reports/Research/PublEastTimorPrint.htm.

[35] Randall Garrison, The Role of Constitution-Building Processes in Democratization, Case Study/East Timor, 2005, at 10, available at http://www.idea.int/conflict/cbp/upload/CBP-Timor-Leste.pdf (last accessed January 27, 2006).

to the CNRT draft highlights a concern expressed by a number of UN officials, who feared the eventual emergence of a one-party state, dominated by Fretilin, the main party in CNRT.[36]

In May 2002, East Timor achieved independence, with Xanana Gusmao as its first president. But it remains an open question whether East Timor will function effectively as a democratic state with a workable rule of law culture. Jarat Chopra argues that UNTAET's centralized, top-down approach failed to include East Timorese at more than a superficial level in the construction of their new state and that UNTAET therefore had only a superficial impact on East Timor's evolving political culture and institutions.[37] As he observes, "[s]uperficiality is the result of mandates vast in scope implemented by missions minimal in capacity and deployments of relatively short duration, with six-month personnel contracts among a population who are there for good."[38] The result is that local politics evolve in ways that displace the "minimal and weak state structures left behind" by interveners.[39] In East Timor, that has meant an increasing trend toward one-party rule.

As this book was going to press in May 2006, concerns over East Timor's post-independence political stability increased sharply. Disgruntled former Timorese soldiers (600 members of the 1400-strong East Timorese army were fired in March 2006) clashed with government forces in violence that escalated rapidly. President Gusmao was forced to declare a state of emergency, and at the government's request, Australia, Malaysia, and New Zealand sent over 2000 peacekeeping troops to Dili, and Portugal provided a contingent of military police, to help the government restore order. The violence highlighted the inadequacy of the pre-independence capacity-building efforts, and leave East Timor's future an open question.

Ironically, UNTAET's principle advantage over UNMIK and other UN missions facing sharp internal divisions – local agreement on the end state – may have made the electoral exit strategy appear more likely to achieve its aims than it actually was and therefore undermined UNTAET's ability to remain in place long enough to foster a broader-based democratic political culture. Certainly, inappropriately early exits seem to plague the democratic reform model in general. In such cases, the blueprint is simpler than in identity-based conflicts but deceptively so. Because interveners do not need to balance power among competing groups, elections are easier to organize and easier to adopt as an exit strategy. In too many cases, that leads interveners to exit before the conditions necessary for elections to succeed are put in place.

[36] *See* Chesterman, *supra* note 34.
[37] Chopra, *supra* note 32, at 995.
[38] Id.
[39] Id.

III. BLUEPRINTS FOR RESOLVING IDENTITY-BASED CONFLICTS

In deeply divided societies such as Bosnia and Kosovo, identity politics makes the task of blueprint design considerably more difficult than in countries torn primarily by struggles over state resources. Indeed, perhaps the single most important variable in the development of a post-conflict reconstruction blueprint is the cohesiveness of the state in which intervention has taken place. When ethnic identities serve as the basis for political mobilization and large-scale intergroup violence, the task of constructing a viable polity becomes much more difficult. In such cases, group aspirations are incompatible and zero sum. This is most apparent on the overriding issue of the integrity of the state itself, because some groups want to form their own state or join with another state, whereas others insist on keeping the existing state intact. But similar problems occur with respect to most major issues associated with future governance arrangements, including the form and composition of any government, the relative powers of the central government and local authorities, the process for electing officials, the control of state resources, and protections to be afforded members of minority groups.

In such cases, the political architects of the post-intervention order must find a way to balance competing group interests without impairing the viability of the new state or violating international standards. As a result, interveners often find that they cannot simply modernize a preexisting constitution; instead, they must start from scratch (as in Bosnia), temporize (as in Kosovo), or radically adapt (as in Iraq) to deal with the underlying reluctance of some groups to remain part of the same state.

A. Blueprints for Identity-Based Conflicts: From Power Sharing to Minority Rights

The range of options in designing blueprints for deeply divided societies may be illustrated by two cases from the former Yugoslavia: Bosnia and Kosovo. The very different approach taken in each reflects a combination of factors, including the demographic makeup of the state, the history of the conflict and its outcome, the involvement of neighboring states, and the circumstances dictating external intervention.

1. Consociationalism in Bosnia

Prior to independence, Bosnia was a "mini-Yugoslavia," with a prewar population approximately 40 percent Muslim, 30 percent Serb, and 17 percent Croat, interspersed in complicated and discontiguous patterns throughout the country. This "ethnic mélange was stable so long as each ethnic community could ally with its siblings in other republics – Bosnian Croats with

Croatia, Bosnian Serbs with Serbia."[40] But the outbreak of war solidified ethnic identities and forced Bosnians into independence as part of a state divided against itself.

The Dayton Agreement had a single, overriding end: termination of the fighting in Bosnia. To achieve this goal, the negotiators felt compelled to meet the minimum demands of each party while rejecting their maximalist and fundamentally irreconcilable aims. The net result was an agreement that satisfied no one, with multiple provisions working at cross-purposes. The Serbs sought recognition of their proclaimed independence and a future right to merge with Serbia, which could not be granted without legitimizing ethnic cleansing and rejecting Bosnian Muslims' demands for a unitary state. Accordingly, the Serbs were denied independence, but given "entity" status within Bosnia with autonomy falling just short of statehood and a right to enter into a "special parallel relationship" with Yugoslavia. Bosnian Croats, already linked to Bosnian Muslims through a paper Federation negotiated at Washington's behest in 1993, retained substantial control over traditionally Croat areas through the division of the Federation into ethnic cantons. Bosnian Muslims, though denied the strong central government they had sought, were given formal recognition of Bosnia's existence as a sovereign state within its republic borders and a set of provisions calling for return of refugees and respect for human rights.

In many respects, the agreement follows consociational principles. Consociationalism is a form of government intended to mitigate conflict in societies in which voting behavior turns on ethnic group affiliation. In such societies, minorities can be outvoted and therefore marginalized. Majorities need not fear that a subsequent election will generate a new and different majority; accordingly, they have few incentives for moderation in dealing with minorities.[41]

To address these problems, Arend Lijphart and others have urged adoption of constitutional structures designed to share power. Lijphart has identified four basic principles of consociational democracy: grand coalition, mutual veto, proportionality, and segmental autonomy.[42] The grand coalition principle calls for inclusion of all major political parties in executive decision-making; in this way, "majority rule is replaced by joint consensual rule."[43] The mutual veto permits each ethnic group (or segment, in Lijphart's

---

[40] Ruth Wedgwood, *Introduction, After Dayton: Lessons of the Bosnia Peace Process* 5 (Council on Foreign Relations Symposium 1999).

[41] *See* Donald Horowitz, ETHNIC GROUPS IN CONFLICT (1985), at 84.

[42] Arend Lijphart, DEMOCRACY IN PLURAL SOCIETIES: A COMPARATIVE EXPLORATION (1977), at 25. For Lijphart, executive power-sharing and group autonomy are the two "primary characteristics" of consociational democracy. Arend Lijphart, *The Wave of Power-Sharing Democracy,* in THE ARCHITECTURE OF DEMOCRACY (A. Reynolds, ed., 2002) at 37, 39.

[43] Lijphart, *supra* note 13, at 118.

terminology) to block legislation it deems inimical to its vital interests. Proportionality displaces the winner-take-all principle as the "basic standard of
political representation, civil service appointments, and allocation of public
funds."[44] Finally, segmental autonomy grants each ethnic group "as much
decision-making autonomy as possible" on areas of "exclusive concern" to
it.[45] In theory, consociationalism offers a way for politically mobilized ethnic
groups to cooperate on issues of common concern while affording each group
assurances that it cannot be outvoted on issues of particular concern to it.

The constitution in Annex 4 of the Dayton Agreement is explicitly consociational. It mandates executive power sharing (the grand coalition principle), makes ethnicity the standard for political representation, confers autonomy on geographically concentrated minorities, and grants them extensive
veto powers to insulate each group from the potentially adverse effects of
majoritarian rule. In theory, the constitution seeks to create a democratic,
pluralist society with a commitment to human rights and employs consociational power-sharing mechanisms as the "constitutional adhesive" designed
to "cement the multiethnic Bosnian state together."[46]

The constitution divides Bosnia into two entities, the nominal Croat-
Muslim Federation and the Republika Sprska. At least until recently, each
entity has exercised nearly complete autonomy over most areas of governance, including education, policing, the media, and the economy. The central government was given control over only those functions absolutely necessary to a single state nominally speaking with one voice in international
affairs, such as foreign policy, customs, monetary policy, immigration, and
air traffic control. Executive and legislative power was shared evenly among
the three principal ethnic groups.

Each group has multiple mechanisms permitting it to veto any executive
action or legislative decision contrary to its interests, warranting compar-
isons of Bosnia to a car with three brakes. Indeed, the constitution was so
heavily weighted toward the protection of ethnic group interests that many
assumed it was simply a mechanism for a disguised transition to the partition of Bosnia. Although the warring parties may well have rejected any
constitution that did not make ethnic group interests its guiding principle,
it was at best an open question in 1995 whether a state burdened with such
an unwieldy political structure could function at all. Certainly, all of the
problems commonly ascribed to consociational arrangements have surfaced
in Bosnia.

---

[44] Id., at 119.

[45] Id.

[46] Patrick J. O'Halloran, *Post-Conflict Reconstruction: Constitutional and Transitional Power-
sharing Arrangements in Bosnia and Kosovo*, in FROM POWER SHARING TO DEMOCRACY:
POST-CONFLICT INSTITUTIONS IN ETHNICALLY DIVIDED SOCIETIES (Sid Noel, ed., 2005) at 104,
106.

The most obvious problem is that consociationalism depends on interelite cooperation, which has been notably absent in Bosnia. The reason for its absence is simple. The war in Bosnia strengthened nationalist parties, exacerbated intergroup animosities, and fostered a pervasive zero-sum politics. Dayton papered over the underlying and incompatible aspirations of Bosnia's national communities but did not resolve them. The central government, intended to create a "thin roof" over the three communities, has been generally ineffective. Bosnian Serbs in particular have consistently opposed efforts by Bosnian Muslims to strengthen the central government and render Bosnia a more cohesive state.

Autonomy affords each principal ethnic group almost complete control over the day-to-day life of its members. Thus, it gives the three major nationalist parties, particularly the Serbs, much of what they want, even if they lack the formal trappings of statehood.[47] Among other things, control of the "key wealth-producing industries" lies with the entities;[48] so does control over most sources of government revenue. But under the guise of protecting group interests, nationalist politicians in fact have primarily protected their own interests through corruption, patronage networks, and continued demonization of the other ethnic communities. Autonomy has fostered continued separation of the three national communities and hindered cooperation across entity lines on law enforcement, communications, public utilities, health care, and economic policy.

The veto provisions in the constitution enable nationalist politicians to pursue continued division by blocking any legislation inconsistent with their group's political program. For Serb representatives, that has meant almost all measures that might strengthen or unify the state and thereby undercut the nationalists' power. Thus, Srpska's representatives have largely opposed the creation or enhanced operation of common institutions, including courts, police, and a national army, or a common infrastructure, including shared transportation, utilities, and communications.

In this kind of environment, the rule of law cannot thrive, because the institutions that make and implement law, at least at the national level, are ineffective, needlessly duplicative, and expensive.[49] Moreover, the focus on

---

[47] The problem is not confined to Srpska: "even within the Federation Bosniaks and Croats maintain separate parallel lines of authority. All three parties, but especially Croats and Serbs, have blocked efforts to develop central institutions...." U.S. Institute of Peace, *Bosnia's Next Five Years: Dayton and Beyond*, at 2, *available at* http://www.usip.org/pubs/specialreports/sr001103.pdf (last accessed January 27, 2006).

[48] Id., at 6.

[49] According to High Representative Paddy Ashdown, Bosnia "is not functional as a state, since 65% [of its budget] is spent on administration and only 35% on the citizens." Interview with Paddy Ashdown, *Nacional* (Zagreb), January 18, 2005, *excerpted at* http://www.bosnia.org.uk/news/news_body.cfm?newsid=2009 (last accessed January 27, 2006).

ethnicity as the guiding principle for the distribution of political power denies equal rights to many Bosnian citizens, particularly the "others" who are entirely neglected in the constitution beyond a brief preambular mention. The centrifugal effects of the Dayton constitution are thus powerful and plainly visible.

Without more, there would be little hope for a viable and multiethnic Bosnia, much less a democratic Bosnia committed to the rule of law. But Dayton also contains a number of potentially unifying provisions. For example, the Dayton Agreement expressly mandates the right of refugees to return to their prewar residences. Effective implementation of this right would go far toward undermining the power of the nationalist parties. Returning refugees might trigger shifts in voting patterns sufficient to support the formation of moderate political parties seeking to build support on common interests other than ethnicity. Returns might also foster intergroup reconciliation.

Even more important is the power of the international community, acting through the Office of the High Representative, to force changes on the recalcitrant local parties. Under the Dayton Agreement, the High Representative is the final authority in theater on the interpretation of the agreement and the implementation of its civilian aspects. Under the original vision of Dayton, the High Representative was expected to monitor and assist local actors in carrying out the terms of the agreement. As the International Crisis Group put it, Dayton opted for a "helping hand" model. Local authorities and institutions already existed, and the agreement had to take their interests into account. As time passed, however, it became apparent that Bosnia's nationalist politicians could not agree even on the simplest things. Progress seemed possible only when the international community insisted and backed its insistence with economic or other leverage. In 1997, a frustrated Peace Implementation Council, meeting in Bonn, Germany, enlarged the High Representative's powers to enable him to force decisions (or take them unilaterally), as he saw fit. Under his "Bonn powers," the High Representative may enact laws by decree, remove politicians from office, ban political parties, and take other measures deemed necessary to implement Dayton. Because of the continuing recalcitrance of the nationalist parties, the High Representative has resorted to these powers with increasing frequency, becoming Bosnia's "principal legislator" and "imposing laws to strengthen the state that could never otherwise be passed."[50] The High Representative has used these powers to create new state institutions, pass new laws and reform old ones, marginalize or remove extremist politicians (including the Serb member of the tripartite presidency), and press for the formation of interethnic parties and alliances.

[50] International Crisis Group, *Bosnia's Alliance for (Smallish) Change*, August 2, 2002, at 16.

To some extent, the imposition of reforms runs counter to the norms of democratic accountability that the international community seeks to instill in Bosnia. And it has permitted Bosnians to resist the fundamental shifts in political culture and attitudes necessary to make Bosnia a viable state. But paradoxically, "[i]n order to abjure use of the Bonn powers," High Representative Paddy Ashdown has needed "to use them more intensively" and "to lift the ceiling of what is meant to be permissible under the Dayton constitution."[51] Ashdown has worked hard to transform Bosnia into a viable, self-sustaining democracy by using his Bonn powers, and the requirements for Euro-Atlantic integration set by the United States and the European Union, to induce the nationalist parties in power in Bosnia to accept reforms designed to transfer power from the entities to state-level institutions. Ashdown has established several internationally chaired commissions to find ways to reassess what the Dayton constitution permits, in the hope that this will lead eventually to a "fully-fledged domestic revision of BiH's constitutional architecture."[52] Significant reforms have been adopted, at least on paper, in the areas of defense, intelligence, and policing, and more are contemplated under the Office of the High Representative's Mission Implementation Plan. Moreover, much of Bosnia's infrastructure has been repaired, the currency is stable, and many refugees have returned.[53] And in November 2005, on the tenth anniversary of the Dayton Agreement, the United States joined Ashdown and others in calling on Bosnia's political leadership to accept fundamental constitutional reforms.

Whether the reform effort will succeed remains to be seen. What is clear is that the power-sharing provisions that permitted the Dayton Agreement to succeed in the first place are now themselves obstacles to further transition. Had interveners been willing to run the risks of a significant military engagement in Bosnia, they could have insisted on a more workable blueprint at the outset.

2. Kosovo and Minority Rights

Although conflict in Kosovo, as in Bosnia, centered on identity politics, Kosovo's very different demographic and political situation mandated a very different blueprint. With the dissolution of the Socialist Federal Republic of Yugoslavia (FRY) in 1991, Kosovo had a plausible claim to independence, along with the various Yugoslav republics. But most states then viewed Kosovo as an integral part of the FRY, one that could not be split off

---

[51] International Crisis Group, *Bosnia's Nationalist Governments: Paddy Ashdown and the Paradoxes of State Building*, July 22, 2003, at ii.

[52] Id.

[53] *See* Office of the High Representative, General Information, *Our Mission Implementation Plan*, *available at* http://www.ohr.int/ohr-info/gen-info/ (last accessed January 27, 2006).

without violating the latter's territorial integrity. Moreover, the demographic imbalance between Kosovar Serbs (some 90 percent of the population) and Kosovar Albanians (approximately 10 percent) rendered a Bosnian-style consociationialist solution unworkable. Under the circumstances, reinstatement of Kosovo's preexisting autonomy coupled with legal protections for minorities seemed to the international community to be the best available means to balance the legitimate interests of both Serbs and Albanians.

In January 1999, the Contact Group (consisting of representatives of the United States, Russia, the United Kingdom, Germany, and France) demanded that FRY and Kosovar Albanian leaders accept a detailed "Interim Agreement for Peace and Self-Government in Kosovo" (the "Rambouillet Agreement"). Belgrade, unhappy with the agreement and with the prospect of NATO troops roaming FRY territory to monitor it, would not agree. Instead, Belgrade intensified its military and paramilitary activities in Kosovo and thereby triggered NATO's three-month bombing campaign.

The bombing ended with Belgrade's capitulation. On June 10, 1999, the Security Council adopted Resolution 1244, which (together with the subsequent constitutional agreement) continues to serve as the blueprint for Kosovo's future. Resolution 1244 authorized the Kosovo Force (KFOR) to use force to establish a secure environment and carry out related tasks. It also authorized the Secretary-General, with assistance from international organizations, to establish a transitional civil administration, to facilitate "a political process designed to determine Kosovo's future status," and eventually to oversee "the transfer of authority from Kosovo's provisional institutions to institutions established under a political settlement."

The withdrawal of Serb authorities from Kosovo following NATO's victory left UNMIK with a ruined infrastructure and a large and rapidly returning refugee population. From the start, then, UNMIK has had to rebuild governing institutions from the ground up. To enable UNMIK to carry out this job (and to avoid the mistakes made in Bosnia), the Security Council "vested in UNMIK all legislative and executive powers as well as the administration of the judiciary" and gave it the authority to repeal or suspend existing laws as it saw fit.[54] Thus, Kosovo has been treated more or less as an international protectorate, with the Special Representative of the Secretary-General (SRSG) exercising essentially proconsul powers.

The advantages to this approach were substantial. The withdrawal of Serb forces left a political and security vacuum that Kosovo Liberation Army (KLA) fighters and others sought to fill. The alternative to UNMIK rule

---

[54] Daan Everts, *Review of the OSCE Mission in Kosovo's Activities, 1999–2000*, at 1, *available at* http://www.reliefweb.int/rw/rwb.nsf/AllDocsByUNID/022a44866c823864c 1256a550032d38c (last accessed January 6, 2006).

would have been, at least in significant part, rule by paramilitary forces with little interest in western notions of liberal democratic governance or the rule of law or, in Serb areas, continued rule by Belgrade. To achieve a transition to democratic self-governance in Kosovo paradoxically required a commanding international role. Among other things, UNMIK needed time to restore basic services, organize governing institutions, deal with refugee returns, and assist Kosovars in organizing for elections. Even more importantly, UNMIK needed time to work on transforming the political culture in Kosovo. At a minimum, UNMIK needed to look for ways to reconcile Kosovar Albanians and Kosovar Serbs to living together. Rule by decree was in many respects an efficient way to proceed.

But necessary as it may have been, treating Kosovo as a protectorate carried its own set of problems. Most important, rule by decree often appeared arbitrary to the Kosovars and sometimes culturally insensitive. At a minimum, it ran counter to basic democratic and rule of law principles, such as transparency and accountability in government decision-making, that UNMIK has sought to build into the Kosovar political system. As discussed in later chapters, this problem has run the gamut from the very first UNMIK regulation selecting the law to be applied in Kosovo to some of the SRSG's most recent decisions.

The crux of the problem, though, has been the uncertainty regarding Kosovo's final status. Resolution 1244 deferred resolution of this issue indefinitely, for the simple reason that agreement on the resolution itself "could only be reached by recourse to a deliberate ambiguity over status."[55] The United States, at least, has been quietly sympathetic to Kosovar Albanian demands for independence; Russia and many European states want Kosovo to remain part of the FRY. As a result, Resolution 1244 stipulated that Kosovo is part of the FRY but directed UNMIK to "facilitat[e] a political process designed to determine Kosovo's future status." The drafters of Resolution 1244 envisioned that this determination would be made within three years, but 1244 carries no time limit. Until recently, little progress was made on this issue, because many international actors feared that attempts to resolve it would jeopardize the progress of democratic reform in Serbia, incite further unrest among Albanian populations in neighboring states, encourage the Republika Srpska to demand independence, and divide the international community.

These concerns were not without foundation. But the uncertainty regarding final status meant that the international community drafted a blueprint for Kosovo's future with no clear idea what the completed structure should look like. Kosovar Albanians insisted that they would accept nothing less

---

[55] International Crisis Group, *A Kosovo Roadmap (I), Addressing Final Status*, March 1, 2002, at 2.

than independence. Kosovar Serbs feared, with considerable justification, that they would be subject to discrimination and worse in an independent Kosovo. Possible solutions are numerous, but all of them are problematic.[56]

Unfortunately, the failure to resolve the final status question has undermined much of UNMIK's work. The Assembly, for example, one of the key institutions of self-governance established in 2001, has wasted much of its time pushing measures designed directly or indirectly to establish independence as Kosovo's end-state, even though this is outside the Assembly's mandate and invariably blocked by the SRSG. Even fundamental rule of law reforms, such as efforts to approve new legal codes, have been stalled by UN officials wary of suggesting that Kosovo's legal system should be wholly divorced from that of the FRY. Uncertainty about final status has also "constrain[ed] the privatization process and hinder[ed] economic development,"[57] because no one can be confident of the future legal and political framework. It has interfered with efforts "to deal with borders and border controls, citizenship, drug and other trafficking, regional cooperation on organized crime, and a host of other issues.... "[58] In short, though the failure to resolve Kosovo's final status is readily understandable, the uncertainty has been "itself a key source of instability."[59]

The goal of intervention in Kosovo was to end the fighting between Serbs and Albanians and to construct a stable and democratic polity in which the rights of each group would be respected. KFOR has ended the fighting. But UNMIK can't construct the polity that would permit the interveners to leave without resolving the issue at the heart of the conflict. Leaving the status issue unresolved encourages each side to view the conflict in zero-sum terms. All efforts at reform are viewed through the lens of their possible effects on final status. As long as that issue "remains open, each side will continue to regard the other as a threat"[60] and each side will continue to maneuver with final status in mind. Serbs, for example, will continue periodically to boycott elections and seek to maintain Belgrade-financed parallel government structures; Albanians will resist cooperation with Belgrade on issues of joint concern and oppose the return of Serb refugees.[61] Nationalists on

---

[56] For discussion of the full range of options, from long-term protectorate to partition, *see* United States Institute of Peace, *Kosovo Final Status: Options and Cross-Border Requirements, available at* http://www.usip.org/pubs/specialreports/sr91.pdf (last accessed January 27, 2006).

[57] Id., at 2.

[58] Id.

[59] *A Kosovo Roadmap (I), supra* note 55, at ii.

[60] Id.

[61] Albanians "see the selection of return locations...as working to fulfil Serbia's political objective: the partition or cantonization of Kosovo. Many also regard returnees as Serbia's Trojan horse – a mechanism to bring the control and influence of the Serbian government

both sides "are able to use the lack of clarity on final status as a rallying point...."[62]

Although well aware of this problem, UNMIK has, at least until recently, focused on pursuing "standards before status." UNMIK established benchmarks on a series of issues, from a functioning economy to an impartial legal system, which once achieved would facilitate resolution of Kosovo's final status. UNMIK hoped in this way to use the status issue as leverage to promote politically moderate behavior. It also hoped that the gradual process of transferring political power and control over the institutions of governance would foster "the emergence of politically moderate parties and credible leaders" and a general "political maturity" conducive to an acceptable final status resolution.[63]

But the process of developing the Constitutional Framework for Provisional Self-Government in Kosovo (the second half of the blueprint) illustrates the difficulties involved. From the start, Albanians fought to create a constitutional framework "as close to an independent state as possible."[64] Serbs, fearing the final status implications, largely boycotted the two-month consultation process.[65] Even the name of the document was contentious. Kosovar Albanians wanted to call it a constitution; the SRSG and other internationals saw that as implying a judgment on Kosovo's final status. "Constitutional Framework" was the compromise.[66] More importantly, "none of the local participants agreed to the text as finally adopted – a 'compromise' that had to be forced on them by Haekkerup [then the SRSG]."[67]

The Constitutional Framework provided for the "gradual transfer of responsibilities to Provisional Institutions of Self-Government" in a broad range of internal areas, from economic policy to good governance and human rights. The hope has been that the transfer would "enhance democratic governance and respect for the rule of law." But the Framework is an UNMIK regulation, and ultimate authority continues to reside with the

back to some parts of Kosovo." International Crisis Group, *Return to Uncertainty: Kosovo's Internally Displaced and the Return Process*, December 13, 2002, at 3. Conversely, Serbs are reluctant to return to what may be a future independent state in which they will be a minority. Id.

[62] United States Institute of Peace, *Kosovo Decision Time: How and When?*, February 2003, at 4, *available at* http://www.usip.org/pubs/specialreports/sr100.pdf (last accessed January 27, 2006).

[63] Chesterman, *supra* note 31, at 6.

[64] International Crisis Group, *Kosovo: Landmark Election*, November 21, 2001, at 3.

[65] Id.

[66] Id.

[67] Simon Chesterman, *Kosovo in Limbo: State Building and "Substantial Autonomy,"* August 2001, at 6–7, *available at* http://216.239.51.104/search?q=cache:8qTa6VyvODYJ:staff.bath.ac.uk/mlssaw/cep/resources/kosovo-in-limbo.pdf+chesterman+forced+on+them+by+Haekkerup+&hl=en&gl=us&ct=clnk&cd=3.

SRSG, who retains a "virtually unlimited prerogative to override" the new institutions.[68]

On the critical issue of majority–minority relations, the Constitutional Framework is more minority rights oriented than consociationalist. The new governing institutions include a president (seen by Albanians as a future head of state) and an assembly. The assembly is structured to provide for overrepresentation of minorities, particularly Serbs, but stops well short of affording them veto power. The assembly has 120 seats, 100 to be chosen by proportional representation; 10 are set aside for Serbs and another 10 for other minorities. Thus, if Serbs participated fully, they might command over 20 seats.[69] In theory, Serbs might exercise significant influence given the split between the two major Albanian parties, each of which might wish to secure Serb votes for its programs. In practice, however, the Albanian parties tend to agree on most issues and are unlikely in the foreseeable future to wish to confer much influence on Serbs by courting their votes.[70] Other features of the Assembly attempt to require interethnic compromise. In a vaguely consociational structure, the seven-member presidency of the assembly requires inclusion of Serb and minority representatives. Similarly, at least one Serb and one other minority must be included in ministerial positions in the executive.

The Constitutional Framework also contains a catalog of minority rights, designed "to preserve, protect and express their ethnic, cultural, religious, and linguistic identities." These rights include language, education, cultural, and employment rights, as well as obligations to preserve religious sites and guaranteed access to public media. The Constitutional Framework also provides that the "the SRSG will retain the authority to intervene as necessary in the exercise of self-government for the purpose of protecting the rights of Communities and their members."

Unfortunately, these provisions for minorities do not go far enough to render Serbs secure in an independent Kosovo. At the same time, they do go far enough to reinforce the salience of ethnicity in Kosovo politics, which "continues to be fought strictly along ethnic lines."[71] This is the underlying problem of trying to resolve intercommunal conflict through legal protection of minority rights. It is a viable approach in societies that already have a tradition of democratic accommodation and respect for human rights. But in deeply divided societies that lack such traditions, minority rights simultaneously offer too little and too much. For most Serbs, the paper protections afforded by the Constitutional Framework offer little or no real protection against Albanian animosity. Serb politicians warn that independence will provoke a mass exodus. The end result may be the ethnically homogenous

---

[68] *Kosovo: Landmark Election, supra* note 64, at 4.
[69] Id. at 8.
[70] Id. at 12.
[71] Chesterman, *supra* note 31, at 7.

territory that Albanian separatists have long sought but that would run counter to western insistence on creating a multiethnic Kosovo. At the same time, so long as power and resources are divided along ethnic lines, politics will continue to turn on ethnicity.

Multiethnic harmony, the goal underlying the minority rights instruments of the 1990s and ostensibly the objective of western involvement in the former Yugoslavia, cannot flourish so long as ethnic identity crowds out other interests (such as class, ideology, and profession) and precludes the formation of interethnic coalitions. Put another way, dividing power among ethnic communities represents an acceptance of the logic of nationalism, applied at the (nominally) substate level. This is the paradox at the heart of western efforts to achieve viable political settlements to ethnic conflicts in Bosnia, Kosovo, and other deeply divided societies. The price of such settlements is often the perpetuation of the differences that necessitated the settlements in the first place. In Kosovo, the emphasis on ethnicity in politics is less than in Bosnia, because of the imbalance in ethnic group numbers. The blueprints are therefore different, but the underlying obstacle in each case is the same, getting hostile national communities to live together on equitable terms.

Despite continuing interethnic antagonism, the status issue is clearly coming to a head. In November 2005, the UN Secretary-General appointed former Finnish President Martti Ahtisaari as his special envoy for final status talks. The two most prominent options remain autonomy and independence. But Ahtisaari and others have called for further progress on building democratic institutions and protecting minority rights as a precondition. Thus, at the time of writing this chapter, the blueprint for Kosovo remains incomplete.

IV. MIXED CASES: AFGHANISTAN AND IRAQ

Afghanistan and Iraq do not fit neatly into the blueprint categories described above. Intervention was not driven by large-scale internal conflict over resources or the identity of the state but rather by the perceived security interests of the United States and its coalition partners. Nonetheless, conditions associated with the identity- and resource-driven conflict models exist in both Afghanistan and Iraq and raise many of the same issues seen in other post-conflict environments. In Afghanistan, the power base of most political elites largely tracks ethnic and tribal affiliations, rendering aspects of the identity-conflict models relevant. Nonetheless, ethnicity does not dominate political behavior in the way it does in places such as Bosnia and Kosovo. Thus, the blueprint for Afghanistan emphasizes majoritarian elections and institution-building. By contrast, in Iraq, Kurdish desires for independence, and increasing tensions between Shiites and Sunnis, have brought to the fore many of the issues associated with identity-based conflicts, producing a complicated constitutional politics that renders straight majoritarian arrangements untenable.

A. Afghanistan: Center and Periphery

On October 7, 2001, the United States responded to the September 11 terrorist attacks on the World Trade Center and the Pentagon by launching Operation Enduring Freedom to eliminate al-Qaeda forces from their bases in Afghanistan and to drive their Taliban hosts from power. Working closely with Northern Alliance forces, the United States and its allies quickly took control of most of the country. After twenty-five years of nearly unremitting warfare, state institutions were in shambles, the country's infrastructure was decaying or destroyed, millions of Afghans lived abroad as refugees, and the country was riven by ethnic, tribal, ideological, and religious fissures. The interveners, especially the United States, feared a deep and protracted involvement in Afghanistan and consciously rejected the transitional administration model employed in Kosovo and East Timor. Where in Kosovo the UN and other international actors played a dominant role in rebuilding the state, taking the lead in pursuing security, reconstruction, and democratization, the United States insisted in Afghanistan on a "light footprint." The goal of this approach was "local ownership of the revival process as much as possible...."[72]

The U.S. motives for the light-footprint approach were clear. The United States did not want to tie down large numbers of troops attempting to secure and rebuild the country. Instead, the United States wanted to help establish a new Afghan government, one sympathetic to U.S. interests, and to place on it primary responsibility for post-conflict reconstruction. Other international actors, including the United Nations, did not want to undertake large-scale nation-building activities without full U.S. involvement and support. In particular, they did not want to attempt to restore security outside Kabul without U.S. military backing.

Instead, the goal, as articulated at a November 2001 meeting of the "Six plus Two" group (the six states bordering Afghanistan, the United States, and the Russian Federation), was to create "a broad-based, freely chosen Afghan government," through which international assistance could be channeled.[73] Under UN auspices, and with active encouragement from the United States and other coalition members, various Afghan factions met in Bonn in late November to hammer out an agreement on transitional arrangements. The participating parties included Afghan military commanders, ethnic

---

[72] Robert McMahon, UN: 'Light Footprint' in Afghanistan Could Hold Lessons for Iraq, Radio Free Europe/Radio Liberty, April 7, 2003, available at http://www.rferl.org/features/2003/04/07042003115224.asp.

[73] See UNAMA/OCPI, The United Nations in Afghanistan: 11 September 2001–11 September 2002, August 31, 2002, at 2.

group leaders, expatriate Afghans, and representatives of Afghanistan's exiled king.[74] On December 6, under considerable pressure from the United States and other interested states, the negotiating factions adopted the Bonn Agreement on Provisional Arrangements in Afghanistan Pending The Re-establishment of Permanent Government Institutions.[75] The Security Council endorsed the agreement the following day.

The Bonn Agreement offered a simple blueprint for Afghanistan's future. The agreement provided for an immediate transfer of power to an Interim Authority, chosen by participants in the Bonn negotiations. The Interim Authority was charged with convening an emergency loya jirga within six months, which in turn was tasked with creating a broad-based Transitional Authority "to lead Afghanistan until such time as a fully representative government can be elected through free and fair elections to be held no later than two years from the date of the convening of the Emergency Loya Jirga."[76] The agreement also provided for the convening of a constitutional loya jirga within eighteen months of the establishment of the Transitional Authority, to adopt a new constitution for Afghanistan. The agreement recognized the need for "broad representation in these interim arrangements of all segments of the Afghan population" and noted that "these interim arrangements are intended as a first step toward the establishment of a broad-based, gender-sensitive, multi-ethnic and fully representative government...."[77] Annex I requested the Security Council to deploy a UN-mandated force to "assist in the maintenance of security for Kabul and its surrounding areas" and "as appropriate" to expand "to other urban centres and areas."[78] As far as it went, the Afghanistan blueprint was reasonably sound. It offered a chance for Afghans, backed by international support, to establish a democratic government in Kabul and to begin the reconstruction process working from the center out.

At the outset, the political process launched with the Bonn agreement was not representative of Afghan society as a whole. The Northern Alliance dominated the talks leading to adoption of the Bonn Agreement and took control of the ministry of defense and other key security services at the conclusion of those talks.[79] The Emergency Loya Jirga, most of whose 1600 members

---

[74] Human Rights Watch, *Afghanistan's Bonn Agreement One Year Later: A Catalog of Missed Opportunities*, December 5, 2002, *available at* http://www.hrw.org/backgrounder/asia/afghanistan/bonn1yr-bck.htm accessed through http://www.hrw.org/press/2002/12/afghan-1205.htm (last accessed January 28, 2006).

[75] *Available at* http://www.unama-afg.org/docs/_nonUN%20Docs/_Internation-Conferences& Forums/Bonn-Talks/bonn.htm (last accessed January 28, 2006).

[76] Id., para. 4. A loya jirga, or national assembly, has been used at various times in modern Afghan history to resolve political crises.

[77] Id., Preamble.

[78] Id., Annex I.

[79] McCool, *supra* note 6, at 8.

were elected under sometimes questionable conditions, constituted a more broadly representative body, but it "was a rowdy, disorganized, politically combative affair operating generally without regard to the rules of proce- dure that had been developed."[80] The Constitutional Loya Jirga was itself reasonably representative of Afghanistan's fractured society and managed to reach consensus on a new constitution, but it had little time to review and reach agreement on an extremely complex set of issues and opened the door to perhaps excessive executive branch input. Still, the results of the process can be deemed "within tolerance levels" for a country emerging from total collapse.[81]

Most of the steps outlined in the blueprint have now been completed. On December 15, 2001, the first troops of the UN-mandated International Security Assistance Force (ISAF) arrived in Kabul.[82] A week later, the Interim Administration, headed by Hamid Karzai, took office. In late January 2002, prospective donors meeting in Tokyo pledged $5 billion in reconstruction assistance over a six-year period.[83] For the next few months, the Special Inde- pendent Commission for the Convening of an Emergency Loya Jirga, with help from the United Nations Assistance Mission in Afghanistan (UNAMA), engaged in a broad-based consultative process leading to the election of can- didates for the Loya Jirga, which was held in June in Kabul. The Loya Jirga elected Karzai as president of the new Transitional Administration. At the same time, work proceeded on a draft constitution, which was adopted in December 2003, with elections for a permanent government set for June 2004. To date, the political reform timetable set out in the Bonn Agreement has largely held, although elections were conducted in October rather than June 2004.

Moreover, Afghanistan has not relapsed into large-scale civil war; more than two million refugees have returned; efforts to rebuild schools, clinics, and markets are underway; international aid has helped ameliorate a dire humanitarian situation; and the Karzai government has grown increasingly coherent.[84] Further, the currency is reasonably stable, the Afghan National Army is improving, and approximately 60,000 former combatants have demobilized.[85] But this apparent march toward a revived political life in Afghanistan masks deep structural problems. Afghanistan is still a country

---

[80] Id., at 10.

[81] Id., at 5.

[82] UNAMA/OCPI, *supra* note 73, at 3. In August 2003, NATO took over ISAF's role.

[83] Id.

[84] Ray Salvatore Jennings, United States Institute of Peace, *The Road Ahead: Lessons in Nation Building from Japan, Germany, and Afghanistan for Postwar Iraq*, April 2003, at 20, avail- able at http://ics.leeds.ac.uk/papers/pmt/exhibits/2165/pwks49.pdf (last accessed January 28, 2006).

[85] International Crisis Group, *Rebuilding the Afghan State: The European Union's Role*, November 30, 2005, at 4.

with minimal state institutions, an average life expectancy of forty-five, a population that is 70 percent illiterate, little domestic revenue or economic growth outside the drug economy, and a continuing insurgency.[86]

By all accounts, the core problem in Afghanistan is insecurity. ISAF, with some 4500 troops (later expanded to 9000), has been of only modest help. By way of comparison, "in Kosovo, Bosnia, and East Timor the international peacekeeping force amounted to one peacekeeper per seventy or so people," whereas "in Afghanistan that ratio was one peacekeeper per five thousand people."[87] Worse, U.S. and international timidity largely confined ISAF to Kabul, at least in the early post-conflict period. To promote stability in rural areas, the United States and other countries dispatched civil–military provincial reconstruction teams (PRTs) to various cities around the country. Although their impact has been positive in some cases, they have not as yet provided the Karzai government with a substantial lever by which to rein in and marginalize warlord activity, and their ultimate success will be measured by the extent to which they can hand their jobs off to provincial and district governments.

The efforts of the United States and its coalition partners to help the Afghan government extend its authority throughout the country have been complicated by the United States's continued pursuit of Taliban and al-Qaeda elements operating in the hinterlands. Although keeping the extremists at bay has given some provinces and districts more breathing space than they would otherwise have, it is also true that the United States has enlisted the support of some of the same warlords who defy central authority and intimidate the local populace. The United States and the Karzai government are attempting to marginalize these warlords gradually, and in a few cases (such as Herat province) they have succeeded. But armed illegal groups still operate with impunity in some areas.

The continued power of local warlords renders uncertain the long-term prospects for the Afghan transition. The central government's writ is still weak or directly challenged in many rural areas. Insecurity and lack of funding continue to undermine reconstruction efforts.[88] "And as infrastructure decays from lack of maintenance, so the status of local Afghan authorities who have unilaterally identified the community's needs is enhanced," even though the same individuals are "often part of the architecture of insecurity and oppression."[89] Farmers unable to obtain access to credit have

---

[86] Id.

[87] Sam Zia-Zarifi, Human Rights Watch Report, *Losing the Peace in Afghanistan*, at 6–7 (2004), *available at* http://hrw.org/wr2k4/download/5.pdf (last accessed January 28, 2006).

[88] "[I]n Kosovo the international community spent twenty-five times more money, on a per capita basis, than it has pledged in Afghanistan. . . . [W]hile Iraq received U.S. $26 billion in reconstruction aid in 2003, Afghanistan received less than $1 billion." Id., at 2.

[89] Jennings, *supra* note 84, at 24.

increasingly turned back to poppy cultivation, and the heroin trade "has blossomed again in Afghanistan, generating billions of dollars for forces outside the control of any legitimate authority," including local warlords "who use this money to increase their military capability and gain independence from the central government and any international troops working with them."[90] In this environment, many worry that the government and constitution created through the Bonn process will rule on paper only.

The new constitution, and the process that created it, are not without their strengths. The Constitutional Review Commission, a diverse body of experts, community leaders, religious leaders, and others, held nationwide consultations, soliciting the views of some 150,000 Afghans at over 500 public meetings. The draft was the subject of vigorous debate in the Constitutional Loya Jirga among a diverse group representing a broad spectrum of Afghan society. On its face, the constitution establishes a modern, democratic presidential system with a bicameral legislature. Although the constitution declares Islam to be the state religion, it also promises to respect religious freedom, free speech, and other internationally protected human rights. The constitution eschews the consociationalist approach to ethnic divisions but recognizes the equality of all ethnic groups and tribes and promises "balanced development in all areas of the country."[91] Women and men are to be treated equally.[92]

Underneath the surface, however, problems are apparent in both constitutional process and substance. Although the Constitutional Review Commission was mandated to consult widely with the public, and a serious public education and consultation process was conducted, the time allotted for consultations was insufficient in a country with little infrastructure and many isolated communities. Moreover, the draft constitution was prepared in relative secrecy and released late, and the members of the Constitutional Loya Jirga had only three weeks to consider it. Perhaps more importantly, President Karzai, a Pashtun, had a strong hand in determining the membership of the drafting committee, and the draft not surprisingly concentrated power in the president's hands.[93] Karzai and his allies (with support from the United States) argued that a strong presidency was essential to restore order in a country riven by factionalism. This approach favored Pashtuns as the largest ethnic group and revived fears among regional leaders and smaller

---

[90] Zia-Zarifi, *supra* note 87, at 9.

[91] Afghan Constitution, Ch. 1, Art. 6, *available at* http://www.unama-afg.org/docs/Docs.htm (last accessed January 28, 2006).

[92] Chapter 2, Article 1 of the constitution provides: "Any kind of discrimination and distinction between citizens of Afghanistan shall be forbidden. The citizens of Afghanistan, man and woman, have equal rights and duties before the law."

[93] *See* International Crisis Group, *Afghanistan: The Constitutional Loya Jirga*, December 12, 2003, at 1.

ethnic groups of renewed Pashtun domination. Ultimately, a compromise was reached, giving the legislature the power to approve key presidential appointments but otherwise retaining a powerful executive.

The draft constitution favored Pashtuns in other respects as well. Pashto and Dari, the languages of the largest ethnic groups, were listed as the two official languages, and apart from general language about proportional representation by region, the draft contained few provisions designed to ensure that ethnic group interests were accommodated. Indeed, the constitution as adopted forbids the formation of political parties on ethnic, linguistic, or regional bases.[94] Up to a point, this approach makes sense. Overt organization or distribution of political power on ethnic lines can aggravate rather than ameliorate ethnic divisions. At the same time, integrative provisions could have been included to ensure that minority group interests are taken into account in governance. The Constitutional Loya Jirga almost collapsed over the national language issue, until a last-minute compromise yielded a provision specifying that other minority group languages could be designated as national languages in regions in which the speakers of that language were in a majority. The exclusion of ethnicity as a basis for political organization appears to reflect the political self-interest of the Karzai government but will likely pose long-term problems in a country fragmented in part on ethnic lines.[95]

A related problem is the relation between the center and the provinces in Afghanistan. Many regional and ethnic group leaders favored a federal structure or at least substantial devolution of power. The constitution instead focuses on the central government and its powers, in significant part because the Karzai government was reluctant "to formalise a situation in which regional administrations . . . retain significant independence."[96] Although this approach has the advantage of lessening the prospects of regional and ethnic division, it also heightens the prospect of a too-powerful and perhaps ultimately authoritarian presidency.

The role of religion in governance proved another contentious issue during the Constitutional Loya Jirga. The inability to resolve differences between religious hardliners and reformers produced constitutional provisions that appear at odds with each other. The constitution mandates respect for international human rights, including religious freedom and equality for women. But it also precludes political parties with a program that "contravene[s] the Holy religion of Islam"[97] and provides that "no law shall contravene the tenets and provisions of the holy religion of Islam."[98] The latter provision

[94] Afghan Constitution, Ch. 2, Art. 14.
[95] See Afghanistan: The Constitutional Loya Jirga, supra note 93, at 5.
[96] Id.
[97] Afghan Constitution, Ch. 2, Art. 14.
[98] Id., Ch. 1, Art. 3.

in particular may open the door for Afghanistan's conservative judiciary to invalidate laws incompatible with a strict interpretation of Shari'a. In an apparently deliberate ambiguity, the constitution does not specify the outcome of a conflict between Islamic law and human rights.

If Afghanistan's past constitutional history is a guide, these possible flaws may pale in significance in the face of a larger problem. Afghanistan's numerous previous constitutions (seven since 1923) either concentrated near total power in the head of state or "were products of governments that never exercised significant control of the Afghan hinterland, and that between 1977 and 1992 were bogged down in fierce and unsuccessful counter-insurgency efforts."[99] The September 2005 parliamentary elections sent mixed signals concerning Afghanistan's future. The elections went relatively smoothly, and although voter turnout was lower than in the 2004 presidential elections, represented the culmination of the Bonn transitional process. But weak political parties combined with ethnic, sectarian, and other divides to produce a National Assembly with little coherence, no clear mandate, and little capacity to balance executive power.[100] Unless the Afghan transition can achieve greater momentum, the country may find itself with a paper democracy in which central government institutions are weak, fractious, and unable to exert much positive influence over large sections of the country.

The present level of international commitment seems inadequate to challenge fundamentally Afghanistan's centrifugal forces. Although the government has registered some successes, Afghanistan's warlords continue to be a major problem in some areas; the Taliban remains a threat; reconstruction efforts are moving at a glacial pace; the efforts to build a national army and police will take years to have a lasting impact; and meanwhile, the opium trade, with its corrupting influence, is booming. The blueprint adopted at Bonn, though reasonably sound, requires much stronger international support than has yet been provided. The Bush Administration and other international actors routinely proclaim that failure is not an option in Afghanistan. But absent the political will to provide greater security and reconstruction assistance over the long haul, success is by no means assured.

B. Iraq: Braking Constitutionalism

Iraq's history, geography, size, political makeup, and religious and ethnic divisions render it an enormously difficult challenge for a democratic rule of law makeover. Indeed, Iraq "has all the characteristics that have impeded

---

[99] International Crisis Group, *Afghanistan's Flawed Constitutional Process*, June 12, 2003, at 2.

[100] For a detailed look at the divisions in National Assembly following the voting, *see* Andrew Wilder, *A House Divided? Analyzing the 2005 Afghan Elections, available at* http://www.areu.org.af/publications/A%20House%20Divided.pdf.

democratic transitions elsewhere: a large, impoverished population deeply divided along ethnic and religious lines; no previous experience with democracy; and a track record of maintaining stability only under the grip of a strongly autocratic government."[101] Unlike Afghanistan, however, Iraq is at least a modern state, with a "population [that] is largely educated, sophisticated, and urban," a previously functioning government and bureaucracy, and "little history of inter-ethnic or communal violence."[102] Moreover, although Iraq is currently burdened with a large foreign debt and even larger reparations obligations stemming from Iraq's 1990 invasion of Kuwait, Iraq also possesses the world's second-largest oil reserves and, despite a crumbling infrastructure, at least the future possibility of economic strength. But even with these advantages, Iraq poses a more difficult challenge than any of the cases previously discussed.

The second Gulf War ended just weeks after it began on March 19, 2003. The political and security vacuum created by the rapid collapse of Iraq's government and military left the United States and the United Kingdom, as occupying powers, with enormous and interrelated challenges. They had to provide security, restore basic services, organize a transitional administration, and devise a strategy for the ultimate transfer of power back to Iraqis. Moreover, they had to do so in a deeply divided country, with competing groups espousing incompatible visions of the country's future. Minority Arab Sunnis, approximately 20 percent of the population but long dominant politically and economically, feared the loss of power and privilege democratic rule might bring. Iraqi Shiites, perhaps 55 percent of the population, welcomed the opportunity to assume a role in governance commensurate with their numbers but were divided themselves on what a future Iraq should look like and how closely it should be aligned with a theocratic Iran. Ethnic Kurds, perhaps another 20 percent of the population, were prepared to remain part of Iraq only if they could count on autonomy at least as complete as currently exercised in northern Iraq. Other fault lines, within and across each group (including tribal, family, and economic ties), and the varied pattern of geographic concentration and intermingling of these groups, rendered the task of forging a cohesive, democratic whole mind-numbingly complex.

Yet before the war, the United States had bold plans for the democratic transformation and economic reconstruction of Iraq. In the weeks leading up to the war, "[t]he plans presented ... exuded confidence that the United States had the capacity not only to replace Iraqi President Saddam Hussein's

---

[101] Marina Ottaway, From Victory to Success: *One Country, Two Plans*, 135 FOREIGN POLICY 55 (2003).

[102] Center for Strategic and International Studies, *A Wiser Peace: An Action Strategy for a Post-Conflict Iraq*, at 10 (January 2003).

regime but to alter the character of the state and the very social fabric of Iraq."[103] The U.S. forces and contractors would "vet the Iraqi civil service," "create and train a Baath-free military and police force," rapidly restore basic services, and rehabilitate Iraq's physical infrastructure.[104] The blueprint for political reconstruction was even more ambitious. The United States would appoint a transitional U.S.-led administration (first military, later civilian) to run the country, and it would quickly transform Iraq "from a centralized, hierarchical country into a model of participatory democracy."[105] A new constitution would be drafted, one in which the national government would "be limited to essential national functions, such as defense and security, monetary and fiscal matters, justice, foreign affairs, and strategic interests such as oil and gas."[106] The rest would be left to local government, which would be "required to operate in an open, transparent, and accountable manner."[107] The transfer of sovereignty to an elected government would occur only after a constitution had been drafted and ratified by referendum.[108]

Unfortunately, this plan for Iraq rested on a set of assumptions having no grounding in local conditions. The United States thought it could remove Saddam Hussein and the most senior Iraqi officials, but that most of the government bureaucracy would remain in place and continue to operate.[109] The United States also expected that organized resistance would end quickly. In fact, the Iraqi government evaporated almost overnight. Occupying forces encountered sustained opposition, and efforts to restore basic services and provide minimal security floundered. As a result, the United States soon began talking about "a short, light-handed occupation and the swift transfer of power to an Iraqi interim authority."[110]

Unlike many of the other cases considered, the conflict in Iraq did not end in a peace agreement or a compact among warring parties, leading naturally to the formation of an interim government. Nor was there a victorious internal faction prepared to assume power. The United States might have attempted to pull together a broad cross-section of Iraqi political leaders to form an interim government, along the lines of the All Liberia Conference that created Liberia's 1990 Interim Government of National Unity. But years of repression by the Baath party left little in the way of credible political leaders or civil society organizations to participate in such a conference.

---

[103] Ottaway, *supra* note 101, at 56.
[104] Id.
[105] Id.
[106] Id. (quoting a statement from USAID).
[107] Id. (quoting a statement from USAID).
[108] The term *sovereignty* is employed here in a political rather than a legal sense.
[109] Celeste Ward, USIP Report, *The Coalition Provisional Authority's Experience with Governance in Iraq Lessons Identified*, May 2005, at 2.
[110] Ottaway, *supra* note 101, at 56.

As a coalition of Iraqi opposition figures accurately predicted in a report prepared as part of a State Department planning project in November 2002:

As a result [of the oppressive rule of Saddam Hussein], there are no recognized domestic political institutions, groups or individuals that can step forward, invoke national legitimacy and assume power.... Many groups and individuals will eventually emerge and compete for power, but this will only happen gradually, as the environment becomes safe for public participation.[111]

The United States recognized that "premature elections risked empowering forces seen as most hostile to it – the Islamists and remnants of the old regime."[112] Appointing an interim government dominated by Iraqi exiles, as some in the Pentagon wished to do, would have been equally problematic, because the exiles lacked any genuine internal constituency.[113] Thus, the United States understandably wanted to allow time for moderate political forces to emerge before surrendering significant power to Iraqis. Accordingly, the United States decided to continue to exercise plenary executive and legislative powers, notwithstanding its rhetoric about a "light-handed occupation," until such time as a national constitution could be drafted and a new government elected, a process expected to last at least two years. With this in mind, and after a brief experiment with military administration, Washington established the Coalition Provisional Authority (CPA) with Paul Bremer as the lead civilian administrator and de facto proconsul.

The CPA's work was hampered from the start by inadequate security, communications and logistical problems, poor planning, lack of knowledge of Iraq and Iraqis, insufficient advance preparation, chaotic local conditions, and a substantial legitimacy deficit. Ill-conceived decrees (especially the abrupt dismantling of the Iraqi army and clumsy efforts at de-Baathification of the civil service) poorly communicated to the people of Iraq made matters worse. As local expectations of rapid progress went unmet, the United States came under growing pressure, from Iraqis, the UN, and the international community, to increase Iraqi responsibility for governance and to establish a legitimate interim Iraqi authority.

In July 2003, the CPA responded by creating the twenty-five-member Iraqi Interim Governing Council (IGC). In choosing council members, the CPA was driven by conflicting imperatives. On the one hand, the United States

---

[111] Democratic Principles Working Group, *Final Report on the Transition to Democracy in Iraq*, November 2002, at 16, *quoted in* Thomas R. Pickering, James R. Schlesinger, & Eric P. Schwartz, Report of an Independent Task Force Sponsored by the Council on Foreign Relations, *Iraq: The Day After*, April 16, 2003, at 28.

[112] International Crisis Group, *Governing Iraq*, August 25, 2003, at 10, *available at* http://www.crisisweb.org//library/documents/report_archive/A401098_25082003.pdf. Early elections in post-intervention Bosnia, which entrenched intransigent nationalists, offered a clear lesson in the dangers of early elections.

[113] Id.

wanted to "develop an interim authority that would have legitimacy in Iraq and abroad, appease the population and deflect criticism of the occupation forces."[114] On the other hand, the United States did not want to empower groups overtly hostile to U.S. political goals in Iraq.[115] In an effort to strike an appropriate balance, the CPA "consulted broadly not only with Iraqi political and social forces, but also with the UK and the once-suspect UN."[116] At the same time, "both the CPA and major Iraqi political groups" were given a tacit veto over the Governing Council's final membership. The result was "a broadly diverse body, including various strands of Iraqi society – Islamist and secular, modern and traditional, old notable families and tribes."[117] But it was also an unelected body that consisted principally of "political leaders with weak popular followings, very little in common between them, no bureaucratic apparatus and a clumsy nine-person rotating presidency."[118] Worse, in an understandable and in some respects laudable effort to reflect Iraq's diverse population, it was a body whose members were chosen in significant part on the basis of ethnic and religious affiliations, leading observers to warn that "[e]thnic and religious conflict, for the most part absent from Iraq's modern history, is likely to be exacerbated as its people increasingly organize along these divisive lines."[119] Not surprisingly, most Iraqis perceived the Governing Council as a tool of the United States, and insofar as Bremer retained final executive and legislative authority, they were not far wrong.

But as attacks on coalition forces mounted, some Bush Administration officials pushed for a quick transfer of power "to lessen the U.S. footprint and diminish popular resistance to the occupation."[120] They were joined by disgruntled Iraqis of "all shades," and by "governments that opposed the U.S. war in Iraq such as France and Germany...."[121] In October 2003, the Security Council, in Resolution 1511, urged the CPA "to return governing responsibilities and authorities to the people of Iraq as soon as practicable" and "invited" the Governing Council to produce a timetable and program for drafting a constitution and holding elections under it "no later than 15 December 2003." Yielding to the pressure, the CPA agreed with the Governing Council to a phased transition involving the adoption of interim governing principles, the selection of a constitutional convention, and eventual election of a government to assume power under a new constitution.

---

[114] Id., at ii.
[115] For an insightful discussion of U.S. legitimacy problems in Iraq, caused in part by U.S. efforts to maintain control of the political process there, *see* Larry Diamond, *What Went Wrong in Iraq?*, 83 FOREIGN AFFAIRS 34 (2004).
[116] *Governing Iraq*, *supra* note 112, at 12.
[117] Id.
[118] Id., at ii.
[119] Id.
[120] International Crisis Group, *Iraq's Constitutional Challenge*, November 13, 2003, at 7.
[121] Id., at 6.

But the CPA's plans, however well intentioned, did not dovetail with the aspirations of much of Iraq's population. A late June 2003 edict issued by Grand Ayatollah Ali Sistani, the most respected Iraqi Shiite cleric, urged Iraqis to press the coalition for early general elections. Direct elections would favor the majority Shiites and give them a decisive influence on the drafting of a constitution and the future governance of Iraq. Sistani's stance helped force the CPA to abandon its original strategy of holding elections after a constitution was put in place. Instead, the Iraqi Governing Council, with the CPA's acquiescence, invited Lakhdar Brahimi, the Special Advisor to the UN Secretary-General, to consult with Iraqi leaders on the feasibility of conducting early elections and on possible candidates for senior positions in a new Iraqi interim government. On March 8, 2004, after extensive negotiations, the Iraqi Governing Council adopted a Transitional Administrative Law (TAL) designed to set out the basics of a future constitution and lay the groundwork for the election of a new government by the end of January 2005. The new government, selected on the basis of Brahimi's recommendations, negotiations among the competing parties, and vigorous (some say heavy-handed) U.S. input, assumed power on June 28, 2005.

The TAL, and the organization of the interim government, represented compromises among the competing interests of Iraq's principal ethnic and sectarian groups. The central fault line involved the nature of federalism in Iraq and the extent of autonomy to be given to Iraqi Kurds. In theory, virtually all parties in Iraq rejected the idea that the state should be structured along ethnic or sectarian lines. They were aware of the difficulties that have frustrated similar efforts in places such as Lebanon, Cyprus, and Bosnia. In practice, however, Iraqi Kurds insisted that only near total autonomy could protect their interests. Although they were willing "to cede matters of foreign, monetary and national defense policy to the Iraqi national government," they were adamant about retaining most of their current autonomy and governing structure.[122] In response, the TAL insisted that government in Iraq shall be "republican, federal, democratic, and pluralistic" and that federalism "shall be based upon geographic and historical realities and the separation of powers, and not upon origin, race, ethnicity, nationality, or confession." At the same time, the TAL authorized any three governorates in Iraq to amalgamate as a political unit and to block adoption of a permanent constitution.

The TAL was problematic in various respects. In particular, it emphasized Iraq's ethnic and sectarian divisions. But it nonetheless offered a set of principles that might be adapted to a new constitution, which in turn might serve as a vehicle for resisting the centrifugal forces that threatened to tear Iraq apart. Many hoped that the process of drafting a constitution would

---

[122] Edward Wong, *Governing Council Parties Are Said to Back Broad Autonomy for Kurds*, THE NEW YORK TIMES, January 10, 2004, at A6.

help heal some of Iraq's divisions and pave the way for the emergence of a national consensus on the future of the state. Unfortunately, the process operated instead to exacerbate Iraq's divisions,[123] and the adoption of the constitution, whatever its merits viewed in the abstract, may yet come to be seen as a turning point on the road to dissolution and possibly civil war.

The problems with Iraq's constitutional process began when Sunni Arabs largely boycotted elections to the Transitional National Assembly (TNA) in January 2005. Although fifteen Sunni Arabs were added to the fifty-five existing members of the Constitutional Committee in July, they had little influence over the course of the subsequent negotiations and were often wholly excluded from key discussions between Kurds and Shiites. The Sunni negotiators charged that their Kurdish and Shiite counterparts refused to accommodate core Sunni interests on key issues, including federalism, Iraq's national identity, and de-Baathification; Shiite and Kurdish negotiators viewed the Sunnis as obstructionist. When the Committee failed to reach consensus by August 15, the TAL deadline for submitting a draft to the TNA, the drafters secured a one-week extension and then an additional three-day extension. When that proved insufficient, negotiations continued, without any clear legal basis.[124] The delays stemmed from belated efforts to devise last-minute compromises that would attract Sunni support, but when that failed, the draft was approved by the TNA over the strong objections of the Sunni negotiators. The TNA could have taken an additional six months under the TAL, but the United States and some interim government officials insisted on adherence to the original timetable.

As the October 15 referendum drew near, and concerns over Sunni opposition grew, the TNA approved modest amendments to the constitutional draft that would, among other things, permit changes to the constitution to be adopted by the parliament even after the referendum. But the changes were too little, too late for most Sunnis, who voted against adoption of the constitution in large numbers. For Sunnis, the constitution represented a bargain between Shiites and Kurds; the marginalization of Sunnis during the drafting process confirmed their fears that even the most basic Sunni interests would not be protected in the new order. As a result, the constitution-formation process, far from healing rifts among Iraqis, exacerbated ethnic and sectarian divisions.

The process problems were matched by problems in constitutional substance. Although Kurds have long been persecuted in Iraq, and Shiites denied political power proportionate to their numbers, ethnic and sectarian divides

---

[123] *See, e.g.,* Jonathan Morrow, *Iraq's Constitutional Process II: An Opportunity Lost*, November 2005, *available at* http://www.usip.org/pubs/specialreports/sr155.pdf (last accessed January 28, 2006).

[124] International Crisis Group, *Unmaking Iraq: A Constitutional Process Gone Awry*, September 26, 2005, at 2.

have not in the past dominated Iraqi politics to the extent that would render a Bosnian-style solution inevitable. Nonetheless, the constitution, though formally eschewing ethnic federalism, permits both Kurdish and Shiite governorates to amalgamate into autonomous regions, with control over most aspects of daily life within them. Sunnis feared that allowing the three Kurdish provinces to form a region in the oil-rich north and the nine or so Shiite provinces to form a region in the oil-rich south would pave the way for the partition of Iraq, with Sunnis left in charge of a resource-poor center. Even if Iraq does not break apart, Sunnis fear that ambiguous language relating to the disposition of Iraq's oil resources might be interpreted by a Shiite-dominated government in ways that would leave Sunnis with little. Sunnis also objected to provisions on national identity and de-Baathification, among others, fearing they were further steps to marginalize the Sunnis.

In both process and substance, Iraq's new constitution reflects a "growing ethno-sectarianism in which Iraqis identify strictly with their own preferred, self-defined community and interpret events exclusively through an ethno-sectarian lens."[125] This trend is extraordinarily dangerous. Geography in Iraq does not lend itself to ethnic federalism as easily as might be supposed. Although northern Iraq is primarily Kurdish, whereas central Iraq is predominantly Sunni and southern Iraq largely Shiite, the reality is that all three groups live interspersed to a significant degree throughout Iraq. Views concerning the borders of these regions are heavily colored by economic and strategic interests, especially the location of contested oil fields. As a result, any effort to divide Iraq along ethnic lines is likely to deteriorate quickly.

Discussions between Kurds, Sunnis, and Shiites on the possibility of a coalition government in early 2006 hold out at least the possibility of compromise and cooperation among Iraq's contending communities. But in the absence of any fundamental consensus on the future of the state or the legitimacy of its new constitution, it remains an open question whether Iraq will slide into full-scale civil war.

CONCLUSION

What should be evident from this chapter's review of post-conflict blueprints is that no general template exists and that every approach carries substantial risks. At the same time, the nature and extent of the risks vary with the type of conflict and the extent to which interveners are prepared to insist on a workable blueprint. Identity-based conflicts present greater political engineering challenges than resource-driven conflicts, but blueprints for both

[125] Id., at 11.

will fail if interveners place higher priority on satisfaction of short-term conflict termination interests over long-term political settlement interests.

- The process of designing a blueprint may be as important as the substance of the blueprint. A poorly managed process will exacerbate rather than mitigate the internal divisions that produce conflict in the first place. The problem is particularly acute when it comes to designing post-conflict constitutions.
- Post-conflict blueprints are not the product of a single, coherent design. Instead, they emerge through a process of bargaining among actors with widely varying goals, sharply differing degrees of commitment, and limited information. The substantive viability of a blueprint will therefore vary depending on the difficulty of the case, the degree to which interveners are prepared to insist on a workable design, and the willingness of the principal local actors to cooperate. Too often, the temptation is to pursue a quick end to the fighting through unstable accommodations of powerful local actors.
- When a state is divided against itself, and its population lacks a shared commitment to a single national identity, blueprint options are limited and unattractive. Unless one party to the conflict wins outright (as in Rwanda), or can be separated from other parties through autonomy (as in Kosovo) or independence (as in East Timor), interveners must find ways to promote power-sharing among the contending groups. This presents an almost irresolvable dilemma: consociationalist blueprint provisions sufficient to insulate minorities from the threat of majoritarian power perpetuate the differences that precipitated conflict in the first place and render government at the center cumbersome or unworkable. But more limited minority rights measures more conducive to effective governance are likely to be rejected as insufficient by minority groups whose cooperation is essential to the construction of a viable, rule of law oriented state.
- Blueprints for resource-driven conflicts and other instances of state failure that do not center on state identity are easier to create and implement. But the temptation in such cases is to rush to an early electoral exit, before combatants are disarmed and viable state institutions and normative commitments to democracy and the rule of law are in place. Elections by themselves are not a blueprint for success.

The better that interveners understand the risks of different blueprint options, the easier it will be to avoid the pitfalls associated with each, and the easier it may be for interveners to resist seemingly attractive short-term options with disastrous long-term consequences.

Post-conflict blueprints provide the foundation, for better or worse, for subsequent efforts to build and strengthen the rule of law. Without such a foundation, interveners and local reformers will lack a framework for transitioning to effective governance, for building justice systems, for providing security for the population, and for working to strengthen and reinforce cultural commitments to the rule of law. Subsequent chapters examine in detail a number of specific aspects and challenges of blueprint implementation. The next chapter, in particular, will examine the enormous challenge of establishing security as the essential precondition – the sine qua non – for building the rule of law after conflict.

CHAPTER FIVE

Security as Sine Qua Non

As George Tanham, an international security and counterinsurgency expert, wrote of Vietnam, "[s]trange as it may seem, the military victory is the easiest part of the struggle. After this has been attained, the real challenge begins: the reestablishment of a secure environment opens a new opportunity for nation building."[1] Tanham's observation could just as easily be applied to the cases studied in this book. The terminology has evolved – the United States, in particular, now prefers "stability operations" to "nation building." But Tanham's point still holds. Military intervention marks only the first, and usually the simplest, phase of the much larger and more complex task of restructuring the governing institutions of the affected state and encouraging the ascendance of actors and social norms capable of making those institutions successful.

As Tanham suggests, the reestablishment of a secure environment is "the sine qua non of post-conflict reconstruction."[2] Absent basic security, efforts to reform political institutions, adopt new laws, promote national reconciliation, and jump-start economic growth are destined to fail. In most cases, however, military victory does not, as Tanham seemed to assume, correlate directly with the establishment of the secure environment that in turn "opens a new opportunity for nation building." In fact, most of the cases studied in this book do not entail a clear military victory. In many cases, interveners used force selectively against one or more parties to the conflict, but their primary goal was to compel a negotiated settlement rather than to achieve an outright military victory. Even when interveners did seek and secure a clear

---

[1] George K. Tanham, War without Guns: American Civilians in Rural Vietnam (1966), at 138, *quoted in* Erwin Schmidl, *Police Functions in Peace Operations: An Historical Overview,* in Policing the New World Disorder: Peace Operations and Public Security (Robert Oakley, Michael Dziedzic, & Eliot Goldberg eds., 1998), at 19, 35.

[2] Center for Strategic and International Studies and the Association of the U.S. Army, *Play to Win: Final Report of the bi-partisan Commission on Post-Conflict Reconstruction,* January, 2003.

military victory, as in Afghanistan and Iraq, "winning" marked only a shift from major combat operations against fielded forces to counterinsurgency campaigns and low-intensity conflict against hit-and-run enemies.

In almost all cases, then, post-intervention security efforts take place in a demanding and often hostile environment. Internal warring factions typically retain considerable power and weaponry and pose a danger to the larger blueprint implementation process even when not engaged in open conflict with interveners and their local allies. Moreover, in the immediate post-intervention period, internal security forces, to the extent they remain intact, are more likely to be part of the problem than part of the solution. In most of the cases studied, the pre-intervention security and police forces of the state operated primarily to impose or support the ruling elite's hold on power (or, in the case of Afghanistan, its draconian social vision); far from following the idealized serve-and-protect mandate familiar to viewers of U.S. television police dramas, these security forces terrorized regime opponents, persecuted minorities, and instilled lasting distrust of state authority in the general population. Such forces can scarcely be relied on to maintain order in a manner consistent with respect for the rule of law. In a few cases, as in Somalia, local police may retain considerable popular support. But even then, the police cannot maintain order in a vacuum; their efforts must be supported by well-functioning courts and prisons and by a government minimally capable of providing its population with basic services.

In general, for post-conflict security efforts to succeed, four conditions must be met. First, security cannot depend solely or even primarily on coercion. Force or the threat of force is often essential to the maintenance of order, particularly in the first days of an intervention. But in the long term, public order, at least outside of a police state, rests on a societal consensus about the legitimacy of state institutions and confidence in the capacity of such institutions to deliver basic services. Accordingly, long-term progress on security depends on and must be matched by progress in political and economic reconstruction. Even a government that protects its people from attack cannot function effectively, at least not from a rule of law standpoint, if the same people are starving, freezing, or dying of easily preventable disease. To achieve lasting security, interveners and their local allies must therefore do more than restore order and protect civilians from crime. They must also provide minimally acceptable levels of basic public goods, including functioning infrastructure (such as power, water, sewage treatment, health care, telecommunications, and the like) and basic humanitarian assistance (such as food and medicine) until the local governing institutions and economy can be restored sufficiently to provide those goods on their own. Otherwise, spoilers will flourish, public support for the interveners and their reforms will dwindle, local elites cooperating with the interveners will be discredited, and demobilized fighters will likely return to their former livelihood.

Second, security requires from interveners a mix of capabilities significantly different from the war-fighting mix required for an initially successful military intervention. Winning wars and maintaining order are two very different tasks. The mix of forces needed for the latter will vary widely from one country to another, depending on the status and capabilities of local security forces and the nature and extent of post-intervention political violence and criminal activity. In some cases, the appropriate force mix will vary widely in different locations and at different times within the same country, as the intensity of opposition to the establishment of a new political order waxes and wanes. In general, however, the demand for security is particularly acute in the immediate post-intervention period, when local belligerents retain their combat capabilities and indigenous security institutions are in disarray; at that point, only the military can provide order. As the situation stabilizes, different skills are required, and interveners must deploy some mix of international civilian police and indigenous police.

Third, efforts to promote security must be part of and subordinate to the larger peace process. When spoilers threaten to derail the peace process through violence, interveners cannot remain neutral. Instead, early and vigorous opposition to spoilers may prove essential to building a lasting peace. At the same time, decisions on whether and when to combat spoilers remain political decisions, to be taken by those managing the overall peace process. Premature attempts to disarm a warring faction, for example, may undermine or derail diplomatic efforts designed to engage key local actors in support of an evolving peace process.[3] In short, security is part of but not a substitute for efforts to implement the overall blueprint for post-conflict reconstruction.

Fourth, interveners must work with local actors from the beginning to rebuild indigenous security institutions. Even the most determined interveners typically seek to leave as quickly as local conditions permit, and only the establishment of an effective indigenous security capability offers interveners a legitimate exit option. Moreover, although interveners can impose order temporarily, interveners lack the knowledge of local laws, customs, and culture required for effective policing over the long term. Ideally, local actors will participate fully in all decision-making pertaining to security from the outset and assume at every stage of the post-conflict period as much of the security responsibilities for their state as circumstances permit. Involving local actors can help interveners adapt security practices to conform to local norms and simultaneously build capacity for the eventual full transfer of security responsibilities to local forces. Moreover, fostering local ownership of security measures will contribute to the social consensus that underpins

---

[3] *See* Michael Dziedzic & Benjamin Lovelock, *An Evolving "Post-Conflict" Role for the Military: Providing a Secure Environment and Supporting the Rule of Law*, in POST-CONFLICT JUSTICE (M. Cherif Bassiouni, ed., 2002), at 851, 851.

order in democratic societies. At the same time, great care must be taken to avoid empowering political elites whose interests are not consistent with long-term rule of law objectives.

Meeting the challenge of providing security is a complex, costly, and time-consuming task. In pursuing security, the synergistic approach outlined in Chapter 3 should be kept in mind. Too often, interveners focus on numeric outputs – numbers of police deployed, judges trained, and spoilers killed or incarcerated – without articulating adequately the overall strategic objectives sought and ensuring that resources are deployed in a coherent and mutually reinforcing way. Similarly, the immediate demands of a hostile post-intervention environment often distract interveners from focusing adequately on how to adapt western models of policing and law enforcement to local conditions and norms, even though security institutions that lack popular legitimacy are unlikely to endure. Finally, interveners often fail to approach security issues systemically, focusing instead on individual components. But rapid progress in one area, such as police reform, will soon be undercut if judges are corrupt, incompetent, or intimidated or if prison facilities cannot keep pace with arrests. Just as security must move forward in tandem with political and economic reform to ensure public order, so too must the individual components of an effective security system move forward in a mutually supportive fashion.

Notwithstanding the difficulty of achieving basic security in a post-conflict environment, substantial progress in restoring public order and rebuilding basic rule of law institutions has been achieved in several post-conflict societies, including Kosovo, East Timor, Bosnia, and Sierra Leone. Although the establishment of a secure environment does not guarantee success, the inability to establish a secure environment does guarantee failure.

I. UNDERSTANDING SECURITY BROADLY

The provision of order is the first task of any government. No government, least of all one committed to the rule of law, can function effectively if its people cannot go about their daily life without fear of being shot, tortured, raped, robbed, or bombed. Unfortunately, post-intervention conditions render the task of ensuring physical security extremely difficult. The task is doubly difficult in states such as Iraq and Afghanistan, where armed conflict continues even after interveners secure their initial military victory.

A. Causes and Consequences of Government Collapse
In all of the cases considered in this book, with the possible exception of Iraq, intervention took place in "failed states" or "quasi-states,"[4] that is, states

---

[4] For a discussion of "quasi-states," *see* Robert H. Jackson, QUASI-STATES: SOVEREIGNTY, INTERNATIONAL RELATIONS AND THE THIRD WORLD (1993).

that lacked not only effective governments but also the underlying social and political cohesion that makes effective governance possible without undue reliance on coercion. States in the industrialized west have "set the standard for effective statehood . . . by their demonstrated success in simultaneously meeting the basic needs of the large majority of their populations, protecting their human rights, and promoting and guaranteeing political participation."[5] But these are states that "have, by and large, successfully completed their state-building process, are politically satiated and economically affluent, and possess unconditional legitimacy in the eyes of the overwhelming majority of their populations."[6]

By contrast, many states in which military intervention typically occurs have not completed the state-building process; their governments cannot meet the basic needs of most of their population and do not possess broad and unquestioned legitimacy. These are states with ineffective governments that have not consolidated their authority over much of the territory of their state, have not succeeded in maintaining order within the territory they do control, and have not managed to use state resources to support security and policing activities that serve the public interest or "to carry on routine administration, deepen the state's penetration of society, and serve symbolic purposes (taxation)."[7] Most importantly, these are states that lack the core identifying characteristic of an effective state: a government with a monopoly over coercive power. Many lack a sense of common citizenship or a political culture that dictates peaceful resolution of disputes.[8] In these states, civil society is weak and disorganized, security forces serve regime rather than state interests, legal codes are outdated and inadequate, and courts are corrupt, politicized, and ineffective.[9] It is not just that law and political institutions in these states are ineffective; it is that the faith in law and political institutions that underpins policing and order in effective states does not exist.

---

[5] Mohammed Ayoob, *State Making, State Breaking, and State Failure*, in TURBULENT PEACE (Chester Crocker, Fen Hampson, & Pamela Aall, eds., 2001), at 127, 133.

[6] Id.

[7] Id., at 128. Ayoob points out that European states took centuries to form, and argues that developing countries have lacked both the time and the free coercive hand necessary to induce or compel "disparate populations under their nominal rule to accept the legitimacy of state boundaries and institutions" and to tax and otherwise regulate their lives. Id., at 130.

[8] *See* J. 'Kayode Fayemi, *Governing Insecurity in Post-Conflict States: the Case of Sierra Leone and Liberia*, in REFORM AND RECONSTRUCTION OF THE SECURITY SECTOR (Alan Bryden & Heinder Hänggi, eds., 2004), at 179, 182–183.

[9] *See, e.g.*, James Dobbins et al., Rand, *America's Role in Nation-Building: From Germany to Iraq*, September, 2003, at xxviii, *available at* http://www.rand.org/pubs/monograph_reports/MR1753/MR1753.pref.pdf (noting that after the "rapid and utter collapse of central state authority" in Somalia, Haiti, Kosovo, and Afghanistan, the "local police, courts, penal services, and militaries were destroyed, disrupted, disbanded, or discredited and consequently unable to fill the post-conflict security gap").

When state institutions are this weak, opportunistic elements in society are quick to take advantage. Warlords and political entrepreneurs flourish and often finance their private militias through criminal activity, including trafficking in arms and drugs. Simple banditry, "fueled by military desertion, the breakdown of social structures, and demobilization" of government forces, "is endemic."[10] Ordinary crime also escalates sharply because of a "combination of economic necessity, social breakdown, the focus of police forces on political and regime security, and the proliferation of weapons."[11] In some states, a "war economy" takes hold, in which political elites and conflict entrepreneurs support continuing violence and political instability for personal gain.

States that lack the political and social cohesion that stem from a fully realized state-building process are perpetually vulnerable to government collapse, easily triggered by any shock to the system. Somalia is perhaps the most obvious example. Somalia never possessed an effective government, and when the end of the Cold War eliminated U.S. and Soviet incentives to prop up any particular regime, anarchy quickly followed. But Somalia was far from unique. Samuel Doe's government in Liberia disintegrated in the face of a few hundred fighters; Sierra Leone's government disappeared when its military joined forces with the rebels; and Afghanistan's government collapsed in the face of the student-inspired Taliban. Even in states with apparently effective governments, as in former Yugoslavia and Iraq, authoritarian rule only masked the weakness of state institutions and an underlying lack of social cohesion.

The collapse of Somalia's government in the early 1990s, and the prospect that much of Somalia's population might starve in the ensuing conflict, precipitated a western military intervention with an unrealistically narrow aim: to establish a secure environment for the distribution of food. The interveners quickly discovered that security and the provision of food could not be achieved on a sustainable basis in the absence of viable governing institutions, and the mission soon morphed into a more ambitious nation-building effort. But the interveners failed to appreciate the magnitude of the task they faced. Somalia's descent into an anarchic maelstrom of warring clans reflected the weakness of the state itself, which never commanded a monopoly on coercive power or a coherent social order legitimate in the eyes of the varied populations inhabiting the state. In this context, superficial efforts to impose order and hold elections held no chance of success, and it was not long before a chastened United States fled Somalia, with the United Nations not far behind.

---

[10] Id., at 178 (Dobbins et al. make the point in the context of a discussion of Iraq, but the point holds true in other cases as well.).

[11] Id.

What is true of Somalia holds true, albeit to a lesser degree, of the other cases under consideration. Restoring sustainable order in the aftermath of intervention in a failed or failing state requires not just the establishment of the security institutions of an effective state; it requires building the state itself. The post–World War II reconstruction efforts in Germany and Japan, the only two unambiguously successful instances of large-scale post-war reconstruction, had the advantage of taking place in effective states in which underlying questions about statehood had already long since been addressed. Although order can be established in contemporary failed or failing states, it is likely to be transitory unless underlying deficiencies in state structures are also addressed. Thus, in Haiti, for example, the 1994 U.S.-led restoration of Jean Bertrand Aristide to office following his ouster by the military in 1991, and the follow-on UN peacekeeping and peacebuilding efforts, succeeded only temporarily in restoring order. The new and vetted police put back on the streets gradually melted away or ceased to matter, because there was no real change in the underlying political culture and little in the way of effective or politically legitimate state institutions. As a result, in February 2004, Aristide was once again forced to flee the country by rebel forces with poor human rights records and in the face of general popular discontent.

Attempting to build a viable political and legal order in a state that has never completed an effective state-building process is a daunting challenge. In the west, particularly in Europe, the process of building effective states lasted many years and, in most cases, centuries. Yet, as Charles Call points out, "in today's postconflict societies, international actors are attempting to take shortcuts through those historical processes, creating public police forces and revamped judicial systems in a few months, while external resources are supplanting internal tax revenues and globalized communications are transmitting new ideas and expectations."[12] It does not follow that interveners in such states face a hopeless task. Order can be restored. And the restoration of order can pave the way for a successful political reconstruction effort. But the process is long, arduous, and expensive.

B. Seeing Security in Context

Because sustainable security requires at least minimally functioning state institutions, security efforts are meaningful only if undertaken as part of a larger post-conflict reconstruction and rule of law project. That larger post-conflict project is now often conceived of as involving four distinct but interdependent and related tasks, commonly referred to as the four "pillars":

---

[12] Charles T. Call, *Introduction: What We Know and Don't Know about Post-Conflict Justice and Security Reform*, in CONSTRUCTING JUSTICE AND SECURITY AFTER WAR (Charles T. Call, ed., 2006), at 9–10.

security, justice and reconciliation, social and economic well-being, and governance and participation. In this framework, security is defined to include "all aspects of public safety, in particular, creating a safe and secure environment and developing legitimate and effective security institutions."[13] Security includes not just the protection of civilians from violence, but also the protection of the territorial integrity of the state.[14] Although security forms the foundation on which all other reconstruction tasks must build, efforts at establishing security in turn depend critically on progress with the other pillars.

The justice and reconciliation pillar "addresses the need to deal with past abuses through formal and informal mechanisms for resolving grievances arising from conflict and to create an impartial and accountable legal system for the future...."[15] Although Chapter 7 of this book examines the challenges of transitional justice, it is worth noting here that there is an intimate but not necessarily straightforward connection between accountability and security. Accountability mechanisms may help marginalize or deter politicians and other actors opposed to the post-conflict blueprint, mitigate pressure for violent redress of past grievances, and foster reconciliation in some cases, but in other circumstances, the pursuit of accountability may also provoke violent backlash and jeopardize fragile political bargains and nascent government institutions.

The government and participation pillar "addresses the need to create legitimate, effective political and administrative institutions and participatory processes, in particular, establishing a representative constitutional structure, strengthening public-sector management and administration, and ensuring the active and open participation of civil society in the formulation of the country's government and its policies."[16] Inevitably, military intervention takes place in support of political goals. Often, those goals include support of a negotiated peace settlement or support for an agreed set of political processes to form a new government. Although "[n]o peace force can compel reconciliation if the power brokers involved are unalterably opposed,"[17] most cases involve relatively fluid situations in which security and progress on governance are directly linked. If basic security is not ensured, the parties to the conflict face an internal security dilemma: any steps they take toward peace, for example, by disarming, may leave them vulnerable to their opponents. More generally, absent effective security measures, parties

---

[13] John Hamre & Gordon Sullivan, *Toward Post-Conflict Reconstruction*, 25 WASH. Q. 85, 91 (2002), *available at* http://www.twq.com/02autumn/hamre.pdf.

[14] Id.

[15] Id.

[16] Id., at 92.

[17] Robert B. Oakley & Michael J. Dziedzic, *Conclusions*, in POLICING THE NEW WORLD DISORDER, *supra* note 1, at 509, 535.

not committed to the larger peace or reconstruction process can easily sabotage any progress on political and economic reconstruction through violence;
in countries emerging from civil war, spoilers will be free to restart the war if
their demands are not met. Conversely, a lack of progress on achieving political institutions broadly acceptable to the most powerful actors in society may
induce those actors to seek power through potentially violent means.

The fourth pillar, social and economic well-being, also correlates closely
with security. Social and economic well-being "addresses fundamental social
and economic needs, in particular, providing emergency relief, restoring
essential services to the population in areas such as health and education,
laying the foundation for a viable economy, and initiating an inclusive and
sustainable development program."[18] At the outset, it entails "protecting
the population from starvation, disease, and the elements"; later, it involves
"long-term social and economic development."[19] Absent progress in this
area, combatants and criminal elements have little reason to forego political
violence.

Thus, in addition to deploying military and police forces to maintain
public order, interveners must simultaneously work with local authorities
to deploy the civilian specialists who can restore electricity, rebuild damaged or destroyed basic infrastructure, and jump-start the country's economy. In Iraq, General Franks, the commander of coalition ground forces,
and Paul Bremer, head of the Coalition Provisional Authority, argued back
and forth over which took precedence – security or reconstruction. Bremer
complained that reconstruction could not proceed effectively without better
security; Franks argued that delays in reconstruction undermined efforts to
restore security.[20] Both tasks are clearly interrelated and to some extent must
proceed simultaneously.

Overall, though, progress on all four pillars begins with basic security. In
the short term, interveners must control looting, separate antagonists, limit
public violence, and generally maintain a minimally secure environment,
pending the reestablishment of indigenous police and security forces. Unless
and until this happens, everything else gets put on hold. New political parties
cannot take hold, civil society cannot function, and economic activity cannot
flourish. As Scott Feil notes,

A return to any sense of normalcy depends on the provision of security. Refugees
and internally displaced persons will wait until they feel safe to go home; former
combatants will wait until they feel safe to lay down their arms and reintegrate into
civilian life or a legitimate, restructured military organization; farmers and merchants

[18] Hamre & Sullivan, *supra* note 13, at 91.
[19] Id.
[20] Michael R. Gordon, *The Strategy to Secure Iraq Did Not Foresee a 2nd War*, THE NEW YORK
TIMES, October 19, 2004, at A1.

will wait until they feel that fields, roads, and markets are safe before engaging in food production and business activity; and parents will wait until they feel safe to send their children to school, tend to their families, and seek economic opportunities.[21]

For the same reasons, an insecure environment "is extremely hostile to long-term development initiatives."[22] Just as individuals "will think twice about investing scarce capital into something that is likely to be taken away the next day by armed bandits," so too will foreign investors shy away from putting capital into an economy vulnerable to an imminent renewal of hostilities.[23] In a vicious circle, insecurity undermines ordinary political and business activity in a way that breeds further insecurity.[24]

II. SECURITY IN THE SHORT TERM

Security tasks vary from one post-conflict environment to another, depending on the outcome of the conflict, the status and interests of the belligerents, the size and geography of the state, the extent to which state institutions and security forces have disintegrated, local political and economic conditions, the involvement of neighboring states, and the capacity, commitment, and goals of the interveners. Moreover, security tasks will vary by time and place. In some states, events may follow a more or less linear trajectory, moving from combat operations against belligerents to peacekeeping operations intended to separate warring parties to more traditional police operations as the post-conflict situation stabilizes. In other cases, traditional policing in some areas of the state may coincide with active combat operations in others. In many cases, the demand for security may transform from protection against overt political violence to protection from organized economic crime. In general, however, security tasks usually entail the following roles: separation, control, and eventual demobilization of belligerents; protection of the civilian population; protection of political leaders, especially local partners in an ongoing peace process; protection of mission participants and the security forces themselves; protection of local infrastructure and institutions; and control of crime and localized violence.[25]

[21] Scott Feil, *Building Better Foundations: Security in Post-conflict Reconstruction*, 25 WASH. Q. 100 (2002).

[22] Espen Barthe Eide & Thorstein Bratteland, *Norwegian Experiences with U.N. Civilian Police Operations*, in POLICING THE NEW WORLD DISORDER, *supra* note 1, at 437, 438.

[23] Id., at 438–439.

[24] Id., at 439.

[25] *See, e.g.*, Feil, *supra* note 21, at 98–99. Security Council Resolution 1244, which established an international security force for Kosovo, identified the relevant security tasks to include: "Deterring renewed hostilities, maintaining and where necessary enforcing a ceasefire, and ensuring the withdrawal and preventing the return into Kosovo of Federal and Republic military, police and paramilitary forces"; "[d]emilitarizing the Kosovo Liberation Army (KLA)

At the outset of the post-intervention period, the dominant task is usually to control belligerents and maintain basic order. Rapid progress on this front is vital, because security efforts at the outset set the tone for the entire post-conflict reconstruction effort. Failure to establish a modicum of order quickly undermines public confidence and invites the entrenchment of forces opposed to the larger peace process or intent on taking personal advantage of the political and security vacuum created by the collapse of the governing regime.[26] In most cases under study, the initial effort to restore order has been principally a military task for two reasons. First, the restoration of order often requires combat capabilities that only the military can provide. Military forces "are heavily armed, train and deploy as a unit" and "operate under rules of engagement" suitable to the control of local belligerents.[27] Second, the military is already in place when post-conflict operations begin and, to the extent specialized military forces not present are needed, they can be deployed quickly. Recruiting and deploying international civilian police, and vetting and restoring indigenous military and police forces, takes much longer, creating a "deployment gap" that usually only the military can fill.[28]

At the same time, the military is generally not well prepared for the demands of a major post-conflict security role. Military forces are trained and equipped principally to fight and win wars. Maintaining the peace in the aftermath of war requires a different mix of forces, different doctrine, different training, and different equipment than fighting the war itself. The U.S. military in particular has been slow to adjust to the different demands of the post-conflict security role, in large part because of the reluctance of military leaders to let the military get drawn too deeply into nation-building activities. Although considerable progress has been made in recent years, much remains to be done, including greater attention to constabulary forces and improved training for the post-conflict environment.

---

and other armed Kosovo-Albanian groups"; "[e]stablishing a secure environment in which refugees and displaced persons can return home in safety, the international civil presence can operate, a transitional administration can be established, and humanitarian aid can be delivered"; "[e]nsuring public safety and order"; "[s]upervising demining"; "[s]upporting, as appropriate, and coordinating closely with the work of the international civil presence"; "[c]onducting border monitoring duties as required"; "[e]nsuring the protection and freedom of movement of itself, the international civil presence, and other international organizations." S.C. Res. 1244, para. 9, U.N. Doc. S/RES/1244, June 10, 1999.

[26] U.S. Institute of Peace, *Establishing the Rule of Law in Iraq*, Special Report No. 104, April 2003, at 3 (noting that without immediate progress on security, "international engagement will be jeopardized by a loss of credibility and an entrenchment of organized crime, extrajudicial processes, and terrorist activities") (hereinafter *USIP Report*).

[27] U.S. Army Peacekeeping & Stability Operations Institute, *Partnership for Effective Peace Operations Briefing Note*, January 2004 (hereinafter *Briefing Note*).

[28] *See, e.g.*, Alton L. Gwaltney III & Cody M. Weston, *Soldiers as Cops, Judges, and Jailers: Law Enforcement by the U.S. Military in Peace Operations*, in Bassiouni, *supra* note 3, at 863, 875.

A. The Post-Intervention Window of Opportunity

Timing in peace operations is a "crucial determinant of success or failure."[29] When fighting ends, or at least moderates to the point that security becomes a priority, a critical window of opportunity opens. Interveners have a chance to demonstrate that a new sheriff is in town and that it is no longer "business as usual." Belligerents and other spoilers may be intimidated by the arrival of professional military forces. Depending on the stage at which intervention takes place, belligerents may be weakened from the fighting, demoralized, and prepared to accept disarmament and demobilization. The general population, exhausted by years of warfare, crime, and disorder, will often be prepared and even eager to cooperate with international forces promising order and a gradual restoration of normalcy. As Robert Oakley and Michael Dziedzic observe, "[t]his phase of the intervention should not be squandered, because military presence in significant numbers and the initial positive impact on public opinion are of limited duration. The longer an external military force remains deployed on the ground, the more it is apt to be perceived as an occupation army."[30] Indeed, the window of opportunity may last only a few weeks.[31]

In Iraq, the United States and its coalition partners learned the hard way the importance of securing order quickly:

In April 2003 U.S. soldiers stood by and watched as looters rampaged through the streets of Baghdad, and throughout Iraq, demolishing government offices and destroying valuable records.... Looters also damaged hospitals, schools, and basic infrastructure. As a result, post-war electricity supply in much of Iraq was worse than before the war. Food and water distribution was heavily disrupted; hospitals were unable to provide basic services; and children were unable to return to school.[32]

Not surprisingly, the looting rendered subsequent reconstruction efforts much more difficult than they might otherwise have been. Efforts to restore basic infrastructure, already in shambles from years of war, sanctions, and neglect, have taken considerably longer than they might have because everything from generators to copper wire had been systematically stripped and carted away. Moreover, the looting and postwar chaos had a cascading effect. Loss of electrical power, for example, shut down water treatment facilities, thus exacerbating an already existing public health crisis. According

---

[29] *Play to Win, supra* note 2, at 9.
[30] Oakley & Dziedzic, *supra* note 17, at 529–530.
[31] Seth Jones, Jeremy Wilson, Andrew Rathmell, & K. Jack Riley, Establishing Law and Order After Conflict (2005), at xii (noting that the "golden hour" may last "several weeks to several months").
[32] *Briefing Note, supra* note 27.

to one U.S. official, looting and sabotage doubled the cost of postwar reconstruction.[33]

The rampant postwar disorder also sharply undermined public attitudes toward coalition forces and their claim to be liberators rather than occupiers. Ironically, the United States was initially hesitant to shoot looters for fear of reinforcing negative images of the United States in the Arab world.[34] But the failure to take aggressive steps to establish security at the outset emboldened a host of forces hostile to the occupation, including remnants of the Iraqi army, terrorists, and Sunni militants alarmed at their loss of status within Iraq. These forces carried out increasingly bold and destructive attacks on coalition forces and reconstruction projects, further impairing efforts to restore order. Iraqis inclined to be supportive of coalition efforts to rebuild Iraq had to hedge their bets for fear that the coalition either could not protect them or might abandon the whole reconstruction project.

Much, of course, depends on the way in which conflict ends. In Haiti, because there were no warring belligerents to separate, the U.S.-led multi-national force focused on creation of a secure environment through the dismantling of the existing Haitian military and the creation of a new civilian police force. Instead of seizing the initiative and using U.S. soldiers to impose order, the United States initially "intended to rely on existing Haitian army units ... to maintain law and order until a sufficient number of international civilian police could be deployed."[35] The flaw in this approach became evident when Haitian soldiers beat civilians gathered to welcome arriving U.S. forces, while U.S. soldiers stood passively by.[36] As a result, the United States was forced to send hundreds of additional military police to Haiti as a stop-gap measure pending the arrival of international civilian police.[37]

In many cases, intervention takes place in support of negotiated settlements to civil wars. In these circumstances, intervention precludes a decisive military victory by any of the parties to the conflict. Belligerents must then decide whether to demobilize and pursue their aims through political processes or to retain their arms in anticipation of either renewed fighting or the possibility of exercising local control over particular regions of the country. When interveners are timid or incapable of imposing their will, belligerents are unlikely to stand down. In such cases, they are likely to see both risk and opportunity. The risk takes the form of a prisoner's dilemma. Even if demobilization is the best course, the risk that other belligerents may choose

---

[33] Jeffrey Sparshot, *Iraq Reconstruction Costs Said to Have Doubled*, THE WASHINGTON TIMES, July 2, 2003.

[34] Eric Schmitt & David E. Sanger, *Looting Disrupts Detailed U.S. Plan to Restore Iraq*, THE NEW YORK TIMES, May 19, 2003, at A1.

[35] Dobbins et al., *supra* note 9, at 76.

[36] Id.

[37] Id.

to retain their military options puts any belligerent who unilaterally demo-bilizes in serious jeopardy, especially if the intevenors cannot be counted on for protection. The opportunity consists of the possibility to achieve some or all of the belligerent's earlier objectives or to enter lucrative criminal enter-prises fostered by war-time conditions and the absence of effective police or security forces.

Belligerents' calculations of risk and opportunity will necessarily vary depending on a host of factors, including the relative strengths of the bel-ligerents and interveners, the willingness of interveners to use coercion, and the evolution of post-conflict reconstruction plans. Intervention and post-conflict reconstruction efforts create winners and losers among local forces, strengthening some and marginalizing others. Those who fear marginaliza-tion and have the capacity to resist it will do so. In the immediate aftermath of intervention, however, they and their supporters may doubt their abil-ity to resist effectively. Thus, prompt action by interveners to sideline or coopt belligerents and potential spoilers can undercut their will to resist and undermine their sources of local support.

Conversely, failure to establish security quickly emboldens spoilers and invites further attacks on interveners and their local partners. As a result, efforts to restore basic services slow or grind to a halt and local support dwindles even further. This creates a dilemma for interveners. To restore order, they must either escalate their own security measures or rely on local allies or security forces with ties to particular factions or poor human rights records. Either approach may alienate key segments of the local population. A vicious circle may take hold, as attempts to suppress spoiler attacks assume an increasingly draconian form, including air strikes that kill innocent civil-ians, roadblocks, security checkpoints, house-to-house searches, and similar measures. Such coercive security actions may in turn generate local resent-ment of the interveners and support for the spoilers, leading to yet more spoiler attacks and even more draconian security measures. Conversely, rapid progress on security at the outset may avoid the vicious circle problem and greatly ease the post-conflict reconstruction process.

B. The Security Gap

Effective states rely principally on police to maintain domestic order, because police are accustomed to living and working within local communities and are trained and equipped to investigate criminal activity and carry out domes-tic security tasks. Conversely, effective states rely on their military forces prin-cipally to fight wars against foreign adversaries and train and equip them accordingly. In post-conflict states, however, indigenous police often either disappear along with the collapse of the state or cannot be relied on to per-form domestic security tasks because they have been associated with a party to the conflict and are seen by the population as repressive and corrupt.

Either way, the absence of acceptable indigenous security forces creates a "security gap" that interveners must fill until indigenous security personnel can be vetted, trained, equipped, and deployed, a process that takes months even under the best of circumstances and typically much longer.

At the outset, that gap must be filled by military rather than police forces, for two compelling reasons. First, it often takes months to recruit, train, equip, and deploy international civilian police forces. In "the developed Western countries, law enforcement personnel are in short supply," and police officers may have to retire or resign to join an international civilian police mission.[38] Moreover, unlike military forces, which train and deploy as units and which exist principally for use abroad, police personnel must be recruited individually from diverse units and pulled from their usual duties. Police recruited in this fashion must be organized into coherent units despite wide variations in language, training, background, and skills and then deployed where needed. In some instances, police recruited for a particular operation are rejected on arrival for lack of training and adequate language skills; many return home early when they find "difficult conditions" and an "inability to perform what is considered real police work."[39] The result is substantial delay in putting adequate numbers of international civilian police on the ground. In Kosovo, for example, the civilian police (CIVPOL) component of the UN mission had achieved only 40 percent of its authorized strength one year after the mission began. Police units requested in 1999 "were still arriving in 2002."[40]

Second, civilian police often lack many of the skills and capabilities needed at the outset of post-conflict security operations. When active combat operations come to a close, heavily armed belligerents often remain in place, pending implementation of a disarmament, demobilization, and reintegration program (DDR). Such forces pose a threat to public order that lightly armed or unarmed civilian police cannot be expected to manage. Although high-intensity combat capabilities generally are not needed at this stage, only military forces can provide many of the diverse capabilities the immediate post-conflict security environment requires. These capabilities include the ability to separate and control armed belligerents; to "shape" the post-conflict environment with preemptive strikes against spoilers; to patrol international borders to stop arms trafficking, smuggling, and terrorist infiltration; to establish and operate security checkpoints; to search for and collect or destroy heavy weapons and explosives; and to apprehend or deter members of armed opposition groups.

---

[38] Frederick M. Lorenz, *Civil–Military Cooperation in Restoring the Rule of Law: Case Studies from Mogadishu toMitrovica*, in Bassiouni, *supra* note 3, at 829, 842.

[39] Id.

[40] *Briefing Note, supra* note 27.

1. Enhancing the Military's Security Capabilities

Although military forces can restore order in the short term, and are often the only ones who can do so, they cannot provide a medium-term, much less a long-term, solution to a post-conflict society's security needs. Military forces are usually trained and equipped to apply overwhelming force against adversaries to secure quick and decisive victories; most soldiers are not trained or equipped to investigate crimes, secure evidence, make arrests, control crowds, direct traffic, ensure public safety, or conduct a host of other specialized police tasks.[41]

In general, western militaries seeking to prepare for the transitional environment in the immediate post-intervention period need forces trained and equipped for roles that blend the requirements of combat and policing. There are two ways to approach this need for transitional forces and capabilities. One is to train soldiers widely in policing and crowd-control techniques and to develop improved doctrine and logistics plans for post-conflict security operations. This approach would be particularly valuable in post-conflict situations such as Iraq, where rapidly changing conditions may demand that the same unit handle crowd control and policing duties one week and combat operations the next.[42]

Within limits, existing military forces have already proven adept at adapting to policing and other traditionally civilian roles. In Iraq, for example, "young lieutenants and captains in the U.S. army [played] the roles of mayor, town council, and police chief."[43] Moreover, arguments that military forces are not trained or equipped to carry out law enforcement functions are often overstated. Majors Gwaltney and Weston note that the U.S. military "has a sizeable number of personnel and units specifically trained to fulfill a law enforcement function," including military police (MP) units and criminal investigation units such as the Army Criminal Investigation Command.[44] Further, they contest the widely held view that individual soldiers lack the training, equipment, and judgment to carry out policing tasks:

Reflecting the reality of today's environment of multiple contingency operations, individual soldiers receive a great deal of instruction on ROE [rules of engagement] and appropriate levels of force, particularly geared towards missions that fall short of full-scale armed conflict. Some soldiers also receive training on law enforcement skills, such as securing a crime scene, taking witness statements, operating checkpoints, and

---

[41] *See* Schmidl, *supra* note 1, at 20; Michael Dziedzic, *Introduction*, in POLICING THE NEW WORLD DISORDER, *supra* note 1, at 12.

[42] We are indebted to Major Ike Wilson for pointing this out.

[43] Peter Gantz, *The United Nations and Post-Conflict Iraq*, September 8, 2003, *available at* http://www.refugeesinternational.org/cgi-bin/ri/bulletin?bc=00645.

[44] Gwaltney & Weston, *supra* note 28, at 876–877. The criminal investigation units "provide the full range of investigative capabilities that one would typically expect out of a comparable civilian agency, to include forensic laboratories, ballistics experts, narcotics experts, computer crimes specialists, and polygraphers." Id.

interacting with interpreters and civil authorities. In addition to such generalized training, the military provides tailored training for law enforcement in specific peace operations.[45]

This trend toward increased training for individual soldiers in the demands associated with post-conflict environments may heighten substantially the capacity of the average ground unit to respond appropriately to post-conflict security challenges.

But in most post-conflict environments, enhanced training for the average soldier or the average ground forces unit, although valuable, is not enough. Of necessity, most ground forces will be trained and equipped primarily for war fighting. Providing members of a tank battalion some instruction in police techniques will not enable that battalion to respond with graduated force and crowd control techniques when a mob attacks a police station.

Instead, and in addition to enhanced training in post-conflict security operations for the average soldier, interveners need to develop and deploy constabulary forces whose primary mission is not war fighting but the maintenance of public order. Such units are specially equipped and trained to perform "both law enforcement and light infantry operations."[46] Examples include the Italian Carabinieri, the Spanish Guardia Civil, and the French Gendarmerie Nationale. These standing units are ideally suited to assist regular military forces in security operations in post-conflict states. As noted in a USIP Special Report:

They are equipped with armored vehicles and mounted weapons and can fight as light infrantry, if required. They are trained to maintain public order and are specially equipped to deal with civil disturbances. They are also trained to conduct investigations, make arrests, direct traffic, and perform other police functions. These units are able to deploy rapidly, are highly mobile, and, in Bosnia, Kosovo, and East Timor, have proven extremely versatile in responding to unforeseen requirements.[47]

Constabulary forces may be particularly useful in dealing with the "rent-a-mob" problem – the use by political elites of large groups of civilians to create civil disturbances difficult for heavily armed soldiers to control without unacceptable levels of violence.[48]

Unfortunately, both approaches – training large numbers of soldiers for policing duties or developing and deploying special constabulary units – run contrary to the dominant philosophy within the U.S. Department of Defense.[49] Although the Pentagon has recently issued new guidance that,

---

[45] Id., at 878. See also Schmidl, supra note 1, at 20–21 (noting that "professional officers and military forces usually adjust remarkably well to the required 'constabulary ethic'").

[46] Oakley & Dziedzic, supra note 17, at 519.

[47] USIP Report, supra note 26, at 11.

[48] See Robert M. Perito, WHERE IS THE LONE RANGER WHEN WE NEED HIM?: AMERICA'S SEARCH FOR A POST-CONFLICT STABILITY FORCE (2004), at 30–31.

[49] See id., at 238–239.

henceforth, stability operations will be considered a core mission, on par with conflict operations,[50] the fact remains that the military services have traditionally regarded dedicated post-conflict capabilities as detracting from their primary war-fighting purpose. The military leadership also has worried that to prepare for peacekeeping and nation-building duties by training forces for the unique demands of those kinds of missions would make it easier for elected officials to use the military in situations in which national security interests were only peripherally at stake. Partly for that reason, the Department of Defense has rejected proposals to develop constabulary forces, even though the United States has deployed such forces in the past. Instead, the United States prefers to look to allies with existing constabulary forces when such capacities are needed. However, these constabulary forces are limited in number and not always available.[51] Even when they are available, the time required to persuade their home countries to deploy them "can delay effective action in country for far too long."[52] As a result, the United States has sometimes been forced to rely on special forces teams to carry out policing functions in peace operations in Haiti, Afghanistan, and elsewhere when constabulary forces from mission partners were not available.[53]

But reliance on special forces, military police, and enhanced training for the average soldier should not serve as a substitute for a fully developed security force capability. The United States should work closely with its NATO partners and other willing states to map out the force levels and equipment needed to provide effective post-conflict security. Some division of labor may be appropriate, with states already experienced in constabulary operations taking the lead on developing those forces. But given that the United States cannot count on the ready availability of constabulary forces, particularly when it engages in interventions that lack a UN mandate or broad international support, it should also develop such capabilities itself.[54]

2. Enhancing CIVPOL Capabilities

But even if military capabilities for post-conflict security operations improve substantially, military forces must still be complemented by more traditional

[50] Department of Defense Directive, No. 3000.05, November 28, 2005, *available at* http://www.fas.org/irp/doddir/dod/d3000_05.pdf.

[51] *See* Oakley & Dziedzic, *supra* note 17, at 520 (noting that frequent use of constabulary forces in peace operations "could overtax the finite number of member states currently possessing such a 'constabulary' capability").

[52] James O'Brien, *Lawyers, Guns, and Money: Warlords and Reconstruction after Iraq*, 11 U.C. DAVIS J. INT'L L. & POL'Y 99, 111 (2004).

[53] *USIP Report, supra* note 26, at 11.

[54] Several European states are already working to create a European Gendarmerie Force (EGF). For discussion of progress in Europe and options for the United States, *see* David Armitage and Anne M. Moisin, Constabulary Forces and Post-Conflict Transition: The Euro-Atlantic Dimension, November 2005, NDU Strategic Forum, *available at* http://www.ndu.edu/inss/strforum/SF218/SF218.pdf.

international civilian police forces over the medium term and supplanted by indigenous police forces over the long term. As the post-conflict environment stabilizes, international civilian police (CIVPOL) can take over from the military much of the basic security work, freeing the military to concentrate on more exclusively military tasks, such as disarming belligerents and securing borders. Among other things, CIVPOL can help monitor, train, and mentor local police forces and where necessary carry out basic law enforcement functions.[55] CIVPOL are not only better trained for such work, but they are also much less expensive to deploy than military forces and less likely to appear to host countries as an occupation force.[56]

But CIVPOL can only complement military forces and local police, not replace them. Even when recruitment and deployment problems can be overcome, CIVPOL are often unarmed, poorly equipped, loosely organized, and hampered by poor unit cohesion. In Bosnia, for example, the International Police Task Force was unarmed and understaffed. It also was not mandated to enforce local law. As a result, it could "operate only with the consent of the parties."[57] In fact, in most peace operations, CIVPOL units are not armed or assigned direct law enforcement responsibilities; the fear is that "law enforcement activity by CIVPOL would run the risk of seriously antagonizing at least one of the former disputants and potentially the indigenous population, as well."[58] The obvious problem with this approach is that CIVPOL often prove ineffective in post-conflict societies where the potential for violence and organized criminal activity is high and commitment to a political settlement is weak.

Proposals to improve CIVPOL capabilities are well known and have been circulated for years. The *Brahimi Report*, for example, urged the United Nations to create on-call lists comparable to those used for rapid deployment of military forces and urged member states to create national pools of individuals eligible to fill quickly police and other civilian rule of law specialist positions. But little progress has been made.[59] Only a few states have moved to create pools of qualified candidates. Many either do not understand what is needed or are unable or unwilling to provide it. Thus, when the UN sought to fill civilian police positions for the deployment to Liberia in fall 2003, many of the candidates presented "failed to meet basic UN standards, which include skills such as driving an automobile and speaking English (the mission language)."[60] Accordingly, in most post-conflict situations, qualified

---

[55] *See* Schmidl, *supra* note 1, at 23.
[56] Perito, *supra* note 48, at 87.
[57] Lorenz, *supra* note 38, at 839.
[58] Oakley & Dziedzic, *supra* note 17, at 528.
[59] William J. Durch, Victoria K. Holt, Caroline R. Earle, & Moira K. Shanahan, *The Brahimi Report and the Future of UN Peace Operations* 80, December 1, 2003, *available at* http://www.stimson.org/fopo/pubs.cfm?ID=90.
[60] Id.

international civilian police are simply unavailable in the requisite numbers when first needed.[61]

Ideally, states with long traditions of effective and democratic policing should develop a surplus police capacity and conduct regular joint training exercises so that international police could be deployed as formed units with common doctrine and training and appropriate equipment. Doing so is harder for countries such as the United States, which do not have national police forces, but not impossible. One could imagine federal support for state and local police agencies willing to take on additional personnel in return for a commitment to make some number of police available for periodic training and deployment in emergencies, a sort of police equivalent to the national guard. At a minimum, on-call lists of the sort recommended by the *Brahimi Report* should be created.

Of course, even if CIVPOL can be recruited and deployed in a timely way; can overcome problems of unit cohesion created by the diverse languages, background, and training of the individually recruited CIVPOL unit members; and can be appropriately armed and mandated to enforce locally applicable law, they are still only at best a medium-term expedient. In the long term, as discussed in Part IV of this chapter, only local police can maintain order. As Erwin Schmidl points out,

"[C]ommunity policing" as we now know it in Western Europe and North America is quite different from military operations engaged in filling the initial public security gap. It can only be performed by officers living in the community who are able to communicate directly with the people – preferably without interpreters – gaining their trust and confidence. Local laws, customs, and institutions must be understood in their cultural context. Peacekeepers are often hampered by their lack of knowledge of local culture. Language alone can be a serious problem.[62]

Accordingly, as considered more fully in Chapter 6, interveners must help rebuild indigenous police capabilities by vetting, training, and reorganizing existing police forces or recruiting and building new forces from scratch. Until such forces can take over, interveners must take on the job of providing order themselves. In most cases, that means first and foremost that interveners must find a way to manage threats to the peace process from powerful local actors who fear that a successful peace process will disadvantage them.

[61] *See* id., at 81, 83. The *Brahimi Report* acknowledges that there is no existing standard timeline for deployment of civilian police. The report recommends that the United Nations develop the ability to deploy peacekeepers (including civilian police) to "traditional" peace operations (i.e., those in which the UN role is principally to serve as a neutral interposition force) within thirty days, and to "complex" operations (involving potentially aggressive peacebuilding measures) within ninety days. Even if the United Nations develops such a rapid deployment capability, a "deployment gap" will still exist at the outset of the mission, which military forces will still have to fill. *See* Gwaltney & Weston, *supra* note 28, at 876.

[62] Schmidl, *supra* note 1, at 23–24.

III. DEALING WITH SPOILERS: THE WARLORD CHALLENGE

During the Cold War, in what are now often referred to as "first-generation" peacekeeping operations, peacekeepers typically deployed only after the parties to a conflict accepted a negotiated peace agreement, and then only with the consent of the previously warring parties. To maintain that consent, peacekeepers followed a strict policy of neutrality and used force only in self-defense. Their job was to assist the parties in maintaining their agreement, not to coerce compliance. Taking sides in particular disputes would inevitably alienate one or more parties and might embroil peacekeepers in fighting for which they were not equipped or mandated.

Peace operations evolved dramatically in the post–Cold War period, however. As the U.S. military puts it, peace operations now are typically "designed to create or sustain the conditions in which political and diplomatic activities may be conducted."[63] This shift "has necessitated a fundamental revision of earlier principles of peace operations."[64] In peace enforcement operations, peacekeepers "may have to fight their way into the conflict area and use force to separate the combatants physically."[65] Moreover, "[c]onflict, violence, disorder, and possibly even chaos, rather than peace, describe the environment" and "one or more of the parties to the conflict prefers it that way."[66] In this context, "[a] neutral posture toward local actors who seek to obstruct the peace process through violence and intimidation is no longer appropriate. Peace implementers must take active measures to support those who support the peace and sanction those who oppose it."[67]

At the same time, the primary goal of peace operations remains the same: to support a political resolution to the underlying dispute. Even the most determined interveners will find it difficult if not impossible to achieve a sustainable peace through the use of force or to "solve the underlying problems that caused peaceful relations to dissolve."[68] Accordingly, the principal post-conflict role for the military must be to create "the necessary security conditions so that the efforts of civilian counterparts can bear fruit."[69] With this in mind, military doctrine for peace enforcement (at least in the United

---

[63] U.S. Joint Warfighting Center, *Joint Task Force Commander's Handbook for Peace Operations*, June 16, 1997, *available at* http://www.dtic.mil/doctrine/jel/research_pubs/k516.pdf, *quoted in* Dziedzic & Lovelock, *supra* note 3, at 854 (hereinafter *Peace Operations Handbook*).

[64] Dziedzic & Lovelock, *supra* note 3, at 853.

[65] Joint Chiefs of Staff, *Joint Tactics, Techniques and Procedures for Peace Operations*, February 12, 1999, at III-3, *available at* http://www.apan-info.net/peace_operations/uploads/jp3_07_3.pdf (hereinafter *Joint Tactics*).

[66] Id., at III-2.

[67] Dziedzic & Lovelock, *supra* note 3, at 853.

[68] *Joint Tactics*, *supra* note 65, at III-2.

[69] Id.

States and the United Kingdom) calls for restraint in the use of force and impartiality to the extent it can be employed consistently with the overall mission objectives.[70] Impartiality, however, does not mean neutrality; it means that interveners may choose to act against individuals or groups who seek to obstruct efforts to promote a political resolution to the underlying conflict or to build a functioning rule of law-oriented state.[71] As Jock Covey, then Principal Deputy Special Representative of the Secretary-General in Kosovo, succinctly put it, "[w]e support those who support UNSCR 1244 [the UN Security Council resolution setting out the principles for a political solution in Kosovo], and we oppose those who act against it."[72] In practice, this means that coercion must sometimes be used to "make the political embrace of peace more attractive than continuance of the conflict."[73] In particular, interveners must be prepared to use force against spoilers, that is, political elites who will benefit from the failure of the mission and who are prepared to use violence to pursue their goals.

Although the use of coercion to support internal political settlements evolved principally in the context of peace operations in places such as Bosnia and Kosovo, the same general principles apply to the post-conflict environments in Afghanistan and Iraq. In fact, in all of the cases examined in this book, interveners have struggled to find the right balance between accommodating and confronting potential spoilers.

A. Fight or Coopt?

Because the military's role in peace operations is to assist the relevant political actors in achieving a political resolution to the conflict, determining who is a spoiler and whether and when to act against a spoiler should be a political rather than a military decision.[74] The intentions, capabilities, and tactics of spoilers will vary significantly from one case to the next and so too will the resolve, capabilities, and tactics of the interveners and their local allies. Thus, in each case, interveners must make a political judgment on whether to work with or oppose potential spoilers and whether and when to employ inducements, sanctions, force, or some combination of each.

In most cases, confronting spoilers vigorously and early will greatly enhance the prospects for successful peace implementation efforts. Spoilers who conclude that interveners lack the political will to confront them

---

[70] Id.; *see also* Dziedzic & Lovelock, *supra* note 3, at 853.

[71] *See Report of the Panel on UN Peace Operations (Brahimi Report)*, at 9, *available at* http://www.un.org/peace/reports/peace_operations/.

[72] The Quest for a Durable Peace in Kosovo: Evolving Strategies of Peace Implementation (Jock Covey, Michael Dziedzic, & Leonard Hawley, eds.) (forthcoming), *quoted in* Dziedzic & Lovelock, *supra* note 3, at 856.

[73] *Joint Tactics, supra* note 65, at III-2.

[74] *See* Dziedzic & Lovelock, *supra* note 3, at 856.

will invariably take advantage. Unlike interveners, spoilers are there for the long haul. If given a chance, they will sabotage peace efforts or simply stall until interveners give up in frustration. But when spoilers prevail, the result is often the resumption of conflict and the collapse of whatever the interveners have previously managed to accomplish.

Unfortunately, it is often difficult for interveners to muster the political will to support aggressive measures against spoilers in the post-conflict intervention phase. Public attention wanes quickly in the aftermath of a military intervention, and political support and associated resources dwindle accordingly. Tolerance for casualties similarly declines, particularly in interventions viewed as elective, that is, those undertaken principally for humanitarian rather than strategic or national security reasons. Mission leaders who lack strong mandates and find themselves strapped for resources and personnel often elect to pursue polices of accommodation rather than confrontation. Painful experience demonstrates, however, that such policies usually fail, often catastrophically.

1. Somalia: Bungling the Warlord Challenge

Somalia is a case in point. The overthrow of Siad Barre's regime in 1991 marked the failure of the Somali state, which quickly "translated into chronic and destructive civil war, predatory banditry, famine, warlord fiefdoms and general lawlessness."[75] Bitter fighting among clans and a protracted drought combined to produce a massive humanitarian crisis. In response, the United Nations dispatched a small, lightly armed mission (UNOSOM I) in 1992 to monitor a negotiated cease-fire but soon realized that a more vigorous mission was needed to confront recalcitrant warlords such as Mohamed Farah Aideed. In late 1992, the Security Council authorized the U.S.-led Unified Task Force (UNITAF I) to use all necessary means to create a secure environment for the delivery of food and other humanitarian assistance. Because UNITAF included a substantial contingent of U.S. troops, local warlords initially concluded that "challenging the U.S.-led operation would lead to disastrous results for their forces."[76] Thus, UNITAF's arrival presaged "a substantial diminution of conflict between warlords and a period of relative quiescence," during which UNITAF was able to carry out its humanitarian relief mission.[77]

But UNITAF failed to pursue its initial advantage. Fearing "mission creep," the United States resisted efforts to expand UNITAF's mandate to

---

[75] International Crisis Group, *Somalia: Countering Terrorism in a Failed State*, May 23, 2002, at 2, *available at* http://www.crisisweb.org//library/documents/report_archive/ A400662_23052002.pdf.
[76] Dobbins, *supra* note 9, at 61.
[77] Id.

deal with the obstructionist tactics of some Somali warlords. As a result, UNITAF did not attempt to disarm local militias, which soon grew bolder and began increasingly to obstruct relief efforts. In May 1993, UNITAF was replaced by UNOSOM II, in keeping with U.S. insistence on an early exit for most U.S. forces. UNOSOM II had a mandate to use force more aggressively against spoilers, but the substitution of "poorly equipped Pakistanis" for well-equipped U.S. forces left UNOSOM a much weaker force than UNITAF.[78] Recognizing the mismatch between mission and forces, the United Nations insisted that UNITAF should disarm local militias prior to UNOSOM's takeover. The United States refused, arguing that disarmament was not part of UNITAF's mission.[79]

As security deteriorated, Somali warlords became increasingly aggressive. In June 1993, fighters associated with Aideed attacked Pakistani peacekeepers, killing twenty-five. In the ensuing hunt for Aideed, U.S. Rangers became embroiled in the street battle depicted in the movie *Black Hawk Down*; the deaths of nineteen U.S. soldiers in that incident prompted the withdrawal of U.S. forces in March 1994. The United Nations then decided it could not maintain an effective humanitarian operation with the forces provided to it, and UNOSOM II withdrew in 1995. Thus, the failure to confront warlords at the outset and with adequate forces resulted in the collapse of the entire relief effort. Moreover, it haunted humanitarian intervention prospects for years; most notably, memories of Somalia helped persuade the Clinton Administration to resist demands for UN-authorized military intervention to end the 1994 genocide in Rwanda.

2. Liberia: If You Can't Beat 'Em, Elect 'Em

Unfortunately, similar mistakes have been made in numerous other cases. In Liberia, ECOMOG forces in 1991 managed to drive Charles Taylor's National Patriotic Front of Liberia (NPFL) troops out of Monrovia and more or less secure the capital. But constrained by sharp political divisions within the Economic Community of West African States (ECOWAS), the nominal sponsor of the ECOMOG intervention, ECOMOG troops did not follow up. As a result, Taylor was able to reorganize, establish his own capital city, strip the country of its resources, and render future international efforts at political reform largely illusory. Elections held in 1997 put an electoral imprimatur on Taylor's rule, but the inability of ECOMOG and the UN to demobilize the various belligerents rendered the election a farce. Liberians voted for Taylor because they knew that to do otherwise would mean the renewal of civil war, something that Taylor's subsequent misrule ensured would occur anyway.

[78] Id., at 62.
[79] Id.

The ripple effects of the refusal to confront Taylor in the early years of the Liberian conflict were felt throughout the region. Even as he worked to secure control over Liberia for his own ends, Taylor supported rebel movements in neighboring countries. Most notably, he assisted the Revolutionary United Front (RUF), which launched a brutal civil war in Sierra Leone in 1991 and eventually joined forces with elements of the Sierra Leonean military to oust the elected government of Ahmad Tejan Kabbah in 1996. Taylor also supported insurgencies in Guinea and Cote D'Ivoire, states that in turn supported rebel movements fighting Taylor's government.[80] Although decisive action in 1991 might have overwhelmed Taylor's forces, inaction led inexorably to a proliferation of rebel movements and the migration of conflict back and forth across state borders in an escalating cycle of violence.

3. Sierra Leone: If You Can't Beat 'Em, Join 'Em

In Sierra Leone, President Kabbah, instead of confronting the RUF, concluded a peace agreement with it less than a year after his election.[81] Six months later, low-level military officers acting with support from the RUF staged a coup, forcing Kabbah from office despite almost universal condemnation of the coup both inside and outside of Sierra Leone. ECOMOG forces (dominated by Nigeria) intervened, and after heavy fighting, managed to force the junta leaders to flee the country. But Nigeria was unable or unwilling to defeat the RUF; in 1999, the RUF again invaded Freetown, "killing, mutilating, and abducting thousands of people."[82] The attack galvanized the international community, but Nigeria under a new democratically elected president wanted to withdraw, and no country wanted to assume its role. As a result, the United States, the United Kingdom, and Sierra Leone's neighbors pressured Kabbah to negotiate another agreement with the RUF and its leader, Foday Sankoh.[83] In this agreement, the Lomé accord, "Sankoh was, astonishingly, given the status of vice president and put in charge of the strategic minerals" that had fueled the war, including diamonds.[84] Notwithstanding the horrific nature of their crimes, RUF members were given amnesty,[85] and a UN peacekeeping force, the United

---

[80] *See* International Crisis Group, *Liberia: The Key to Ending Regional Instability*, Africa Report No. 62, April 30, 2003, at 8.

[81] The prior government hired Executive Outcomes (EO), a South African mercenary outfit, to secure Freetown and Sierra Leone's diamond fields. Executive Outcomes's success in fighting the RUF rendered the 1996 elections possible, but Kabbah unwisely agreed to the RUF's demand for EO's departure, leading to his own ouster a few months later. International Crisis Group, *Sierra Leone: Time for a New Political and Military Strategy*, Africa Report No. 28, at 2 (hereafter *Time for a New Strategy*).

[82] Id., at 2.

[83] Id., at 12.

[84] Id., *at* Appendix A.

[85] *See* Kenneth Roth, Wall Street Journal Europe, *International Injustice: The Tragedy of Sierra Leone*, August 2002, *available at* http://www.hrw.org/editorials/2000/ken-sl-aug.htm.

Nations Assistance Mission for Sierra Leone (UNAMSIL), was dispatched to oversee implementation of the accord. Not surprisingly, the Lomé agreement soon collapsed, in large part because the RUF sabotaged the peace process.[86]

Thus, the attempt to treat as political partners warlords who "lacked a coherent political agenda and almost any political base" proved to be "a vain exercise motivated largely by international expediency."[87] Progress in Sierra Leone did not occur until the international community abandoned the strategy of trying to coopt the RUF and other warring groups and instead applied sustained political and military pressure to the RUF and its supporters. In 2001, the British sent a small military force to Sierra Leone and demonstrated a willingness to use it against spoilers.[88] Pressure on Charles Taylor, a strengthened UNAMSIL, and a successful campaign by Guinea against RUF soldiers on its western border combined with the psychological impact of the British government's "extraordinary campaign of intimidation" over time forced the RUF to accept demobilization and paved the way for the progressive extension of government authority throughout much of Sierra Leone.[89]

4. Bosnia: Entrenching Spoilers

In Bosnia, NATO confronted a variation on the entrenched belligerents problem. Instead of a failed state, Bosnia in 1995 consisted of three distinct and antagonistic mini-states, each with its own military and police. In keeping with the Dayton Agreement that ended the fighting among those contending proto-states, NATO ensured the physical separation of the previously warring forces but otherwise left them intact and in control of agreed territories. As a result, Bosnia post-Dayton remained a divided country with three armies and multiple overlapping jurisdictions with little police cooperation across jurisdictional lines. Extremist nationalist politicians have since frustrated many peacebuilding initiatives. Moreover, the reluctance of NATO to confront spoilers fostered an environment in which organized crime has flourished and become part of the political fabric of the state.

To a substantial extent, Bosnia's inability to function as a modern, effective state reflects the bargain struck at Dayton. The decision in 1995 to accept Bosnia's division into three ethnic mini-states with an ineffective central

---

In response to sharp protests over the amnesty, the UN indicated that it did not consider the amnesty binding on international tribunals. Id.

[86] *Time for a New Strategy, supra* note 81, at 3. Among other things, the RUF captured and held hostage some 500 UN peacekeepers.

[87] Id.

[88] *See* International Crisis Group, *Managing Uncertainty*, Africa Report No. 35, October 24, 2001, at 1–2.

[89] Id.

government serving as a thin common roof provided political and legal cover for nationalist politicians intent on blocking genuine reunification and building personal fiefdoms through corruption and organized criminal activity. Coercing spoilers in Bosnia is thus a much more complex task than in places such as Liberia or Sierra Leone. Opportunities for spoilers to frustrate reform efforts were built into the constitution of postwar Bosnia, making it difficult for interveners to confront spoilers without undermining their own rule of law message. Still, NATO could have pursued indicted war criminals much more aggressively than it has throughout most of the post-Dayton period. And the High Representative could have used his nearly proconsul powers more vigorously in the early post-Dayton period to undermine nationalist politicians (whose return to power through elections in 2002 "was widely assessed as a calamity" by observers of the Bosnian peace process).[90]

Nonetheless, considerable progress has been made in recent years. As discussed in Chapter 4, the Office of the High Representative has taken many steps, including the removal of obstructionist politicians from office, to transform Bosnia into a functioning state eligible for entry into the European Union. A variety of factors, including the economic attraction of integration into Europe, the passage of time, political change within the Federal Republic of Yugoslavia, and vigorous action by the High Representative have helped position Bosnia for negotiations on a Stabilization and Association Agreement with the European Union. But limited progress on police reform, as a result of obstruction by nationalist politicians in the Republika Srpska, remains a major stumbling block.[91]

5. Afghanistan: Divide and Misrule

Everything accomplished in Afghanistan stands in jeopardy partly because of the reluctance of the interveners, principally the United States, to confront the warlords and military commanders who run much of the country. In the early post-intervention period, the failure to disarm Afghanistan's numerous armed factions made it "inconceivable that any of the key elements" of the Bonn political process could "be meaningfully implemented."[92] As Lakhdar Brahimi, the former Special Representative of the Secretary-General for Afghanistan, reported to the Security Council in January 2003, the new constitutional order established through the Bonn process "will only have meaning for the average Afghan if security improves and the rule of law is

[90] International Crisis Group, *Bosnia's Nationalist Governments: Paddy Ashdown and the Paradoxes of State Building*, Balkans Report No. 146, July 22, 2003, at i.

[91] International Crisis Group, *Bosnia's Stalled Police Reform: No Progress, No EU*, Report No. 164, September 6, 2005, at 1.

[92] International Crisis Group, *Disarmament and Reintegration in Afghanistan*, Asia Report No. 65, September 30, 2003, at i (hereinafter *Disarmament and Reintegration*).

strengthened."[93] But until 2005, little progress on security was made; if any-thing, movement was in the other direction, as warlords consolidated their power in the Afghan countryside.[94]

The coalition's intervention in Afghanistan ended temporarily more than twenty years of internecine fighting. But it also crystallized the division of Afghanistan into "a patchwork of militia fiefdoms, with varying levels of internal organisation."[95] Coalition forces working with the Northern Alliance ousted the Taliban but simultaneously empowered Northern Alliance commanders and other anti-Taliban militia groups, some of which have taken control of regions throughout the country. Some of the stronger commanders took control of key government ministries, including the defense ministry, and used these ministries to develop their own power bases largely outside the control of the national government.[96]

These many and loosely organized regional warlords stand a great deal to lose from the success of the Bonn political process. With little effective central authority outside Kabul, they were free to siphon off reconstruction aid, collect "taxes," run smuggling operations, and collect the vast revenues associated with Afghanistan's booming trade in opium. As a result, "for too many Afghans, the daily insecurity they face comes not from resurgent extremism associated with the Taliban, destabilizing as that is, but from the predatory behaviour of local commanders and officials who nominally claim to represent the government."[97] Growing insecurity in turn impeded reconstruction efforts and jeopardized the political, institutional, and legal reforms needed for long-term stability.

For obvious reasons, the United States initially focused its efforts on com-bating Taliban and al-Qaeda forces along the border with Pakistan. The downside of this strategy, however, was that the United States used war-lord proxies to assist its ongoing military campaign, helping some warlords entrench themselves even further. Only recently has the United States begun to ramp up its security efforts. In 2004, the United States almost doubled its force size in Afghanistan, from 11,000 to 20,000. In anticipation of the

---

[93] Statement of Lakhdar Brahimi to the UN Security Council, January 15, 2003, *available at* http://www.unama-afg.org/docs/_UN-Docs/sc/briefings/03.jan15.htm.

[94] *See* S/2003/1212, *Report of the Secretary-General on the Situation in Afghanistan and Its Implication for International Peace and Security*, December, 2003, at 15 (noting that "inse-curity in the south and south-east, particularly, has had the effect of shrinking the area in which the Government, the United Nations and the international community can effectively operate").

[95] *Disarmament and Reintegration, supra* note 92, at 2.

[96] *See, e.g.*, Brahimi, *supra* note 93 (noting the need for security institutions that are "truly national, rather than factionally dominated"); Anja Manuel & P. W. Singer, *A New Model Afghan Army*, 81 FOREIGN AFFAIRS 44, 46 (2002) (noting that a "subset of Tajiks control[led] key ministries and the former secret police").

[97] Brahimi, *supra* note 93.

elections held in October 2004, the United States also pressed Pakistan to step up its efforts to control the infiltration of Taliban forces into Afghanistan. As a result, Taliban threats to disrupt the elections through violence came to little, and voter turnout demonstrated a broad-based desire for continued political reform. Moreover, the United States and NATO have also significantly expanded the number and range of ISAF forces, which work with the Karzai government to help it extend its authority to rural areas. Progress has been greatest in the north and west of the country, though as of January 2006, ISAF had plans to expand gradually into the south as well.

Nonetheless, Afghanistan remains an unstable and fractured place, and the explosive growth in the drug trade threatens to turn Afghanistan into a narco-state in which the rule of law cannot take hold.[98] Unfortunately, forcibly subordinating Afghanistan's warlords, defeating the Taliban, and curtailing the drug trade would require more troops and resources than the United States or others appear ready to commit, and in the short term may run counter to efforts to overcome ethnic tensions. Unless that changes, the strength of spoilers may continue to dictate efforts to coopt rather than subdue them,[99] even though continuing along that path seems a prescription for future instability.

6. Iraq: Pursuing Spoilers and Making Enemies

Iraq is one of the few cases in which interveners have made a concerted effort to pursue spoilers. The mixed results achieved so far illustrate the difficulties and dangers of this approach, at least when dealing with insurgents commanding some degree of popular support. Postwar Iraq is currently a breeding ground for spoilers of all sorts. Years of authoritarian misrule, international sanctions, and war have divided the population along sectarian, ethnic, tribal, and clan lines. In this environment, Sunni, Shiite, and Kurdish leaders jockey for power, and remnants of the former regime, militant Islamist groups, and foreign terrorists carry out deadly attacks on coalition forces, Iraqi police, and anyone working with them on an almost daily basis.[100]

---

[98] *See* Jones et al., *supra* note 31, at 88, 99 (concluding that "there is little security in notable parts of the country," and that "Afghanistan still has one of the most ineffective justice systems in the world").

[99] *See* Manuel & Singer, *supra* note 96, at 53 ("[g]iven the warlords' deep-rooted hold over local power structures, the government probably could not crush them – indeed, it would be injudicious even to try").

[100] *See* International Crisis Group, *Governing Iraq,* Middle East Report No. 17, August 25, 2003, at ii (noting that opposition "comes in various shades: Baathist loyalists; nationalists; Islamists, who for the time being are predominantly Sunni; tribal members motivated by revenge or anger at the occupiers' violation of basic cultural norms; criminal elements; Islamist and other militants from Arab and other countries").

The United States and its coalition partners misjudged the extent to which occupation forces would encounter violent resistance and then compounded the misjudgment by several ill-advised decisions taken at the outset of the occupation. The United States failed to deploy sufficient troops to seal off Iraq's borders or to impose order in the so-called Sunni Triangle and the capital.[101] Moreover, the decision to disband the Iraqi army, though later modified, initially put hundreds of thousand of soldiers, many with little loyalty to Saddam Hussein's regime, out on the streets with their arms but "without pay, future, and honour."[102] This step, along with heavy-handed de-Baathification efforts, also alienated many Iraqis, particularly Sunnis, who were disproportionately represented in both the army and the civil service.[103]

Within limits, coalition forces have vigorously pursued individuals suspected of attacks, using both counterinsurgency and policing methods. But in doing so, the coalition has angered many Iraqis, and in the process arguably compounded an already potent security crisis. As the International Crisis Group notes, "as in any foreign occupation, checkpoints, searches, [and] raids have a cumulative negative effect, strengthening the forces of resistance they are designed to suppress."[104] Moreover, U.S. tactics have often displayed an inadequate understanding of local culture:

[M]any Iraqis accuse U.S. forces of heavy-handedness and insufficient cultural sensitivity. Civilians have been killed as a result of egregious U.S. errors or in cross fire; Iraqis claim that U.S. soldiers leave behind considerable material damage, breaking furniture and doors in their attempts to snuff out resistance; U.S. soldiers also have been blamed for stealing money and jewelry during their weapons searches. Coalition forces' raids against mosques – at times used as hideouts or as staging areas for attacks against U.S. soldiers – and alleged confiscation of alms or zakat, have fuelled anger. The use of police dogs – considered by observant Muslims as sources of impurity – has provoked similar protests. Physical searches by male soldiers of women and the storming of their private bedrooms (without giving them a chance to cover themselves properly) are experienced by Iraqis as dreadful breaches of local norms and sinful transgressions of Islamic law.[105]

To achieve its security goals, the coalition must not simply pursue spoilers; it must do so in a culturally acceptable way, while simultaneously building the capacity of and political support for the Iraqi government. Shifting security responsibilities to indigenous military and security forces, with coalition forces acting in a support role and ensuring adherence to international norms, may offer the best way to combat spoilers without generating new enemies.

---

[101] *See* Michael R. Gordon, *The Strategy to Secure Iraq Did Not Foresee a 2nd War*, THE NEW YORK TIMES, October 19, 2004, at A1.

[102] International Crisis Group, *Iraq: Building a New Security Structure*, Middle East Report No. 20, December 23, 2003, at i.

[103] Id.

[104] *Governing Iraq*, *supra* note 100, at 5.

[105] Id., at 4–5.

But making that transition, something coalition forces hope to do sooner rather than later, requires rebuilding the indigenous security forces and fostering a political climate in which those forces will act in the public interest. This is necessarily a time-consuming process, rendered more difficult by the coalition's early missteps in disbanding the army and stripping all national institutions, including the army and police, of their senior leadership through wholesale de-Baathification efforts. After a series of false starts, the coalition has trained a number of Iraqi military units, which have assisted with mixed results in counterinsurgency and general security efforts.[106] In time, these units may serve as the nucleus of a new and professional Iraqi Armed Forces. Similarly, the coalition has trained and deployed thousands of Iraqi police. But the late start to security efforts, and the overwhelming political pressure to deploy indigenous forces quickly, have in some cases led to premature deployment of Iraqi units that are not fully trained or equipped. Moreover, it is not at all clear that Iraqi government leaders are committed to democratically accountable security forces and that those forces will not revert to protection of regime rather than state interests.[107] Thus, ground lost early in the fight against spoilers has proven extraordinarily difficult to make up.

The way in which interveners deal with spoilers will necessarily depend on the interveners' political objectives, commitment, and capacity as well as the nature, objectives, and strength of the spoilers the interveners confront. As in Somalia, Liberia, and Sierra Leone, a weak intervention force hobbled by political dissension among the interveners will have little choice but to attempt to work with spoilers, however unattractive and unlikely to succeed such an approach may be. A strong intervention force at least has the choice of working with potential spoilers (as in Afghanistan) or pursuing them aggressively (as in Iraq). In general, attempts to co-opt spoilers are unlikely to produce more than short-term gains in the form of a temporary cessation of conflict. When interveners later attempt to pursue their long-term objectives of establishing central government authority throughout the state and instituting the rule of law, spoilers whose power and resources are threatened will disrupt or derail the process.

When spoilers consist principally of warring factions seeking personal enrichment and lack broad popular support, aggressive efforts to defeat or sideline them may offer substantial and quick benefits to the larger post-conflict rehabilitation effort, as occurred when the British used force against spoilers in Sierra Leone. When spoilers take the form of ideologically

---

[106] The U.S. political and security strategy for Iraq is outlined in the National Security Council's National Strategy for Victory in Iraq, November 2005, at 18–22, *available at* http://www.whitehouse.gov/infocus/iraq/iraq_national_strategy_20051130.pdf.

[107] *See* Jones et al., *supra* note 31, at 173.

motivated insurgents with significant popular support, as in Afghanistan and Iraq, aggressive military tactics may prove insufficient and even counterproductive. In such cases, even more so than in places such as Somalia, Liberia, and Sierra Leone, the real struggle is political rather than military.[108] The establishment of effective and respected domestic political institutions and indigenous security capabilities is the only long-term solution, and "long-term" means years, sometimes many years. In the interim, foreign military actions against spoilers must be designed to assist indigenous security forces in their efforts to extend government control over contested areas gradually while minimizing civilian casualties to avoid generating a backlash against the interveners and the government they support.[109]

B. DDR and Its Discontents

In most post-conflict environments, dealing with spoilers requires the disarmament, demobilization, and reintegration (DDR) of combatants into civil society. In a nutshell, the goal is to "give the central government a monopoly over military force in the country."[110] The failure to demobilize and reintegrate ex-combatants gives faction leaders leverage to obstruct any aspect of the peace process they deem inimical to their interests and renders resumption of warfare an easy option in the event that it seems to offer greater benefits to one or more parties than pursuit of peace. The long string of broken peace accords and continued warfare in places such as Liberia and Sierra Leone illustrates the fragility of any peace agreement that is not accompanied by an effective DDR program. In short, unless politics is demilitarized, and warring factions are transformed into political parties or interest groups, "civil wars cannot be brought to an end, and the consolidation of democracy and the protection of human rights have little chance of success."[111]

Unfortunately, achieving effective DDR is extraordinarily difficult. In most cases, international peace operations are launched to compel or to support an agreed political process for post-conflict reconciliation and reconstruction. In such cases, interveners seek if at all possible to treat the previously warring factions, many of whom signed the relevant peace agreement, as partners in the peace process rather than spoilers. DDR is encouraged, but seldom coerced, because coercion risks dragging interveners into a civil war

---

[108] *See* Thomas X. Hammes, *Real Victory Will Come with Political Control*, INTERNATIONAL HERALD TRIBUNE, October 6, 2004, at 6.

[109] Id.

[110] Michael Bhatia, Kevin Lanigan, & Philip Wilkinson, *Minimal Investments, Minimal Results: The Failure of Security Policy in Afghanistan*, 6 TIDSKRIFT 59, 83 (2004).

[111] Stephen John Steadman, *Implementing Peace Agreements in Civil Wars: Lessons and Recommendations for Policymakers*, IPA Policy Paper Series on Peace Implementation, May 2001, at 3, *available at* http://www.ipacademy.org/PDF_Reports/Pdf_Report_Implementing.pdf.

they lack sufficient national interest incentive to fight. For many interveners, this is the lesson of Somalia. Attempts to disarm Mohamed Farah Aideed's faction by force ended in disaster because interveners did not have sufficient reason to devote the troops and resources necessary to succeed.

Accordingly, interveners typically attempt to induce DDR through political pressure and economic incentives. But faction leaders often conclude that they are better off retaining a military capability, for several reasons. First, retaining fighting forces provides leverage in post-conflict decision-making on the distribution of political power and the other spoils of governance. In Afghanistan, for example, some militia leaders have been rewarded with district governorships and other political posts. Second, faction leaders distrust one another. They recognize that disarmament may render them vulnerable to adversaries who do not disarm, particularly when interveners lack the capacity and the will to protect them. Interveners can attempt to overcome this factional security dilemma by staging demobilization and disarmament in phases keyed to simultaneous compliance by each of the major warring parties. The difficulty with this approach is that cheating is pervasive and difficult to prevent. Third, faction leaders often seek to take advantage of those who do disarm by threatening to resume fighting (or actually doing so) whenever it is to their advantage. In short, for faction leaders, "DDR is first and foremost a political exercise. To shut down one's war machine is to close an option for reaching one's political goals."[112]

Individual fighters also often prove reluctant to lay down their arms. For some, it may be the only life they have known. With few skills and few community ties, they may justly fear rejection, loss of status, and unemployment. Thus, absent strong outside pressure or incentives, both faction leaders and rank-and-file fighters will keep their options open.

But generating the necessary pressure or incentives is difficult. In many cases, DDR programs are slighted in post-conflict planning and implementation. When fighting dies down, international interest wanes. Raising funds to support DDR programs proves difficult, and local economic conditions typically make post-conflict employment for former combatants hard if not impossible to find. When interveners attempt to proceed with inadequately resourced DDR programs, the results may be worse than failing to pursue DDR at all. The promise of DDR often generates high expectations on the part of ex-combatants, followed by a backlash when those expectations cannot be met.

---

[112] Jean-Marie Guéhenno, Under-Secretary-General for Peacekeeping, *Disarmament, Demobilisation, and Reintegration in Peace Operations*, NGO/DPI Workshop on Demobilising War Machines – Making Peace Last, September 11, 2002, at 2, *available at* http://www.un.org/dpi/ngosection/annualconfs/55/guehenno.pdf.

Further, DDR programs are notoriously difficult to monitor and verify. Interveners usually lack sophisticated local intelligence capabilities. As a result, "information on the numbers of combatants and their location is often available only from the parties."[113] Even when interveners learn of violations of DDR agreements, interveners may be reluctant to report them for fear of alienating the factions whose cooperation they seek to carry out their mission. In Angola, for example, peacekeepers falsely verified UNITAF's demobilization claims to characterize their mission as successful.[114]

Thus, from the standpoint of the belligerents, the risks and opportunity costs of DDR are high, the benefits are speculative, and the chances of being caught, much less sanctioned, for reneging on demobilization promises are slight. As a result, "cheating is pervasive in the demobilization of soldiers."[115] In some cases, belligerents turn in only old or badly functioning weapons, often only the least combat-capable belligerents demobilize, or belligerents demobilize but cache their arms and remain together, ready to mobilize again as circumstances dictate.

DDR can succeed, but only when it is part of a holistic enterprise. Interveners must back demands for DDR with meaningful incentives and a realistic threat of coercion. DDR programs must be comprehensive and long term and must be integrated into the larger blueprint for post-conflict reconstruction. Ex-combatants must receive adequate training and reorientation programs to prepare them for the return to civilian life.[116] They also need adequate "reinsertion" packages to ensure that they have food, clothing, and shelter for the period required to transition to self-sustaining employment in local communities. Moreover, DDR must be accompanied by efforts to restart the broader economy so that demobilized combatants will have economic opportunities to replace those lost when they give up their weapons. DDR programs should also include efforts to assist ex-combatants to integrate into communities that may regard them with fear, suspicion, and anger and that may resent the special privileges given to those who "earned" them only by waging war and killing civilians.

Special attention must be paid to gender issues in DDR. Marginalized groups in society, particularly women and children, usually suffer the most during internal conflicts of the sort that trigger external military intervention. In Sierra Leone and Liberia, for example, women were often treated as a commodity, to be taken forcibly to serve as bush wives or reluctant

---

[113] Id., at 3.
[114] Steadman, *supra* note 111, at 16.
[115] Id.
[116] UN Department of Peacekeeping Operations, *Disarmament, Demobilization, and Reintegration of Ex-Combatants in a Peacekeeping Environment: Principles and Guidelines*, December, 1999, at 9.

low-level combatants. In Bosnia, rape was intentionally used as a vehicle for ethnic cleansing. Unfortunately, women also suffer disproportionately when organized violence ends. Returning male combatants, long removed from conventional social settings, may lapse readily into domestic violence.[117] Moreover, returning but unemployed combatants may displace women from economic roles assumed during the height of the conflict. In Sierra Leone, scarce resources for DDR went disproportionately to male combatants, with little for women combatants and less for women who served for years in the bush, willingly or not, as camp followers.[118] Few women, and few organizations that specialize in women's issues, are typically included in discussions on how to design and implement DDR programs. Including a gender perspective in future DDR efforts will help ensure a more balanced and, in the long run, more successful DDR process.

As difficult as it is to carry out successful DDR programs, the alternatives – leaving combatant forces intact or simply disbanding them by fiat – are even worse. Liberia illustrates the folly of leaving warring factions intact. In Liberia, political divisions among the interveners, and ties between the warring factions and neighboring states, frustrated any hope for disarmament and demobilization in the early years of Liberia's long civil war. ECOMOG's unwillingness or inability to force disarmament left Charles Taylor in place to spread insurrection to neighboring states even as warring factions proliferated within Liberia itself. DDR efforts stood no chance of success until 2003, when the United Nations returned peacekeepers to Liberia in force and started to approach DDR as a regional rather than a purely local problem; even then, the UN mission lacked the coercive mandate that may yet prove essential to successful DDR.[119]

Iraq illustrates the difficulty of simply disbanding combatant forces without providing them with alternative avenues to status and employment. Before the war began in March 2003, U.S. plans called for enlisting most Iraqi soldiers in security and reconstruction tasks.[120] But shortly after assuming power in Baghdad, the Coalition Provisional Authority (CPA) discovered that state institutions had "evaporated overnight"; most soldiers and police simply went home, in effect "self-demobilizing."[121] The CPA then decided formally to dissolve the army in its entirety. Enlisted men lost their

---

[117] *See* Tracy Fitzsimmons, *Engendering Justice and Security after War,* in Call, *supra* note 12, at 351–352.

[118] In Sierra Leone, many women and child combatants were left out of DDR efforts in part because of "the absence of credible data in relation to children and women associated with the fighting factions." Bengt Ljunggren and Desmond Molloy, *Some Lessons in DDR: The Sierra Leone Experience,* June 2004, at 1 (paper on file with authors).

[119] *See* S.C. Res. 1509 (2003) (deciding that UNMIL should develop an action plan for DDR, and "carry out voluntary disarmament" as part of a DDR program).

[120] *Iraq: Building a New Security Structure, supra* note 102, at 5.

[121] Jones et al., *supra* note 31, at 112.

employment; high-ranking officers in addition lost status and eligibility for future public service.[122] The CPA's decision effectively to ratify self-demobilization is now widely regarded as a serious mistake. Iraqi soldiers could instead have been given paid leave and recalled as conditions stabilized; indeed, the CPA was soon forced to resume payments to the Iraqi military in the face of escalating demonstrations by demobilized soldiers and attacks on coalition forces.[123]

Despite the difficulties, a comprehensive DDR program, properly implemented, can make a vital contribution to the success of post-conflict stability and reconstruction efforts. Relative success stories include Sierra Leone and Kosovo, though each remains a work in varying stages of progress. Liberia may yet join the potential successes, but it has further to go.

In Sierra Leone, military pressure compelled the RUF to agree to disarm and demobilize in 2001. The process was carried out in stages. First, a strengthened UNAMSIL gradually deployed throughout the country, working to secure Sierra Leone's borders, cut off the RUF's supply routes, and gain the confidence of the combatants.[124] Second, disarmament and demobilization efforts followed in UNAMSIL's wake as fighters were encouraged to turn in their weapons in exchange for modest payments and benefits such as access to vocational training.[125] Third, as fighters demobilized, the Sierra Leone government gradually extended its own authority through deployment of army and police forces and eventually civil administrators.

At first the process was replete with problems. Many hard-core RUF fighters refused to disarm; weapons turned in were often of low quality; and civilians sometimes posed as fighters to claim DDR benefits.[126] Over time, however, the DDR process gained momentum. By December 2001, most RUF fighters had either "disarmed and accepted the programs on offer for reintegration into society" or left "to take up lucrative mercenary jobs with Charles Taylor."[127] By January 2002, the DDR process was largely complete, and by May 2002, Sierra Leone, after eleven years of civil war, managed to hold its first genuinely nonviolent elections.

The Sierra Leone DDR process was flawed in many ways and left a significant number of ex-combatants without assistance. But through active cooperation, the Sierra Leone government and various international partners managed to find innovative ways to keep the process moving, including targeted grants and micro-finance schemes aimed at individual entrepreneurs,

---

[122] Id., at 5–6.
[123] Id., at 8.
[124] *Managing Uncertainty*, *supra* note 88, at 4.
[125] Id.
[126] Id.
[127] International Crisis Group, *Sierra Leone: Ripe for Elections?*, Africa Briefing, December 19, 2001, at 1.

efforts to involve youth in sports, and a "StopGaps" system to "offer labor intensive, quick impact" programs to employ ex-combatants when such intervention seemed necessary to avoid renewed conflict.[128]

Much remains to be done before Sierra Leone can be declared a success story. Governance reforms are vital, and security remains uncertain. Problems with the army persist, the community-based civil defense forces could easily remobilize, and many ex-combatants remain frustrated with the often poor quality of the reintegration training and assistance available.[129] Thus, the durability of Sierra Leone's transition remains uncertain. Still, Sierra Leone has made extraordinary progress, enough for the Security Council to declare UNAMSIL's mandate concluded in December 2005 and to replace UNAMSIL with a follow-on mission, the United Nations Integrated Office for Sierra Leone, intended to help consolidate the peace.

Considerable progress has also been made in Kosovo, though the expulsion of FRY security forces and the perception of NATO forces as liberators among most Kosovars helped immeasurably in laying the groundwork for demobilizing KLA forces. In June 1999, shortly after the FRY accepted NATO's terms for ending the conflict over Kosovo, the KLA agreed to its own demilitarization, and by September 20, the NATO-led Kosovo Force (KFOR) declared that the demilitarization was complete.[130] Some KLA forces joined the newly formed Kosovo Protection Corps, a mostly unarmed quasi-national guard force established as a compromise between NATO's desire to dispense with any local military entity and the desire of most Kosovars for their own army. Other KLA members joined the newly constituted Kosovo Police Service (KPS). Still others entered politics as members of a KLA political party. Although these developments are largely positive, they have a dark side. KLA leaders retain influence in ways that render them a "new kind of nomenklatura which is exclusive and hard to join."[131] Moreover, some members of this nomenklatura have become involved in organized crime, of the sort that now festers throughout the war-torn areas of former Yugoslavia. Thus, demobilization, although generally positive, is no guarantee of stability in Kosovo, particularly given continuing uncertainties regarding Kosovo's future status and still strong animosities between Kosovo's ethnic Albanians and Kosovo's dwindling number of ethnic Serbs.

After years of warfare in which almost 400,000 of its three million people died, Liberia faces a much tougher challenge than Kosovo. Like Sierra

---

[128] See Ljunggren and Molloy, *supra* note 118, at 3.

[129] International Crisis Group, *Sierra Leone: The State of Security and Governance,* Africa Report No. 67, September 2, 2003, at 1, 6–8.

[130] International Crisis Group, *What Happened to the KLA?*, Balkans Report No. 88, March 3, 2000, at 1.

[131] Id., at 2.

Leone, Liberia has been torn apart by multiple warring factions. Its political and factional leaders remain committed to advancing their personal interests rather than any conception of the national interest. The country is awash in arms from over a dozen years of warfare. Although all this bodes ill for the success of ongoing DDR efforts, there are some positive elements. The United Nations Mission in Liberia (UNMIL) has 15,000 troops and a Chapter VII mandate, and most Liberians are desperate for peace. UNMIL's early DDR efforts in December 2003 collapsed because UNMIL was not ready for the number of combatants who wished to participate,[132] but more UNMIL troops have since deployed and UNMIL has learned from its mistakes. UNMIL recognizes that combatants must be disarmed for peace to have any chance of taking hold and is attempting to emulate the success achieved in Sierra Leone by securing Liberia's borders and detaching fighters from their corrupt and self-serving commanders.

To succeed, UNMIL and others must come up with effective reintegration packages while simultaneously attempting to reform Liberia's security sector, rebuild state institutions, overcome endemic corruption, and promote good governance in a country that has never known it.[133] Efforts so far have yielded mixed results. The formal disarmament and demobilization period ended in November 2004. According to UNMIL, over 100,000 Liberians turned in their arms, including over 20,000 women and over 10,000 children.[134] The sheer number of those seeking reintegration packages (many of them not genuinely entitled) has strained the system beyond its capacity. As of September 2005, some 26,000 ex-combatants were still waiting to participate in reintegration programs.[135] Some have rioted to demand payments due them; others have been rerecruited into conflicts in neighboring states. The program faces continuing funding shortfalls and delays. In a country where most people live on less than a dollar a day, opportunities for employment are bleak. Thus, the prospects for a stable peace, much less for the rule of law, remain tenuous.

In Liberia, as in other cases examined here, reconstruction must be a holistic process. Providing security, combating spoilers, and demobilizing combatants are only essential first steps in the larger process of governance reform, economic recovery, and state rebuilding. Moreover, these efforts cannot proceed in a vacuum. Although interveners can establish order and demobilize combatants in the short term, the longer-term success of those

---

[132] See International Crisis Group, *Rebuilding Liberia: Prospects and Perils*, Africa Report No. 75, January 30, 2004, at 5.

[133] See generally id.

[134] S/2005/177, *Sixth Progress Report of the Secretary-General on the UN Mission in Liberia*, March 17, 2005, at 5.

[135] S/2005/560, *Eighth Progress Report of the Secretary-General on the UN Mission in Liberia*, September 1, 2005, at 5.

efforts requires the reconstitution of domestic security and justice institutions. In particular, states need effective and reasonably apolitical police,
courts, and prisons for security genuinely to take hold.

IV. REBUILDING DOMESTIC SECURITY AND JUSTICE CAPABILITIES

The need for functioning police, courts and prisons is never greater than in the
immediate aftermath of intervention. With the collapse of existing security
institutions, crime flourishes; if nothing is done quickly, organized criminal
activity can become woven tightly into the political fabric and almost impossible to eradicate later. As Hansjeorg Strohmeyer notes with reference to the
aftermath of NATO's intervention in Kosovo:

> Looting, arson, forced expropriation of apartments belonging to Serbs and other
> non-Albanians ... became daily phenomena. Moreover, organized crime, including
> smuggling, drug trafficking, and trafficking in women, soon flourished. It was appar-
> ent, within the first few days, that the previous law enforcement and judicial system in
> Kosovo had collapsed. Criminal gangs competing for control of the scarce resources
> immediately started to exploit the emerging void.[136]

Six years later, organized crime remains one of the greatest threats to the
rule of law in Kosovo.

Moreover, because of the often close links between organized crime and
political leaders in some post-conflict societies, the resources generated by
criminal activity are often used to fund further conflict.[137] In Bosnia, for
example, "the exigencies of the war drove political leaders from all three
warring factions to rely on the criminal underworld to perform various
essential functions," including smuggling of military equipment banned by
the then applicable UN arms embargo and raising revenue to prosecute the
war.[138] At times, political leaders relied "upon local thugs and armed gangs
to prosecute the war effort" and conduct ethnic cleansing.[139] The continuing
postwar interpenetration of crime and politics makes building an effective
justice system an urgent priority if efforts at governance reforms are to have
any chance of success.

When judicial systems in post-conflict societies have collapsed, interveners face a dilemma. Quick action is required to combat spoilers, limit crime,
restore public confidence, and protect the intervention forces. But carrying

---

[136] Hansjörg Strohmeyer, *Collapse and Reconstruction of a Judicial System: The United Nations
    Missions in Kosovo and East Timor*, 95 AM. J. INT'L L. 46, 8–49 (2001).
[137] *See* Speech by NATO Secretary-General Lord Robertson, *International Security and Law
    Enforcement – A Look Ahead*, June 19, 2001, *available at* http://www.nato.int/docu/speech/
    2001/s010619a.htm.
[138] Michael J. Dziedzic and Andrew Bair, *Bosnia and the International Police Task Force*, in
    POLICING THE NEW WORLD DISORDER, *supra* note 1, at 253, 260.
[139] Id.

out large-scale arrests with no clear legal authority by troops from multiple states using widely varying procedures and doing so in the absence of functioning courts and in violation of international standards sends a message of arbitrary rule that threatens to undermine the rule of law norms interveners hope to promote.

The experience of interveners in the immediate aftermath of the Kosovo intervention illustrates the problem. Confronted with the complete collapse of the preconflict judicial system and the rapid spread of organized crime, interveners scrambled to restore minimum public order. Because the UN needed months to deploy civilian police and administrators, KFOR of necessity took the lead initially on security. Immediately after deploying to Kosovo, KFOR began to arrest dozens of individuals. KFOR detained those caught in the act of committing serious crimes even while releasing most suspects with only a warning. In two weeks, KFOR was holding over 200 detainees in makeshift NATO and UN jails,[140] with no functioning courts in which to try them or adequate prisons in which to hold them. Because KFOR forces came from multiple countries, the policing and arrests were not done "according to a uniform standard."[141] Moreover, by holding suspects indefinitely and in many cases without charge, KFOR ran afoul of the human rights prohibition on prolonged, arbitrary detention. Thus, KFOR at the outset undercut its own rule of law message. But the alternative, releasing violent offenders, would have undercut rule of law efforts even more.

Many of the problems encountered by UNMIK at the outset of its administration of Kosovo might have been prevented or at least minimized by better advance preparation. In December 2000, Bernard Kouchner, the highest-ranking UN official in Kosovo at the time, declared that the "lesson to be learned from Kosovo" is that "peacekeeping missions need a judicial or law-and-order 'kit' made up of trained police officers, judges and prosecutors, plus a set of draconian security laws or regulations that are available on their arrival. This is the only way to stop criminal behavior from flourishing in a postwar vacuum of authority."[142] Kouchner's call for a law-and-order kit parallels other proposals for creation of law-and-order teams available for rapid deployment to conflict zones.[143] These proposals make considerable

---

[140] *See* Strohmeyer, *supra* note 136, at 49.

[141] Wendy S. Betts, Scott N. Carlson, Gregory Gisvold, *The Post-Conflict Transitional Administration of Kosovo and the Lessons Learned in Efforts to Establish a Judiciary and Rule of Law*, 22 MICH. J. INT'L L. 371, 374 (2001).

[142] R. Jeffrey Smith, *Kosovo Still Seethes as UN Official Nears Exit*, THE WASHINGTON POST, December 18, 2000, at A20.

[143] For example, the "Winning the Peace Act of 2003," legislation introduced in the U.S. Congress based on the report of the bipartisan Commission on Post-Conflict Reconstruction, calls for the United States to "present to the North Atlantic Council a proposal to establish within the North Atlantic Treaty Organization an Integrated Security Support Component to train and equip selected units within the North Atlantic Treaty Organization to execute security tasks in countries or regions that require reconstruction services." H.R. 2616, 108th

sense, and the expense of maintaining such teams would likely fall far short of the costs incurred by missions that must jump-start security from scratch. Nonetheless, governments have exhibited little interest in developing and maintaining rapid deployment legal teams. But more limited steps in this direction might prove feasible. Oakley and Dziedzic, for example, argue that "[t]he standby force concept currently used to assemble military troop contributions for peace operations should be adapted for use in CIVPOL mobilization" and that similar standby arrangements, or rosters of potentially available experts, could be developed for judicial and other needed legal personnel.[144] Implementing such proposals might help interveners avoid or surmount the initial legal vacuum created by the collapse of local security institutions.

Historically, interveners have been reluctant to shoulder the burden of ensuring domestic security for any extended period of time. Policing duties are dangerous and complex, and international civilian police, which must often be pulled from their domestic responsibilities, are in short supply.[145] Moreover, assuming security functions risks drawing interveners ever more deeply into the internal politics, and conflicts, of the affected state. Accordingly, "[o]nly in exceptional, emergency situations will states be convinced that is in their interest to submit their own domestic order to further pressure in order to take on the burdens of the internal order of another state."[146]

Until recently, most peace operations confined international policing efforts to monitoring, advising, and training local police, with particular attention to human rights practices.[147] But growing demands for more effective responses to internal disorder, and growing recognition that the failure to establish effective indigenous security institutions jeopardizes the entire intervention effort, led inexorably to expanding international involvement in security matters. These efforts culminated with the decisions of the interveners in Kosovo and East Timor to assume full responsibility for providing security in the short term and for establishing effective indigenous security forces.

But the trend toward greater assumption of security responsibilities may already have peaked. In Kosovo and East Timor, UN missions were given full executive policing authority; unlike most earlier missions, international

Cong., 1st Sess., June 26, 2003. In a similar vein, Presidential Decision Directive 71 (2000) calls for creation of a U.S. rapid deployment force of 500 to 2000 civilian police.

[144] Oakley & Dziedzic, *supra* note 17, at 513.

[145] Renata Dwan, *Introduction*, in EXECUTIVE POLICE (Renata Dwan, ed., 2002) at 1, 2.

[146] Id.

[147] Id., at 3 ("By 1995 these tasks were encapsulated by the DPKO in the 'SMART' concept – Supporting human rights; Monitoring the performance of the local enforcement authority; Advising the local police on best practices; Reporting on situations and incidents; and Training local enforcement in best practice for policing and human rights.").

police officers could make arrests and enforce the law. But "enthusiasm for this approach cooled rapidly" along with nation-building ambitions generally and "no full-scale executive authority operations have been authorized since."[148] Much depends on the problems interveners confront and their perceived national interests. Both Kosovo and East Timor are small territories with small populations, and large majorities of those populations welcomed the interveners as liberators, rendering international executive policing feasible at a reasonable cost.[149] Moreover, in Kosovo, NATO wanted to justify its intervention and stabilize the Balkans.[150] In East Timor, the UN and its members felt pressure to act stemming in part from the UN's long involvement with East Timor and its inability to avert predictable violence there. But other cases present a quite different balance of interests. In Afghanistan, for example, the United States and many of its allies resisted broad stabilization efforts because of the difficulties presented by the country's size, "legendary xenophobia," and many well-armed and potentially hostile factions, as well as the U.S. desire to avoid tying down large numbers of troops in the opening phase of the larger war on terror.[151]

Although international military and civilian police must of necessity often initially fill the security void in post-conflict societies, they are a poor substitute for an effective indigenous police force. Unlike interveners, indigenous police know local languages, customs, and laws. They can speak directly to the local populace without relying on interpreters, "who are not always perceived as neutral by the population."[152] They live in the community and know the people they are asked to police "down to the neighborhood and gang level."[153] Moreover, interveners will eventually leave, and it will then be up to indigenous police to provide security fairly and effectively. As the post-conflict environment stabilizes, and as efforts to establish and reform local police forces bear fruit, security responsibilities can be progressively turned over to local actors. This not only reduces the personal risks run by international forces, but it also minimizes the danger that interveners will be seen as occupiers.

The speed with which local police can assume security responsibilities varies considerably. It depends on the extent to which local security institutions have decayed, the resources interveners are prepared to commit to

---

[148] Anja Kaspersen, Espen Barth Eide, & Annika Hansen, *International Policing and the Rule of Law in Transitions from War to Peace*, Norwegian Institute of International Affairs Working Paper No. 4, October, 2004, at 11, *available at* http://pbpu.unlb.org/pbpu/library/International%20Policing.pdf.

[149] Dwan, *supra* note 145, at 5.

[150] Id.

[151] *See* Dobbins et al., *supra* note 9, at 133.

[152] Schmidl, *supra* note 1, at 24.

[153] Lynn Thomas & Steve Spataro, *Peacekeeping and Police in Somalia*, in POLICING THE NEW WORLD DISORDER, *supra* note 1, at 175, 211.

providing security and to rebuilding domestic security capabilities, and the nature of local attitudes toward indigenous police.

Increasingly, however, interveners and domestic reformers alike have come to realize that long-term security requires not only effective indigenous police but also fair and functioning domestic justice systems. Effective security can only be provided when police, courts, and prisons all function together as elements of an integrated justice system. If police arrest suspects, they need functioning courts for the conduct of prosecutions and functioning prisons for the incarceration of those convicted. The failure of any one component of the justice system necessarily jeopardizes the work of the others. Even the best designed and resourced efforts at rebuilding indigenous justice institutions can falter, moreover, in the absence of broader systemic reform. In the next chapter, we explore the critical and difficult task of rebuilding justice systems in the wake of military intervention

CONCLUSION

Reestablishment of a secure environment constitutes an essential first step on the road to reconfiguring the political institutions of a state and building the rule of law after military intervention. Interveners must separate and if possible disarm previously warring factions, control public violence, and start the process of turning over security to indigenous forces. In thinking about post-conflict security, interveners should consider the following points:

- Security efforts cannot succeed in a vacuum. Providing physical security is a necessary component of effective and accountable governance, but progress in security will not prove durable unless it is accompanied by progress in political and economic reconstruction. This means that security must be seen as part of a larger state-building enterprise.
- Establishing a secure environment in the immediate aftermath of military intervention should be a primary objective. The window of opportunity closes quickly, sometimes in a matter of weeks.
- To establish security quickly, interveners need to commit the necessary resources and deploy the right force mix at the outset. This means enhancing existing capabilities, long in advance of the next major military intervention. Prospective interveners should step up efforts to train individual soldiers in doctrine and tactics associated with post-conflict security efforts and train, equip, and deploy additional constabulary forces. In addition, long-standing calls for the establishment of effective standby arrangements for fast deployment of international civilian police should finally be heeded.

- Interveners must be prepared to confront spoilers proactively and in ways that support implementation of the overall political blueprint. Dealing with spoilers requires, among other things, greater commitment and resources for effective DDR programs and a willingness to use force as well as economic incentives to compel compliance.
- Interveners must recognize that police, courts, and prisons are part of a system and that no component of the system can function effectively unless the others are also functioning well. Accordingly, progress in one area must be matched by progress in the other two, as we discuss more fully in Chapter 6.
- Finally, interveners must work closely with local actors to adapt western security models to local conditions and to develop effective and respected indigenous security institutions. Security institutions that lack popular legitimacy will not survive the departure of the interveners that put such institutions in place.

CHAPTER SIX

The Challenge of Justice System Reform

As we argued in earlier chapters, building the rule of law requires not only basic security and functioning institutions but also a strong degree of public support and confidence. People need to know that they can resolve disputes without resorting to violence, that the law will protect them from abusive government officials and predatory nonstate actors alike, and that their fundamental rights will be secure. But for people to have good reason for confidence in the rule of law as a cultural matter, we also emphasized the need for laws and law-making processes that enjoy legitimacy, for legal institutions that function fairly, and for a government that is prepared to be bound by law. Strengthening the rule of law, in short, is both a practical project of institution-building and a cultural project of shaping attitudes and commitments.

This chapter examines one piece of this mosaic: building fair, effective justice systems in the wake of military interventions. Beyond the immediate task of establishing security, longer-term efforts to strengthen a country's justice system – including its courts, police, and prisons – are a vital part of building the rule of law after intervention. In countries as diverse as Afghanistan, Iraq, East Timor, Kosovo, Bosnia, Haiti, and Sierra Leone, among others, interveners have worked with local leaders to recruit and train police, appoint and train judges, build and furnish courthouses, and improve often deplorable prison conditions. These efforts are all the more daunting because in so many instances these institutions not only were decimated by conflict, but they also functioned poorly for years and were widely viewed by the population as tools of oppression and corrupt rule rather than of justice.

Of the many issues covered in this book, those in this chapter may be most familiar to readers with prior experience in rule of law programs. For many programs, courts, police, and prisons are the bread and butter of rule of law promotion. Yet as important as functioning justice institutions are, interveners sometimes focus on institution-building in a far too narrow way. Post-conflict rule of law assistance typically has concentrated mainly on formal institutions, political elites, and urban areas, paying insufficient attention to the perceptions of ordinary people or to ways of nurturing a social and political environment in which justice institutions can grow and thrive. We call this "institutional insularity." Rule of law assistance is also often highly segmented. Different experts, government agencies, and nongovernmental organizations (NGOs) naturally tend to concentrate on the components of justice systems within their core competencies, such as police or courts. But developing a reasonably functioning justice system requires astute attention to how the various components relate to one another and to the larger political system and culture in which they are embedded. If reformers miss these larger links and interactions, their reform effort as a whole will be a good deal less than the sum of its parts.

The risks posed by the twin problems of institutional insularity and segmentation manifest themselves in a variety of ways. The first risk is that reforms will be piecemeal and consequently have little enduring impact. Efforts to build a credible community-based police system to enforce the law, for example, will be undermined if courts are dysfunctional or largely controlled by local power-holders who use the courts to perpetuate their own interests, or if there are no decent prisons to detain those accused and convicted of crimes.

A second risk is the possibility of a continuing deficit in public support. Standard assistance to improve courts, for instance – to train judges, to refurbish courthouses, to provide legal materials and administrative support – may be squandered if public distrust of judicial independence remains deeply rooted or courts are available only to those with resources in urban areas. A broader array of programs and forms of assistance will be needed to nurture credible and accountable legal institutions, to ensure greater access to them, and to build public confidence that grievances can be fairly resolved through these institutions.

A third risk concerns the vulnerability of justice institutions to predatory politics. Unless interveners understand how these institutions function within the larger political system, the institutions may simply end up providing political elites with an effective apparatus for manipulating and perpetrating injustices against marginalized segments of society. If interveners focus solely on building up state institutions such as courts and police, for example – particularly in the absence of meaningful governance reform or accountability mechanisms – they may inadvertently give self-interested power-holders more effective institutional tools to advance their own agendas rather than creating genuine rule of law.

The intervention in Haiti in the mid-1990s illustrates all three of these hazards, as we elaborate in this chapter. Enormous progress was made early on in vetting and training the Haitian National Police during the UN mission following Aristide's return to power. But other parts of the justice system did not receive the same degree of assistance or pressure for reform. Corrupt judges could be bribed to release suspects, and bad governance generally undermined the larger political system in which police operated. Little was done, moreover, to address the widespread suspicion among ordinary people that law is a vehicle of control and repression rather than of justice. In the end, international reform efforts were undermined by Aristide's own political agenda, revealing the risks of strengthening state institutions that can be manipulated and misused by the powerful before building a more accountable political system more generally.

As the experience in Haiti attests, building and sustaining justice systems in the wake of military interventions is extraordinarily difficult. To be sure, each post-conflict situation presents unique obstacles and opportunities. Because of these unique cultural and political circumstances, applying "lessons learned" or common approaches from one situation to another may be ineffectual or even counterproductive. But recent experience also suggests some recurring challenges and potentially useful practices, as well as common traps to avoid, all of which we explore here. These lessons from experience are both conceptual and practical.

In this chapter we focus on the multifaceted challenges of strengthening justice systems in the aftermath of military intervention. We highlight and explore three main capacities that we take to be essential to a functioning justice system – capacities for law-making, law enforcement, and adjudication – and we stress the importance of building these capacities on solid foundations. We also highlight the importance of building an effective capacity for legal education (broadly construed), an issue we take up again in Chapter 8. Within this framework, and using examples from different countries, we examine specific challenges that arise, as well as pitfalls to avoid, in reforming laws and in improving police, prisons, and courts. Throughout the analysis, we attend to the uniqueness of each post-conflict situation as well as to the culture and history of the country involved, but we also make a special effort to bring out the common problems, themes, and lessons that emerge in examining recent efforts to build justice systems after intervention. Finally, we stress the need to understand the role that informal, traditional dispute resolution mechanisms play in some post-conflict societies, a theme that we explore more fully in Chapter 8.

Before presenting our analysis of law-making, enforcement, and adjudicative capacities and how to build and strengthen them, it will be helpful to expand our earlier discussion (see Chapter 3) of a *synergistic approach* to promoting the rule of law, and to bring it to bear specifically on matters of justice system reform – a centrally important element in advancing the rule of law.

I. THE "SYNERGISTIC" APPROACH TO JUSTICE SYSTEM REFORM

Substantively, the synergistic approach is ends-based and strategic, adaptive and dynamic, and systemic. Methodologically, this approach demands that we look at justice institutions holistically, that we understand how the different institutions relate to each other and to the larger culture and political system, and that, in pursuing reform on the ground, we seek to strengthen institutional capacities in a balanced and mutually reinforcing way. The immediate task, then – as a preliminary to discussing the particulars of law-making, enforcement, and adjudication – is to determine what these different elements of the synergistic approach entail in the specific context of justice system reform.

A. An Ends-Based, Strategic Approach

One of the three elements of the synergistic approach is that the building and strengthening of justice systems needs to be *ends-based and strategic*. This approach focuses on the ultimate goals of building an effective justice system and resists an overly narrow concentration on institutions alone. Thus, we find much value in Rachel Kleinfeld's argument for an explicitly ends-based understanding of the rule of law.[1] She argues that there are five fundamental and relatively well-established goals, or ends, that the rule of law should serve in society: (1) law and order, (2) a government bound by law, (3) equality before the law, (4) predictable and efficient justice, and (5) protection of human rights.[2] Although ultimately and ideally, these goals should be mutually reinforcing in developed legal systems, Kleinfeld emphasizes that in transitional societies clear tensions may exist between them. These goals are desired aims of the rule of law generally and of justice systems in particular. And in the context of our discussion of post-conflict societies, they can serve as overarching goals for justice system reform.

In the aftermath of violent conflict, securing basic *law and order* is certainly a vital goal both immediately and in the longer term. Building a functioning justice system that can help support a stable social order – permitting people to plan and live their lives without constant fear of predation by private actors or state officials – is fundamental to achieving basic law and order. In a sense, it makes all other things possible. But maintaining law and order, though urgent and critically important in post-conflict societies, is not the only priority.

Another fundamental objective in strengthening justice systems is the overarching goal of a *government bound by law*. A government prepared to

---

[1] Rachel Kleinfeld, *Competing Definitions of the Rule of Law,* in PROMOTING THE RULE OF LAW ABROAD: IN SEARCH OF KNOWLEDGE (Thomas Carothers, ed., 2006), at 31.

[2] Id., at 34–47.

enforce the law against its own leaders – and officials prepared to abide by the law rather than simply using their power to seek preferential treatment for themselves and their allies – is a fundamental part of a stable rule of law and guards against arbitrary and capricious rule. In strengthening courts, police, and other justice institutions, the goal of government bound by law must be a clear aim of reform efforts and will require building account-ability and oversight mechanisms as justice institutions are strengthened. If not, interveners may inadvertently enable government officials to use their authority (and newly built legal institutions) to aggrandize themselves rather than serve the public interest.

A key goal that has both formal and substantive dimensions is *equality before the law*. The idea that the law should be blind – that one should be treated equally whether one is a political leader or an ordinary citizen, whether one is rich or poor – is part of a long-standing understanding of what the rule of law means. Beyond formal notions of equality, the goal of "equal protection of the law" is an important, substantive, though often culturally contentious one. We view equal protection of the law as one of the fundamental goals that justice systems should aim to achieve: regardless of one's ethnic group, minority status, or gender, individuals should be treated fairly and consistently with fundamental human rights.

Another end of the rule of law is what Kleinfeld refers to as *predictable, efficient justice*.[3] By this she, like many other commentators, primarily means principled and predictable decisions by courts and other components of the justice system that enable people to plan their affairs and to resolve disputes nonviolently with confidence and consistency. We would add another ele-ment to this, however: beyond simply predictable and efficient court rulings and enforcement of the law, the basic substantive rules being enforced must themselves be widely viewed as fair and legitimate by the population if they are to command public support.

A final goal of the rule of law generally – and of justice systems in par-ticular – is the *protection of universally recognized human rights*. Although specific details of this goal may be contested among different groups and cultures, basic protection of at least the most fundamental human rights is essential to any justice system that we would recognize as respecting the rule of law. These rights include, among others, the right of anyone "accused of a crime . . . to a fair, prompt hearing and [to be] presumed innocent until proved guilty."[4] Fundamental human rights also include the prohibition against torture, basic rights of due process, and the right to freedom of opinion and belief.[5]

---

[3] Id., at 42–44.

[4] Thomas Carothers, *The Rule of Law Revival*, 77 FOREIGN AFFAIRS (1998), at 96.

[5] *See International Covenant on Civil and Political Rights* and *Convention against Torture and Other Cruel, Inhuman or Degrading Treatment or Punishment, available at* http://www. ohchr.org/english/law/index.htm.

In particular post-conflict situations, it may prove challenging indeed to forge agreement on strategic, overarching rule of law goals such as those discussed above. Nevertheless, keeping a clear focus on such ultimate goals is crucial in designing effective programs to strengthen justice systems, whether in post-conflict settings or more generally. Reformers, at the same time, need to be honest about the tensions that may exist, at least in the near term, between some of their objectives, recognizing that, particularly in post-conflict settings with limited resources and fragile stability, they may not be able to advance each goal equally at the same pace.

B. An Adaptive, Dynamic Process with a Systemic Focus

The second element of the synergistic approach is the recognition that justice system reform is *adaptive and dynamic*. Justice institutions cannot be imposed or imported wholesale; to be sustainable they must be built on existing cultural foundations and they must enjoy public legitimacy. Adaptive reform also recognizes that building support for the rule of law is a long-term, dynamic process that often requires transforming attitudes of officials and power-holders and ordinary people alike, nurturing grassroots demand for sustainable reform, and providing better access to justice for disadvantaged groups. Those engaged in building justice systems also need to understand both the limitations and the appeal of customary systems of dispute resolution and how they might be adapted and moved in constructive directions.

The third element is that the process of improving justice institutions needs to be *systemic in focus*. Understanding how justice institutions interconnect and operate *as a system* is crucial to designing effective and balanced programs for reform. Reformers need to work toward a balanced development of the parts of a functioning legal system, including: laws and law-making processes that enjoy legitimacy among the people and are responsive to their needs; functioning courts, police, and prisons that adhere to basic human rights standards; effective education; and outreach to the people. The priorities in specific post-conflict situations will depend on the areas of greatest need, with the overall aim of balanced and mutually reinforcing improvements.

Taking a step back from the immediate focus on justice system reform per se, it would be a serious mistake to forget that justice institutions are embedded and function within a larger political system. Building up state institutions without corresponding governance reforms or adequate accountability mechanisms may simply give governmental elites more effective means to advance their own interests at the expense of the general public. An overly technical focus on reforming institutions – without sufficient understanding of the political stakes and interests of officials or adequate attention to the needs and perceptions of ordinary citizens – will undermine the prospects for achieving the desired objectives.

In short, the problem with many programs for promoting the rule of law is not that they focus on institutions per se. Rather, the problem is an overly narrow and insular focus on building justice institutions, with insufficient attention to connections between them or to the cultural and political conditions necessary for those institutions to effectively serve the goals of the rule of law.

But what, concretely, does this mean for specific initiatives to strengthen justice systems in post-conflict situations, as part of larger efforts to build the rule of law?

C. Getting Concrete: Building Core Capacities on Solid Foundations

Practitioners and scholars often refer to the "justice triad" of police, courts, and prisons – sometimes called the public "security triad" – as critical components of a functioning criminal justice system. Understandably, when confronted with urgent problems of crime and security, interveners generally place priority on criminal justice reform and on reestablishing law and order. But, as they work to strengthen the basic institutional building blocks of a functioning justice system, reformers must not neglect other goals, such as protection of fundamental human rights and a government bound by law, as they design assistance programs. Furthermore, familiar conceptual lenses can be restricting; and we believe it is useful to rethink the now-familiar "justice triad" concept in light of additional, overarching goals of promoting the rule of law. The "justice triad" focus is too narrow for longer-term, more comprehensive efforts to strengthen justice systems after conflict.

We find it helpful to think of a broader set of *critical, interrelated capacities* that are needed in an effective justice system: a law-making capacity, law enforcement capacity, adjudicatory capacity, and legal education capacity. Reframing the "triad" in broader functional terms helps to highlight the wider web of supporting institutions and capabilities that are needed to build and sustain an effective justice system.

The first leg of a functioning legal system – an effective, legitimate capacity to make laws – is fundamental, yet it sometimes is shortchanged in post-conflict assistance. Interveners focus, of course, on revising existing substantive laws in post-conflict societies, but these new or revised laws are sometimes imposed from on high or adopted by executive decree; strengthening *a sustainable indigenous capacity for effective law-making* often is not given the attention it requires. Any fully functioning legal system requires not only laws that enjoy legitimacy and address urgent public needs, but also fair and inclusive domestic procedures for making and revising laws.

Effective law enforcement is also critical, but it depends on more than just the police. It depends also on capable prosecutors and defense attorneys, decent prisons, functioning courts, and public support, cooperation, and confidence. An effective adjudicatory capacity requires not only judges and courthouses but also lawyers and administrative support. It requires, moreover, a cultural and political context in which judges are able to decide cases relatively free from political intimidation and external control.

Legal education, an issue discussed further in Chapter 8, is too often a missing element in post-conflict rule of law assistance.[6] Pressured to show early progress, donors tend to focus more attention on short-term training programs of various kinds. Yet, in the long term, effective indigenous legal education is critical to training a new generation of lawyers, judges, prosecutors, and other legal professionals, and it should be the focus of more systematic assistance from the start. Also critical is educating the public about their rights in a developing legal system.

In short, reframing the "justice triad" more broadly in functional terms underscores the vital point that supporting institutions and capacities are needed to develop and sustain an effective justice system – and that law and order is only one of many key goals.

Even so, efforts to build effective law-making, law enforcement, adjudicatory, and educational capacity will not serve the deeper goals of the rule of law unless they rest on solid foundations. Just as a house built on sand will not be stable or enduring, so too a justice system requires solid underpinnings:

Legitimacy. Does the local population view the laws and the developing institutions as legitimate and responsive to their needs and concerns? In societies that have been wracked by conflict, law and order often have completely broken down, and institutions are devastated or minimally functional. A deep and pervasive popular skepticism about government institutions may be widespread – and for good reason. Police and courts may be permeated by political influence and corruption. Local methods of dispute resolution, rooted in customary practices and traditional authorities, may provide some stability but may not extend fair treatment to vulnerable segments of the population, such as women and minorities. As new institutions to provide law and order are developed, public concerns about the legitimacy of these institutions need to be a major focus, and their relationship to traditional practices carefully considered. Outreach and education programs geared to the larger population and responsive to their needs and concerns should complement training of police, judges, and other legal professionals, as we elaborate in Chapter 8. Such programs should be integrated into overarching strategic plans for strengthening justice institutions.

---

[6] *See* Erik G. Jensen, *The Rule of Law and Judicial Reform: The Political Economy of Diverse Institutional Patterns and Reformers' Responses*, in BEYOND COMMON KNOWLEDGE: EMPIRICAL APPROACHES TO THE RULE OF LAW (Erik G. Jensen & Thomas C. Heller, eds., 2003), at 359–360.

Accountability. Are the developing justice institutions – and the actors within them, such as police, judges, executive officials, law-makers – accountable under the law? Justice institutions should be developed not for their own sake, nor to provide opportunities for self-aggrandizement and perks to office holders, but rather to promote a more just and stable society in which governmental officials and private actors alike are accountable under the law. All too often, in societies marked by long-standing conflict and instability, governmental positions are viewed by many office-seekers as opportunities to secure personal benefits rather than to serve the public good. Low pay and desperate conditions can tempt even well-meaning individuals into a wide range of corrupt practices. As institutions are developed, programs to monitor and promote accountability need to be built in tandem in order to improve the prospects for a government bound by law and to reduce the chances of institutional positions being used to aggrandize office holders at the expense of vulnerable and less advantaged members of the population.

Human Rights. Are reforms helping to advance fundamental human rights and justice within society? By this we mean two things in particular. First, do the institutions and officials within them abide by basic human rights standards? For instance, have police been trained regarding fundamental human rights, and are mechanisms in place to monitor their behavior and enable aggrieved citizens to file complaints? Do judges follow civil and criminal procedures that respect fundamental human rights? Do prisons observe fundamental standards of human rights, such as the prohibition against torture and other cruel, inhuman or degrading treatment, as well as the separation of incarcerated men and women? Even in the face of extremely limited resources, basic protections must be in place, and training and monitoring programs established. Second, do the reforms underway help, more broadly, to promote fundamental human rights and justice within society? Are the rights of women and minorities being advanced, not only through formal justice institutions but also through other initiatives, such as programs to improve access to justice and efforts to move customary law practices in constructive directions? As Rama Mani cautions, too often international assistance programs "and their sponsors are largely silent as to whether the rule of law is designed to provide citizens with their right to justice and to safeguard their dignity, or merely to provide order in society."[7]

Sustainability. Are the developing justice institutions sustainable once interveners leave? Are supporting programs and national capacities being developed (for example, necessary legal professionals and civil society

---

[7] Rama Mani, BEYOND RETRIBUTION: SEEKING JUSTICE IN THE SHADOWS OF WAR (2002), at 76. She criticizes the "programmatic minimalism" of rule of law assistance that concentrates "on the institutions and mechanics, the form and structure, of the rule of law, while evading the substantive content – the *ethos* of that rule of law." Id.

organizations), and is a public demand for credible justice institutions being nurtured? Justice institutions are embedded in a larger social and political system, and sustainable reforms depend on the commitment of local leaders and ordinary people alike, on local involvement in decision-making, and on strengthening cultural foundations for the rule of law. (Chapters 8 and 9 take up these themes in detail.)

None of this is easy. Strengthening the rule of law is hard enough in countries that have not been wracked by armed conflict. In post-conflict situations that have triggered international military intervention, the challenges are usually even greater. Conflict may have devastated institutions, destroyed infrastructure, and led skilled professionals to flee the country, and, after a legacy of repression, citizens may be deeply distrustful of legal institutions.

Some concrete examples are telling. In East Timor, during the years of Indonesian occupation, local distrust of the police, courts, and prisons was pervasive, and the East Timorese frequently turned to alternative locally based mechanisms to resolve disputes.[8] Later, during the militia-led violence following East Timor's referendum for independence from Indonesia, the "preexisting judicial infrastructure ... was virtually destroyed."[9] In a scorched-earth campaign led by forces opposed to independence, court buildings, equipment, records, law books, case files, and furniture were all burned or stolen. Fearing retaliation as perceived Indonesian government sympathizers, pre-intervention judges, lawyers, prosecutors, and court staff all fled. As a result, fewer than ten lawyers remained.[10] Starting virtually from scratch – literally "rising from the ashes," a new justice system had to be created.[11]

The circumstances in Kosovo were also daunting. Systematic pre-intervention discrimination precluded all but a handful of Kosovar Albanians from serving as judges, lawyers, court administrators, or police. As a result, "only 30 out of 756 judges and prosecutors were Kosovar Albanian."[12] When NATO forced Serb military and paramilitary forces out of Kosovo, virtually all the qualified and trained judicial and police personnel left with them. Moreover, many court buildings as well as "equipment, legal texts, and other materials necessary for an operating legal system had been destroyed."[13]

[8] Ronald A. West, *Lawyers, Guns, and Money: Justice and Security Reform in East Timor*, in CONSTRUCTING JUSTICE AND SECURITY AFTER WAR (Charles T. Call, ed., 2006), at 329–330.

[9] Hansjorg Strohmeyer, *Collapse and Reconstruction of a Judicial System: The United Nations Missions in Kosovo and East Timor*, 95 AM. J. INT'L L. 46, 50 (2001).

[10] Id.

[11] Suzannah Linton, *Rising from the Ashes: The Creation of a Viable Criminal Justice System in East Timor*, 25 MELB. U. L. REV. 122 (2001).

[12] Strohmeyer, *Collapse and Reconstruction of a Judicial System, supra* note 9, at 50.

[13] Wendy S. Betts, Scott N. Carlson, & Gregory Gisvold, *The Post-Conflict Transitional Administration of Kosovo and the Lessons Learned in Efforts to Establish a Judiciary and Rule of Law*, 22 MICH. J. INT'L L. 371, 377 (2001).

In Afghanistan, it was much the same story. The Ministry of Justice had few trained staff and little electricity or heat. Those willing to apply the law did not know what law to apply, because "[i]n its zeal to establish a fundamentalist Islamic state, the Taliban had burned all the law books . . . as well as copies of the Official Gazette, the record of enacted laws."[14] Over two decades of armed conflict had devastated the justice system, with many Afghans relying instead on local *shuras* and *jirgas* (or councils of elders) to resolve disputes.[15] Public fear and distrust of Taliban-era security forces was deep and pervasive.

The unique combination of challenges that interveners and local leaders confront in building justice systems after conflict underscores the importance of taking a broad, synergistic approach to reform – an approach rooted in a deep understanding of the particular cultural and political context.

II. UNDERSTANDING THE ENVIRONMENT: THE IMPORTANCE OF STRATEGIC ASSESSMENT

Knowledge and understanding of local culture, history, and politics is essential to designing effective reforms. Despite frequent and fair criticism of a "one size fits all" approach to rule of law reform, interveners tend to fall back on a basic template of reforms that may not be optimal for the unique political and cultural terrain in a given country.[16] No matter how devastated by conflict, every society generally has its own dispute-resolution mechanisms and practices and distinctive cultural and institutional resources for the rule of law. By the same token, however, the extent to which existing legal institutions function or enjoy any degree of public support will vary substantially in different countries. It is also true that public attitudes toward intervening states will differ and may profoundly affect subsequent outside efforts to build justice systems. Consequently, "transplanting" lessons and approaches from one context to another, without sufficient cultural and historical knowledge, can be ineffective at best or deeply counterproductive.

On the positive side, however, a *window of opportunity* for significant change frequently exists after intervention.[17] Although this window closes

---

[14] *See* Kimberly Bayley, *On Bringing Law to Damaged Lands*, 13 BUS. L. TODAY, 29 (2004).

[15] Amnesty International, *Afghanistan: Re-establishing the Rule of Law,* August 14, 2003, at 48–49.

[16] Mani, BEYOND RETRIBUTION, *supra* note 7, at 72.

[17] Charles T. Call, *Introduction: What We Know and Don't Know about Post-Conflict Justice and Security Reform*, in CONSTRUCTING JUSTICE AND SECURITY AFTER WAR, *supra* note 8, at 10–11; Charles T. Call, *War Transitions and the New Civilian Security in Latin America*, 35 COMP. POL. 1 (2002), at 7, 13; and Seth G. Jones, Jeremy M. Wilson, Andrew Rathmell, & K. Jack Riley, ESTABLISHING LAW AND ORDER AFTER CONFLICT (2005), at xi (referring to "golden hour").

quickly, the opportunity to significantly alter the status quo, to provide new opportunities for previously disadvantaged and disempowered groups (such as women and minorities), and to reform institutions generally exists in a more dramatic way in the wake of an international military intervention than in more traditional reform programs in countries that have not experienced such intervention. A rapid infusion of international resources and organizations can assist opportunities for change and social transformation, although they may also work at cross-purposes with competing agendas. The opportunity for change provides interveners and local leaders with an occasion to consider broad strategic objectives rather than just incremental tinkering. This puts a considerable premium on timely and effective strategic assessment – in effect, to keep the "window" open long enough for well-designed reforms to begin. But if an early strategic assessment of a country's justice system is a vital starting point for planning effective reforms, how should this be done?

A thorough strategic assessment by a diverse team of personnel, asking broad strategic questions, is critical to yield useful information for identifying needs and priorities. Anthropologists and country experts – as well as individuals with functional expertise in rule of law assistance – should participate in the effort. Including local participation and perspectives is also critical to gaining a comprehensive understanding of the unique needs and resources of the country at issue and to designing reforms that are more likely to enjoy local support and buy-in. Assessment is clearly an area where the international community could do better.[18]

A comprehensive strategic assessment needs to address a series of interrelated issues, the most fundamental of which relates to the causes and consequences of the conflict – the *conflict legacy.* Without an understanding of such matters, no effort at justice system reform has any likelihood of succeeding. And yet the pressure of action often preempts thorough assessment. In its retrospective evaluation, Sierra Leone's Truth and Reconciliation Commission emphasized how poor governance and a breakdown in the rule of law contributed to that country's devastating conflict. The Commission's Report emphasized that "it was years of bad governance, endemic corruption and the denial of basic human rights that created the deplorable conditions that made conflict inevitable," that "[d]emocracy and the rule of law were dead" by the start of the conflict, and that only the "slightest spark" was required for "violence to be ignited."[19] Stressing that many of these causes of conflict have not yet been adequately addressed, the Commission recommended

---

[18] *See generally* Thomas Carothers, *The Problem of Knowledge,* in Promoting the Rule of Law Abroad, *supra* note 1, at 15; Shelby R. Quast, *Rule of Law in Post-Conflict Societies: What Is the Role of the International Community?,* 39 New Eng. L. Rev. 45, 48–49 (2004).

[19] Introduction, *Final Report of the Truth & Reconciliation Commission of Sierra Leone,* Vol. I, para. 11, *available at* http://www.trcsierraleone.org/drwebsite/publish/intro.shtml.

reforms to strengthen Sierra Leone's legal and political system, including "introduction of a new transparent regime in which citizens will have reasonable access to government information" such as what is "being spent on services and amenities" and in which "senior public officials disclose their financial interests."[20] Failure to appreciate such systemic problems may lead to forms of assistance that only superficially address the real needs in building the rule of law.[21]

In addition, the tangible and continuing consequences of long-standing conflict must be understood. The most outwardly visible sign of war damage may be decimated formal justice institutions. At a deeper level, however, the public may have little or no confidence in state institutions or officials; indeed, they may be widely discredited and viewed as part of the problem more than the solution to urgent needs. Thus, understanding what ordinary people view as urgent priorities is a critical part of a valuable strategic assessment. Common disputes – for example, over property or concerning domestic violence – may not be addressed at all or effectively. Yet they may be a major source of continuing conflict and grievance in society. Interveners and their domestic allies need to focus not only on the producers of law and on building institutions; they also need to focus on the consumers – the demand side, on ordinary people and the parts of the law that they come in contact with – and to identify the major substantive problems that developing justice institutions will need to address.

Even with a firm understanding of the origins of conflict, no plans for reform can succeed without a realistic, strategic assessment of existing local *resources* for the rule of law. Such an assessment will help to identify what resources – cultural, human, material, and, indeed, legal – are available and also how best to make use of them. Starting with the positives may help reformers think in new ways. What positive cultural resources and practices already exist for resolving disputes? What is available, functioning, and a potential foundation for moving in constructive directions? Are existing institutions abusive, however, and discriminatory toward vulnerable segments of the population? To the extent that formal justice institutions exist – including courts and police – a careful assessment of their relative condition and their strengths and weaknesses is essential. Moreover, an astute assessment of how

---

[20] Id., para. 12.

[21] Regarding Sierra Leone, astute practitioners and commentators emphasize that problems of abuse of power and lack of accountability continue, despite considerable funds spent on the "hardware" of justice system reform. Abdul Tejan Cole & Mohamed Gibril Sesay, *Traditional Justice Systems and the Rule of Law in Post-Conflict Sierra Leone*, prepared for the project The Role of Nonstate Justice Systems in Fostering the Rule of Law in Post-Conflict Societies, United States Institute of Peace, August 2005, at 25; International Crisis Group, *Sierra Leone: The State of Security and Governance*, September 2, 2003, at 21–22.

these various institutions interrelate can help subsequently in establishing reform priorities that maximize prospects for balanced progress and synergies. Interveners should also seek to understand the role and impact (both positive and negative) of informal or customary dispute resolution mechanisms – and their relationship, de jure or de facto, to formal justice institutions. In addition, available human resources for justice reform must be identified – not only personnel that could serve in strengthened institutions but also potential allies in sustaining reform, such as local NGOs and other supportive domestic actors.

The opposite side of the above question about available resources concerns resources that are lacking and that cannot be relied on in justice system reform. That is, the *obstacles and threats* to strengthening the rule of law must be identified and analyzed systematically. Human resource limitations – such as lack of trained legal personnel – and material resource limitations, such as lack of basic facilities or funds, must be catalogued. The more elusive issue for analysis will focus on political and self-interested threats to the process of rule of law reform. These threats must be clearly identified: whose interests are served by current arrangements? Who may have a stake in resisting or sabotaging reform? Can incentives for, and stakes in, reform be developed? As experienced practitioners will attest, developing effective human relationships with constructive domestic actors is often the critical ingredient in successful reforms.

Finally, and most difficult of all, a strategic assessment must identify *promising external interventions to promote and buttress reform* – including key priorities and also opportunities for synergies among different reform efforts. A good way to start this component of the assessment is to highlight the major substantive problems (such as disputes over property, and crime) that developing justice institutions will need to address, always keeping the ultimate goals of the rule of law (such as government bound by law, and human rights protection) firmly in mind. Then key capacities that need strengthening and reform (law-making, law enforcement, adjudication, and education) and acute institutional needs and priorities can be identified, recognizing that balanced reform and attention to interrelationships between institutions are critical. Also, strategic ways to reinforce and sustain reform should be identified, such as developing capacities among local NGOs and civil society organizations to monitor and scrutinize progress, and developing effective external scrutiny and monitoring.

As noted earlier, the pressure for taking immediate action may leave interveners with little apparent time or energy to put together a systematic, strategic assessment. Nevertheless, without one, and without a further understanding of the challenges, opportunities, and pitfalls of reforming particular justice institutions, interventions are all too likely to go awry and fall short of even modest sustainable goals.

We now turn to the hardest part of all: transforming good diagnosis into an effective remedy. In what follows we consider critical capacities – those for effective law-making, law enforcement, and adjudication – that need to be strengthened in order to build the rule of law based on synergistic principles. Though the result is a chapter of some length, we believe that addressing the three capacities together in a systematic way helps to highlight the interconnections that are crucial for successful justice system reform. The related capacity for legal education (broadly defined) is also critical; we address it here and take it up more fully in Chapter 8.

III. STRENGTHENING CRITICAL CAPACITIES IN LAW AND LAW-MAKING

As assessment challenges are overcome, reformers face a basic predicament in translating knowledge into action: one cannot really build the rule of law without there being some minimally acceptable law already in place. The question of "applicable law" is thus critically important in the initial phase of post-conflict intervention. Criminal law issues are particularly urgent. Substantive criminal law must be available to address common crimes, and procedural law governing the arrest, detention, and trial of suspects is needed in order to enforce the law effectively and fairly. After all, those charged with enforcing the law, and with adjudicating disputes, must know what law to apply, or insecurity may spiral and popular hopes for a better future may be undermined, as criminal activity becomes more embedded and difficult to address.

A. The Potential Role of Temporary Codes

Interveners will need law to apply from day one as they confront criminal activity, and this may entail use of temporary legal codes. The Australian forces that led the UN-authorized military intervention in East Timor in 1999, for instance, developed and applied an "interim criminal justice package" based on the Indonesian criminal law then in effect and "international legal standards."[22] They also adopted an ordinance on detention, which established a legal framework for handling various categories of detainees and provided for review of detention decisions by military legal officers.[23]

Temporary measures such as these may be necessary in addressing immediate intervention exigencies. In the absence of a clear understanding of applicable law and procedures, international civilian police may simply fall back

---

[22] Bruce M. Oswald, *Model Codes for Criminal Justice and Peace Operations: Some Legal Issues*, 9 J. CONFLICT & SEC. L. 253, 269–270 & note 75 (2004).

[23] Id. *See also* Michael J. Kelly, Timothy L. H. McCormack, Paul Muggleton, & Bruce M. Oswald, *Legal Aspects of Australia's Involvement in the International Force for East Timor*, 841 INT'L REV. RED CROSS 101–139 (2001).

on their own diverse home country's procedures, as occurred in both Kosovo and East Timor.[24] Moreover, crime can escalate in the face of delays in clarifying or developing applicable law. In light of these and other challenges, the UN's *Brahimi Report* urged the potential development of an "interim criminal code" to address basic substantive offenses and criminal procedure in transitional administrations "pending the re-establishment of local rule of law and local law enforcement capacity."[25] In some situations, the use of interim, so-called "skinny codes" of criminal law and procedure – codes that meet international standards and can be applied by trained international personnel on a temporary basis – may help to address immediate criminal law issues in the early phases of a multinational intervention.[26]

But working with national actors in a longer-term process of domestic "law reform" will be essential to address the many, varied substantive and procedural legal needs in particular post-conflict societies. The UN Secretary-General's 2004 Report on The Rule of Law and Transitional Justice in Conflict and Post-Conflict Societies correctly stresses the importance of supporting "domestic reform constituencies" and strengthening national capacity to "help fill the rule of law vacuum evident in so many post-conflict societies."[27]

B. Law Reform: Goals and Challenges

Protecting the basic rights of the population through substantive and procedural law is a fundamental goal of the rule of law. The law must be responsive to the needs of the population and must address the kinds of conflicts and crimes that threaten security in society. The law must also be clear and accessible to those who must enforce it, if it is to be a stable foundation for a government bound by law. Moreover, effective national law-making processes must be nurtured that are transparent and ultimately accountable to the people.

The capacity of international interveners to contribute to domestic legal reform will depend, in part, on the interveners' own authority or legal

---

[24] Colette Rausch, *The Assumption of Authority in Kosovo and East Timor: Legal and Practical Implications*, in EXECUTIVE POLICING: ENFORCING THE LAW IN PEACE OPERATIONS (Renata Dwan, ed., 2002), at 17–18; West, *Lawyers, Guns, and Money: Justice and Security Reform in East Timor, supra* note 8, at 336.

[25] *Report of the Panel on United Nations Peace Operations* (hereinafter *Brahimi Report*), UN Doc. A/55/305-S/2000/809, August 21, 2000, para. 83, *available at* http://www.un.org/peace/reports/peace_operations/.

[26] But more far-reaching use of temporary codes is a controversial issue. *See* Vivienne O'Connor & Colette Rausch, *A Tool Box to Tackle Law Reform Challenges in Post Conflict Countries: The Model Codes for Post Conflict Criminal Justice*, 10 INT'L PEACEKEEPING: THE YEARBOOK OF INT'L PEACE OPERATIONS (2006), at 9, 16–17 (discussing critiques of *Brahimi Report's* recommendations). *See also* Oswald, *Model Codes for Criminal Justice and Peace Operations, supra* note 22, at 258–264.

[27] *Report of the Secretary-General on the Rule of Law and Transitional Justice in Conflict and Post-Conflict Societies*, UN Doc. S/2004/616, August 23, 2004, Summary.

mandate.[28] At one end of the spectrum are "executive" missions, as in Kosovo and East Timor, where UN-authorized transitional administrations were empowered by the Security Council to administer justice, maintain law and order, and determine applicable law.[29] At the other end of the spectrum are more common "assistance" missions, as in Afghanistan, where the United Nations and other international actors provide assistance to national authorities, including rule of law assistance, under a UN umbrella.

Beyond the question of legal mandate, each post-conflict situation presents unique domestic challenges and needs in the domain of law and law reform. Careful attention to the particular cultural and legal traditions is the touchstone of any effective international effort to work with local leaders to evaluate existing laws and identify areas in need of reform, as we discuss more fully below.

Nevertheless, some distinctive challenges have recurred in numerous countries emerging from violent conflict, as scholar Vivienne O'Connor has discussed.[30]

- Accessing and identifying existing law in a clear and authoritative way can be exceedingly difficult. In East Timor, for example, law books, case files, and court records were burned, and "very few people had copies of the Indonesian Criminal Code in a language they understood, let alone the Indonesian Code of Criminal Procedure."[31] In Afghanistan, because "all existing significant collections of legal texts were destroyed," it took time for various organizations to collect "authenticated versions" of critical legal codes and distribute them.[32]
- Existing law may not enjoy widespread public legitimacy. Indeed, many citizens may view the law as an instrument of oppression. Kosovo's Albanian population, for instance, widely regarded the Yugoslavian law in effect after Belgrade revoked Kosovo's autonomy in 1989 as a vehicle of discrimination and repression.[33] Efforts at law reform have the greatest chance for success if they are seen as responsive to deeply felt public views concerning the law's legitimacy.

[28] *See* Oswald, *Model Codes for Criminal Justice and Peace Operations, supra* note 22, at 265–275 (discussing authority based on host country consent, Chapter VII authorization by the Security Council, and occupation law).

[29] *See* S.C. Res. 1244 (1999); S.C. Res. 1272 (1999); Rausch, *The Assumption of Authority in Kosovo and East Timor, supra* note 24.

[30] This discussion draws on the very thoughtful treatment by Vivienne O'Connor, *Traversing the Rocky Road of Law Reform in Conflict and Post Conflict States: Model Codes for Post Conflict Criminal Justice as a Tool of Assistance*, 16 CRIMINAL LAW FORUM 231 (2006).

[31] Linton, *Rising from the Ashes: The Creation of a Viable Criminal Justice System in East Timor, supra* note 11, at 140.

[32] Laurel Miller & Robert Perito, USIP Special Report 117, *Establishing the Rule of Law in Afghanistan,* March 2004, at 9.

[33] Strohmeyer, *Collapse and Reconstruction of a Judicial System, supra* note 9, at 58–59.

- Existing law may flagrantly violate basic standards of international human rights. Discrimination against women and minorities is especially common. Law in Afghanistan under the Taliban, for example, denied women basic, fundamental rights. In various post-conflict settings, provisions of criminal law and procedure may fail to protect the basic rights of criminal defendants.

- The law may be "outdated" and therefore "unresponsive to contemporary social realities."[34] The law may have critical gaps, for instance. It may not address crimes such as trafficking in persons or organized crime – crimes that may mushroom in post-conflict environments. The law may also, for example, be unclear, unduly complex, or in need of updating. In Sierra Leone, for instance, many of the laws based originally on British law have not been updated for decades or modernized to take account of advancements in women's rights.

Such problems with the law itself present formidable challenges to strengthening the rule of law in post-conflict societies, quite apart from the difficulties of actually enforcing the law fairly or consistently. Furthermore, existing national law-making processes may be deeply discredited, poorly functioning, and in need of fundamental reform.

Despite all these problems, interveners cannot simply impose law from "on high" if the law is to enjoy local legitimacy and support. In a fundamental sense, law is "gelled" culture: it reflects cultural and political realities, and ideally, it should reflect the agreed values and priorities of a society. Indeed, to be accepted and followed, law must rest on a foundation of public legitimacy, and local involvement in law reform is essential.

Even (or especially) in executive missions that possess broad authority over applicable law, the local population's perception of the law's legitimacy is critical to building domestic support for the rule of law. (In Chapter 8, this issue is discussed in more detail.) A case in point is the initial failure of the United Nations Interim Administration Mission in Kosovo (UNMIK) to provide for applicable law that Kosovo's Albanian population regarded as legitimate.

1. Trap to Avoid: Failure to Provide for Applicable Law That Enjoys Local Legitimacy

In Kosovo, the international interveners encountered serious problems in determining the applicable law. Following NATO's intervention, there was a legal limbo, and the Security Council gave UNMIK a mandate to maintain law and order and protect human rights.[35] UNMIK initially issued a

---

[34] O'Connor, *Traversing the Rocky Road of Law Reform in Conflict and Post Conflict States,* supra note 30, at 236.

[35] S.C. Res. 1244 (1999), para. 11(i) and para. 11(j).

regulation declaring that applicable law in Kosovo would be pre-intervention law insofar as it conformed to international human rights standards. This made perfect sense from a formalist standpoint. But the decision outraged Kosovar Albanians generally, and the Kosovar Albanian legal community – the group expected to apply the law – in particular. To them, pre-intervention law was anathema as "one of the most potent tools of a decade-long policy of discrimination against and repression of the Kosovar Albanian population."[36] Moreover, UNMIK failed to specify the ways in which pre-intervention law fell short of international human rights standards, leaving poorly trained police, lawyers, and judges to reach their own conclusions. The result was confusion and delay as judges, lawyers, and police "applied a diverse collection of legal provisions and standards, including FRY/Serbian law, pre-1989 criminal law, and Albanian criminal law.... "[37] Worse, UNMIK's failure to consult with local lawyers and politicians prior to issuing its first regulation sent the message to a population long accustomed to arbitrary rule that UNMIK's rule of law rhetoric might be just that – rhetoric only. In the face of domestic opposition, UNMIK ultimately reversed itself, learning a difficult lesson about the importance of domestic perceptions of the law's legitimacy.

2. Improving National Law: Domestic Legitimacy and Beyond
Yet as critical as domestic legitimacy is for sustainable legal reform, legitimacy is often not straightforward. On the contrary, if domestic views are disaggregated, different groups and constituencies are likely to have quite different perceptions of whether a particular law or reform is "legitimate." In Afghanistan, for instance, a number of brave women ran for parliament – thanks in part to a constitutional provision reserving 68 of the 249 elected seats in parliament for women.[38] Many female parliamentary candidates persisted in their campaigns despite intimidation, harassment, death threats, and worse, and despite opposition by some tribal leaders and others, who presumably regarded the law mandating women in parliament as illegitimate.[39]

---

[36] Strohmeyer, *Collapse and Reconstruction of a Judicial System, supra* note 9, at 58–59.

[37] Betts et al., *The Post-Conflict Transitional Administration of Kosovo, supra* note 13, at 375.

[38] Elizabeth Rubin, *Women's Work,* THE NEW YORK TIMES MAGAZINE, October 9, 2005, at 54. More precisely, Article 83(6) of Afghanistan's constitution provides that "at least two female delegates should be elected from each province" to the lower house of parliament; and Article 84 provides that the president appoints one-third of the members of the upper house of parliament, "50 percent of these people from among women." Arts. 84(4), 84(5). The Constitution is available at http://www.oefre.unibe.ch/law/icl/af00000.html.

[39] N. C. Aizenman, *Afghan Women Put Lives on Line to Run for Office,* THE WASHINGTON POST, July 29, 2005, at A1. On the other hand, a recent public opinion survey in Afghanistan reports that over 82 percent of those surveyed (including 77 percent of male respondents) said they think reserving some seats in parliament for women representatives is "a good idea." *New WPO Poll: Afghan Public Overwhelmingly Rejects al-Qaeda, Taliban,* January 11, 2006, *available at* http://www.worldpublicopinion.org.

Though without triggering such opposition, East Timor's Commission on Reception, Truth and Reconciliation likewise reserved a certain number of places for women in the community-based reconciliation panels, providing a leadership opportunity for women that otherwise would have been unlikely to occur. Such provisions for female participation – usually pressed by internationals with the support of some domestic reformers – aim to promote greater equality for women and to advance women's fundamental rights. In Afghanistan and elsewhere, the provisions were a critical, though not universally popular, means of empowering women who otherwise would have far more limited chances to play a role in governance or community leadership.

This underscores that domestic legitimacy is not the only touchstone for law reform in post-conflict societies. Helping to develop national laws and procedures that meet basic *international* standards is a major focus of UN agencies and other international actors. The Secretary-General of the United Nations has made clear that international standards, including international human rights law, provide the foundation for UN assistance and "serve as the normative basis for all United Nations activities in support of justice and the rule of law."[40] The UN Transitional Administration in East Timor (UNTAET) and UNMIK in Kosovo thus both determined that local law would not apply if it was inconsistent with international human rights standards. Many NGOs likewise work to promote laws and procedures that are consistent with, and help to advance, fundamental human rights.

But even the most well-intentioned and culturally sensitive law reform efforts can run up against difficult dilemmas. In particular, limited domestic resources and capacity can make it difficult, and sometimes impossible, to fully satisfy basic international standards. Adopting new laws consistent with international standards is one thing; gaining local acceptance of those laws – or developing the capacity to implement them effectively – is quite another. Are there some constructive ways to address these dilemmas in the law reform process?

3. The Potential Role of Model Codes
Recently developed "model codes" provide one potential resource for law reform efforts in challenging post-conflict environments. Particularly in the field of criminal law and procedure, significant progress has been made in developing model legislation that meets basic international standards but is also designed with the exigencies of post-conflict societies in mind. The United States Institute of Peace (USIP) and the Irish Centre for Human Rights

---

[40] *Report of the Secretary-General on the Rule of Law and Transitional Justice in Conflict and Post-Conflict Societies, supra* note 27, para. 9. Moreover, the report continues, "where we are mandated to undertake executive or judicial functions, United Nations-operated facilities must scrupulously comply with international standards for human rights in the administration of justice." Id., at para. 10.

(ICHR), in cooperation with the Office of the UN High Commissioner for Human Rights and the UN Office on Drugs and Crime, have worked with legal experts and practitioners from around the world to develop four such "model codes." These include a substantive criminal code, a criminal procedure code, a detention act, and a police powers act.[41]

The criminal code, which includes over eighty articles, covers basic principles of criminal law as well as substantive offenses such as murder, rape, assault, and offenses against property, among others, and crimes that often arise in post-conflict settings, such as trafficking in persons and organized crime. The code also addresses genocide, war crimes, and crimes against humanity. The criminal procedure code, which includes over 225 articles, covers the range of issues from investigation of crimes to indictment, trial, and appellate proceedings, as well as matters such as witness protection.[42] In addition, recognizing the enormous challenges of policing and detention in post-conflict settings, the USIP/ICHR project is developing two additional model codes: a detention act and a police powers act. The codes are due to be published by USIP by 2007, and they will be accompanied by commentary and guidelines to assist those who might make use of them.

Two features of the model codes project in particular stand out. First, the model codes are designed with post-conflict environments firmly in mind, and they strive to translate human rights standards into *concrete legal provisions potentially achievable in post-conflict settings*. Recognizing limitations such as lack of resources, judges, or means of transport, for instance, the codes provide that arrested persons be brought before a judge within seventy-two hours, which is consistent with international standards but also cognizant of post-conflict impediments.[43] Second, the model codes are a self-conscious *hybrid* that incorporates features from both civil and common law legal systems.

The codes are not expected to be adopted in their entirety. On the contrary, they are designed to be a *resource* for reformers to use and adapt to the needs of particular countries and legal systems. Although many of the model codes' provisions may enjoy acceptance in different post-conflict settings, sharply differing views regarding appropriate punishments and substantive offenses clearly exist in different cultures, and the codes do not purport to resolve these difficult issues. However, they do aim to assist law reform

---

[41] *See* O'Connor & Rausch, *A Tool Box to Tackle Law Reform Challenges in Post Conflict Countries: The Model Codes for Post Conflict Criminal Justice*, *supra* note 26, at 12–14; United States Institute of Peace, Rule of Law, Current Projects: Model Transitional Codes for Post-Conflict Criminal Justice, *available at* http://www.usip.org/ruleoflaw/ projects/codes.html.

[42] O'Connor, *Traversing the Rocky Road of Law Reform in Conflict and Post Conflict States*, *supra* note 30, at 252.

[43] *Model Codes for Post-Conflict Justice: Guidelines for Application* (draft as of October 2004), at 37.

efforts in a number of ways.[44] For one, the codes can be used for specific gap-filling: reformers could potentially borrow and adapt a particular provision, as needed, to fill a concrete need in existing law. More ambitiously, the codes could serve as a resource for those developing transitional or temporary legal codes in different settings. Finally, the codes could serve as a resource for longer-term projects of national legal reform in the criminal justice area.

The model codes reflect an enormous commitment of time and energy and are indeed a useful resource for law reform projects both large and small. Also helpful are the commentary and guidelines accompanying the codes, which can assist reformers as well as judges, prosecutors, and others who might be responsible for implementing particular provisions. The challenge will be whether these codes can be used effectively and adapted appropriately in law reform initiatives in specific countries. The codes cannot and should not be imposed; on the contrary, sustainable law reform will require a process that involves national leaders and reform-minded civil society organizations and that seeks to build national consensus over the law.

C. Reforming Law-Making Processes

Rather than giving careful attention to the process by which laws are revised and enacted, interveners often focus far more, or even exclusively, on the substance of law reform initiatives. In Afghanistan, for instance, an Italian initiative led to the promulgation of a new criminal procedure code with little local consultation or participation.[45] Likewise in Kosovo, "local input was marginalized" in law reform and the UN "often chose to rely almost exclusively on its own legal advisors and outside experts who submitted various draft regulations."[46] Eager for results, international actors are sometimes impatient with processes that involve extensive local participation and feedback. Yet, in the long run, the process of law reform can be as important as the substantive output.

To the extent possible, the process of law-making should be transparent and accountable to the people. Especially after a period of autocratic rule and corruption, sustainable law reform will depend critically on strengthening

---

[44] The codes' developers highlight several possibilities. O'Connor & Rausch, *A Tool Box to Tackle Law Reform Challenges in Post Conflict Countries, supra* note 26, at 16–21; O'Connor, *Traversing the Rocky Road of Law Reform in Conflict and Post Conflict States, supra* note 30, at 14–20; United States Institute of Peace, *Current Projects: Model Transitional Codes for Post-Conflict Criminal Justice, available at* http://www.usip.org/ruleoflaw/projects/codes.html.

[45] Miller & Perito, *Establishing the Rule of Law in Afghanistan, supra* note 32, at 8.

[46] Colette Rausch, *From Elation to Disappointment: Justice and Security Reform in Kosovo,* in CONSTRUCTING JUSTICE AND SECURITY AFTER WAR, *supra* note 8, at 279. *See also* David Marshall & Shelley Inglis, *The Disempowerment of Human Rights-Based Justice in the United Nations Mission in Kosovo,* 16 HARV. HUM. RTS. J. 95, 117–119, 145 (2003).

domestic law-making processes to include a role for civil society and relevant stakeholders. Promulgating top-down reforms will do little to empower national reformers or to nurture domestic constituencies that can keep constructive pressure on government actors. Law reform by decree also fails to nurture the habits and practice of compromise so critical to the nonviolent resolution of conflict. As a U.S. Agency for International Development assessment mission in Bosnia concluded:

[T]he Bosnian legal community is not deeply enough involved in the process of reform and could even be said, at least in some instances, to be alienated from it, a situation to which parts of the international community contribute. . . . There are at least two serious repercussions: first, developing the capacity for true self-governance, including the messy democratic business of reaching compromises, is stilted. Second, the citizens, who feel that they are not consulted in the development of the law, have little ownership in it, and do not feel bound by it.[47]

Different strategies may be needed in different political contexts but, after bitter conflicts involving ethnic and intergroup hostility, nurturing and encouraging domestic capacity for compromise and moderation are essential.

Also vital is more effective assistance (in various forms) to legislative bodies in post-conflict environments. Though it is somewhat at odds with the international focus on elections as a benchmark for progress, donors often provide less aid to legislatures than to the executive branch or to civil society organizations in post-conflict societies.[48] Nevertheless, assistance to legislatures can provide tangible dividends by strengthening the separation of powers and improving oversight of executive action. Training in how to review and assess budgets can help promote greater transparency of government programs and more effective legislative oversight – all the more important because executive departments and agencies typically have considerable

---

[47] U.S. Agency for International Development, *Priorities and Partners: Developing the Rule of Law in Bosnia and Herzegovina* (2003), at i, *available at* http://bosnia.usaid.gov/rol_report_english_june2003.doc. For additional critiques of "top-down" law reform in Bosnia, *see* David Chandler, *Imposing the 'Rule of Law': The Lessons of BiH for Peacebuilding in Iraq*, 11 INT'L PEACEKEEPING 312 (2004); Patrice C. McMahon, *Rebuilding Bosnia: A Model to Emulate or Avoid?*, 119 POL. SCI. Q. 569 (2004–2005). For a discussion more generally of the "mistaken assumption" that "new laws are the answer" with insufficient attention to promoting "underlying policy dialogues and processes," *see* Wade Channell, *Lessons Not Learned: Problems with Western Aid for Law Reform in Postcommunist Countries*, Democracy and Rule of Law Project, Carnegie Papers No. 77, May 2005, at 8.

[48] UN Development Programme, *Conference Report, A Policy Dialogue on Legislative Development* (2002), at section II, *available at* http://www.undp.org/governance/eventsites/policy_dialog/index.htm; UN Development Programme, *Summary of Discussion, Enhancing the Role of Parliaments in Conflict/Post-Conflict Settings*, Geneva, March 24, 2004, at 1, *available at* http://www.undp.org/governance/eventsites/PARLgeneva04/summdisc.doc. As the *Summary of Discussion* noted: "Often, the international community focuses inordinate attention on organizing elections and does not pay adequate attention to the sustenance of the institutions born of those elections." Id., at 1.

control over the disbursement of aid funds.[49] Assistance and training to political parties can help strengthen domestic capacity for effective law-making, representation, and compromise, so long as it is provided in a balanced and even-handed way.[50] Legislative strengthening can also help reassert civilian control over military and security forces. Among the possibilities here are supporting parliamentary committees on national defense and the military (especially with committee members that cut across social cleavages), and conditioning military aid on legislative oversight.[51] To neglect legislatures is thus to lose a valuable opportunity to build capacity in domestic law-making and in civilian oversight of the military.

That said, legislative assistance programs cannot be provided in a technical, "cookie-cutter" way. Instead, they must be carefully tailored to the local political and cultural environment. Aid to political parties can be particularly delicate and must take careful account of local realities if it is to strengthen the capacity for democratic politics and compromise. In East Timor, for instance, the relative weakness of opposition parties, coupled with rigid party discipline in the ruling party, threatens to undermine the long-term democratic vitality and legitimacy of East Timor's political process. Legislative assistance and training must therefore not only navigate sensitive political terrain but also take into account that reform may be needed in how elections are conducted, how party lists are structured, and in other matters, too, that are essential for the development of effective and stable legislative processes. Designing effective legislative assistance programs is consequently a delicate and context-specific matter that warrants greater and more systematic attention in post-conflict reconstruction.

Taking a slight step back from the legislative arena, support for non-government organizations can also be a critical investment in improving domestic law-making capacity. East Timor's Judicial System Monitoring Programme (JSMP), for instance, is an NGO that monitors and reports on the justice system and that also plays an important role in law reform by

---

[49] UN Development Programme, *Summary of Discussion, Enhancing The Role of Parliaments in Conflict/Post-Conflict Settings, supra* note 48, at 5. U.S. Agency for International Development studies also emphasize the value of strengthening the legislative role in the budget process. Hal Lippman & Jan Emmert, U.S. Agency for International Development, *Assisting Legislatures in Developing Countries: A Framework for Program Planning and Implementation,* Program and Operations Assessment Report No. 20, October 1997, at 24.

[50] For discussion of challenges in aid to political parties, *see* John K. Johnson with Jessie Biddle, PN-ACR-217, U.S. Agency for International Development, *Understanding Representation: Implications for Legislative Strengthening, Second International Conference on Legislative Strengthening,* November 2000, at 11, *available at* http://www.usaid.gov/our_work/democracy_and_governance/publications/pdfs/pnacr217.pdf; UN Development Programme, *Conference Report, A Policy Dialogue on Legislative Development, supra* note 48, at section II.

[51] UN Development Programme, *Summary of Discussion, Enhancing the Role of Parliaments in Conflict/Post-Conflict Settings, supra* note 48, at 4.

evaluating pending legislation and advocating reforms.[52] A valuable source of public information, the JSMP has helped introduce greater transparency in the law reform process. More generally, supporting such organizations can help to strengthen domestic law-making processes and make them more accountable to public concerns.

Also important is meaningful *dissemination* of the law. Even making the law available to critical actors within the justice system – judges, prosecutors, police, defense counsel – can be a major challenge in many post-conflict countries. Quite apart from a lack of libraries or computers, resources as basic as paper and pens can be in short supply. Yet not only public officials but also civil society organizations and ordinary people need greater access to legal materials and wider awareness of the law.

Finally, adopting new law is, by itself, only half the story; the larger question is whether an adequate capacity to *implement* the law exists or can be developed. As Linn Hammergren cautions based on experience in Latin America, "code reform has intrinsic limitations as to what it can change"; law reform focusing on the justice sector "will be of little help if the major obstacles to improved performance are such external factors as political intervention, formal or informal restrictions on institutional powers, or inadequate funding."[53] Moreover, without adequate attention to strengthening "institutional capacity," code reform is unlikely to have enduring positive effects. In post-conflict societies, the challenge of developing an institutional capacity for fair and effective law enforcement can be particularly difficult, as we now examine.

IV. STRENGTHENING LAW ENFORCEMENT CAPACITY

A decent law enforcement capacity is part of an effective justice system and essential to the rule of law. Adequate and functioning state institutions – police, prisons, and courts – are needed. Each of these components, moreover,

[52] The Judicial System Monitoring Programme Web site can be found at http://www.jsmp. minihub.org. We discuss the JSMP and the importance of NGOs more fully in Chapter 8.

[53] Linn Hammergren, *Code Reform and Law Revision*, PN-ACD-022, Executive Summary, U.S. Agency for International Development, Center for Democracy and Governance, Bureau for Global Programs, Field Support, and Research, August 1998, at 2. More emphasis on effective implementation of new laws is needed in many post-conflict societies. In Bosnia, for instance, a USAID assessment team concluded: "While drafting new legislation is relatively simple, the changes that are being introduced in some cases, such as with the criminal procedure code, are almost seismic in nature. Implementation requires not only training of judges, prosecutors, lawyers, and police (as is being done, to a large degree), but also the embedding of experts into key institutions, and engaging in public education." U.S. Agency for International Development, *Priorities and Partners: Developing the Rule of Law in Bosnia and Herzegovina, supra* note 47, at ii.

is mutually dependent and must work well together as a system. We examine the particular challenges of post-conflict reform of police and prisons in this section, and of judiciaries in the next.

A. Police Reform in Post-Conflict Societies

Police reform has long received the lion's share of attention from post-conflict capacity-builders. Even so, creating an effective police force that enjoys public legitimacy can be enormously difficult. This should come as no surprise, given the legacy of police abuse and public mistrust that pervades many countries racked by conflict. All too often the police have functioned as instruments of control, repression, and intimidation rather than of justice. Poorly paid, if paid at all, they were often corrupt, depending on bribes and side payments for their livelihood. Poorly educated and trained, police often used abusive methods of interrogation in preference to investigation. Moreover, police often were highly discriminatory, favoring "a narrow segment of the population – ethnically, religiously or politically defined" – rather than serving "the general public welfare."[54] As a result, regime opponents, minorities, women – in short, anyone lacking power and influence – quickly learned to expect ill treatment from the very institutions that should protect individual rights in a functioning legal system operating under the rule of law.

A few concrete examples are illustrative. In East Timor under Indonesian occupation, the police, together with courts and prisons, served "as tools of the occupation regime."[55] Likewise, in Kosovo, the police historically "have been viewed as oppressors and bribe takers."[56] In Iraq under Saddam Hussein, police were despised and feared, perpetrating abuses, engaging in torture, and preserving the government's hold on power. In Haiti prior to the 1994 intervention, there were no civilian police separate from the thuggish, brutal, and feared armed forces. In circumstances such as these, as William O'Neill points out, successful police reform will require far more than "technical" changes in "police doctrine or practice"; it will entail "transforming power relations in a society."[57]

Yet there are also significant counterexamples. In Somalia, the police were "well-trained, disciplined, and generally nontribal" and largely well

---

[54] Eric Scheye, *Transitions to Local Authority,* in EXECUTIVE POLICING, *supra* note 24, at 105.

[55] West, *Lawyers, Guns, and Money: Justice and Security Reform in East Timor, supra* note 8, at 316.

[56] Rausch, *From Elation to Disappointment: Justice and Security Reform in Kosovo, supra* note 46, at 295.

[57] William G. O'Neill, *Police Reform in Post-Conflict Societies: What We Know and What We Still Need to Know*, International Peace Academy Policy Paper, April 2005 at 2, *available at* http://www.ipacademy.org/Programs/Research/ProgReseSecDev_Pub.htm.

respected.[58] Thus, following the 1992 intervention, "[t]he nucleus for a Somali police force already existed, acceptable to Somalis in regions where they were stationed," although UN and donor support to train and equip the police persistently fell short.[59]

Interveners thus need to start by asking some fundamental questions: What is the historical baseline in the particular society at issue? How do police view their role and their loyalties? How do citizens view the police? Once reformers understand the social and political context in which police operate, they can begin to ask what kinds of police reforms are needed to advance the goals of the rule of law – goals that include not only maintaining law and order but also protecting human rights, a government bound by law, and equality before the law. More concretely, is there some combination of inputs that can help build a fair and effective law enforcement capacity that will be affordable and sustainable once interveners leave?

Much has been written on the challenges of reforming and strengthening police in transitioning and post-conflict societies.[60] We can't possibly address all the complex issues involved here. Instead, our goal is to emphasize some central and recurring issues that reformers should keep in mind while grappling with the unique needs and circumstances of specific post-conflict societies. These issues include: the critical overarching challenge of transforming police–society relations; the need to define goals clearly and to develop a systematic plan for realizing them; challenges in constructing a police force that enjoys local legitimacy and that protects the rights of vulnerable populations, including women, after conflict; challenges in training police effectively; the critical importance and difficulty of changing organizational culture and building accountability; and the fundamental need for corresponding reforms in the larger legal and political system in which police operate.

1. Transforming Police–Society Relations: The Overarching Challenge

Probably the most important point for reformers to keep in mind is that effective police reform in post-conflict societies generally requires "transforming

---

[58] Martin R. Ganzglass, *Then Restoration of the Somali Justice System*, in LEARNING FROM SOMALIA: THE LESSONS OF ARMED HUMANITARIAN INTERVENTION (Walter M. Clarke & Jeffrey M. Herbst, eds., 1997), at 22.

[59] Id.

[60] *See, e.g.*, CONSTRUCTING JUSTICE AND SECURITY AFTER WAR, *supra* note 8; Jones et al., ESTABLISHING LAW AND ORDER AFTER CONFLICT, *supra* note 17, at 23–24; Robert M. Perito, WHERE IS THE LONE RANGER WHEN WE NEED HIM?: AMERICA'S SEARCH FOR A POSTCONFLICT STABILITY FORCE (2004); David H. Bayley, *Democratizing the Police Abroad: What to Do and How to Do It*, June 2001, *available at* http://www.ojp.usdoj.gov/nij; O'Neill, *Police Reform in Post-Conflict Societies, supra* note 57.

the relationship between police institutions and society."[61] The relationship between police and citizens, between the police and other components of the justice system, and between the police and the government all may require fundamental transformation.

Transforming the relationship between communities and police requires changing *both* sides of the equation. Police will need to be trained and reoriented to view their job as serving the community, not simply serving powerful political or economic actors or naked self-interest. Moreover, as police reform experts emphasize, the organizational culture of police – including the incentives, expectations, and rewards – must be reoriented to encourage a public service orientation, accountability to the law, respect for human rights, and transparency.[62]

Citizens, in turn, may be understandably dubious about turning to the police for fair or reliable protection. Transforming this situation requires international monitoring, and community outreach and education regarding what citizens should expect of the police, and what to do in the face of abusive or corrupt behavior. Community outreach programs and complaint mechanisms should be developed in tandem with police restructuring – not as an afterthought. Furthermore, as Rama Mani emphasizes, interveners should think of police not simply as part of the "security sector" but as part of a system that aims to provide justice and to protect the rights of citizens.[63] All of this depends, of course, on reforms in the broader political system of which police are but a part.

2. Goals of Police Reform

"Democratic policing" is a fundamental objective of many police reform programs. It has several key elements, as expert David Bayley explains. These include giving priority to serving the needs of the public, accountability to the law rather than to the arbitrary dictates of particular regimes and leaders, protection of human rights, and transparency of police operations.[64] The central idea is a police force that understands itself as functioning in the public interest, with the aim of fair enforcement of the law and protection of basic rights, within a system of government that is accountable under the law.

"Community policing" has also been a goal in a number of post-conflict settings – or at least the capacity to employ some techniques of community

---

[61] Charles T. Call, *Conclusion: Constructing Justice and Security after War*, in CONSTRUCTING JUSTICE AND SECURITY AFTER WAR, *supra* note 8, at 387.

[62] Bayley, *Democratizing the Police Abroad*, *supra* note 60, at 13–15; O'Neill, *Police Reform in Post-Conflict Societies*, *supra* note 57, at 9–10.

[63] Mani, BEYOND RETRIBUTION, *supra* note 7, at 77.

[64] Bayley, *Democratizing the Police Abroad*, *supra* note 60, at 13–15.

policing. Definitions vary, but the central idea of community policing is that "law enforcement works in partnership with a community to solve the problems of crime and disorder. . . ."[65] Community policing generally involves police that are based locally in the community, with a continuous presence such as a police station and regular patrolling, and a capacity to respond to local problems in a nonthreatening manner, with the assistance of the community.[66]

But community policing is not a panacea. It is sometimes adopted as a goal without a clear understanding of what it means, concretely.[67] Furthermore, locally recruited police may be more susceptible to corruption and favoritism than those drawn from other parts of a country. Particularly in diverse societies that have experienced police abuse in the past, safeguards imposed from outside the immediate community may be essential to protect minority rights, to defuse ethnic tension, and to counter corruption.

Quite apart from the corruption problems, community police may simply not be capable of safeguarding the local populations they are meant to serve. In situations of active insurgency, as in parts of Iraq, it is practically impossible to operate police as a lightly armed presence in communities without making them attractive targets for heavily armed militia units. "Policing" in such difficult circumstances devolves into a commando operation aimed at hunting down insurgent groups and their supporters.

In Iraq, the absence of safeguards on constabulary or commando operations has been plainly evident. The police organizations of Basra – Iraq's second largest city – reportedly have been infiltrated by local Shiite militia to such an extent that they have become a force unto themselves, based in the community but answerable to commanders with factional loyalties outside the formal police structure.[68] Indeed, in Basra and elsewhere, some "police" units reportedly have perpetrated kidnapping, torture and summary execution against rival sectarian groups, against a wider background of insecurity, insurgency, and sectarian violence.[69] Given the level of civil

---

[65] International Association of Chiefs of Police, *quoted in* Eirin Mobekk, *Policing from Below: Community Policing as an Objective in Peace Operations*, in EXECUTIVE POLICING, *supra* note 24, at 54.

[66] Interview, James A. Schear, November 13, 2005.

[67] In East Timor, for instance, community policing was adopted as an objective without a clear understanding (among reformers, CIVPOL, local police, or citizens) of exactly what this meant or should mean. Mobekk, *Policing from Below: Community Policing as an Objective in Peace Operations*, *supra* note 65, at 56–58.

[68] Richard A. Oppel, Jr., *Basra Chaos Reflects Militia Infiltration of Police*, THE NEW YORK TIMES, October 9, 2005, at 1.

[69] Id. *See also* Michael Moss (with David Rohde & Kirk Semple), *How Iraq Police Reform Became Casualty of War*, THE NEW YORK TIMES, May 22, 2006, at A1; Nir Rosen, *Killing Fields*, THE WASHINGTON POST, May 28, 2006, at B3. For additional analysis of the difficulties in developing effective, accountable police and security forces in Iraq, see Michael Moss & David Rohde, *Misjudgments Marred U.S. Plans for Iraqi Police*, THE NEW YORK TIMES,

violence in present-day Iraq, it is impossible to predict how Basra or other militia-dominated municipalities could navigate toward more stable systems of community police, absent a major imposition of external control, which seems scarcely likely. What is clear is that even in far more auspicious and stable circumstances, building police forces that are capable of effective democratic and community policing takes considerable time and resources.

Police experts frequently argue that five years is a minimum period of time required to develop such a capability.[70] Moreover, the cost of building and staffing police academies, providing classroom and field training, and equipping police and police stations is significant. Even when the international community has been willing to commit substantial resources to building police forces – in Kosovo and East Timor, and in Haiti in the mid- to late 1990s, for instance – the program was generally more rushed and the resources more limited than experts would have liked. In addition to confronting tough choices about how best to use resources in the time frame available, interveners and their domestic allies also face difficult questions regarding the sustainability of reforms. Interveners can jump-start a program of training, restructuring, infrastructure support, and community outreach; but planning for how to sustain the momentum of reform – including how to support it as international resources taper off – requires far more attention from the outset.

All this underscores the need for clear goals and astute strategic planning in police reform efforts. A more concerted effort to forge agreement not only on basic objectives but also on the methods, techniques, and timetables to achieve them should be part of systematic police reform, up front.[71]

3. Constructing a Balanced Police Force That Enjoys Legitimacy

In many post-conflict societies, building a functioning police force that enjoys public legitimacy may require a brand new police force – created either from scratch, by vetting and retraining some existing forces, or through some combination of the two. It may be tempting to work with existing police because security needs are usually pressing, and recruiting, training, and equipping wholly new forces takes considerable time and effort. In some cases, as in Somalia, this may be a viable approach: the pre-civil war Somali police (unlike the Somali military) were well trained and respected, with "an

May 21, 2006, at 1; Dexter Filkins, *Shadows, Armed Groups Propel Iraq Toward Chaos*, THE NEW YORK TIMES, May 24, 2006, at A1.

[70] Perito, *National Police Training within an Executive Police Operation*, in EXECUTIVE POLICING, *supra* note 24, at 100; Jones et al., ESTABLISHING LAW AND ORDER AFTER CONFLICT, *supra* note 17, at xiii.

[71] Bayley, *Democratizing the Police Abroad, supra* note 60, at 37 (stressing the need for advance planning, "clearly specifying objectives, implementation actions, resource requirements, and timetables").

undisputed reputation for professionalism," so they could be quickly and usefully deployed with relatively little vetting and retraining.[72]

More often, however, existing police forces are poorly trained and disciplined, distrusted by the public, and often notorious for criminal activity and abuse of human rights.[73] In such cases, the police forces must be carefully vetted to screen out corrupt personnel and human rights violators, and reorganized, retrained, and, to the extent possible, imbued "with an ethos of public service and impartiality. . . ."[74] In some circumstances, it may be simplest to disband entire units, especially elite units, and require individuals to apply for positions and, if accepted, to undergo full retraining in legitimate police techniques.

The United Nations and some other international organizations and individual states now have substantial experience with vetting and reforming police forces. In Kosovo, UNMIK supervises Kosovo Police Service (KPS) operations while the Organization for Security and Co-operation in Europe (OSCE) provides training and professional development. The Kosovo Police Service School (KPSS) began training police within two months of KFOR's arrival in Kosovo, and it has since put thousands of trained and vetted police on the streets, operating with UNMIK monitors and KFOR backup.[75] For the most part, this program has been successful, and violent crime in Kosovo generally has diminished substantially over the last several years. Although overcoming historical mistrust of police takes time, public perceptions of the KPS are quite positive.[76] Nevertheless, the ability of the KPS to withstand pressure "when confronted with organized crime or crimes involving blood feuds within families" remains a concern both of locals and internationals.[77]

A predicament for interveners in Kosovo and elsewhere is eliciting support from those who fought and ultimately prevailed in the conflict and now seek jobs. In East Timor, for example, community resentments still fester over the inclusion of some prior police from the period of Indonesian occupation, particularly when so many who actively supported the anti-occupation resistance remain unemployed.[78] In Kosovo, the Kosovo Liberation Army

---

[72] Lynn Thomas & Steve Spataro, *Peacekeeping and Policing in Somalia*, in POLICING THE NEW WORLD DISORDER: PEACE OPERATIONS AND PUBLIC SECURITY (Robert B. Oakley, Michael J. Dziedzic, & Eliot M. Goldberg, eds., 1998), at 176.

[73] Michael J. Dziedzic, *Introduction*, in POLICING THE NEW WORLD DISORDER, *supra* note 72, at 14.

[74] Robert B. Oakley & Michael J. Dziedzic, *Conclusions*, in POLICING THE NEW WORLD DISORDER, *supra* note 72, at 524 (italics omitted), 521.

[75] Perito, *National Police Training within an Executive Police Operation, supra* note 70, at 87.

[76] O'Neill, *Police Reform in Post-conflict Societies, supra* note 57, at 8; Rausch, *From Elation to Disappointment: Justice and Security Reform in Kosovo, supra* note 46, at 295.

[77] Rausch, id., at 295.

[78] West, *Lawyers, Guns, and Money: Justice and Security Reform in East Timor, supra* note 8, at 335.

(KLA) "insisted on a role in vetting applicants" and 50 percent of the new police positions initially were set aside for former KLA. With another 20 percent of seats designated for former police dismissed after Kosovo's loss of autonomy in 1989, and 20 percent for women, this left only 10 percent for otherwise qualified males, including many scoring highly on the qualifying exams.[79] Partly for this reason, "the application process was restructured in Spring 2001, ending the quota and preferential consideration for ex-KLA candidates."[80]

Another recurring challenge is constructing a balanced police force that fairly reflects the composition and diversity of the larger community in which it functions. In Kosovo, for example, as of January 2002, graduates of the KPSS included 16 percent minorities (of which 8 percent were Serb); but despite efforts to overcome Kosovo's ethnic divide, problems persist, including "reports of harassment of Serb KPS officers."[81] Moreover, "in Albanian-dominant areas, KPS units had virtually no minorities," whereas in Serb-dominated areas, "KPS units tended to be almost entirely Serb," perpetuating largely separate or parallel systems.[82] This kind of problem is hardly unique to Kosovo. In Afghanistan, the government of Hamid Karzai has struggled mightily to reestablish a truly national corps of professional police (the Afghan National Police or ANP) by drawing inclusively from across the various ethnic groups – the Pashtuns, Tajiks, Uzbeks, Hazaras, and other groups – that comprise the country's present-day population of roughly thirty million. With strong encouragement from international donors, this effort at multiethnicity has achieved some success within national-level ANP institutions, such as the Ministry of Interior in Kabul, despite the difficulties of finding adequate experience among traditionally disadvantaged groups, such as the Hazaras, to fill managerial jobs. Even so, at provincial and district levels, the task of deploying ethnically balanced police forces has lagged behind, especially in areas of the country where the ANP finds itself operating in close proximity to local, tribal "police" elements whose level of public acceptance within a given area may be higher. In Iraq, as noted earlier, the barriers to a balanced national police force are even higher as continued civil conflict is abetting a process of ethnic and sectarian separation.

---

[79] Rausch, *From Elation to Disappointment: Justice and Security Reform in Kosovo, supra* note 46, at 292; Perito, *National Police Training within an Executive Police Operation, supra* note 70, at 95.

[80] Rausch, *From Elation to Disappointment: Justice and Security Reform in Kosovo, supra* note 46, at 293.

[81] Id., at 294.

[82] Id., at 303. As Charles Call notes, in Kosovo and elsewhere, the inclusion of minorities within police forces, although very important, often has not translated into fundamental changes in social practices. Call, *Conclusion: Constructing Justice and Security after War, supra* note 61, at 389.

Achieving greater gender balance in police forces has been possible in some post-conflict settings but extremely difficult in others. In both Kosovo and East Timor, increasing the presence of women on the police force has been an explicit goal. With the aim of 20 percent, women comprised 18 percent of the first sixteen classes of the Kosovo Police Service, which is "higher than the average percentage in U.S. police forces."[83] In East Timor, over 30 percent of the police force are women.[84] In Haiti, in contrast, targets were not set when training began in 1995 and only 7 percent of the initial police force were women.[85] Even more difficult, in Afghanistan, only about 4 percent of basic recruits and 1 percent of officer cadets were women as of November 2003.[86]

Increasing the number of female police is a critical goal and, at least in a few countries, a notable achievement. But even so, women are often sidelined into lower-status positions or face widespread discrimination from male officers.[87] Furthermore, increasing numbers, although extremely important, by itself is insufficient to address the deep problems of violence and insecurity that women often confront on a daily basis in post-conflict settings.

4. Protecting and Empowering Women

Violence against women often increases in the aftermath of war. Domestic violence, in particular, has spiked in a number of post-conflict societies as demobilized soldiers return home from the battlefield with limited job prospects and years of experience in violent conflict.[88] Disarmament, demobilization, and reintegration (DDR) programs focus on integrating combatants back into their communities, but the reintegration component is often shortchanged and the particular circumstances and needs of women given less attention.

Much more is required to effectively address the violence and insecurity that women in post-conflict societies often face. Better training for all police, male or female, in responding effectively to domestic violence and other

---

[83] Tracy Fitzsimmons, *Engendering Justice and Security after War*, in CONSTRUCTING JUSTICE AND SECURITY AFTER WAR, *supra* note 8, at 358.

[84] Id., at 361. In the first wave of police recruits, women comprised 40 percent, but more recent classes have averaged 20 percent. *See* Judicial System Monitoring Programme, *Police Treatment of Women in Timor Leste*, January 2005, at 12; UNIFEM, *The Impact of the Conflict on East Timorese Women*, available at http://www.womenwarpeace.org/timor_leste/timor_leste.htm.

[85] Fitzsimmons, *Engendering Justice and Security after War*, *supra* note 83, at 355.

[86] Miller & Perito, *Establishing the Rule of Law in Afghanistan*, *supra* note 32, at 11 (11 of the 1000 officer cadets were women, and 22 of the 500 noncommissioned officers were women).

[87] Rausch, *From Elation to Disappointment: Justice and Security Reform in Kosovo*, *supra* note 46, at 294 ("discrimination against female officers remains widespread"); Fitzsimmons, *Engendering Justice and Security after War*, *supra* note 83, at 355, 359; Interviews in East Timor, November 2003; Amnesty International, *Afghanistan: Police Reconstruction Essential for the Protection of Human Rights*, March 2003, at 21–22.

[88] Call, *Conclusions: Constructing Justice and Security after War*, *supra* note 61, at 381–382.

violent crimes against women is necessary. Haiti's four-month training course for new police officers "included less than half a day on rape and domestic sexual violence, and nothing more generally on gender issues or the treatment of women."[89] In contrast, in Kosovo, the training of the KPS "included more modules on domestic violence, rape, and women's issues" than in any previous international civilian police (CIVPOL) mission.[90] Beyond training, far more sensitivity to victims of violence is needed, and innovations such as "women's police stations or women's sections within police stations" can "encourage higher reporting levels and more citizen confidence in the police."[91] But preventing violence against women requires more systematic effort and a wider array of initiatives, as Tracy Fitzsimmons argues, including changes in criminal law, early socialization of new police forces, and development of effective reform coalitions, among others.[92]

5. Police Training and Professionalism

In the effort to build police organizations that can maintain law and order but also protect basic rights, effective training is always a core element. In post-conflict settings, however, classroom training is usually rushed and field training is often inadequate. Although police experts argue that a program of basic training "designed to give raw recruits a minimum understanding of policing skills and the law" generally takes between six months and a year, limited funds and the need to deploy police quickly typically result in truncated training.[93] In Kosovo, classroom training for the first KPS class was limited to only five weeks, and later classes received only eight weeks.[94] In East Timor, recruits received twelve weeks of basic training at the East Timor Police Training College.[95] In Afghanistan, police recruits receive three months of training, whereas officers attend a five-year training course.[96] Although a number of Iraqi police recruits received eight weeks of training at the International Police Training Center in Jordan, the urgent need for police led to shorter training programs at the Baghdad Public Safety Academy and other training centers in Iraq.[97]

Much of the police training provided in post-conflict settings consists of basic and essential police skills. These include arrest procedures, criminal investigation techniques, patrolling, report writing, defensive tactics,

---

[89] Fitzsimmons, *Engendering Justice and Security after War, supra* note 83, at 355.
[90] Id., at 358.
[91] Id., at 365.
[92] Id., at 359–366.
[93] Perito, *National Police Training within an Executive Police Operation, supra* note 70, at 93.
[94] Id.
[95] Id., at 91.
[96] Miller & Perito, *Establishing the Rule of Law in Afghanistan, supra* note 32, at 11; Jones et al., Establishing Law and Order after Conflict, *supra* note 17, at 73–75.
[97] Jones et al., Establishing Law and Order after Conflict, *supra* note 17, at 119.

firearms use, and first aid, among others.[98] Training in supervision and management – as a means of developing future leaders – is also critical. Another
component of training that is vital, but sometimes shortchanged, is educating police about their role in relationship to other components of the justice
system. Professional education also requires training of a more transformative character, including training in human rights standards and in effective
community relations. Integrating human rights and professional skills training together is important in order to underscore that effective policing and
respecting human rights go hand in hand.[99]

After initial classroom instruction, adequate field training and follow-on
in-service training has been a consistent problem in many post-conflict settings. In East Timor, three months of field training, supervised by CIVPOL
field training officers, was to follow classroom training of recruits.[100] But the
quality of CIVPOL mentoring varied enormously, and the "lack of a field
training protocol" and the limited number of CIVPOL available for this
task resulted in uneven, and often insufficient "field training," compounded
by a subsequent lack of "in-service training."[101] As former CIVPOL officer Ronald West argues, this shows the need "for donors and host country
nationals to agree upon a realistic time frame" for a program of police development and "for greater rigor in promulgating standards once initial training
has ended."[102] Yet East Timor was at the relatively high end in terms of police
field training: in Afghanistan, for instance, field training outside of Kabul has
been limited.[103] Experts agree, however, that good field training is critically
important to developing and reinforcing police skills and good practices.[104]

Effective training both in the classroom and in the field requires competent
and committed teachers and mentors. Policymakers cannot simply "assume
that CivPol missions will be able to train the local police in addition to per-
forming their other duties."[105] On the contrary, a better capacity to assemble
teams of rapidly deployable specialists – including police trainers with special
skills and experience but also experts in the culture and legal system of the
host country – is needed within regional and international organizations and

[98] Perito, *National Police Training within an Executive Police Operation, supra* note 70, at 88,
91.
[99] O'Neill, *Police Reform in Post-Conflict Societies, supra* note 57, at 2.
[100] Perito, *National Police Training within an Executive Police Operation, supra* note 70, at 91.
[101] West, *Lawyers, Guns, and Money: Justice and Security Reform in East Timor, supra* note 8,
at 342.
[102] Id.
[103] U.S. Government Accounting Office, *Afghanistan Security: Efforts to Establish Army and
Police Have Made Progress, but Future Plans Need to Be Better Defined,* June 2005, at
24–25. U.S. officials "cited the high costs, the security threat to training personnel stationed
in the field, and the difficulty of recruiting sufficient numbers of international police as
impediments to implementing a countrywide field-based program." Id., at 25.
[104] Id., at 24.
[105] Perito, *National Police Training within an Executive Police Operation, supra* note 70, at 96.

within key states. These teams can work with domestic reformers in designing and implementing training programs that take account of the particular cultural conditions and needs of the host country in order to maximize the effectiveness of educating new police.

But training is, of course, only part of the picture. Another even more difficult challenge is changing the "culture" of police organizations to inculcate a public service orientation and related norms of democratic policing.[106]

6. Changing Organizational Culture and Building Accountability

In post-conflict countries where the police previously functioned as agents of governmental control and repression, building a new organizational culture is essential. Indeed, the "entire system of incentives and rewards needs to reflect the new police ethos of serving and protecting the public."[107] The organizational culture – or what police "themselves think is expected of them" – needs to encourage and reward positive behavior, and tangible ways must be found to communicate and reinforce the view that reform is in the self-interest of police.[108] Recruitment and promotion, for instance, "must be based on objective criteria and not on nepotism or political favoritism."[109] Merit promotion, in particular, is critical to reinforce new norms of accountable, democratic policing. Adequate salaries must also be established and maintained in order to help thwart destructive patterns of corruption and extortion by police. Unfortunately, doing so has often proven difficult. In Afghanistan, for example, low and erratic pay has contributed to "widespread corruption" among police, "who are generally regarded with a mixture of fear and disdain."[110]

Effective disciplinary and oversight mechanisms are also a vital part of changing organizational culture. If police are not subject to discipline for abusive behavior, reformers may simply empower unaccountable state actors who violate human rights with impunity and use their power in arbitrary and capricious ways. Concretely, before pouring intensive resources into capacity-building programs for police, reformers should develop disciplinary and accountability mechanisms that can be used to remove officials who are corrupt and abusive. Establishing effective controls is much harder to do after state actors are already empowered and entrenched in their new positions. Independent oversight bodies, both internal and external, must be established and given the resources and authority to do an effective job.[111]

---

[106] Bayley, *Democratizing the Police Abroad, supra* note 60, at 20–21.
[107] O'Neill, *Police Reform in Post-Conflict Societies, supra* note 57, at 9.
[108] Bayley, *Democratizing the Police Abroad, supra* note 60, at 20–21.
[109] O'Neill, *Police Reform in Post-Conflict Societies, supra* note 57, at 9.
[110] Miller & Perito, *Establishing the Rule of Law in Afghanistan, supra* note 32, at 11. *See also* U.S. General Accounting Office, *Afghanistan Security, supra* note 103, at 25.
[111] O'Neill, *Police Reform in Post-Conflict Societies, supra* note 57, at 7.

International police must themselves set a positive example and be accountable for their conduct. Regrettably, beyond the typical problem of wide disparity in CIVPOL quality, a far more pernicious problem of serious misconduct by some CIVPOL officers has plagued several interventions. In Bosnia, for instance, CIVPOL involvement in trafficking and prostitution of women set a horrendous example and undermined public confidence and respect for police.[112] Monitoring and accountability for misconduct must apply to international as well as domestic police.

B. Police–State Relations: The Critical Larger System

The ultimate impact of even far-reaching organizational reform depends critically on the larger political system in which the police function. Even the most impressive recruiting and training programs and organizational reforms are unlikely to yield sustainable police reform if political conditions are not hospitable. As we have pointed out earlier, the synergistic approach to legal reform emphasizes the vital importance of the larger political system in which state institutions function. It also cautions against reforming one part of the justice system without adequate attention to the other essential components. Haiti's experience illustrates why.

1. Haiti's Mixed Record of Police Reform

Haiti's mixed record of police reform following the 1994 U.S-led intervention shows the importance of reforming the broader political and legal system in which police operate. Initially off to a promising start, the Haitian National Police "became for a time the most honest and effective component of the Haitian bureaucracy, only to find itself slowly sucked back into the culture of corruption, incompetence, and politicization in which it was embedded."[113] This experience highlights some positive lessons but also some traps to avoid in police reform after intervention.

When the United States launched Operation Uphold Democracy in 1994, U.S., Haitian, and international policymakers made reform of Haiti's corrupt and brutal security forces a high priority. Haiti had no police force separate from the much-feared military, and, with U.S. assistance, a minimally trained and quickly vetted Interim Public Security Force (IPSF) was deployed as a temporary measure. The presence of former military in this force undermined its credibility among the Haitian public, long accustomed to abuse by security

---

[112] Fitzsimmons, Engendering Justice and Security after War, *supra* note 83, at 365–366; Perito, WHERE IS THE LONE RANGER WHEN WE NEED HIM?, *supra* note 60, at 281–288. Regarding similar problems in Kosovo, *see* Rausch, *From Elation to Disappointment: Justice and Security Reform in Kosovo*, *supra* note 46, at 288, 291.

[113] James Dobbins et al., *America's Role in Nation-Building: From Germany to Iraq* Rand, September, 2003, at 77, *available at* http://www.rand.org/pubs/monograph_reports/MR1753/MR1753.pref.pdf.

forces; a new, well-trained police force was clearly needed. Shortly after President Aristide resumed office, he abolished Haiti's thuggish military and supported implementation of a major international effort to develop and train a new police force, the Haitian National Police (HNP). Over 5000 new police were recruited, trained, and eventually deployed.[114]

A number of factors help explain the initial success in developing a credible and broadly respected police force in Haiti. For one, substantial international resources were devoted to selecting and training the force. Beginning from scratch and setting high standards for admission into the force were also critical: members of the much-feared military were largely excluded from the new force, which was vital to gaining public confidence and establishing new patterns of behavior. In addition to high selection standards – high school graduation, physical and written exams, interviews, screening for war crimes, among other things – an intensive four-month course of training was provided by experienced U.S., Canadian, and French personnel. International CIVPOL then acted as field training officers, going on joint patrols and helping to mentor and monitor HNP officers. In addition, the office of the Inspector General provided domestic oversight, receiving and investigating complaints regarding police misconduct. Although some of the new recruits followed the pattern of their predecessors in committing human rights violations, many who did so were investigated and punished, a "revolutionary" development in a country where impunity was long the norm.[115] Moreover, despite ongoing problems, the Haitian police gradually improved and began to operate in a reasonably professional manner.

But the failure to make comparable gains in the courts and the political system more generally undermined improvements in policing. Haiti's corrupt and easily intimidated judges quickly released suspects with political influence or money, while other suspects languished in pretrial detention for months or even years. Moreover, Haiti's government and other powerful local actors increasingly pressured the senior police leadership to serve political ends.[116] Such political pressure was particularly intense in the lead up to the 2000 elections. Seeing much of their work prove fruitless, and lacking the numbers and resources to do their job effectively, Haiti's newly trained police soon became demoralized. Some quit, and many of those who remained were tempted to take the law into their own hands in the face of judicial corruption and inefficiency, or returned to old practices of accepting bribes and mistreating prisoners.

[114] Washington Office on Latin America, *Haiti's Police Reform: Can Slow Progress be Sustained?*, December 1997, Executive Summary, at 1, *available at* http://www.wola.org/publications/haiti_police_reform_sustained.pdf.
[115] Id.
[116] *See* Elizabeth Farnsworth, Online Newshour, *Policing Haiti*, January 11, 2000, *available at* http://www.pbs.org/newshour/bb/international/jan–june00/haiti_1–11.html.

When a new UN mission deployed in Haiti in 2004, following Aristide's departure, much of the earlier progress in developing the HNP had been severely undermined by years of politicization, demoralization, and bad habits. An International Crisis Group (ICG) report in 2005 found that public distrust of the police in the capital's poor neighborhoods was extremely high, that a significant number of police were involved in crime and human rights violations, largely with impunity, and that the HNP "seems unable to protect Haiti's citizens" or sustain their confidence.[117] Although "[t]here are still competent HNP officers who perform their duties with extreme dedication under difficult conditions," the ICG warns that former military members have been integrated into the police "without proper screening or training" and that the HNP has resorted to "military-style operations in the capital's poor neighborhoods with little regard for collateral damage to civilians."[118] There is a compelling need for better, more enduring international and domestic oversight of the police, and for additional recruitment and training of qualified new HNP officers; but today – compared to the mid- to late 1990s – international resources and attention are in far shorter supply.

Haiti's difficult experience with police reform illustrates a fundamental reality: sustainable police reform depends on reforms in the broader political system of which police are a part. Indeed, in the absence of political reform, intervener assistance in building up indigenous police forces can even be counterproductive. Two traps are especially important to avoid.

2. Trap to Avoid: Institution-Building without Corresponding Political Reform

Reformers need to be wary of prematurely building up state institutions – such as the police – in the absence of corresponding governance reforms. Institution-building should not get ahead of political reform or efforts to build effective checks and balances. Otherwise, interveners may unwittingly build up potential instruments of state oppression. If a self-serving leader uses police and courts to protect and bolster his own power and to engage in political vendettas, for instance, or to oppress disadvantaged groups, then building up those institutions and providing them with more resources will not strengthen "the rule of law." Effective institution-building, in short, must be part of a larger political strategy of governance reform.

Avoiding giving institutional tools to abusive power-holders is a challenge that can take very different forms in different societies. In Afghanistan, for example, the lack of central government oversight and authority in many areas outside the capital has often left police in the provinces subject to

---

[117] International Crisis Group, *Spoiling Security in Haiti*, May 2005, at 10–12.
[118] Id., at 13.

control or intimidation by local warlords and militia commanders.[119] Furthermore, a shortfall in international funding "means that the central government lacks the resources to fund the police outside of the capital, and thus the ability to reduce the influence of regional leaders."[120] A program for police training at seven regional training centers is being developed, but the continuing lack of central government oversight in the provinces, coupled with corruption and political influence over the judiciary by regional commanders, has severely undermined efforts to strengthen the rule of law outside the capital. Changing behavior is extraordinarily difficult when newly trained police officers are deployed to local police stations often "staffed by poorly trained, illiterate conscripts or former militia members who have little loyalty to the central government" and when local commanders pressure trained police to practice extortion.[121] Afghanistan's predicament underscores the difficulty of making progress on justice system reform – beyond Kabul, in this case – when background or regional political conditions are hostile.

3. Another Trap to Avoid: Unbalanced Reform in the Justice System

Reformers also need to avoid unbalanced reforms that focus on one component of the justice system without sufficient attention to the others – one of the problems in Haiti. Police reform often receives more early attention and funding than judicial reform, and efforts to restore order and improve justice have often faltered for lack of broader systemic reform.[122] Yet, as Robert Perito explains, the "most serious challenges to fledgling police services derive from weak judicial institutions and from traditions of intimidation and authoritarianism in society."[123] Even if police reform progresses more quickly than other justice system reforms, it is "not itself sufficient to remedy a paralyzed judicial system, an inadequate legal code, an overcrowded penal system, or political manipulation of the judicial process."[124] Rather, all aspects of the "investigation to incarceration" continuum must be working well for justice system reform to prove sustainable.

[119] Police in the provinces often "owe their allegiance to local warlords and militia commanders and not to the central government" and many are "former Mujahedeen who have experienced a lifetime of armed conflict and are accustomed to acting with impunity." Miller & Perito, *Establishing the Rule of Law in Afghanistan, supra* note 32, at 10–11.

[120] Id., at 11.

[121] U.S. Government Accounting Office, *Afghanistan Security, supra* note 103, at 22. GAO investigators were informed "that many police resort to corrupt practices, in part because their salaries are low and inconsistently paid." Id.

[122] *See* Miller & Perito, *Establishing the Rule of Law in Afghanistan, supra* note 32, at 2, regarding this problem in Afghanistan.

[123] Perito, *National Police Training within an Executive Police Operation, supra* note 70, at 97.

[124] Mark S. Ellis, *International Legal Assistance*, in POST-CONFLICT JUSTICE (M. Cherif Bassiouni, ed., 2002), at 922.

The need for a holistic and integrated approach to justice system reform is now well understood, at least intellectually. Police, prisons, and courts must function effectively together. "If unreformed, any one of these elements can diminish the effects and even undo reforms in the other parts of the justice system."[125] If reformed police forces arrest criminal suspects only to have them released by corrupt and intimidated judges, for instance, or if suspects languish in squalid prisons for months or years without access to judicial process, the entire law enforcement system is undermined.

Yet developing integrated, functional teams – and planning processes – is often extremely difficult in practice. Different donors and organizations focus on their particular priority projects often without sufficient coordination with other actors, as we discuss further in Chapter 9. Also, finding sufficient funds to support reform in some components of the justice system – particularly prisons – has frequently proven especially difficult, as we will now examine.

C. Prison Reform: Too Often Neglected

Prisons generally get the short end of the stick in post-conflict legal reform. International attention and donor resources typically flow far more readily to police and judicial reform.[126] In post-conflict societies, the prison "systems" are often devastated and squalid, poorly equipped, and poorly run. The task of bringing them up to even basic standards can be so daunting that donors – faced with many needs crying out for resources and attention – prefer to focus on other more "attractive" and more quickly achievable projects.

Domestic attitudes can also complicate support for prison reform. In desperately poor countries, ordinary citizens struggle daily to feed and sustain their families. "When foreign assistance is directed at prisoners and prison conditions, locals view this as favoring 'criminals' over 'victims,' and increasing the legitimacy of prisoners."[127] If prisoners have better food and living conditions than ordinary people in surrounding areas, the public resentment may be considerable. As a U.S. military officer in charge of one prison in Haiti told a foreign visitor in 1995, she was more worried about people from the surrounding neighborhood wanting to break in to the prison (which served decent and regular meals) than about anyone breaking out.[128]

Yet neglect of prisons can have profoundly negative consequences. As a matter of basic humanity, the potential for human beings to abuse other human beings, sadly, is enormous in prison situations where guards wield

---

[125] Dobbins et al., *America's Role in Nation-Building: From Germany to Iraq, supra* note 113, at 84–85.

[126] Mani, BEYOND RETRIBUTION, *supra* note 16, at 66 ("As recently as 1992, donors were unaware of or unwilling to address this issue").

[127] Id., at 67.

[128] Interview with James A. Schear, November 5, 2005.

virtually total control over detainees. Without adequate standards, training, and monitoring, the potential for serious abuse is always present. To complicate matters further, in many post-conflict situations, the rudimentary prisons and jails include many detainees (perhaps even a majority) who have never been tried or convicted of offenses. Moreover, because of inadequate review of pretrial detention, they may languish there, uncharged and untried, for months or even years. And if violent and nonviolent offenders, adults and children, men and women, are placed together, the risk to detainees and the potential for abuse is even greater.

Beyond the inherent concern for the basic rights of detainees, prison abuse can cause enormous harm to the credibility of interveners. If interveners themselves are running prisons and fail to comply with basic standards, the public outrage and fallout can be profound. Instances of abuse of detainees at Abu Ghraib prison in Iraq have had severe consequences for the United States. The abuse has profoundly undermined U.S. stature in the region and around the world, and it has served as a recruiting tool for insurgents fighting against U.S. efforts to bring stability to Iraq. It has also undermined the credibility of U.S. advocacy for the rule of law and humane treatment of prisoners in Iraq and elsewhere, impairing the rule of law message the United States hoped to promote.

Abuse of detainees by Iraqis in Iraqi-run detention centers has also generated enormous concern and anger, especially among Iraq's Sunni population. Several raids on Iraqi government detention centers in November and December 2005 uncovered instances of severe abuse by Iraqis of scores of Iraqi detainees.[129] The United States subsequently announced that the U.S. military will not turn over detainees or detention centers under U.S. control to Iraqi custody until improved standards are in place in Iraqi facilities and adequate training of Iraqi prison personnel has taken place.[130]

As a long-term systemic matter, the effective administration of justice depends on prisons that are humane and well run. Efforts to reform justice institutions and develop public confidence in them will be undermined if prisons remain largely immune from decent standards and government oversight. In Afghanistan, for instance, outside Kabul "it appears that all or most actually functioning prisons and detention facilities" are controlled

---

[129] John F. Burns, *Torture Alleged at Ministry Site Outside Baghdad*, THE NEW YORK TIMES, November 16, 2005, at A1; Dexter Filkins, *Sunnis Accuse Iraqi Military of Executions*, THE NEW YORK TIMES, November 29, 2005, at A1; John F. Burns, *To Halt Abuses, U.S. Will Inspect Jails Run by Iraq*, THE NEW YORK TIMES, December 14, 2005, at A1. Problems of Iraqi mistreatment of detainees preceded these raids. *See, e.g.*, Human Rights Watch, *The New Iraq: Torture and Ill-Treatment of Detainees in Iraqi Custody*, January 2005, *available at* http://hrw.org/reports/2005/iraq0105/.

[130] Eric Schmitt & Thom Shanker, *U.S., Citing Abuse in Iraqi Prisons, Holds Detainees*, THE NEW YORK TIMES, December 25, 2005, at 1.

not by the central government but "by commanders or other regional power-holders."[131]

Interveners will immediately face a number of issues concerning detention. In the initial, emergency phase of an intervention, the interveners themselves will need procedures and basic facilities in place to handle arrests and detention. In Kosovo, for example, the gap between the deployment of military forces and the arrival of international police meant that within two weeks, KFOR was holding over 200 detainees in makeshift NATO and UN jails, with no functioning courts in which to try them or adequate prisons in which to hold them.[132] Because KFOR forces came from multiple countries, the policing and arrests were not done "according to a uniform standard."[133] Moreover, by holding suspects indefinitely and in many cases without charge, KFOR undercut its own rule of law message.

In Afghanistan and Iraq, the problems of detention confronting interveners have been magnified many times over. In both cases, the United States launched an intervention to topple a regime and now finds itself waging a protracted conflict against insurgent elements. Thus, the population of detainees includes not only ordinary criminals but also a mix of insurgents and terrorist operatives (who, if released, would continue to pose threats to both U.S. forces and the national governments of Iraq and Afghanistan), as well as potential terrorist suspects and, very likely, ordinary people who simply happened to be in the wrong place at the wrong time. The complex and dangerous security environment, coupled with the sheer numbers of detainees and the difficult process of determining the degree of threat posed by individual detainees, has presented a set of issues far beyond those faced in the earlier interventions of the 1990s.

Not only must interveners do better planning on detention procedures and arrangements, but they also must secure existing prison facilities or face the prospect of prison breaks, looting, and destruction of needed infrastructure. Moreover, because managing these institutions eventually will be the responsibility of the domestic government, interveners need to work closely with local authorities to improve domestic prison facilities and procedures and to pave the way for a transition in the control and administration of prisons. At the most fundamental level, goals should include a prison system that is secure, nonabusive, and in accord with basic standards. In addition

---

[131] Miller & Perito, *Establishing the Rule of Law in Afghanistan, supra* note 32, at 12.

[132] Strohmeyer, *Collapse and Reconstruction of a Judicial System, supra* note 9, at 49; Captain Alton L. Gwaltney III, *Law and Order in Kosovo: A Look at Criminal Justice During the First Year of Operation Joint Guardian*, in LESSONS FROM KOSOVO: THE KFOR EXPERIENCE 233 (Larry Wentz, ed., 2002); Rausch, *The Assumption of Authority in Kosovo and East Timor, supra* note 24, at 28 note 32.

[133] Betts, Carlson, & Gisvold, *The Post-Conflict Transitional Administration of Kosovo and the Lessons-Learned in Efforts to Establish a Judiciary and Rule of Law, supra* note 13, at 374.

to providing acceptable living conditions for all detainees, the system should segregate women from men, adults from juveniles, violent from mild offenders, and pretrial detainees from convicted persons. How can such basic goals be achieved? The truly hard issue is balancing a progressive handoff to local authorities with the countervailing requirement for sufficient international oversight to support and sustain reform.

1. Critical Elements of Prison Reform: Rules, Training, and Accountability

Three key elements – rules, training, and accountability – are essential to developing an effective and nonabusive prison system. Even if ample resources are available, clear rules, effective training, oversight, and accountability are needed to protect against abuse in prisons and other detention facilities.

In post-conflict societies, establishing *rules* for prisons that meet basic international standards but are potentially achievable in resource-poor environments is a fundamental challenge. The UN Standard Minimum Rules for the Treatment of Prisoners provide a helpful starting point.[134] In establishing a prison service in East Timor, for example, UNTAET stipulated that every penal institution would operate in accordance with these rules as well as with international human rights conventions and other relevant principles.[135] Another resource (and potential guide) for international and national reformers is the "Model Detention Act" being developed by the U.S. Institute of Peace and the Irish Centre for Human Rights, in cooperation with the Office of the UN High Commissioner for Human Rights and the UN Office on Drugs and Crime. This act addresses a full spectrum of issues from procedures for detention, release, and transfer, to maintaining adequate records, to conditions of detention (such as food, accommodation, sanitation, exercise, medical assistance, separation of female detainees from male detainees, exercise of religion, handling of juvenile detainees, among other important issues), to mechanisms for complaints and oversight.[136]

Even with agreed basic rules and procedures, providing *training* to relevant prison personnel regarding those standards and procedures will be critical to successful reform. The personnel to be trained should include

---

[134] *United Nations Standard Minimum Rules for the Treatment of Prisoners, available at* http://www.unhchr.ch/html/menu3/b/h_comp34.htm.

[135] UNTAET/REG/2001/23, August 28, 2001, at section 2.1. The UN mission in Kosovo also used these and other standards, and, in Afghanistan, the UN assistance mission (UNAMA) translated and distributed copies of the standard minimum rules. Amnesty International, *Afghanistan: Crumbling Prison System Desperately in Need of Repair,* July 2003, at 43, *available at* http://web.amnesty.org/library/index/ENGASA110172003; Rausch, *From Elation to Disappointment: Justice and Security Reform in Kosovo, supra* note 46, at 297.

[136] The Model Detention Act, scheduled to be published by USIP by 2007, is discussed in O'Connor & Rausch, *A Tool Box to Tackle Law Reform Challenges in Post Conflict Countries, supra* note 26, at 13.

wardens and those in leadership positions as well as prison guards and other prison staff.

Finally, an *oversight* capacity is needed. Of critical importance here is the ability to effectively *monitor* compliance with basic rules and procedures, to hold individuals *accountable* for compliance, and to receive and respond to complaints. The UN Standard Minimum Rules for the Treatment of Prisoners provide that prisoners should be notified of their rights and of complaint mechanisms upon admission.[137] Effective internal procedures for addressing complaints are also needed, as are external oversight mechanisms to monitor prison conditions and ensure that prison staff are accountable.[138] In addition, independent monitoring bodies including diverse personnel (such as judges, lawyers, and human rights experts) should visit prisons and assess conditions.[139]

2. Key Additional Factors in Sustaining Prison Reform

The impact of efforts to improve prisons by establishing reasonable rules, training, and oversight will depend critically in the long term on three additional factors. First and fundamentally is the adequacy of *resources*. Satisfying even the most basic standards of decent treatment in prisons – food, clean water, sanitation, health care, avoidance of overcrowding, and so forth – requires resources. This problem is hardly unique to post-conflict countries. In many developing regions, where the shortage of resources (financial and otherwise) is commonplace, prisons are often characterized by horrific overcrowding, poor sanitation, and lack of basic nutrition.[140]

A second key factor is the *adequacy of the other components of the justice system*. A common problem in post-conflict societies is the huge percentage of detainees who have never been charged or tried for offenses, but instead languish for months or years in prison awaiting some kind of legal process. Nearly 80 percent of Haiti's prison population from 1995 to 2001 was in pretrial detention.[141] Similarly, in East Timor, the UN Development Programme found that about 77 percent of detainees in 2002 had not been tried.[142] As a means of addressing the problem of prolonged pretrial detention,

---

[137] Rule No. 35, *Standard Minimum Rules for the Treatment of Prisoners*.

[138] Amnesty International, *Afghanistan: Crumbling Prison System Desperately in Need of Repair, supra* note 135, at 31–32.

[139] Id., at 32.

[140] Michael Wines, *Wasting Away, a Million Wait in African Jails, Many Were Never Tried – Crowding Is Rife*, THE NEW YORK TIMES, November 6, 2005, at 1.

[141] Anne Fuller et al., *Prolonged Pretrial Detention in Haiti*, Vera Institute of Justice, July 2002, at 1, *available at* www.vera.org. This is a national figure, and the study found that the pretrial detention rate was higher in the capital, Port-au-Prince, than in the provinces. Id., at i, 1.

[142] West, *Lawyers, Guns, and Money: Justice and Security Reform in East Timor, supra* note 8, at 340 note 84 (citing UNDP, *Timor-Leste Correctional Service: Setting the Course,* August 2002).

a U.S.-funded project in Haiti brought rotating judicial teams into prisons to review pretrial detention cases, which helped reduce backlogged cases at least for awhile.[143] If prisons are not to be overcrowded wastelands lacking in due process, programs such as this – and improving pretrial review and court systems more generally – will be critical.

A third key factor in prison reform over the longer term is the *commitment of local officials to reform*. Not only the attitude and commitment of domestic officials but also *a positive systemic environment* – political and cultural – will be critical to sustaining reforms. Indeed, interveners need to focus on the issue of sustainability early on as they design and initiate prison reform programs. Local authorities will also need to grapple with the long-term goals of incarceration and prison reform.

In both Kosovo and East Timor, prison reform efforts have enjoyed some relative success. In both situations, international interveners managed the prison system initially and, at least in comparison to other recent interventions, committed fairly significant resources and attention to the effort. Even so, the road has sometimes been rocky and challenges remain. But the positives are worth highlighting.

In Kosovo, neither the United Nations nor international donors put correctional services high on their radar screen initially. Responsibility for overseeing detention fell first on KFOR's shoulders; and UNMIK's delays in planning, budgeting, or securing funding for correctional services revealed a preliminary lack of appreciation of the importance of this task. But in October 1999, the UN mission established a Penal Management Division (PMD) and, soon thereafter, the Kosovo Correctional Service (KCS). The PMD/KCS gradually assumed responsibility for corrections and applied, among other things, the UN minimum standards for the treatment of prisoners.[144] International experts provided leadership and training, and nearly 600 KCS staff were trained and posted in prison facilities by November 2000.[145] On balance, international observers credit PMD for improving conditions in prisons, for working with other components of the justice system to address issues such as "illegal detention" and "alternative penalties," and for "striving to maintain positive relations with the prisoners, for instance, by simply taking time to explain the process and rules and what could be expected in detention as well as in court."[146] Nevertheless, challenges remain, including to improve arrangements for mentally ill and juvenile offenders and to

---

[143] Fuller et al., *Prolonged Pretrial Detention in Haiti, supra* note 141, at 10.

[144] Rausch, *From Elation to Disappointment: Justice and Security Reform in Kosovo, supra* note 46, at 297.

[145] Id. Raush explains that "correctional officers attend[] a four-week Corrections Officer Course at the Kosovo Police Service School" and that by January 2002, "[s]ome 700 officers had been trained and deployed." Id., at 298.

[146] Id., at 297–298.

maintain adequate resources, oversight, and training to sustain the local corrections capacity that has been developed.

International involvement in managing prisons and building local capacity was also significant in East Timor. The United Nations ran the prisons prior to Timor-Leste's independence in 2002, and international corrections personnel, primarily from New Zealand and Australia, provided leadership and expertise. New Zealand Department of Corrections officers provided training to Timorese prison staff.[147] UNTAET enacted a comprehensive regulation in 2001 providing for the establishment and management of penal institutions in East Timor, laying out institutional arrangements, procedures for the admission and treatment of inmates, and complaint mechanisms, among other things.[148]

Despite international efforts to reform prisons in East Timor, a long history during the Indonesian occupation of forced disappearances and of use of legal process to punish dissenters has left many Timorese deeply distrustful of prisons and "fearful of what happens to prisoners."[149] In the longer run, sustaining adequate standards in East Timor's prisons will depend on the willingness and ability of the government to commit the necessary funds and effort. Furthermore, the problem of prolonged pretrial detention remains extremely serious, and finding effective ways to expedite judicial review of pending matters is an urgent need.[150]

Haiti's uneven experience with prison reform illustrates the difficulty of sustaining progress without continued outside involvement, resources, and pressure. Penal reform in Haiti was off to a relatively promising start under the UN mission in the mid- to late 1990s. International donors contributed resources, UNDP provided training to penitentiary personnel, new facilities were built, a separate prison for women and minors was opened, and, with international support, prison procedures, including maintaining prisoner records and prison registers, were improved.[151] An innovative program to cut down on pretrial detention brought court personnel to the National Penitentiary to review cases.[152] Later, however, international support, training, and monitoring were cut back, and prisons stagnated, with persistent problems of overcrowding, unhealthy living conditions, and prolonged

---

[147] West, *Lawyers, Guns, and Money: Justice and Security Reform in East Timor, supra* note 8, at 329.

[148] UNTAET/REG/2001/23, August 28, 2001.

[149] West, *Lawyers, Guns, and Money: Justice and Security Reform in East Timor, supra* note 8, at 339, 329.

[150] Id., at 340. UNDP estimated in 2002 that about 77 percent of prisoners in East Timor were awaiting trial. UNDP, *Timor-Leste Correctional Service: Setting the Course*, August 2002.

[151] Fuller et al., *Prolonged Pretrial Detention in Haiti, supra* note 141, at 6, 15–17; Amnesty International, *Haiti: Unfinished Business: Justice and Liberties at Risk*, March 2000, at 16.

[152] Fuller et al., *Prolonged Pretrial Detention in Haiti, supra* note 141, at 10.

pretrial detention.[153] Early reforms clearly were not sufficient to secure enduring change, particularly without greater corresponding reforms in the justice system more broadly.

Afghanistan illustrates, yet again, the relative neglect of prisons and correctional reform that too often occurs in post-conflict societies. After over twenty-three years of conflict, Afghanistan's prisons, which frequently had served as places of mistreatment and torture, were in desperate shape.[154] But despite glaring problems, little was done to address prisons in the first year of the UN Assistance Mission in Afghanistan (UNAMA). Only in 2003, after prisons were transferred from the Ministry of the Interior to the Ministry of Justice, did one of the countries involved in UNAMA (Italy) assume a lead role as part of its justice system responsibilities.[155] The UN Office on Drugs and Crime has provided most of the international support on prisons, including assistance in drafting a new Afghan law of prisons and detention centers consistent with the UN minimum standards for the treatment of prisoners, training in implementing the law and on methods to monitor prison institutions, improving prison facilities in Kabul, and strengthening management capability within the Ministry of Justice.[156] Still, the remaining problems are daunting – especially the lack of central government oversight of prisons and detention centers outside the capital, many of which are controlled by regional commanders with no monitoring or accountability at all.[157]

The mixed experiences with post-conflict prison reform highlight several recurring issues. First is the risk of neglecting prisons relative to other components of the justice system, at least early on. Second is the frequent

---

[153] A 2002 study found that the vast majority of detainees had not been tried, with most waiting for months and many for years. Id., at i, 4. Nationwide, "as many as 400 to 500 people have been [stuck in] pretrial detention since 1999 or earlier." Id., at 4.

[154] Prison conditions were appalling, including lack of food, clean water, or sanitation; prison personnel were largely unaware of basic rights of prisoners and often had not been paid for months; many detainees were held for long periods without charge or trial; and, outside Kabul, regional commanders or warlords reportedly control abusive detention facilities without any supervision by the central government. Amnesty International, *Afghanistan: Crumbling Prison System Desperately in Need of Repair, supra* note 135, at 16, 25, 29–30, 36, 38, 41, 43. *See also* Miller & Perito, *Establishing the Rule of Law in Afghanistan, supra* note 32, at 12.

[155] Amnesty International, *Afghanistan: Crumbling Prison System Desperately in Need of Repair, supra* note 135, at 13.

[156] Id.; Jones et al., ESTABLISHING LAW AND ORDER AFTER CONFLICT, *supra* note 17, at 80; UNODC press release, *Afghan and International Legal Experts Meet to Discuss the New Prison Law and Relation to Human Rights Principles*, June 13, 2005, *available at* http://www.reliefweb.int/rw/RWB.NSF/db900SID/EVOD-6DBH56?Open Document.

[157] As Amnesty International stresses, "[t]he widespread existence of such unofficial systems jeopardizes the attempts of the [Afghan authorities] to establish the legitimacy of the formal law enforcement apparatus and the provincial government system as a whole." Amnesty International, *Afghanistan: Crumbling Prison System Desperately in Need of Repair, supra* note 135, at 41.

need for substantial international involvement, expertise, and resources to begin to bring prison conditions and procedures up to even rudimentary standards – and the need for continuing international involvement to help sustain reforms. Third and finally, as we have emphasized throughout this chapter, is the need for a systemic approach to reform: many of the serious problems in prisons – notably chronic overcrowding and prolonged detention of individuals awaiting trial – will not be solved without improvements in the justice system more broadly.

This brings us to the next component of an effective justice system: courts and the capacity for fair and efficient adjudication.

V. STRENGTHENING THE COURTS

It practically goes without saying that fair and functioning courts are essential to an effective justice system. If courts are dysfunctional, corruptible, or manipulated by powerful interests, government will not be bound by law; there will be no equality under the law; little recourse will exist for arbitrary and capricious behavior; litigants will not receive due process; arrested individuals may languish in pretrial detention; wealthy criminals will go free; and the public will have little confidence in the justice system.

Building a court system unblemished by these problems would be a difficult task even under good conditions. Yet, in countries transitioning out of conflict, where the courts may suffer from damaged infrastructure, an ill-trained, politicized, or corrupted judiciary, and ingrained public mistrust, the barriers can seem impossibly high. Many aspects of the judicial system are likely to require simultaneous reform, each of which can take considerable time, and critical reforms often run up against entrenched interests at the highest levels of government and society. Unfortunately, post-conflict judicial reform efforts often only scratch the surface of these deeper problems.

A. The Complexities of Post-Conflict Court Reform

The struggle to rebuild the Bosnian judicial and legal system provides one illustration of the magnitude and complexity of court reform. Since adoption of the Dayton Agreement, an alphabet soup of international organizations and NGOs has worked to promote judicial reform and respect for the rule of law in Bosnia. Foreign experts descended on the country en masse to offer technical assistance on drafting legislation (on everything from corruption to human rights to criminal procedure), improving court administration, and training of judges and lawyers to international standards. Under the aegis of the Office of the High Representative (OHR), the Independent Judicial Commission (IJC) took the lead on judicial reform, with the assistance of numerous international agencies and NGOs. To strengthen the independence of judges and prosecutors, OHR mandated salary raises and a comprehensive peer review process designed to weed out corrupt, incompetent, and biased judges.[158] When peer review failed (because local judges lacked the incentive and capacity to vet their peers and because the IJC lacked adequate supervisory capabilities), a new process of general reappointment replaced it, forcing all would-be judges to receive approval from a judicial body with both foreign and domestic members.[159] OHR pushed through a host of new laws and legal reforms, created a new State Court, strengthened the Bosnian Human Rights Chamber, and worked to combat spreading corruption. The United Nations initiated a program to monitor criminal court proceedings and to provide other assistance, and the OSCE and the Council of Europe both provided training programs and advice on legislative drafting.

Despite all this effort and the millions of dollars spent, the International Crisis Group (ICG) concluded in 2002 that "[i]n comparison to the sums expended, the results achieved have been pitiful."[160] Even though the number of courts doubled after the war, the courts have been "swamped on all levels with a backlog of cases reckoned in the tens of thousands."[161] The court system is "inefficient, bloated and very expensive,"[162] legislation is still outdated, reversal rates are high, efforts to punish members of the political elite or their associates for corruption and other crimes are futile, and the participation of foreign judges remains essential to combat open ethnic bias. In short, despite years of intensive international efforts, the ICG concluded that the "law does not yet rule" in Bosnia: "What prevail instead are nationally defined politics, inconsistency in the application of law, corrupt and incompetent courts, a fragmented judicial space, half-baked or half-implemented reforms, and sheer negligence."[163]

The problems in Bosnia stem from many factors, including the nature of the conflict, the prewar state of the legal system, the havoc caused by the war itself, the postwar entrenchment of organized crime, and ongoing interethnic tensions. Moreover, efforts at reform have been complicated and in some respects impeded by the Dayton Agreement, which in addition to creating a framework for peace also created a fractured judicial and political space. By recognizing lines drawn during the conflict, the Dayton Agreement ensures that law-making in Bosnia takes place inconsistently and often haphazardly among "one state, two entities, ten cantons in the Federation, and Brcko

---

[158] *See* International Crisis Group, *Courting Disaster: The Misrule of Law in Bosnia and Herzegovina*, Balkans Report No. 127, March 25, 2002, at 6–7.

[159] Id., at 7.

[160] Id., at 3.

[161] Id., at 12.

[162] Id.

[163] Id., at i.

District."[164] Attempts to prosecute crime across entity and cantonal boundaries often founder for want of cooperation. More fundamentally, because competing visions about the identity and unity of the state were not resolved at Dayton, efforts at reform of the legal system constantly run up against the political implications of every decision. Political leaders in the Republic of Srpska, for example, resist every effort at unifying the legal system for fear it will undermine Srpska's autonomy.

International reform efforts, though well intentioned and successful in particular areas, have thus had at best a modest impact overall. In part, those efforts have suffered from inadequate coordination, inadequate resources, insufficient familiarity with local norms, and lack of overall strategic direction. More importantly, those efforts have suffered from an internal contradiction: efforts to impose uniformity and international standards through the broad decision-making powers accorded to the High Representative, although substantively desirable, always run into the problem of attempting to build the rule of law through what appears to be its procedural antithesis – the unreviewable exercise of power.

But the experience in Bosnia has not been all negative. In Brcko District, a coordinated and systematic reform effort produced dramatic improvements within two years. Rather than vetting and reviewing existing judges, all candidates for the judiciary and prosecution had to reapply, resulting "in the replacement of 80 per cent of the previous office holders"; moreover, judges and prosecutors were appointed only for a probationary one-year period, followed by a performance review for long-term tenure.[165] A modernized criminal code and other reforms improved the efficiency of the courts, and the ICG reports that "corruption and bribery have been banished from Brcko's courts": the "old milieu in which judges and prosecutors could be bought by the new rich, by politicians and by lawyers has gone."[166] At the national level, the Bosnian Human Rights Chamber, which operated from 1999 to 2003 and was composed of both national and international judges, provided a valuable and respected forum for addressing human rights abuses.[167] And the Special War Crimes Chamber within Bosnia's State Court, composed of national and international jurists, is beginning to make progress, as we discuss in Chapter 7. Finally, the possible rewriting of Bosnia's constitution holds out promise for constructing a less complex and divided legal and judicial system.

---

[164] Id., at 4.
[165] Id., at 49.
[166] Id., at 50.
[167] See J. David Yeager, *The Human Rights Chamber for Bosnia and Herzegovina: A Case Study in Transitional Justice*, 14 INT'L LEGAL PERSP. 44 (2004); Timothy Cornell & Lance Salisbury, *The Importance of Civil Law in the Transition to Peace: Lessons From the Human Rights Chamber for Bosnia and Herzegovina*, 35 CORNELL INT'L L. J. 389 (2002).

If Bosnia's experience provides a sobering illustration of the challenges involved in building a functioning judiciary, it is hardly alone in that respect. In Afghanistan, for example, the poor qualifications of many judges, the lack of central government oversight outside the capital, and the influence that warlords, regional commanders, and other powerful actors exercise over judges (complicated by the enormous corrupting influence of drug trafficking), are fundamental obstacles to effective judicial reform. In Kosovo, continuing ethnic tensions and the uncertainty about the territory's ultimate political status have greatly complicated efforts to strengthen the justice system. Across a variety of unique post-conflict situations, there is a clear need for more ambitious and strategic approaches to judicial reform.

Probably the single greatest challenge to building an independent and impartial judiciary in many post-conflict societies is the problem of political influence and entrenched corruption. Faced with devastated court systems, interveners and local reformers focus understandably on immediate needs such as vetting, appointing, and training judges; rebuilding destroyed or looted courthouses; and providing furniture, electricity, and basic supplies. But for long-term success, reformers must also address the harder, more intractable challenges. The legal framework itself must be clear and well understood; structural protections to encourage independent, impartial judicial decision-making must be put in place; judicial appointment processes must be transparent and based on merit and qualifications rather than cronyism and patronage; court operations and judicial proceedings must be made more transparent; and disciplinary and judicial system monitoring mechanisms are needed. Above all, the larger political system must permit and encourage impartial adjudication rather than manipulation and control of judicial decision-making by government elites, self-interested litigants, or other powerful local actors.

Much can be learned from a growing literature of case studies and reports exploring in detail the particular difficulties and accomplishments of judicial reform efforts in a wide variety of post-conflict settings.[168] Our goal here is to highlight some of the most significant, recurring challenges that reformers are likely to face – as well as traps to avoid – as they contend with the specific needs and circumstances of particular post-conflict societies. We focus first on the crucial importance of transparent and merit-based appointment processes. We then examine challenges in providing appropriate training, in creating effective disciplinary and monitoring mechanisms, and in finding an effective mix of international and local jurists to support domestic

---

[168] *See, e.g.,* the chapters in CONSTRUCTING JUSTICE AND SECURITY AFTER WAR, *supra* note 8, and country studies and reports by the International Crisis Group, Amnesty International, the Asia Foundation, the United States Institute of Peace, and other organizations and agencies engaged in judicial and rule of law reform, among the many helpful sources by scholars and practitioners.

capacity-building. We also examine the critically important problems of reducing corruption and external pressure, increasing transparency in judicial operations and proceedings, improving access to justice, and investing in education and civil society.

B. Strengthening Judiciaries after Conflict

As with other elements of rule of law reform, a baseline assessment of judicial system capacity is a vital first step.[169] Reformers need a clear sense of the skills, experience, and quality of existing judges – and of other legal personnel, including prosecutors, defense attorneys, and administrators. Also, as Erik Jensen argues, reformers need good empirical information about "what courts actually do" in particular societies and how they relate to other "noncourt" dispute resolution mechanisms.[170] Interveners and donors, moreover, need to assess "the degree of receptivity to change" and the political will of local leaders to build a fair and competent judicial system.[171]

In many post-conflict societies, judiciaries have functioned as "an extension of executive branch, elite, or military domination of the country."[172] Poorly trained, demoralized, and sometimes corrupt judges do not tend to view themselves – nor does the public view them – as agents of impartial justice. All too often, the process of appointment and promotion was based not on legal qualifications or competence but on loyalty and subservience to those in political control. In such circumstances, what are the reforms needed to build a competent and impartial judiciary – a judiciary largely composed of judges who decide cases fairly based on the facts and the law, not on the basis of political influence or other external pressure?[173]

1. Merit-Based Appointment: A Fundamental Reform

Few reforms are more fundamental than establishing a transparent, merit-based appointment process. Indeed, if the existing process was "designed to facilitate the exercise of influence by outside parties, as is true in many countries, it will be difficult to overcome that flaw with checks farther down in the system."[174] Even when appointment processes appear designed to check

---

[169] As Mark Ellis points out, a prompt assessment is needed to "identify which areas of the judicial system are intact and functional, and which areas need to be redeployed, recreated, or redesigned." Ellis, *International Legal Assistance, supra* note 124, at 928.

[170] Jensen, *The Rule of Law and Judicial Reform, supra* note 6, at 337, 362–364.

[171] U.S. Agency for International Development, Office of Democracy and Governance, *Guidance for Promoting Judicial Independence and Impartiality*, revised edition, January 2002, at 40 (hereinafter AID, *Guidance for Promoting Judicial Independence and Impartiality*), *available at* http://www.usaid.gov/our_work/democracy_and_governance/publications/pdfs/pnacm007.pdf.

[172] Id., at 6.

[173] For helpful analysis, *see* id; Ellis, *International Legal Assistance, supra* note 124, at 927–933.

[174] AID, *Guidance for Promoting Judicial Independence and Impartiality, supra* note 171, at 12.

political influence, they may not work that way in practice. For example, although Sierra Leone's constitution provides for executive appointment of judges subject to legislative confirmation, the impact of these structural safeguards is undercut by practical realities, including: executive domination of the legislature, an executive practice of appointing judges on short-term contracts, a pattern of executive removal of judges who buck executive wishes, difficulty in recruiting judicial candidates because of poor pay and working conditions, and lack of public esteem for the judiciary.[175]

Developing transparent and merit-based appointment procedures – and recruiting and selecting qualified judges – has been a central challenge in many post-conflict societies. Civil law and common law countries typically use different appointment mechanisms, but the particular method used is less important than the transparency of the process and the selection of judges based on qualifications.[176] Also critical is ensuring that qualified women and minority lawyers are part of the candidate pool and that the ultimate composition of the judiciary is inclusive and representative of the society at large. Achieving even basic objectives such as these can be particularly challenging in post-conflict environments where judges are needed urgently and must be appointed quickly.

Kosovo is one example. Faced with escalating crime, a total collapse of the previous judicial and law enforcement system, and a growing number of pretrial detainees, UNMIK quickly established a seven-member commission of local and international legal experts to review and recommend judicial and prosecutorial candidates; shortly thereafter, the head of the UN mission appointed nine judges and prosecutors who served in mobile units and conducted detention hearings throughout Kosovo.[177] But local controversy flared over the commission's composition and over some appointments. By July 1999, as more candidates were identified, UNMIK appointed twenty-eight judges and prosecutors, including "twenty-one Kosovar Albanians, four Serbs, one Roma, one member of the Turkish community in Kosovo, and one Bosniak."[178] Although a number of Kosovar Albanians had served as judges or prosecutors prior to 1989 or had other relevant legal background, their lack of experience in an impartial system of justice, coupled with external threats, intimidation, and pressure upon some judges posed significant challenges to building an independent judiciary.[179] Moreover, UNMIK's efforts to create a multiethnic judiciary have faced severe

---

[175] Cole & Sesay, *Traditional Justice Systems and the Rule of Law in Post-Conflict Sierra Leone*, *supra* note 21.

[176] AID, *Guidance for Promoting Judicial Independence and Impartiality*, *supra* note 171, at 13, 17, 47.

[177] Strohmeyer, *Collapse and Reconstruction of a Judicial System*, *supra* note 9, at 52–53.

[178] Id., at 53.

[179] International Crisis Group, *Finding the Balance: The Scales of Justice in Kosovo*, ICG Balkans Report No. 134, September 12, 2002, at 5.

obstacles: Serb judges have been reluctant to serve for political, economic, and security reasons, and parallel Serbian courts continue to function.[180]

In East Timor, a judiciary has literally been built from scratch, on the smoldering devastation left by fleeing Indonesian military and militia forces. Systematic discrimination during Indonesia's occupation denied Timorese lawyers the opportunity to serve as judges and prosecutors, leaving "a huge void in experienced legal personnel."[181] Upon its arrival, UNTAET sought to identify Timorese "lawyers, law graduates, and law students" (including by dropping leaflets from INTERFET aircraft), and it established the Transitional Judicial Service Commission, composed of three Timorese and two international experts, to review, interview, and recommend candidates for the judiciary based on merit. The UN transitional administrator then appointed East Timorese judges and prosecutors beginning in January 2000, although "only a few of these jurists had any practical legal experience, some in law firms and legal aid organizations in Java and other parts of the Indonesian archipelago, and others as paralegals with Timorese human rights organizations and resistance groups."[182] Despite their lack of prior judicial or prosecutorial experience, UNTAET provided only "a series of one-week, compulsory 'quick impact' training courses" before these judges and prosecutors took office, with subsequent on-the-job training and international mentoring to follow.[183]

Rather than starting from scratch, just the opposite process was followed in Bosnia. In 1996, Bosnia's judges and prosecutors received "initial five-year mandates" to be followed later by a review process for long-term appointment.[184] However, the comprehensive peer-review process was ill-conceived, underresourced, and ineffective, resulting in a replacement rate of less than 2.5 percent before it was ultimately terminated.[185] Far more effective was the "general reappointment" procedure followed in Brcko District, where all judges and prosecutors were required to resign followed by a general process of reapplication and reappointment of qualified candidates – based on transparent and merit-based criteria – for a probationary period of one year.[186]

---

[180] Id., at 10; *Kosovo Judicial System: Assessment & Proposed Options, 2003–2004*, Report prepared pursuant to a request of the Special Representative of the Secretary-General United Nation Mission in Kosovo and the Kosovo Judicial and Prosecutorial Council, at 8.

[181] Strohmeyer, *Collapse and Reconstruction of a Judicial System, supra* note 9, at 53–54.

[182] Id., at 54. Judge Ximenes, however, who is the President of East Timor's Court of Appeal, had served as a judge in Portugal.

[183] Id., at 55, 56.

[184] International Crisis Group, *Courting Disaster: The Misrule of Law in Bosnia & Herzegovina, supra* note 158, at 39.

[185] Id., at 36. As the International Crisis Group concluded: "The Bosnian context of a highly politicised, war-inflated, post-socialist, nationally divided, financially dependent and institutionally deficient judiciary made peer review a virtual contradiction in terms." Id., at 37.

[186] Id., at 49.

Despite the benefits of such an approach, it is not always politically possible. In Afghanistan, for instance, efforts to introduce more transparent and merit-based appointment procedures have run up against entrenched resistance. Judges of the Supreme Court are appointed by the president subject to approval by the lower house of Afghanistan's parliament; but the appointment of other judges does not have this check. Instead, these judges are appointed by the president based on nominations by the Supreme Court (with the Chief Justice playing the major role).[187] Although Afghan law sets out the qualifications required for judicial office, many judges do not possess these qualifications.[188] Indeed, "many judges appointed in the post-Taliban period, including some on the Supreme Court, do not have a legal education (secular or *Shari'a*)" at all.[189] Amnesty International reports, moreover, that "the judicial appointment process has been marred with political manipulation and bias, including pressure from armed groups," with many judges voicing concern about the nomination and selection of unqualified individuals based on "political manipulation within the Supreme Court."[190] Furthermore, neither the Supreme Court nor the president's office have shown much willingness to initiate proceedings to remove unqualified judges.

At the same time, the opportunities for qualified women in the Afghan judiciary are limited. "With the exception of the heads of the juvenile and family courts in Kabul, women are excluded from key positions within the judiciary" and "are rarely involved in the adjudication of cases."[191] With all these problems, improving the quality of Afghanistan's judges is, by most accounts, the single greatest need in building its judicial system.[192] There are at least some recent signs of change: the lower house of parliament, for instance, rejected the president's renomination of a conservative mullah to serve as Chief Justice – a significant development given this individual's enormous influence over the judiciary and resistance to a number of

---

[187] Miller & Perito, *Establishing the Rule of Law in Afghanistan, supra* note 32, at 7. The Constitution of Afghanistan, adopted in 2004, provides in Article 117 for a nine-member Supreme Court appointed by the president with the approval of the lower house of Afghanistan's parliament. Qualifications for members of the Supreme Court are set forth in Article 118. Article 132 provides that lower court judges "are appointed with the recommendation of the Supreme Court and approval of the President" and the "appointment, transfer, promotion, punishment, and proposals to retire judges are within the authority of the Supreme Court in accordance with the law." The Constitution is available at http://www.oefre.unibe.ch/law/icl/af00000.html.

[188] Amnesty International, *Afghanistan: Re-establishing the Rule of Law, supra* note 15, at 13–14.

[189] Miller & Perito, *Establishing the Rule of Law in Afghanistan, supra* note 32, at 7.

[190] Amnesty International, *Afghanistan: Re-establishing the Rule of Law, supra* note 15, at 13–14.

[191] Id., at 16.

[192] Miller & Perito, *Establishing the Rule of Law in Afghanistan, supra* note 32, at 7.

reforms.[193] But the process of judicial reform more broadly will require years of sustained effort and pressure.

In Iraq, the process of vetting existing judges and prosecutors was relatively effective. Although the courts under Saddam Hussein's rule "had been politicized and subordinated to the intelligence services and Ba'ath Party, Iraq had a body of judges and prosecutors who were relatively honest, educated, and professional."[194] The Coalition Provisional Authority established a Judicial Review Committee (JRC) to vet existing judges and remove "those found to be corrupt or guilty of human rights abuses."[195] By 2004, the JRC "reviewed the files of all 860 judges and prosecutors in Iraq, removed 176 staff, reappointed 82 judges and prosecutors who had been removed by Saddam, and appointed 123 new judges and prosecutors."[196] Even so, Iraq still faces enormous challenges in building a fair, effective justice system that enjoys public confidence.

2. Effective Training and Education: A Critical Need

Short-term training is typically provided to judges and prosecutors in post-conflict settings, but it is rarely sufficient. In Kosovo and East Timor, for instance, only minimal training was provided initially, with judicial training institutes established only later.[197] Training has proven to be a particularly difficult issue in East Timor. Inexperienced judges were put on the job after only limited "quick-impact" training courses – on the assumption that they would later receive "mandatory ongoing training" while already working as judges.[198] Once busy with daily responsibilities, however, enthusiasm for training waned, at least among some judges, while others wished for more practical training on matters such as writing opinions and managing a courtroom. A group of judges did eventually travel to Portugal for a year-long training program, but this created a large gap in the already small Timorese judiciary. Meanwhile, within East Timor itself, the issue of language has greatly complicated training for a number of judges: the training is conducted in Portuguese even though many Timorese judges are not yet fluent,

---

[193] BBC News, *Afghan Assembly Rejects Top Judge*, May 27, 2006, *available at* http://news.bbc.co.uk/2/hi/south_asia/5023392.stm; Carlotta Gall, *Afghan Lawmakers Review Court Nominees*, THE NEW YORK TIMES, May 17, 2006, at A1; Scott Baldauf, *The West Pushes to Reform Traditionalist Afghan Courts*, THE CHRISTIAN SCIENCE MONITOR, February 21, 2006, *available at* http://www.csmonitor.com/2006/0221/p01s04-wosc.html.

[194] Jones et al., ESTABLISHING LAW AND ORDER AFTER CONFLICT, *supra* note 17, at 137.

[195] Id., at 137, 143.

[196] Id., at 143.

[197] David Marshall & Shelley Inglis, *The Disempowerment of Human Rights-Based Justice in the United Nations Mission in Kosovo*, 16 HARV. HUM. RTS. J. 95, 123–125 (2003); Strohmeyer, *Collapse and Reconstruction of a Judicial System*, *supra* note 9, at 55–57; International Crisis Group, *Finding the Balance: The Scales of Justice in Kosovo*, *supra* note 179, at 8.

[198] Strohmeyer, *Collapse and Reconstruction of a Judicial System*, *supra* note 9, at 55.

and their requests for translation into Bahasa Indonesian or Tetum generally have been denied. Thus, it is perhaps not surprising that in January 2005, the President of the Court of Appeal announced that all the Timorese judges and prosecutors had failed their qualifying exams for permanent appointment. As a result, they began a full-time, year-long training program at the Judicial Training Center in Dili, while international judges stepped in to serve as the judiciary of East Timor.[199] Given this difficult history, it would have been far more efficient to have provided more sustained and systematic training for Timor's judges and prosecutors *before* they assumed their professional duties.

The particular kind of training that is most needed will, of course, be country specific. Judges, as well as prosecutors and public defenders, need to be educated on applicable law, including criminal law and procedure. Training in fundamental international human rights principles can also be an important and valuable investment. Some practical training, too, is likely to be invaluable – such as training in opinion writing and courtroom management. In Afghanistan, for instance, participants in judicial training sessions "have no experience in producing written opinions, no experience with defense advocates in the courtroom, and are accustomed to disposing of issues without any reference to legal texts."[200] As a result, "[w]orking to impart the basic idea of making judicial decisions based on actual law has been an important element of the training."[201]

3. Trap to Avoid: Premature Empowerment of Judges, before Adequate Training and before Credible Disciplinary and Removal Mechanisms Established

The experiences in several post-conflict societies underscore a trap to avoid: premature empowerment of judges. In East Timor, as discussed above, judges were appointed and deployed without adequate training and support, and they have been struggling with the consequences ever since.

Equally problematic is the appointment of judges before credible disciplinary, removal, and complaint mechanisms are established. In Kosovo, for instance, when allegations of judicial misconduct arose, "the necessary transparent judicial disciplinary procedures were nonexistent."[202] Although UNMIK regulations outlined the grounds for judicial dismissal, they did not

---

[199] Judicial System Monitoring Programme, *Overview of the Justice Sector: March 2005*, at 7, 12, 27–28; *Progress Report of the Secretary-General on the United Nations Mission of Support in East Timor*, February 18, 2005, UN Doc. S/2005/99, at 5–6.

[200] Miller & Perito, *Establishing the Rule of Law in Afghanisan, supra* note 32, at 10.

[201] Id.

[202] Betts, Carlson, & Gisvold, *The Post-Conflict Transitional Administration of Kosovo and the Lessons-Learned in Efforts to Establish a Judiciary and Rule of Law, supra* note 13, at 379 (footnote omitted).

spell out "specific, transparent complaint procedures."[203] In Afghanistan, although the Supreme Court is responsible for investigation of judicial misconduct, the procedure is not sufficiently transparent. An Amnesty International study found that: allegations of misconduct and corruption were not effectively investigated, particularly outside of Kabul; a potential conflict existed between the Supreme Court's role in recommending judicial candidates and also investigating misconduct; the Supreme Court itself was not subject to effective oversight; and there was no functioning mechanism for public complaints.[204] Amnesty International thus urged that a judicial services commission be established in Afghanistan with a mandate to investigate judicial and prosecutorial misconduct and also to create a public complaint mechanism.[205]

Although there can be "a delicate balance between judicial independence and accountability, a strong mechanism for oversight and discipline is critical particularly in the formative stages" of a judiciary.[206] In a country that has a weak rule of law tradition, poorly trained and compensated judges, and no politically neutral mechanism for removing judges, an "independent judiciary" can end up meaning little more than a judiciary that is free to be as corrupt and incompetent as it can be. Effective disciplinary, removal, and complaint mechanisms are therefore crucial. Charles Call argues that it may, in fact, be necessary to focus on accountability *first* in order to achieve a more impartial and independent judiciary in the longer run.[207]

C. A Good Practice: Finding an Effective Mix of International and Local Jurists

One method for strengthening judiciaries after conflict has been to blend international with domestic jurists. On the one hand, building local capacity, ownership, leadership, and responsibility is fundamental. On the other hand, experienced judges, prosecutors, and defense counsel from other countries can provide an infusion of skills that can assist new domestic legal personnel. International judges, for instance, can provide valuable balance in highly charged, ethnically divided post-conflict settings. But finding an

---

[203] Id. (discussing UNMIK Regulations 1999/7 & 2000/6).

[204] Amnesty International, *Afghanistan: Reestablishing the Rule of Law, supra* note 15, at 23–24.

[205] Id., at 25.

[206] International Crisis Group, *Finding the Balance: The Scales of Justice in Kosovo, supra* note 179, at 7. For a thoughtful discussion of the challenges of advancing independence and accountability, *see* Linn Hammergren, *Judicial Independence and Judicial Accountability: The Shifting Balance in Reform Goals,* in AID, *Guidance for Promoting Judicial Independence and Impartiality, supra* note 171, at 149–157.

[207] Call, *Conclusion: Constructing Justice and Security After War, supra* note 61, at 394 (stressing the need to promote "both judicial independence *and* accountability" and the need to establish "mechanisms of accountability *before* judicial autonomy becomes entrenched").

effective mix of international and local personnel is highly context specific, and it has proven difficult in a number of post-conflict situations. The uneven experience highlights the need for more systematic thinking up-front about designing effective international/national arrangements and partnerships.

To start with, finding experienced judges who can deploy to post-conflict settings in a timely manner has not been easy. In some instances, international judges lacked necessary experience in critical areas, such as criminal law, and had limited knowledge of, or sensitivity toward, local law, culture, and practice. Also, even experienced judges did not necessarily have effective mentoring skills. Judging and mentoring are two quite different activities, and not everyone is good at both. In some instances, patronizing attitudes, coupled with differential pay and benefits, have engendered resentments on the part of national judges. Language difficulties have also impeded effective give-and-take between international and national jurists.

But international judges have also made enormously positive contributions to domestic justice systems. Judge Teresa Doherty is a case in point. An Irish national who spent years as a magistrate and Supreme Court judge in Papua, New Guinea, Judge Doherty also served in Sierra Leone's domestic justice system as a judge of the Court of Appeal and High Court. Her intelligence and efficiency, the high standards she expected of the lawyers in her courtroom, and her well-reasoned rulings earned her enormous respect among the bar in Sierra Leone and served as an impressive model of fair and impartial justice. While in Sierra Leone, Judge Doherty also visited prisons and made recommendations to the Chief Justice of the Supreme Court for addressing delays in appeals and other urgent problems. Judge Doherty is now serving as a judge on the Special Court for Sierra Leone – the hybrid war crimes tribunal based in Sierra Leone composed of national and international judges, prosecutors, defense attorneys, and other personnel.

In East Timor, greater reliance on international judges in the domestic justice system at the beginning could have helped avoid difficult problems later on. Instead, as discussed above, Timorese judges were appointed without adequate experience or training and expected to function as judges from day one, only to later fail their qualifying exams for continued service as judges. In the words of one international prosecutor, Suzannah Linton:

The task of institution-building would undoubtedly have been better served by having international expertise brought in for the transitional period, with East Timorese appointed as deputies on probation in order to receive the appropriate training on the job. At the end of the transitional period, their training would have empowered them to assume full responsibility as judges, prosecutors and public defenders.[208]

[208] Linton, *Rising from the Ashes: The Creation of a Viable Criminal Justice System in East Timor, supra* note 11, at 134.

Today, senior Timorese officials likewise say that international jurists should have staffed the justice system initially, giving Timorese judge-designates the opportunity for meaningful training before undertaking their duties.[209]

At the time, of course, the choice was not easy. The decision to immediately appoint Timorese judges and prosecutors was influenced by a number of factors: the desire to empower Timorese and build local ownership; the urgent need for judicial personnel to address the growing number of pretrial detainees and other problems of law and order; the need for judges familiar with Indonesian law (which was the controlling law to the extent that it did not contravene international law); and the enormous expense of deploying international jurists, dependent on translators and other support, and the likely delay in doing so.[210] But once Timorese judges and prosecutors were appointed by UNTAET, the failure to provide adequate training and mentoring in a language understandable to the jurists was an enormous setback to the development of East Timor's judicial system.

In Kosovo, many argue that UNMIK was also too slow in deploying international judges and prosecutors.[211] UNMIK ultimately did provide explicitly for panels with a majority of international judges "if it determines that this is necessary to ensure the independence and impartiality of the judiciary or the proper administration of justice."[212] The open-endedness in the criteria for appointing international prosecutors or majority judicial panels, however, coupled with the considerable discretion in their application, undermined public confidence about the fairness of the system.[213]

All in all, international judges and prosecutors have made a valuable contribution to Kosovo's justice system. They have helped address sensitive criminal cases, and they play a vital role in combating organized crime and in prosecuting war crimes and "ethnically motivated crimes."[214] Nevertheless, their continuing involvement has some costs. For one, if internationals continue to address all cases of any sensitivity, local jurists "will not be given the opportunity to take on difficult cases to build their competence and test their impartiality."[215] International judges are also very expensive, and they

---

[209] Interviews with senior Timorese officials, Dili, November 2003.

[210] Strohmeyer, *Collapse and Reconstruction of a Judicial System, supra* note 9, at 54–55; Simon Chesterman, You, THE PEOPLE: THE UNITED NATIONS, TRANSITIONAL ADMINISTRATION, AND STATE-BUILDING (2004), at 170–171.

[211] *See, e.g.,* Michael E. Hartmann, *International Judges and Prosecutors in Kosovo: A New Model for Post-Conflict Peacekeeping,* United States Institute of Peace Special Report 112, October 2003.

[212] UNMIK Regulation 2000/64, *On the Assignment of International Judges and Prosecutors and/or Change of Venue,* December 15, 2000.

[213] International Crisis Group, *Finding the Balance: The Scales of Justice in Kosovo, supra* note 179, at 8–9. We discuss this more fully in Chapter 7.

[214] Id., at 8.

[215] Id., at 9.

have contributed less to domestic capacity-building than initially hoped. As the ICG reports, "there is no mechanism for the mentoring of local judges by internationals"; international and national judges in Pristina are located in different buildings; and even in the districts "there is little interaction" between them.[216]

In Bosnia and Herzegovina, however, judges in Brcko credit international judges and prosecutors for making vital contributions to the general reappointment process and to legal reform more generally. As one Brcko judge put it: "If the internationals were not involved during and after the judicial reform to assure the integrity of the process and fend off attacks after the reform, there would have been an open run at the judiciary."[217] In Bosnia more broadly, particularly in war crimes trials, international judges have helped provide "balance, independence and expertise" in cases that otherwise "test local judges' disinterestedness and ability to resist political and tribal pressures."[218] International judges likewise played an essential role in Bosnia's successful Human Rights Chamber, and they continue to be critical in Bosnia's hybrid War Crimes Chamber in the State Court.

No one model or approach for combining international and national jurists will work across the board. In some settings, national leaders may reject the idea of deploying international judges altogether. Iraqi leaders, for instance, had no interest in international judges serving on Iraq's war crimes tribunal. The point here is simply that *finding an effective mix of national and international jurists and other experts is a complex and context-specific matter that requires systematic thinking from the start.*

In addition, a more effective international capacity to deploy interested and experienced jurists to post-conflict settings is needed. Finding suitable judges (as well as prosecutors and defense counsel) who are familiar with civil law or common law systems (as the case may be), knowledgeable about criminal law or international law, fluent in a relevant language or languages, willing to live in often difficult environments, and are culturally sensitive – and who ideally also have a capacity to relate well, to mentor, and to learn from local judges – is exceedingly difficult.[219] Finding them and deploying them quickly in time-urgent circumstances is even harder. Yet having a greater network of potentially available jurists is vital, and a number of organizations are well-placed to create and update rosters of such individuals. The International Association of Women Judges, ABA/CEELI, and the International Legal Assistance Consortium, to name only three, could potentially

---

[216] Id.

[217] International Crisis Group, *Courting Disaster: The Misrule of Law in Bosnia & Herzegovina, supra* note 158, at 54.

[218] Id., at 34.

[219] International Crisis Group, *Finding the Balance: The Scales of Justice in Kosovo, supra* note 179, at 5–6.

coordinate with other organizations to maintain active rosters of interested judges and other legal personnel, which could be provided to the United Nations as well as to other organizations and states involved in justice system reform in post-conflict societies.[220]

D. Additional Reforms to Encourage Impartial Adjudication

A fair and effective justice system requires more than qualified and honest judges selected in a transparent manner; it depends, too, on a legal and political system that supports and permits impartial adjudication. Moving away from long-standing practices of corruption and, more generally, of external pressure on judges – an endemic problem in many post-conflict societies – is a particularly daunting challenge. The obstacles to greater judicial independence and impartiality "are generally embedded in a country's history and culture and are not easily eradicated," with the consequence that changes made in the judicial system will typically "need to go hand-in-hand with broader societal changes."[221] Although it must always be remembered that a particular model for judicial reform that works well in one country may not work well in another,[222] a number of key reforms are likely to be necessary in most post-conflict situations. Among other things, the legal framework itself must be clear and provide adequate procedural protections to litigants; the judiciary must have an adequate budget and resources; and court operations and proceedings must be transparent to the public. Attitudinal changes – among judges, powerful elites, and ordinary citizens alike – concerning the role and purpose of courts within the justice system can take years, but such changes are indeed possible – as the reform efforts in Brcko District in Bosnia suggest.

1. Resources and Budgets

The adequacy of resources and the question of control over budgets are key factors in developing an impartial judiciary that decides cases based on the law rather than on external pressure, intimidation, and corruption. Without adequate resources, judiciaries cannot offer salaries sufficient to attract good candidates or to reduce the prospects of corruption; courts may lack

---

[220] A number of these organizations already have membership directories and rosters of judges available to assist with training and other matters; but more attention could be devoted to developing rosters of jurists potentially able to deploy into post-conflict settings on short notice. A potential resource for such an effort is the global database that the International Association of Women Judges (IAWJ) is developing. This database, the IAWJ notes, "will be a useful tool to identify qualified women judges when vacancies arise on international judicial and investigative bodies, or when speakers or trainers are needed to address various legal topics, and for serving as a resource to governments, NGOs and international organizations." See IAWJ Web site at http://www.iawj.org/what/other.asp.

[221] AID, *Guidance for Promoting Judicial Independence and Impartiality, supra* note 171, at 40.

[222] Id.

basic legal materials, such as laws and higher-court decisions, necessary for principled decision-making; and adequate records of judicial proceedings cannot be compiled, "undermining the appeal process and transparency and accountability."[223] Insufficient resources can also result in severely "inadequate physical working conditions that undermine respect for the judiciary both in the judges' own eyes and in the eyes of the public."[224] Lack of resources may also mean that the physical security of judges is compromised, making them more vulnerable to intimidation.

All of these problems are apparent in Afghanistan. Despite legal guarantees of judicial independence, pressure and interference from "armed groups, persons holding public office and private individuals" are a major problem, aggravated by a lack of physical security for judges, increasing their susceptibility to external threats and pressure.[225] Low and irregular salaries contribute to widespread corruption among judges and prosecutors.[226] Many courts have little access to basic legal materials, including statutes, and "many judges are unfamiliar with the law and make decisions without reference to it."[227] In this environment, examples of corruption and intimidation in the judiciary are all too common, and "certain individuals remain above the law because of their place in the community or because they are able to use threats, intimidation and other forms of pressure to influence judicial proceedings."[228]

Problems of political and economic influence and corruption are not limited to Afghanistan. In Bosnia, domestic prosecutors and judges are vulnerable to influence and intimidation by powerful individuals, particularly in the absence of adequate security measures, and prosecutors are sometimes reluctant to pursue war crimes and other cases against politically prominent suspects.[229] In Sierra Leone, the judicial system is perceived by the public

---

[223] Id. at 25.

[224] Id.

[225] Amnesty International, *Afghanistan: Re-establishing the Rule of Law, supra* note 15, at 18, 24.

[226] Id., at 21. Miller & Perito, *Establishing the Rule of Law in Afghanisan, supra* note 32, at 7. Amnesty International reports: "Judges in Afghanistan currently receive approximately $50 a month" and in some provincial regions, "judges and prosecutors had not received their salaries for three months," evidently because of difficulties in a "safe method of salary distribution." Amnesty International, *Afghanistan: Re-establishing the Rule of Law, supra* note 15, at 22–23.

[227] Miller & Perito, *Establishing the Rule of Law in Afghanisan, supra* note 32, at 7.

[228] Amnesty International, *Afghanistan: Re-establishing the Rule of Law, supra* note 15, at 19. Examples include extrajudicial detention of individuals without charge on the order of regional commanders or wealthy individuals, intimidation against prosecutors and judges to drop cases involving serious crimes, pressure from family members to incarcerate young girls who resist forced marriages, and bribes to judges and prosecutors to not proceed with cases or to secure release of detainees. Id., at 19–22.

[229] International Crisis Group, *Courting Disaster: The Misrule of Law in Bosnia & Herzegovina, supra* note 158, at i–ii.

"to be slow, ineffective, and corrupt – 'as long as you have money you can walk away'" is a common refrain.[230]

Yet the solutions are not simple. While decent and regular salaries can certainly help by providing an adequate living for judges and attracting better-qualified candidates, "reducing corruption appears to be much more closely linked to increasing transparency and meritocracy in hiring, promotions, and discipline."[231] More generally, transforming practices, attitudes, and expectations among powerful actors, litigants, and members of the judiciary can be a daunting endeavor requiring many separate, but mutually reinforcing reforms. Greater transparency of court proceedings, and adequate and transparent budgets for court operations, among others, may be critical.

The very structure of budgetary arrangements, which differ significantly among judicial systems, can make a difference. The two main models are a judiciary dependent on the executive (often the justice ministry) for budgetary and administrative support, and a judiciary that is a separate branch of government with "the same degree of self-government and budgetary control over its operations" as that enjoyed by the executive branch.[232] "Although there are clear examples of independent judicial decision-making under executive branch administration, the trend" is away from this model and toward placing greater budgetary and administrative responsibility within the judiciary itself.[233] Yet even this is no panacea. Court presidents can gain enormous influence over their colleagues through their control over resources and – if they are not reform-minded – can substantially undermine efforts to develop a more independent and impartial judiciary. Indeed, sometimes pressure from senior or higher-level judges on more junior judges can be as great a barrier to impartial decision-making as pressure from litigants or other power-holders.

2. Increasing Transparency

One of the most effective ways to strengthen the impartiality of a judiciary is to increase the transparency of its activities. If court procedures are shrouded in uncertainty, if trial proceedings are not open to the public, if judicial decisions are not explained publicly or in writing, and if the public has no recourse in the face of judicial corruption and misconduct, then the

---

[230] International Crisis Group, *Sierra Leone: The State of Security and Governance, supra* note 21, at 21.

[231] AID, *Guidance for Promoting Judicial Independence and Impartiality, supra* note 171, at 32 (discussing World Bank study). Salary increases in Bosnia, although "welcome and necessary," could not alone "assure the independence of judges and prosecutors." International Crisis Group, *Courting Disaster: The Misrule of Law in Bosnia & Herzegovina, supra* note 158, at 6.

[232] AID, *Guidance for Promoting Judicial Independence and Impartiality, supra* note 171, at 23.

[233] Id., at 24.

prospects for increasing judicial impartiality are dim. Judicial reform expert Linn Hammergren stresses the importance of greater transparency in four key areas: in the selection of judges, in court operations, in judicial decisions, and in public complaint mechanisms.[234]

Greater transparency in these areas can increase public confidence in the justice system and help reduce the occasions for corruption. More transparent court operations, clear procedures, and good management of court records, for instance, can decrease opportunities "for bribery, intimidation, or manipulation."[235] Criminal procedure reforms that introduce greater transparency – such as proceedings that are adversarial and public – increase public awareness and scrutiny and judicial accountability.

The publication of judicial decisions is also of crucial importance.[236] All too often, judges don't provide any public explanation of the grounds for their decisions. Even when limited resources in post-conflict societies do not permit publication of all judicial decisions, a clear public statement of reasons is critical to help deter rulings "based on considerations other than law and facts."[237]

Greater transparency facilitates more effective monitoring of courts by NGOs, bar associations, and the public. A court system with "structured, transparent practices" is far easier to monitor "than one that is either intentionally opaque or merely disorganized and chaotic."[238] Yet credible monitoring also depends on effective NGOs that can focus on the justice system, highlight problems, recommend reforms, and keep up pressure on the government.

E. Good Practice: Nurture Sustainable Justice System Reforms by Investing in Civil Society, Legal Education, and Programs to Increase Access to Justice

Transforming a justice system is a long-term effort that requires investment in institutions and programs far beyond the judiciary itself, as we elaborate more fully in Chapter 8. Supporting local NGOs, such as East Timor's

---

[234] Hammergren, *Judicial Independence and Judicial Accountability, supra* note 206, at 153. *See also* Ellis, *International Legal Assistance, supra* note 124, at 930, on the importance of transparency.

[235] AID, *Guidance for Promoting Judicial Independence and Impartiality, supra* note 171, at 33.

[236] Jensen, *The Rule of Law and Judicial Reform, supra* note 6, at 360; Ellis, *International Legal Assistance, supra* note 124, at 930. The publication, in East Timor, of two volumes of Court of Appeals decisions in 2005 is an important step in making judicial decision-making more transparent and accessible to the public and to other legal actors in the justice system. Judicial System Monitoring Programme, *Justice Update*, October/November 2005, Issue 22/2005.

[237] AID, *Guidance for Promoting Judicial Independence and Impartiality, supra* note 171, at 34.

[238] Id., at 35.

Judicial System Monitoring Programme, can be indispensable in helping to build a more transparent, effective, and fair justice system.[239] Supporting legal education is also a critical investment. Although interveners typically focus on short-term training and immediate needs, inadequate university legal education can be a serious obstacle to the development of a fair and effective justice system staffed by competent defense counsel, prosecutors, judges, and other legal personnel.[240] Educating ordinary citizens about their legal rights plays a critical role by empowering them to make more effective use of developing justice institutions.

Serious problems of access to justice must also be addressed. All too often, in building justice institutions after conflict, interveners pay too little attention to issues of access to justice by marginalized populations or to the needs of rural areas.[241] Basic institution-building, particularly in the capital and major cities, is an understandable focus of reform when time and resources are limited. But ignoring problems of access to justice can mean that vulnerable and economically disadvantaged segments of the population have little recourse to justice at all. The legal institutions being developed may serve only the needs of the powerful and privileged few. The impact on women and other vulnerable segments of the population may be especially harsh.[242]

Access to justice can be especially difficult in rural areas. In East Timor, for instance, where a majority of the population lives in villages in the countryside, judges and prosecutors have been reluctant to reside in rural districts, with the consequence that court proceedings remain infrequent. The resulting options for litigants are to travel to the capital city, which few can afford, or to seek a hearing during the few days a month that judges travel to the districts to hold proceedings. Gradually, the situation is improving, but court schedules in the districts remain extremely limited.[243] In Afghanistan, the

---

[239] For information about the JSMP, *see* its Web site, *available at* http://www.jsmp.minihub.org. The JSMP has a Women's Justice Unit that examines the impact of the justice system on women and a Victim Support Service focused especially on victims of domestic violence. The JSMP also has evaluated traditional justice mechanisms in East Timor and has examined the work of the Commission on Reception, Truth and Reconciliation (CAVR) and the work of the Special Panels for Serious Crimes, among other things.

[240] AID, *Guidance for Promoting Judicial Independence and Impartiality, supra* note 171, at 29. *See also* Jensen, *The Rule of Law and Judicial Reform, supra* note 6, at 350, 359–360.

[241] Jensen, *The Rule of Law and Judicial Reform, supra* note 6, at 350, 354–355.

[242] In Afghanistan, for instance, young girls, often underage, who resist forced marriages or run away from abusive husbands are frequently charged with crimes with no adequate opportunity to prepare a defense or protect their rights. Without internationally supported programs and reforms to provide assistance and to stand up for their interests, these young girls are at the mercy of a harsh and discriminatory system. Amnesty International, *Afghanistan: Re-establishing the Rule of Law, supra* note 15, at 43–48.

[243] As the JSMP reports, "resumption of the courts in the districts is still limited in that the judges only travel to the districts for a few days, one or two times a month." Judicial System Monitoring Programme, *Overview of the Justice Sector: March 2005*, at 12. Moreover, "prior to the employment of international judges, the district Courts (Bacau, Suai and

challenge of strengthening the rule of law outside the capital or major cities is especially acute because of the lack of central government authority and oversight. In addition to the difficulties of policing in areas dominated by local warlords and regional commanders, as we discussed earlier, there are problems of access to courts in rural areas.[244] The limited presence of courts outside of provincial capitals means that for many Afghans, few, if any, alternatives exist to "heavy reliance on informal justice mechanisms."[245]

Justice system reformers thus must understand the significant role that traditional dispute resolution mechanisms continue to play in many post-conflict societies. These informal mechanisms and practices may enjoy considerable local support and, for many citizens, are the only "law the people see."[246] Yet these traditional dispute settlement practices may also disadvantage segments of the population, especially women.[247] Given the delays and difficulties in extending formal justice institutions into rural areas in many post-conflict societies, reliance on informal mechanisms will persist. As a result, reformers will need to grapple with a number of issues, including how state justice institutions should relate to traditional mechanisms of dispute resolution, and whether those mechanisms can be built upon in constructive directions (and modified if they conflict with fundamental human rights). In Chapter 8, which focuses on building rule of law cultures, we will take up these issues explicitly and also address other factors that can affect the success or failure of justice system reforms.

Throughout the current chapter, and indeed throughout this book, we have repeatedly stressed the importance of a synergistic approach to the rule of law, which emphasizes, among other things, the interrelations between formal legal institutions, such as courts, and other societal institutions, ranging from NGOs and universities to informal or traditional dispute-resolution practices. We have also emphasized the critical importance of finding ways to

---

Oecussi) had been basically non-operational in their respective districts for many months due to lack of personnel." Id., at 28, note 19. *See also* Judicial System Monitoring Programme, *Justice in the Districts 2003*, December 2003.

[244] Miller & Perito, *Establishing the Rule of Law in Afghanistan, supra* note 32, at 10–11. *See also* Amnesty International, *Afghanistan: Police Reconstruction Essential for the Protection of Human Rights*, March 2003, at 7, 48–49.

[245] Amnesty International, *Afghanistan: Re-establishing the Rule of Law, supra* note 15, at 7.

[246] *See* Owen Alterman, Aneta Binienda, Sophie Rodella, & Kimyia Varzi, *The Law People See: The Status of Dispute Resolution in the Provinces of Sierra Leone in 2002*, National Forum for Human Rights, January 2003.

[247] The ability of women to participate and protect their interests in these largely patriarchal systems is often limited. *See* Amnesty International, *Afghanistan: Re-establishing the Rule of Law, supra* note 15, at 50–51. In East Timor, although women have more limited rights than men to present their cases to the traditional system, a majority surveyed "support women advocating for themselves" in the customary dispute settlement process. The Asia Foundation, *Law and Justice in East Timor: A Survey of Citizen Awareness and Attitudes Regarding Law and Justice in East Timor*, February 2004, at 3.

give ordinary people a stake in rule of law reforms. In Chapter 8, we focus on those issues in detail, looking in particular at the crucial role of civil society, education, customary and informal dispute resolution, and other seemingly "nonlegal" issues such as community organizing and economic development. As we argue, these tend to be marginalized or forgotten when interveners conceptualize rule of law programs – but, in practice, linking more traditional rule of law programs to a broader array of reforms can be integral to their success or failure.

CONCLUSION

As this chapter has argued, building fair and effective justice systems after conflict is an exceptionally difficult, long-term process that usually requires many far-reaching reforms. Recruiting and training capable police, judges, and other justice system personnel is necessary for success, but it is not suffi-cient. Building up a basic institutional infrastructure and providing resources is also critical, but it, too, is not sufficient. None of this will result in a justice system that advances the goals of the rule of law unless the larger legal and political system supports fair, effective enforcement of the law and impartial adjudication.

Significant systemic reforms will often be crucial: a workable legal frame-work that protects basic rights; transparent and merit-based appointment procedures rather than appointments based on patronage and cronyism; greater transparency and accountability in the components of the justice system; more effective monitoring, disciplinary, and oversight arrangements; better education for legal professionals, and public education to make citi-zens aware of their rights and better able to demand justice, among others. Changing attitudes and expectations – of officials, police, judges, the public – regarding how the system should operate may be the hardest challenge of all, particularly in societies in which police and courts previously served as tools of self-interested leaders and other powerful actors rather than as instruments of justice.

The obstacles to justice system reform and the accomplishments have varied significantly in different countries, as we have discussed. But we have also tried to highlight some of the more positive and effective practices – as well as recurring challenges and traps to avoid. To sum up:

- Reformers must go beyond surface reforms and work to build solid polit-ical foundations for the justice system. This requires addressing prob-lems of political influence, factional control, and corruption that may be deeply rooted in the political and legal system. Unless such problems are addressed, interveners risk simply providing institutional tools to power-ful elites rather than genuinely building the rule of law.

- As the synergistic approach to justice system reform stresses, a clear articulation of goals, an adaptive strategy that builds upon existing cultural foundations, and systemic reforms that address connections and build synergies between key institutions (such as police, prisons, and courts) are essential.
- Each post-conflict society presents unique obstacles and opportunities for strengthening justice systems after conflict. A critical starting point for reform is a strategic assessment that takes account of the conflict legacy in that society, the available human, cultural, and material resources, and the obstacles and threats to reform, and that identifies promising external interventions to promote and buttress reform. Core capacities – including law-making, law enforcement, and adjudication – need to be built on solid foundations of legitimacy, accountability, human rights protection, and sustainability.
- Law reform is usually a critical task in post-conflict societies. Existing law – or parts of it – may lack public legitimacy, fail to address complex criminal activity, and fall short of international human rights standards. Reform of criminal law and procedure is often particularly urgent. Although model codes can be helpful resources in law reform, the process of law reform can be just as important as the substance. Building domestic capacity for compromise is crucial. More effective assistance to legislatures in post-conflict societies is needed to help build this and related law-making skills.
- Police reform often moves more quickly than reforms in other parts of the justice system, but without corresponding reforms in prisons and the judiciary, problems such as extended pretrial detention, lack of due process, and unfairness in treatment of suspects will undermine the impact of police reform. Changing organizational culture in police organizations is critical to sustain reform. Necessary elements include fair and transparent selection and promotion criteria, adequate pay, good training, incentives for good performance, and improved police–society relations.
- Prisons are usually shortchanged in post-conflict justice reform. Yet, as experience in Iraq and elsewhere has shown, neglecting prisons can result in severe abuse and can have devastating long-term costs. Effective prison reform requires clear rules, good training, competent personnel, credible monitoring and accountability, adequate resources, and often sustained international interest and support.
- Judicial reform – building more impartial and competent judiciaries – is probably the most complex and difficult aspect of justice system reform. The specific challenges and obstacles vary in different countries, but critical reforms generally include transparent and merit-based appointments procedures; good training; building structural protections for impartial

decision-making by increasing the transparency and accountability of judicial operations; providing adequate resources and budgets; supporting independent court monitoring organizations; investing in legal education; and, above all, addressing larger systemic problems of external influence, political control, and corruption that prevent impartial adjudication.

- Although reformers will face a variety of unique obstacles in particular societies, there are also some common and recurring traps to avoid. These include the failure to provide for applicable law that enjoys local legitimacy or to involve local decision-makers sufficiently in law reform; premature institution-building without corresponding political reform; premature empowerment of judges or other justice system officials, before adequate training and before credible disciplinary and removal mechanisms are established; failure to address sufficiently the needs of vulnerable segments of the population, including women and girls, who often face increased violence after conflicts; neglecting rural areas and problems of access to justice more generally; and focusing on institutional building blocks – and surface indicators – with insufficient attention to building the solid political foundations of a fair justice system.

- We also highlighted a number of positive practices, including looking for mutually reinforcing synergies in reform efforts; deploying an effective mix of national and international actors in the justice system; promoting greater transparency in the justice system; instituting merit-based selection and promotion standards and procedures; working to develop inclusive and representative composition in justice institutions; working to promote sustainable reforms by investing in civil society organizations and legal education; and paying greater attention to problems of access to justice, as we discuss more fully in Chapter 8.

Ultimately, building a fair and effective justice system will depend on a political framework and culture that supports such a system. It will require long-term, synergistic efforts to reform many interrelated components of the justice system and to nurture attitudes and expectations – among those who work in the system and those who turn to it for help – that the system should serve the goals of the rule of law. To change attitudes and expectations can be especially hard in societies that have endured horrific atrocities and human rights abuses, leaving deep pain, devastation, and anger in their wake. In Chapter 7, we examine the challenges of pursuing meaningful accountability for atrocities after conflict. We explore, in particular, the impact these efforts can have on building domestic capacity for the rule of law.

CHAPTER SEVEN

Accountability for Atrocities:
Moving Forward by Looking Backward?

Atrocities cast a long shadow. In post-intervention societies, reestablishing security, reconstructing governance institutions, and reforming the justice system are all crucial steps in promoting the rule of law, but important as they are, they are rarely sufficient to grapple with the legacy of past abuses. In most of the post-conflict societies discussed in this book, severe abuses were widespread in the period prior to intervention. The Balkan wars, for instance, were characterized by brutal massacres, mass rapes, and ethnic cleansing. Sierra Leone's civil war was characterized by the forced recruitment of child soldiers, widespread rapes and murders, and the gruesome mutilation of civilians. Afghanistan, Iraq, and East Timor also have had bloody pasts marked by severe abuses.

In such societies, the traumatization caused by widespread past atrocities does not end when the guns fall silent. Although nothing can undo the suffering caused by atrocities, ensuring that perpetrators face some reckoning may be critical to moving forward in countries recovering from violent conflict. Ensuring accountability may help victims move on and can also help signal to all members of post-conflict societies that, henceforth, such abuses will not be permitted to recur. Just as important, the process of ensuring accountability may, in some circumstances, reinforce broader efforts to reform the justice system.

As with every challenge discussed in this book, however, "ensuring accountability" is more easily said than done. In the wake of violent conflicts, national justice systems, if they function effectively at all, usually have only limited ability to address the claims and needs of victims or render fair justice. More often than not, citizens may view existing legal institutions skeptically because of corruption, systematic bias, association with abusive past regimes, failure to effectively address past grievances, or severe shortfalls in human and other resources. Those who have committed atrocities, moreover, may still wield political power or exert influence behind the scenes. Even when criminal trials are initiated against perpetrators, those facing trial and their political allies may view the proceedings as illegitimate forms of "victor's justice." And in some situations accountability mechanisms may actually trigger further violence. Meanwhile, it is not always clear how victims can best be served: although some victims may demand trial and punishment of perpetrators, others may place greater emphasis on public acknowledgment of their suffering and on reparations or some tangible form of assistance. In such contexts, both interveners and domestic leaders – confronted by limited resources and other urgent reconstruction challenges – must struggle to balance justice, reconciliation, and other compelling goals.

Yet the challenge of accountability cannot be ignored. As we argued in Chapter 6, establishing a credible and functioning justice system that serves the goals of the rule of law is a central part of the challenge of moving forward after violent conflict. Even more fundamentally, strengthening the rule of law depends on building the public's confidence that they will be protected from predatory state and nonstate actors, that they can resolve disagreements fairly and reliably without resorting to violence, and that legal and political institutions will function in ways that protect rather than violate basic human rights. Only then is the rule of law, as we defined it in Chapter 3, likely to take hold: a state of affairs in which most people, most of the time, choose to resolve disputes in a manner that is consistent with fair rules and fundamental human rights norms, in which modern legal institutions and laws exist, and in which there is a widely shared cultural and political commitment to the values underlying those institutions and laws.

This chapter explores the following question: can the pursuit of accountability for atrocities through criminal prosecutions and other supplementary methods help build the rule of law and strengthen domestic justice systems?

At a broad level, this question has divided scholars and practitioners alike. A *rights-based approach* argues that major perpetrators of atrocities must be held legally accountable if a country is to make an effective transition to a society marked by the rule of law. Defenders of criminal prosecutions see the biggest barrier to sustainable peace as legal impunity and argue that vigorous prosecution of at least major offenders is the only real way to remove the stain of impunity from traumatized societies. Fair trials affirm that atrocities are wrong and unacceptable – drawing a clear line for all to see – and incarceration prevents the guilty from repeat offenses and potentially serves as a deterrent to others.[1] Trials can also give victims a sense of justice that helps them move forward without a need to seek personal vengeance. Truth

---

[1] *See, e.g.*, M. Cherif Bassiouni, *Accountability for Violations of International Humanitarian Law and Other Serious Violations of Human Rights*, in POST-CONFLICT JUSTICE (M. Cherif Bassiouni, ed., 2003) at 3, 4, 54.

commissions can supplement trials and acknowledge more fully the truth of what occurred and the pain and needs of victims and, many argue, may potentially contribute to reconciliation over time.[2] Even if accountability efforts are inevitably imperfect responses to the suffering caused by atrocities, they can symbolize a society's desire to confront its past, to reject patterns of impunity, and to move in a new direction.

An alternative, *realist view* disputes the beneficial impacts of trials and argues instead that criminal prosecution of major perpetrators can be destabilizing. Proponents of this view argue that conditional amnesties may be necessary to remove "spoilers" and thus help create a better prospect for peace and long-term development of the rule of law. Once political bargains are struck among contending groups, they argue, "institutions based on the rule of law become more feasible."[3] Pursuing accountability without establishing "political and institutional preconditions," they contend, "risks weakening norms of justice by revealing their ineffectiveness and hindering necessary political bargaining."[4]

Neither camp is without its vulnerabilities. If some proponents of the rights-based approach are at times too starry-eyed about the practical benefits of trials and truth commissions or sometimes unpragmatic in acknowledging real-world constraints, the realists are prone to overstate the downsides of prosecution by focusing on the perspectives of self-interested ruling elites rather than on a broader segment of post-conflict societies, including victims and civil society organizations. The realists also tend to overstate the practical benefits of amnesties: even if high-ranking individuals are given an amnesty as the price for peace, there is no assurance that the amnesty will in fact be sufficient to sustain peace. In Sierra Leone, for instance, the amnesty given to Revolutionary United Front (RUF) forces and other groups in the 1999 Lome Agreement did not stop the conflict, rooted in greed and self-interest, from continuing.[5] An international intervention led by Britain was

---

[2] *See* Priscilla B. Hayner, UNSPEAKABLE TRUTHS: CONFRONTING STATE TERROR AND ATROCITY (2001), for an extremely thoughtful discussion of truth commissions. In both East Timor and Sierra Leone, truth commissions sought to contribute to reconciliation through community-based reconciliation procedures that we examine in this chapter.

[3] Jack Snyder & Leslie Vinjamuri, *Trials and Errors: Principle and Pragmatism in Strategies of International Justice*, 28 INT'L SEC. 5, 6 (Winter 2003/04). Snyder and Vinjamuri argue that "[j]ustice does not lead; it follows... [and] a norm-governed political order must be based on a political bargain among contending groups and on the creation of robust administrative institutions that can predictably enforce the law." Id. Although they "agree that the ultimate goal is to prevent atrocities by effectively institutionalizing appropriate standards of criminal justice," they argue that "the initial steps toward that goal must usually travel down the path of political expediency." Id., at 6–7.

[4] Id., at 6–7.

[5] The text of the Lome Agreement is *available at* http://www.sierra-leone.org/lomeaccord. html. Article IX of the agreement provided that "[i]n order to bring lasting peace to Sierra Leone, the Government of Sierra Leone shall take appropriate legal steps to grant Corporal

necessary. Realist critics also understate the degree of innovation and pragmatism that is already reflected in more recent efforts to link accountability
for past atrocities to forward-looking reforms.

Trends on the ground, to some degree, are overtaking this broad theoretical debate. Advocates of the rights-based approach increasingly have
recognized the need to supplement trials with noncriminal accountability
mechanisms that offer alternatives to trials for lesser offenders. The community reconciliation process in East Timor (now Timor Leste) is one recent
example.[6] Furthermore, the normative acceptability of amnesties for serious offenses is more contested today, both internationally and domestically.[7] In Afghanistan, for instance, amnesty provisions proposed by the
Northern Alliance were not included in the Bonn Agreement, and a majority of Afghans surveyed oppose amnesties for serious offenses.[8] Furthermore, devising amnesty arrangements that effectively remove spoilers and

Foday Sankoh absolute and free pardon." That article also provided for the Government
of Sierra Leone to "grant absolute and free pardon and reprieve to all combatants and
collaborators in respect of anything done by them in pursuit of their objectives, up to the
time of the signing" of the Lome Agreement. In addition, "the Government of Sierra Leone
shall ensure that no official or judicial action is taken against any member of the RUF/SL,
ex-AFRC, ex-SLA or CDF in respect of anything done by them in pursuit of their objectives
as members of those organizations, since March 1991, up to the time of the signing of the
present Agreement."

[6] Upon attaining independence in May 2002, East Timor became the Democratic Republic of Timor Leste. Because this book and chapter refer to multiple time periods, pre and
post independence, we use the term East Timor for ease of reference, but we recognize that
Timor Leste is the country's preferred English name today. The community-based reconciliation procedures developed by the Commission for Reception, Truth and Reconciliation
are discussed in detail in its report, *Chega!: Final Report of the Commission for Reception,
Truth and Reconciliation in East Timor* (2005), *available at* http://www.etan.org/news/2006/
cavr.htm (hereinafter *Chega!: Final Report of the CAVR*). "Chega!" means "Enough!" in
Portuguese.

[7] *See* The Secretary-General, *Report of the Secretary-General on the Rule of Law and Transitional Justice in Conflict and Post-Conflict Societies*, para.10, *delivered to the Security
Council*, U.N. Doc. S/2004/616 (August 3, 2004) ("United Nations-endorsed peace agreements can never promise amnesties for genocide, war crimes, crimes against humanity or
gross violations of human rights"); Charles T. Call, *Conclusions*, in CONSTRUCTING JUSTICE
AND SECURITY AFTER WAR (Charles T. Call, ed., 2006).

[8] *See* Afghan Independent Human Rights Commission, *A Call for Justice: A National Consultation on Past Human Rights Violations in Afghanistan* (hereinafter *A Call for Justice*), at 21,
41–43, *available at* http://www.aihrc.org.af/rep_Eng_29_01_05.htm (noting that views varied
regionally, but that 60.5 per cent overall of those surveyed rejected the idea of "amnesties or
pardons for anyone who confessed their crimes before an institution created for transitional
justice"). As the report explains, the Bonn Agreement "affirms accountability as a principle"
but provides for no particular mechanisms. Although an amnesty provision proposed by the
Northern Alliance was not adopted, a clause prohibiting amnesty for war crimes and crimes
against humanity supported by the United Nations "was deleted." Id., at 43. More recently,
however, the Afghan government has agreed that "no amnesty will be granted for gross violations of human rights." Press release, Afghan Independent Human Rights Commission,
Truth-seeking and Reconciliation in Afghanistan (December 15, 2005), at 2.

genuinely help to create conditions for strengthening the rule of law – rather than just permitting impunity – is enormously difficult in practice.

Nevertheless, the realists do have an important point. Moving forward after atrocities does require a clear-eyed assessment of the underlying forces that impede stability and reform. Holding key perpetrators criminally accountable – especially before international tribunals miles away – may advance international standards of justice; but it may have very little, if any, impact on strengthening the domestic rule of law in a post-conflict society. Just as we cannot assume that such trials will be destabilizing domestically – or that amnesties will effectively neutralize spoilers and clear the way for genuine reform – neither can we assume a positive spillover effect on domestic rule of law-building from criminal trials.

Indeed, the question of whether and how accountability proceedings can contribute to strengthening domestic justice systems and to building the rule of law in post-conflict societies is surprisingly underanalyzed.[9] For too long, the practical division of the fields of "transitional justice" and "rule of law reform" into two largely separate communities of scholars and practitioners has impeded efforts to explore systematically how accountability processes might, concretely, contribute to forward-looking rule of law reforms.[10] If this gap can be overcome, opportunities for valuable synergies between accountability efforts and rule of law reform programs can be pursued more effectively. To be sure, we are relatively early in the process of understanding the longer-term impacts of accountability processes – such as criminal prosecutions, truth commissions, reconciliation proceedings, vetting – in different post-conflict societies; furthermore, the unique circumstances and obstacles in each society attempting to overcome horrific atrocities make generalizations risky. Still, more systematic thinking and empirical research on the impact of accountability proceedings in specific post-conflict societies is a critical need and an increasingly important area of inquiry.[11]

---

[9] Scholars advocating a variety of approaches to accountability acknowledge that we need more systematic analysis of the impact of accountability proceedings on strengthening the rule of law prospectively. For a helpful recent effort to explore the potential impact of accountability efforts on forward-looking justice reform, *see* CONSTRUCTING JUSTICE AND SECURITY AFTER WAR, *supra* note 7, especially the Introduction and Conclusion by Charles T. Call.

[10] One scholar and practitioner who spans both fields and has worked hard to bring them together is Neil Kritz of the U.S. Institute of Peace. *See, e.g.,* Neil J. Kritz, *The Rule of Law in the Postconflict Phase: Building a Stable Peace,* in TURBULENT PEACE: THE CHALLENGE OF MANAGING INTERNATIONAL CONFLICT (Chester A. Crocker et al., eds., 2001); Neil J. Kritz, *Progress and Humility: The Ongoing Search for Post-Conflict Justice,* in POST-CONFLICT JUSTICE, *supra* note 1, at 84–87.

[11] For thoughtful recent assessments of East Timor's community reconciliation proceedings, for example, *see* Spencer Zifcak, The Asia Foundation, *Restorative Justice in East Timor: An Evaluation of the Community Reconciliation Process of the CAVR* (2004); Piers Pigou, United Nations Development Programme, *The Community Reconciliation Process of the Commission for Reception, Truth and Reconciliation* (2004).

This chapter aims to clarify what we know – and don't know – about the impact of accountability processes on domestic justice systems and the rule of law in post-intervention societies. We aim to look backward and forward at the same time and to explore systematically the relationships, if any, between retrospective accountability proceedings and prospective domestic capacity-building and reform. Before examining the experiences in a number of post-intervention societies, we first consider some of the broad trends that have influenced choices made in these situations regarding particular accountability mechanisms and goals. We then offer a theory about how accountability processes may contribute to building the rule of law in post-conflict societies through their demonstration and capacity-building effects. The chapter then examines the empirical record, looking in particular at the practical impact of the international tribunals for former Yugoslavia and for Rwanda; at the hybrid national/international tribunals in Kosovo, East Timor, and Sierra Leone; at domestic prosecutions particularly in Bosnia; and at the truth and reconciliation commissions in a number of post-intervention societies. We also discuss the trials only just beginning in Iraq's special tribunal for crimes against humanity, as well as the prospects for accountability in Afghanistan.

We argue that the long-term impact of accountability proceedings on the rule of law depends critically on three factors: first, the effective disempowerment of key perpetrators who threaten stability and undermine public confidence in the rule of law; second, the character of the accountability proceedings pursued, particularly whether they demonstrate credibly that previous patterns of abuse and impunity are rejected and that justice can be fair; and third, the extent to which systematic and meaningful efforts at domestic capacity-building are included as part of the accountability process. In a number of countries studied here, we argue that trials have not been as influential as advocates had hoped and seem to have had little impact at all on forward-looking efforts to strengthen justice systems and the rule of law. But in other cases, accountability processes, particularly those located within affected countries that enjoy considerable public support and engage in systematic outreach, are contributing to national capacity-building and may be reinforcing domestic expectations of accountability and demands for fairer justice processes in the future. We identify some of the features of the more effective processes, such as Sierra Leone's Special Court and East Timor's Commission for Reception, Truth and Reconciliation, but we also acknowledge their limitations and emphasize the challenge of sustaining their impact and legacy.

First, however, we must provide some essential background – on broad trends in efforts to seek accountability for atrocities since the 1990s, and on key goals and specific mechanisms that have been pursued in different cases.

I. "TRANSITIONAL JUSTICE" IN EVOLUTION:
THE ACCOUNTABILITY LEARNING CURVE

When international and local leaders pursue accountability for atrocities, they have many goals in mind beyond contributing to domestic legal reform.[12] Bringing major perpetrators to justice – demonstrating that their conduct is wrong and unacceptable – is an immediate and fundamental goal. Prosecuting and punishing major offenders affirms and reinforces the core international legal rules prohibiting genocide, crimes against humanity, and war crimes.[13] Holding individual perpetrators legally accountable can also provide some sense of justice and relief to victims and their families and potentially help to defuse grievances and curtail cycles of vengeance.

Prosecution of major offenders, it is also hoped, may help to deter future perpetrators by setting an example and making clear that wrong-doers will be held accountable. But because prosecutions inevitably are selective and because many factors contribute to individual decisions to commit atrocities, the issue of deterring future abuses is a complex and often uncertain matter.[14] Although it would be a mistake to claim too much for accountability proceedings, alone, in preventing future atrocities, they can be a central part of a larger effort to strengthen and to begin institutionalizing normative commitments to accountability – rather than impunity – in post-conflict societies.

The selective and focused nature of criminal trials after massive atrocities, however, means that they are limited mechanisms for achieving a number

---

[12] *See* Jane E. Stromseth, *Introduction: Goals and Challenges in the Pursuit of Accountability*, in ACCOUNTABILITY FOR ATROCITIES: NATIONAL AND INTERNATIONAL RESPONSES (Jane E. Stromseth, ed., 2003) at 1, 5–13. For analysis of accountability goals, methods, and concrete experiences, *see* POST-CONFLICT JUSTICE, *supra* note 1; Martha Minow, BETWEEN VENGEANCE AND FORGIVENESS: FACING HISTORY AFTER MASS VIOLENCE (1998); Hayner, UNSPEAKABLE TRUTHS, *supra* note 2; Steven R. Ratner & Jason S. Abrams, ACCOUNTABILITY FOR HUMAN RIGHTS VIOLATIONS IN INTERNATIONAL LAW: BEYOND THE NUREMBERG LEGACY (2nd ed. 2001); Ruti G. Teitel, TRANSITIONAL JUSTICE (2000); Miriam J. Aukerman, *Extraordinary Evil, Ordinary Crime: A Framework for Understanding Transitional Justice*, 15 HARV. HUM. RTS. J. 39 (2002); David A. Crocker, *Reckoning with Past Wrongs: A Normative Framework*, 13 ETHICS & INT'L AFF. 43 (1999); Neil J. Kritz, *Coming to Terms with Atrocities: A Review of Mechanisms for Mass Violations of Human Rights*, 59 LAW & CONTEMP. PROBS. 127 (1996).

[13] *See generally* Ratner & Abrams, ACCOUNTABILITY FOR HUMAN RIGHTS VIOLATIONS IN INTERNATIONAL LAW, *supra* note 12; Bassiouni, *Accountability for Violations of International Humanitarian Law and Other Serious Violations of Human Rights, supra* note 1.

[14] On the difficulties of deterrence, *see* David Wippman, *Atrocities, Deterrence, and the Limits of International Justice*, 23 FORDHAM INT'L L. J. 473 (1999); David Wippman, *Exaggerating the ICC*, in BRINGING POWER TO JUSTICE: THE PROSPECTS OF THE INTERNATIONAL CRIMINAL COURT (Joanna Harrington, ed., 2005); Gary Jonathan Bass, STAY THE HAND OF VENGEANCE: THE POLITICS OF WAR CRIMES TRIBUNALS (2000), at 290–295; Payam Akhavan, *Beyond Impunity: Can International Criminal Justice Prevent Future Atrocities*, 95 AM. J. INT'L L. 7 (2001).

of other important goals, such as a comprehensive account of a conflict and its causes. In contrast, truth commissions are more likely than trials to be effective in compiling a comprehensive "truth" that addresses the broader context of a conflict and provides a fuller account of the factors contributing to atrocities. Truth commissions can provide a greater opportunity for direct participation by a larger number of victims and may also – as in East Timor and Sierra Leone – seek to promote reconciliation and reintegration of lesser perpetrators into the community through reconciliation agreements and rituals. Unlike trials, truth commissions can make far-reaching policy recommendations, and they may be better able to advance goals of "restorative" or "reparative" justice by focusing directly on the concrete needs of victims.[15] Sierra Leone's truth commission, for instance, has recommended free health care and education for amputees, victims of sexual violence, and other injured by the conflict.[16] East Timor's Commission for Reception, Truth and Reconciliation likewise has proposed an ambitious reparations program (calling on Indonesia and other states to contribute), as well as a broad array of innovative reforms.[17]

No single mechanism or approach can satisfy the many – sometimes conflicting – goals of justice, truth, prevention and deterrence, reconciliation, and domestic capacity-building in the aftermath of severe atrocities. Recognition of this fact has contributed to a significant recent trend toward "mixed" approaches to accountability that combine multiple mechanisms designed to advance a number of different goals. These mechanisms may include criminal prosecutions but also truth commissions, reconciliation procedures for lesser offenders, and vetting (restrictions on access to government positions), for instance. Generally, the more deeply rooted the causes of atrocities, the more pressures accountability processes will face to be not only the arbiter of justice in specific cases but also to become an agent for achieving more systemic social change.

A second trend in transitional justice is to move away from remotely located international tribunals toward hybrid courts with national participation situated directly in affected countries. In both East Timor and Sierra Leone, for instance, defendants have been prosecuted for war crimes and crimes against humanity before mixed panels of national and international judges, with the prosecutorial staff likewise composed of international and national lawyers. Although purely international tribunals may sometimes be necessary, international courts – like the international criminal

---

[15] For a thoughtful discussion of reparative justice, *see* Rama Mani, BEYOND RETRIBUTION: SEEKING JUSTICE IN THE SHADOWS OF WAR (2002), at 173–178.

[16] *See Witness To Truth: Report of the Sierra Leone Truth and Reconciliation Commission,* Vol. 1, para. 51 (2004), *available at* http://www.trcsierraleone.org/drwebsite/publish/index.shtml (hereinafter *Witness to Truth*).

[17] *See Chega!: Final Report of the CAVR, supra note 6, Part 11: Recommendations.*

tribunals for former Yugoslavia and for Rwanda – are physically and often psychologically distant from the people most affected by the atrocities they are prosecuting; these tribunals are also not designed to contribute resources or training directly to the domestic justice system. In contrast, hybrid tribunals located within post-conflict societies may be viewed as more legitimate by domestic audiences, have greater potential for domestic capacity-building by involving domestic jurists directly in the work of the court, and may be better able to demonstrate the importance of accountability and fair justice to local populations.[18] These potential benefits, in theory at least, have contributed to the trend toward hybrid arrangements, a trend that may well continue even with the arrival of the International Criminal Court.[19]

A third, and overdue, trend is a more systematic effort to understand the specific goals and priorities of domestic populations who, after all, are the people who endured the atrocities and must chart a new future. The question of how best to face the past – and what forms of accountability to pursue – is a difficult one, and different societies ultimately may have quite different goals and priorities. Within those societies, moreover, various actors and groups may disagree, possibly quite strongly, over priorities. In East Timor, for example, President Xanana Gusmao has long stressed the importance of reconciliation and forward-looking social justice, whereas others (including the Commission for Reception, Truth and Reconciliation in its recent report) also emphasize the continuing importance of criminal prosecution of major offenders.

International actors, moreover, have their own priorities. Even when international commitment to accountability is reasonably strong, which it sometimes is not, international actors may not give sufficient attention to the concrete problems and obstacles to achieving meaningful accountability in specific post-conflict countries. Domestic leaders often perceive international leaders and donors as more concerned about sending a general deterrent message regarding atrocities than about the specific, long-term needs of the particular post-conflict society directly involved.[20] Yet these needs, as well as the often deep-seated grievances, inequalities, and systemic problems that contribute to violence and instability, must be addressed if a stable rule of law is to take root.

The growing recognition of the importance of understanding local goals and priorities is evident in Afghanistan. With international support, the Afghan Independent Human Rights Commission (AIHRC) conducted a

[18] See Laura A. Dickinson, *The Promise of Hybrid Courts*, 97 Am. J. Int'l L. 295 (2003).

[19] See Jenia Iontcheva Turner, *Nationalizing International Criminal Law*, 41 Stan. J. Int'l L. 1 (2005); Stromseth, *Introduction: Goals and Challenges in the Pursuit of Accountability*, in Accountability for Atrocities, *supra* note 12, at 32.

[20] See, e.g., Jason Strain & Elizabeth Keyes, *Accountability in the Aftermath of Rwanda's Genocide*, in Accountability for Atrocities, *supra* note 12, at 98–99, 130.

countrywide survey and series of 200 focus groups to determine the priorities of the Afghan people regarding accountability. In its report, *A Call for Justice*, the AIHRC documents overwhelming Afghan support for removing from power those who committed serious abuses during Afghanistan's long years of conflict, many of whom continue to wield power today.[21] Strong public support for criminal trials for the most serious offenders is accompanied by widespread support for vetting and removing other offenders from power. Afghans, though generally unfamiliar with "truth commissions" as such, also expressed a strong desire for some truth-seeking mechanism as well as deep support for "reparations" or compensation to those victims most in need. Afghans also expressed a strong preference for conducting criminal trials in Afghanistan – not outside the country – and for a hybrid tribunal that includes both Afghan as well as international jurists. This impressive effort to understand what the people of Afghanistan want holds out the potential for tailoring accountability processes to fulfill deep domestic aspirations; but whether, in fact, these aspirations will be fulfilled remains an open question fraught with obstacles, as we discuss below.

II. THE CHALLENGE OF DEMONSTRATING AND INSTITUTIONALIZING ACCOUNTABILITY NORMS

If the trends discussed above underscore the need for multifaceted accountability procedures, they also signify a growing determination on the part of both international and domestic actors to leave behind a continuing legacy – facilities, skills, new habits of thought and practice – when accountability proceedings conclude. But the impact of different accountability initiatives on strengthening the domestic rule of law in post-conflict societies is not straightforward. Much depends on how accountability processes are conducted, the uncertainties of unintended consequences, and the extent to which local perceptions of justice are altered by the proceedings. The potentially salutary impacts of accountability proceedings fall into at least two categories: their demonstration effects and their capacity-building effects. We consider each in turn.

A. Demonstration Effects
First, accountability proceedings can contribute to strengthening the rule of law in post-conflict societies through their *demonstration effects*.[22] Most

---

[21] *A Call for Justice, supra* note 8, at 17–21, 27–29, 34, 46–47.

[22] The idea of "demonstration effects" has been discussed by others as well. *See* International Center for Transitional Justice & United Nations Development Programme, *The "Legacy" of the Special Court for Sierra Leone*, 2003, at 12, *available at* http://www.ictj.org/downloads/LegacyReport.pdf. We try in this chapter to develop the concept and amplify the ways in which accountability proceedings can have positive demonstration effects on

tangibly and directly, by removing perpetrators of atrocities from positions in which they can control and abuse others, criminal trials (and processes such as rigorous vetting) can have a cathartic impact by assuring the population that old patterns of impunity and exploitation are no longer tolerable. Barring known perpetrators from again committing atrocities and delegitimizing them in the eyes of the public helps to break patterns of rule by fear and begins to build public confidence that justice can be fair. Many Afghans, for instance, have made clear that their trust in justice and in government institutions depends on removing serious abusers from positions of power and that they view this as essential for, not contrary to, security and long-term stability.[23]

Such cathartic processes can, nevertheless, be wrenching and traumatic in the near term. As powerful figures and their allies see their authority slip away, they may choose to mount resistance, which can aggravate existing instabilities. Also, in circumstances where vetting processes have been extensive, if inconsistent, as in Iraq, there is a risk that so many individuals may be removed from their positions that it undermines the stability of existing institutions or the prospects for building new ones in a timely manner.

In addition to disempowering perpetrators, the demonstration effects of accountability processes will depend on their character and credibility. Accountability proceedings – particularly trials but also truth commissions – aim to demonstrate that atrocities are unacceptable, condemned, and not to be repeated. They aim to substantiate concretely, and to demonstrate, a norm of accountability. If the proceedings that lead to conviction for major offenses – or the reconciliation rituals for lesser offenses – are widely viewed as fair and legitimate, they are more likely to demonstrate credibly that previous patterns of impunity have been rejected, that law can be fair, and that political position or economic clout does not immunize a person from accountability. If a norm of accountability is demonstrated credibly, it may provide meaningful justice to victims, reducing the chances of personal vengeance-seeking and eliminating impunity as a source of grievance more broadly. Providing a model of fair justice – through fair criminal prosecutions or through balanced reconciliation agreements for lesser offenders, for instance – can give citizens legitimate reason to expect (and to demand) better accountability and fairer processes in the future in other areas of life as well.

Of course, if accountability proceedings are widely viewed as biased, or if big fish go free while much lesser offenders are held accountable, those

building the rule of law in post-conflict societies. For an interesting analysis of the "political effects" of criminal tribunals, including their impact in delegitimating offenders and their possible stabilizing or destabilizing effects, *see* William W. Burke-White, A SYSTEM OF MULTILEVEL GLOBAL GOVERNANCE IN THE ENFORCEMENT OF INTERNATIONAL CRIMINAL LAW (forthcoming), Chapter IV.

[23] *A Call for Justice, supra* note 8, at 17, 41–44.

proceedings may have negative, counterproductive demonstration effects. They may send a message that justice is not fair, that previous patterns of impunity are continuing, and that deep-seated grievances will not be addressed. The complete failure to pursue accountability at all can send a similar message. In Afghanistan, for example, impunity is still rampant in those parts of the country where regional commanders and warlords function as a law unto themselves. Accountability for current abuses is probably of greater immediate concern for many Afghans than accountability for the past, but the two are clearly related when, in many instances, warlords who grew accustomed to operating with impunity in the past brazenly continue to do so in the present.[24]

Pursuing accountability fairly and credibly can have *empowering ripple effects* in a post-conflict society. By putting the issue of accountability on the national agenda, credible accountability proceedings can be a focal point for local and international nongovernmental organizations who advocate for related domestic reforms. Interveners involved in accountability proceedings can stress the importance of accountability norms to local elites generally,[25] and local and international NGOs can magnify these effects by working to inform and empower ordinary citizens about the importance of accountability and fair justice and by keeping pressure on post-conflict governments.[26] To effectively strengthen the domestic rule of law in the long term, accountability proceedings must demonstrate the value and importance of accountability and fair justice to local leaders and ordinary citizens alike: positive domestic change is more likely if pressure can be applied both from above and below.[27]

---

[24] On the problem of impunity in Afghanistan, *see* Rama Mani, Afghanistan Research and Evaluation Unit, *Ending Impunity and Building Justice in Afghanistan* (2003); *A Call for Justice, supra* note 8, at 17 ("Many persons who committed gross human rights violations remain in power today. This has provoked a profound disappointment in Afghans together with an almost total breakdown of trust in authority and public institutions").

[25] For a helpful general discussion of the importance of socializing elites in achieving norm change, *see* G. John Ikenberry & Charles A. Kupchan, *Socialization and Hegemonic Power*, 44 INT'L ORG. 2283 (1990).

[26] Political scientists have developed various models of norm diffusion and human rights advocacy. These include a "spiral model" through which local and international NGOs put pressure on domestic governments – from above and below – to abide by human rights principles, and a process of "norm cascades" as values gain credence broadly through a society after reaching a certain "tipping point." *See* Thomas Risse & Kathryn Sikkink, *The Socialization of International Human Rights Norms into Domestic Practice*, in THE POWER OF HUMAN RIGHTS: INTERNATIONAL NORMS AND DOMESTIC CHANGE (Thomas Risse, ed., 1999), at 1 (spiral model); Martha Finnemore & Kathryn Sikkink, *International Norm Dynamics and Political Change*, 52 INT'L ORG. 887 (1998) (norm cascades).

[27] This analysis is consistent with Risse and Sikkink's "spiral model." On the critical importance of socializing elites, *see* Ikenberry & Kupchan, *Socialization and Hegemonic Power, supra* note 25. On the importance of empowering citizens, especially the poor, in building the

Accountability proceedings, in short, can strengthen the fabric of a post-conflict society by helping to build and spread domestic support for a norm of accountability. As political scientists have argued, at some point in the development of a new norm, a "tipping point" is reached where the norm, enjoying broad acceptance, "cascades" through a society.[28] Before this point is reached, active efforts at persuasion by norm advocates, including local and international NGOs, are essential. Accountability proceedings can serve as a focal point for these efforts. Indeed, building toward an accountability cascade – in which expectations of accountability become the norm – is critical to overcome the legacy of a previous and pervasive impunity cascade in which order and accountability simply broke down (an example of an impunity cascade is Sierra Leone's situation in 1991, when many factors together tipped the country toward violence with impunity).[29] The slow and enormously hard work of building new normative expectations of accountability – rooted in a real capacity to deliver it, at least at a basic level – is often the key to establishing a viable domestic rule of law after conflict. The demonstration effect of accountability proceedings can be an essential, though not sufficient, component of that long-term effort.

B. Capacity-Building Effects

A second, related way that accountability proceedings can influence development of the rule of law domestically is through concrete *capacity-building*. Accountability proceedings cannot simply be an "aside" – standing totally apart from ordinary and ongoing processes of reform. Instead, over time, accountability norms – the condemnation of brutal atrocities, the importance of fair proceedings for determining responsibility, and the need for effective and impartial procedures for resolving future disputes more generally – must become *embedded in domestic practices*. Some accountability mechanisms,

---

rule of law, *see* Stephen Golub, *Beyond Rule of Law Orthodoxy: The Legal Empowerment Alternative,* Carnegie Endowment for International Peace, Democracy & Rule of Law Project, Rule of Law Series, No. 41, 2003.

[28] *See* Finnemore & Sikkink, *International Norm Dynamics and Political Change, supra* note 26, at 895.

[29] Sierra Leone's Truth and Reconciliation Commission has argued as follows: "While there were many factors, both internal and external, that explain the cause of the civil war, the Commission came to the conclusion that it was years of bad governance, endemic corruption and the denial of basic human rights that created the deplorable conditions that made the conflict inevitable. Successive regimes became increasingly impervious to the wishes and needs of the majority.... Government accountability was non-existent. Political expression and dissent had been crushed. Democracy and the rule of law were dead. By 1991, Sierra Leone was a deeply divided society and full of the potential for violence. It required only the slightest spark for this violence to be ignited." *Witness to Truth, supra* note 16, Vol. 1, para. 11, at 10.

by virtue of their location and degree of local participation, can help build domestic capacity directly by increasing the skills and experience of local professionals and through outreach efforts designed to educate and empower citizens and civil society organizations more broadly. International tribunals can serve important goals – such as providing justice for victims and conveying a strong international statement about fundamental international principles, including due process – even if their domestic impact in post-conflict societies is less clear. But unless norms of accountability are *institutionalized domestically* in a sustainable manner by strengthening national legal institutions and encouraging fairer processes and greater substantive accountability more broadly, the longer-term impact of accountability proceedings for past atrocities is likely to be uncertain.

Even though accountability proceedings can contribute to such domestic capacity-building, they also can compete with and divert resources from domestic legal systems. Prosecutions for serious violations of international humanitarian law are complex, costly, and time consuming, and competing priorities – for example, between international and domestic actors – can generate sharp tensions. In Rwanda, for instance, the government and ordinary citizens alike resent the millions of dollars spent on the international tribunal in Arusha, Tanzania, while Rwanda's own domestic legal system languishes desperately in need of aid. Even when hybrid courts are established, as in Sierra Leone and East Timor, the contrast between the facilities and resources of war crimes tribunals and the regular justice system is stark and sobering. The long-term needs of "ordinary" justice institutions generally cry out for attention, while international funding typically flows more generously to the more dramatic accountability proceedings.

This potential tension highlights the need to think more systematically from the start about designing processes that can both advance fundamental goals of accountability and develop domestic capacity for fair justice. Criminal trials, of course, must focus on their core purpose of bringing individual perpetrators to justice in fair and impartial proceedings. But modest efforts to enhance their domestic rule of law impact (for example, through early and well-planned outreach to local populations explaining the proceedings and the principles underlying them) can potentially make a real difference.

Based on the framework we have outlined here, one would expect that international trials held far from the people most affected by atrocities – and lacking in any direct domestic capacity-building or outreach efforts – are unlikely to have a substantial impact on strengthening the domestic rule of law in post-conflict societies. Even if they prosecute and thereby remove major perpetrators from domestic power structures, these trials must also be seen domestically to be doing justice if they are to have positive demonstration effects. Hybrid tribunals or truth commissions located in the affected country – with strong domestic participation and outreach – are more likely to leave a tangible legacy, at least if the bulk of the population views them as legitimate and fair. Either approach will have a limited long-term impact, however, if strategic efforts at domestic capacity-building are never undertaken or if underlying domestic conflicts (whether ethnic tensions or deep-seated perceived injustices) are simply left to fester or are even exacerbated by proceedings regarded as biased.

But what more specific conclusions can we draw, from recent experience, regarding the impact of accountability proceedings on building the rule of law domestically? It is to this challenging question that we now turn.

III. INTERNATIONAL TRIBUNALS AND THEIR IMPACT ON DOMESTIC RULE OF LAW: THE ICTY AND THE ICTR

The international community had good reason, at the time, to establish special international tribunals for Yugoslavia and Rwanda. Both conflicts involved egregious and widespread violations of international humanitarian law, and many states were determined to convey an emphatic international message that such conduct was unacceptable. In neither case were domestic legal systems in a position to provide fair and impartial justice. The Balkans were in the throes of a bitter conflict, and violence and ethnic hostilities precluded chances of fair and unbiased domestic prosecutions. Rwanda's legal system was devastated and overwhelmed in the face of massive genocide. The risks of "victor's justice" in both situations were substantial. In these circumstances, international tribunals held out a better prospect of independent and impartial proceedings and also of gaining custody over perpetrators beyond national borders.[30]

Established by the UN Security Council and funded largely by member states, the International Criminal Tribunal for the former Yugoslavia (ICTY)[31] and the International Criminal Tribunal for Rwanda (ICTR)[32] both have accomplished a great deal. They have each brought to justice, in fair trials, at least some of the individuals most responsible for egregious atrocities. Rwanda's former prime minister, Jean Kambanda, for instance, pled guilty and was convicted of genocide before the ICTR and is serving a life

[30] *See* Kritz, *The Rule of Law in the Postconflict Phase, supra* note 10, at 816.
[31] S.C. Res. 827, U.N. Doc. S/Res/827, May 25, 1993; *see* International Criminal Tribunal for the Former Yugoslavia, *ICTY at a Glance*, General Information, *available at* http://www.un.org/icty/glance-e/index.htm (last accessed February 4, 2006).
[32] S.C. Res. 955, U.N. Doc. S/Res/955 (November 8, 1994).

sentence.[33] At the ICTY, General Radislav Krstic – Commander of the Drina Corps – was found guilty of genocide in the 1995 Srebrenica massacres of as many as 8000 Muslim men and boys. The trial of former Yugoslav president Slobodan Milosevic before the ICTY was plagued by delay and other difficulties before his death in March 2006 brought the proceedings to an end without a final verdict; but his indictment for crimes committed in Bosnia, Croatia, and Kosovo – the first indictment ever to be brought against a sitting head of state – sent a clear message that nobody is above the law and contributed to his ultimate fall from power.[34] Both tribunals have also set some groundbreaking legal precedents contributing to the development of international criminal law, and they have played an educational role in focusing world attention on fundamental rules of international law. In bringing major perpetrators to justice, both tribunals have established an official record of the horrendous crimes committed and the criminal responsibilities of those involved.

Yet, despite these significant steps, both international tribunals may be remembered in the end as much for their shortcomings as their accomplishments. For one, they are geographically and psychologically distant from those most affected by the atrocities they are investigating and prosecuting. This distance, coupled with only belated and limited attempts at outreach, has undercut their legitimacy in the eyes of critical domestic audiences. Limited accurate information about the tribunals' proceedings, at least at first, undermined the tribunals' potential impact among local populations. For example, despite working hard to provide an impartial forum, the ICTY has suffered from a crisis of legitimacy – especially among Serbs – many of whom do not regard the tribunal as an embodiment of neutral justice.[35] These various factors have limited the ability of the international tribunals

---

[33] He was also convicted of conspiracy to commit genocide, direct and public incitement to commit genocide, complicity in genocide, and crimes against humanity. The ICTR also has brought a number of other high-level perpetrators to justice, including cabinet members and mayors.

[34] See Case Information Sheet: Milosevic (IT-02–54), *available at* http://www.un.org/icty/cases-e/index-e.htm (last accessed February 5, 2006). For a discussion of the indictment's impact, *see* Burke-White, A System of Multilevel Global Governance in the Enforcement of International Criminal Law, *supra* note 22, Chapter IV, at 231–234. For information on the Krstic case, see Prosecutor v. Krstic, Case No. IT-98-33-A, Judgment in the Appeals Chamber, April 19, 2004, *available at* http://www.un.org/icty/krstic/Appeal/judgment/index.htm. As of May 2006, important ICTY indictees – such as Ratko Mladic and Radovan Karadzic – still remained at large.

[35] See Jelena Pejic, *The Yugoslav Truth and Reconciliation Commission: A Shaky Start*, 25 Fordham Int'l L. J. 1 note 6 (2001). Others, including a group of Bosnian Serb and Bosnian Croat judges and prosecutors, have also expressed skepticism regarding the neutrality of the ICTY. *See* Report, *Justice, Accountability and Social Reconstruction: An Interview Study of Bosnian Judges and Prosecutors*, 18 Berkley J. Int'l L. 102, 104 (2000) (hereinafter *Justice, Accountability, and Social Reconstruction*).

to demonstrate fair justice and accountability for atrocities in a way that resonates with the people most directly affected.

The ICTY and the ICTR also have contributed very little to building domestic judicial capacity in the Balkans or Rwanda, respectively. Although this was never their main purpose or preoccupation, both tribunals could have done much more to assist domestic capacity-building. The ICTY and ICTR are in a position to try only a limited number of high-level cases, so domestic legal systems have a critical role to play if significant accountability for atrocities is to be realized. But neither tribunal, until they began focusing systematically on their completion strategies (for wrapping up their own trials and investigations), had done very much to help strengthen the ability of local courts to deal with the substantial number of potential suspects remaining to be tried. More has been done since 2003, when the Security Council called for greater international assistance to improve the domestic capacity in relevant states and encouraged the ICTY and ICTR "to develop and improve" their outreach programs.[36]

A. The ICTY's Impact on Domestic Rule of Law: Kosovo and Bosnia

The ICTY's limited impact on domestic capacity-building is especially unfortunate in light of the more than a billion dollars spent on the tribunal.[37] Despite the start of an outreach program in 1999 and other periodic contacts between ICTY personnel and legal communities in the region, systematic and sustained efforts to share the tribunal's technical expertise with justice systems in the region were not pursued, illustrating a general lack of priority placed on such efforts.[38] As David Tolbert, former senior legal adviser at the ICTY and later deputy prosecutor, put it: "principally due to a failure in design and, to a lesser extent, in implementation, the tribunal's long-term impact on the systems of justice in the area of conflict has been minimal."[39]

Take the situation in Kosovo, for instance. The ICTY has devoted enormous energy and resources to investigating war crimes committed in Kosovo in 1998–1999, but so far the ICTY and the UN Mission in Kosovo (UNMIK) have not developed formal arrangements for sharing information or

---

[36] S.C. Res. 1503, U.N. Doc. S/Res./1503 (August 28, 2003), para 1. For discussion of ICTR outreach, *see* Victor Peskin, *Courting Rwanda: The Promises and Pitfalls of the ICTR's Outreach Program*, 3 J. INT'L CRIM. JUS. 950 (2005). For examples of ICTY outreach, *see* the Calendar of Events at http://www.un.org/icty/bhs/outreach/events.htm (hereinafter *ICTY Calendar of Events*).

[37] Total expenditures through 2005 equaled slightly more than $1 billion. An additional $276.5 million has been authorized for 2006 and 2007. *See* ICTY at a Glance, *supra* note 31.

[38] David Tolbert, *The International Criminal Tribunal for the Former Yugoslavia: Unforeseen Successes and Foreseeable Shortcomings*, 26 FLETCHER F. WORLD AFF. 7, 13–15 (2002).

[39] Id., at 8.

enhancing cooperation.[40] And although ICTY staff have shared their expertise with Kosovo jurists in periodic outreach activities, the ICTY failed to develop systematic, formalized plans to help enhance the capacity of local institutions to try such complex cases.[41] Because of the substantial funds invested in the Tribunal's work, its "lack of impact on at least preparing and buttressing the local courts" to conduct war crimes prosecutions is "troubling,"[42] leaving more recent efforts associated with ICTY's completion strategy with considerable ground to cover.

The ICTY has played a somewhat greater role in Bosnia. To provide some ICTY oversight of domestic prosecutions, Rules of the Road were agreed on in 1996 between the ICTY and Bosnia, Serbia, and Croatia, respectively. Under this arrangement, ICTY prosecutors review domestic warrants and indictments to ensure their fairness.[43] On this basis, trials of lesser war crimes suspects have been taking place in the two entities of Bosnia-Herzegovina.[44] The number of cases handled domestically is expected to increase sharply as the ICTY progresses with its completion strategy, putting an already weak domestic justice system under serious strain.

[40] Legislation evidently is being developed. *See* press release, UNMIK/PR/1123, United Nations Mission in Kosovo, Legislation on Cooperation with ICTY Can Only Be Promulgated by UNMIK, February 20, 2004.

[41] The outreach program in Kosovo has included ad hoc seminars and information sessions during which specialists from The Hague share their expertise with Kosovar jurists. *See* Int'l Crisis Group, *Finding the Balance: The Scales of Justice in Kosovo* 23 (2003); ICTY Calendar of Events, *supra* note 36.

[42] Tolbert, *The International Criminal Tribunal for the Former Yugoslavia, supra* note 38, at 12. Tolbert argues that with modest resources, the ICTY could have helped build domestic capacity by training local prosecutors, monitoring court proceedings in war crimes cases, training judges, and providing advice on victims' issues. Id., at 16. Instead, despite all the money spent on the ICTY, "there is virtually no effective enforcement of these important laws in the courts that ultimately matter the most, i.e., the region's domestic courts." Id., at 8.

[43] Paragraph 5 of the Rome Agreement of February 18, 1996, provides that "Persons, other than those already indicted by the International Tribunal, may be arrested and detained for serious violations of international humanitarian law only pursuant to a previously issued order, warrant, or indictment that has been reviewed and deemed consistent with international legal standards by the International Tribunal," *available at* www.ohr.int/ohr-dept/hr-rol/thedept/war-crime-tr/default.asp?content_id=6093.

[44] As of November 2003, thirteen war crimes trials were taking place before entity courts. *See* Amnesty International, *Shelving Justice: War Crimes Prosecutions in Paralysis* 5 (2003), *available at* http://web.amnesty.org/library/Index/ENGEUR630182003?open&of=ENG-BIH (hereinafter *Shelving Justice*). *See also* International Crisis Group, *Courting Disaster: The Misrule of Law in Bosnia and Herzegovina* 31 (2002) (hereinafter *Courting Disaster*) (reporting that, as of March 2002, approximately thirty-five verdicts had been entered against accused in courts of the Federation). As of May 2002, an estimated 3000 people in the Republika Srpska and 6000 in the Federation were suspected of war crimes. *Shelving Justice*, at note 1. By February 2006, the cantonal prosecutor for Sarajevo and the surrounding area reported about 2100 war crimes suspects in the region and about 1600 individuals were the subject of requests for investigation by local authorities. *Bosnian TV Reports Prosecutor Outlines Progress in War Crimes Processing*, BBC INTERNATIONAL REPORTS, February 6, 2006.

Yet concerns about fairness and about impunity have been endemic in Bosnia from the start. Bosnian cantonal or entity courts have dispensed justice that has proven highly inadequate, triggering frequent allegations that trials have been tainted by "ethnic justice" and are being used to exact revenge.[45] All too often, instead of promoting justice, war crimes prosecutions in Bosnian courts have been yet another means of continuing ethnic conflict, undermining the goals of justice both for victims and for the accused.[46] With a few notable exceptions, a disturbing pattern has emerged with members of each of the three ethnic groups engaged in attempts to arrest, prosecute, and punish for war crimes members of their rival ethnic groups, who often are still viewed as heroes by their respective communities.[47] Thus far, the majority of war crimes trials have taken place in the Federation, with Muslim areas targeting almost exclusively Bosnian Serbs and Croats, and Croatian areas targeting primarily Serbs and Muslims.[48] Rather than promoting healing and confidence-building among the parties, trials often end up exacerbating divisions and mutual suspicion.[49] The record so far has been discouraging but some improvements have occurred.[50] Moreover, the creation of a special hybrid War Crimes Chamber within the national State Court of Bosnia and Herzegovina holds real promise.

This special War Crimes Chamber is now composed of national and international judges, prosecutors, and other staff, but the international participation will gradually phase out over a period of years.[51] This arrangement is designed to build local capacity to conduct fair trials in accordance with international standards, and ICTY staff have provided briefings and materials to judges and lawyers. The tribunal's location in Sarajevo means that

---

[45] *See* Michael Bohlander, *Last Exit Bosnia: Transferring War Crimes Prosecution from the International Tribunal to Domestic Courts*, 14 CRIM. L. F. 59, 67 (2003). According to the International Crisis Group, "[p]ublic debates and mutual accusations of pursuing 'ethnic justice' with the aim of eliminating political competitors or protecting one's brethren continue[s], involving a wide range of politicians, judges and human rights' activists," and "[a] leitmotif of the controversy [is] a widely shared recognition that the local judiciary [is] incapable of handling war crimes cases either competently or fairly." *Courting Disaster, supra* note 44, at 33.

[46] Aram A. Schvey, *Striving for Accountability in the Former Yugoslavia*, in Stromseth, ACCOUNTABILITY FOR ATROCITIES, *supra* note 12, at 67.

[47] Id., at 48–49.

[48] Id. The first war crimes trial in the Republika Srpska started only in September 2003. *See* Human Rights Watch, *Bosnia: Massacre Trial Highlights Obstacles to Justice in the Balkans*, January, 2004, *available at* http://hrw.org/english/docs/2004/01/15/bosher6939.htm.

[49] *See* Kritz, *Coming to Terms with Atrocities, supra* note 12, at 136–137.

[50] *See* OSCE, *War Crimes Trials before the Domestic Courts of Bosnia and Herzegovina: Progress and Obstacles*, March 2005, at 51.

[51] For a description of the special War Crimes Chamber, *see* S/2005/458, *Report to the Secretary-General of the Commission of Experts to Review the Prosecution of Serious Violations of Human Rights in Timor-Leste (then East Timor) in 1999*, May 26, 2005 (hereinafter *Commission of Experts Report*), Annex II to letter dated June 24, 2005, from the Secretary-General addressed to the president of the Security Council, July 15, 2005, at 109–110, 112–113.

its proceedings are more accessible to the local population and the prospects for direct outreach are greater. Compared to the problems that have plagued local trials, the special War Crimes Chamber has a greater capacity to render, and to be seen as rendering, impartial justice. The court began its first trial in September 2005 and received its first transfer of an indictee from the ICTY two weeks later.[52] The ICTY prosecutor's office has sought the transfer of an additional twelve defendants, and the local courts continue to send sensitive war crimes prosecutions to the special chamber.[53] Hybrid panels within the State Court also address difficult cases involving organized crime, economic crime, and corruption, with international participation and assistance that will gradually be phased out leaving purely domestic actors in place.

Compared to the distant ICTY and the often problematic local trials, the trials before the State Court's special chamber may be able to demonstrate impartial justice more directly and effectively to domestic audiences. The capacity-building effects of this arrangement are also substantial and vitally important. Even so, several concerns remain. For one, the schedule for the phase-out of international participation, driven substantially by funding realities, may be more rapid than is ideal for effective capacity-building. Furthermore, the entity-level Bosnian courts, rather than the State Court's special chamber, will continue to handle the bulk of war crimes cases, and if they do not receive greater assistance, there is a risk that some of the same problems that have confronted the ICTY may be "replicated at the national level."[54] Finally, although trials before the State Court's special chamber can help provide a model of fair and effective justice at the national level, systematic outreach and dialogue will still be needed as different segments of Bosnian society react to the prosecutions, including of figures who retain substantial loyalty and support within their respective communities.

B. The ICTY and Serbia

The ICTY's contribution to improving the domestic justice system and building the rule of law has been even more complicated in the case of Serbia. For many Serbs, the international prosecution of Milosevic robbed Serbia of the opportunity to hold him accountable in domestic courts. Milosevic's decision to defend himself and to challenge the very terms of reference of the international tribunal resonated in many quarters within Serbia, and a substantial segment of the public questioned whether he was getting a fair trial.[55]

---

[52] Council of Europe, *Bosnia and Herzegovina: Compliance With Obligations and Commitments and Implementation of the Post-Accession Co-Operation Program*, SG/Inf(2005)21, November 3, 2005, para. 54.

[53] Id.

[54] Amnesty International, *Shelving Justice, supra* note 44, at 8.

[55] According to opinion polls, less than one-fourth of Serbs believed Milosevic was getting a fair trial, and his approval rating doubled at the outset of his trial; he went from being a

Several factors have undercut the ICTY's ability to demonstrate to the Serbian population that the tribunal has been fair and impartial in its pursuit of accountability for atrocities. For one, many Serbs take a different view of the history of the breakup of the former Yugoslavia, rejecting the view of predominant Serb responsibility taken by NATO states supporting the ICTY. The tribunal's failure to indict leaders such as Croatian President Tudjman, who is now dead, has left the ICTY open to perceptions within Serbia of an anti-Serb bias. For many Serbs, this perception was reinforced by the tribunal's decision not to investigate NATO's actions during the Kosovo war. The circumstances surrounding the domestic handover of Milosevic to the ICTY also remain controversial, and many Serbs view the government's cooperation with the tribunal as strictly a function of monetary pressures rather than of justice. Finally, Milosevic sought to use his trial as a platform to influence public opinion in Serbia and was surprisingly effective in representing himself in court and portraying himself as an underdog.

All of these perceptions have been compounded by the ICTY's lack of effective outreach within Serbia. If the ICTY had provided Serbs with a clearer idea of its operations and purpose, early on, they might have been less prone to view the tribunal so skeptically. The ICTY did establish an outreach office in 1999 to inform people of the region about its work, but in crucial earlier phases, the ICTY's work was subject to "gross distortions and disinformation" in many parts of the former Yugoslavia.[56] As ICTY official David Tolbert notes, "the tribunal became a political football for certain unscrupulous politicians in the region who cynically manipulated...misunderstandings."[57] The ICTY should have anticipated this potential opposition and taken steps to ensure that the Serbian population would hear the truth about its operations from the very start.

The ICTY's contribution to capacity-building within Serbia has also been sorely lacking. Although more than a billion dollars has supported the ICTY since its inception,[58] relatively little has been done to share the tribunal's technical expertise or to assist local courts, even though they are expected to bring to justice many perpetrators not tried in The Hague. Even though

---

reviled individual to the fourth most admired Serb. Michael P. Scharf, *The ICTY at Ten: A Critical Assessment of the Major Rulings of the International Criminal Tribunal Over the Past Decade*, 37 NEW ENG. L. REV. 915, 930–931 (2003). Public opinion within Serbia has varied over the years, and there is some indication that public opposition to the ICTY diminished after release of the Scorpions video showing members of a Serbian police unit executing Bosnian Muslims in cold blood. *See, e.g.*, Nicholas Wood, *Videotape of Serbian Police Killing 6 Muslims From Srebrenica Grips Balkans*, THE NEW YORK TIMES, June 12, 2005, at A1.

[56] Tolbert, *The International Criminal Tribunal for the Former Yugoslavia, supra* note 38, at 13.

[57] Id.

[58] *See* ICTY at a Glance, *supra* note 31.

sharing its expertise and assisting local courts is not formally part of ICTY's mandate, more efforts to do this could have earned the ICTY considerable goodwill in Serbia and helped to better prepare local courts to continue prosecutions after the ICTY concludes its operations.

Yet, despite these problems, attitudes in Serbia – at least among some groups – may gradually be changing, and the ICTY may yet have a positive impact over the longer term. Although Serbia had completed only four domestic war crimes trials by January 2003, despite a large number of suspected war criminals within its borders, Serbia created a new Special Court for Organized Crimes and War Crimes later that year.[59] An exclusively domestic court, Serbia's Special Court receives international support, and the law establishing the Court provides for cooperation with the ICTY. In the Special Court's first case, the "Ovcara trial," in which a number of Serbs were accused of executing 192 Croatian prisoners of war at the Ovcara pig farm in the Croatian city of Vukovar in 1991, ICTY's prosecutor Carla del Ponte provided at least eight boxes of evidence to the Court, and Croatia provided exhumation records.[60] The ICTY's support to the Special Court in this case and in other potential cases is an important development as the ICTY begins to bring its own work to a close over the next few years. In December 2005, the Special Court completed the Ovcara trial, handing down lengthy prison sentences for fourteen of the sixteen defendants.[61]

Also in 2005, the emergence of a videotape showing members of the Serbian police unit known as the Scorpions callously executing Muslims at Srebrenica was aired extensively in Serbia and internationally after first being played at the Milosevic trial on June 1, 2005.[62] As of late 2005, one member of the unit depicted on the tape had been convicted in Croatia, and five others were on trial in Serbia.[63]

Serbia's Special Court has only recently begun its work and its long-term impact within Serbia remains to be seen. The Ovcara trial, at least initially, received considerable domestic attention, and it may have helped to encourage greater public dialogue and awareness regarding war crimes, at least to

---

[59] The law, passed on July 2003, is *available at* http://www.osce.org/documents/fry/2003/07/446_en.pdf

[60] Milanka Saponja Hadzic, Institute for War and Peace Reporting, *Serbian Judiciary Facing Key Test* (2004), *available at* http://www.iwpr.net. The Ovcara trial began on March 9, 2004. Press release, *Humanitarian Law Center, "Ovcara" Case: A Trial Is Professional but the Indictment Is Amiss*, April 6, 2005, *available at* http://www.hlc.org.yu/english/War_Crimes_Trials_Before_National_Courts/index.php.

[61] *Serbian Court Jails 14 Over 1991 "Execution" of Prisoners in Croatia*, BBC NEWSFILE, December 12, 2005.

[62] Nicholas Wood, *Videotape of Serbian Police Killing 6 Muslims from Srebrenica Grips Balkans*, THE NEW YORK TIMES, June 12, 2005, at A12.

[63] *Serb Jailed over Srebrenica Video*, BBC NEWS, December 29, 2005, *available at* http://news.bbc.co.uk/2/hi/europe/4567704.stm.

some extent. The release and repeated broadcast in Serbia of the Scorpions video has added to that public discussion. Domestic debates over the ICTY still remain highly charged – and prone to opportunistic manipulation by political factions – but the ICTY's legal support to domestic prosecutions like the Ovcara case may help, over time, to demonstrate accountability and build domestic capacity in a manner more widely viewed as credible within Serbia.

C. The ICTR: An Ambivalent Domestic Impact

The ICTR's impact within Rwanda has likewise been a mixed one.[64] The tribunal's relationship with the Rwandan government was uneasy from the start. After seeking international assistance in bringing perpetrators of Rwanda's devastating genocide to justice, Rwanda was the only state on the UN Security Council to vote against establishing the ICTR. Rwanda's objections – which still fester – included the failure to locate the tribunal within Rwanda, the lack of a provision for capital punishment, and limits on the time frame of the court's jurisdiction.[65] Significant management problems early on at the ICTR, coupled with the over one billion dollars spent on the ICTR while Rwanda's domestic system struggles to try thousands of suspects, have also been a source of resentment and tension. The limited number of individuals that the ICTR is able to try, the slow pace of proceedings at the tribunal, and the limited role for, and attention to, needs of victims have all been criticisms raised by Rwandan political leaders.[66]

In the face of these criticisms, the ICTR has had a difficult time establishing broad credibility among the Rwandan public. "Constantly exposed to such bitter criticism highlighting the imperfections of the Tribunal, many Rwandans tend to hold an overwhelmingly negative opinion of international justice," notes Aloys Habimana.[67] For many Rwandans, moreover, the individuals who directly committed atrocities in front of their own eyes matter as much as the more distant architects of the genocide.

The ICTR should have done more from the start to explain its purpose and its proceedings broadly within Rwanda and to address concerns raised by citizens. Instead, the tribunal's outreach has been belated and its physical

---

[64] Although Rwanda is not a case involving a major international military intervention (quite to the contrary) and therefore is not the focus of other chapters of this book, we discuss it here because of its importance for understanding the potential impact of accountability processes on building the rule of law.

[65] Aloys Habimana, *Judicial Responses to Mass Violence: Is the International Criminal Tribunal for Rwanda Making a Difference Towards Reconciliation in Rwanda?*, in INTERNATIONAL WAR CRIMES TRIALS: MAKING A DIFFERENCE? 83, 84–85 (Steven R. Ratner & James L. Bischoff, eds., 2003).

[66] Id., at 85.

[67] Id., at 86.

presence within Rwanda is limited.[68] Created in 1994, with its first trials commencing in 1997, the ICTR established an outreach project only in 1998 and an Information Center in Rwanda in 2000.[69] The ICTR's own Web site has improved, and several Web sites managed by international NGOs publish good information and analysis on the ICTR, but very few Rwandans have Internet access, so this information is largely available only to foreigners.[70] Radio Rwanda reports from the tribunal in Arusha, Tanzania, and a number of organizations, including the European Commission and some NGOs, support outreach efforts that include distributing documents and showing documentary films about the ICTR in the Rwandan countryside.[71] But much more needs to be done if the ICTR expects to have a longer-term impact within Rwanda.

Still, despite a slow start, the ICTR has the potential to demonstrate the importance of accountability and fair justice to audiences within Rwanda in a number of ways. For one, the tribunal has brought high-level perpetrators of genocide to justice. This sends "a clear message to victims, victimizers, and bystanders that leaders who commit gross violations of human rights are not always invincible," which is a message that "is fundamental for ensuring the rule of law in a post-conflict society like that of Rwanda," as Aloys Habimana argues.[72] In addition, these trials reveal how self-interested leaders exploited ethnic differences for their own purposes – which

---

[68] All of the courtrooms for the ICTR are in Arusha, Tanzania, and the ICTR's main formal presence in Rwanda is with the Office of the Prosecutor (formerly Carla del Ponte, now Hassan Jallow from the Gambia). The ICTY opened an Information Center in Kigali in 2000.

[69] Peter Uvin & Charles Mironko, *Western and Local Approaches to Justice in Rwanda*, 9 GLOBAL GOVERNANCE 219, 221 (2003). The Information Center, *Umusanzu mu Bwiyunge* ("Contribution to reconciliation"), in Rwanda's capital, Kigali, is open to "students, journalists, civil servants, judges and lawyers, as well as ordinary citizens." U.N. Doc. S/2003/707, A/58/140, International Criminal Tribunal for Rwanda, *Report of the International Criminal Tribunal for the Prosecution of Persons Responsible for Genocide and Other Serious Violations of International Humanitarian Law Committed in the Territory of Rwanda and Rwandan Citizens Responsible for Genocide and Other Such Violations Committed in the Territory of Neighbouring States between 1 January and 31 December 1994*, July 11, 2003, *available at* http://65.18.216.88/ENGLISH/annualreports/a58/140e.pdf (hereinafter *ICTR Report*).

[70] Uvin & Mironko, *Western and Local Approaches to Justice in Rwanda*, *supra* note 69, at 219.

[71] Id. The U.S.-based Internews media organization, for example, has produced documentary films about ICTR and domestic war crimes trials, which are then shown in rural communities, sometimes accompanied by Rwandan ICTR outreach officers. Peskin, *Courting Rwanda: The Promises and Pitfalls of the ICTR's Outreach Program*, *supra* note 36, at 960. Peskin urges the ICTR to establish partnerships with Rwandan civil society leaders and academics, some of whom have tried to secure ICTR's commitment, so far unsuccessfully, "to hold post-trial seminars in Rwanda with ICTR officials to discuss the significance of recent trials," which could be a foundation for further Rwandan-initiated outreach. Id.

[72] Habimana, *Judicial Responses to Mass Violence*, *supra* note 65, at 88.

may contribute to a greater domestic understanding of the causes of the genocide and possibly lay some foundation for reconciliation over time.[73] Finally, through fair trials that follow fundamental principles of due process, the tribunal can help demonstrate to Rwandans "what 'fair justice' should look like,"[74] potentially providing a point of reference for future domestic reforms.

But to have any sustainable long-term impacts along these lines will require more effective and convincing outreach within Rwanda than has occurred thus far. This is an uphill battle given the skepticism about the tribunal among many audiences in Rwanda. The tribunal, in short, faces a major challenge "not only to render justice, but also to make sure that Rwandans, in all their complex categories, see that justice is being done."[75] Yet, so far, the ICTR has been reluctant to partner with independent civil society organizations to engage in sustained outreach, thereby missing opportunities for empowering ripple effects; instead, the ICTR has preferred to interact with the Rwandan government and "government-backed survivor groups," whose cooperation the tribunal needs.[76]

The ICTR also needs to do more, before its work comes to an end, to contribute to capacity-building within the domestic justice system. But, to date, the ICTR has done almost nothing to contribute to the capacity of the Rwandan judiciary.[77] One of the few activities led by the ICTR involving the Rwandan judiciary was a September 2003 visit by twenty senior Rwandan judicial officials (judges, prosecutors, and senior officials) to the tribunal in Arusha.[78] The focus was primarily on issues related to the pursuit of justice at the ICTR (e.g., witness protection, pace of proceedings, and completion strategy) rather than on capacity-building for the Rwandan justice system itself.[79] One is left wondering whether some of the millions of dollars spent annually on the ICTR could have been better spent on direct domestic

---

[73] Id., at 89.

[74] Id.

[75] Id., at 90.

[76] Peskin, *Courting Rwanda: The Promises and Pitfalls of the ICTR's Outreach Program, supra* note 36, at 961. Peskin notes that despite overtures from leading academics and human rights activists, including Aloys Habimana, the ICTR has not embarked on cooperative partnerships with them to engage in more extensive outreach. Id., at 960–961.

[77] Id., at 957–958.

[78] The ICTR Registrar extended the invitation, and two groups of ten officials spent one week each at the tribunal. The purpose was "to strengthen the co-operation between the Rwandan judicial system and the Tribunal in what is called *appui judiciaire* to the national Rwandese judicial bodies." Press Release, ICTR/INFO-9-2-360. EN, International Criminal Tribunal for Rwanda, *Rwandan Judicial Officials Visit the ICTR,* September 26, 2003, *available at* http://65.18.216.88/ENGLISH/PRESSREL/2003/360.htm. The ICTR has also organized visits to the tribunal by Rwandan law students, as well as some internships. Peskin, *Courting Rwanda, supra* note 36, at 955–956.

[79] Press release, *supra* note 78.

capacity-building, particularly given Rwanda's desire to undertake domestic criminal prosecutions and community-based accountability proceedings.

In short, both the ICTR and the ICTY have faced obstacles in leaving a positive, long-term legacy in the countries most affected by the atrocities they are prosecuting. In future international prosecutions, some of these difficulties could be addressed by earlier, more effective outreach to domestic audiences, and by more systematic efforts to design focused, well-conceived domestic capacity-building programs. Still, international tribunals located far from the affected country with little or no involvement by national judges, prosecutors, and defense counsel are inherently limited in the direct impact they are likely to have domestically in post-conflict societies. But purely domestic proceedings may not be the answer either – at least in cases where national justice systems are devastated by conflict or unlikely to deliver fair or impartial justice. Hybrid, or mixed, tribunals with both national and international participation may, in some instances, hold more promise.

IV. HYBRID TRIBUNALS AND THEIR IMPACT ON DOMESTIC RULE OF LAW

Hybrid tribunals first emerged toward the end of the 1990s as an alternative to purely international or purely domestic courts. In a number of countries – Kosovo, East Timor, Sierra Leone, and Bosnia – hybrid arrangements have been established to try individuals for violations of international and sometimes also domestic law. In addition to combining national and international staff – judges and prosecutors, among others – these hybrids are located directly in the country that experienced the atrocities.

Hybrids, in many ways, are like a piece of clay that can be molded to fit the challenges and circumstances at hand. But they have been shaped by political necessity and compromise as much as by any grand theory. In the case of Kosovo, for instance, biased domestic trials provoked outcries from Kosovo's Serbian population and led the United Nations to design a hybrid system in which panels comprised of a majority of international judges would address war crimes and other sensitive cases and international prosecutors could revive cases dismissed by domestic prosecutors.[80] In other situations – East Timor and Cambodia – hybrids were negotiated because key states simply did not want to create new international tribunals even in the face of major atrocities.[81]

---

[80] Michael E. Hartmann, U.S. Institute of Peace, *International Judges and Prosecutors in Kosovo* 13 (2003), *available at* http://www.usip.org/pubs/specialreports/sr112.html. Hartmann was the first international prosecutor to serve under this arrangement.

[81] The Cambodian government together with China, for instance, rejected calls by a group of experts for an international tribunal to try former Khmer Rouge leaders. Yet Cambodian domestic courts were in no position to provide impartial justice in such cases. So the United

Though they differ in form and origins, hybrids have at least the potential to overcome some of the limitations of purely international or purely domestic proceedings.[82] They may, for instance, enjoy greater legitimacy among affected local populations than either international prosecutions far away or domestic prosecutions before a justice system of limited means or credibility. International participation and resources can help ensure that the proceedings satisfy international standards of due process, while domestic participation can give citizens of the country most affected a greater stake and sense of ownership. Thus, hybrids may demonstrate accountability in a way that resonates more effectively with local populations.

Second, hybrids may have advantages in contributing to domestic capacity-building and institutionalization of accountability norms. Locating tribunals directly in countries that endured atrocities – and including national participation in their work at all levels – provides an opportunity to build capacity and leave behind a tangible contribution to the national justice system, including resources, facilities, and training. Finally, by providing for direct interaction between national and international jurists and by enhancing opportunities for outreach to the local population, hybrids may be more effective than either international or national processes alone in fostering awareness of, and encouraging respect for, fundamental principles of international law and human rights at the domestic level among citizens and officials of the country involved. They may, to borrow from political science terminology, be more effective at "norm diffusion."[83]

But whether recent hybrids are actually achieving these results is a much more complicated question. The demonstration effects and capacity-building impact of these diverse hybrids, in fact, have varied widely.

A. Kosovo's Hybrid Arrangement: Mixed Results

In Kosovo, UNMIK established a hybrid judicial arrangement in 2000 to prosecute and try war crimes cases. The ICTY has primacy over such cases arising in the conflict in the former Yugoslavia, but it cannot try them all, so domestic courts also have a critical role to play in achieving

Nations and Cambodia – with U.S. involvement along the way – negotiated a compromise hybrid tribunal with a majority of Cambodian judges, although this agreement is only now slowly being implemented. *See* Rachel S. Taylor, *Better Late Than Never: Cambodia's Joint Tribunal*, in Stromseth, ACCOUNTABILITY FOR ATROCITIES, *supra* note 12, at 237. In East Timor, the United Nations together with key states opted for a hybrid arrangement – joint national/international judicial panels within East Timor and domestic prosecutions in Indonesia – even though there were good reasons to doubt whether high-level Indonesian military officials would ultimately face justice under such an arrangement, at least absent sustained international pressure on Indonesia.

[82] For a thoughtful analysis, *see* Dickinson, *The Promise of Hybrid Courts, supra* note 18.

[83] For a discussion of norm diffusion, *see generally* Finnemore & Sikkink, *International Norm Dynamics and Political Change, supra* note 26.

accountability.[84] In Kosovo's case, however, the local judicial system was seriously incapacitated. Most of the local judges and lawyers – of predominantly Serb ethnicity – fled the province or refused to serve in the UN-established judicial system, and newly appointed Kosovar Albanian judges lacked professional experience because of their decade-long exclusion as a result of officially sanctioned discrimination. But in ethnically divided Kosovo, the virtually monoethnic, UN-appointed judiciary was not perceived as providing – nor could it deliver – impartial justice. Only after mounting pressure from ethnic Serbs in what was increasingly viewed as a biased justice system did UNMIK introduce international judges and prosecutors to serve in Kosovo's judicial system.

The initial deployment of these international jurists in 2000 was "crisis driven" and improvised, rather than the result of a carefully designed and implemented strategy.[85] Appointed to most, but not all, war crimes and other sensitive cases, including ethnic crimes and high-level organized crime, the international jurists initially had little impact: they were in the minority on judicial panels and were invariably outvoted by Kosovar Albanian judges. This only reinforced perceptions of "victor's justice" among Kosovo's Serbian population – now with the involvement of the international community – which reinforced resentments and ethnic tensions rather than helping to defuse them. In the face of these clear shortcomings, UNMIK issued regulations in December 2000 providing for the introduction of majority international judicial panels and empowering international prosecutors to reactivate cases abandoned by their Kosovar counterparts.

These "64 panels" – named after UNMIK's Regulation 2000/64 establishing them – have helped to reduce perceptions of bias in the justice system and have redressed some earlier miscarriages of justice. Nevertheless, shortcomings in implementation and some subjective aspects of this arrangement have undermined their potential impact. Introduced by UNMIK without consulting and involving local judges, the arrangement has faced widespread resistance by local judges, and some have refused to participate in majority international panels.[86] Moreover, the grounds for participation of international judges and prosecutors have been criticized as overly vague and subjective,

[84] The ICTY has jurisdiction over serious violations of international humanitarian law committed in the former Yugoslavia since January 1, 1991, including war crimes, genocide, and crimes against humanity. The ICTY's jurisdiction is concurrent with national courts, but it enjoys primacy and can request a national court to defer to it. Statute of the International Criminal Tribunal for the Former Yugoslavia, Art. 9, *annexed to Report of the Secretary General Pursuant to Paragraph 2 of Security Council Resolution 808 (1993)*, UN SCOR, 48th Sess., U.N. Doc. S/25704 (1993) (hereinafter ICTY Statute); ICTY R.P. & Evid. 9–11 (July 21, 2005), *available at* http://www.un.org/icty/legaldoc-e/index.htm.

[85] Hartmann, *International Judges and Prosecutors in Kosovo, supra* note 80.

[86] David Marshall & Shelley Inglis, *The Disempowerment of Human Rights-Based Justice in the United Nations Mission in Kosovo*, 16 HARV. HUM. RTS. J. 95, 130 (2003).

contributing to a perception, especially among Albanians, that the system is a "parallel justice system" vulnerable to political influence and maneuvering. Also, because the regulation does not guarantee prosecution by an international prosecutor before a majority international panel, Kosovo Serb defendants also view the arrangement as vulnerable to double standards and unequal treatment.[87] Thus, the "64 panels" have only partially been able to address public perceptions of bias in ethnically charged Kosovo.

Viewed over the long term, the demonstration effects of the hybrid panels within Kosovo clearly have been mixed. On the one hand, the majority international panels' ability to consider particularly delicate and divisive cases, coupled with the international prosecutors' ability to revive and pursue cases abandoned by local counterparts, has, over time, helped to address systemic biases and miscarriages of justice in the largely monoethnic local justice system. On the other hand, UNMIK's belated, ad hoc introduction of the "64 panels" was a missed opportunity to demonstrate a commitment and a capacity for impartial justice from the start. As the first international prosecutor in Kosovo, Michael Hartmann, has observed, international participation in the judiciary would have been more successful had it been "immediate and bold" rather than "incremental and crisis driven."[88] Early prosecutions and trials before majority international panels could have enhanced the real and perceived impartiality of the judiciary, increasing its legitimacy among the different sectors of the population. Rather than empowering local jurists and belatedly stripping them of their "monopoly" over sensitive cases, such a policy also would have been easier and likely less contentious to implement. Finally, beginning with a more systematic international role in the local judicial system could have had a broader impact by helping to limit the destructive influence and entrenchment of criminal power structures and their linkages to extremist ethnic and nationalist groups.[89]

Not surprisingly, the capacity-building results of Kosovo's hybrid panels also have been less than hoped for. Despite the potential for mutual learning when international jurists serve besides local judges, a number of the international judges, especially early on, had little background or training in international humanitarian law, which limited their ability to contribute to local capacity-building in this area.[90] Language barriers, the intensive workload, and the lack of systematic mentoring mechanisms all hampered potential capacity-building more generally. The hybrid arrangement in

[87] Id., at 134.

[88] Hartmann, *International Judges and Prosecutors in Kosovo, supra* note 80, at 13.

[89] Id.

[90] Marshall & Inglis, *The Disempowerment of Human Rights-Based Justice in the United Nations Mission in Kosovo, supra* note 86, at 129 ("Of the internationals that were appointed between 1999 and 2001, few had conducted trials involving serious criminal offenses and none had any practical experience in, or knowledge of, international humanitarian law . . . ").

Kosovo – which places the most sensitive cases before the "64 panels" – also has delayed the day when Kosovo's local judges have to take full responsibility for adjudicating such cases.

All of this suggests that hybrids are more likely to be effective in demonstrating accountability and fair justice – and in developing local capacity – if they are designed in a more strategic way than was the case with Kosovo's early experiment. It may well be, at least in circumstances where local legal capacity is absent or devastated, that turning to international jurists early on – if they possess the necessary legal background and skills – makes sense as an initial response, while local jurists are trained effectively and expeditiously to join, as soon as possible, in the task of adjudicating sensitive and difficult war crimes cases. In any event, creating standing panels with clear jurisdiction – rather than ad hoc discretionary panels – to address war crimes and other sensitive cases may be less vulnerable to perceptions of political malleability by affected populations.

B. Timor Leste: "Independence Is a Form of Justice"

East Timor's hybrid tribunal for serious crimes has faced tough challenges in pursuing accountability amidst the political complexities associated with the nation's transition to independence, yielding deeply ambivalent demonstration effects. During East Timor's historic referendum in 1999, militias operating with the aid and support of the Indonesian army perpetrated atrocities – murders, rapes, looting, burning – against Timorese independence supporters. An international commission of inquiry established at the UN Human Rights Commission in 1999 called for an international tribunal to bring those responsible to justice. But critical states and UN leaders – involved in delicate negotiations with Indonesia to secure its consent to the deployment of an international military force, INTERFET, to stabilize East Timor after the referendum – instead pressed Indonesia to bring those responsible for the violence to justice domestically.[91] In opting not to establish an international tribunal for this purpose, many no doubt hoped that persistent international pressure on Indonesia might produce meaningful domestic accountability; but, at the same time, the absence of an international accountability mechanism with clear enforcement authority undermined the prospects of trying leading Indonesian suspects if Indonesia itself chose not to do so.

---

[91] In an April 2000 MOU between Indonesia and the UN, Indonesia agreed to share information and transfer indictees to East Timor. *Memorandum of Understanding Between the Republic of Indonesia and the United Nations Transitional Administration in East Timor Regarding Cooperation in Legal, Judicial and Human Rights Related Matters*, Indon.-UNTAET, April 6, 2000, *available at* http://www.jsmp.minihub.org/Reports/MOU.htm. INTERFET, a UN-authorized military force (with Indonesian consent) led by Australia deployed in August 1999 to restore stability to East Timor, followed by a UN provisional administration – the UN Transitional Administration in East Timor (or UNTAET) together with a UN peacekeeping force. S.C. Res. 1272, U.N. Doc. S/RES/1272, October 25, 1999.

Within East Timor, the UN Transitional Administration (UNTAET) established an innovative hybrid tribunal in June 2000 (in lieu of an international tribunal per se). The Special Panels for Serious Crimes – hybrid judicial panels within the Dili District Court consisting of two international judges and one Timorese judge – were created to try cases of crimes against humanity, war crimes, and other atrocities.[92] UNTAET also established the Serious Crimes Unit, a UN-funded prosecutorial and investigatory office for serious crimes, to serve as the prosecutorial and investigations arm of the hybrid tribunal.[93] Although both the Special Panels and Serious Crimes Unit received UN funding, defense counsel received more limited, ad hoc support – an imbalance of concern from the start.[94] In 2002, the successor UN mission (UNMISET) established a Defense Lawyer's Unit to provide more resources and expertise to assist in defense of suspects before the Special Panels.[95] Overall, however, neither political support (international or domestic) nor resources for East Timor's hybrid tribunal were ever as forthcoming as many originally had hoped.

These limitations seriously constrained the tribunal's impact both in achieving accountability for the atrocities surrounding the referendum and in capacity-building. The special tribunal faced chronic shortages of administrative, legal, and linguistic support, particularly at the beginning. In early trials, for instance, no court reporters or other means were available to produce records of the proceedings.[96] Interpreters frequently were unavailable in some of the four languages (Portuguese, Bahasa Indonesia, Tetum, and English) in which proceedings were conducted. Resources for defense counsel were particularly limited, and no defense witnesses were called at all in a number of the early trials.[97] Significant improvements certainly occurred over time, but a shortage of resources and support personnel continued to

---

[92] The panels were given jurisdiction over genocide, torture, crimes against humanity, and war crimes; in addition, they had jurisdiction over murder and sexual offenses committed from January 1, 1999, through October 25, 1999 – the period leading up to and following the referendum and before the UN became administering authority in East Timor. UNTAET Reg. 2000/15, U.N. Doc. UNTAET/REG/2000/15, June 6, 2000. Although the jurisdiction over crimes against humanity and the other international crimes was not time limited, the Serious Crimes Unit focused its prosecutions on the crimes surrounding the 1999 referendum.

[93] UNTAET Reg. 2000/16, U.N. Doc. UNTAET/REG/2000/16, June 6, 2000.

[94] See David Cohen, *Seeking Justice on the Cheap: Is the East Timor Tribunal Really a Model for the Future?*, ASIA PACIFIC ISSUES (August 2002) at 5, *available at* http://www.eastwestcenter.org/stored/pdfs/api061.pdf; Suzanne Katzenstein, *Hybrid Tribunals: Searching for Justice in East Timor*, 16 HARV. HUM. RTS. J. 245, 251, 262–264 (2003).

[95] For analysis of the Defense Lawyer's Unit, *see* Commission of Experts Report, *supra* note 51, at 36–37.

[96] Cohen, *Seeking Justice on the Cheap, supra* note 94, at 5; Katzenstein, *Hybrid Tribunals, supra* note 94, at 260.

[97] Cohen, *Seeking Justice on the Cheap, supra* note 94, at 5–6; Katzenstein, *Hybrid Tribunals, supra* note 94, at 253.

hamper the tribunal, which concluded its last trials in 2005, with appeals to be completed in 2006.[98]

Substantively, the hybrid tribunal's impact in terms of demonstrating accountability and fair justice has been ambiguous, at best. On the one hand, the tribunal tried a significant number of individuals for crimes against humanity and other offenses in proceedings that an international commission of experts concluded generally accorded with international standards.[99] A total of eighty-seven defendants were tried, with eighty-four convicted and three acquitted.[100] The Serious Crimes Unit also issued many indictments – a total of 95 against 440 defendants – including some against high-level Indonesian military officials.[101] On the other hand, the vast majority of the accused (339 individuals) are beyond the physical jurisdiction of the court (mostly in Indonesia), and they are unlikely ever to be either extradited to East Timor for trial or credibly tried in Indonesia – absent sustained international pressure on Indonesia, which has not been forthcoming, particularly since 9/11. The net result is that East Timor's hybrid tribunal tried only mid- and lower-level indictees, mostly Timorese ex-militia members involved in the violence surrounding the referendum, but did not reach the higher-level suspects in Indonesia. When those at the top never face justice, it sends a very mixed message about accountability to Timorese citizens.

The situation of Indonesia's General Wiranto illustrates this dilemma. Wiranto, who was defense minister and commander of the armed forces of Indonesia at the time of the Timorese referendum, is charged, along with six

---

[98] The UN Security Council decided to conclude the mandate of the special panels in May 2005 when UNMISET's mandate ended, and it urged that all trials be concluded by then. S.C. Res. 1543, U.N. Doc. S/RES/1543, May 14, 2004. In fact, some appeals were handled subsequently and, as of February 2006, two defendants still had appeals pending. *See* Judicial System Monitoring Programme, *available at* http://www.jsmp.minihub.org/ (follow hyperlinks under SPSC Case Information).

[99] Commission of Experts Report, *supra* note 51, para. 357, at 86.

[100] *See* Judicial System Monitoring Programme, *The Special Panels for Serious Crimes Hear Their Final Case, Justice Update*, May 12–May 20, Issue 12/2005, *available at* http://www. jsmp.minihub.org (hereinafter *JSMP Justice Update*). For information on cases, *see* the JSMP Web site, as well as American University, War Crimes Research Office, Special Panels for Serious Crimes in East Timor Status Updates, *available at* http://www.wcl. american.edu/warcrimes/easttimor_status.cfm.

[101] *JSMP Justice Update*, *supra* note 100. Those indicted include General Wiranto (former Defense Minister and Commander of the Armed Forces of Indonesia), Major General Zacky Anwar Makarim (Security Task Force Advisor), Major General Adam Damiri (former chief of the Regional Military Command), Brigadier General Suhartono Suratman (former Military Commander for East Timor), Colonel Mohmanned Noer Muis (Commander of the Sub-Regional Command 164), Brigadier General Timbul Silaen (former Chief of Police for East Timor), and Lieutenant Colonel Yayat Sudrajat (Commander of the Intelligence Task Force of Sub-Regional Command 164). Amnesty International & Judicial System Monitoring Programme, *Justice for Timor-Leste: The Way Forward*, April 2004, *available at*: http://news.amnesty.org/library/index/engasa210062004.

other high-ranking Indonesian military officers and the former governor of East Timor, with committing crimes against humanity – murder, deportation, and persecution – in 1999.[102] After many months, the special court issued a warrant for his arrest, but East Timorese officials refrained from handing the warrant to Interpol for international action. Key Timorese leaders, including President Xanana Gusmao, have placed a higher priority on forward-looking reconciliation and on building a strong relationship with Indonesia than on seeking judicial accountability for the 1999 atrocities.[103] Gusmao, in particular, has argued that pressing Indonesia might produce a military backlash just at a moment when the country was struggling to solidify its own democratic reforms.[104] Indeed, Gusmao met with Wiranto – then a candidate for president of Indonesia – in 2004, just before the Indonesian elections, proclaiming that bygones should be bygones.[105] Although other Timorese officials, such as Foreign Minister Jose Ramos-Horta, were critical of this meeting and its timing,[106] few Timorese leaders are comfortable pressuring their powerful neighbor to hand over top figures given their strong desire to improve East Timor's economy, to resolve border issues, and generally to build cordial relations with Indonesia. Even East Timor's prosecutor-general, who earlier had emphasized the importance of bringing Wiranto to justice, later backed off.[107]

Timorese political leaders consistently have emphasized the importance of consolidating East Timor's independence and building a strong relationship with Indonesia. Ramos-Horta has stressed, moreover, that "independence is a form of justice."[108] This is an important point from someone who, along with Gusmao and many others, devoted his career to East Timor's long and historic struggle for independence. Independence for the Timorese people

---

[102] Wiranto is charged under the principle of command responsibility. The February 2003 indictment is available on the JSMP Web site at http://www.jsmp.minihub.org/index.htm (follow link to SPSC Case Information for 2003).

[103] President Gusmao was elected overwhelmingly as East Timor's first president, and he has placed a strong emphasis on looking forward. Gusmao has focused on pursuing economic development and "social justice" in East Timor – and on achieving reconciliation and reintegrating resistance fighters and remaining remnants of opposing militias into Timorese society. *See* Rachel S. Taylor, *Justice and Reconciliation in East Timor, Interview: East Timorese President Xanana Gusmao*, WORLD PRESS REVIEW, October 1, 2002, *available at* http://www.worldpress.org/Asia/743.cfm. Gusmao has also sought to establish constructive relations with Indonesia – East Timor's powerful neighbor and key trading partner.

[104] *See, e.g.,* Letter dated June 22, 2005 from the President of Timor-Leste to the Secretary-General, Annex I to letter dated July 14, 2005 from the Secretary-General addressed to the President of the Security Council, U.N. Doc. S/2005/459, July 15, 2005, at 3.

[105] *East Timor's Foreign Minister Questions Gusmao's Meeting With Wiranto*, ASSOCIATED PRESS (May 30, 2004).

[106] Id.

[107] *Forwarding Wiranto Warrant to Interpol Not in E. Timor Interest: Prosecutor*, AGENCE FRANCE PRESS (May 25, 2004).

[108] Interview with Foreign Minister Jose Ramos-Horta in Dili, Timor Leste (November 2003).

does provide tangible vindication for their struggle and their suffering. And East Timor clearly needs to consolidate its long-sought independence and to build constructive relationships with its neighbors.

Yet lack of accountability has been a bitter pill to swallow. As many human rights advocates, church leaders, and civil society organizations in East Timor and elsewhere emphasize, the victims and survivors of the brutal atrocities in 1999 – and during the much longer quarter century of Indonesian occupation – deserve to know the truth about who was responsible, and those who bear the greatest responsibility need to be held accountable in some way. East Timor's Commission for Reception, Truth and Reconciliation has argued that "the crimes committed in 1999 were far outweighed by those committed during the previous 24 years of occupation and cannot be properly understood or addressed without acknowledging the truth of the long conflict"; the Commission also urges that the mandate of the Special Panels and Serious Crimes Unit be renewed so that they can concentrate on key cases from the longer period of 1975–1999, and it calls for a serious effort on Indonesia's part to hold major perpetrators accountable as well.[109] Realistically, this will only happen if there is much stronger and more consistent international pressure on Indonesia to live up to its earlier commitment to pursue accountability domestically, as well as international support for an international accountability mechanism of some kind if this does not occur.

Within Indonesia, however, the recent trend has been in the exact opposite direction. In August 2004, an Indonesian court overturned the convictions of four Indonesian security officials previously found guilty of crimes against humanity in the violence in East Timor.[110] No reasons were given for the court's reversal. These acquittals mean that no Indonesian security officials are serving time for the horrific violence and brutality perpetrated against the East Timorese in the period surrounding its referendum.[111]

---

[109] *Chega!: Final Report of the CAVR, supra* note 6, Part 11: Recommendations, at 23–25.

[110] Evelyn Rusli, *Indonesia Court Voids 4 Convictions in 1999 East Timor Strife,* THE NEW YORK TIMES, August 7, 2004, at A2.

[111] In the end, all those tried before Indonesia's Ad Hoc Human Rights Court "were acquitted either at trial or on appeal except for one, Eurico Guterres, whose appeal has yet to be heard." Commission of Experts Report, *supra* note 51, at para.171. The August 2004 acquittals triggered sharply divergent reactions. They caused an outcry among human rights NGOs, both domestic and international, and provoked strong statements by a number of governments. But many Timorese officials took a very different view. Foreign Minister Ramos-Horta expressed support for an international truth commission but opposed an international criminal tribunal. Prosecution of Indonesian officials, he argued, could be destabilizing within Indonesia and would undermine East Timor's efforts to improve its relations with Indonesia. Dan Eaton, *East Timor Urges End to Push for UN Tribunal,* REUTERS, August 9, 2004; *East Timor's Foreign Minister Opposes Rights Tribunal,* ASSOCIATED PRESS, September 8, 2004. For a discussion and critique of the Indonesian prosecutions before the Ad Hoc Human Rights Court, *see* Commission of Experts Report, *supra* note 51, at 38–80.

Meanwhile, in East Timor, the capacity-building impact of the hybrid tribunal, like its accountability record, has been mixed. Valuable experience clearly has been gained by Timorese judges serving on the Special Panels and by Timorese investigators and prosecutors working in the Serious Crimes Unit. The fact that the Timorese judges serving on the trial and appellate panels are also part of the domestic justice system and likely will continue to serve there means that their experience on the Special Panels – in trial procedures, opinion-drafting, and so forth – will be of direct benefit to the national courts.[112] This is valuable capacity-building. Nevertheless, language barriers among the national and international judges limited the opportunities for exchange of ideas and mutual learning. Also, salary and support arrangements made Timorese judges on the Special Panels sometimes feel like second-class citizens.[113] A lack of systematic and well-planned training early on also constrained the capacity-building potential of the hybrid tribunal.[114]

On the prosecution side, few Timorese were integrated into top positions in the serious crimes prosecutorial office. More generally, the stark contrast in resources between the Serious Crimes Unit and East Timor's "ordinary crimes" capacity presented a constant struggle for East Timor's prosecutor-general, Longuinhos Monteiro, who headed both components and whose five district prosecutors had no land phone lines by which to communicate.[115] Monteiro expressed concern that when the tribunal's mandate ended (as it did in 2005) and the UN departed, equipment and resources on which Timorese prosecutors in the Serious Crimes Unit had come to depend would also leave with the UN, despite the considerable domestic legal challenges that would remain.[116] As of February 2006, the wrap-up arrangements, including provisions for storage of the Serious Crime Unit's files, were being

---

[112] Although, as we discussed in Chapter 6, Timorese judges failed their exams to move beyond probationary status, they are engaged in intensive training programs and many passed their midterm evaluation. *See* U.N. Doc. S/2006/24, *Progress Report of the Secretary-General on the United Nations Office in Timor-Leste,* January 17, 2006, para. 19.

[113] The United Nations pays the salaries of international judges, prosecutors, and investigators. Timorese counterparts are paid at local rates by the Timorese government. It is not so much salary differentials but rather some differences in basic support – such as computers and other resources – that has grated on some Timorese judges, for instance.

[114] This has been a more general problem in the East Timorese judicial system. *See* Katzenstein, *Hybrid Tribunals, supra* note 94, at 265–268.

[115] Interview with Prosecutor-General Longuinhos Monteiro in Dili, Timor-Leste (November 2003).

[116] Id. In the end, the UN-funded Serious Crimes Unit was able to investigate only less "than half of the estimated 1,450 murders committed in 1999." U.N. Doc. S/2005/533, *Progress Report of the Secretary-General on the United Nations Office in Timor-Leste,* August 18, 2005, para. 49. Arrangements for storing the Serious Crime Unit's original files in Timor Leste, and for storing a complete copy of these records at the United Nations are being finalized. Id., at paras. 12–14. For discussion of the conclusion of the tribunal's mandate, see *supra* note 98.

finalized. On the defense side, the capacity-building has been more limited. Internationals largely handled the defense in serious crimes cases, while providing some training for Timorese public defenders.[117] In short, important local capacity-building clearly has taken place, but the potential offered by East Timor's hybrid arrangement has been realized only partially.

To sum up: The mixed results of East Timor's Special Panels reflect the broader ambivalence of Timorese leaders, UN officials, and major governments about pressing Indonesia too hard. Other goals – consolidating independence, forging political and economic ties, resolving outstanding border issues, counterterrorism cooperation – have consistently taken higher priority. Given how closely East Timor's fate is tied to that of Indonesia, and taking into account the broader international unwillingness to pressure Jakarta, the path chosen by East Timor's leaders is understandable. Nevertheless, disappointment within East Timor about the limited accountability for the 1999 atrocities, and more broadly for atrocities throughout the long Indonesian occupation, may fester unless more is done to seek meaningful accountability.[118] Furthermore, Indonesia's unwillingness to acknowledge the responsibility of specific Indonesian military leaders and militia forces for the violence in East Timor perpetuates a pattern of impunity that bodes poorly for its human rights accountability in other contexts.

Against this background, it is hardly surprising that the decision of East Timor and Indonesia to establish a bilateral Commission of Truth and Friendship (CTF) in late 2004 has evoked ambivalent responses within East Timor.[119] According to its terms of reference, the CTF aims to "resolve residual problems of the past" and to "establish the conclusive truth" regarding "the events prior to and immediately after the popular consultations," including the "nature, causes and the extent" of the human rights violations, and to do so through "a forward looking and reconciliatory approach"

---

[117] Katzenstein, *Hybrid Tribunals, supra* note 94, at 263, 267. *See also* Commission of Experts Report, *supra* note 51, at 36–37.

[118] As we discuss below, many Timorese participating in the community-based reconciliation proceedings have expressed strong disappointment that many of those who committed serious crimes have not been prosecuted at all. *See Chega!: Final Report of the CAVR, supra* note 6, Part 9: Community Reconciliation, at 48 (para. 170); Zifcak, *Restorative Justice in East Timor, supra* note 11, at 41; Pigou, *An Evaluation of the Community Reconciliation Process, supra* note 11, at 100–101; Commission of Experts Report, *supra* note 51, at 89 (para. 381) (citing 2004 opinion poll in which "52 per cent of the population responded that justice must be sought even if it slows down reconciliation with Indonesia, while 39 per cent favoured reconciliation even if that meant significantly reducing efforts to seek justice").

[119] The leaders of Indonesia and East Timor met in Bali on December 14, 2004, to establish the Commission of Truth and Friendship. Information about the Commission, including its terms of reference and members, is available on its Web site at http://www.ctf-ri-tl.org. The Commission has ten members, five of whom are Indonesian and five Timorese, including the Chair of East Timor's CAVR.

that "will not lead to prosecution and will emphasize institutional respon-sibilities."[120] The CTF ultimately will issue a report that will establish a "shared historical record" and recommend measures to "heal the wounds of the past." Human rights and victims groups in East Timor, however, have expressed deep concern about aspects of the CTF's mandate, partic-ularly the idea of "amnesty for those involved in human rights violations who cooperate fully in revealing the truth."[121] There is also concern that the Commission will face pressure from the Indonesian side not to call senior military leaders at all, and that it will backtrack on what has already been accomplished thus far in documenting the historical record and issuing indictments.

C. East Timor's Innovative Community Reconciliation Procedures

Within East Timor, it is the Commission for Reception, Truth and Rec-onciliation (CAVR) that may ultimately have the greater domestic impact, particularly through its innovative community reconciliation procedures and through its comprehensive report and recommendations. An indepen-dent body supported by voluntary contributions, the CAVR included seven national commissioners and twenty-nine regional commissioners and was chaired by Aniceto Guterres Lopes, an accomplished and widely respected Timorese human rights lawyer.[122] From 2001 until it completed its over-2000 page report in 2005, the Commission worked diligently to seek the truth regarding human rights violations in East Timor during the period between April 1974 and October 1999, reaching out to citizens throughout East Timor, gathering testimony from victims, and holding a series of major public hearings.[123] The CAVR was also charged with assisting the reception and reintegration of individuals into their communities after the long period of political conflict in East Timor.

The Commission's community reconciliation process made a unique con-tribution to this goal. The Commission's staff traveled throughout the country to visit communities affected by violence during the Indonesian

---

[120] Terms of Reference for the Commission of Truth and Friendship, paras. 7–14, *available at* http://www.ctf-ri-tl.org.

[121] Id., at para. 14.b.i.

[122] The commission was supported by voluntary contributions from states, nongovernmen-tal organizations, and individuals. Established by UNTAET in 2001, the commission's mandate was negotiated with Timorese leaders. *See* UNTAET Reg. 2001/10, U.N. Doc. UNTAET/REG/2001/10, July 13, 2001; Carsten Stahn, *Accommodating Individual Crimi-nal Responsibility and National Reconciliation: The UN Truth Commission for East Timor*, 95 AM. J. INT'L L. 952 (2001). The commission was headquartered at Dili's former Balide Prison, the site of horrific torture and atrocities during Indonesian rule – a location that will become a museum once the commission's work is finished.

[123] *See Chega!: Final Report of the CAVR, supra* note 6.

occupation. Working with community leaders, the Commission established panels composed of a regional commissioner and local leaders before which community-based reconciliation proceedings took place. The involvement of traditional local leaders helped provided legitimacy within communities, but the Commission also took pains to ensure that women and young people were included in the process.[124] This helped to empower some new voices in traditional community settings.

Under a carefully devised procedure, individuals who committed lesser offenses – such as looting or minor assault – were able to acknowledge what they had done in a public hearing before their community, express contrition, and enter into a "community reconciliation agreement" (CRA). Prosecutors in the Serious Crimes Unit reviewed written statements from these individuals before the community hearings even took place in order to determine whether the person was eligible to participate or, instead, potentially liable for prosecution for more serious crimes. Eligible individuals who concluded CRAs are immune from civil liability or criminal prosecution for the acts underlying the agreement. The CRAs were registered with district courts, however, providing a link to the formal justice system in the event of noncompliance.

The Commission received more than 1500 statements from individuals (called deponents) wishing to participate in the process. Ultimately, 1371 deponents completed the community reconciliation process, and the CAVR estimates that up to 3000 more might have participated had the process continued for a longer time. Over 40,000 Timorese – nearly 5 percent of the total population – attended the community hearings held throughout the country.[125]

These community reconciliation proceedings have had three results or accomplishments, in the view of the Commission's chair, Aniceto Guterres Lopes.[126] First, they helped to stabilize the situation in rural areas after a turbulent period. Second, they provided a sense of justice processes in communities throughout the country that have limited access to formal courts. The proceedings "reinforced the value of the rule of law, and contributed to the fight against impunity by resolving a significant number of cases that could not realistically have been dealt with through the formal justice system."[127] Third, the community reconciliation process encouraged local cultural traditions of reconciliation and conflict resolution. They

---

[124] The CAVR followed the requirement of its mandate "that a minimum 30% of all Regional Commissioners be women" and that community reconciliation panels have "appropriate gender representation." Id. Part 9: Community Reconciliation, at 43 (para. 154).

[125] *Chega!: Final Report of the CAVR, supra* note 6, Part 9: Community Reconciliation, at 29, 43, 47.

[126] Interview with CAVR Chair Aniceto Guterres Lopes in Dili, Timor-Leste (Nov. 2003).

[127] *Chega!: Final Report of the CAVR, supra* note 6, Part 9: Community Reconciliation, at 47.

also provided some valuable mediation training and capacity-building to panel members and other participants. These accomplishments are steps in building a foundation for further development of the rule of law in East Timor.

Not surprisingly, the community-based reconciliation procedures were more successful in some communities than in others. The hearings attracted significant numbers of people in many communities. Some participants confessed to specific offenses such as looting, whereas others acknowledged only a general association with Indonesian police or authorities. Some community reconciliation agreements required individuals to provide concrete restitution to victims – such as rebuilding a destroyed home, returning stolen goods, or repaying a victim for lost livestock – or to engage in forms of community service such as working on damaged school buildings or assisting orphanages or churches.[128] Many CRAs, however, simply involved a formal, public apology before the community.[129] Some individuals seemed genuinely contrite in these reconciliation proceedings, others far less so. The impact of the proceedings thus no doubt has varied in different communities and among different participants.

Most of the deponents who entered into community reconciliation agreements have expressed clear satisfaction with the process. A number of former militia members, for instance, have felt that the procedures helped them integrate more effectively into their communities.[130]

The response among victims has been more mixed, however, for a number of reasons. For some, the confessions of the deponents were not as forthright as hoped for, and the CRAs in many cases were not very demanding.[131] Victims hoping for more information about the fate of their loved ones were sometimes disappointed. Some victims found the proceedings and the public apology before the community to be a constructive and affirming experience, but others felt a certain sense of pressure or community expectation that they

---

[128] Pigou, *The Community Reconciliation Process of the Commission for Reception, Truth and Reconciliation, supra* note 11, at 56.

[129] Id. As Zifcak explains, as the reconciliation process unfolded over time, "simple apology" became more common as the basis of reconciliation agreements: "A straightforward apology embodied in a legal document signed by all parties combined with a commitment not to take part in any similar activities became, then, the quickest and easiest means of obtaining some form of closure, which in turn signaled 'success.'" Zifcak, *Restorative Justice in East Timor, supra* note 11, at 22. For additional reflections on why only apology was required in many CRAs, *see Chega!: Final Report of the CAVR, supra* note 6, Part 9: Community Reconciliation, at 33.

[130] Pigou, *The Community Reconciliation Process of the Commission for Reception, Truth and Reconciliation, supra* note 11, at 81; *Chega!: Final Report of the CAVR, supra* note 6, Part 9: Community Reconciliation, at 33–34.

[131] Pigou, *The Community Reconciliation Process of the Commission for Reception, Truth and Reconciliation, supra* note 11, at 81–83; Zifcak, *Restorative Justice in East Timor, supra* note 11, at 20–22, 25–26.

would reconcile with perpetrators.[132] The CAVR acknowledges that clearer guidelines regarding the role of victims in the proceedings and a greater focus on their needs would have been beneficial.[133]

Despite the range of reactions to the community reconciliation procedures, they do seem to have brought some sense of justice procedures to rural communities that have little access to the country's formal justice system. The emphasis on confession, forgiveness, and reconciliation also had deep cultural resonance in predominantly Catholic East Timor. Problematic, however, is a lingering sense of injustice and inequity that many Timorese feel because of the failure of the Serious Crimes Unit and Special Panels to bring to justice many who committed more serious offenses. For many Timorese, support for the community reconciliation process was tied to expectations that serious offenders living within their communities would be brought to justice. Yet the vast majority have not been investigated or charged. When lesser offenders conclude reconciliation agreements but more serious offenders often face no process at all, the resulting "justice deficit" has disappointed public expectations of fair accountability.[134]

Unfortunately, the circumstances surrounding the release of the CAVR's final report have also created a sense of injustice in East Timor. In late 2005, the CAVR completed and presented its report to President Gusmao, who subsequently presented it to the Timorese parliament. But, as of February 2006, the report had not been publicly released within East Timor, despite the fact that it had been presented to UN Secretary-General Annan and was available in full or in part on various Web sites.[135] The fact that the

---

[132] Zifcak, *Restorative Justice in East Timor, supra* note 11, at 20–22, 25–26. *See also Chega!, Final Report of the* CAVR, *supra* note 6, Part 9: Community Reconciliation, at 39.

[133] *Chega!: Final Report of the CAVR, supra* note 6, Part 9: Community Reconciliation, at 39 (para. 33) (noting that "[g]uidelines establishing a right of victims to a say in the decision on what 'acts of reconciliation' the perpetrator should perform, and a stronger place for victims in the formal decision-making structure of the CRP would have helped to ensure that their interests were not overlooked.").

[134] For analysis of this problem, *see Chega!: Final Report of the CAVR, supra* note 6, Part 9: Community Reconciliation, at 48 (para. 170); Zifcak, *Restorative Justice in East Timor, supra* note 11, at 41; Pigou, *The Community Reconciliation Process of the Commission for Reception, Truth and Reconciliation, supra* note 11, at 100–101. Less than half of the 1450 murders estimated to have been committed in 1999 were ultimately investigated by the Serious Crimes Unit. U.N. Doc. S/2005/533, *Progress Report of the Secretary-General on the United Nations Office in Timor-Leste,* August 18, 2005, para. 49.

[135] The commission submitted its report to President Gusmao on October 31, 2005, who presented it to East Timor's parliament and cabinet in November 2005. In January 2006, President Gusmao presented the report to UN Secretary-General Annan. Yet, as of February 2006, the report had not been publicly released in East Timor, even though the CAVR's mandate provides that the report "shall be immediately available to the public and shall be published in the Official Gazette." UNTAET Reg. 2001/10, U.N. Doc. UNTAET/REG/2001/10, July 13, 2001, section 21.3. The report has been available in full on the Web site of the International Center for Transitional Justice since January 30, 2006, *see* http://www.ictj.org in

report has not been presented publicly in East Timor – when it is otherwise widely available – is perplexing and upsetting to many Timorese human rights and victims organizations and to members of the public. It remains to be seen whether and how this will be rectified, and whether many of the Commission's important and innovative recommendations are taken up by the Timorese government and by other states.

D. Sierra Leone's Special Court: A Promising Hybrid

Though it faces many challenges, Sierra Leone's Special Court is probably the criminal tribunal that has been best able, thus far, to begin realizing in practice the potential benefits of a hybrid accountability mechanism. The tribunal has made a reasonably strong start in its primary mission of seeking justice and accountability for the brutal atrocities that marked Sierra Leone's decade-long civil war – a war that claimed the lives of an estimated 75,000 people and displaced a third of the country's population.[136] Two major trials began in summer 2004. These include the trial of three leaders of the RUF – the Revolutionary United Front – who are accused of horrific crimes against humanity and war crimes, including terrorizing the civilian population, rape, murder, amputations, abduction of women into forced "marriages," and forced recruitment of child soldiers.[137] Also on trial are three leaders of the CDF – Civilian Defense Forces – who are on trial for multiple counts of crimes against humanity and war crimes, including murder, inhumane acts, terrorizing the civilian population, and conscripting child soldiers.[138] A third trial against three members of the AFRC – Armed Forces Revolutionary Council – for similar crimes began in March 2005. One year later, in March 2006, former Liberian President Charles Taylor was finally taken into custody by the Special Court, where he stands charged with eleven

---

English and Bahasa Indonesia, but, as of February 2006, translation of the Report's introduction into Tetum had not been completed.

[136] Institute for Transitional Justice, *The Special Court for Sierra Leone: The First Eighteen Months*, 2004, at 1, *available at* http://www.ictj.org/downloads/SC_SL_Case_Study_designed.pdf. For a discussion of the conflict, *see* Avril D. Haines, *Accountability in Sierra Leone: The Role of the Special Court*, in ACCOUNTABILITY FOR ATROCITIES, *supra* note 12, at 176.

[137] The RUF leaders on trial are Issa Hassan Sesay, Morris Kallon, and Augustine Gbao. *See* http://www.sc-sl.org/RUF.html. In his opening statement, Special Court prosecutor David Crane described a meeting on February 27, 1991, in which Liberia's Charles Taylor, along with RUF General Foday Sankoh and others, planned the invasion of Sierra Leone and the capture of its diamond-rich areas – an invasion that set in motion the devastating decade-long conflict in Sierra Leone.

[138] Sam Hinga Norman, former Commander of the Civilian Defense Force (CDF) and former Deputy Defense Minister and Minister of Internal Affairs, is one of the three accused in this case. The other two accused are Allieu Kondewa and Moinina Fofana. *See* http://www.sc-sl.org/CDF.html. The three members of the AFRC on trial are Alex Tamba Brima, Brima Bazzy Kamara, and Santigie Borbor Kanu. *See* http://www.sc-sl.org/AFRC.html.

counts of crimes against humanity, war crimes, and other serious violations of international humanitarian law, including terrorizing the civilian population, murder, rape, sexual slavery, and use of child soldiers.[139]

The Special Court, established in 2002 by agreement between the government of Sierra Leone and the United Nations, was a deliberate effort to design a tribunal that could overcome some of the limitations of purely international or purely domestic proceedings.[140] In many ways, the Court's structure and mandate reflected the lessons – the "accountability learning curve" – of the previous decade. As a hybrid tribunal supported by the United Nations – with both international and domestic judges, prosecutors, investigators, defense counsel, and administrators – the Special Court has greater resources and credibility than Sierra Leone's struggling domestic justice system.[141] Yet the Court's physical location in Sierra Leone, with nationals participating in each of its components, provides important opportunities for building domestic capacity – and for extensive outreach efforts designed to deepen public understanding and expectations of accountability and fair justice, producing a more direct impact on the local population. In contrast to the enormous expense and open-ended time frames of the ICTY and ICTR, Sierra Leone's Special Court has a mandate focused on those who bear "the greatest responsibility" for serious violations of international humanitarian law – a mandate that the Court's original prosecutor, David Crane, argued is manageable and achievable in a time frame that he believes should allow both justice to be done and wounds to begin to heal as Sierra Leone moves forward.[142]

---

[139] Taylor's indictment, and a summary of the charges against him, are available on the Web site of the Special Court for Sierra Leone, *available at* http://www.sc-sl.org/Taylor.html. Taylor was taken into custody by the Special Court on March 29, 2006, and he was arraigned on April 3, 2006.

[140] The court's design also reflected political compromises as, for example, in the time frame of its jurisdiction. Haines, *Accountability in Sierra Leone, supra* note 136, at 214–215; *see also* J. Peter Pham, *Politics and International Justice in a World of States*, 4 HUM. RTS. & HUM. WELFARE 119, 131–32 (2004).

[141] The court has primacy over Sierra Leone's domestic courts and is a "mixed" or "hybrid" tribunal in at least two ways: its staff includes both international and national personnel, and it has authority to prosecute certain offenses under international law and under Sierra Leonean law. As a treaty-based court explicitly empowered to try those bearing "the greatest responsibility for violations of international humanitarian law" committed in Sierra Leone since November 30, 1996, the tribunal can prosecute those shielded from domestic prosecution by the amnesty of the 1999 Lome Agreement. Haines, *Accountability in Sierra Leone, supra* note 136, at 213.

[142] Interview with prosecutor David Crane in Freetown, Sierra Leone (June 2004). Crane argued that the mandate, in his view, was achievable within a time frame of three to five years. Id. *See also* David Crane, *Dancing with the Devil: Prosecuting West Africa's Warlords, Current Lessons Learned and Challenges*, in COLLOQUIUM OF PROSECUTORS OF INTERNATIONAL CRIMINAL TRIBUNALS, ARUSHA (2004) at 4–5, *available at* http://65/18/216/88/ENGLISH/colloquimo4/04 (hereinafter Crane, *Dancing*).

The Special Court has faced some but not all of the practical challenges of earlier hybrid tribunals. Maintaining adequate and reliable funding has been an ongoing concern, because the Special Court depends primarily on voluntary donations.[143] Nevertheless, starting up its operations with voluntary rather than UN-assessed funding actually proved to be beneficial because it gave the Court flexibility in hiring, enabling it to assemble an extremely talented staff very quickly. The Court has also managed to blend national and international staff quite well,[144] avoiding some of the disparities in salaries and support that created tensions, for instance, in East Timor.[145] Language barriers between international and national staff have not been an issue here, so easier exchange and give-and-take between staff is more possible. The Special Court's Defense Office also represents an important (and earlier) effort to achieve greater equality between the prosecution and the defense than has been the case in other tribunals.[146] Still, the many practical disparities between support for the prosecution and for the defense have been a continuing issue.[147]

---

[143] For instance, insufficient voluntary contributions led to a budget shortfall of about US $20 million in the tribunal's third year of operations, requiring a one-time UN contribution of over $16 million. Commission of Experts Report, *supra* note 51, at 29, para. 103.

[144] Each of the Special Court's four components – chambers, office of the prosecutor, defense office, and registry – is an interesting blend of international and national staff. As of June 2004, for example, the Trial Chambers included three judges: a Sierra Leonean national appointed by the government of Sierra Leone and a Canadian and a Cameroonean appointed by UN Secretary-General Annan. The Appeals Chamber included five judges: a Sierra Leonean and a British/Australian jurist, both appointed by Sierra Leone, and three judges – a Nigerian, a Sri Lankan, and an Austrian – appointed by the Secretary-General. The prosecutor was an American, and approximately 50 percent of the prosecutor's office (which includes investigators) was Sierra Leonean. The first registrar was an experienced British court administrator. The head of outreach is a Sierra Leonean, as are almost all of her staff. The defense office, an innovative component of the court, includes as part of its structure three duty counsel (two were Sierra Leonean and one Gambian, as of June 2004).

[145] The fact that living allowances for local Sierra Leonean jurists are less than for international judges has nevertheless been criticized by some Sierra Leoneans.

[146] The Special Court's registrar, Robin Vincent, was a strong early advocate of establishing a defense component modeled on a public defender's office. His evaluation of the ICTR influenced his views about the need for a more robust defense capacity in Sierra Leone. At Sierra Leone's Special Court, duty counsel in the defense office assist defendants before they have obtained independent counsel; they also provide research support to defense counsel and assist in building a defense and formulating arguments. In addition, the defense office has established a list of qualified defense counsel, and it administers contracts for attorneys appointed to represent indigent defendants and for defense investigators. Still, the Court's administrators will frankly acknowledge that they wish they had built up the defense office earlier and provided it with a greater budget. Nevertheless, it is a considerable and dramatic improvement over the limited support offered to the defense in other tribunals, both hybrid and international.

[147] *See* James Cockayne, *The Fraying Shoestring: Rethinking War Crimes Tribunals*, 28 FORDHAM INT'L L. J. 616, 699–674 (2005).

Sierra Leone's Special Court is very much a work in progress, so it is too early to determine whether, in fact, it will ultimately succeed in delivering meaningful justice to the people of Sierra Leone or in helping to improve domestic capacity for fair justice and the rule of law. A number of positive signs already exist, but there are also areas of concern. In any event, the theoretical benefits of an in-country hybrid do not flow automatically; they require astute planning, considerable resources, and sensitivity to the many practical and political challenges that can arise when a tribunal locates directly in the country most affected by the atrocities.[148]

So far, the glass is at least half full. By indicting those who bear the greatest responsibility for starting and orchestrating the brutal conflict in Sierra Leone, the tribunal helped to disempower and prevent them from again committing such atrocities. Sierra Leoneans agree to a remarkable extent who these people are. In outreach meetings all across the country held by the Special Court's prosecutor, Sierra Leoneans put former Liberian president Charles Taylor at the top of the list. He was followed by two others: RUF commander Foday Sankoh and General Sam Bockarie. All three have been indicted, but only Taylor is still alive to stand trial. (Sankoh died of natural causes in custody; Bockarie was killed in Liberia as was his family, allegedly on Taylor's orders.[149])

Charles Taylor presents the biggest challenge in the struggle for accountability and for peace in West Africa. Virtually everyone agrees that he bears the greatest responsibility for the violence that engulfed Sierra Leone and much of the rest of West Africa. Preventing him from ever again exercising power directly in Liberia – or behind the scenes – is a critical goal in bringing lasting peace to the region. Throughout Sierra Leone, people overwhelmingly support prosecuting him before the Special Court. [150] For two and a half years, however, Taylor was in Nigeria under a grant of asylum brokered as part of his departure from power in Liberia. During this period, the Nigerian government, along with some other African and international leaders, resisted handing Taylor over, arguing that to do so would undermine

---

[148] *See, e.g.,* id., at 674–675.

[149] The chief of investigations for the Special Court stated in May 2003 that he had "credible information" that Bockarie's family had been killed on orders from Taylor, which "casts serious doubts about [Taylor's] claims regarding the circumstances of Sam Bockarie's death." Press release, *Bockarie's Family Alleged Murdered; Office of the Prosecutor Demands Full Cooperation from Taylor,* Special Court for Sierra Leone, Office of the Prosecutor, May 15, 2003, *available at* http://www.sc-sl.org/Press/prosecutor-051503.html. *See also* U.S. State Department, Bureau of Intelligence & Research, *Background Note on Sierra Leone,* May, 2006, *available at* http://www.state.gov/r/pa/ei/bgn/5475.htm (stating Taylor "probably" directed Bockarie's killing to keep him from testifying).

[150] Sierra Leone's Parliament in February 2006 unanimously adopted a resolution calling for Taylor's trial before the Special Court. Press release, *Prosecutor Welcomes Sierra Leone Parliamentary Resolution Supporting Taylor's Trial at the Special Court,* Special Court for Sierra Leone, Office of the Prosecutor, February 9, 2006, *available at* http://www.sc-sl.org/Press/prosecutor-020906.pdf.

future negotiated departures of dictators as a way to end conflicts.[151] Others, in contrast, argued strongly that ending the impunity of high-level leaders for atrocities – such as those of which Taylor is accused – is an essential step in preventing their recurrence in the region.[152] In the end, as international pressure grew for holding Taylor to account, and after a newly elected government in Liberia called for his prosecution, Nigeria handed Taylor over to the Special Court in March 2006.

As Taylor arrived and was taken into custody in Sierra Leone, hundreds of Sierra Leoneans gathered in the hills of Freetown near the Special Court to commemorate this dramatic day. Yet, whether Taylor's trial would, in fact, be held in Sierra Leone, as many hoped, or instead would take place in The Hague before a panel of the Special Court for Sierra Leone assembled there, was yet to be determined. Taylor's trial raises special issues of security and stability as a result of his role in West Africa's conflicts. In the end, the Special Court and the government of Sierra Leone requested that his trial be held at The Hague, and Taylor was transferred there in June 2006.

Although it has made considerable progress, the Special Court faces some distinct challenges in demonstrating meaningful accountability for atrocities to the people of Sierra Leone. To demonstrate credibly that justice is fair, the court's proceedings much be widely viewed as legitimate both in terms of their substance (who is being prosecuted for what offenses) and in terms of process. The fact that the prosecution indicted Charles Taylor as well as leaders from all the major groups in Sierra Leone's conflict – the RUF, the AFRC, and the CDF – is important in demonstrating that no one is above the law and in avoiding the perception of victor's justice.

Still, there are difficult, lingering issues that may affect the perceived legitimacy of the trials among the Sierra Leonean population. For one, Charles Taylor's long-awaited prosecution before the Special Court has raised public expectations of accountability that may be disappointed, at least to some extent, by the decision to hold the trial outside of Sierra Leone, thus making the proceedings less accessible to the local population.[153] Second, the trial of CDF leader and former Interior Minister Sam Hinga Norman has generated controversy, at least initially: many regard him as a hero who acted to

---

[151] For discussion of the controversy over the Special Court's unveiling of the sealed indictment against Taylor during a peace negotiation in Ghana and subsequent differences of view over Nigeria's offer of amnesty to Taylor, see Pham, *Politics and International Justice in a World of States, supra* note 140, at 131–133.

[152] *See* Zainab Bangura, op-ed., *Flouting the Rule of Law,* THE WASHINGTON POST, June 25, 2004, at A29.

[153] *See* John E. Leigh, op-ed, *Bringing It All Back Home,* THE NEW YORK TIMES, April 17, 2006, at A25. Leigh, who is Sierra Leone's former ambassador to the United States, argues that transferring Taylor to The Hague for trial "would defeat a principal purpose behind the establishment of the special court in Sierra Leone – namely, to teach Africans, firsthand and in their own countries, the fundamentals of justice and to drive home that no one is above the law." Id.

defend Sierra Leone from the RUF, and the court's outreach staff has had to work hard to explain that he is being tried for serious atrocities in violation of international law – that regardless of one's cause, there are clear limits on how one can fight. Third, many Sierra Leoneans express frustration that many individuals who did the actual chopping, raping, and killing remain free. As one amputee put it, "the person who chopped off my hand lives down the street; if there is no justice, my children may seek vengeance."[154] Or as one local TV journalist, critical of the peacekeeping forces of the Economic Community of West African States, exclaimed: "ECOMOG forces killed my brother and raped my sister, so why aren't they being tried?"[155] In other words, although Sierra Leoneans support trying those who bear "the greatest responsibility" for the atrocities, there remains frustration that other, lower-level offenders are not being held accountable as well.

The Special Court's processes also need to be perceived as fair to credibly demonstrate a norm of accountability and impartial justice. The fact that both international and national jurists and staff participate in the work of the Special Court has enhanced its legitimacy among the local population. But even so, the Special Court's local outreach officers have encountered skepticism in both directions: some Sierra Leoneans, based on negative perceptions of the country's own judicial system, needed reassurance that the Sierra Leonean jurists on the court would, in fact, be impartial; others wondered whether the court was being forced upon Sierra Leone by international actors. Still, the tribunal seems to enjoy considerable support and legitimacy in Sierra Leone.[156]

To sustain this perception, the tribunal needs to conduct demonstrably fair trials. The prosecution team is extremely skilled and well resourced. A significant concern is whether defense counsel will be effective enough and have sufficient resources to mount a high-quality defense or to effectively assist defendants who have opted to represent themselves, such as former Interior Minister Sam Hinga Norman. Ensuring that the defense has the personnel and resources to present a credible defense will be important to the legitimacy of the proceedings. But beyond the issue of a technically skilled defense, whether Sierra Leoneans ultimately will regard the Special Court

---

[154] Town hall meeting with Amputee Association in Freetown, Sierra Leone, June 2004.

[155] Interview in Freetown, Sierra Leone, June 2004. ECOMOG is the acronym for forces of the Economic Community of West African States (ECOWAS) that deployed to Sierra Leone in response to the conflict. See ECOMOG: Peacekeeper or Participant?, BBC NEWSFILE, February 11, 1998, available at http://news.bbc.co.uk/2/hi/africa/55719.stm.

[156] For example, in one poll conducted by the Campaign for Good Governance (CGG), a Sierra Leonean NGO, before the trials even began, 67 percent of those surveyed had heard of the court, 62 percent found it necessary, and 61 percent thought the court was intended to benefit the people of Sierra Leone. Cited in International Crisis Group, The Special Court for Sierra Leone: Promises and Pitfalls of a "New Model," 2003), at 17, available at http://www.crisisgroup.org/home/index.cfm?id=1803&l=1.

as demonstrating meaningful accountability and fair justice will depend on whether they are convinced – through outreach and other efforts – that defendants such as Sam Hinga Norman are fairly and appropriately being tried for conduct that violates agreed rules.[157] Finally, the trial of Charles Taylor raises a whole host of issues that will demand an extremely disciplined handling of the proceedings by the Special Court's judiciary. The tumultous trials of former leaders Slobodan Milosevic and Saddam Hussein have made clear that such proceedings face the ever-present risk of turning into highly-charged political drama, and thus require judges who can walk a fine line between protecting the accused's rights to speak and maintaining courtroom dignity, order, and efficiency.

1. Outreach: Demonstrating Accountability and Fair Justice

Even though Charles Taylor's trial poses special challenges, it also provides a long-awaited opportunity to demonstrate meaningful accountability and fair justice to the people of Sierra Leone. In fact, systematic outreach to the population of Sierra Leone has been central to the Special Court's work from the very beginning. In September 2002, shortly after he arrived in Freetown, prosecutor David Crane began traveling throughout the country to hear what the Sierra Leonean people had to say about who bore "the greatest responsibility" for the atrocities committed during the brutal conflict. A month later, the office of the prosecutor and the registry conducted outreach together. In the spring of 2003, a chief of outreach was hired, and the outreach office, under the registry, now also has ten district offices throughout Sierra Leone. This substantial outreach program has been vital in engaging the Sierra Leonean people in the work of the court and stands in contrast to the lack of systematic outreach in other post-conflict contexts.

The explicit goal of the Special Court's countrywide outreach program is to "promote understanding of the Special Court and respect for human rights and the rule of law in Sierra Leone."[158] Thus, in addition to providing basic information about the court – how it came about, its authority, structure and procedures, who is indicted for what offenses, and an update on the trials – the outreach office raises broader issues as well. In community town hall meetings and focused workshops around the country, outreach officers aim to demonstrate and illustrate, based on the actual proceedings before

---

[157] For a skeptical assessment emphasizing the political nature of accountability proceedings, *see* Tim Kelsall, *Politics, Anti-Politics, International Justice: Notes on the Special Court for Sierra Leone*, October 15, 2004 (Submitted at the conference "Settling Accounts: Truth, Justice and Redress in Post-Conflict Societies," Weatherhead Centre for International Affairs, Harvard University, November 1–3, 2004, *available at* http://www.wcfia.harvard.edu/conferences/truthjustice/Papers/KelsallFullPAPER.pdf).

[158] Special Court for Sierra Leone, Outreach Mission Statement.

the court, that no one is above the law, that law can and should be fair, and ultimately that the rule of law is more powerful than the rule of the gun.[159] In a society with limited mass media and a strong oral tradition, these meetings are critical to convey the importance of accountability.

Outreach meetings and workshops frequently involve lively, intense, and wide-ranging conversations on vital, difficult issues. The court's outreach officers work hard, for example, to explain what "fair justice" looks like. A prosecution and defense before an impartial tribunal is an important concept to convey to a population deeply skeptical of the fairness of justice systems and inclined, from bitter experience, to believe that people are simply "on the take." The outreach staff uses the concrete cases before the Special Court to illustrate key principles. For instance, when the appellate chamber ruled that Charles Taylor was not entitled to immunity from prosecution as head of state, this illustrated the concept that no one is above the law. The indictment and trial of former Interior Minister Sam Hinga Norman – controversial in some quarters – illustrates, the outreach officers stress, that the Special Court is not a court controlled by the government. When pressed – as they often are – by victims who ask why the person who chopped off their hand is not being prosecuted, the outreach staff discusses the principle of command responsibility to explain that somebody is answering for the crime. These discussions – led by dynamic Sierra Leoneon outreach officers – are often not easy, but they do wrestle forthrightly with the difficult challenges of justice and accountability.

There is no doubt that these outreach efforts are having an impact. In a society where travel to rural areas is difficult and access to media is limited, the outreach staff has reached out to engage the population on critically important issues. Opinion polls indicate that significant majorities are aware of the court and view its work positively.[160] As the three combined trials of RUF, CDF, and AFRC leaders have proceeded, moreover, the Special Court's public affairs office has produced weekly audio summaries highlighting critical developments in the proceedings, which are widely broadcast over the radio throughout Sierra Leone.

The outreach and public affairs efforts have not been immune from criticism. Some members of the defense staff at the Special Court have expressed

---

[159] With a chief of outreach and substantial staff in Freetown and ten district offices, the Special Court's outreach office conducts its outreach in a variety of ways. These include "community townhall meetings," held after making arrangements with local chiefs; workshops for special groups (for instance, school pupils and university students, military forces, police, market women, victims, ex-combatants, youths, teachers); and radio discussion programs, among others. Sierra Leonean outreach officers lead these discussions in the local dialects that allow them to best communicate with the participants. Interviews with the chief of outreach and with district outreach officers, Freetown, Sierra Leone, June 2004. *See also* http://www.sc-sl.org/outreach.html.

[160] *See The Special Court for Sierra Leone, supra* note 156, at 17.

frustration that they have not had more opportunity to engage in outreach, particularly after the early efforts by the prosecution.[161] The weekly radio broadcasts of trial proceedings have not been as frequent as some observers would like. And the ability of most Sierra Leoneans to actually attend Special Court proceedings in the capital remains limited, despite court-sponsored programs to bring groups of citizens to Freetown to attend the trials.[162]

More fundamentally, whether the demonstration effects of the trials – and the outreach office's efforts to convey norms of accountability and fair justice throughout the country – will have a longer-term impact within Sierra Leone remains to be seen and is linked to the broader issue of capacity-building and institutionalization of accountability norms.

2. Capacity-Building in Sierra Leone

The Special Court, by virtue of its location and substantial local participation, is in a position to help build domestic capacity directly by increasing the skills and experience of local professionals. The Sierra Leoneans who work at the court as prosecutors, investigators, defense counsel, judges, administrators, outreach officers, and other staff are learning a great deal about international humanitarian law and its basic principles, about the conduct of fair trials, and about substantive issues in their specific areas of responsibility. Interactions between international and national staff are a valuable two-way street of mutual learning – as the international investigators who work hand in hand with their Sierra Leonean counterparts are the first to attest. The unanswered question, however, is how many of the local judges, prosecutors, defense counsel, investigators, and other court staff actually will remain in Sierra Leone after the court completes its work – and consequently continue to use their valuable skills in the national justice system.

The Special Court engages in a second kind of capacity-building, namely, working with NGOs that share a common commitment to accountability. By linking up with organizations committed to advancing fundamental human rights principles, the court can potentially have larger ripple effects within Sierra Leone and help to educate and empower citizens and civil society organizations more broadly.

Two examples illustrate these effects. First, the Special Court's outreach officers worked hard to help establish "Accountability Now Clubs" across the country – clubs of university students to discuss issues of accountability, justice, human rights, and good governance, with the expectation that club members will visit secondary and elementary schools to address these issues and communicate the critical importance of accountability past, present,

---

[161] Cockayne, *The Fraying Shoestring, supra* note 147, at 672–673.

[162] Human Rights Watch, *Bringing Justice: The Special Court for Sierra Leone: Accessibility and Legacy,* 2004, at 2, *available at* http://hrw.org/reports/2004/sierraleone0904/8.htm.

and future.[163] Second, the outreach staff, along with other court personnel, participate in the Special Court Interactive Forum, a gathering of local and international NGOs that focus primarily on the work of the court and how it can be improved, but that also can network on additional accountability and human rights issues.

Finally, the Special Court is in a position to contribute expertise and training to Sierra Leone's domestic justice system. International investigators at the Special Court, for instance, have trained a number of Sierra Leonean police officers in witness management and protection – a critical issue given the long-term dangers that witnesses take on in coming forward to testify before the Special Court. A number of the court's judges and other legal professionals have lectured on law reform and related topics at local universities and bar associations. More generally, the Special Court has worked with the Sierra Leone Bar Association and with various organizations, both domestic and international, to identify and develop projects aimed at "helping to rebuild a devastated judiciary."[164] The Special Court's resources and the time of its personnel are understandably focused on its core mission of trying those who bear the greatest responsibility for the atrocities committed in Sierra Leone; but there is no doubt that more systematic efforts to provide training and to share expertise with participants in the local justice system would be beneficial.[165]

Ultimately, however, whether the Special Court's capacity-building efforts – the professional skills development of its own staff, the ripple effects of working with local NGOs, and the training and sharing of expertise with local jurists and legal personnel – will make a lasting and sustainable impact on Sierra Leone's domestic justice system and political culture will depend on longer-term reforms within Sierra Leone. The jury clearly is still out on

---

[163] These clubs exist at eight universities throughout Sierra Leone. *See* http://www.sc-sl.org/outreach.html.

[164] Crane, *Dancing, supra* note 142, at 6–7.

[165] A joint UNDP/ICTJ report recommends that as part of its "legacy" efforts, the Special Court should focus additional attention on substantive law reform in Sierra Leone, on professional development for domestic justice personnel, and on programs to raise greater awareness in the provinces of the Special Court as an example of fair, effective legal process. ICTJ & UNDP, *The "Legacy" of the Special Court for Sierra Leone, supra* note 22, at 1–2. The Special Court's outreach staff has provided training, for instance, to lay personnel working in the customary law system. Working together with the UN Development Programme, the Special Court's outreach staff offered training on fundamental human rights principles to lay magistrates, court clerks, court bailiffs, and other participants in the customary law system. The outreach staff provided information on the Special Court and linked principles that are supposed to govern the application of customary law ("equity, good conscience, and natural justice") to human rights principles of equality, independence, and impartiality. Interview with the director of outreach, Special Court for Sierra Leone, Freetown, Sierra Leone (June 2004). Developing a fairer, more transparent, more equitable system of dispute settlement in the customary law system remains a very long-term challenge, however.

this, and the challenges are immense, as the previous chapter discussed. The degree of outreach and serious dialogue about accountability that the Special Court has inspired is impressive and has indeed sent some ripples of hope through Sierra Leonean society. But the enormous challenge of institutionalizing principles of accountability – including strengthening a weak and underresourced domestic justice system and addressing deep and pervasive problems of corruption and governance – ultimately will determine how sustainable these efforts prove to be.

E. Sierra Leone's Truth and Reconciliation Commission

Sierra Leone's Truth and Reconciliation Commission (TRC) highlighted these broader challenges in its final report. The commission focused on the deeper and more systemic causes of grievance in Sierra Leone – such as lack of transparency and accountability in the use of governmental power, few opportunities for young people, and pervasive corruption.[166] Stressing that many of these causes of conflict have not yet been addressed adequately, the commission recommended reforms to strengthen Sierra Leone's legal and political system, including greater transparency and public access to information and greater accountability of government officials.[167]

As in East Timor, Sierra Leone's TRC gained significant national participation in its work, collecting over 8000 statements from civilians and combatants in Sierra Leone and neighboring countries.[168] Local NGOs and human rights leaders supported creation of the TRC, in part to address the complexity of the conflict and its devastating effects, including on children who often were victimized and forced to take up arms. A Sierra Leonean NGO estimates that up to 70 percent of combatants were children.[169] Moreover, 72 percent of combatants claimed to have been forcibly conscripted, with more than 80 percent of the female soldiers reporting that status.[170]

---

[166] The commission emphasized that "it was years of bad governance, endemic corruption and the denial of basic human rights that created the deplorable conditions that made conflict inevitable," that "[d]emocracy and the rule of law were dead" by the start of the conflict, and that only the "slightest spark" was required for "violence to be ignited." *Witness to Truth, supra* note 16, Vol. 1, para. 11. Sierra Leone's TRC submitted its report to the Security Council in October 2004, *available at* http://www.trcsierraleone.org/drwebsite/publish/index.shtml.

[167] Id., para 12.

[168] International Center for Transitional Justice, *The Sierra Leone Truth and Reconciliation Commission: Reviewing the First Year* (2004), at 3, *available at* http://www.ictj.org/downloads/SL_TRC_Case_Study_designed.pdf; *The Special Court for Sierra Leone, supra* note 156, at 10.

[169] International Center for Transitional Justice & Post-Conflict Reintegration Initiative for Development and Empowerment, *Ex-Combatant Views of the Truth and Reconciliation Commission and the Special Court in Sierra Leone,* September, 2002, at 13, *available at* http://www.ictj.org/images/content/0/9/090.pdf.

[170] Id.

The Special Court's prosecutor made clear early on that he did not intend to prosecute child soldiers, so other approaches to accountability – such as the TRC's emphasis on truth-telling, restorative justice, and reconciliation – were a means to engage this large and significant group of former combatants and to provide a forum for addressing the needs of victims.[171]

At least in some areas, the commission had some success in promoting community-based healing ceremonies and in helping to reintegrate perpetrators into society through symbolic acts of reconciliation.[172] Moreover, in response to the specific concerns and needs of victims, the commission recommended a reparations program that would include free health care to amputees, war wounded, and victims of sexual violence; monthly pensions; and free education to the senior secondary level for specific groups affected by the conflict, such as amputees, children of amputees, children who were abducted or conscripted, victims of sexual violence, and other groups.[173]

But the impact of the TRC remains uncertain and indeed contested. No government reparations program had yet been implemented as of early 2006. Moreover, some scholars dispute whether the public hearings and reconciliation proceedings were, in fact, beneficial to many Sierra Leoneans. Anthropologist Rosalind Shaw argues, based on her extensive research throughout the country, that many communities had already engaged in reconciliation in their own way before the TRC's hearings began and that asking people to publicly recount and relive their war-time experiences disrupted ongoing efforts to heal and move on.[174] Scholar Tim Kelsall, who observed a number of public reconciliation proceedings, questions whether the truth emerged in any clear or full way, although in some instances the rituals that concluded

---

[171] The TRC and the Special Court operated concurrently and tensions developed between the two bodies on various matters, highlighting the need for careful planning regarding the relationship between such different accountability mechanisms. In the case of East Timor, the relationship between the Special Panels and the CAVR was addressed much more systematically and was more constructive.

[172] Unlike in East Timor, the mandate of Sierra Leone's commission did not explicitly create a community reconciliation mechanism. However, the act establishing the TRC did provide, that the commission "may seek assistance from traditional and religious leaders to facilitate its public sessions and in resolving local conflicts arising from past violations or abuses or in support of healing and reconciliation." See Truth and Reconciliation Commission Act 2000, section 7(2), *available at* http://www.sierra-leone.org/trcact2000.html. Thus, after building relationships with community leaders, the TRC's hearings in the districts often concluded with symbolic, customary, and religious healing ceremonies in which perpetrators "came forward to ask their communities for forgiveness, which was granted by local traditional leaders." Elizabeth M. Evenson, Note, *Truth and Justice in Sierra Leone: Coordination Between Commission and Court*, 104 COLUM. L. REV. 730, 763 (2004).

[173] *Witness to Truth, supra* note 16, Vol. 1, paras. 51–52.

[174] Rosalind Shaw, *Rethinking Truth and Reconciliation Commissions: Lessons from Sierra Leone,* United States Institute of Peace Special Report, February 2005.

the proceedings did, in his view, suggest an opening for some degree of reconciliation.[175] These scholarly reports highlight the importance of understanding the aspirations and cultural traditions of the people most affected by atrocities in order to design accountability mechanisms that will be responsive and constructive. The mixed reports regarding the TRC's impact also underscore the continuing need for careful study of the actual effects of such accountability mechanisms on the ground.

V. DOMESTIC APPROACHES TO ACCOUNTABILITY AND THE POTENTIAL IMPACT OF THE ICC

The explicitly hybrid tribunals established in Sierra Leone and East Timor, coupled with truth and reconciliation commissions, have not proven possible in many other situations. Rwanda, disappointed that the ICTR was located elsewhere, has tried thousands of individuals for genocide and related crimes before its underresourced domestic courts, and it is beginning to try large numbers of people in a community-based process that builds upon traditional dispute settlement practices known as *gacaca*.[176] Indonesia largely insisted on handling cases arising out of the violence in East Timor on its own in a special domestic ad hoc human rights court, but a lack of political commitment ultimately undermined these efforts, yielding no effective accountability in the Indonesian domestic courts.[177]

---

[175] Based on his observations, Kelsall questions whether perpetrators presented a fully truthful account of their role or even whether victims have been willing to tell the whole truth of their experience. *See* Tim Kelsall, *Truth, Lies, Ritual: Preliminary Reflections on the Truth and Reconciliation Commission in Sierra Leone*, 27 HUM. RTS. Q. 361 (2005). Nevertheless, he argues that "the addition of a carefully staged reconciliation ceremony to the proceedings, a ritual that created an emotionally charged atmosphere that succeeded in moving many of the participants and spectators...arguably opened an avenue for reconciliation" in a number of communities. Id., at 363.

[176] For a discussion of both the potential benefits and due process concerns raised by the *gacaca* proceedings, *see* Strain & Keyes, *Accountability in the Aftermath of Rwanda's Genocide*, *supra* note 20, at 117–122; Maya Goldstein-Bolocan, *Rwandan Gacaca: An Experiment in Transitional Justice*, 2004 J. DISP. RESOL. 355 (2004). As the process has unfolded, suicide has increased among suspected perpetrators. Craig Timberg, *In Rwanda, Suicides Impede Road to Justice and Closure*, THE WASHINGTON POST, February 17, 2006, at A1.

[177] *See* Commission of Experts Report, *supra* note 51, at 38–80. Early on, when international pressure was stronger, Indonesia did take some initial positive steps toward accountability, including an investigation and report by a national commission of inquiry, KPP-HAM. Laura A. Dickinson, *The Dance of Complementarity: Relationships among Domestic, International, and Transnational Accountability Mechanisms in East Timor and Indonesia*, in ACCOUNTABILITY FOR ATROCITIES, *supra* note 12, at 332–335, 352, 358–360. Although the terms of reference for the Commission of Truth and Friendship established by Indonesia and Timor Leste indicate a clear focus away from criminal prosecution, paragraph 8 states that the "unprecedented judicial process" in Indonesia "has not yet come to its completion." Terms of Reference, *supra* note 120.

Domestic prosecutions, if they are conducted in a credible manner that is widely viewed as legitimate and fair, can help demonstrate accountability in a very direct way to domestic audiences. But a lack of resources, an unwillingness to pursue accountability in a serious and balanced way, or both, can undermine these domestic efforts. International assistance – and pressure – may be critical to bolster both domestic will and capacity.

A. Iraq's Special Tribunal: Trying Saddam Hussein

Iraq is proceeding to try Saddam Hussein and others accused of serious crimes, and the Iraqi Special Tribunal for Crimes Against Humanity was established for this purpose.[178] Iraqis serve as the tribunal's judges and prosecutors, although the Iraqi government can, "if it deems necessary," appoint non-Iraqis to serve as judges as well.[179] The tribunal's statute requires the appointment of international experts to serve as advisors or observers, however, "to provide assistance to the judges with respect to international law and the experience of similar tribunals . . . and to monitor the protection by the Tribunal of general due process of law standards."[180] International advisors also assist investigators and prosecutors.[181] American lawyers have been working closely with Iraqis, for instance, in reviewing and preparing evidence, but European and UN officials generally have declined to assist,

---

[178] The Iraqi Governing Council, working closely with the U.S.-led Coalition Provisional Authority (CPA), in December 2003 issued a statute creating the Iraqi Special Tribunal for Crimes Against Humanity ("Tribunal"), *available at* http://www.cpa-iraq.org/human_rights/Statute.htm. The statute was issued and took effect on December 10, 2003. The elected Iraqi government reaffirmed the statute in 2005. The tribunal has jurisdiction over Iraqi nationals or residents accused of genocide, crimes against humanity, war crimes, and certain violations of Iraqi law (manipulation of the judiciary, waste of national resources and squandering of public assets, and abuse of position leading to war against an Arab county) committed between July 17, 1968, and May 1, 2003. Statute of the Iraqi Special Tribunal, Arts. 1, 11–14 (2003). The definitions of the international crimes are taken from the Statute for the International Criminal Court (ICC), and in interpreting those provisions, "the Trial Chambers and the Appellate Chamber may resort to the relevant decisions of international courts or tribunals as persuasive authority for their decisions." Id. Art. 17(b). Article 35 provides that "[t]he expenses of the Tribunal shall be borne by the regular budget of the Government of Iraq."

[179] Id. Art. 4(d). The Tribunal's Trial Chambers will consist of five judges. Id. Art. 4. The Appeals Chamber will consist of nine judges. Id. Article 28 provides that: "[t]he judges, investigative judges, prosecutors and the Director of the Administration Department shall be Iraqi nationals." Article 33 further provides that "No officer, prosecutor, investigative judge, judge or other personnel of the Tribunal shall have been a member of the Ba'ath Party."

[180] Id. Art. 6(b). Article 6(b) further provides that "[i]n appointing such non-Iraqi experts, the President of the Tribunal shall be entitled to request assistance from the international community, including the United Nations."

[181] Id. Arts. 7(n), 8(j).

largely because they oppose the tribunal's authority to impose the death penalty.[182]

This essentially domestic tribunal may allow for prosecutions that Iraqis view as more legitimate than trials before an explicitly hybrid court in which international jurists play a major and visible role. Iraqi leaders have emphasized the importance of bringing Saddam Hussein to justice in order to "heal[] the wounds" in Iraqi society,[183] and large numbers of Iraqis from families and groups victimized by his regime are following the trials with great interest. But the tribunal has faced extraordinary obstacles from the start: several defense counsel were murdered, the presiding judge stepped down and was replaced by a judge initially contested by the defense, and Saddam Hussein has stridently mocked and challenged the court's authority. The trial of Saddam and other defendants accused of the torture and murder of more than 140 Iraqi men and boys in the town of Dujail following a 1982 assassination attempt has been marked by turmoil since it began. Nevertheless, the proceedings have taken on a more sober tone since the court affirmed that the defendants would face charges for crimes against humanity, which carry a possible death sentence.[184]

At this point, it remains to be seen whether this and subsequent prosecutions of Saddam Hussein and other major figures before the tribunal will be conducted in a fair and credible manner,[185] and whether the proceedings will have a positive domestic impact. Furthermore, as instability, sectarian violence, and insurgency continue to wrack so much of the country, new atrocities – murders, kidnapping, torture, rape – are perpetrated with impunity on a daily basis, undermining prospects for a stable rule of law built on a reliable system of accountability. Instead, a spiral of violence and impunity

---

[182] Marlise Simons, *Iraqis Not Ready for Trials; U.N. to Withhold Training*, THE NEW YORK TIMES, October 22, 2004, at A11.

[183] John F. Burns, *For Hussein, A Spartan Life at His Former Palace*, THE NEW YORK TIMES, September 19, 2004, at 1, 6 (quoting human rights minister Bakhtiar Amin: "Without justice, I don't see any possibility of healing the wounds in this society").

[184] John F. Burns, *Surprise. Hussein Acts as if He's on Trial.*, THE NEW YORK TIMES, May 21, 2006, at 3.

[185] The statute affirms fundamental due process rights of the accused, including the presumption of innocence. Statute of the Iraqi Special Tribunal, Art. 20 (2003). That article explicitly affirms the right of the accused "to defend himself in person or through legal assistance of his own choosing" and "to have legal assistance assigned to him, in any case where the interests of justice so require." Id. Art. 20(4). It also provides that the "accused is entitled to have non-Iraqi legal representation, so long as the principal lawyer of such accused is Iraqi." Id. Art. 20(2). As of mid-September 2004, "the tribunal ha[d] found no Iraqi lawyers to defend Mr. Hussein and his associates." Burns, *supra* note 183, at 6. Currently, Hussein's primary defense counsel is Baghdad-based Khalil Dulaimi, though his trial has undergone significant turmoil since it began in 2005. *See, e.g.*, Jamal Halaby, *Saddam Lawyer: U.S. Blocking Meeting*, ASSOCIATED PRESS, February 5, 2006; Sabrina Tavernise, *Hussein Trial Resumes, But He Stays Away*, THE NEW YORK TIMES, February 2, 2006, at A10.

is profoundly eroding public confidence in the rule of law throughout Iraq, overshadowing the significance and potential impact of Saddam Hussein's trial.

B. Afghanistan: Evolving Prospects for Accountability

In Afghanistan, the public has expressed strong support for accountability processes that can remove from power those who have committed serious human rights abuses.[186] Criminal trials for the most serious offenders accompanied by vetting and removal from power of lesser offenders are cited by many Afghans as essential to stability, security, and public trust in the rule of law. Afghanistan's government has shown more ambivalence about this path – not surprising when some of those who wield power, including in Afghanistan's parliament, are among those widely viewed as responsible for serious human rights abuses.[187] The Karzai government did take an important step forward in December 2005, however, when it adopted a five-point plan for accountability. Although the issue of criminal prosecution was finessed for the time being, the government did affirm that "no amnesty will be granted for gross violations of human rights."[188] Moreover, drawing on an action plan developed by Afghan officials and the Afghan Independent Human Rights Commission, with international and UN support, the government affirmed a five-part strategy for peace, justice, and reconciliation in Afghanistan. The plan includes measures to tangibly acknowledge and commemorate the suffering of the Afghan people during the long period of civil war; measures to increase public confidence in state institutions through fair and transparent vetting procedures and institutional reform; development of a truth-seeking mechanism, after fuller consideration of the potential contours of such an effort; exploration of measures to promote reconciliation and national unity; and strengthening of Afghanistan's criminal justice system, along with an affirmation that amnesty will not be granted for gross human rights violations.[189]

---

[186] See A Call for Justice, supra note 8, at 17–21, 27–29, 34, 46–47, reporting on the surveys and focus groups conducted by the Afghan Independent Human Rights Commission (AIHRC).

[187] See Afghanistan: Where's the Justice?, THE ECONOMIST, January 21, 2006.

[188] Afghan Independent Human Rights Commission, press release, Truth-seeking and Reconciliation in Afghanistan, December 15, 2005, at 2, available at http://www.aihrc.org.af/pre_truthseeking_22_12_05.htm.

[189] Id. The government-adopted plan was based on a plan developed by the Government of Afghanistan together with the Afghan Independent Human Rights Commission with assistance from the United Nations Mission in Afghanistan. See Peace, Reconciliation and Justice in Afghanistan, Action Plan of the Government of the Islamic Republic of Afghanistan, June 6–7, 2005, available at http://www.aihrc.org.af/tj_actionplan_19_dec_05.htm. The issue of criminal prosecutions – and the question of a possible hybrid tribunal for this purpose – was not addressed directly by the government in adopting its five-part plan. The AIHRC survey found considerable support among the Afghan population for a hybrid tribunal within Afghanistan. See A Call for Justice, supra note 8, at 24–26.

The challenge, of course, will be how seriously these goals are pursued, and whether major offenders are ever held accountable and removed from positions of power and intimidation. These are hard issues that will depend on the commitment and priorities of Afghanistan's leaders, in both government and civil society, on international support for accountability, and on the success of gradual efforts to extend governmental authority to remote areas of Afghanistan where local commanders and warlords still operate largely with impunity. What is clear is that the people of Afghanistan regard meaningful accountability for abuses – past and present – as critical to their trust and confidence in the country's developing legal and political institutions. Demonstrating accountability, in short, although complicated and difficult, is an integral part of moving forward to build the rule of law.

C. The Potential Impact of the ICC

Most of the interventions we have studied in this book took place before the International Criminal Court (ICC) was up and running.[190] In future conflicts, however, the ICC may have some leverage in encouraging credible national investigations and prosecutions of major atrocities. The ICC is designed explicitly to complement and encourage domestic legal action – not replace it. The Court will have jurisdiction over individuals accused of genocide, crimes against humanity, or war crimes only if states with jurisdiction are "unable or unwilling" "genuinely" to investigate or prosecute these cases.[191] The primacy of national jurisdiction – and the principle that the ICC is to be complementary to, not a substitute for, national action – reflects a realist core at the heart of the ICC statute: awareness that effective national action, including domestic political will and capacity, is an essential component of lasting accountability. The ICC does provide a potential check, however – and a judicial forum – if domestic action falls short.

In principle, the threat of possible ICC prosecution can help to prod and encourage responsible domestic investigation and prosecution of atrocities.

---

[190] The jurisdiction of the ICC took effect on July 1, 2002. Our discussion of the ICC draws directly on Stromseth, *Introduction: Goals and Challenges in the Pursuit of Accountability*, *supra* note 12, at 3–4, 26–32, 36.

[191] Rome Statute of the International Criminal Court, Art. 17, July 17, 1998, 2187 U.N.T.S. 90. Under the complementarity provisions of the ICC, a case is inadmissible if a state with jurisdiction has genuinely investigated the matter and prosecuted or made a good faith determination not to prosecute. States wishing to avoid ICC jurisdiction under the Rome Statute thus can take steps to ensure that they are able and willing to investigate and, if appropriate, to prosecute individuals domestically for ICC crimes. So ideally the impulses of sovereignty should combine with the prospect of international action to produce more effective national accountability efforts. For discussions of complementarity, *see* Michael A. Newton, *Comparative Complementarity: Domestic Jurisdiction Consistent with the Rome Statute of the International Criminal Court*, 167 MIL L. REV. 20 (2001); David J. Scheffer, *Fourteenth Waldemar A. Solf Lecture in International Law: A Negotiator's Perspective on the International Criminal Court*, 167 MIL. L. REV. 1, 10–11 (2001).

Many states already have adapted their domestic criminal law to provide for national prosecution of genocide, crimes against humanity, and war crimes. This may be the ICC's most significant impact to date on strengthening domestic rule of law. In practice, however, the effectiveness of the ICC's prodding abilities will depend on the court's own credibility and legitimacy – and on domestic will and capacity in particular states.

Domestic reformers may sometimes welcome the threat of international action as a means to spur and support their own indigenous efforts.[192] But "there is a fine line between pressure that strengthens the hand of internal reformers and pressure that results in greater domestic resistance to perceived foreign interference."[193] Also, domestic reformers must be in a position to translate international pressure into influence and effective national action. Even when there is domestic will to prosecute and to prevent atrocities, national capacity to do so effectively may be sorely lacking.

Gaps will exist, in any event, in the ICC's ability to serve as a lever to prod and encourage responsible domestic accountability processes. Many of the worst atrocities in recent memory occurred during internal conflicts. When perpetrators of atrocities come from the state on whose territory the crimes occurred, the ICC will be in a position to assert jurisdiction only if that state is a party to the ICC statute or otherwise consents.[194] Thus, many situations of internal conflict in which atrocities occur may not be amenable to the ICC's prodding function. In addition, atrocities committed before the ICC's jurisdiction took effect on July 1, 2002, will not be subject to prosecution before the Court – which includes most of the situations studied in this book.

Thus other mechanisms and initiatives will continue to be needed to encourage effective domestic accountability for atrocities. States will continue to differ profoundly in their willingness and their capacity to hold individuals accountable for atrocities or to take effective measures to prevent future atrocities. Different methods of strengthening and reinforcing domestic capacity – and different combinations of mechanisms and of national and international roles – will be needed, moreover, in response to the particular goals, needs, and circumstances of specific states in the aftermath of grave atrocities. Finding an optimal relationship between domestic and international actors will not be easy in many cases, but the need for innovative hybrid accountability mechanisms will surely continue.[195]

---

[192] See Dickinson, *The Dance of Complementarity, supra* note 177, at 358–365.

[193] Id., *at* 372. As in Indonesia, internal reformers can play the "nationalist card" in encouraging domestic accountability processes as an alternative to international action, but those resisting reform can do so as well.

[194] Rome Statute of the International Criminal Court, Art. 12, July 17, 1998, 2187 U.N.T.S. 90.

[195] For a discussion of potential national and international roles and relationships in the pursuit of accountability, *see* Kritz, *Coming to Terms with Atrocities, supra* note 12, at 144–152; Turner, *Nationalizing International Criminal Law, supra* note 19; Stromseth, *Introduction:*

CONCLUSION

To revisit this chapter's basic question: can the pursuit of accountability for atrocities through criminal prosecutions and other methods help to build the rule of law and strengthen domestic justice systems in post-intervention societies? The answer is "yes, but." As we have argued here, accountability processes clearly are having a positive impact in a number of societies, but the effects of these efforts on domestic rule of law have been mixed, complex, and often unclear, and more research is needed to fully understand their longer-term impact.

Whether accountability processes have helped to strengthen the rule of law domestically depends, in part, as we have argued, on their demonstration effects and their capacity-building impact. On the positive side, criminal trials of major perpetrators can help disempower destructive actors and, if widely viewed as fair, can demonstrate that even leaders with political and economic clout are not above the law and that pervasive impunity for serious atrocities will no longer be tolerated. Trials can also provide some solace to victims or their families and help to remove impunity as a source of grievance more broadly. But if trials are seen as biased, they can have negative demonstration effects, reinforcing rather than diluting skepticism that law can be fair and reinforcing grounds for grievance. On the issue of capacity-building, an infusion of international resources can have positive effects, especially in hybrid tribunal arrangements that provide valuable direct experience to participating judges, prosecutors, investigators, defense counsel, and other staff, many of whom may then contribute to the domestic legal system. But, in the case of purely international tribunals, about two billon dollars have been spent with little discernible impact on domestic capacity-building. More specifically:

- The ICTY and the ICTR have accomplished a great deal in terms of bringing to justice, in fair legal proceedings, individuals accused of major atrocities. Nevertheless, these tribunals have had only a limited impact on demonstrating the importance of accountability and fair justice to critical domestic audiences or on helping to build capacity in the relevant national justice systems. With earlier and more effective outreach to local populations and more systematic capacity-building programs, these tribunals could have accomplished much more. They still have an opportunity to make a greater domestic impact if their completion strategies focus more attention and resources on the systematic strengthening of domestic capacities to handle complex war crimes cases.

Goals and Challenges in the Pursuit of Accountability, supra note 12, at 26–36. For a cautionary account of the potential pitfalls of national efforts, *see* Bass, STAY THE HAND OF VENGEANCE, *supra* note 14, at 304–310.

- Even the hybrid tribunals have struggled to realize in practice their theoretical potential. By combining national and international staff and operating in the country that directly experienced the atrocities, hybrids – in principle at least – offer important benefits. But if they are not given adequate resources and support, hybrid arrangements may fall short of satisfying standards of legitimacy and credibility among international and domestic audiences alike. At a practical level, language barriers and less-than-systematic efforts at cross-fertilization and training can limit the prospects for genuine capacity-building. Kosovo's hybrid arrangement has suffered from a lack of legitimacy among domestic audiences. In East Timor, the hybrid tribunal's contributions both in accountability and capacity-building have been constrained significantly by limited resources and by lack of political support.
- If they are designed and implemented well, however, hybrid tribunals can have significant, positive domestic effects. As the experience in Sierra Leone suggests, hybrid tribunals can pursue accountability fairly and credibly while strengthening local capacity and reaching out systematically to local populations. The longer-term impact of the Special Court's work of course remains to be seen, especially the impact of the trial of Charles Taylor. Although more remains to be done, the Special Court and its innovative outreach program have strengthened public awareness of the importance of accountability and contributed to domestic capacity-building.
- Still, criminal trials alone, even with ambitious outreach programs, are – at best – only part of what is needed to grapple with past atrocities or to build local capacity for justice. Combined approaches that also include truth and reconciliation mechanisms are more likely to produce more effective and far-reaching demonstration effects and capacity-building than trials alone. The truth and reconciliation commissions in East Timor and Sierra Leone – which operated contemporaneously with the hybrid criminal tribunals – played a critical role in addressing the larger factors that led to atrocities, reaching out to victims, and recommending systemic reforms.
- Particularly in post-conflict societies where formal justice systems have limited geographic reach, community-based accountability proceedings that both enjoy local legitimacy and respect human rights can have an important immediate impact and also contribute to the longer-term goal of strengthening the rule of law. East Timor's Commission for Reception, Truth and Reconciliation, in particular, has made a difference in rural areas with limited access to formal justice: the commission's innovative reconciliation procedures have helped integrate individuals back into their communities, and the commission's deliberate effort to involve women and young people alongside traditional community leaders helped cultivate some potential new leaders.

Our exploration of the links between accountability processes for past atrocities and forward-looking rule of law reform leads us to offer two final thoughts. First, more research is needed on the impact of accountability proceedings in different post-conflict societies. Seeking justice by holding major perpetrators legally accountable, of course, can and should be pursued as a matter of principle. Yet knowing more about the impact of different kinds of accountability mechanisms can help in designing approaches that can seek justice fairly and also contribute more effectively to building the rule of law domestically and to strengthening justice systems in post-conflict societies.

Second, international actors involved in designing accountability processes need to be both more bold and more humble at the same time. They need to be bolder in working to link accountability proceedings more clearly to longer-term efforts to build domestic capacity for the rule of law. Accountability processes should not be simply an endeavor totally apart from ongoing processes of reform: fair justice can be provided while also working to engage in innovative outreach to local communities, to build local legal capacity, and to develop synergies with local NGOs. What's required are vision, energy, and resources to press ahead on multiple fronts.

Yet international actors also need to show more humility and modesty regarding the ability of accountability processes to bind up the wounds of those who have suffered atrocities. The needs and aspirations of the people who endured the atrocities must be appreciated more fully, and their goals must be given greater attention in designing accountability efforts. Meaningful accountability for atrocities takes time, and communities may in fact need to move forward for awhile before they can effectively look backward. Furthermore, claiming too much for accountability processes alone in meeting the often complex expectations of local communities can lead to deep disappointment. Even the fairest and most credible trials of those responsible for severe atrocities, the most systematic efforts at judicial capacity-building, or the best-designed reconciliation procedures will have only a limited long-term impact if the deeper cultural underpinnings of the rule of law – and the deeper obstacles to strengthening the rule of law – are not understood or addressed. This difficult and essential topic is taken up in Chapter 8.

CHAPTER EIGHT

Creating Rule of Law Cultures

Over the past decades, most international and U.S. efforts to promote the rule of law have focused primarily on the "formal" dimensions of the rule of law: fostering new or improved courts, prison systems, constitutions, statutes, and so forth. In this book, we have repeatedly emphasized that such programs, though valuable, are unlikely to reap lasting benefits unless they are integrated into the far broader project of ensuring peace, stability, and security and unless rule of law programs proceed more or less simultaneously rather than consecutively.

Without security, neither governance nor economic development programs can hope to succeed. Without viable macro-level blueprints for governance, legal and judicial reform projects may be impossible, incoherent, or self-undermining. Without moderately effective police, criminals cannot be arrested; without an adequate prison system, they cannot be detained; without courts, they cannot be tried; without lawyers, they probably cannot be tried fairly; without functioning law schools, there can be no lawyers or judges. Promoting the rule of law requires interveners to keep many balls in the air at once, and doing so presents monumental challenges.

But the challenges for interveners do not end there. However one chooses to define the rule of law, the rule of law can neither be created nor sustained unless most people in a given society recognize its value and have a reasonable amount of faith in its efficacy. The rule of law is as much a culture as a set of institutions, as much a matter of the habits, commitments, and beliefs of ordinary people as of legal codes. Institutions and codes are important, but without the cultural and political commitment to back them up, they are rarely more than window dressing.

This is as true in stable, democratic societies as it is in post-conflict settings. Much of the psychological and sociolegal work that has been done on why people obey the law in the United States reminds us that factors such as the perceived morality of the substantive law and the perceived legitimacy and procedural fairness of legislative and judicial processes are often of paramount importance in explaining why people do (or do not) behave in accordance with law.[1] When people believe that law and legal institutions are fair and effective, they will use them and allow their actions to be constrained by them. When people doubt law's fairness or efficacy, they will seek alternative methods of ordering their lives and settling problems, and changes in the law or in institutions will consequently have less of an effect on their behavior.

Persuading people to believe in the rule of law is a difficult task in any context and one that is particularly difficult in post-conflict societies. In post-conflict societies, prior to international interventions and subsequent reconstruction efforts, the institutions meant to buttress the rule of law were often badly discredited. In repressive states, legal institutions generally lose credibility because they are used to further the political agenda of those with power. In weak states, legal institutions may simply be too corrupt and inefficient to garner much loyalty.

In weak or repressive states where the rule of law does not exist, people develop alternative means of resolving conflict. Depending on the society, they may look to informal mediation, to religious leaders, to tribal elders, or to local warlords to settle their differences; they may rely on nepotism or bribery to get what they need, or they may turn to violence and vigilante activity if that appears the simplest way to resolve problems. Such nonlegal ways of resolving disputes may be neither efficient nor equitable, but they are often the only avenues available for ordinary people.

In the wake of international military interventions, many people may be reluctant to give up these methods in favor of new and untried institutions of the sort that did not help them much in the past. Interveners eager to foster the rule of law must thus seek ways to persuade both elites and ordinary people to value the rule of law over the alternative (and often violent) ways of settling disputes that have been most effective for many people prior to the intervention.

To put it differently, interveners must seek to create a rule of law culture, one in which a reasonably large percentage of people come to believe in the value of legal institutions. The wisest constitutional arrangements, the most modern and sophisticated statutes, and the most well-organized judicial system will be of little use if most people lack faith in them and turn instead to warlords or vigilante activity to resolve disputes.

One could, in principle, imagine a peaceful and stable society without elaborate modern legal institutions, and historically many such societies

---

[1] Tom Tyler, WHY PEOPLE OBEY THE LAW (1995). *See also* Raymond Paternoster, *Decisions to Participate in and Desist from Four Types of Common Delinquency: Deterrence and the Rational Choice Perspective*, 23 LAW & SOC'Y REV. 7 (1989) (noting that moral beliefs were more central to decisions about whether to break the law than assessments of the likelihood and seriousness of punishment).

have existed, particularly on a small scale. Today, however, in our globalized and interdependent world, no state is likely to prosper without a
modern legal regime, because this is necessary both to comply with international legal obligations under various treaty regimes and to participate
effectively in the global economy. This means that modernized legal institutions and codes are a practical necessity in post-conflict societies. But as we
have noted, the mere existence of these institutions and codes will not necessarily translate into "the rule of law" in any nonsuperficial sense. They will
only make a difference if both elites and ordinary people are committed to
them.

But this creates something of a chicken-and-egg problem in post-conflict
societies. When people already believe law matters, it will matter; when
people think law doesn't matter, it rarely can, and few rule of law programs
pay explicit attention to the conundrum of how to go from the latter state
to the former.[2]

Changing entrenched attitudes toward the law is made even more difficult
by the inherently contradictory aspects of most post-intervention rule of law
efforts. The idea of the rule of law, though complex, rests significantly on the
assumption that legal process is superior to violence as a means of resolving
conflicts and that even the most powerful must respect legal process and the
rights of those with less power. The rule of law elevates reason over force
and rights over mere might. This creates a difficult irony. Regardless of the
specific background to any given intervention, interveners have the capacity
to intervene for one overriding reason: the possession of superior military
might.

Much of the time, this is no doubt as it should be: we see no reason
to doubt that NATO's military control over Kosovo was a better thing for
Kosovars and for the world than Slobodan Milosevic's military control over
Kosovo. But even when a particular intervention is widely seen as legitimate,
the fact remains that on the ground, interveners are present because they have
greater military power than other contenders. From Bosnia and East Timor
to Afghanistan and Iraq, interveners are in a position to promote the rule of
law mainly because they have a superior capacity to capture, disable, or kill
most of those who get in the way. Although they may not possess a complete
monopoly on the use of force, they certainly have the biggest guns on the
block, and they can use those guns, directly or indirectly, to coerce local
actors into cooperating with rule of law initiatives.

---

[2] Cf. Paul Kahn, THE CULTURAL STUDY OF LAW: RECONSTRUCTING LEGAL SCHOLARSHIP 36 (1999).
("The rule of law is a social practice: it is a way of being in the world. To live under the rule
of law is to maintain a set of beliefs about the self and community, time and space, authority
and representation. It is to understand the actions of others and the possible actions of the
self as expressions of these beliefs. Without these beliefs, the rule of law appears as just
another form of coercive governmental authority.")

To be sure, the relation between law and sheer coercion is uneasy even in peaceful, democratic societies with strong rule of law traditions. This is a problem that has preoccupied jurisprudential theorists from Hobbes through Austen and Hart. Law seeks to appeal to reason, but always relies in part on the threat of coercion for its efficacy. This seeming paradox can never be completely eliminated in any society. Nonetheless, in democratic societies, the state holds a monopoly on force through the consent of the governed. Although that consent may be tacit, most ordinary people in democratic societies readily accept the legitimacy of the state's monopolization of violence. The notion of the social compact, however mythical, remains a powerful legitimating factor in democracies.

In post-intervention societies, however, the tension between the law's appeal to reason and the realities of coercion is particularly glaring, and greatly complicates efforts to create rule of law cultures. In these societies, interveners have an opportunity to convince local people to believe in the value of law, reason, and rights as an alternative to sheer power and violence, but they are in a position to hold the floor only because they have just provided an object lesson in the ability of force to settle arguments (however temporarily).

Possession of superior force thus creates both opportunities and challenges for interveners. On the one hand, interveners have perhaps a unique capacity to foster positive change. Rule of law initiatives in societies that have *not* gone through major conflicts or interventions inevitably proceed in a piecemeal fashion, because it is hardly feasible or desirable to wholly dismantle state and civic institutions to start from scratch with "better" ones. But in post-intervention societies, the very degree of breakdown creates unique opportunities for renewal and change. In post-intervention societies, the "old" institutions have often collapsed, and local stakeholders may be willing, even eager, to make an entirely new start, rethinking every civic verity from how they understand nationality and ethnicity to how they want their society to function. They may simply be tired of conflict, and willing to let outside actors take the lead. In the absence of credible and functioning local governance institutions, interveners can set the conditions under which local people can participate in governing their own society. Because interveners can compel cooperation – or at least the outward forms of cooperation – they can easily spearhead the creation of new institutions or reformed legal codes.

But in other ways, possession of superior force only increases the difficulties faced by interveners eager to help foster a rule of law culture. The example of the intervention itself tends to undercut subsequent arguments made by interveners about the value of reason and legal process over force, particularly if the intervention was of contested legality, as in Iraq. If the intervention itself is read as an object lesson about the irrelevance of law as a constraint on power, people on the ground may be particularly resistant to efforts to convince them of the virtues of the rule of law. Even when local people initially called for or welcomed the intervention, possession of superior force can nonetheless reduce the credibility of the interveners once they are on the ground, as they may themselves be inclined (or appear to be inclined) to fall back on superior force when reasoned argument does not suffice to convince local people to do things the "right" way.

The challenge for interveners who want to promote the rule of law thus goes far beyond the challenge of ensuring security and designing sensible governance blueprints, judicial reform programs, and accountability mechanisms. The challenge for interveners is to foster – or even create from scratch – a rule of law culture, and to do so in the face of the enormous inherent difficulties and paradoxes described above.

What's more, just as judicial reform will have little value if it is not accompanied by simultaneous legal reform, police reform, prison reform, and so on, the project of creating a rule of law culture must similarly be undertaken from day one, in parallel with all of the other critical post-intervention projects.

Although its intangible nature may tempt interveners to relegate it to the back burner, creating a rule of law culture cannot be put off until some vague future time when the institutional framework is already in place, because by then it is already too late. In the immediate wake of crisis and intervention, there is a brief window in which people may be willing to give new alternatives a chance; that window closes rapidly as time passes with little or no evidence that things are changing for the better.

To date, few international and U.S. efforts to create the rule of law in post-conflict settings have paid explicit attention to the challenge of creating rule of law cultures. Perhaps "culture" appears to many policymakers like a matter most appropriately left to anthropologists; the term may seem too soft and ill-defined to suit hard-nosed political realists. Rule of law programs are generally assigned to lawyers, who are trained to think in terms of codes and institutions rather than in terms of cultural change. And changes to laws and institutions are indeed a critical part of creating the rule of law, as the preceding chapters of this book have emphasized. But on their own, they are insufficient.

The task of creating rule of law cultures requires interveners to enter into largely uncharted territory, but it is territory that can't be neglected and that requires interveners to go beyond the traditional skill sets normally considered essential in post-conflict planning. As one thoughtful critic puts it, rule of law practitioners "need to think less like lawyers and more like agents of social change."[3]

---

[3] Stephen Golub, *Beyond Rule of Law Orthodoxy: The Legal Empowerment Alternative,* Carnegie Endowment for International Peace, Paper No. 41, October 2003.

Promoting social change requires creativity, openness to alternative and nontraditional approaches, and a willingness to move beyond political elites to focus as well on grassroots efforts. It requires demonstrating to ordinary people the concrete advantages of turning to law rather than some other dispute resolution methods, and it also requires the creation of narratives about law that capture imaginations. This in turn requires a willingness to consider the role of media, civil society, and even popular culture as well as the role of institutions and political elites.

So far, the international community's track record in this area is not impressive, and it is difficult to feel optimistic that future interventions will excel where past interventions have fallen so far short. As previous chapters have already noted, promoting the rule of law involves keeping track of so many moving parts that even the wisest and best-prepared interveners may often be stymied. (And this is to say nothing of the problem of resources and coordination on the part of the interveners, a subject that will be taken up in the next chapter.) Nonetheless, although there is little reason to imagine that creating rule of law cultures will be easy or even wholly possible in all post-conflict societies, this book would not exist if we did not think we can do better in the future than we have in the past. The remainder of this chapter focuses on how interveners might do a better job in the future.

For interveners as for physicians, the most fundamental duty might be construed as "do no harm." In keeping with that principle, the first part of this chapter looks at how interveners sometimes unintentionally undermine their own efforts to promote the rule of law through cultural insensitivity or apparent arbitrariness. We suggest that to avoid undermining their own efforts, interveners must *acknowledge and address the paradoxes created by trying to pull the rule of law from the barrel of a gun* and shore up their own legitimacy as much as possible. This requires *linguistic and cultural know-how* on the part of interveners; the *ability to plan carefully and avoid early errors* that will require seemingly arbitrary about-faces; a *willingness to act collaboratively and multilaterally*; and, perhaps most important, a *commitment to transparency and accountability*. Only if interveners are seen to hold themselves to the same high standards they demand of others can they hope to gain public trust.

The second part of this chapter takes a different course. Because rule of law efforts that are unduly formalistic have a very poor track record, the second part of this chapter examines the kinds of programs that seem most likely to help affirmatively create a widely shared cultural commitment to the rule of law in post-intervention societies.

It emphasizes the *importance of moving beyond political elites and beyond the strictly "legal" to design programs that reach rural citizens, the poor, the disempowered, and the disaffected; that build on preexisting informal dispute resolution mechanisms; that are integrated into local-level development*

and antipoverty programs, and that creatively use media and popular cul-
ture techniques to educate and inspire ordinary people. It also emphasizes the
importance of civil society and education to the long-term project of building the rule of law. Although nothing described in this chapter is a panacea,
what empirical work has been done so far suggests that such an emphasis is
likely to be more productive than programs that focus solely on elites and
institutions.

I. DOING NO HARM: HOW INTERVENERS CAN AVOID UNDERMINING THEIR OWN EFFORTS

Chapter 6 briefly introduced several examples from Kosovo that suggest the
ways in which well-intentioned rule of law promotion efforts can sometimes
inadvertently undermine the rule of law. These examples are discussed here
in somewhat greater detail.

In 1999, the ethnic cleansing campaign by Serbs against Kosovar Albanians led ultimately to NATO military intervention and to Security Council
Resolution 1244,[4] which created an international civilian administration in
Kosovo (UNMIK) under the auspices of the United Nations. In post-conflict
Kosovo, UNMIK faced the daunting challenge of governing 1.8 million people in a devastated region with no functioning courts, no functioning prisons,
no police, and a legacy of ethnic bitterness between the Serbs and the Kosovar Albanians, who for a decade had been unable to participate in Kosovo's
governance.

In the wake of NATO's military intervention, Kosovo also lacked an
agreed-on body of law. With Serbia no longer in control, and the UN running
the show, it was unclear what body of law was applicable in Kosovo. The
uncertainty about applicable law caused confusion on numerous fronts: no
one knew what laws should govern the apprehension and trial of criminal
suspects; the thorny problem of disputed property claims; or, for that matter,
the actions of UNMIK itself.

The route UNMIK took to resolve these issues helps demonstrate that
a simplistic formalism can be a dead end for rule of law reformers when
more culturally potent symbolic issues are at stake. UNMIK head Bernard
Kouchner decided to resolve the problem of applicable law by making the
applicable law in UN-administered Kosovo the same as the law that was
applicable *before* the NATO air campaign began. He issued UNMIK Regulation One, which stated that "the laws applicable in the territory of Kosovo
prior to 24 March 1999 shall continue to apply in Kosovo," insofar as those
pre-March 1999 laws did not conflict with internationally recognized human

---

[4] S.C. Res. 1244, UN Doc. S/RES/1244 (June 10, 1999).

rights standards, the UNMIK mandate under UNSC Resolution 1244, or any other UNMIK regulation.[5]

This seemingly efficient solution backfired badly. To Kosovo's 1.5 million ethnic Albanians, the applicable laws in Kosovo before the bombing campaign began were "Serb laws," a key symbol of Serbian oppression against the Albanians. To the policymakers at UNMIK, the fact that the pre-1999 laws had been promulgated by Serbs seemed purely academic – but to many Kosovars, after ten years of Serb oppression, an ethnic cleansing campaign, and an armed struggle, the idea that the UN would issue a decree requiring the Kosovar Albanians to continue to live under "Serb law" was profoundly insulting. It made no difference that UNMIK Regulation 1 said that human rights standards would trump the laws on the books in the event of a conflict. Nearly all of the fifty-five people sworn in by UNMIK to serve as judges and prosecutors in UNMIK's new "emergency judicial system" declared that they would not apply "Serb law."

A crisis ensued, complete with angry editorials and dozens of stormy meetings in Pristina, UN headquarters, the State Department, and other sites. UNMIK refused to rescind Regulation 1. At the same time, because most prosecutors and judges refused to accept Regulation 1, few judicial proceedings began in Kosovo's makeshift courts. Most Kosovar judges insisted that the applicable law should by right be the laws in force before 1989, because these laws were passed with the approval of the Albanian-dominated Kosovo parliamentarians before the Serbs ended Kosovo's autonomy.

The controversy ended in defeat for UNMIK. Six months after issuing Regulation 1, UNMIK (without official comment) made a full about-face in the form of UNMIK Regulation 24.[6] This new regulation declared that the law applicable in Kosovo would henceforth be the law in force on March 22, 1989, immediately prior to the ending of Kosovar autonomy. Regulation 24 in fact permitted Kosovar judges to pick and choose whatever law they liked best: when the pre-1989 laws failed to cover a given situation, Regulation 24 gave judges the freedom to apply any nondiscriminatory legal provision applicable in Kosovo after March 22, 1999. And, of course, all law applied had to be consistent with international human rights standards – although Regulation 24, like Regulation 1, neglected to identify sections of the law inconsistent with human rights standards or lay out the procedures to be followed in the event of perceived conflict between a provision of the law and human rights standards.

This was not a trivial oversight. Ironically, the pre-1989 laws so dear to the Kosovar Albanian community were far less consistent with modern

---

[5] UNMIK Regulation 1, *reprinted in* U.S. DEPARTMENT OF STATE: KOSOVO JUDICIAL ASSESSMENT, by Rosa Ehrenreich & William Spencer (2000), Appendix. Much of what follows is drawn from personal experiences in Kosovo in 1999 and 2000.

[6] UNMIK Regulation 24, *reprinted in* Ehrenreich & Spencer, *supra* note 5.

international human rights norms than the post-1989 "Serb law" they had so vehemently rejected. The pre-1989 laws were designed in the communist era, before the fall of the Berlin Wall and the advent of greater openness in Yugoslavia.[7] Not only did the pre-1989 laws fail to conform to international human rights standards in numerous ways, but the property and civil law regime they created also reflected a very different set of assumptions about how social life should be organized than those most Kosovars held a decade later. On their face, the post-1989 "Serb laws" appeared an improvement on their predecessors. It was primarily the *implementation* of these post-1989 laws that had been discriminatory and oppressive.[8]

This is a small example of how a well-intentioned but overly formalistic approach to law foundered when it came up against powerful local cultural understandings. Although this dispute seems trivial in many ways, its consequences were major. If UNMIK read the Kosovar Albanian rejection of Regulation 1 as irrational and obstructionist, the Kosovar Albanian community read UNMIK's initial refusal to take their objections seriously as evidence that the international community had insufficient respect for their history, fears, and aspirations. Furthermore, UNMIK's ultimate reversal on the question of applying the pre-1989 laws suggested to the Kosovars that law UNMIK-style was a matter of arbitrary decrees that could be issued and reversed by an unaccountable appointed bureaucracy.

The dispute over Regulation 1 was a small part of a larger problem that plagued efforts to foster the rule of law in Kosovo. As Chapter 4 noted, the final status of Kosovo was not determined by Resolution 1244. In part as a result, UNMIK's policymakers could never entirely decide whether their ultimate goal was to promote self-determination or to promote and ensure human rights. For that matter, UNMIK did not truly confront the question of whether a commitment to human rights requires a commitment to democratic decision-making, what truly constitutes democratic decision-making in a society with no obviously legitimate representatives, or how to resolve crises in which majoritarian democracy seemed likely to trample on minority and individual rights.[9] These are complex issues without easy answers, but UNMIK's early failure to confront them at all was particularly damaging given that UNMIK's whole *raison d'etre* in Kosovo involved protecting the Kosovars' right to self-determination and promoting human rights. Indeed, NATO went to war in Kosovo with the stated aim of protecting the Kosovars from Serb domination and human rights abuses.

---

[7] For a readable history of Yugoslavia, *see generally* Tim Judah, THE SERBS: HISTORY, MYTH AND THE DESTRUCTION OF YUGOSLAVIA (2000).

[8] *See generally* Ehrenreich & Spencer, *supra* note 5.

[9] Cf. Owen Fiss, *The Autonomy of Law*, in SELA 2000, SEMINARIO EN LATINOAMERICA DE TEROIA CONSTITUCIONAL Y POLITICA: THE RULE OF LAW (June 8–11, 2000) (discussing the inherent conflict between justice and autonomy, despite the tendency of human rights discourse to conflate the two).

In the first years after the intervention, UNMIK proved unable to come up with any coherent mechanism for addressing these sometimes conflicting imperatives. In the early days of the UN administration, UNMIK established a variety of consultative bodies designed to include the Kosovars in decisions about the all-important project of reestablishing the rule of law. Including prominent Kosovar lawyers, academics, and political figures, these bodies were meant to help appoint judges, revitalize legal education, and produce legal codes. But time and time again, this consultative process foundered, as quarrels broke out over substantive issues and over who should serve on the advisory bodies (no clear criteria existed, and the different ethnic groups and political parties clashed both with UNMIK and with each other over how to divvy up the seats) and what language the proceedings should be conducted in. (The Serbs insisted on Serbian and the Albanians on Albanian. Because the UN personnel generally spoke neither, this forced meetings to include multiple translators, leading to further inefficiency and misunderstanding.)

The consultative process also faltered on more substantive issues: not infrequently, for instance, Albanian participants would express the view that there should be no Serb judges, as all Serbs were complicit in war crimes, or that the property code should give Serbian property to Albanians, since it had been stolen from them in the first place, even if decades or centuries before, or that revenge killings of Serbs by Albanians should be treated more leniently than other kinds of killings.

Such disputes did not bode well for the due process of law that UNMIK hoped to see emerge, and UNMIK frequently responded by dismissing its advisory councils in frustration and making key decisions itself. In other words, when a majoritarian form of self-determination came up against human rights, self-determination lost. This may be appropriate, but the sequence of events leading to those decisions hardly looked like due process. In essence, UNMIK wanted the decision-making process to be as participatory and democratic as possible, but when the Kosovar participants came up with suggestions or demands that UNMIK found unpalatable, UNMIK simply dismissed them and made the decisions on its own. Unsurprisingly, this did little to enhance UNMIK's reputation with the Kosovars, as they saw UNMIK as increasingly arbitrary and unaccountable in its rule. Ultimately, the advisory councils became semipermanent battlegrounds, frequently dissolved by UNMIK, just as frequently boycotted by one or more Kosovar or Serb groups, and nearly always locked in angry paralysis.

UNMIK's credibility was also damaged by its own difficulty in abiding by the international human rights standards it sought to impose on Kosovo. In Regulation 1, UNMIK effectively incorporated international human rights standards into Kosovo's law, and this was affirmed in Regulation 24. Although UNMIK's regulations never specified precisely how to identify a norm of international human rights law, UNMIK legal advisers, other international actors, and Kosovars all took "international human rights" to include, at a minimum, the core rights at the heart of the Universal Declaration of Human Rights, the International Covenant on Civil and Political Rights (ICCPR), the European Charter, and decisions of the European Court of Human Rights (because Kosovo was, after all, part of Europe, and the EU and the Organization for Security and Co-operation both had major roles in Kosovo under the UNMIK umbrella). Under each of these overlapping regimes, core rights include (among others) the rights to equal protection, due process, fair and expeditious judicial proceedings, freedom from arbitrary detention, adequate detention conditions, and representation by counsel.[10]

The police, prison, and judicial systems initially established by UNMIK were unable to comply with those standards, however, or even with the generally less stringent standards that had been laid out in pre-1989 or post-1989 Kosovo, Serbian, and Yugoslavian law. An international civilian police force for Kosovo got up and running only slowly. In the first post-intervention years, in some regions of Kosovo, UN civilian police from around the world apprehended suspects and investigated crimes, using their own diverse home-country procedures. In other regions, Kosovars who had gone through a basic training course at a UN police school patrolled the streets. In some areas, NATO soldiers acted as the police. In still other areas, all three shared de facto responsibility for policing. These various policing agents spoke different languages and applied widely varying methods and standards for stopping, questioning, and detaining suspects.[11]

Detention facilities in Kosovo were equally variable. Most prewar prisons were damaged by bombs or arson, and some detainees ended up in police holding cells or in NATO tents behind barbed wire. Few are held in facilities that were purpose-built for long-term detention, which means that many detainees had no health care facilities, no exercise areas, no private visitation areas (or set standards for determining when to allow access for visitors), and no access to legal materials. Few facilities allowed full separation of men from women, juveniles from adults, or pretrial detainees from convicted criminals. There were few adequately trained prison and detention facility guards, and detention facility officials were in several well-publicized cases unable to prevent ethnic violence among detainees or escapes by well-organized groups of prisoners assisted by outsiders.

Court resources varied as well. Most courts used Kosovar judges appointed by the UN or by the fledgling Kosovar government. Some courts made partial use of international judges (who were paid more than ten times as much as local counterparts and given far better resources and security,

---

[10] For a basic introductory text on core international human rights principles and regimes, *see generally* Thomas Buergenthal, INTERNATIONAL HUMAN RIGHTS IN A NUTSHELL (2002).

[11] *See generally* Ehrenreich & Spencer, *supra* note 5.

which unsurprisingly bred resentment). Many courts still lacked law libraries or basic equipment several years after the intervention. (Indeed, for many judges the issue of applicable law remained moot for well over a year after UNMIK took over. Until summer 2000, most Kosovar judges lacked copies of either the pre-1989 statutes or the post-1989 statutes, as well as copies of international human rights treaties, UNMIK regulations, and European Court of Human Rights caselaw.) For eighteen months after the NATO air campaign ended, most courts and prosecutors' offices also lacked vehicles, office equipment, furniture, and full staffs.[12]

As a result of resource limitations, unresolved jurisdictional issues, and the dispute over the applicable law, most courts were slow to begin hearing cases. In many areas, no judicial proceedings were held at all for more than eight months after the beginning of the UNMIK administration. But NATO and UN civilian police began arresting criminal suspects as soon as they were deployed, because the restoration of "law and order," in the sense of stopping the widespread violence, was rightly viewed as a key priority.

But though it was appropriate for NATO and UNMIK to treat the reestablishment of security as a top priority, planners and funders failed to make plans for detaining and trying the hundreds of people who were soon detained by intervention authorities. Within months after the UN administration started, hundreds of criminal suspects were detained in makeshift NATO and UN jails. For the most part, these detainees could not be tried or even indicted because the courts were so slow. Although virtually any straight reading of the applicable law (pre-1989 or post-1999 Kosovo law, European human rights law, whatever) made it clear that detainees could certainly not be held indefinitely without charge, many detainees were not released, although they were not charged, either.[13] Some suspects were also detained pursuant to the UN Special Representative's executive powers.[14]

The UN administration's commitment to upholding human rights and the rule of law thus created another conundrum: holding hundreds of people for indefinite periods without charge was surely a problem under anyone's reading of the law, but letting dangerous suspects – including a number of people accused of war crimes – back out into the streets also seemed unacceptable to NATO and UNMIK. Allowing criminals to run free would

---

[12] Id. In spring and summer 2000, a $2 million grant from the U.S. State Department's Bureau of Human Rights, Democracy and Labor ultimately rectified some of these resource problems.

[13] *See* Ehrenreich & Spencer, *supra* note 5.

[14] *See Organization for Security and Cooperation in Europe, Mission in Kosovo Department of Human Rights and Rule of Law,* THE RESPONSE OF THE JUSTICE SYSTEM TO THE MARCH 2004 RIOTS (December 2005), *available at* http://www.osce.org/documents/mik/2005/ 12/17177_en.pdf; *see also Organization for Security and Cooperation in Europe, Mission in Kosovo Department of Human Rights and rule of law, Review of the Criminal Justice System, April 2003–October 2004, available at* http://www.osce.org/documents/ mik/2004/12/3984_en.pdf.

undermine all of the UNMIK and NATO efforts to restore order, reduce violence, and increase public confidence in the international community's commitment to good governance in Kosovo.

UNMIK ultimately resolved this conundrum by issuing UNMIK Regulation 26, which noted blithely that "in order to ensure the proper administration of justice," pretrial detainees could be held for a *full year* if they were suspected of serious crimes.[15] Meanwhile, many Kosovars and international observers claimed that those suspects who were released (either through the exercise of prosecutorial discretion or because a judge determined that they had been held for excessive periods without charge) tended to be disproportionately Albanians who either had "connections" to powerful people or who had committed revenge crimes against Serbs and other minorities, whereas those who continued to be detained were often minorities or those without powerful friends.

The story of missteps in creating the rule of law in Kosovo does not end here – further and more recent instances of ethnic bias, corruption, and intimidation in the courtroom, prison escapes, and so on could all be cited.[16] But this is probably enough to show how easy it is for well-intentioned rule of law reforms to backfire and become self-undermining. UNMIK and NATO authorities did their best, but lack of resources, lack of advance planning, and poor coordination and communication undermined efforts to send consistent messages about the rule of law.

Recent events in Iraq suggest that many of the lessons of Kosovo remain unlearned today, at least by the United States. In Iraq, similar missteps and misunderstandings have exacerbated tensions between Iraqis and the U.S.-led coalition. As in Kosovo, the tensions between pursuing security and pursuing political reconstruction goals continues to create problems. Without security, political reconstruction is difficult, if not impossible, but heavy-handedness in pursuit of security can alienate citizens and make them less willing to participate in later reconstruction projects urged by interveners. As discussed in Chapter 5, the coalition and ordinary Iraqis are still paying a heavy price for the coalition's ongoing inability to guarantee a secure environment, and this affects Iraqi trust of coalition efforts across a wide range of sectors. Given the poor security environment, "getting it right" in other ways becomes both more difficult and even more crucial.

So much has been written recently about American mistakes in Iraq that it is hardly necessary to discuss them at length here. In Iraq as in Kosovo, linguistic and cultural differences continue to compound the difficulties that coalition officials encounter as they try to build rule of law institutions in Iraq. Both military and civilian officials charged with working to reform the Iraqi legal and judicial system generally have little background in Iraqi law

---

[15] UNMIK Regulation 26, *reprinted in* Ehrenreich & Spencer, *supra* note 5, Appendix.
[16] *See supra* note 14.

or even in civil law systems. This lack of background rankles with many Iraqis lawyers and judges, who – though fully aware of their system's many problems – often take pride in their country's ancient legal traditions, which date back to the Code of Hammurabi from the 18th century B.C.

Also as in Kosovo, the coalition's substantive commitment to rule of law values sometimes clashes with the formal aspects of the rule of law. Tensions have emerged, for instance, over detentions policy, with many Iraqi judges complaining that coalition officials detain Iraqi suspects who have been ordered released by Iraqi judges and equally arbitrarily release suspects who had been ordered detained by the judges. From the perspective of the judges, this is sheer arbitrariness and disrespectful of Iraqi legal process. From the perspective of coalition officials, many of whom are U.S. officers with the Judge Advocate General's Corps (JAG), this represents an effort to correct substantive defects in the Iraqi judicial process. As a coalition official explained to one of this book's authors, at times coalition officials free suspects because they are convinced that the evidence against them was obtained through coerced confessions elicited after beatings or torture; at other times, coalition officials order the continued detention of suspects when they are convinced that judicial release orders were influenced by nepotism, bribery, or intimidation.

These coalition acts may be well intentioned, and in accordance with the substantive values we associate with the rule of law, but inevitably they appear arbitrary and hypocritical to some Iraqi observers. Iraqi judges also complain about the frequent failure of coalition officials to produce detainees for court proceedings when requested. Here too, coalition officials defend such failures, attributing them in part to concerns about detainee security (convoys transporting detainees have frequently been targeted by insurgents) and in part to simple linguistic confusion. Difficulties transliterating Arabic names often mean that coalition authorities lose track of suspects or confuse one suspect with another who has a similar name. But when coalition officials seem unable or unwilling to cooperate with properly issued court orders, coalition credibility is undermined.

Needless to say, the much-publicized abuses at Abu Ghraib prison in Baghdad dealt a particularly devastating blow to coalition efforts to promote the rule of law in Iraq. When photos surfaced in the spring of 2004 depicting American soldiers abusing and humiliating Iraqi detainees (many of whom were acknowledged by the coalition to be civilians with no known connection to terrorists or insurgents), coalition efforts to convince Iraqis to accept U.S. efforts to reform Iraqi police and prisons were badly undermined. To the extent that the Abu Ghraib abuses have come to be seen as linked to broader U.S. government disregard for the Geneva Conventions, the Convention Against Torture, and other international legal norms and institutions, Iraqis can hardly be blamed for questioning the genuineness of the U.S. commitment to the rule of law.

Many Americans, both military personnel and civilians, have worked sensitively and respectfully with Iraqi counterparts to foster shared rule of law goals. But the good work and good intentions of these individuals are badly undermined whenever other Americans commit abuses or simply behave in an arrogant or culturally inappropriate way. American military practices such as house-to-house searches have, in some towns, led to enormous ill-feeling between soldiers and Iraqi civilians, and poor conditions at American-run detention facilities have also created substantial bitterness. "Collateral damage" in the form of civilian deaths have also generated anticoalition sentiment in Iraq.

In a poll of Iraqi public opinion done just prior to the Abu Ghraib scandal, 80 percent of Iraqis said they lacked confidence in the coalition, and 82 percent disapproved of the coalition. By May 2004, a survey commissioned by the Coalition Provisional Authority found confidence in the coalition down to a mere 11 percent. Ninety-two percent of Iraqis told coalition pollsters that they viewed the United States as an occupying force, and 54 percent said they believed that all Americans behaved like the American guards portrayed in the Abu Ghraib prison abuse photos. Iraqi attitudes toward the coalition and the intervention itself have fluctuated over time, and a Time–ABC poll conducted in October and November of 2005 suggested continuing ambivalence: although 46 percent of Iraqis said they felt "the US was right to invade Iraq," 64 percent said they "oppose Coalition forces."[17] But different segments of the Iraqi population view the situation differently. Support for the invasion was highest in Kurdish areas (80 percent), where only 22 percent said they "oppose Coalition forces"; these figures were 58 percent and 59 percent, respectively, in Shiite areas; in Sunni areas, only 16 percent said "the US was right to invade," and 85 percent opposed coalition forces. Overall, 51 percent of Iraqis surveyed said "life is better since the war," with the numbers again varying substantially among the different groups.[18]

These ambivalent results point again to the inherent contradiction that plagues virtually all post-intervention rule of law efforts. Although there is, as Chapter 3 noted, much disagreement about precisely how to define the rule of law, at its heart lies the idea that processes based on rules and reasons must trump force, that rights are more important than might. Yet in Iraq today, American efforts to create the rule of law encounter an immediate paradox. The United States governed Iraq because its coalition had the military muscle to defeat Saddam Hussein's demoralized army and because its status as the world's sole superpower kept other nations from interfering, despite much global skepticism about the legality and legitimacy of the intervention.

---

[17] Brookings Iraq Index, January 17, 2006, at 38, *available at* http://www.brookings.edu/fp/saban/iraq/index.pdf (October/November 2005 Time-ABC News Poll).

[18] Id.

As we have noted, this inherent contradiction complicates *all* post-intervention rule of law efforts to a greater or lesser degree. By definition, interveners are in a position to promote the rule of law in post-conflict societies because the balance of force is in their favor. Interveners can impose governance blueprints and institutional reform because local populations must cooperate, at least to some degree, to survive and prosper. But imposed reforms rarely generate the genuine popular support that will enable them to endure in the longer-term, and popular support is particularly difficult to come by if the interveners are seen as hypocritical or motivated by less-than-altruistic concerns.

How acute this problem is will depend on the context. In East Timor, this problem was relatively unimportant, because interveners enjoyed both a clear legal mandate from the UN Security Council and significant local support. Likewise, in Afghanistan, 82 percent of Afghans surveyed told researchers that "overthrowing the Taliban government was a good thing for Afghanistan" and 83 percent have a favorable view of U.S. forces there.[19] In Kosovo, the situation was somewhat murkier: NATO's military intervention was widely welcomed by Kosovar Albanians, although its legality was contested by some key states. Even so, as the examples above suggest, the initial goodwill the intervention enjoyed was undercut by some early decisions, leaving interveners vulnerable to charges that their own authority in Kosovo was itself in tension with rule of law values. In Iraq, in the face of a deeply divided international community and strongly divided domestic views, the disconnect between the coalition's rule of law rhetoric and its sometimes discordant actions was particularly glaring.

There is no way to wish these difficulties away. Nonetheless, once we recognize that the rule of law is a matter of cultural commitments as much as a matter of formal institutions and legal codes, the lessons from past mistakes are fairly straightforward. Policymakers who want to promote the rule of law in post-intervention societies can avoid some of the pitfalls illustrated here by the examples from Kosovo and Iraq. Avoiding these pitfalls won't guarantee success in creating the rule of law – but it can help protect against catastrophic failures.

Six ways to minimize harm:

• First, and most obviously, interveners need to *acknowledge the paradox inherent in the project of trying to pull the rule of law from the barrel of a gun,* and the ways in which the very fact of the intervention itself may undermine their claims about the value of the rule of law. There's no way around this problem, but acknowledging it at least makes the nature of the challenge clearer.

---

[19] New WPO Poll: Afghan Public Overwhelmingly Rejects al-Qaeda, Taliban, January 11, 2006, *available at* http://www.worldpublicopinion.org.

- Second, interveners need to *be committed to transparency in their own actions*. It's better to acknowledge it when a particular program or policy is being forced on a society or group. When interveners seek to create consultative processes, as was done in Kosovo, but then ignore advice they don't like, it undermines their credibility. Acknowledging that certain policies and principles are nonnegotiable, at least in the short term, may make interveners unpopular – but hardly more unpopular than they are when they feign a willingness to allow local societies to make their own choices but then veto their choices.

  Being transparent also means acknowledging that problems and mistakes are inevitable: innocent people may be detained or even killed; foolish regulations may be promulgated and then rescinded; rash policies may be enforced and altered only after complaints. Acknowledging all this cannot eliminate the frustration, anger, and grief local residents will feel over the mistakes of the interveners, but it can ameliorate it to some extent. Interveners should acknowledge and accept responsibility for errors past and future.

- Third, and relatedly, interveners need to *be accountable for their own actions*. When interveners insist that legal codes in a post-conflict society must reflect international human rights standards, but interveners themselves seem unable or unwilling to comply with those same standards, their credibility suffers. Announcing – in advance – a scheme for retroactively adjudicating claims against the interveners and compensating those who are wronged may help diffuse popular resentment about missteps made by interveners. Those detained wrongly or for excessive periods should be entitled to compensation, as should anyone wrongfully physically harmed by police or military forces or anyone whose property was wrongly damaged.

  It is particularly important for interveners to demonstrate that they do not have a double standard. When anyone affiliated with an intervening power behaves inappropriately or commits crimes, interveners need to ensure that investigation, trial, and punishment are prompt, fair, and public.

- Fourth, interveners need to *be better educated about the language and culture* of the societies in which they are working. Although it is unrealistic to expect every policymaker or soldier in post-conflict societies to be fluent in local languages and deeply familiar with local history and customs, it is not unrealistic for governments, NGOs, and intergovernmental agencies to create and require crash courses for those new to a region and culture. Some of the mistakes that plagued rule of law efforts in societies like Kosovo and Iraq could have been avoided with a minimum of cultural sensitivity.

- Fifth, interveners need to *plan rule of law programs carefully* before they begin. It is easier to prevent damage than to undo it, and poor planning often leads only to a need for embarrassing about-faces further down the road. Of course, planning is useful only if authorities make use of it: one of the numerous tragedies associated with the U.S. invasion of Iraq was the failure of Defense Department planners to make use of the extensive planning done by State Department experts in consultation with Iraqis. As a result, Defense Department officials were unprepared to protect the crucial infrastructure that was sabotaged by opposition forces in the early days after the invasion, although attacks on this infrastructure had been predicted by many.

- Sixth, interveners should *act multilaterally and collaboratively* in designing and implementing rule of law programs. Given the paradoxes inherent in trying to create the rule of law in the wake of military interventions, interveners need to gain as much legitimacy as possible: rule of law cannot always be fostered effectively by soldiers with guns. Interventions that are perceived as unilateral run particular risks, because it is easy for local (or international) hostility toward a particular intervening state to evolve into general hostility to the reconstruction projects favored by that intervening state. This risk can be minimized, to some extent, if post-conflict tasks are shared by a broad and multilateral coalition able to promote international NGO involvement and offer civilian experts as well as military troops.

Here again, Iraq offers a negative example: the U.S.-led military coalition was narrow to begin with, because many states normally allied with the United States opposed the invasion, which lacked a clear Security Council mandate. The United States compounded this problem by insisting in the immediate post-invasion period that coalition military forces and associated government contractors could handle post-conflict reconstruction tasks without substantial help from the United Nations, NGOs, or other experienced actors. (Indeed, U.S. contracting rules initially froze out potential contractors from states that had not supported the invasion.) This "go it alone" approach meant that many intergovernmental actors and civilians with relevant skills and experiences were excluded from early post-intervention activities, and it also focused Iraqi resentment on the coalition. Ensuring that no one state or religion or ethnicity is seen as behind all rule of law programs can help diminish resentment and skepticism about the motives of interveners.

II. DOING SOME GOOD: FOSTERING A RULE OF LAW CULTURE

Rule of law promotion efforts stumble when they come up against countervailing cultural commitments that are resistant to clumsy and formalistic efforts to change them. At their worst, rule of law programs may do as much harm as good, if interveners themselves act in ways that seem counter to rule of law values. When this happens, rule of law programs can actually undermine the rule of law. This chapter has suggested that interveners, like physicians, have a minimum duty to do no harm and urged interveners to be honest, transparent, accountable, culturally informed and sensitive, well-prepared, and collaborative in their approaches to rule of law programs. By heeding the lessons of past failure, future interveners can help avoid unintentionally undermining their own efforts.

But this tells us little about how to actually go about creating rule of law cultures in post-conflict societies. This remainder of this chapter will focus on some of the affirmative steps interveners can take to create rule of law cultures. In previous chapters, we described, first, many of the essential background conditions that must be present for rule of law programs to succeed: the creation of viable post-conflict governance arrangements, the establishment of basic human security, functioning police, prisons, and courts. We turn now to the challenge of taking these building blocks and turning them into something that actually works.

It is worth returning briefly to the pragmatic definition of the rule of law we laid out in Chapter 3:

> The "rule of law" describes a state of affairs in which the state successfully monopolizes the means of violence, and in which most people, most of the time, choose to resolve disputes in a manner consistent with procedurally fair, neutral, and universally applicable rules, and in a manner that respects fundamental human rights norms (prohibitions on racial, ethnic, religious and gender discrimination, torture, slavery, prolonged arbitrary detentions, and extrajudicial killings). In the context of today's globally interconnected world, this requires modern and effective legal institutions and codes, and it also requires a widely shared cultural and political commitment to the values underlying these institutions and codes.

In keeping with this understanding of the rule of law, throughout this book we have urged a more nuanced approach to promoting the rule of law, built on the recognition that the rule of law is also a particular set of cultural commitments. For the rule of law to exist, more is needed than courthouses and statutes. In fact, from a purely theoretical perspective, the rule of law could exist even in a society with no courthouses and no statutes. The rule of law is valuable because it protects people from the arbitrary exercise of power by public officials, allows people to plan their affairs with confidence, and helps shield people from abuses. Theoretically, a wide range of different institutions and norms could accomplish these ends. As this chapter has already noted, modern legal institutions are neither essential to accomplishing these ends nor can they guarantee that these ends will be achieved.

But, as the second part of our definition suggests, the sheer interconnectedness of today's global society makes the development of modern legal institutions necessary in post-intervention settings. Every successful, prosperous and peaceful country in the world has some roughly similar legal institutions, and if post-intervention societies are to take their place as equal players on the world stage, they too need to improve or develop modern legal institutions similar to those that thrive elsewhere.

Nonetheless, it is important to distinguish between means and ends. The rule of law is an end; our familiar modern legal institutions are one means of achieving that end, but not the only means, and at times not even the most effective means in the shorter term. Particularly in the immediate wake of violent conflicts, law reform may not be the only way to develop a culture of procedural fairness and respect for human dignity and rights. There may be times when "nonlegal" approaches, such as informal or traditional dispute resolution, do more to quickly establish the rule of law than any number of courthouse refurbishments or judicial training programs.

Realistically, as noted above, all post-intervention societies will be under pressure to develop modern legal institutions, so throughout this book we have assumed that such institutions must and will be developed along lines familiar to inhabitants of most developed nations. In the 21st century, it is no longer feasible for successful states to ignore the norms and institutions of other successful states. Nonetheless, making modern legal institutions successful in post-conflict societies requires going far beyond the approaches taken by traditional rule of law programs.

The rule of law requires people to know what law is and believe in its worth. Building rule of law cultures in post-conflict societies thus requires interveners to develop programs that seek to integrate legal norms into all aspects of life and into all sectors of society. This means a willingness to focus on longer-term initiatives designed to improve legal education and to strengthen civil society, and it also means moving beyond state institutions, beyond major urban areas, and beyond political elites. It also means moving beyond the obviously "legal" and recognizing the value of seemingly "peripheral" activities such as informal dispute resolution, media campaigns, education, and antipoverty programs.

We now turn to some of the kinds of programs critical to creating rule of law cultures. We first highlight several particularly important and promising kinds of initiatives: those that focus on strengthening supportive civil society institutions, those that focus on legal education, including law clinics; those that seek to link formal legal institutions to informal and customary law practices; and those that focus on transferring law-related skills to non-lawyers, including paralegals and trained mediators.

It is beyond the scope of this chapter to do more than highlight some of the most promising ways interveners can help foster long-term rule of law cultures: whole chapters, or even books, could be written about each of the programs mentioned above. Our hope is that by identifying and briefly describing some of these programs, this chapter will inspire practitioners to investigate these approaches more deeply and adapt them creatively.

At the end of the chapter, we summarize what we see as key factors in creating robust rule of law cultures: getting to the grassroots; strengthening civil society; shaping the next generation; giving people a stake in rule of law reform, including marginalized groups such as women, minorities, and youth; and creativity and willingness to use untraditional tools, such as the media and pop culture.

A. Good Practice: Nurture a Rule of Law Culture by Investing in Civil Society

1. Investing in Civil Society Organizations

Legal institutions do not exist in isolation. If fair and efficient courts will be ineffective without decent legislation, honest and effective police, good lawyers, and a decent prison system, all of these institutions depend equally on supportive social institutions such as media, civic associations, and NGOs. These social actors help educate people about legal institutions and also help educate legal institutions about the broader society: as watchdogs and advocates, they can help keep legal institutions honest and ensure that injustices and institutional failures can be remedied.

Local NGOs that are well designed and supported can play an indispensable role in helping to build a more transparent, effective, and fair justice system.[20] One example is the Judicial System Monitoring Programme (JSMP), an East Timor NGO, which monitors and provides independent information on East Timor's judicial system.[21] Established in 2001, the JSMP's mission is "to contribute to the ongoing evaluation and building of the justice system in East Timor" through "court monitoring, the provision of legal analysis and thematic reports on the development of the judicial system, and outreach activities."[22] In addition to evaluating progress in East Timor's district courts and court of appeal, the JSMP has a Women's Justice Unit that examines the particular impact of the system on women. The JSMP also has evaluated traditional justice mechanisms in East Timor; it has examined the work of the Commission for Reception, Truth and Reconciliation (CAVR) and the work of the Special Panels for Serious Crimes; and it has established a Victim Support Service focused especially on victims of domestic violence.

This organization, with both Timorese and international staffs, has highlighted problems in the justice system, recommended concrete reforms in legislation and practice, and provided much-needed public information and scrutiny of the developing justice system in East Timor. Organizations such as

---

[20] Stephen Golub, *Civil Society Contributions to Judicial Independence*, in U.S. Agency for International Development, Office of Democracy and Governance, *Guidance for Promoting Judicial Independence and Impartiality*, revised edition, January 2002, at 166–175.

[21] Judicial System Monitoring Programme, http://www.jsmp.minihub.org (last accessed Jan. 31, 2006).

[22] Id., mission statement.

this can play a vital role in monitoring and strengthening justice institutions in post-conflict societies and should be well supported and funded.[23]

In many post-intervention societies, similar NGOs either exist or can be developed relatively quickly once minimal political stability is restored. NGOs can, of course, be narrow in their focus or extremely broad. Some may be explicitly legal in their focus, conducting legal research, urging law reform, raising awareness of violations of the law, or initiating impact litigation in an effort to redress rights abuses or draw attention to gaps in the law. But NGOs not explicitly focused on law and legal institutions can also play valuable roles in fostering the rule of law: they can be a critical means of citizen mobilization and participation on a wide range of issues; they can help educate members and constituents about new law-related initiatives; they can conduct research and generate policy proposals in ways that ultimately foster rule of law goals of civic engagement and reasoned settlement of disputes.

When considering how NGOs can foster rule of law cultures, practitioners should keep in mind that "nonlegal" civil society organizations can be just as important to the rule of law as more obviously law-oriented NGOs. An NGO that focuses on the status of women through education and health care may be as important in rule of law efforts as a women's legal rights NGO, for instance: just as post-conflict societies as a whole cannot realize rule of law goals without basic physical security, so too it is difficult to meaningfully vindicate women's legal rights when women lack education and access to basic health care. Similarly, well-functioning neighborhood associations or religious associations can help identify needs, disseminate information, prevent disputes from getting out of hand, and be a locus for community-based initiatives. Which civil society groups are most important will vary from society to society, and from region to region, and for different demographic groups as well. What we want to emphasize, here as throughout this book, is that practitioners should avoid adopting a narrow understanding of the rule of law and a consequent cookie-cutter approach to supporting programs and organizations. Instead, practitioners should be open-minded, creative, and willing to work with what they find rather than import their own assumptions.

One reason for caution is that NGOs can be destructive as well as constructive. In post-conflict environments, where unemployment levels may be high and where foreign donors may be anxious to support fledgling civil society initiatives, the entrepreneurially minded have a strong incentive to form NGOs that are likely to appeal to interveners and donors. This in itself

---

[23] The JSMP's funders include international NGOs, foundations, UN agencies, and government agencies, such as the U.S. Agency for International Development. Id. Donors Page. In Afghanistan, Amnesty International urges that the Afghan Independent Human Rights Commission (AIHRC) be supported to engage in "independent monitoring of the criminal justice system from a human rights law perspective." Amnesty International, *Afghanistan: Re-establishing the Rule of Law*, August 14, 2003, at 58–59, 5.

is not necessarily a bad thing, but interveners and funders need to be alert to the structure of post-conflict incentives. In a context in which interveners may be eager to identify and fund local NGOs operating in the rule of law sector, NGOs may deliberately or inadvertently overstate their capacities. A few may be actually fraudulent, designed mainly to siphon off donor funds. All NGOs, no matter how competent and ethical, may face a strong temptation to tell interveners what they want to hear – and interveners face a strong temptation to accept even implausible claims as true, in order to send positive progress reports back to their own domestic constituencies.

This has two implications for interveners. First, interveners are well advised to do careful research before supporting or relying on a particular NGO, because appearing to uncritically support an NGO that is weak, biased, or fraudulent will undermine intervener credibility with other local stakeholders, as well as waste time and money. But, second, interveners should also give attention to helping NGOs and other civil society organizations build capacity and develop internal and external accountability mechanisms. In Iraq, for instance, where repression under Saddam Hussein had thwarted the development of a lively NGO sector, the U.S. Agency for International Devlopment developed an innovative project called "NGO in a box," which was designed to help local NGOs spring up and develop their capacity. In essence, the project sought to provide fledgling NGOs with everything needed to get started quickly, providing everything from basic office equipment to a series of workshops on issues ranging from budgeting to accountability. Similar programs have been undertaken in Liberia and other post-conflict settings as well. Although such programs cannot guarantee healthy, transparent, and accountable NGOs, they can nonetheless make such outcomes more likely.

Support for bar associations and judges associations can also be a valuable long-term investment. Independent bar associations, among other things, can develop codes of conduct for lawyers, serve as a source of advice on legislation and judicial reform, and, if resources permit, potentially organize mechanisms for legal representation of indigent defendants.[24] Similarly, judges' associations can potentially develop codes of conduct for jurists and provide a vehicle for training programs, judicial exchanges, and other opportunities to interact with judges from well-established judicial systems. Given the difficult working conditions of judges in many post-conflict settings, financial and technical support for judges' associations can, over time, help reinforce the importance and value of an impartial judiciary.

---

[24] Mark S. Ellis, *International Legal Assistance*, in POST-CONFLICT JUSTICE (M. Cherif Bassiouni, ed., 2002), at 932–933. In Afghanistan, for instance, Amnesty International recommends "creation of an independent bar association, capable of overseeing and organizing the work of defense lawyers" as "an essential component of the judicial reform program." Amnesty International, *Afghanistan, Re-establishing the Rule of Law, supra* note 23, at 35.

Here too, a word of caution is in order. As with NGOs, bar and judicial associations can play valuable roles, or destructive roles, depending on their degree of capacity and degree of accountability, transparency, and commitment to high ethical standards. In some societies, lawyers and judges are respected for their learning and integrity and legal and judicial associations can quickly play constructive roles if given financial or technical support. In other societies, however, where the quality of the bar and the judiciary is low, or where lawyers and judges are seen as corrupt or complicit in abuses, external support for such associations can backfire. Of course, bar and judicial organizations can be reformed, or new organizations started, in ways that raise professional standards – but here as elsewhere, interveners need to do their homework before leaping to support organizations that may look good on paper. The only thing worse than ignoring such potentially critical civil society allies is rushing in blindly before understanding how local players regard a given organization or professional group.

2. Investing in Legal Education

Supporting legal education is a critical investment in a sound justice system.[25] Interveners and donors typically focus on short-term training for lawyers, judges, and other groups, but in the longer run, building a rule of law culture will depend in part on nurturing the next generation of legal professionals. In many post-conflict settings, law schools are underfunded and understaffed; curricula may not have been updated for decades. Although investing in law schools may not be the immediate priority after an intervention, it should not spend too much time on the back burner, for the relative neglect of legal education can have long-term costs. As the International Crisis Group warns, in Bosnia, "The international community's failure to address legal education systematically in its law reform programs means that Bosnia risks being unable to sustain the structures and standards that its foreign patrons aim to bequeath."[26]

Investing in legal education also creates possible synergies with other programs that help foster rule of law cultures. For instance, well-designed clinical legal education programs can provide valuable professional training to law students while also providing much-needed assistance to underserved groups as well.[27] Legal aid clinics can focus on gaps in the legal system, such

---

[25] Erik G. Jensen, *The Rule of Law and Judicial Reform: The Political Economy of Diverse Institutional Patterns*, in BEYOND COMMON KNOWLEDGE: EMPIRICAL APPROACHES TO THE RULE OF LAW (Erik G. Jensen & Thomas C. Heller, eds., 2003), at 359–360.

[26] International Crisis Group, *Courting Disaster: The Misrule of Law in Bosnia & Herzegovina*, ICG Balkans Report No. 127, 25 March 2002, at 48.

[27] For discussion of efforts to develop clinical legal education programs at several Iraqi law schools, *see* Haider Ala Hamoudi, *Toward a Rule of Law Society in Iraq: Introducing Clinical Legal Education into Iraqi Law Schools*, 23 BERK. J. INT'L L. 112 (2005).

as inadequate criminal defense services,[28] or on impact litigation or even on community organizing or legal and policy research.

Outside of post-conflict settings, clinics have played important roles in helping build rule of law cultures. In South Africa, legal clinics at nonwhite universities helped draw attention to abuses during the apartheid era, while nurturing a generation of educated African lawyers who were poised to take on leadership positions when apartheid ended. After the transition away from apartheid, South African legal clinics have continued to play an important role in providing legal services for the indigent, in keeping the spotlight on structural inequalities in postapartheid society, and in seeking to ensure that rights declared in the postapartheid South African constitution have practical meaning for ordinary people. From Argentina to China, experimental clinics have sprung up in the past decade and have often been important legal innovators.[29]

Although there are fewer examples of successful clinics in post-intervention settings, there is every reason to think they can play a similarly valuable role there. In Sierra Leone, for instance, a human rights clinic sprang up at Freetown's Fourah Bay College (FBC) even before many other important post-conflict institutions had come into being (it slightly predated the Truth and Reconciliation Commission and the Special Court, for instance). Founded by a group of young Sierra Leonean law professors and students with funding and technical support from the Open Society Institute, the FBC Human Rights Clinic undertook a mix of projects, from free representation of the poor to human rights education programs in local high schools. Clinic students work closely with local and national NGOs, and the clinic also places students as holiday interns with NGOs.

The potential benefits of such clinical programs are enormous. Indigent people and NGOs benefit by receiving free assistance from students. Students benefit by learning advocacy skills and substantive law, and, perhaps as important, clinics can help students get into the habit of seeing pro bono work, rather than only profit-seeking, as crucial to the lawyer's role.

B. Traditional Dispute Settlement Mechanisms and Their Relationship to Formal Justice Institutions

When considering ways to foster rule of law cultures, interveners should also examine the degree to which formal legal institutions are utilized in a given society. In some societies educated urbanites may have made extensive use of formal legal institutions prior to an intervention, and be ready to use them again once stability is restored, but these same institutions may

---

[28] Amnesty International, *Afghanistan: Re-establishing the Rule of Law, supra* note 23, at 35–36.
[29] *See generally* Aubrey McCutcheon, *University Legal Aid Clinics: A Growing Presence with Manifold Benefits,* in MANY ROADS TO JUSTICE (Ford Foundation, 2000).

have been virtually irrelevant in rural areas or among less educated and less affluent people. In such contexts, many people may be more accustomed to turning to traditional or informal dispute settlement mechanisms. These may range in complexity and legitimacy, but in some societies, traditional dispute resolution mechanisms enjoy considerable local support.

In East Timor, customary conflict resolution practices are diverse, but many involve community-based processes of arbitration in which village elders and "Lia-nains" (or custodians of traditional law) serve as neutral third parties. Such traditional processes differ from the formal legal system in the high emphasis they place on maintaining harmony and on restorative justice,[30] and a recent Asia Foundation survey found that most Timorese were "most comfortable and familiar" with customary dispute resolution processes and viewed the formal legal system as "less fair, less accessible, more complex, and a greater financial risk."[31] The survey found substantial public support for reliance on traditional dispute resolution processes to settle conflicts over land and "minor" offenses such as theft.[32]

Local and tribally based dispute mechanisms also play a significant role in rural Sierra Leone.[33] Traditional mechanisms, which vary considerably among different groups and regions, generally include an ascending hierarchy from family-based mechanisms to dispute resolution by community elders and/or religious leaders to "chiefs' barray" (chiefs assisted by elders), to local courts in the provinces presided over by chairmen appointed by (and removable by) the Interior Minister.[34] Even before the civil war, courthouses

---

[30] Christian Ranheim, *Legal Pluralism in East Timor: The Formal Judicial System and Community-based Customary Law,* prepared for the project, The Role of Non-State Justice Systems in Fostering the Rule of Law in Post-Conflict Societies, United States Institute of Peace, February 2005, at 12. On customary dispute settlement in East Timor, *see also* Tanya Hohe & Rod Nixon, *Reconciling Justice: "Traditional" Law and State Judiciary in East Timor,* Report prepared for the United States Institute of Peace, January 2003, *available at* http://www.jsmp.minihub.org/Traditional%20Justice/Indextraditional.htm; David Mearns, *Looking Both Ways: Models for Justice in East Timor,* AUSTRALIAN LEGAL RESOURCES. INT'L (2002), *available at* http://www.jsmp.minihub.org/Traditional%20Justice/Indextraditional.htm; Aisling Swaine, *Traditional Justice and Gender Based Violence,* International Rescue Committee Research Report, August 2003, *available at* http://www.jsmp.minihub.org/Traditional%20Justice/Indextraditional.htm; Judicial System Monitoring Programme, *Findings and Recommendations: Workshop on Formal and Local Justice Systems in East Timor,* July 2002, *available at* http://www.jsmp.minihub.org/Traditional%20Justice/Indextraditional.htm.

[31] Ranheim, *Legal Pluralism in East Timor, supra* note 30, at 2.

[32] The Asia Foundation, *Law and Justice In East Timor, A Survey of Citizen Awareness and Attitudes Regarding Law and Justice in East Timor,* February 2004, at 3.

[33] Abdul Tejan Cole & Mohamed Gibril Sesay, *Traditional Justice Systems and the Rule of Law in Post Conflict Sierra Leone,* prepared for the project, The Role of Non-State Justice Systems in Fostering the Rule of Law in Post-Conflict Societies, United States Institute of Peace, August 2005.

[34] Id.

only existed in major cities. As a result, the vast majority of "legal" problems (from crime to divorce to real estate transactions) were handled informally or through tribal elders and chiefs. As a result, changes to the formal law and formal legal institutions had little relevance to most people's lives.

So too in rural Afghanistan. As a recent USIP report noted, "[o]utside of the major cities, village councils or tribal elders have for generations played the predominant role in resolving disputes and meting out justice."[35] Dispute settlement practices by *jirgas* or *shuras* vary considerably among Afghanistan's different ethnic groups and regions. Some features that tend to recur, however, are a focus on restorative damages and formal apology rituals, with some notably severe penalties for offenses such as adultery.[36]

In such contexts, interveners need to understand that focusing solely on formal legal institutions may have only a very limited impact, perhaps only on urban elites. Reaching rural and less affluent people may require finding creative ways to engage with traditional and customary dispute settlement regimes. Sometimes, where traditional processes are viewed by local people as highly credible and fair, interveners may wish to import some features of traditional processes into formal legal institutions, because these formal institutions may become less irrelevant to ordinary people if they borrow from preexisting rules and procedures.

Here too, however, interveners need to exercise caution. On the one hand, rule of law efforts should not ignore the role of traditional and informal dispute settlement mechanisms, because these may command substantial loyalty and may offer useful models for more formal institutions. On the other hand, traditional dispute settlement mechanisms may be substantively or procedurally problematic: they may privilege men over women, or one ethnic group over another, and interveners may confront difficult instances in which long-standing customary practices violate fundamental rights.

In Sierra Leone, for instance, the customary system is highly patriarchal and tends to favor males and older disputants, which "stack[s] the system against youths, women, the poor and members of weak lineages."[37] Yet for the majority of citizens, lack of access to the formal court system means that this, for better or worse, is primarily "the law people see."[38]

---

[35] Laurel Miller & Robert Perito, *Establishing the Rule of Law in Afghanistan*, United States Institute of Peace Special Report 117, March 2004, at 10.

[36] International Legal Foundation, *The Customary Laws of Afghanistan*, September 2004, *available at* http://216.239.51.104/search?q=cache:Aw5XW8xWGvkJ:www.theilf.org/ILF_cust_law_afgh_10-15.doc+International+Legal+Foundation,+The+Customary+Laws+of+Afghanistan&hl=en&gl=us&ct=clnk&cd=2.

[37] Cole & Sesay, *Traditional Justice Systems and the Rule of Law in Post Conflict Sierra Leone*, *supra* note 33, at 50.

[38] *See* Owen Alterman, Aneta Binienda, Sophie Rodella, & Kimyia Varzi, National Forum for Human Rights, *The Law People See: The Status of Dispute Resolution in the Provinces of Sierra Leone in 2002*, January 2003.

In Afghanistan, the same is true in many regions. In Pashtun areas, for example, *jirgas* consider and adjudicate even the most serious crimes, and damages can include "cash, services, animals, and also the transfer of women."[39] In an Afghan customary practice, known as "Bad," *jirgas* can resolve murder cases "by ordering that the alleged perpetrator provide the family of the alleged victim with a young girl or girls, usually below the legal marriage age, in order to compensate for the alleged crime" and "the girl, who is 'exchanged,'" may then be forced to marry "a male member of the victim's family."[40] Needless to say, this practice conflicts with internationally accepted human rights norms, and like other traditional laws and practices that run counter to international human rights norms, it creates a quandary for interveners. On the one hand, interveners may wish to work with traditional authorities or find ways to piggyback reforms onto traditional institutions and may thus be reluctant to challenge long-standing and locally accepted practices. But on the other hand, interveners need to make every effort to end abusive practices such as coerced marriages: failing to end the practice not only harms the women and girls who are treated as chattel or forced into unwanted marriages but also undermines broader rule of law messages about the equal dignity and worth of men and women, which interveners need to support. As a result of these challenges, working with traditional dispute resolution mechanisms can be difficult and sensitive, and interveners who are only superficially familiar with local customs and institutions may find themselves inadvertently propping up practices they oppose. This does not make efforts to work with traditional dispute resolution mechanisms worthless: well-designed and sensitive programs can empower local reformers to change traditional norms themselves (there is some evidence that support within Afghanistan for "limiting the authority of customary law mechanisms, particularly in areas of criminal justice," may, in fact, be growing, for instance).[41]

While interveners engaged in justice system reform are becoming more attentive to the role of traditional dispute settlement practices, gaining a detailed understanding can be difficult and time consuming. Good empirical information is needed to understand how such practices operate in particular post-conflict societies and communities,[42] as well as their impact on different

---

[39] Mark A. Drumbl, *Rights, Culture, and Crime: The Role of Rule of Law for the Women of Afghanistan*, 42 COLUM. J. TRANS'L L. 349, 384 (2004).

[40] Amnesty International, *Afghanistan: Re-establishing the Rule of Law, supra* note 23, at 50.

[41] Miller & Perito, *Establishing the Rule of Law in Afghanistan, supra* note 35, at 10; Afghan Independent Human Rights Commission, Program on Humanitarian Policy and Conflict Research, *Human Rights and the Rule of Law: Constitutional and Legal Reform* (Roundtable) (2003), at 13.

[42] *See* Erik Jensen, *The Rule of Law and Judicial Reform*, in BEYOND COMMON KNOWLEDGE, *supra* note 25, at 336, 362–363. In Pakistan, for instance, "[t]raditional community-based ADR ... were regarded as speedy and inexpensive but largely unjust, mostly owing to the fact that they were easily captured by local elites." Id. at 363.

segments of the population, including women and other vulnerable groups; their perceived legitimacy; and their consistency with fundamental human rights. Given the frequent delays and difficulties in extending formal justice institutions into rural areas in many resource-poor post-conflict societies, reliance on informal mechanisms is likely to persist and reformers will need to address a number of key issues.

In the long run, both interveners and local residents need to consider how traditional dispute settlement mechanisms will relate to developing state justice institutions. What is their relationship and what should it be? More specifically, should the customary system be *recognized but restricted* (limited to certain issues or kinds of disputes, with safeguards to protect human rights) and allowed to coexist in its designated sphere? Alternatively, should the formal justice system *incorporate (and constrain)* some aspects of customary practice? Or should the customary system be incrementally *abolished* as the formal system expands in geographic scope?

Different societies have dealt with this issue in different ways. East Timor's constitution leaves open the status of traditional dispute settlement, providing that "[t]he State shall recognize and value the norms and customs of East Timor that are not contrary to the Constitution and to any legislation dealing specifically with customary law";[43] Sierra Leone permits some aspects of customary practice and limits others.[44] In Afghanistan, however, "the relationship between the formal and informal justice systems and the competence of the informal system is largely unregulated" and unresolved, resulting in diverse and inconsistent arrangements in different parts of the country.[45]

In the best of all possible worlds, interveners would find ways to build on the positive aspects of informal and customary dispute resolution mechanisms, without encouraging their negative aspects. Interveners should not sacrifice core human rights standards and should work with local reformers to protect vulnerable segments of the population. But inevitably, this is complex and difficult: as reformers work to build local acceptance of rights-protecting reforms, they may face deeply entrenched obstacles, especially in the area of women's rights.

---

[43] Constitution of the Democratic Republic of East Timor, Section 2.
[44] Cole & Sesay, *Justice Systems and the Rule of Law in Post Conflict Sierra Leone*, *supra* note 33, at 42, 47–50.
[45] Amnesty International, *Afghanistan: Re-establishing the Rule of Law*, *supra* note 23, at 49. In parts of Afghanistan, for instance, courts have declined to address some criminal and civil matters until they have been considered in local dispute mechanisms. Id. But there is no uniformity on this, and the role that these mechanisms should play has yet to be resolved. But, in light of their significance, Amnesty International urges that the "competence of informal justice systems must be clearly set out in the law in order to remove any ambiguity regarding" their role, that their relationship to the formal justice system be clarified by law, and that the Afghan authorities "ensure that the jirgas and shuras, if they are allowed to function, fully conform to international human rights law." Id. at 51.

In East Timor, for example, UNTAET sought to encourage the Timorese to refer crimes of gender-based violence, such as rape, to the formal justice system rather than to informal dispute mechanisms. But UNTAET's efforts ran up against difficulties caused not only by long-standing practices and cultural attitudes but also by economic realities. In East Timor, a woman who has been raped may face social stigmatization and be unable to marry. As a result, traditional dispute mechanisms tend to include a practical focus on locating alternative means of economic support for a rape victim, because, after a rape, she may be unable to find a husband to help support her.[46] Given these social and economic realities, Timorese women may be reluctant to turn to formal legal institutions in cases of rape, since although these formal institutions may be more respectful of women's equal rights, they don't encompass the kinds of community-enforced economic remedies offered by traditional mechanisms. Interveners committed to protecting fundamental human rights thus need to appreciate the larger social and economic context to design reforms likely to effectively advance those rights over time.

But at least in some cases, interveners may be able to identify innovative ways to accommodate local traditions without compromising human rights. In the case described above, there is no inherent reason the formal legal system could not provide remedies that take equal account of women's economic situation. Reparations could be provided in addition to criminal penalties, for instance: within East Timor, reparations in the form of animals and food are a form of sanction that is deeply rooted in cultural practices; such practices could be incorporated as part of punishments in the criminal justice system without sacrificing core human rights standards.

C. The Role of Paralegals and Mediators

Supporting programs that make use of paralegals and trained mediators is another way interveners may be able to develop useful synergies (and even healthy competition) between the formal justice system and informal dispute settlement mechanisms. In Sierra Leone, for example, the introduction of community-based paralegals in rural areas, supported by NGOs, has provided a valuable (and free) alternative dispute settlement resource. By educating citizens about their legal rights within the formal justice system, and advocating for their interests with local chiefdom authorities, these paralegals have provided valuable pressure for reform, serving "as bridges between the two legal regimes" and helping citizens pursue the most effective options among those available.[47] With citizens more aware of their rights

---

[46] Erica Harper, *The Effectiveness and Sustainability of UN Legal Codes in Post-Conflict Situations* (2005 draft, on file with authors).

[47] Vivek Maru, *The Challenges of African Legal Dualism: an Experiment in Sierra Leone*, JUSTICE INITIATIVES, February 1, 2005, at 21–22, *available at* www.justiceinitiative.org/db/resource2/fs/?file_id=15277.

and options, traditional authorities may face greater incentives to offer reasonable dispute settlement arrangements if they wish to continue to attract customers for their services.

The rule of law is not the exclusive province of lawyers; in some societies, paralegals and mediators drawn from within poor and rural communities may be far more effective than lawyers would be in spreading awareness of legal remedies and in encouraging people to use legal institutions. And regardless of the role played by traditional dispute resolution mechanisms in a given society, access to justice is a major problem for the poor, the less educated, and the less urban populations of many societies. Supporting paralegals and mediators can be an efficient and cost-effective way to spread information and skills beyond elite sectors of society. Training a lawyer or a judge takes several years, but equipping nonprofessionals with basic legal advocacy skills, information, and/or mediation skills can be done far more quickly.

III. PUTTING IT ALL TOGETHER

Every society is different, and there is no "one size fits all" approach to creating rule of law cultures. Building on traditional dispute-resolution mechanisms may be an excellent idea in societies in which such mechanisms are popular and seen as credible and fair; in another society, however, traditional mechanisms may be viewed by many as part of an unjust hierarchy, and interveners who become associated with these mechanisms may quickly lose credibility. Similarly, supporting a judges' association may be just the right approach in a society with capable, ethical judges who are respected by other stakeholders, but it may backfire if judges are viewed as corrupt, incompetent, or complicit in abuses.

The first part of this chapter discussed some the ways in which interveners can unwittingly undermine their own rule of law efforts and urged interveners to be honest, transparent, accountable, educated about the societies in which they work, careful in their research and planning, and collaborative in their approaches to developing rule of law programs. In the second part of the chapter, we discussed some affirmative approaches to building rule of law cultures. Here as elsewhere in this book, we won't conclude by offering a list of "best practices"; what is best in one context may be a disaster in another setting. Similarly, offering "lessons learned" is too optimistic: the international community is only beginning to recognize the lessons of past successes and failures, and it would be premature to assume that any lasting learning has taken place.

Instead, the remainder of this chapter simply outlines some of the *key issues that interveners should consider when seeking to foster a durable cultural commitment to the rule of law.*

A. Getting to the Grassroots

Most traditional rule of law programs focus on political and economic elites: judges, lawyers, and politicians are targeted by training programs and reform efforts. But this elite focus overlooks the fact that for the rule of law to exist, the law's "consumers" – ordinary people as well as elites – need to be convinced of the value of legal institutions. It also overlooks the fact that in many troubled societies, the formal institutions of the law often draw their consumers from only a tiny slice of society. Interveners need to find ways to reach beyond cities, state institutions, and elites.

This can be done in a number of ways:

- *Programs that seek more broadly to educate nonelites about law, human rights, and governance can have significant spillover effects on more traditional justice sector programs.* The same is true for programs that train citizens in community organizing and advocacy techniques. Such programs can often work with and through preexisting NGOs or civil society groups (from churches to teachers' associations). Such programs can have benefits across sectors, enabling nonelites to lobby more effectively for beneficial health and economic programs, for instance, as well as simply educating them about the law.
- Similarly, *programs that help nonelites gain access to courts and other governance institutions to resolve problems can increase public confidence in justice sector institutions.* Such projects may include "access to justice" programs such as legal aid offices and clinics that offer free or low-cost legal advice and representation, pro se projects that train people to represent themselves, and paralegal-based projects that train and utilize nonlawyers with some legal training to serve as advocates and mediators.
- *In its broad sense, the rule of law is also strengthened by programs that offer conflict resolution services such as mediation to enable people to resolve disputes without using formal legal institutions.* In societies with strong preexisting traditions of informal dispute resolution, these programs may often be most effective if they can be tied into credible existing dispute resolution methods, involving, as appropriate, religious or tribal figures, for instance.

B. Strengthening Civil Society

Building and sustaining a rule of law culture also requires a strong civil society. Since a critical goal of the rule of law is to protect citizens from official arbitrariness and abuse, strong nongovernmental organizations play a major role in keeping government officials accountable. Strengthening media, NGOs, and other civil institutions is often seen as a task that is distinct from rule of law promotion, but it should instead be seen as part and parcel of promoting the rule of law.

- *Strengthening responsible and independent media* helps discourage corruption and abuse. In particular, programs that focus on training journalists in ethics and investigative techniques can be helpful.
- *NGOs of all sorts (from human rights organizations to youth associations to women's groups) can help foster the rule of law,* both by serving as watchdogs and advocates and by helping to ensure an educated and engaged citizenry. In post-conflict settings with a history of government repression, there may be little tradition of independent NGOs; NGOs, if they exist at all, may mainly be linked to political parties or religious entities. In such settings, interveners can play a useful role by giving fledgling NGOs the resources and training necessary to get up and running. In Iraq, for instance, USAID started a series of NGO training sessions to help NGOs get started. USAID was able to deliver "NGO in a box" packages, including both start-up funding and logistical and technical assistance.
- Particular attention should be given by interveners to *strengthening indigenous policy development capacity* in post-conflict societies. Particularly in societies that have suffered significant "brain drain" as a result of conflict or lack of economic opportunity, policy-development capacity may be minimal. As a result, elites may resent interveners, but be unable to formulate viable policy alternatives themselves. Interveners should provide resources to encourage serious policy research and development.

C. Shaping the Next Generation

Building a durable rule of law culture is a long-term project. Especially in post-conflict societies with little or no prior rule of law tradition, years – even centuries – of skepticism about law may need to be "unlearned" before the rule of law can flourish. Inevitably, there is a limit to the degree to which people can unlearn the habits and assumptions of a lifetime. For that reason, interveners need to find ways to encourage younger people in particular to have a stake in the rule of law.

- *Education at every level is crucial to fostering the rule of law.* From primary school onward, lessons about law, legal institutions, governance, and human rights need to be integrated into texts and curricula. In societies where secondary schooling is a luxury few can afford, special emphasis should be placed on integrating civic and legal education into primary curricula. Working with teachers' associations and teacher training programs can be a crucial tool.
- Training programs for judges and lawyers who have already developed their own professional habits and identities will not be as effective in the long run as *university programs designed to shape the next generation of legal professionals.* Law schools and law school clinics can play a particularly important role in inculcating rule of law values in emerging professionals.

- *Cultural and educational exchange programs can also play a key role,* especially (though not exclusively) for students and young professionals. Time spent in other societies with strong rule of law traditions can encourage and inspire younger people to revitalize rule of law traditions at home.

D. Giving People a Stake

In post-conflict settings with little previous rule of law tradition, rule of law programs that engage only a tiny slice of the population are unlikely to have much lasting impact. Interveners need to find ways to give large numbers of people a stake in laws, legal institutions, and the institutions of governance more broadly. This can be done both through programs that seek to give ordinary people a sense of "ownership" over the law and through the creation of concrete incentives to make use of law and legal institutions.

- *Innovative outreach programs* can help create a sense of shared ownership if they solicit ideas for new laws and institutions from across a broad spectrum of society. Perhaps the most successful example of this (though not from a post-intervention society) involves effort made by South Africa's first postapartheid government to involve ordinary people in designing the nation's new constitution. Billboards, pop songs, and cartoons all explained the constitution-creation process and urged people to write or call special toll-free numbers with their thoughts on what the new constitution should say. Millions of South Africans offered their ideas to the constitutional assembly, and the inclusiveness of the process seems to have paid off in the loyalty South Africans of all races feel toward their new constitution.
- Programs that *link access to justice, citizens education, and dispute mediation to other kinds of development and antipoverty initiatives* may offer double benefits, with each kind of work having a multiplier effect on the other. First, they can create a concrete incentive for people to get involved with organizations that do law-related work by linking the law-related services to issues that have an immediate and clear effect on people's lives (such as agrarian reform or micro-credit programs). Second, combining traditional community-level development programs with a focus on advocacy, law, and policy can help ensure that development gains are sustained by a hospitable political and legal climate (by property, contract, and financial laws that ensure equitable and sustainable growth, for instance).

E. Including Marginalized Groups

Traditional rule of law programs focus mainly on the "supply side" of the law: judges, lawyers, law students, legislators, and so on. For durable and broad-based rule of law cultures to be created, interveners need to move beyond elites, but it is particularly important to focus on marginalized groups, who will otherwise remain vulnerable to abuse – and possibly disaffected enough to pose a significant threat to stability.

- *Programs that seek to empower women are particularly important and can have spillover effects on economic development and peace-related initiatives.* Study after study suggests the crucial role of women in development and peacebuilding; education for girls, for instance, has a strong multiplier effect on every other indicator. Women in post-conflict settings face unique challenges; they may have been targeted for sexual violence before, during, and after the conflict, and they usually have primary responsibility for children. They are often left out of post-conflict reforms and are the last to benefit from new economic and political opportunities. In part for these reasons, women are often more engaged participants than are men in development and advocacy initiatives, and women are also more likely than men to share benefits they receive with broader communities. Law-related services that target women not only help protect women from violence and marginalization but also make it more likely that the programs will effect children and men.
- Rule of law programs should also seek to *involve young people, particularly young people who are undereducated and underemployed.* The percentage of a population that consists of young men is a good predictor of social conflict; when those young men are unemployed, they make prime recruiting prospects for armed and criminal groups. Giving such young men the tools to participate more constructively in social and political life is an important part of creating rule of law cultures. (This issue should be considered in tandem with the issue of giving people a stake in the rule of law. Programs that offer economic benefits for constructive civic participation – such as DDR programs – can be effective when they offer durable advantages to disaffected populations, but the very benefits they offer to the disaffected can increase resentment among other segments of the population, who see bad actors apparently being "rewarded." Innovative programs should seek to spread the benefits of involving marginalized people throughout communities.)
- *Minorities also need to be a prime focus of rule of law programs.* Like unemployed youths, minorities are extremely vulnerable; they may be seen as expendable by elites from the majority and left out of any power-sharing. In some post-conflict settings, actual or feared marginalization and abuse drives minority groups into the role of spoilers. Targeting minorities in rule of law programming helps give these otherwise vulnerable groups the tools to protect themselves in ways that do not undermine social stability.

F. Being Creative

Since the rule of law is a culture as much as a set of institutions and legal codes, interveners need to be willing to use the tools of "culture" as well as the tools of law and development. If the rule of law and its associated institutions and rules are to capture the imagination and loyalty of citizens in any society, interveners need to consider the role of the media and the role of popular and folk culture.

- The media can help get messages across to broad audiences, and *interveners should build a media strategy into their planning.* Depending on the society, television, radio, and print media may play an important role in educating and informing the public. At a minimum, enlisting the help of the media can help ensure that the public is well informed about law-related initiatives. It is critical, however, that any media messages be targeted and culturally appropriate; clumsy media messages risk being either irrelevant or damaging.
- For most Americans, cop shows and shows like "Judge Judy" or "West Wing" shape and inform popular understandings of law and the political process. Although these shows are "entertainment," they also play an important role in cultural transmission. Because interveners tend themselves to be legal or policy professionals, rather than scriptwriters, poets, or singers, they rarely *consider strategies involving popular culture.* Yet in many societies, the arts, including the popular arts, are critical means of disseminating new ideas and forging cultural solidarity. Creative advertising campaigns can also be effective ways to inform and inspire the public.
- Rule of law promotion efforts may be most effective when they *link "new" or reformed legal institutions and rules to traditional dispute resolution methods and narratives.* This can help create a sense of continuity with the past and engender loyalty to newer forms. It can also help keep "traditional" constituencies, such as tribal elders, from becoming disaffected (and possibly being spoilers) by giving them an ongoing role in rule of law programs.

CONCLUSION

Throughout this book, we have emphasized the difficulty of building the rule of law in post-intervention societies. But despite the relatively disappointing results of many rule of law efforts undertaken so far, there is some empirical basis for believing that the approaches outlined above offer considerable promise. In a relatively small-scale way, donors and interveners – from Bangladesh and Ecuador to Malawi and Nepal – have begun to experiment with programs that reach beyond elites and legal institutions and focus on the long-term project of building deep cultural commitments to the rule of law. Most of these experiments were not done in post-intervention or post-conflict settings. Nonetheless, the evidence is that such "legal empowerment" programs, as commentator Stephen Golub has dubbed them, may be a crucial complement to traditional rule of law programs.

CHAPTER NINE

Enhancing Rule of Law Efforts:
Planning, Funding, and Local Ownership

Evaluating the effectiveness of rule of law assistance is complicated because rule of law promotion efforts are tied to the fate of the larger post-intervention reconstruction effort. Whether one defines rule of law assistance broadly, to encompass macro-political efforts such as forging the conflict settlement blueprint, or narrowly, to include only justice-sector-related assistance, failures in governance reforms, economic reconstruction, or security measures will undermine or defeat even well-designed rule of law assistance efforts.

But as noted, even when viewed in the most favorable light, rule of law assistance has frequently yielded only very modest results. For example, in a 2001 study, the U.S. General Accounting Office (GAO) reported on the limited impact of eight years of U.S. aid intended to assist the states of the former Soviet Union to develop sustainable rule of law institutions and traditions. The report concluded that progress was slow, that conditions in key states (Russia and the Ukraine) had deteriorated, and that the limited results elsewhere in the former Soviet Union "may not be sustainable in many cases."[1] The study correctly noted that "establishing the rule of law is a complex and long-term undertaking in the new independent states" and that impediments to success included "limited political consensus on the need to reform laws and institutions," "a shortage of domestic resources," and problems in the design and management of assistance programs by U.S. agencies.[2]

Conditions in post-intervention states are typically far less hospitable to rule of law efforts than those in the former Soviet Union. War-torn societies commonly remain sharply divided. In such countries, it is usually a misnomer to refer to "post-conflict reconstruction," because the conflict that

---

[1] GAO, Report to Congressional Requesters, *Former Soviet Union: U.S. Rule of Law Assistance Has Had Limited Impact and Sustainability*, May 17, 2001, at 3, *available at* http://www.gao.gov/new.items/d01354.pdf.

[2] Id.

precipitated intervention often continues at lower levels of intensity.[3] Infrastructure is shattered, spoilers contend for power and resources, economic activity is minimal, security is lacking, neighboring states interfere for their own ends, the populace lacks any experience with well-functioning legal systems, and the judicial sector is in tatters. Moreover, local leaders often oppose reforms and "seek to manipulate the law enforcement and judicial systems to suppress opposition."[4] Thus, structural barriers independent of the design and implementation of assistance programs often scuttle rule of law efforts.

But deficiencies in the design and delivery of peace implementation programs in general, and rule of law aid in particular, are also partly to blame. We have already identified some of the key problems associated with post-conflict rule of law efforts. In Chapter 3, we highlighted the problems caused by conflating the rule of law with the formal legal institutions characteristic of mature democracies. In Chapter 4, we considered the dangers of poorly designed post-conflict blueprints, and in Chapters 5 and 6, we identified problems with existing approaches to restoring order and building effective justice systems. Chapter 7 discussed the challenges associated with various approaches to accountability for past atrocities. And in Chapter 8, we examined the critical importance of thinking creatively about building rule of law cultures.

This chapter focuses on pragmatic and technical problems in post-conflict recovery and rule of law assistance efforts. These problems include poor to nonexistent overarching strategies for reconstruction, governance reform, and rule of law delivery; inadequate assessment of post-intervention needs and poor advance planning of rule of law and other programs; failure to scale resources to need; a focus on short-term outputs instead of sustainable results; poor coordination among rule of law service providers, donors, and other actors; insufficient involvement of local actors in designing and implementing rule of law reforms; a mismatch between the years and even decades required to build a functioning rule of law system and the short attention spans of interveners and donors; and inadequate understanding of local cultures and institutions.

The United Nations, the UN Secretary-General, the Organization on Security and Co-operation in Europe (OSCE), the European Union (EU), the United States, the international financial institutions, and other key actors have made considerable progress in recent years in identifying and starting

---

[3] Cf. S/2000/809, para. 20, *Report of the Panel on United Nations Peace Operations*, August 21, 2000 (hereinafter *Brahimi Report*) (noting that interveners must "work to divert the unfinished conflict . . . from the military to the political arena. . . ."), *available at* http://www.itcm.org/pdf/s_2000_809.pdf.

[4] Comments from the Department of State [on draft GAO Report at note 1 *supra*], March 16, 2001, *available at* http://www.gao.gov/new.items/d01354.pdf.

to address some of these problems, especially as they pertain to the technical aspects of peace implementation and rule of law delivery. But major hurdles remain to be crossed.

As emphasized in earlier chapters, rule of law assistance is part and parcel of the larger post-intervention rebuilding effort. Just as the larger effort will not succeed unless rule of law takes hold, so too will rule of law efforts fail if the larger effort to restore peace and foster democratic governance does not succeed. As Secretary-General Kofi Annan has observed, "[j]ustice, peace, and democracy are...mutually reinforcing imperatives."[5] Accordingly, this chapter examines several ways in which international actors can strengthen post-conflict reconstruction efforts in areas critical to fostering effective governments operating under the rule of law. In particular, the chapter focuses on three key themes: first, the critical importance of adequate *advance planning and coordination of efforts* among the multiple actors attempting to provide governance and rule of law aid; second, the necessity of *matching resources and commitment to the nature and extent of the problems* to be confronted; and, third – building on the discussion in Chapter 8 – the often neglected requirement of *involving local actors* constructively in the design and implementation of governance and rule of law reforms.

In thinking about these themes, it is important to bear in mind that the rule of law cannot be fostered in a vacuum. We argued earlier that building an effective justice system requires a synergistic approach. For the same reasons, the overall peace implementation effort must also be synergistic to be effective. Failure in efforts to restore security, promote economic opportunities, build effective governance institutions, or reconcile a deeply divided population will likely doom even the best designed and delivered rule of law programs.

We noted in earlier chapters that a synergistic approach is ends-based and strategic. In the context of the overall peace implementation effort, that means that a coherent, overarching strategy should guide post-intervention planning, funding priorities, and efforts to involve local actors. The strategy will necessarily vary from case to case, depending on the nature of the problems to be addressed. In Bosnia, for example, the need to overcome social fragmentation was the primary driver of the peace process and post-intervention peace implementation efforts; in Sierra Leone, the need to restore a secure environment proved the critical issue. But although each case differs, in all cases the political blueprint adopted at the outset should serve as the touchstone for all international actors in developing a coherent, overarching, agreed strategy for the post-intervention period.

---

[5] S/2004/616, Report of the Secretary-General, *The Rule of Law and Transitional Justice in Conflict and Post-Conflict Societies*, August 23, 2004, at 1.

We also argued earlier that a synergistic approach is adaptive; it builds on the cultural, human, and other resources already in place and adapts as conditions change. The political blueprint adopted at the outset of post-intervention rebuilding efforts almost inevitably reflects the social, cultural, political, and material dynamics in play on the ground to some extent, but it is often skewed by the political interests of the interveners and the need to placate the leaders of the principal warring factions. Moreover, even if the political blueprint is well designed initially, efforts to implement the blueprint must continually be adjusted and updated. As we have emphasized, post-intervention reconstruction efforts are not politically neutral. Funding decisions, institutional development, involvement of particular local partners and all other aspects of peace implementation necessarily favor some individuals and groups over others. Interveners must be flexible enough to adjust repeatedly to fast-changing local conditions when planning, funding, and working with local partners on implementing assistance programs generally and rule of law programs in particular.

Finally, we have argued that a synergistic approach is systemic. Interveners must appreciate how the work of different international actors influences the overall effort. Too often, international actors with different mandates and different interests duplicate or actively undermine each other's efforts. Just as the components of an effective judicial system must work in a complementary and mutually reinforcing way, so too should the various components of the overall peace effort work together for any of them to be effective. Thus, efforts to demobilize combatants, for example, must dovetail with efforts to jump-start the local economy and provide new jobs; similarly, building a new army requires simultaneous support for an effective defense ministry to provide civilian control over that army.

I. PLANNING AND COORDINATION

In recent years, there has been "an explosion of the number of actors involved in various aspects of conflict management.... "[6] In many cases, the result is "a veritable 'circus atmosphere' of UN agencies, international organizations, NGOs, and individual donor governments all engaged in the often uncoordinated monitoring of human rights, policing assistance, judicial rehabilitation, investigating war crimes, training police, and administering

---

[6] Bruce Jones, *The Challenges of Strategic Coordination*, in ENDING CIVIL WARS: THE IMPLEMENTATION OF PEACE AGREEMENTS (Stephen Stedman, Donald Rothchild, & Elizabeth Cousens, eds., 2002), at 88, 102. Jones notes that the proliferation stems from the creation of post-conflict units in multilateral and bilateral aid agencies, the creation of emergency response units in development and technical assistance agencies, and the growing number of NGOs involved in post-conflict reconstruction. Id., at 104.

prisons."[7] The problem repeats at the national level. In the United States, for example, "dozens" of agencies participate in post-conflict security, reconstruction, and rule of law efforts.[8] Duplication of effort, confusion, competition for resources, gaps in assistance, mixed messages, and lost time commonly follow. Worse, division among the international actors creates opportunities for spoilers to play different international actors off against each other, and even derail assistance efforts.[9]

These problems exist at all levels of peace implementation efforts, including those aimed at fostering the rule of law. Country studies conducted for a King's College review of peace operations "emphasise the lack of a coherent strategy for the development of rule-of-law institutions and insufficient planning for this, even when the mandate seemed clear."[10] As a result, recent years have witnessed recurring calls for better planning and coordination of peace implementation and rule of law promotion efforts. The U.S. General Accounting Office, for example, noted that thirty-two reports on peacekeeping operations in sixteen countries "came to similar conclusions about the need for comprehensive transition planning in complex emergency situations."[11] The *Brahimi Report* called for strengthening the UN's strategic planning and coordination capacity.[12] Similarly, the Final Report of the Bi-Partisan Commission on Post-Conflict Reconstruction identified strategic planning as a crucial "enabler" of post-conflict reconstruction success and urged the U.S. government to create its own standing comprehensive interagency planning process.[13] The Secretary-General's strategy for effective peacekeeping transitions, endorsed by the Security Council in February 2001, likewise makes planning and coordination a central goal, and the new UN Peacebuilding Commission represents an effort to put planning front and center in future peacebuilding missions.

Considerable progress has been made in responding to these calls for improved planning and coordination, along many fronts. But many

---

[7] The Stanley Foundation, *Post Conflict Justice: The Role of the International Community* 1997, at 7.

[8] Scott Feil, *Building Better Foundations: Security in Post Conflict Reconstruction*, 25 WASH. Q. 97, 101 (2002).

[9] *See* Jones, *supra* note 6, at 8.

[10] Conflict, Security and Development Group, King's College London, *A Review of Peace Operations: A Case for Change, Overall Introduction and Synthesis Report*, March 10, 2003, at 12 para. xx, *available at* http://ipi.sspp.kcl.ac.uk/rep002/index.html (hereinafter *Review of Peace Operations*).

[11] GAO Report, GAO-03–1071, *U.N. Peacekeeping: Transition Strategies for Post Conflict Countries Lack Results-Oriented Measures of Progress*, September 2003, at 8, *available at* http://www.gao.gov/new.items/d031071.pdf (hereafter *Transition Strategies*).

[12] *See Brahimi Report, supra* note 3, at 12.

[13] *Play to Win, Final Report of the Bi-Partisan Commission on Post-Conflict Reconstruction*, January 2003, at 8, *available at* http://www.ausa.org/PDFdocs/PCRFinalReport.pdf.

post-conflict peace implementation and rule of law promotion efforts remain fragmented and correspondingly ineffective.

The basic elements of effective planning are simple in theory and apply both to the larger peace implementation effort and to its component parts, including rule of law assistance. These elements include the following:

- At the outset, the principal interveners, working with local partners, should develop a shared assessment of needs, based on what is required to fulfill the political blueprint for transition.
- The common needs assessment should form the basis for an overarching strategy that will permit the multiplicity of international actors involved in the post-intervention phase to work together rather than at cross-purposes.
- The lead international actors should reach agreement on the key program activities needed to carry out the overall strategy and should agree on coordination mechanisms and a division of responsibilities that should be "planned by and cohere around sectors, themes and/or geographic areas... rather than on the basis of agency mandates solely."[14]
- To the extent possible, all key international and local stakeholders should be included or at least consulted in planning efforts as early and as fully as feasible. Planning must from the outset include strategies for building local capacity and fostering local ownership of post-intervention reconstruction efforts.
- The lead actors should set timetables for achieving critical objectives, with agreed interim benchmarks for reaching post-intervention goals. Progress should be systematically reviewed on a regular basis, and planning should then be adjusted as necessary.
- Steps should be taken to ensure that consistent, multiyear funding is available as needed to carry out various program objectives in a timely and appropriately sequenced fashion.

Although these principles of effective planning are simple to state, they are exceptionally difficult to carry out. We consider below some of the obstacles to effective planning and coordination, and possible improvements to international capabilities in this area.

A. Obstacles to Effective Planning
The obstacles to effective planning and coordination are many and varied. Some are avoidable and subject to control or at least mitigation through development of improved planning processes and institutions. Others are structural, inherent in the nature of the peacebuilding enterprise, and must be compensated for to the extent possible.

---

[14] *Report of the UNDG/ECHA Working Group on Transition Issues*, para. 43, February 2004.

The sheer proliferation of actors noted above, though it brings a wide variety of expertise and capabilities to the post-intervention reconstruction effort, complicates planning and coordination. Each of the relevant actors operates on the basis of its own mandate, interests, and funding sources,[15] rendering cooperation difficult. Disagreements over objectives and methods, bureaucratic inertia, political rivalries, and competition over turf exacerbate the problem. Even when the actors involved recognize the need for planning and coordination, political interests and competition, rather than comparative advantage, often determine which state or organization takes the lead on a given issue.

Peace operations continue to be organized hastily and on a largely ad hoc basis, in response to crises, making comprehensive advance planning difficult. Rule of law promotion efforts suffer in particular because, despite broad recognition of their importance, rule of law still often appears in mission planning almost as an afterthought.[16] The *Brahimi Report* recommended a doctrinal shift in the UN's approach to rule of law, urging commitment to and planning for a complete rule of law package. But despite some improvements in this area, pressing needs, most notably control of belligerents, tend to take priority over long-term needs such as rule of law reform.

In addition, building rule of law norms and institutions requires planning and coordination across different sectors of peace implementation operations. Security, administration of justice, human rights, economic development, and public administration are all interlinked, but different agencies and organizations tend to concentrate on one or the other task, without fully appreciating the extent to which progress in one area is conditioned on progress in another. Efforts to restructure the police and security services, for example, commonly outpace the longer-term task of reforming or rebuilding courts and prisons. In Haiti, for example, early successes in police retraining were undermined and eventually defeated by inadequate progress in judicial and governance reforms. Similarly, in East Timor, efforts to train and equip a new police service initially foundered because of overcrowded prisons, poorly equipped courts, and a shortage of judges and defense counsel.

Even when comprehensive mission planning is attempted, it must necessarily be context sensitive; each mission takes place in a different country at a different stage in that country's conflict cycle. Some international organizations and states now attempt to do "pre-post-conflict planning" – the World Bank, for example, utilizes "watching briefs" to pave the way for post-conflict planning – but interveners usually only begin to understand clearly what is needed and who is needed to do it once the mission has begun.[17]

---

[15] *Review of Peace Operations, supra* note 10, at 11.
[16] Id., at 12 para. xxi.
[17] Id., at 21 para. 27.

Thus, post-conflict intervention inevitably involves a "period of planning 'on the go' on the one hand, and regular and major revision of objectives on the other."[18]

Unfortunately, making these adjustments appropriately assumes that international actors can reliably determine the extent of progress toward meeting rule of law and other mission objectives. But most post-conflict assistance providers, including most rule of law service providers, lack objective measures to make such assessments. The UN transition strategy for peace implementation calls for "developing objectives, linked to the country conditions sought, and measures of progress toward achieving those conditions," an outgrowth of a General Assembly decision in 2000 to adopt results-based budgeting.[19] The objectives at issue include developing institutions that ensure the rule of law. But despite progress in this regard, "most measures are tasks and outputs rather than measures of underlying conditions in the country that the peace operation is to improve."[20] In East Timor, for example, the objective of increasing the ability of the national police to provide security centered on meeting a particular output – 2830 newly trained officers. But the objective was determined using "a standard European police-to-population ratio" and based on "outdated population estimates."[21] Moreover, it did not measure quality. Riots in the capital city forced the United Nations to revise its training procedures and increase the number of police sought by 500.[22] Similarly, in Sierra Leone, the reestablishment of courts was used as a measure of progress toward restoring the rule of law, without application of "any systematic measures or criteria, such as the ability of those filing suit to obtain satisfactory resolution of their cases within a reasonable period of time."[23]

Considerable progress in developing useful indicators has been made in recent years. In fact, as the World Bank notes, "there has been a virtual explosion of datasets measuring quality of institutions, governance and corruption."[24] World Bank researchers, for example, have developed a rule of law index that seeks to measure "perceptions of the incidence of both violent and non-violent crime, the effectiveness and predictability of the judiciary, and the enforceability of contracts," to assess "the success of a society in developing an environment in which fair and predictable rules form the

---

[18] Id.

[19] *Transition Strategies, supra* note 11, at 10.

[20] Id., at 30.

[21] Id., at 31.

[22] Id., at 31–32.

[23] Id., at 32.

[24] World Bank Group, *Governance Data: Web-Interactive Inventory of Datasets and Empirical Tools, available at* http://www.worldbank.org/wbi/governance/govdatasets/ (covering the period from 1996–2004).

basis for economic and social interactions."[25] But much remains to be done to develop, test, and put such indicators into practice in ongoing rule of law assistance efforts.

Planning efforts must also deal with the need to sequence and prioritize post-intervention reconstruction efforts based on urgent needs, while at the same time working in a synergistic way to make mutually reinforcing improvements. Until recently, post-intervention planning assumed an essentially linear movement from a stabilization phase to an institution building/transformation phase to a period of consolidation, with each phase having its own recovery priorities.[26] This view has come under increasing criticism, as some experts argue that "the dynamics of conflict are discontinuous and sequential approaches are far less effective than 'joined up' strategies that combine all policy tools in a coherent package of inducements and restraints."[27] In theory, the "joined up" approach is preferable and more consistent with the synergistic approach advocated in this book. As a practical matter, however, interveners will find it necessary to prioritize and sequence, given limits on resources, personnel, and local capacity. At the same time, decisions on sequencing and priorities must be made collectively and conform to an overall strategy, so that priorities will be chosen and implemented in ways that will render them mutually reinforcing; otherwise, progress on one front will be stymied (and resources wasted) when progress languishes on another front. When choices have to be made because of budget constraints, limited local absorptive capacity, or some other reason, priority should go to programs intended to advance the primary goals of the post-conflict blueprint, even if longer-term development needs must temporarily take second place. Reinsertion programs for ex-combatants, for example, may have to take priority over other employment projects. Certainly, achieving blueprint goals should take priority over the pet projects of particular donors.

Despite the various obstacles summarized above, the need for improved planning and coordination is widely recognized, and considerable progress is being made. There are now many different planning and coordination tools in use or under consideration. Which ones may prove helpful, or essential, depend on the interveners involved and on the conditions in the country

---

[25] *See* D. Kaufmann., A. Kraay, & M. Mastruzzi, World Bank, World Bank Policy Research Working Paper 3106, *Governance Matters III: Governance Indicators for 1996–2002*, 2003, at 4, *available at* http://www.worldbank.org/wbi/governance/pubs/govmatters2001.htm.

[26] For a useful list of priorities divided by phase, *see* Kevelitz et al., *Practical Guide to Multilateral Needs Assessments in Post-Conflict Situations*, August 2004, section 2.3, *available at* http://www.undp.org/documents/4937_-_PCNA_-PracticalGuide_to_Multilateral_Needs_Assessments_in_Post-Conflict_Situations.pdf.

[27] Robert Picciotto, Charles Alao, Eka Ikpe, Martin Kimani, & Roger Slade, *Striking a New Balance: Donor Policy Coherence and Development Cooperation in Difficult Environments*, January 13–14, 2005, at 6, *available at* http://www.oecd.org/dataoecd/31/62/34252747.pdf.

at issue. In general, the more difficult the implementation environment, the more important planning and coordination are (and the more difficult they are to do). Successful coordination usually requires both "a high degree of international commitment and a rough correspondence of interests of the major powers."[28] In Bosnia, for example, despite a relatively high degree of international commitment and various international coordinating mechanisms, implementation was "weakened by competing strategies among key implementing actors and contributing governments, these driven as much by bureaucratic and domestic considerations as by debate over the best way to consolidate peace."[29] Thus, even though the Dayton Accords assigned responsibility among different agencies for implementation of key tasks, and despite establishment of the Office of the High Representative to provide strategic and operational coordination, the absence of a common strategic vision among the principal interveners meant that coordination worked mostly at the margins.[30] Similarly, in Kosovo, there was considerable overlap and sometimes significant tension between UN and OSCE judicial and police reform efforts.

Unfortunately, there is no simple and agreed model for planning and coordination of peace implementation and rule of law promotion. Indeed, no single model is appropriate for all cases. For example, the use of the Kosovo operation as a template for planning the East Timor mission generated substantial criticism for neglecting the unique aspects of the latter and ignoring the wishes of the Timorese.[31] Options for planning and coordination range from friends groups to lead state coordination to integrated missions. Whichever model is chosen, the person or entity selected to lead must actually be given the resources and authority to enforce planning and coordination decisions,[32] a difficult task when states and local actors with different interests and priorities are involved.

B. Enhancing Interveners' Capacity for Planning and Coordination

Although there is now a broad consensus that the myriad states and international organizations engaged in post-conflict reconstruction and rule of law promotion should follow a coherent, agreed plan, there is little agreement on which actor should take the lead in organizing and implementing that plan. The obvious candidate is the United Nations, which by virtue of its

[28] Jones, *supra* note 6, at 90.
[29] Id., at 91 (quoting Elizabeth Cousens).
[30] Id.
[31] *Review of Peace Operations, supra* note 10, at 19 para. 16.
[32] *See* Stanley Foundation report, *Laying a Durable Foundation for Post-Conflict Societies,* June 2002, at 23, *available at* http://www.stanleyfoundation.org/reports/UNND02.pdf (coordination "means empowering the individual with the authority and resources to force the UN specialized agencies and others to rise above the demands of their respective bureaucratic interests") (hereinafter *Durable Foundation*).

broad representation carries a legitimacy and a reputation for impartiality that no other actor can match. The United Nations also "brings a range of capacities across the spectrum of post-conflict assistance that cannot be found elsewhere."[33] For these reasons, the United Nations does often play a lead planning and coordinating role. In some cases, however, UN missions lack the political support, personnel, funding, organization, and military capabilities necessary to play an effective lead role and must be backed by a lead state willing and able to supply what a particular UN mission lacks. In other cases, a lead actor, most notably the United States, takes the lead role itself, leaving the United Nations to play a supporting role. In still other cases, a coalition of international actors shares the planning and coordination functions. Whichever model is followed, there is substantial room for improvement, despite considerable progress in recent years.

The *Brahimi Report* emphasized the importance of improving the UN's strategic planning and coordination capacity. Among other things, it called for creation of a "professional system in the Secretariat for accumulating knowledge about conflict situations, distributing that knowledge efficiently to a wide user base, [and] generating policy analyses and formulating long-term strategies."[34] More importantly, the report called for treating peace-keeping as a core activity of the United Nations, with funding to come through the regular budget of the organization, which would provide for a predictable baseline budget and permit advance planning for "potential contingencies six months to a year down the road."[35] Further, the report called for the creation of Integrated Mission Task Forces (IMTFs), with staff seconded from throughout the UN system, "to plan new missions and help them reach full deployment...."[36] The report also called for a variety of structural adjustments and other reforms, such as new standby arrangements for military and civilian experts, new information technologies, and stronger merit-based hiring.

Some of these reforms have been implemented.[37] The United Nations has consolidated peacekeeping responsibilities in the Department of Peace-keeping Operations (DPKO), increased its staff to permit better planning, required planners to "identify objectives, tasks to be undertaken, resources required, expected timetables, and criteria for measuring success," begun using IMTFs to plan operations, and created a best practices unit in DPKO

---

[33] Id., at 22.

[34] *Brahimi Report, supra* note 3, at 12. The proposed system was to be created as the ECPS Information and Strategic Analysis Secretariat (EISAS). Id.

[35] Id., at 33.

[36] Id., at xiii, 34–37.

[37] For a review of progress on various *Brahimi Report* reforms, *see* William J. Durch, Victoria K. Holt, Caroline R. Earle, & Moira K. Shanahan, *The Brahimi Report and the Future of UN Peace Operations* 2003, at 18, *available at* http://www.stimson.org/fopo/pubs.cfm?ID=90.

to identify lessons learned from past operations and apply them to future operations.[38] The United Nations also established a small Criminal Law and Judicial Advisory Unit in the Department of Peacekeeping Operations to help create comprehensive rule of law transition strategies and created a Rule of Law Focal Point Network at UN headquarters to improve coordination and support for rule of law aspects of peace operations. In addition, the United Nations has increased its efforts to coordinate transition planning with other international organizations and participating states.[39] Although most of these reforms deal with planning and coordination in New York, some reforms focus on planning and coordination in the field. For example, the Secretary-General created the position of Deputy Special Representative of the Secretary-General to "ensure coordination of security and economic reform efforts" in the field.[40]

But many proposed reforms have not been implemented, or have achieved only "mixed results," and operational plans are not yet systematically reviewed and adjusted.[41] Thus, planning and coordination continue to be incomplete and sometimes ad hoc. The problem stems in part from the reluctance of some states, for a variety of domestic political reasons, to give the United Nations the resources necessary for comprehensive planning. In various ways, the Secretariat has sometimes been set up for failure, when it has been given ambitious mandates and inadequate support.[42] In part, the problem stems from the sheer multiplicity of actors involved in post-conflict transitions, each with their own mandates and priorities. And in part, the problem stems from the structure, organization, and nature of the United Nations itself, an organization that for many reasons still lacks "a real culture of planning."[43] Moreover, as a Stanley Foundation report put it,

Simply put, the United Nations is unable to capitalize on its coordinating potential because the UN system is not designed to coordinate well. There are countless structural constraints created by the decentralized nature of the UN system, including numerous component parts with overlapping mandates, separate funding sources and governing boards, and different national constituencies. By its very nature, the intergovernmental system is cumbersome and weighed down by inertia, leading to a culture of indecisiveness and resistance to reform.[44]

[38] *Transition Strategies, supra* note 11, at 11. At the same time, "the level of in-house resources and personnel dedicated to planning continues to be inadequate." *Review of Peace Operations, supra* note 10, at 18 para. 14.

[39] *Transition Strategies, supra* note 11, at 11.

[40] Id., at 17.

[41] Espen Eide, Anja Kaspersen, Randolph Kent, & Karen von Hippel, *Report on Integrated Missions: Practical Perspectives and Recommendations,* May 2005, at 21, *available at* http://pbpu.unlb.org/pbpu/library/Report%20on%20Integrated%20Missions%20May%202005%20Final.pdf (noting that IMTFs "have been used with mixed results thus far").

[42] *Durable Foundation, supra* note 32, at 30.

[43] Eide, *supra* note 41, at 20, *available at* http://pbpu.unlb.org/pbpu/library/Report%20on%20Integrated%20Missions%20May%202005%20Final.pdf.

[44] *Durable Foundation, supra* note 32, at 23.

In the field, the United Nations has experimented with various coordinating structures. In 1999, the General Assembly adopted Generic Guidelines for Strategic Frameworks to facilitate coordination and identify priorities among UN agencies and other actors involved in post-conflict reconstruction and aid work. The guidelines "outline criteria, process, and institutional arrangements for the elaboration and prioritisation of political, assistance and protection objectives including the advancement of human rights. . . . "[45] The guidelines direct the Special Representative of the Secretary-General (SRSG) and the UN Resident Coordinator to chair a set of coordinating bodies designed to bring together UN agencies, donor governments, other international organizations, NGOs, and national authorities to develop and work toward shared objectives and to "ensure that specific programmes and projects adhere to common objectives and priorities."[46]

The strategic framework was first applied in Afghanistan, but became principally a body for aid coordination given the conditions then present in that country.[47] A second strategic framework experiment was then attempted in Sierra Leone, but it fared no better. A year of effort "produced little more than a general statement of existing coordination problems and of the need for greater links between the political, development, and humanitarian coordination mechanisms."[48] This is not to say there were no coordination mechanisms operating. At one point there were no fewer than four "distinct UN coordination structures in Sierra Leone, none of which bore any formal or substantive relationship to the others."[49] UN experts came to conclude that the strategic framework was too "cumbersome" to "generate serious collaboration or flexible coordination" and did "little to actually empower lead coordinators such as the SRSG."[50]

Dissatisfaction with the strategic framework model, as applied in Sierra Leone, led the United Nations to move to the integrated mission model. An early version of the model was used first in the UN Mission in Kosovo (UNMIK), deployed in May 1999.[51] In Kosovo, the United Nations sought to avoid the coordination problems experienced in Bosnia. The challenge was substantial. Departing Serb forces left the province in an administrative and security vacuum and forced the interveners to assume all aspects of public administration. The United Nations had little advance notice of the primary role it was eventually to play. It was not until Security Council Resolution 1244 assigned NATO the lead on military matters, leaving all

[45] *Generic Guidelines for a Strategic Framework Approach for Response to and Recovery from Crisis*, para. 4, *available at* http://coe-dmha.org/PKO/Philippines2003/plenbrfs/day1/unstrat.pdf.
[46] Id., at para. 19.
[47] Jones, *supra* note 6, at 106.
[48] Id., at 107.
[49] Id.
[50] Id.
[51] Id.

civilian responsibilities for the United Nations, with assistance from the OSCE and the European Union, that the scope of the UN's responsibilities became clear.[52] To achieve a unified international effort, it was essential to devise mechanisms to coordinate the work of these major international organizations, while leaving each sufficient flexibility to carry out its assignments.[53]

To meet the challenge, the United Nations established an integrated mission, in which the SRSG headed a joint structure in which each of the principal organizations (the UN, the EU, the OSCE, and UNHCR) took primary responsibility for one pillar: UNHCR took pillar I (humanitarian assistance); the UN took pillar II (civil administration, police, and justice); OSCE took pillar III (institution-building, democratization, human rights, and rule of law); and the EU took pillar IV (reconstruction). This division of responsibility had more to do with international politics than with the comparative advantage of each organization,[54] and encountered some problems in application, but nonetheless constituted an improvement over past practice. Each organization assigned its mission head to serve as a deputy SRSG, thus permitting the SRSG to "manage the overall mission structure" and, in theory, "to ensure policy coherence and an effective division of labor.... "[55] Inevitably, the tasks involved in each pillar overlapped. Thus, for example, there could be no neat division between the UN's law and order responsibilities and NATO's security role.[56] As a result, the pillar structure "proved to be unwieldy when tackling cross-cutting issues,"[57] though some progress was made in sorting out responsibilities through interpillar negotiations as time passed.[58] The effectiveness of this structure, and subordinate coordinating entities established later, varied depending on the performance of the senior officials from each organization and their willingness to respond to the coordination efforts of the SRSG and his deputy.[59] Moreover, the failure of the interested states to reach agreement on an end-state for Kosovo exacerbated policy differences among the interveners.[60] Overall, the integrated mission structure demonstrated "a fairly good ability to coordinate technical

---

[52] At the outset, the general assumption was that the OSCE would take the lead role, in part because of dissatisfaction on the part of key states over the UN's performance in Bosnia. *See* Kings College, London, *A Review of Peace Operations: A Case for Change, Kosovo Report*, paras. 17 & 21, *available at* http://ipi.sspp.kcl.ac.uk/rep005/index.htm (hereinafter *Kosovo Report*). It was only after the OSCE was ruled out by Russia, and the EU by the United States, that the United Nations was assigned primary responsibility. Id. para. 22.

[53] Id.

[54] Jones, *supra* note 6, at 108.

[55] Id., at 109.

[56] Id.; *see also Kosovo Report, supra* note 52.

[57] *Kosovo Report, supra* note 52, para. 26.

[58] Jones, *supra* note 6, at 109.

[59] Id., at 110.

[60] Id.

policy differences between the implementing organizations, but a far more constrained capacity to coordinate overall strategic questions."[61]

A similar structure was utilized in East Timor. As in Sierra Leone, UN planning initially was premised on an unrealistic assumption, that a vote for autonomy would not trigger large-scale violence.[62] The Security Council did not even authorize planning for a transitional administration until an Australian-led coalition of the willing organized to restore order.[63] As a result, the United Nations had only a few weeks to plan for conditions much worse than originally anticipated. Planning was further hampered by disagreements between the UN's Department of Peacekeeping Operations and its Department of Political Affairs and by uncertainty over whether the mission was to be peacekeeping or peacebuilding, problems that plagued the mission throughout its existence.[64]

Formally, the structure for planning and coordination on the ground resembled that adopted in Kosovo. It consisted of four pillars: (1) civil administration, (2) economy and infrastructure, (3) humanitarian, and (4) peacekeeping. But the effort to transplant the Kosovo model was not fully successful. Key aspects of the pillars' various goals were not adequately defined. It was unclear, for example, whether the civil administration pillar was to form the nucleus of an East Timorese government. Moreover, key differences between East Timor and Kosovo were overlooked; for example, the mission did not plan initially for a customs service, because unlike East Timor, Kosovo, as a nonsovereign entity, did not need one.[65] Perhaps most important, the structure did not provide adequately for a role for East Timorese in transition planning and implementation.

Problems in planning and coordination clearly impeded efforts to restore the rule of law in East Timor. "Pre-mission planning on justice issues was minimal at best."[66] No comprehensive assessment of the legal system's needs was undertaken. Even after UNTAET became fully operational and the immediate humanitarian crisis receded, UNTAET did not generate a comprehensive strategy for legal reform. The repercussions were numerous and lasting. For example, UNTAET moved quickly to put in place new police and judges but failed to move forward simultaneously with the creation of new prisons and courts, prerequisites for the effective functioning of the police and judges. At times, the lack of a comprehensive strategy, and the weakness of coordination, created conflicts in implementation efforts. For

---

[61] Id., at 110–111.
[62] See Kings College, London, *A Review of Peace Operations: A Case for Change, East Timor Report*, para. 11, *available at* http://ipi.sspp.kcl.ac.uk/rep006/s01.html.
[63] Id., at para. 18.
[64] Id., at para. 21.
[65] Id., at para. 28.
[66] Id., at para. 222.

example, World Bank efforts to help villagers form local governing councils operating under traditional law clashed with UNTAET efforts to strengthen central government authority and apply consistent regulations throughout the country.[67]

Thus, although the integrated mission structure in East Timor helped avoid some of the planning and coordination problems that have plagued previous missions, many such problems continued to obstruct achievement of UNTAET's goals. The fault lies less in the planning and coordinating structure itself (and the United Nations has continued to refine the integrated mission concept in subsequent missions) than in a host of other considerations. These include the reluctance of Security Council members and other key states to plan for the kind of mission ultimately needed, in part for fear of offending Indonesia; bureaucratic rivalries within the UN system and between the United Nations and other international organizations; a lack of resources; the variable quality of the personnel involved, particularly those with key operational responsibilities; and insufficient understanding of the politics and culture of East Timor itself. Such problems can at best be mitigated but not solved by planning and coordination mechanisms, however well designed.

In March 2005, the UN Secretary-General offered an ambitious proposal to plug what he called the "gaping hole in the United Nations institutional machinery" that precluded it from effectively addressing "the challenge of helping countries with the transition from war to lasting peace."[68] Modifying an earlier proposal offered by the High Level Panel on Threats, Challenges and Change, the Secretary-General urged UN member states to create an intergovernmental Peacebuilding Commission and a Peacebuilding Support Office with a dedicated rule of law unit within the UN Secretariat. The proposal is designed to address many of the specific problems noted above. As the Secretary-General put it,

A Peacebuilding Commission could...improve United Nations planning for sustained recovery...; help to ensure predictable financing for early recovery activities, in part by providing an overview of assessed, voluntary and standing funding mechanisms; improve the coordination of the many post-conflict activities of the United Nations funds, programmes and agencies; provide a forum in which the United Nations, major bilateral donors, troop contributors, relevant regional actors and organizations, the international financial institutions and the national or transitional Government of the country concerned can share information about their respective post-conflict recovery strategies, in the interests of greater coherence; periodically review progress towards medium-term recovery goals; and extend the period of political attention to post-conflict recovery.[69]

---

[67] *Transition Strategies*, *supra* note 11, at 29.
[68] *In Larger Freedom: Towards Development, Security, and Human Rights for All*, *Report of the Secretary-General*, UN Doc. A/59/2005, para. 114, March 21, 2005, *available at* http://www.globalpolicy.org/reform/initiatives/annan/2005/followupreport.pdf.
[69] Id., at para. 115.

An effective peacebuilding commission would substantially improve existing efforts to set priorities, mobilize resources, and coordinate post-conflict planning and implementation. It would provide strategic-level planning and coordination in much the same way that integrated missions are to provide field-level planning and coordination. Such a commission would, at least in theory, have the power and resources to force coherence in post-conflict planning and to ensure that resources are matched to needs in a timely and adequate fashion. The commission would "support – and not attempt to replace – effective country-level planning."[70]

But it is not at all clear that the Peacebuilding Commission as created by the Security Council and the General Assembly in December 2005 can achieve the objectives set for it. The proposed commission was established as an intergovernmental advisory body, with a core membership of thirty-one states, including key Security Council members, donors, troop contributors, and others. When addressing country-specific conflicts, the affected country, its neighbors, and relevant donors and troop contributing countries would be invited to participate as well. The commission is therefore likely to be large, divided by internal politics, and cumbersome in operation.

Moreover, the commission can only offer advice to the Security Council and others; it is not itself a decision-making body. Not only does it lack authority over its members or other states, it "has no executive management responsibility to assure the adherence of the multitude of UN agencies, international institutions, bilateral agencies, national and local agencies, and civil society organizations to an agreed-upon coherent and effective post-conflict plan."[71] Thus, its influence will be determined by the weight powerful states, international organizations, relief agencies, and others choose to place on its advice. Furthermore, the quality of that advice may itself be limited by the UN's reluctance to provide appropriate staff support. The Secretary-General requested twenty-one new positions to staff the new commission, a number barely adequate to "fulfil[l] the PBC's basic secretarial and monitoring needs, let alone provide training to field staff, rigorous analysis of peace-building trends and lessons learned . . . and much-needed substantive and logistical support to field operations."[72] But the request was turned down on budgetary grounds; instead, the Secretariat is supposed to support the new commission from existing Secretariat staff.[73]

[70] A/59/2005/Add. 2, *Addendum, In Larger Freedom, supra* note 68, para. 6.

[71] Katherine Andrews, *New UN Peacebuilding Commission Requires Resources and Authority to be Effective, available at* http://www.refugeesinternational.org/content/article/detail/7634/.

[72] *See* Richard Ponzio, *The Creation and Functioning of the UN Peacebuilding Commission,* November 2005, at 6, *available at* http://www.saferworld.org.uk/publications/Peace%20Builidng%20rep%20Nov05.pdf.

[73] *See UN OKs New Peacebuilding Commission,* Associated Press, December 20, 2005, *available at* http://www.globalpolicy.org/reform/topics/pbc/2005/1220oks.htm.

Further, the Peacebuilding Fund, created along with the commission and intended to finance post-conflict reconstruction, depends entirely on voluntary contributions. The high-level panel recommended a fund "at the level of at least $250 million that can be used to finance the recurrent expenditures of a nascent Government, as well as critical agency programmes in the areas of rehabilitation and reintegration."[74] Even this level of funding would be "woefully inadequate,"[75] and it is not clear states will provide funding even at this level. Although a well-designed and supported Peacebuilding Commission might do much to improve intergovernmental planning and coordination, the Peacebuilding Commission as formed may do relatively little beyond serve as a forum for discussion.

Just as a strong coordinating and planning mechanism is needed at the international level, similar mechanisms are needed at the national level to improve post-conflict response capabilities. The unfortunate U.S. experience in Somalia, in which poor planning contributed substantially to the collapse of the entire post-intervention effort, led the Clinton Administration in 1993 to develop the "first-ever inter-agency political-military plan" for the subsequent intervention in Haiti.[76] The relative (though short-lived) success of that effort led the Clinton Administration in 1997 to promulgate Presidential Decision Directive 56 (PDD 56).[77] PDD 56 made planning for all aspects of "complex contingency operations" a central feature of U.S. efforts to cope with and respond effectively to the rising demand for U.S. involvement in humanitarian interventions and peace operations generally. PDD 56 required preparation of a detailed political–military plan intended to ensure coordination among different U.S. agencies, and with international organizations and other actors, in responding to complex emergencies, and to ensure a match between mission mandates and resources.

The Bush Administration, skeptical about Clinton-era interventions, decided to abandon the PDD 56 process.[78] In January 2003, shortly before the Iraq war, the Administration put the Defense Department in charge of postwar reconstruction planning, assigning it a responsibility that has traditionally rested with (and would later return to) the State Department.[79] Partly as a result of this decision, and its timing, the United States did not accurately anticipate or plan for the security problems it actually encountered

---

[74] *See High-Level Panel on Threats, Challenges and Change: A More Secure World: Our Shared Responsibility* (2004), at 62, *available at* http://www.un.org/secureworld/.

[75] Ponzio, *supra* note 72, at 7.

[76] *Final Report, supra* note 13, at 10.

[77] Id.

[78] Council on Foreign Relations Report, *In the Wake of War: Improving U.S. Post-Conflict Capabilities,* July 2005, at 9, *available at* http://www.cfr.org/publication/8438/in_the_wake_of_war.html.

[79] Id., at 9–10.

in Iraq. Pre-war warnings about the difficulty of rebuilding Iraq were largely ignored.[80] U.S. officials later acknowledged that they had not foreseen either the extent of the lawlessness that plagued postwar Iraq or the extent to which Iraq's infrastructure had deteriorated.[81] Former U.S. lieutenant general Jay Garner, the man initially tasked with leading the reconstruction effort, admitted to Congress that his was "an ad hoc operation, glued together over about four or five weeks' time," and that his team "didn't really have enough time to plan."[82]

In fact, the United States did engage in significant prewar planning for Iraq. In April 2002, the State Department launched an extensive study of key issues likely to arise in the aftermath of an Iraq war. The study, titled the Future of Iraq Project, pulled together a large and diverse team of experts into seventeen working groups to study issues ranging from transitional justice to security to reorganizing the economy.[83] The transitional justice working group explicitly warned of postwar chaos and the potential release of thousands of criminals held in Iraqi jails and noted that "[t]he period immediately after regime change might offer these criminals the opportunity to engage in acts of killing, plunder, and looting."[84] The report went on to urge that the United States should "organize military patrols by coalition forces in all major cities to prevent lawlessness, especially against vital utilities and key government facilities."[85] Similarly, the economy and infrastructure working group recognized the extent of the investment that would be needed to repair Iraq's infrastructure.[86]

The project eventually produced thirteen volumes of reports and supporting documents. But officials at the Pentagon, which assumed the primary role in postwar planning, held a different vision of postwar Iraq, and largely ignored the State Department's work.[87] Indeed, General Garner's Pentagon-based Office of Reconstruction and Humanitarian Assistance (ORHA), which was not established until January 20, 2003, did not even learn of

---

[80] Warren Strobel & John Walcott, *Post-war Planning Non-existent, available at* http://www.realcities.com/mld/krwashington/9927782.htm.

[81] One U.S. military official observed with respect to early security efforts in Iraq, "[w]e're making it up with both hands," and added, "[t]his isn't the operational climate we expected. We never expected such widespread looting, or such a general collapse of authority." Thomas E. Ricks, *U.S. Alters Tactics in Baghdad Occupation; Less Threatening Posture Foreseen,* THE WASHINGTON POST, May 25, 2003, at A1.

[82] Eric Schmitt & David Sanger, *Aftereffects: Reconstruction Policy; Looting Disrupts Detailed U.S. Plan To Restore Iraq,* THE NEW YORK TIMES, May 19, 2003, at A1.

[83] Eric Schmitt & Joel Brinkley, *The Struggle for Iraq: Planning,* THE NEW YORK TIMES, October 19, 2003, at A1.

[84] Id.

[85] Id.

[86] Id.

[87] David Rieff, *Blueprint for a Mess,* THE NEW YORK TIMES MAGAZINE, November 2, 2003, at 28.

the State Department reports until the following month, less than a month before the war began.[88]

Even then, the United States planned for the wrong contingencies. U.S. forces prepared for several problems that largely did not occur, including "numerous fires in the oil fields, a massive humanitarian crisis, widespread revenge attacks...and threats from Iraq's neighbors."[89] The Pentagon hoped that Iraqi police would be able to maintain some order and that Iraqi soldiers would assist in reconstruction.[90] The Pentagon simply did not anticipate the wholesale collapse of the Iraqi military and police (and the resultant security vacuum that created), or the extent of damage to Iraq's infrastructure, and as a result U.S. forces on the ground lacked the mandate, training, equipment, forces, and operational plans for dealing adequately with the looting and general lawlessness.

To improve its planning and response capacity, the United States Department of State created the Office of the Coordinator for Reconstruction and Stabilization in July 2004. This new office is charged with planning and leading the U.S. civilian response to post-conflict situations and with coordinating U.S. participation in multilateral operations. The office is working to develop a framework for stabilization and reconstruction planning in an attempt to ensure that planners set realistic post-conflict goals and that the resources needed to achieve them are made available.[91]

The new State Department office marks an important advance in U.S. efforts to plan and coordinate post-conflict efforts. At the outset, as pointed out by a task force chaired by former U.S. national security advisors Samuel Berger and Brent Scowcroft, the new office lacked the funding, staff support, and institutional clout to play the role of lead interagency actor.[92] The task force recommended that the State Department coordinator be raised to the undersecretary of state level, with the responsibility to oversee civilian post-conflict efforts, and that USAID be given primary responsibility for daily operations, with adequate funding for both agencies. The task force also recommended creation of a new National Security Council directorate to coordinate the roles of the military and civilian agencies.

Instead, in December 2005, President Bush issued National Security Presidential Directive 44 (NSPD 44), which sets out a new framework for managing U.S. government interagency efforts on post-conflict reconstruction and stabilization efforts. NSPD 44 tasks the Secretary of State with primary

---

[88] *See* Schmitt & Brinkley, *supra* note 83.

[89] *See* Eric Schmitt & Joel Brinkley, *State Department Study Foresaw Trouble Now Plaguing Iraq*, THE NEW YORK TIMES, October 19, 2003.

[90] Schmitt & Sanger, *supra* note 82.

[91] Stephen Krasner & Carlos Pascual, *Addressing State Failure*, 84 FOREIGN AFFAIRS 153, 161 (2005).

[92] *See* Report of an Independent Task Force, *In the Wake of War: Improving U.S. Post-Conflict Capabilities*, (2005), at 19, *available at* http://www.cfr.org/content/publications/attachments/Post-Conflict_Capabilities_final.pdf.

responsibility for planning and coordinating U.S. post-conflict reconstruction efforts and for resolving interagency "policy, program, and funding disputes."[93] Moreover, the president's 2006 budget requests $100 million for a Conflict Response Fund and funding to strengthen the Office of the Coordinator for Reconstruction and Stabilization. This "first phase of funding focuses on building core leadership, coordination and response capabilities and providing baseline funding to support rapid field deployments essential to creating positive dynamics on the ground."[94] Thus, on paper at least, the Bush Administration has put in place a system that appears well suited to planning and coordinating future U.S. post-conflict reconstruction efforts.

Whether this approach will live up to its promise remains to be seen. Ideally, State's new role, coupled with the recognition in Defense Department Directive 3000.05 that "[s]tability operations are a core U.S. military mission...[to] be given priority comparable to combat operations" should lead to a greatly strengthened U.S. military–civilian response to post-conflict reconstruction needs.[95] But there is a risk that most of the necessary resources and responsibility will flow to the Defense Department, despite State's central role. Moreover, it is unclear, in a time of budget stress, whether the Office of the Coordinator for Reconstruction and Stabilization will be given sufficient staff or resources to handle the wide range of planning and implementation responsibilities placed on it. But properly supported, the NSPD 44 framework should substantially strengthen U.S. post-conflict planning and implementation capabilities.

II. RESOURCES AND COMMITMENT

It is a truism that peace implementation efforts, of which rule of law reform is a part, work only when the resources and commitment of the interveners are adequate to the challenge posed by conditions in the affected state. Military interventions of the sort considered in this book take place principally in failed or failing states. Thus, although the range of difficulty presented by each case differs widely, all demand substantial commitments of time, money, and personnel.

A. Half Measures Are Often Worse Than None at All

Halfhearted interventions are almost certain to be wasteful and ineffective. As the *Brahimi Report* observed, "Member States must not be led to believe that they are doing something useful for countries in trouble when – by

---

93 NSPD 44, *available at* http://www.fas.org/irp/offdocs/nspd/nspd-44.html.
94 Office of the Coordinator for Reconstruction and Stabilization, *Fact Sheet, available at* http://www.state.gov/s/crs/rls/43327.htm.
95 *See* Directive 3000.05, *available at* http://www.dtic.mil/shs/directives/corres/pdf/d300005-112805/d300005p.pdf.

under-resourcing missions – they are more likely agreeing to a waste of human resources, time and money."[96] Yet time and again, interveners – whether acting through the United Nations, a regional or subregional organization, or ad hoc coalitions of the willing – underestimate the challenges of restoring stable governance and the rule of law, refuse to commit the resources that might foster a successful transition, and exit before reforms have had a chance to take hold. Interveners have been driven out of Somalia, held hostage in Sierra Leone, sidelined in Afghanistan, and attacked in Iraq in substantial part because of a refusal to match resources to the magnitude of the tasks at hand. Even in relatively successful cases, such as East Timor, reforms are often superficial and interveners often withdraw "without having built adequate local capacity."[97] Thus, even though great sums have been spent on post-conflict reconstruction and rule of law assistance, much of it has not borne fruit.

The reasons for failing to devote adequate time and resources vary from case to case. In some cases, pressure to intervene, driven by the "CNN effect," may prompt states to vote for or participate in operations to which they are not fully committed. In such cases, as in Somalia, unexpected casualties or mounting costs can easily reverse domestic political calculations and generate pressure for a premature withdrawal. In other cases, unduly optimistic planning assumptions may shatter against hard realities. In Iraq, for example, the United States sharply underestimated the number of troops and level of commitment required to stabilize the country and establish a rule of law-based government. In still other cases, fostering good governance and inculcating the rule of law is simply not a priority; in Afghanistan, for example, the United States and its allies focused at least initially on pursuing al-Qaeda and Taliban remnants, shortchanging post-intervention reconstruction and reform.

In a nutshell, the failure to match resources and commitment to the problems posed stems from an imbalance between interveners' perceived interests and the magnitude of the problems they confront. A recent study of sixteen efforts to implement peace agreements following civil wars confirms that "the most important variable" in determining whether countries will provide the requisite resources and troops "is whether assisting the affected country is seen as vital to the national interests of a major or regional power," otherwise "the resources and commitment necessary for coercive strategies to succeed will not be forthcoming."[98] The study concludes that in difficult

---

[96] *Brahimi Report, supra* note 3, para. 59.

[97] Jarat Chopra, *The UN's Kingdom of East Timor,* SURVIVAL, Autumn 2000, at 31.

[98] Stephen Stedman, IPA Policy Paper Series on Peace Implementation, *Implementing Peace Agreements in Civil Wars: Lessons and Recommendations for Policymakers,* May 2001, at 2, *available at* http://www.ipacademy.org/PDF_Reports/Pdf_Report_Implementing.pdf. *See also* U.S. General Accounting Office, Letter from Joseph Christoff to Henry Hyde,

environments, characterized among other things by contending multiple parties, the presence of spoilers, the existence of valuable natural resources that can fuel conflict, and hostile neighbors, great or regional power interest should be treated as a "hard constraint."[99] In its absence, international and regional organizations ordinarily should not attempt peace implementation missions and, by extension, major rule of law reform efforts. The *Brahimi Report* makes a similar point. It notes that the complexity of the environment varies considerably, depending on the sources of conflict, the "number of local parties and the divergence of their goals," the "level of casualties," the attitude of local authorities and neighboring states, and similar factors, and concludes: "In less forgiving, more dangerous environments... United Nations missions put not only their own people but peace itself at risk unless they perform their tasks with the competence and efficiency that the situation requires and have serious great power backing."[100]

It does not follow that the Somalias of the world should be ignored because no great power perceives its national interests to be at stake. Lack of great power interest can be at least partially compensated for by securing a robust collective mandate and advance commitments of key states to support it. Problems arise principally when the Security Council or a regional organization directs a mission to assume comprehensive nation-building responsibilities, including rule of law reform, without providing the mission the troops, resources, or political backing necessary to fulfill those responsibilities. When that happens, the UN or regional organization is likely to flounder or worse.

To some extent, the Secretary-General has already acted on the *Brahimi Report's* suggestion that the "Secretariat must tell the Security Council what it needs to know, not what it wants to hear...."[101] Thus, the Secretary-General resisted efforts to deploy a UN peacekeeping operation in Afghanistan in 2001 as too dangerous and successfully urged robust mandates for UN peacekeeping operations in Liberia and in the Democratic Republic of Congo in 2003.[102] More generally, the Secretary-General has articulated a strategy intended to permit effective peacekeeping and to match resources to need, highlighting the need for sustained political support and appropriate mandates, among other things.[103] The Security Council has indicated its support for that strategy, though it continues to decide "on a

May 24, 2002 (comparing the relative success of NATO-led deployments in the Balkans with failed UN-led missions in Somalia and Bosnia), *available at* http://www.gao.gov/new.items/d02707r.pdf.

[99] Stedman, *supra* note 98, at 6.

[100] *Brahimi Report*, *supra* note 3, para. 25.

[101] Id., at para. 64d.

[102] *See* Durch et al., *supra* note 37.

[103] *See* S/2001/138, Letter dated February 12, 2001 from the Secretary-General addressed to the President of the Security Council, February 14, 2001.

case-by-case basis whether to authorize the peacekeepers and resources required to implement it."[104]

Efforts to build effective rule of law institutions (and governance institutions generally) are particularly vulnerable to fluctuations in commitment and resources, because such "activities normally take considerably longer than the average peacekeeping operation."[105] Below some minimum threshold of resources and commitment, a threshold determined by the difficulty of the environment, peace implementation and rule of law efforts will be wasted. Above that threshold, such efforts may have a positive impact, though they will always be vulnerable to problems of design and implementation, and to exogenous factors outside the control of interveners, ranging from natural disasters to spillover effects from nearby conflicts.[106]

B. Finding Funds

Adequate resources are plainly crucial to rule of law promotion and to peace implementation generally. As a participant in a conference on post-conflict reconstruction has observed, "[i]f you don't identify resources, you'll just end up with a checklist."[107] Overall, international donors "pledged over sixty billion dollars in aid to assist the recovery of three dozen war-torn countries" during the 1990s.[108] Although rule of law assistance was only a small part of that total, the success of rule of law promotion efforts is bound up in the success of overall reconstruction efforts. But despite the magnitude of the total aid pledged, often relatively little actually reaches those the funds are ostensibly intended to help.

In all cases, of course, money and interest are limited. Both tend to decline as time passes and new crises emerge to compete for attention and resources. Thus, "while dramatic conflict and emergency will typically mobilize resources and interest from the international community, once a crisis fades from the political radar screen, the international community tends to walk away prematurely."[109] Rapidly waning international interest creates a mismatch between the time and resources needed for an effective transition and the time and resources outside states will commit. Creating conditions for sustainable peace, and by extension, a viable rule of law system, invariably takes longer and costs more than interveners expect.[110]

---

[104] *Transition Strategies, supra* note 11, at 2.

[105] *In Larger Freedom, addendum, supra* note 68, para. 14.

[106] *Cf.* Stedman, *supra* note 98, at 8 (noting the vulnerability of peace implementation efforts generally to "extraneous factors" such as business cycles, famine, and the like).

[107] *Durable Foundation, supra* note 32, at 28.

[108] Stewart Patrick, *The Check Is in the Mail: Improving the Delivery and Coordination of Post-Conflict Assistance* (1998), *available at* http://www.cic.nyu.edu/archive/pdf/the_check_is_in_the_mail.pdf.

[109] *Durable Foundation, supra* note 32, at 7.

[110] *Transition Strategies, supra* note 11, at 27.

The present system of cobbling together resources ad hoc is clearly unsatisfactory and widely recognized as such. Although the process followed varies from case to case, funding efforts often begin with preliminary discussions among a core group of donors, UN and other international organization officials, and national authorities of the affected state. Thereafter, an international donor conference is held, and agreement is reached on the mandate and composition of an in-country needs assessment mission. The mission helps define the post-conflict reconstruction agenda by identifying the country's needs and their magnitude; in some cases, a transitional results matrix is produced, specifying in some detail which projects must be accomplished within given time frames. Pledging conferences often follow, to enlist additional donors and attempt to match funding to assessed needs. Various financing structures, such as multidonor trust funds, may be employed to organize financial assistance efforts in a coherent way.

But the process rarely goes smoothly. Post-conflict needs assessments and joint assessment missions are sometimes fragmented, with different components using different assessment tools. Often, states make financial pledges at donor conferences and then fail to follow through.[111] Even when donors do follow through, the amounts pledged are frequently inadequate, and there is often a substantial delay between pledges and delivery.[112] Moreover, of the amounts allocated for post-conflict missions, only a small portion may actually reach the affected population. In East Timor, for example,

> Of the UN Transitional Administration's annual budget of over $500 million, around one-tenth actually reached the East Timorese. At one point, $27 million was spent annually on bottled water for the international staff – approximately half the budget of the embryonic Timorese government.... [113]

Similarly, in Iraq, only a small percentage of aid allocated has actually been disbursed. At a fall 2003 conference in Madrid, donor governments pledged some $32 billion in reconstruction assistance. The United States pledged $18.4 billion for the Iraq Relief and Reconstruction Fund, which Congress approved in November 2003. More than six months later, less than $400 million of the U.S. allocated funds had actually been disbursed, with more money "spent on administration than all projects related to education, human rights, democracy and governance."[114] As of April 2005, the United States had

---

[111] *See Durable Foundation, supra* note 32, at 29.
[112] United Nations Development Programme, UNDP Background Paper for Working Group Discussions, May 5–7, 2004, at 6, *available at* http://unpan1.un.org/intradoc/groups/public/documents/UNTC/UNPAN016465.pdf.
[113] Simon Chesterman, You, The People: The United Nations, Transitional Administration, and State-Building 183 (2004).
[114] Rajiv Chadrasekaran, *U.S. Funds for Iraq Are Largely Unspent*, The Washington Post, July 4, 2004, at A1.

delivered only about one-fourth of the aid it had allocated, and other states only about 10 percent of the amounts they had pledged.

The reasons for the often wide gap between aid pledged and aid delivered are many and varied. Growing international involvement in complex emergencies comes at a time when resources are relatively scarce. As of July 2005, the United Nations had eleven ongoing "political and peacebuilding" missions and seventeen peacekeeping operations;[115] both types of operations are carried out mostly in impoverished states, in which all manner of post-conflict assistance is required. The demand for post-conflict peacebuilding resources is therefore high, even as international economic conditions have led many states to reduce their outlays.

Further, the plethora of states, international organizations, NGOs, and other actors involved in assistance decisions tends to disperse responsibility and create free-rider incentives. Because interventions of the sort considered in this book usually take place in areas of marginal strategic interest, donors often have only modest incentives to assist, and those incentives dwindle sharply when the burden can be shifted to other actors, and even more so when the affected state falls out of the headlines. Even when interventions engage the strategic interests of important states, as in Iraq or Afghanistan, political differences among potential donors may impede efforts to mobilize substantial resources. In Iraq, for example, many European states have cooperated only grudgingly with U.S. reconstruction efforts, given their opposition to military intervention in the first place.

In addition, post-intervention states seldom have the institutional capacity to absorb the relatively large amounts of aid that typically flow at the outset of reconstruction efforts. As Stewart Patrick notes,

On the demand side, states recovering from war often lack both the absorptive capacity needed to manage considerable sums of money emanating from diverse foreign sources for multiple purposes and the administrative structures required to design and implement comprehensive plans for reconstruction.[116]

To complicate matters, donors invariably have their own priorities and agendas. It is understandable that donors wish to control how their funds are spent. In practice, however, this means that donors "design aid packages to reflect their own political and pecuniary interests – or the interests of their national service providers."[117] As a result, a variety of distortions and inefficiencies appear in aid policies. Countries of strategic interest, or with close ties to powerful states, receive a disproportionately large share of donor attention. Kosovo gets more than Somalia, and Iraq more than Afghanistan. Donors tend to prefer high-visibility projects, which may take years to plan

---

[115] See UN Factsheet, available at http://www.un.org/peace/reports/peace_operations/.
[116] Patrick, supra note 108.
[117] Id.

and put in place, shortchanging less glamorous but more urgent quick-impact projects. Moreover, donors may be reluctant to provide aid to programs, such as security sector reform, that carry significant future political risks or past political taint, however important such aid might be.[118] For example, despite UN appeals, "most donors declined to support a new civilian police in El Salvador,"[119] notwithstanding the critical importance of such aid to larger rule of law reform efforts and to peace implementation overall. Some NGOs are complicit in the misallocation of donor resources, spending much of their time "raising funds from local donor missions and UN agencies" rather than providing services.[120]

Donors' desire to control the uses to which their aid is put, though in substantial part self-interested, also reflects an understandable desire for accountability and transparency in recipients' expenditures. From the donors' standpoint, much of the aid that reaches recipients is wasted, because of incompetence, corruption, mismanagement, inadequate legal frameworks, poor infrastructure, and limited absorptive capacity.[121] Worse, aid badly administered or misdirected can undermine reconstruction efforts by distorting the local economy, fostering dependence, or bolstering corrupt or authoritarian politicians. Accordingly, donors routinely seek to put conditions on satisfaction of performance or behavioral criteria, for example, meeting fiscal targets or basic human rights standards.[122] But the standards are often inconsistent and sometimes contradictory. Where the international financial institutions have traditionally focused on economic conditionality, other donors "use conditionality to consolidate peace."[123] At times, the two conflict. In Bosnia, for example, the Office of the High Representative and the European Union wanted to condition aid on satisfaction of political goals; this conflicted with the World Bank's exclusively economic mandate.[124] Although considerable progress has been made in recent years – the World Bank, for example, has a Conflict Prevention and Reconstruction Unit that improves the bank's capacity to take post-conflict needs into account – the use of conditionality remains inconsistent and confusing to aid recipients and donors alike. Moreover, in many instances, recipient states, "[w]hether through venality, incompetence, or misfortune . . . sometimes fail to meet even the most generous loan conditions."[125]

[118] Salvatore Schiavo-Campo, *Financing and Aid Management in Post-Conflict Situations*, CPR Working Paper No. 6, June 2003, at 15, *available at* http://www.unsudanig.org/JAM/clusters/development/background-docs/FinancingAidMgmtArrangmts.pdf.

[119] Patrick, *supra* note 108.

[120] Chesterman, *supra* note 113, at 186.

[121] *See* Patrick, *supra* note 108.

[122] A particularly stark example is the Governance and Economic Management Assistance Program (GEMAP) imposed on Liberia, as discussed in Chapter 4.

[123] *See* Patrick, *supra* note 108.

[124] Schiavo-Campo, *supra* note 118, at 14.

[125] *See* Patrick, *supra* note 108.

Perhaps most problematic of all is the fact that donors often poorly monitor and coordinate their multiple assistance efforts. "[P]arallel efforts are pursued through diverse pledging initiatives, variegated financing instruments, and sundry implementing partners."[126] As each donor follows its own priorities and procedures, some programs are needlessly duplicated, whereas others are not funded at all. Donors commonly lack adequate systems to track pledges, commitments, and disbursements and so find it difficult to target aid effectively. Pledges that are largely fictitious render planning and resource allocation all the more difficult, forcing service providers to overstate their needs, undermining expectations of recipient populations, and disrupting peace implementation programs of all kinds.

National authorities in the recipient states should, of course, insist on effective donor coordination and tie donor aid to their own national budgets and priorities. But often national authorities lack either the capacity or the incentive to perform this function effectively. "Dueling donors" may provide unscrupulous politicians a desired "nurturing environment for bad policies and corruption."[127]

These problems plague peace implementation efforts generally and rule of law assistance programs specifically. As the Secretary-General's Report on building the rule of law in post-conflict societies observes,

Inadequate coordination in this sector leads to duplication, waste, gaps in assistance and conflicting aid and programme objectives. Worse yet, the uncoordinated intervention of the international community can have the effect of distorting domestic justice agendas, wastefully diverting the valuable time of domestic justice sector actors and consuming precious development resources.[128]

Part of the problem is that complex emergencies have often been treated on an ad hoc and reactive basis. For UN peacekeeping operations, only tasks specifically included in the mission mandate are ordinarily funded from assessments on member states. In the past, much of the funding required for post-conflict reconstruction efforts, including rule of law promotion, has not been included in the mandate and so has had to come from voluntary contributions, with all the problems that entails. In recent UN peace operations, however, the Security Council, urged on by the Secretariat, has made greater efforts to include in the mandate essential peacebuilding tasks, including critical rule of law responsibilities. Thus, in the Afghanistan mission, for example, development of the judicial system was included in the mandate; institution-building and judicial system development were also included in the mandate for East Timor.

---

[126] Id.

[127] USAID, Donor Coordination Strategies, September 22, 200 (copy on file with authors).

[128] Report of the Secretary-General, *supra* note 5, at 20.

Similarly, the trend in DDR funding appears to be toward greater inclusion in UN mandates. In the past, mission mandates have often included funding for disarmament and demobilization, but funds to support reintegration (seen as an economic support issue) had to come from voluntary contributions. The *Brahimi Report* correctly noted that this often created a dangerous gap. As recently as the 2003 UN Mission for the Democratic Republic of Congo, support for reintegration was limited to voluntary funding. But in the more recent UN mission for Liberia, funding for reintegration was included in the mandate.[129] Nonetheless, many states remain reluctant to include important aspects of post-conflict reconstruction, especially humanitarian assistance and economic reconstruction, in mission mandates.

Overall, though donors "are generally more eager to script their own role in post-conflict reconstruction than to coordinate with other international or local actors,"[130] they recognize the problems noted above. Many have taken at least modest steps toward improving existing mechanisms to mobilize and deliver aid. Increasingly, pledging conferences are used by key actors, including donor states, international agencies and lending institutions, and representatives of recipient states, to review and refine proposed reconstruction efforts and to coordinate assistance accordingly. These meetings, often led by the World Bank because of its lead role in economic development, may discourage free riding, promote equitable burden sharing, and mobilize international and domestic political support for reconstruction efforts.[131] Multi-donor trust funds help organize financing efforts under one tent and can be matched more effectively to national government budgets than a plethora of funds and financing vehicles. The Afghanistan Reconstruction Trust Fund, for example, has worked relatively well as a vehicle to coordinate donor programs and Afghan national government priorities across most major budget categories.[132] But pledging conferences and trust funds have their limits. Donors sometimes claim political points by pledging amounts they will never produce; often they "double-count" amounts previously committed or delivered.[133] And donors often lack adequate incentives to submerge their interests in multidonor trust funds or avoid them because of their high overheads and "glacial" operations.[134] Funds focusing on selected sectors or issues may be more flexible in some circumstances.

---

[129] *See* Durch et al., *supra* note 37, at 28.
[130] *Play to Win*, *supra* note 13, at 7.
[131] *See* Patrick, *supra* note 108; Chesterman, *supra* note 113, at 194.
[132] *See* Schiavo-Campo, *supra* note 118, at 27–30.
[133] Patrick, *supra* note 108.
[134] Chesterman, *supra* note 113, at 197. Agency views on the effectiveness of trust funds differ. For example, the World Bank viewed its trust fund for East Timor as a success, whereas UN agencies thought it was inaccessible, cumbersome, and slow. *Report of the UNDG/ECHA Working Group*, *supra* note 14, at 25.

The new UN Peacebuilding Commission, despite its limitations, may do much to overcome some of the obstacles to effective funding of post-conflict activities, including rule of law assistance. As the Secretary-General notes, the commission could "provide a mechanism through which donors could be encouraged to make specific, sustainable commitments to the financing of peacebuilding and recovery activities" and could "help to ensure adequate early attention to and financing for oft-neglected issues, such as building public administration capacity for the rule of law...."[135] The commission could also review planned financing for peacebuilding activities to "identify shortfalls and gaps" and catalyze efforts to fill those gaps.[136] Moreover, the new UN standing Fund for Peacebuilding, if adequately financed, could "provide national authorities with vital support for strengthening institutions of the rule of law, national reconciliation processes and similar efforts to reduce the risk of conflict."[137] In short, the Peacebuilding Commission and its associated fund could, in theory, offer a guaranteed source of funding and centralized direction, review, and coordination of reconstruction aid. But most states remain unwilling to surrender control of the uses to which their funds are put and might be reluctant to commit substantial resources to a voluntary fund. So long as that remains true, it may be necessary to pursue modest, incremental changes to recent practices. Such changes could include steps to increase transparency and donor accountability in aid efforts; tighten the coordination mechanisms currently in place; create standardized systems monitoring pledges, commitments, and disbursements; and develop more consistent conditionality practices.

III. IMPROVING LOCAL PARTICIPATION

"Better to let them do it imperfectly than to do it yourself, for it is their country, their way, and your time is short." T. E. Lawrence[138]

It is almost a truism now to say that local actors "must own the process of reconstruction."[139] The purpose of peace implementation and rule of law reform is, after all, to develop sustainable institutions and a culture of respect for law that will outlast the presence of the interveners.[140]

---

[135] *In Larger Freedom, supra* note 68, para. 10.
[136] Id., at para. 11.
[137] Id., at para. 23.
[138] THE SEVEN PILLARS OF WISDOM (1935).
[139] *See, e.g., Play to Win, supra* note 13, at 6 ("[t]he people of the country in question must own the reconstruction process and be its prime movers").
[140] *See, e.g., Balkans 2010, Report of an Independent Task Force Sponsored by the Council on Foreign Relations Center for Preventive Action 2002,* at 9 ("the ultimate goal for the international community in the region [the Balkans] is to turn over responsibility to local leaders who are accountable to their fellow citizens and who support democratic values"), *available*

From a self-interested standpoint, critical objectives of military intervention – ensuring regional stability and eliminating breeding grounds for migration, terrorism, and international crime – generally will not be accomplished beyond the life of the mission, if at all, unless governance reforms take hold. Early termination of peace implementation efforts in Somalia, Liberia, and Sierra Leone led to protracted warfare and near anarchy and, in the latter two cases, to renewed external interventions. Incomplete institution building in East Timor has left that state with relatively weak state institutions and a fragile capacity for rule of law. Yet, it is, or at least it should be, the goal of interveners engaged in post-conflict peacebuilding to "work themselves out of a job" by helping to build local commitment and capacity.[141]

In determining the role local actors should play in peace implementation generally, and in rule of law efforts specifically, three points should be kept in mind. First, durable social change must come from within; it can be guided but not imposed by external actors.[142] Second, the notion of local "ownership" is complicated; externally driven institution-building and rule of law reforms necessarily entail choosing among competing local actors with different visions of their society and different claims to represent it. Third, international and local priorities, standards, and values will at times conflict, forcing interveners to seek a balance between respect for local preferences and satisfying international norms.

A. Change from Within

Peace implementation and transitional governance efforts require interveners to build democratic governance and respect for the rule of law in societies that have little or no experience with either. The comparative advantage of the international actors is their familiarity with successful governance institutions and rule of law norms, but that advantage is at least partly offset by their lack of familiarity with the political and social structures operating in transitional states and the normative and cultural commitments that underpin those structures. Thus, building sustainable democratic and law-governed institutions and practices requires more than monitored elections and the construction of western-style governance and legal institutions. It demands the establishment of institutions and practices viewed by the

---

at http://unpan1.un.org/intradoc/groups/public/documents/UNTC/UNPAN009978.pdf; Michelle Flournoy & Michael Plan, *Dealing with Demons: Justice and Reconciliation*, 25 WASH. Q. 111, 112 (2002) ("*the guiding principle for international assistance in the justice and reconciliation arena should always be to seek to empower local actors and to promote the building of sustainable indigenous capacity while reinforcing respect for human rights and international norms*") (italics in original).

[141] *See* Project on Justice in Times of Transition, *Incorporating Local Voices into International Rule of Law Strategies: A Policy Dialogue*, 2002, at 11 (hereafter *Policy Dialogue*).

[142] *See Review of Peace Operations*, *supra* note 10, at 33 para. 85.

local population as legitimately constituted and consistent with local norms and preferences. Otherwise, "the population ends up with a government and state bodies that are not accepted within the world view of the local population...."[143]

Rule of law assistance may be particularly sensitive to local variations in culture, values, and preferences. Legal systems rely heavily on precedent and the training in particular approaches of those involved in the system. Participants in the system tend to resist new methods, as the United States discovered in its efforts to promote rule of law in the states of the former Soviet Union. In the early years of those efforts, the United States "emphasized the promotion of western methods and models of reform."[144] But "as it became clear that host country officials often did not consider these to be appropriate to their local contexts, USAID began to foster the development of more 'home-grown' reforms."[145]

Although local actors in post-intervention states may sometimes have little choice but to accept, at least nominally, imposed western models as a condition for aid, local actors can usually find many ways to subvert or resist implementation of those models or to turn them to self-interested ends inconsistent with interveners' purposes. It has taken time to learn this lesson. In some peace implementation operations, such as Cambodia, Liberia, Sierra Leone, and Haiti, interveners concentrated initially on establishing the formal structures and practices of western democratic governance – elections, the separation of power among the executive, legislative, and judicial branches, creation of nominally independent police and courts, and the like. But for a host of reasons, including the interveners' limited mandates, political pressures for early exit, resource constraints, lack of expertise on local conditions, and insufficient attention to local capacity building, as well as the sheer complexity and difficulty of post-intervention environments, the imported structures and practices never took root or did so only superficially. Instead, shortly after the interveners' departure, competition for political power and resources took the form of coups and civil war rather than elections and legal process, in some cases leading to renewed external military intervention.

In the long run, sustainable reforms must have popular support. Such support is contingent on the active involvement of representative local actors in the process of developing the institutions and legal frameworks of governance, so that these institutions and frameworks are perceived as legitimate

---

[143] Id., at para. 86.

[144] *See GAO Report, supra* note 1, at 11. For a discussion of successful U.S. contributions to criminal justice reform efforts in the former Soviet Union, *see* Mathew Spence, *The Complexity of Success: The U.S. Role in Russian Rule of Law Reform, Carnegie Endowment,* July 2005, *available at* http://www.carnegieendowment.org/files/CP60.spence.FINAL.pdf.

[145] Id., at 11.

in origin. Support is also contingent on building local capacity for democratic self-governance and on adapting unfamiliar governance methods and norms to accord with local values.

In recent peace operations, especially the transitional governance operations in Kosovo, East Timor, and Iraq, interveners have taken more seriously the need to involve local actors in decision-making, to build local capacity for governance, and to take into account local values and beliefs. But for many reasons, doing so successfully is extraordinarily difficult. Thus, the UN Transitional Administration in East Timor, for example, despite successfully accomplishing its overall strategic mission of fostering the birth of an independent East Timor, has been criticized for failing, early on, to appreciate adequately the critical importance of local participation. As one observer put it, UNTAET built institutions

based on the assumption that there were no strong concepts and ideas existing on the local level, and that the population just had to be 'taught' democracy.... This ignored the fact that human beings grow up in a social environment with powerful ideas of how to classify and understand their world. Local perceptions and practices were thought of as cultural 'folklore' and were not accorded much significance. Therefore international attempts [at institution building] often failed or had marginal impact.[146]

Although this observation may overstate the case with respect to East Timor, it captures a recurrent problem in peace implementation efforts. In Chapter 8, we discussed ways in which local commitment to a rule of law culture may be fostered. We consider below some of the difficulties involved in attempting to promote local "ownership" of the reform process and in reconciling international and local values and priorities.

B. The Dilemmas of Local Ownership

The notion of local ownership entails both local participation in and, to the extent feasible, local control of the development and operation of institutions and governance practices. The latter necessarily entails the creation of adequate local capacity. But developing local participation and capacity is a project fraught with difficulty, for several reasons.

First, encouraging local participation is not a politically neutral enterprise. To a greater or lesser degree, it means picking winners and losers, empowering some actors and disempowering others. In the aftermath of military intervention, host state governance capacity is typically extremely limited. Infrastructure is in ruins, and local actors with significant government, administrative, or judicial experience – those few who remain in-country – are often viewed as tainted by prior association with a discredited and oppressive former government. In the competition for political power

---

[146] Id., at para. 87 (quoting Tanja Hohe, *The Clash of Paradigms: International Administrations and Local Political Legitimacy in East Timor*, unpublished paper, Brown University, 2001).

that inevitably ensues, interveners' choice of local interlocutors necessarily shifts the local balance of power, for better or worse. As one observer put it, "[c]hoosing which actors to recognize, which ones to work with, and what processes and projects to support can tilt the balance of power either toward or away from a stable peace."[147]

In theory, interveners should work with groups and individuals who collectively are broadly representative of the society at large. In the constitution-drafting process, for example, some broad-based national dialogue of the sort that emerged in Afghanistan, one that includes all or nearly all political parties and viewpoints, constitutes one vehicle for promoting local ownership of the constitution that results. But working with representative local actors in the day-to-day process of transitional governance is extraordinarily difficult, particularly in deeply divided post-intervention states. In Kosovo, for example, western intervention was generally welcomed by Albanian Kosovars, who had self-appointed local authorities in place, ready and willing to consult with transitional administrators on the future governance of the province. But Kosovar Serbs did not welcome the intervention and resisted efforts to draw them into governance decision-making. In East Timor, the National Council for Timorese Resistance (CNRT), a coalition of proindependence groups, seemed the logical interlocutor for UNTAET. But CNRT consisted of diverse parties with widely divergent agendas; moreover, CNRT's leadership "was composed largely of Lusafone expatriates who were, in some respects, out of touch with the youthful Indonesian-speaking majority of the East Timorese population."[148] UNTAET saw CNRT more as a political party than a protogovernment and for the most part "kept its distance."[149] To the extent UNTAET did rely on CNRT as a local partner, it inadvertently advanced "particular individuals and factions through the mechanisms of participation."[150]

In other post-intervention states, interveners intentionally choose local partners on the basis of their likely contribution to the interveners' post-conflict objectives. To the extent those objectives center on building democracy and the rule of law, a selection bias seems appropriate. There is no point to strengthening local warlords or obstructionist nationalists, even if they have a significant popular following. But applying a selection bias in practice is fraught with peril. The United States worked hard to empower local actors in Iraq who were receptive to western political objectives and to

---

[147] Robert Orr, *Post-Conflict Reconstruction Project, Meeting the Challenges of Governance and Participation in Post-Conflict Settings, Draft White Paper* 2002, at 3, *available at* http://www.idlo.int/texts///IDLO//mis6307.pdf.

[148] Joel Beauvais, *Benevolent Despotism: A Critique of U.N. State-Building in East Timor*, 33 N.Y.U. J. INT'L L. & POL. 1101, 1123 (2001).

[149] Schiavo-Campo, *supra* note 118, at 21.

[150] Beauvais, *supra* note 148, at 1123.

marginalize actors hostile to the coalition's presence and goals. For example, the United States put a disproportionate number of exile parties' representatives on the Iraqi Governing Council and worked to exclude groups seen as too radical or too aligned with Iran. But the result was that the governing council's legitimacy in the eyes of the local population, and its effectiveness, were sharply undermined, and the United States was forced to move more quickly than it had intended, and more quickly perhaps than a viable transition required, to an Iraqi-controlled government.

In general, promoting local ownership is a dynamic and variable process. In many cases, it is neither possible nor desirable to include the full spectrum of local actors, because some will be adamantly opposed to the entire reconstruction effort. Instead, it may be necessary to work with key national stakeholders at the outset and then work to broaden the base of support for interveners' efforts over time.[151]

Even assuming interveners can identify and work with representative local actors, including them actively in the early stages of post-intervention governance complicates an already overwhelming task. Inevitably, there exists a tension between interveners' short-term mission, to stabilize and help govern a failed polity, and their longer-term mission, to build sustainable political institutions and practices that will survive the interveners' departure. The extent of the tension will vary widely, depending on a variety of factors, most notably whether the mission is a "light footprint" effort to assist a nascent government or a full-scale transitional administration.

When a national government is in place or being put in place, it is relatively easy to co-locate international staff in national ministries and take other steps to build local capacity and involvement. In particular, the existence of national authorities facilitates preparation of a national budget and disbursement of aid in concert with local priorities. But even then, capacity issues limit the utility of efforts to empower local actors. In Liberia, for example, the United Nations had government ministers chair key sectoral groups in the reconstruction process, but the effort foundered because there was no capacity within the ministries to support the ministers.[152] In such cases, interveners often take over, marginalizing national authorities in an effort to get the task at hand accomplished.

The tension is even greater with transitional administration missions. In such cases, the short-term governance mandate "is predicated on centralized international control and staffing of the transitional administration, whereas preparation for democratic self-government implies broad participation of

---

[151] *See* World Bank, *An Operational Note on Transitional Results Matrices: Using Results-Based Frameworks in Fragile States,* January 2005, at 5, *available at* http://www.undg.org/documents/5532-Operational_Note_on_Transitional_Results_Matrices_-_Results_Matrix_Guide.pdf.

[152] Eide et al., *supra* note 41, at 34.

local stakeholders in decisionmaking and intensive investment in building local capacity."[153] Overstretched and underresourced transitional administrations have only limited capacity to incorporate local actors in decisionmaking. It is simply faster and easier for interveners to make decisions by decree rather than through protracted negotiations with local actors, particularly in deeply divided states and those with little local governance capacity, even though the cost of doing so may be to undercut longer-term efforts at capacity building.

In the emergency environment that characterizes the start-up of most post-intervention missions, whether light footprint or transitional administration, it is usually the "'logic' of peacekeeping and emergency relief" that dominates; a logic that entails "heavy, foreign and largely self-sufficient and self-contained presence, international recruitment and political neutrality, quick results, short time-frame."[154] By contrast, a focus on capacity building entails a "logic of development" – an "emphasis on [local] participation, bottom-up, long time-frames, process-as-result, institution building."[155] In all cases, then, interveners must strike a balance "between the mission's efforts to re-establish a public administration, maintain some control, and monitor quality and progress, on the one hand, and its ultimate responsibility to facilitate local ownership and effect eventual handover on the other."[156]

Ideally, local actors will be actively involved from the outset, starting with needs assessment and mission planning. Their knowledge of local conditions can help interveners avoid major mistakes (such as choosing an applicable law that is anathema to those asked to apply it) and lend legitimacy to what might otherwise appear as foreign encroachment. And their early involvement can build badly needed local capacity from the start. But in practice, it is easier to include local actors as the situation stabilizes and the transitional administration develops its own capacity. Thus, in Kosovo, the Secretary-General envisioned several phases, beginning with direct rule by UNMIK, and followed by gradually increasing delegation of authority to local actors, to joint administration, to a form of assisted self-governance.[157] Similarly, in East Timor, UNTAET initially focused on developing its own governance capacity.

This approach risks marginalizing local actors. In East Timor, for example, a perceived lack of capacity on the Timorese side led UN officials to commit one of the "cardinal sins" of post-intervention assistance: "with a

---

[153] Beauvais, *supra* note 148, at 1106.
[154] Id., at 1113 [*quoting* Astri Suhrke, *Reason and Reconstruction: The Multiple Logics of UNTAET* 2 (2001)] (unpublished manuscript).
[155] Id.
[156] *A Review of Peace Operations, supra* note 10, at 30 para. 69.
[157] *Kosovo Report, supra* note 52, at 15–17.

very few individual exceptions, the expatriate experts focused almost entirely on doing the jobs, instead of also gradually bringing in, training, and empowering local individuals."[158] Only well into the mission, when UNTAET was effectively compelled by East Timorese pressure to concentrate on local participation and capacity building, did UNTAET shift its approach.[159] Even then, UNTAET took a bottom-up approach to the recruitment of Timorese government employees, increasing the time needed for Timorese to reach senior positions and exercise real influence over decision-making; as a result, the Timorese at independence were not nearly as well prepared to govern as they might have been.[160] In retrospect, it would have been preferable at the outset to work toward systematic inclusion of Timorese in governance and decision-making at all levels.

Sierra Leone offers a positive example of efforts to build local capacity. After a series of false starts, interveners worked with the national authorities to devise a "national recovery strategy." The strategy rested heavily on gradually restoring civil administration and rule of law to districts outside the capital, as they became accessible. The approach adopted "placed the government in the driver's seat, with an emphasis on building national capacities from the ground up, district by district.... "[161] Although it is too early to judge the overall success of these efforts, considerable progress has been made.

In other cases, when indigenous national authorities have been ousted or discredited, interveners may be tempted to work principally with "outsider nationals," members of a returning diaspora who speak the language and know the culture of the interveners. Although such individuals may bring much-needed technical skills, they may correspondingly lack familiarity with local conditions. As in Iraq, undue reliance on returning nationals may also generate resentment among those who have remained in-country and may stifle local initiatives.[162]

Overall, the trick is to ensure that the best does not become the enemy of the good and that local actors are involved as much as is reasonably feasible as early as possible, without strengthening those responsible for conflict in the past or likely to resist needed reforms. The tendency of most

---

[158] Schiavo-Campo, *supra* note 118, at 23.
[159] Beauvais, *supra* note 148, at 1114. This is true even though the Secretary-General in an October 1999 report expressly called for employing East Timorese in transitional administration positions "where qualified individuals are available," and when such individuals were not available, for employing a "dual-desk" system in which international staff would pair with local counterparts to build capacity and prepare them to assume full responsibility for the functions at issue. S/1999/1024, *Report of the Secretary-General on the Situation in East Timor*, October 4, 1999.
[160] Schiavo-Campo, *supra* note 118, at 23–24.
[161] *Report of the UNDG/ECHA Working Group on Transition Issues, supra* note 14, at 19–20.
[162] *See* Schiavo-Campo, *supra* note 118, at 45.

post-intervention efforts to date has been to opt for ease of administration by sidelining local perspectives.[163] This approach inappropriately prioritizes short-term over long-term needs. Today's emergency crowds out tomorrow's sustainable development. But given the overall goal of peace implementation, greater attention to inclusion and capacity building are essential; it is local actors, after all, who remain when the interveners depart. At the same time, interveners need to be candid about the extent to which local actors will be involved in decision-making in peace implementation efforts and straightforward about the conditions that will lead to a shift in interveners' approach. Creating and then ignoring vehicles for local ownership of the post-conflict reconstruction process is likely to generate greater opposition than specifying openly the limits of local involvement, the reasons for those limits, and the circumstances that will lead to the gradual assumption by local actors of full decision-making power.

C. Handling Value Conflicts

One of the difficulties of "local ownership" of the peace implementation process is that local and international values and priorities often conflict. Interveners generally engage in governance and rule of law reform with western human rights standards in mind. But the states in which interventions take place almost by definition lack experience with such standards, and local actors in any event have their own priorities.

In some cases, those priorities include finishing unfinished business with adversaries in the conflict that prompted intervention. In Kosovo, for example, many Albanian Kosovars viewed the legal system as a forum in which to continue their conflict with Serbs. In interethnic disputes, local judges frequently displayed "ethnic and political bias . . . as a result of actual or potential security threats, or of their own preference."[164] Moreover, much of the local population refused "to cooperate with the judiciary in cases involving former combatants."[165] Thus, efforts to develop local capacity by employing local judges ran counter to mission objectives (promoting interethnic harmony and protecting basic minority rights). As a result, UNMIK was forced to employ international judges in potentially sensitive cases. While other UNMIK departments were downsizing and transferring responsibility to local actors, UNMIK's Department of Justice was expanding and increasing international control over the legal system.[166] This created a system with

---

[163] *A Review of Peace Operations, supra* note 10, at 18.
[164] *Kosovo Report, supra* note 52, para. 185; *see also* id., para. 202 ("On the one hand there was a trend not to consider evidence in favour of minority community defendants and on the other a trend towards dismissing charges against and releasing former KLA members and other powerful Albanians").
[165] Id.
[166] Id., at para. 190.

international and local components, with control residing primarily with the internationals. As a result, "[t]he local side of the system is developing dependence on the international side in the sense that, despite their initial opposition, local judges are now comfortable with not having to deal with sensitive cases and do not wish to do so in the future, for as long as former KLA members might be involved."[167] In short, the move to international judges, though unavoidable from an international values standpoint, permitted Kosovar judges to escape responsibility for living up to international standards.

In other cases, the clash between international and local standards proves more subtle. In Sierra Leone, for example, "the U.N. strategy for restoring local government . . . included reestablishing both hereditary chieftaincies and elected district councils."[168] But "reliance on hereditary chieftains has always compromised transparency and accountability. . . . "; it also "limits democratic participation because only candidates meeting hereditary lineage requirements" are eligible to fill such posts.[169] Thus, respect for local practices may entail violating the standards interveners are committed to promoting. Moreover, it may also complicate later efforts to strengthen democratically elected local governments.

Similarly, in East Timor, long and unfortunate experience with the Indonesian justice system "had created widespread mistrust and lack of faith in formal state justice processes. . . . "[170] As a result, even after UNTAET attempted to reform the official justice system, there was "continued widespread reliance on traditional or customary justice mechanisms that operated at the village level."[171] Yet these relatively informal local mechanisms sometimes "show little regard for the rights of women," and, at least in some circumstances, their use constituted "a significant obstacle to applying Western norms of judicial conduct and respect for human rights."[172]

Interveners confronted with such value conflicts face difficult choices. On the one hand, they cannot, at least formally, accept local practices that violate international standards. On the other hand, they risk irrelevance, charges of imperialism, or worse, if they push western values too aggressively. Striking the right balance is context sensitive and will necessarily vary from case to case. As a practical matter, however, interveners often have no choice; continued reliance on local justice in East Timor, for example, could not be avoided because no fully functioning justice system existed outside the capital, nor could one be created quickly.

---

[167] Id., at para. 231.
[168] *Transition Strategies, supra* note 11, at 25.
[169] Id.
[170] *East Timor Report, supra* note 62, para. 219.
[171] Id.
[172] *Transition Strategies, supra* note 11, at 26.

At the same time, interveners and local actors both have to remain flexible and be prepared to adapt as conditions change. What might not be possible at the outset of the post-intervention period may become possible as conditions improve and as interveners and local actors work together to adapt imported practices and institutions to local norms and preferences. The post-conflict reconstruction process should be dynamic and evolutionary; not everything can be done at once, and positive changes may be phased in over time.

CONCLUSION

Rule of law assistance efforts can only succeed as part of a larger effort to stabilize the affected country and create a functioning government. To succeed, interveners must plan and coordinate peace implementation and rule of law programs in a systematic way, scale commitment and resources to need, and actively involve local actors in peacebuilding and rule of law efforts. With that in mind, interveners should take the following steps:

- Achieve unity of effort. Key international actors must agree early on a coherent strategic plan for the post-intervention period. This plan should be developed through broad consultations with relevant stakeholders and keyed to the post-conflict political blueprint for the country's future. The plan should set out agreed priorities and foster a genuine partnership among the relevant international and local actors. The UN Peacebuilding Commission offers one obvious forum for planning and coordination at the international level, notwithstanding the limits described earlier. Similarly, NSPD 44 offers a good example of the possibilities for improving national planning and implementation processes.
- Conduct a comprehensive needs assessment mission as early as possible, using common assessment tools and frameworks, to help identify needs and priorities and determine the appropriate sequencing of post-intervention efforts. At the same time, recognize the need to pursue reforms that will prove mutually reinforcing. Utilize a strategic level planning body, such as the new UN Peacebuilding Commission, to foster strategic coherence and resource mobilization at the intergovernmental level. More critical than the planning structure chosen is the need to foster early and coordinated participation of the key actors and to divide responsibility for achieving agreed objectives.
- Create a comparable, field-level planning and coordination mechanism, such as an integrated mission, again recalling that the structure of that mechanism is less important than fostering a genuine partnership among the multiplicity of organizations and government agencies involved in the post-intervention effort.

- At both the strategic and field levels, establish detailed benchmarks and timetables for achievement of mission goals and systematically review progress and revise objectives as needed to reflect changing realities on the ground.
- Particular attention should be paid to coordination of donor activities, utilizing trust funds and other devices to encourage predictable financing of priority projects that address urgent needs. Ensure that donors take a synergistic, systemic approach to identifying financing needs, so that reform efforts reinforce each other. To the maximum extent possible, donors' activities should be transparent to minimize waste, corruption, and misallocation of monies attributable to donor self-interest.
- Involve local actors as early and as fully as feasible in all aspects of planning and implementation of post-intervention efforts from the assessment of needs to the establishment of benchmarks and timetables. But recognize the risks of pursuing inclusion, and be candid when signaling the extent to which local actors will or will not be involved in particular decisions. Where possible, provision of economic assistance should be linked to national development plans and budgets.
- When local capacity is too weak to involve local actors fully, a comprehensive effort should be made as early as possible to build adequate local capacity and to transfer governance responsibility as quickly as practical to local actors.

Ultimately, of course, responsibility for the country's future must rest with its population. But these and other steps outlined above will improve the chances that peace implementation efforts in general, and rule of law assistance in particular, are not derailed or wasted altogether.

CHAPTER TEN

Conclusion

This is not an optimistic book. Throughout the preceding chapters, we have emphasized the enormous challenges associated with building the rule of law after military interventions. The very concept of the "rule of law" is elusive to begin with, and striving for the rule of law requires a constant juggling act on the part of interveners. It is little wonder that so many past efforts in this area have been so disappointing.

But this book is not entirely pessimistic, either. Although the challenges are daunting, we are convinced that modest successes are possible. If the international community has delivered less than was promised in Kosovo, Bosnia, Sierra Leone, East Timor, and Afghanistan, people in these societies are nonetheless probably better off than if there had been no outside interventions and no subsequent rule of law programs. In each case, serious problems remain: security is tenuous, economic development has been slow, serious rights abuses continue, political and legal institutions have struggled to achieve credibility and effectiveness, and many abuses have gone unpunished and uncompensated. Nonetheless, in each case, things could be far worse.

The moral, we think, is that it *is* possible for outside interventions to help foster the rule of law, but only if interveners fully understand the nature and magnitude of the task – and only if interveners understand that the role outsiders can play is crucial but limited.

We can't afford not to face up to the challenges associated with building the rule of law, for the international community will face these issues again and again in the years to come. However much we wish it were not so, the foreseeable future will continue to bring us armed conflicts and interventions driven both by humanitarian concerns and by security imperatives. And for the reasons we emphasized in this book's introductory chapter, interveners will continue to face pressures (both self-imposed and externally imposed) to help repair both the damage they find and the damage they cause in conflict-ridden societies, in part through efforts to restore the rule of law.

388

Interveners will, of course, also continue to have a short-term incentive to do rule of law "on the cheap." But the costs of such penny-wise, pound-foolish approaches are becoming ever more evident. In Iraq, for instance, the failure of the U.S.-led coalition to devote adequate planning and resources to the period immediately following the overthrow of Saddam Hussein badly discredited the coalition. Those early failures allowed insecurity to spiral and brought civil reconstruction projects to a virtual standstill in many parts of Iraq. Progress on rule of law issues has consequently also been uneven and slow. The price inflicted by the unsuppressed civil violence has been paid primarily by the Iraqis, who have lost at least 30,000 civilians in the period since major fighting ended. But the United States and other coalition states have also paid a high price: well over 2000 U.S. soldiers have been killed in Iraq so far, and thousands more have been badly wounded. Hundreds of other foreigners have also been killed in Iraq, including dozens of humanitarian workers such as those who died in the 2003 truck-bombing of the UN office in Baghdad. The Iraq experience has been a painful object lesson in just why interveners need to invest the resources to do things correctly from the start.

In any case, however troubled we may be by unwise, ill-planned, or poorly executed interventions, we cannot wish interventions away; those of us who care about human rights and the rule of law can, however, try to make the best of the situation. Although there is no guarantee that powerful states and institutions will in fact learn from past mistakes, they certainly will not change unless policymakers and analysts are willing to clear-headedly assess just what we know and what we do not know about fostering the rule of law. Armed with the insights gained from this assessment process, we can strive, in the future, both to avoid the most glaring mistakes of the past and to develop innovative new approaches.

If past rule of law programs have been disappointing, one major reason is that far too many past programs have been based on simplistic assumptions about the relationship between formal legal institutions and durable cultural change. As we have emphasized throughout this book, policymakers and interveners have tended to conflate "the rule of law" with the formal legal institutions that support the rule of law in complex democracies. As a result, far too many rule of law programs have focused mainly on judicial training, law reform, and similar forms of technical assistance, failing to understand that these programs alone cannot produce the rule of law.

Thus, a critical first step in avoiding the failures of the past involves recognizing just how nuanced a concept the "rule of law" really is. In Chapter 3, we offered a pragmatic definition of the rule of law, a definition designed to emphasize that the rule of law is a complex bundle of institutions, rules, and cultural commitments. That means that those who wish to design rule of law programs need to think about the rule of law holistically, understanding that there are certain background conditions critical to the success of narrower, institutionally focused reforms.

If interveners are themselves perceived as having acted illegitimately or illegally, for instance, subsequent efforts to promote rule of law values will face challenges to their credibility. This was the case in Iraq, where the legally contested intervention made the subsequent rebuilding efforts a harder sell with multiple audiences. The Abu Ghraib prison abuse scandal also greatly undermined U.S. efforts to promote the rule of law in Iraq and elsewhere. Similarly, an early failure to provide basic human security can also badly undermine rule of law efforts. People too fearful to venture out of their homes can make little use of their legal rights, and hunger and disease similarly take priority over more complex governance issues. Past rule of law efforts have also often been sabotaged by poor planning and coordination, by the failure to think through the likely consequences of different governance blueprints, by inadequate local knowledge, and by inadequate resources.

But fostering rule of law in post-intervention settings has been, and will be, difficult even under the best of circumstances, because rule of law efforts after military interventions are plagued by inherent paradoxes and contradictions. Most obviously, the idea of using coercion to convince people of the value of the rule of law is inherently paradoxical. The paradox is particularly apparent in settings such as Iraq, where a significant sector of the population views the U.S.-led invasion as itself illegitimate, but it also causes difficulties even in settings where interveners are largely welcomed by local citizens. By nature, interveners are in a position to foster the rule of law because of their superior capacity to use coercion: it is this capacity for coercion that can force an end to tyranny or civil conflict and bring opposing groups to the same table. But it is hard to promote a lasting commitment to law through the barrel of a gun.

Efforts to build the rule of law are also inherently difficult because local populations are made up of numerous individuals or groups, who may (and usually do) have wildly varying (and sometimes shifting) interests and incentives. As a result, interveners often face built-in conflicts: ensuring that minorities are protected and represented politically often conflicts with the desire of majorities to exercise control, for instance. Fostering "local owner-ship" and respecting local cultural norms may conflict with efforts to ensure rights for women, children, and religious minorities.

Societies do not stand still, and decisions must often be made quickly. Short-term interests often conflict with long-term interests (for instance, collaboration with local warlords or militias may be useful in establishing basic security in the short term but may dangerously empower spoilers in the long term). In practice, promoting the rule of law is never politically neutral, although interveners often like to imagine that it is: the decisions made by interveners necessarily empower some local actors at the expense of others.

This incites opposition (sometimes violent), which can in turn force interveners to respond with coercion, which then generates more opposition.

Interveners must constantly make choices among imperfect alternatives, and as a result, movement toward the rule of law is rarely linear but rather back and forth. It is this that led us, in this book, to adopt a synergistic account of building the rule of law.

The synergistic approach is described in Chapter 3 and returned to in many of the chapters that follow. To recapitulate, a synergistic approach to building the rule of law is *ends-based and strategic* in that it aims to achieve certain clear overarching objectives or effects rather than focusing narrowly on particular means (such as formal legal institutions) to the exclusion of others. It is *adaptive and dynamic* in that it aims to build on existing cultural and institutional resources for the rule of law and move them in a constructive direction, but it recognizes, at the same time, that the rule of law is always a work in progress, requiring continual maintenance and reevaluation. It is *systemic* because it emphasizes interrelationships between the various components of a functioning justice system, highlighting the necessity of an integrated approach to reform to achieve effects not possible by focusing on single institutions in isolation.

Such an approach, adopted with appropriate modesty, can make a real difference. Progress toward the rule of law is rarely linear but instead involves frequent movement back and forth: a success in reforming legislation may be counterbalanced by a walkout from the political process by a disgruntled groups of stakeholders; a program to train women in effective legal advocacy and community organizing may be counterbalanced by restrictions on women's movements resulting from a surge in insecurity. As with most human endeavors, progress will be uneven and often difficult to measure.

Nonetheless, interveners need to strive to keep the momentum going in the direction of the rule of law. If enough progress is made, sometimes a tipping point is reached, and things begin to come together. But with too many errors and setbacks, the balance can also tip in the other direction. As recent events in Iraq indicate, momentum and goodwill, once lost, can be exceptionally difficult to recover.

In *Alice in Wonderland*, Alice tells the Queen that "one can't believe impossible things." The Queens responds briskly: "I daresay you haven't had much practice.... When I was younger, I always did it for half an hour a day. Why, sometimes I've believed as many as six impossible things before breakfast." In a sense, interveners who wish to build the rule of law after military interventions must not only *believe* in six impossible things before breakfast: they must, in fact, do their best to accomplish the impossible.

At least, it may seem that way. After all, this book has emphasized that to maximize their chances of success, interveners must somehow accomplish all of the following: they must acknowledge the complexity of the rule of law and be clear about what it is that they are trying to achieve. They must develop basic governance blueprints to determine how to create appropriate institutions, while recognizing that the choice of blueprints will inevitably constrain and possibly undermine some rule of law goals. They must seize early opportunities to ensure basic security and reform police, prisons, courts, law schools, and so on, all in tandem. They must ensure that accountability efforts send the right messages and enhance local capacity and avoid undermining rule of law efforts through cultural insensitivity, poor planning, lack of transparency, or the appearance of hypocrisy. They must think creatively about building rule of law cultures, which requires going beyond the traditionally "legal" to consider informal dispute resolution, community organizing and advocacy, civil society, education, media, antipoverty and development initiatives, and ensuring inclusion of nonelites and marginalized groups. Finally, they must contrive to plan and coordinate all of the above, and ensure resources commensurate to the task.

It is, of course, impossible to do all that. Even the most powerful states and institutions in the world can hardly do all that. The United States, for all its global power and ambition, fell badly short of the mark in Iraq, for instance. And most practitioners work on a far smaller scale: they design programs for USAID, coordinate the efforts of an NGO, look for funding opportunities for a foundation, or struggle, on the ground, to work with local actors in small-scale programs.

But as we have said, although we are not overly optimistic, we are not overly pessimistic, either. Although we may each be painting only one small piece of the picture, it will surely be a better work of art if we all know just what the picture is supposed to represent in the end, and if we have all given conscious thought to how our own sketches or brushstrokes may fit into the complex and evolving whole. If we can manage to be both more ambitious and more modest, we may achieve, in the future, far more than we have in the past.

In the world we inhabit, there is no other choice.

Index